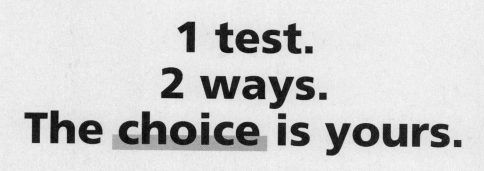

GMAT

GMAT™ Official Guide
Verbal Review
2022

Add over 340 verbal practice questions to your prep.

 Book + Online + Mobile

What's included

Book:

✓ Over 340 practice questions not included in the main Official Guide

✓ Answer explanations

✓ New! Review chapter with 25 practice questions

Online tools:

✓ Question Bank

✓ Flash cards

✓ Mobile app

The ONLY source of real GMAT™ questions from past exams

GMAT™ Official Prep

GMAT™ Official Guide Verbal Review 2022

Published by John Wiley & Sons, Inc., Hoboken, New Jersey.

For general information on our other products and services or to obtain technical support please contact our Customer Care Department within the U.S. at (877) 762-2974, outside the U.S. at (317) 572-3993 or fax (317) 572-4002.

Wiley also publishes its books in a variety of electronic formats. Some content that appears in print may not be available in electronic books. For more information about Wiley products, please visit our Web site at www.wiley.com.

ISBN 978-1-119-79379-3 (pbk); ISBN 978-1-119-79388-5 (ePUB)

Printed in the United States of America

SKY10024666_041221

Table of Contents

Dear GMAT™ Test-Taker,

Thank you for your interest in graduate management education. Today more than 7,000 graduate programs around the world use the GMAT exam to establish their MBA, business master's, and other graduate-level management degree programs as hallmarks of excellence. Nine out of ten new MBA enrollments globally are made using a GMAT score.*

By using the *GMAT™ Official Guide* to prepare for the GMAT exam, you're taking a very important step toward achieving your goals and pursuing admission to the MBA or business master's program that is the best fit for you.

This book, *GMAT™ Official Guide Verbal Review 2022*, is designed to help you prepare for and build confidence to do your best on exam day. It's the only guide that features real questions from past exams published by the Graduate Management Admission Council (GMAC), the makers of the GMAT exam.

For more than 60 years, the GMAT exam has helped candidates like you demonstrate their command of the skills needed for success in the classroom and showcase to schools their commitment to pursuing a graduate business degree. Schools use and trust the GMAT exam as part of their admissions process because it's a proven predictor of classroom success and your ability to excel in your chosen program.

The mission of GMAC is to ensure no talent goes undiscovered. We are driven to continue improving the GMAT exam as well as helping you find and connect with the best-fit schools and programs for you. I applaud your commitment to educational success. This guide and the other GMAT™ Official Prep products available at mba.com will give you the confidence to achieve your personal best on the GMAT exam and launch or reinvigorate a rewarding career.

I wish you the best success on all your future educational and professional endeavors.

Sincerely,

Sangeet Chowfla
President & CEO of the Graduate Management Admission Council

---

* Top 100 *Financial Times* full-time MBA programs

GMAT™ Official Guide
Verbal Review 2022

1.0 What Is the GMAT™ Exam?

1.0 What Is the GMAT™ Exam?

The Graduate Management Admission Test™ (GMAT™) exam is a standardized exam used in admissions decisions by more than 7,000 graduate management programs, at approximately 2,300 graduate business schools worldwide. It helps you gauge, and demonstrate to schools, your academic potential for success in graduate-level management studies.

The four-part exam measures your Analytical Writing, Integrated Reasoning, Verbal Reasoning, and Quantitative Reasoning skills—higher-order reasoning skills that management faculty, admissions professionals, and employers worldwide have identified as important for incoming students to have. "Higher-order" reasoning skills involve complex judgments, and include critical thinking, analysis, and problem solving. Unlike undergraduate grades and curricula, which vary in their meaning across regions and institutions, your GMAT scores provide a standardized, statistically valid and reliable measure of how you are likely to perform academically in the core curriculum of a graduate management program. The GMAT exam's validity, fairness, and value in admissions have been well-established through numerous academic studies.

The GMAT exam is delivered online or at a test center, entirely in English, and solely on a computer. It is not a test of business knowledge, subject-matter mastery, English vocabulary, or advanced computational skills. The GMAT exam also does not measure other factors related to success in graduate management study, such as job experience, leadership ability, motivation, and interpersonal skills. Your GMAT score is intended to be used as one admissions criterion among other, more subjective, criteria, such as admissions essays and interviews.

1.1 Why Take the GMAT™ Exam?

Taking the GMAT exam helps you stand out in the admissions process and demonstrate your readiness and commitment to pursuing graduate management education. Schools use GMAT scores to help them select the most qualified applicants—because they know that candidates who take the GMAT exam are serious about earning a graduate business degree, and it's a proven predictor of a student's ability to succeed in his or her chosen program. When you consider which programs to apply to, you can look at a school's use of the GMAT exam as one indicator of quality. Schools that use the GMAT exam typically list score ranges or average scores in their class profiles, so you may also find these profiles helpful in gauging the academic competitiveness of a program you are considering and how well your performance on the exam compares with that of the students enrolled in the program.

No matter how you perform on the GMAT exam, you should contact the schools that interest you to learn more and to ask how they use GMAT scores and other criteria (such as your undergraduate grades, essays, and letters of recommendation) in their admissions processes. School admissions offices, websites, and materials published by schools are the key sources of information when you are doing research about where you might want to go to business school.

> ## Myth -vs- FACT
>
> 𝓜 – **If I don't achieve a high score on the GMAT exam, I won't get into my top choice schools.**
>
> F – **There are great schools available for candidates at any GMAT score range.**
>
> Fewer than 50 of the ~200,000 people taking the GMAT exam each year get a perfect score of 800; and many more get into top business school programs around the world each year. Admissions Officers use GMAT scores as one component in their admissions decisions, in conjunction with undergraduate records, application essays, interviews, letters of recommendation, and other information when deciding whom to accept into their programs. Visit School Finder on mba.com to learn about schools that are the best fit for you.

For more information on the GMAT exam, test preparation materials, registration, how to use and send your GMAT scores to schools, and applying to business school, please visit mba.com/gmat.

1.2 GMAT™ Exam Format

The GMAT exam consists of four separately timed sections (see the table on the next page). The Analytical Writing Assessment (AWA) section consists of one essay. The Integrated Reasoning section consists of graphical and data analysis questions in multiple response formats. The Quantitative and Verbal Reasoning sections consist of multiple-choice questions.

The Quantitative and Verbal Reasoning sections of the GMAT exam are computer adaptive, which means that the test draws from a large bank of questions to tailor itself to your ability level, and you won't get many questions that are too hard or too easy for you. The first question will be of medium difficulty. As you answer each question, the computer scores your answer and uses it—as well as your responses to all preceding questions—to select the next question.

Computer-adaptive tests become more difficult the more questions you answer correctly, but if you get a question that seems easier than the last one, it does not necessarily mean you answered the last question incorrectly. The test must cover a range of content, both in the type of question asked and the subject matter presented.

> ## Myth -vs- FACT
>
> M – **Getting an easier question means I answered the last one wrong.**
>
> F – **You should not become distracted by the difficulty level of a question.**
>
> Many different factors contribute to the difficulty of a question, so don't worry when taking the test or waste valuable time trying to determine the difficulty of the question you are answering.
>
> To ensure that everyone receives the same content, the test selects a specific number of questions of each type. The test may call for your next problem to be a relatively hard data sufficiency question involving arithmetic operations. But, if there are no more relatively difficult data sufficiency questions involving arithmetic, you might be given an easier question.

Because the computer uses your answers to select your next questions, you may not skip questions or go back and change your answer to a previous question. If you don't know the answer to a question, try to eliminate as many choices as possible, then select the answer you think is best.

Though the individual questions are different, the mix of question types is the same for every GMAT exam. Your score is determined by the difficulty and statistical characteristics of the questions you answer as well as the number of questions you answer correctly. By adapting to each test-taker, the GMAT exam is able to accurately and efficiently gauge skill levels over a full range of abilities, from very high to very low.

The test includes the types of questions found in this book and in the online question bank found at gmat.wiley.com, but the format and presentation of the GMAT exam questions are different.

Five things to know about GMAT exam questions:

- Only one question or question prompt at a time is presented on the computer screen.
- The answer choices for the multiple-choice questions will be preceded by radio buttons, rather than by letters.
- Different question types appear in random order in the multiple-choice and Integrated Reasoning sections.
- You must choose an answer and confirm your choice before moving on to the next question.
- You may not go back to previous screens to change answers to previous questions.

Format of the GMAT™ Exam

	Questions	Timing
Analytical Writing Assessment	1	30 min.

Integrated Reasoning
    Multi-Source Reasoning
    Table Analysis
    Graphics Interpretation
    Two-Part Analysis
	12	30 min.

Quantitative Reasoning
    Problem Solving
    Data Sufficiency
	31	62 min.

Verbal Reasoning
    Reading Comprehension
    Critical Reasoning
    Sentence Correction
	36	65 min.

	Total Time:	187 min.

On exam day, immediately prior to the start of the first exam section, you will have the flexibility to select your section order for the GMAT exam from three order combinations.

Order #1	Order #2	Order #3
Analytical Writing Assessment Integrated Reasoning	Verbal Reasoning	Quantitative Reasoning
Optional 8-minute break		
Quantitative Reasoning	Quantitative Reasoning	Verbal Reasoning
Optional 8-minute break		
Verbal Reasoning	Integrated Reasoning Analytical Writing Assessment	Integrated Reasoning Analytical Writing Assessment

1.3 What Will the Test Experience Be Like?

The GMAT exam offers the flexibility to take the exam either online or at a test center—wherever you feel most comfortable. You may feel more comfortable at home with the online delivery format or prefer the structure and environment of a test center. The choice and flexibility is yours. Both delivery options include the exact same content, structure, two optional 8-minute breaks, scores, and score scales, and scores are uniformly accepted by schools worldwide, so you can choose the option that works best for you.

At the Test Center: The GMAT exam is administered under standardized conditions at over 700 test centers worldwide. Each test center has a proctored testing room with individual computer workstations that allow you to take the exam under quiet conditions and with some privacy. You may not take notes or scratch paper with you into the testing room, but an erasable notepad and marker will be provided for you to use during the test. For more information about exam day visit mba.com/gmat.

Online: The GMAT Online exam is a remote proctored experience in the comfort of your home or office. You will need a quiet workspace with a desktop or laptop computer that meets minimum system requirements, a webcam, and a reliable internet connection. During your exam you will be able to use a physical whiteboard with up to two dry-erase markers and an eraser and/or an online whiteboard to work through the exam questions (no scratch paper is allowed). For more information about exam day visit mba.com/gmatonline.

To learn more about accommodations options for the GMAT exam, visit mba.com/accommodations.

1.4 What Is the Content of the GMAT™ Exam Like?

The GMAT exam measures higher-order analytical skills encompassing several types of reasoning. The Analytical Writing Assessment asks you to analyze the reasoning behind an argument and respond in writing; the Integrated Reasoning section asks you to interpret and synthesize information from multiple sources and in different formats to make reasoned conclusions; the Quantitative Reasoning section includes basic arithmetic, algebra, and geometry; and the Verbal Reasoning section asks you to read and comprehend written material and to reason and evaluate arguments.

Test questions may address a variety of subjects, but all the information you need to answer the questions will be included on the exam, with no outside knowledge of the subject matter necessary. The GMAT exam is not a test of business knowledge, English vocabulary, or advanced computational skills. You will need to read and write in English and have basic math and English skills to perform well on the test, but its difficulty comes from analytical and critical thinking abilities.

> ## *Myth* -vs- **FACT**
>
> M – **My success in business school is not predicted by the GMAT exam.**
>
> F – **False. The GMAT exam measures your critical thinking and reasoning skills, the ones used in business school and beyond in your career.**
>
> The exam measures your ability to make inferences, problem-solve, and analyze data. In fact, some employers even use the GMAT exam to determine your skill sets in these areas. If your program does not require the GMAT exam, you can stand out from the crowd with your performance on the exam and show that you have skills that it takes to succeed in business school.

The questions in this book are organized by question type and from easiest to most difficult, but keep in mind that when you take the test, you may see different types of questions in any order within each section.

1.5 Analytical Writing Assessment Section

The GMAT Analytical Writing Assessment (AWA) section consists of one 30-minute writing task: Analysis of an Argument. The AWA measures your ability to think critically, communicate your ideas, and formulate an appropriate and constructive critique. You will type your essay on a computer keyboard.

1.6 Integrated Reasoning Section

The GMAT Integrated Reasoning section highlights the relevant skills that business managers in today's data-driven world need in order to analyze sophisticated streams of data and solve complex problems. It measures your ability to understand and evaluate multiple sources and types of information—graphic, numeric, and verbal—as they relate to one another. This section will require you to use both quantitative and verbal reasoning to solve complex problems and solve multiple problems in relation to one another.

Four types of questions are used in the Integrated Reasoning section:

- Multi-Source Reasoning
- Table Analysis
- Graphics Interpretation
- Two-Part Analysis

Integrated Reasoning questions may require quantitative or verbal reasoning skills, or a combination of both. You will have to interpret graphics and sort tables to extract meaning from data, but advanced statistical knowledge and spreadsheet manipulation skills are not necessary. For both online and test center exams you will have access to an on-screen calculator with basic functions for the Integrated Reasoning section but note that the calculator is ***not*** available on the Quantitative Reasoning section.

1.7 Quantitative Reasoning Section

The GMAT Quantitative Reasoning section measures your ability to solve quantitative problems and interpret graphic data.

Two types of multiple-choice questions are used in the Quantitative Reasoning section:

- Problem Solving
- Data Sufficiency

Both are intermingled throughout the Quantitative Reasoning section, and require basic knowledge of arithmetic, elementary algebra, and commonly known concepts of geometry.

1.8 Verbal Reasoning Section

The GMAT Verbal Reasoning section measures your ability to read and comprehend written material and to reason and evaluate arguments. The Verbal Reasoning section includes reading sections from several different content areas. Although you may be generally familiar with some of the material, neither the reading passages nor the questions assume detailed knowledge of the topics discussed.

Three types of multiple-choice questions are intermingled throughout the Verbal Reasoning section:

- Reading Comprehension
- Critical Reasoning
- Sentence Correction

For test-taking tips specific to each question type in the Verbal Reasoning section, practice questions, and answer explanations, see chapters 4 through 6.

1.9 How Are Scores Calculated?

Verbal Reasoning and Quantitative Reasoning sections are scored on a scale of 6 to 51, in one-point increments. The Total GMAT score ranges from 200 to 800 and is based on your performance in these two sections. Your score is determined by:

- The number of questions you answer
- The number of questions you answer correctly or incorrectly
- The level of difficulty and other statistical characteristics of each question

Your Verbal Reasoning, Quantitative Reasoning, and Total GMAT scores are determined by an algorithm that takes into account the difficulty of the questions that were presented to you and how you answered them. When you answer the easier questions correctly, you get a chance to answer harder questions, making it possible to earn a higher score. After you have completed all the questions on the exam, or when your time is expired, the computer will calculate your scores.

You will receive five scores: Total Score (which is based on your Quantitative Reasoning and Verbal Reasoning scores), Integrated Reasoning Score, and Analytical Writing Assessment Score. The following table summarizes the different types of scores, the scales, and the increments.

Type of Score	Scale	Increments
Total (based on Quantitative Reasoning and Verbal Reasoning)	200–800	10
Quantitative Reasoning	6–51	1
Verbal Reasoning	6–51	1
Integrated Reasoning	1–8	1
Analytical Writing Assessment	0–6	0.5

Your GMAT scores are valid for five years from the date of the exam.

Your GMAT score includes a percentile ranking that compares your skill level with other test-takers from the past three years. The percentile rank of your score shows the percentage of tests taken with scores lower than your score. Every July, percentile ranking tables are updated. Visit mba.com to view the most recent percentile rankings tables.

2.0 How to Prepare

2.0 How to Prepare

2.1 How Should I Prepare to Take the Test?

The GMAT™ exam is designed specifically to measure reasoning skills needed for management education, and the test contains several question formats unique to the GMAT exam. At a minimum, you should be familiar with the test format and the question formats before you sit for the test. Because the GMAT exam is a timed exam, you should practice answering test questions, not only to better understand the question formats and the skills they require, but also to help you learn to pace yourself so you can finish each section when you sit for the exam.

Because the exam measures reasoning rather than subject-matter knowledge, you most likely will not find it helpful to memorize facts. You do not need to study advanced mathematical concepts, but you should be sure your grasp of basic arithmetic, algebra, and geometry is sound enough that you can use these skills in quantitative problem solving. Likewise, you do not need to study advanced vocabulary words, but you should have a firm understanding of basic English vocabulary and grammar for reading, writing, and reasoning.

> ### *Myth* -vs- **FACT**
>
> **M** – **You need very advanced math skills to get a high GMAT score.**
>
> **F** – **The GMAT exam measures your reasoning and critical thinking abilities, rather than your advanced math skills.**
>
> The GMAT exam only requires basic quantitative skills. You should review the math skills (algebra, geometry, basic arithmetic) presented in this guide (chapter 3) and the *GMAT™ Official Guide Quantitative Review 2022*. The difficulty of GMAT Quantitative Reasoning questions stems from the logic and analysis used to solve the problems and not the underlying math skills.

2.2 Getting Ready for Exam Day

Whether you are testing online or in a test center, it is important to know what to expect to have a successful and worry-free testing experience.

Test Center

While checking into a test center be prepared to:

- Present appropriate identification.
- Provide your palm vein scan (where permitted by law).
- Provide your digital signature stating that you understand and agree to the Test-Taker Rules and Agreement.
- Have a digital photograph taken.

For more information visit mba.com/gmat.

Online

Preparing to take your exam online:

- Check your computer—before your exam day, ensure that your computer meets the minimum system requirements to run the exam.

- Prepare your workspace—identify a quiet place to take your exam and prepare your workspace by ensuring it is clean and all objects are removed except for your computer and whiteboard.

- Whiteboard—if you plan to use a physical whiteboard during your exam, make sure your whiteboard fits the approved dimensions, and you have up to two dry-erase markers, and an eraser.

- Plan ahead—you should plan to begin your check-in process 30 minutes before your scheduled exam time.

For more information visit mba.com/gmatonline.

2.3 How to Use the *GMAT™ Official Guide Verbal Review*

The *GMAT™ Official Guide Verbal Review* is designed for those who have completed the Verbal Reasoning questions in the *GMAT™ Official Guide* and are looking for additional practice questions, as well as those who are interested in practicing only Verbal Reasoning questions. Questions in each chapter are organized by difficulty level from easy to hard, so if you are new to studying, we recommend starting at the beginning of each chapter and working your way through the questions sequentially. You may find certain "easy" questions to be hard and some "hard" questions to be easy; this is not unusual and reflects the fact that different people will often have different perceptions of a question's difficulty level.

You may also find questions in the *GMAT™ Official Guide Verbal Review* to be easier or harder than questions you see on the GMAT™ Official Practice Exams and/or the actual GMAT exam. This is expected because, unlike the Official Practice Exams, the *GMAT™ Official Guide Verbal Review* is not computer-adaptive and does not adjust to your ability. If you were to complete all of the questions in this book, you will encounter roughly one-third easy questions, one-third medium questions, and one-third hard questions, whereas on the actual exam, you will not likely see such an even mix of questions across difficulty levels.

To find questions of a specific type and difficulty level (e.g., easy sentence correction questions), use the index of questions in chapter 7. Note that the ratio of questions across different content areas in the *GMAT™ Official Guide Verbal Review* in no way reflects the ratio of questions across different content areas on the actual GMAT exam.

Finally, because the GMAT exam is administered on a computer, we encourage you to practice the questions in the *GMAT™ Official Guide Verbal Review* using the Online Question Bank at gmat.wiley. com. All of the questions in this book are available there, and you'll be able to create practice sets and track your progress more easily. The Online Question Bank can also be accessed on your mobile device through the Wiley Efficient Learning mobile app. To access the Online Question Bank on your mobile device, first create an account at gmat.wiley.com and then sign in to your account on the mobile app.

2.4 How to Use Other GMAT™ Official Prep Products

In addition to the *GMAT™ Official Guide*, we recommend using our other GMAT™ Official Prep products.

- **For those who want a realistic simulation of the GMAT exam:** GMAT™ Official Practice Exams 1–6 are the only practice exams that use questions from past GMAT exams and feature the same scoring algorithm and user interface as the real exam, including the online whiteboard tool that is used in the online version of the GMAT exam. The first two practice exams are free to all test-takers and available at mba.com/exam-prep.

- **For those who want more practice questions:** GMAT™ Official Practice Questions 1 and 2 offer additional questions that are not available in the *GMAT™ Official Guide* series.

- **For those who are looking for additional practice with challenging questions:** *GMAT™ Official Advanced Questions* is a compilation of 300 hard Quantitative Reasoning and Verbal Reasoning questions, similar in difficulty level to hard questions found in the *GMAT™ Official Guide* series.

To maximize your studying efforts:

1. Start by learning about the GMAT exam and the question types in the *GMAT™ Official Guide*.

2. Take GMAT™ Official Practice Exam 1 to become familiar with the exam and get a baseline score. Don't worry about your score on the first practice exam! The goal is to become familiar with the exam and set a baseline for measuring your progress.

3. Go to gmat.wiley.com and practice the questions in the *GMAT™ Official Guide*, focusing on areas that require your attention. As you continue to practice, take additional GMAT™ Official Practice Exams to gauge your progress.

4. Before your actual GMAT exam, take a final Official Practice Exam to simulate the real test-taking experience and see how you score.

Remember: the first two GMAT™ Official Practice Exams are part of the free GMAT™ Official Starter Kit, which includes 90 free practice questions and is available to everyone with a mba.com account. GMAT™ Official Practice Exams 3 to 6, additional GMAT™ Official Practice Questions, and other Official Prep products are available for purchase through mba.com/prep.

2.5 General Test-Taking Suggestions

Specific test-taking strategies for individual question types are presented later in this book. The following are general suggestions to help you perform your best on the test.

1. **Use your time wisely.**

   Although the GMAT exam stresses accuracy more than speed, it is important to use your time wisely. On average, you will have about $1\frac{3}{4}$ minutes for each Verbal Reasoning question, about 2 minutes for each Quantitative Reasoning question, and about $2\frac{1}{2}$ minutes for each Integrated Reasoning question, some of which have multiple questions. Once you start the test, an onscreen clock will show the time you have left. You can hide this display if you want, but it is a good idea to check the clock periodically to monitor your progress. The clock will automatically alert you when 5 minutes remain for the section you are working on.

2. **Determine your preferred section order before the actual exam.**

   The GMAT exam allows you to select the order in which to take the sections. Use the GMAT™ Official Practice Exams as an opportunity to practice and determine your preferred order. Remember: there is no "right" order in which to take the exam; you can practice each order and see which one works best for you.

Myth -vs- FACT

M – **It is more important to respond correctly to the test questions than it is to finish the test.**

F – **There is a significant penalty for not completing the GMAT exam.**

Pacing is important. If you are stumped by a question, give it your best guess and move on. If you guess incorrectly, the computer program will likely give you an easier question, which you are likely to answer correctly, and the computer will rapidly return to giving you questions matched to your ability. If you don't finish the test, your score will be reduced. Failing to answer five verbal questions, for example, could reduce your score from the 91st percentile to the 77th percentile.

3. **Answer practice questions ahead of time.**

After you become generally familiar with all question types, use the practice questions in this book and online at gmat.wiley.com to prepare for the actual test (note that Integrated Reasoning questions are only available online). It may be useful to time yourself as you answer the practice questions to get an idea of how long you will have for each question when you sit for the actual test, as well as to determine whether you are answering quickly enough to finish the test in the allotted time.

4. **Read all test directions carefully.**

The directions explain exactly what is required to answer each question type. If you read hastily, you may miss important instructions and impact your ability to answer correctly. To review directions during the test, click on the Help icon. But be aware that the time you spend reviewing directions will count against your time allotment for that section of the test.

5. **Read each question carefully and thoroughly.**

Before you answer a question, determine exactly what is being asked and then select the best choice. Never skim a question or the possible answers; skimming may cause you to miss important information or nuances.

6. **Do not spend too much time on any one question.**

If you do not know the correct answer, or if the question is too time consuming, try to eliminate answer choices you know are wrong, select the best of the remaining answer choices, and move on to the next question.

Not completing sections and randomly guessing answers to questions at the end of each test section can significantly lower your score. As long as you have worked on each section, you will receive a score even if you do not finish one or more sections in the allotted time. You will not earn points for questions you never get to see.

7. **Confirm your answers ONLY when you are ready to move on.**

On the Quantitative Reasoning and Verbal Reasoning sections, once you have selected your answer to a multiple-choice question, you will be asked to confirm it. Once you confirm your response, you cannot go back and change it. You may not skip questions. In the Integrated Reasoning section, there may be several questions based on information provided in the same question prompt. When there is more than one response on a single screen, you can change your response to any of the questions on the screen before moving on to the next screen. However, you may not navigate back to a previous screen to change any responses.

8. **Plan your essay answer before you begin to write.**

The best way to approach the Analytical Writing Assessment (AWA) section is to read the directions carefully, take a few minutes to think about the question, and plan a response before you begin writing. Take time to organize your ideas and develop them fully but leave time to reread your response and make any revisions that you think would improve it.

This book and other study materials released by the Graduate Management Admission Council (GMAC) are the ONLY source of real questions that have been used on the GMAT exam. All questions that appear or have appeared on the GMAT exam are copyrighted and owned by GMAC, which does not license them to be reprinted elsewhere. Accessing live Integrated Reasoning, Quantitative Reasoning, and/or Verbal Reasoning test questions in advance or sharing test content during or after you take the test is a serious violation, which could cause your scores to be canceled and schools to be notified. In cases of a serious violation, you may be banned from future testing and other legal remedies may be pursued.

Myth -vs- **FACT**

M – **The first 10 questions are critical, and you should invest the most time on those.**

F – **All questions count.**

The computer-adaptive testing algorithm uses each answered question to obtain an *initial* estimate. However, as you continue to answer questions, the algorithm self-corrects by computing an updated estimate on the basis of all the questions you have answered, and then administers questions that are closely matched to this new estimate of your ability. Your final score is based on all your responses and considers the difficulty of all the questions you answered. Taking additional time on the first 10 questions will not game the system and can hurt your ability to finish the test.

3.0   Verbal Review

3.0 Verbal Reasoning

The Verbal Reasoning section of the GMAT™ exam uses multiple-choice questions to measure your skills in reading and comprehending written material, reasoning, evaluating arguments, and correcting written material to conform to standard written English. This section includes content on a variety of topics, but neither the passages nor the questions assume knowledge of the topics discussed. Intermingled throughout the section are three main types of questions: Reading Comprehension, Critical Reasoning, and Sentence Correction.

Reading Comprehension questions are based on passages consisting of generally between 200 to 350 words. Each passage is followed by several questions that require you to understand, analyze, apply, and evaluate information and concepts presented in the passage.

Critical Reasoning questions are based on passages typically less than 100 words in length. Unlike Reading Comprehension passages, each Critical Reasoning passage is associated with just one question. This question requires you to logically analyze, evaluate, or reason about an argument, situation, or plan presented in the passage.

Sentence Correction questions are not based on passages. Instead, each Sentence Correction question presents a single sentence in which words are underlined. This question asks you to replace the underlined section with an answer choice—either the original underlined wording or a substitute for that wording—that makes the sentence as a whole express its intended meaning most correctly and effectively. This task requires you to know and apply the stylistic conventions and grammatical rules of standard written English.

You will have 65 minutes to complete the Verbal Reasoning section, or an average of about $1\frac{3}{4}$ minutes to answer each question. Including the time needed to read the Reading Comprehension passages, the average time you require to answer each Reading Comprehension question will probably be slightly longer than the overall Verbal Reasoning section average. On the other hand, the average time you require to answer a Sentence Correction question will probably be shorter than the Verbal Reasoning section average if you work efficiently and manage your time wisely.

To prepare for the Verbal Reasoning section, you may wish to first review basic concepts of textual analysis and logical reasoning to ensure that you have the foundational skills needed to answer the questions, before moving on to practice applying this knowledge on retired questions from past GMAT exams.

3.1 Verbal Review

To prepare for the Verbal Reasoning section and to succeed in graduate business programs, you will need some basic skills in analyzing and evaluating written texts and the ideas they express. This chapter explains some basic concepts that are useful in developing these skills. Only a high-level summary is provided, so if you find unfamiliar terms or concepts, you should consult other resources for a more detailed discussion and explanation.

The following concepts will help you develop different skills you may require in answering questions in the Verbal Reasoning section of the GMAT exam.

Section 3.2, "Analyzing Passages," includes the following topics:

1. Arguments
2. Explanations
3. Narratives and Descriptions

Section 3.3, "Inductive Reasoning," includes the following topics:

1. Inductive Arguments
2. Generalizations and Predictions
3. Causal Reasoning
4. Analogies

Section 3.4, "Deductive Reasoning," includes the following topics:

1. Deductive Arguments
2. Logical Operators
3. Reasoning with Logical Operators
4. Necessity, Probability, and Possibility
5. Quantifiers
6. Reasoning with Quantifiers

Section 3.5, "Grammar and Style," includes the following topics:

1. Subjects and Objects
2. Number and Person
3. Tense and Mood
4. Modifiers
5. Clauses and Conjunctions
6. Style

3.2 Analyzing Passages

1. Arguments

A. An *argument* presents one or more ideas as reasons to accept one or more other ideas. Often some of these ideas are not explicitly expressed, but are to be implicitly understood.

> *Example:*
> The sidewalk is dry, so it must not have rained last night.
> In this example, the observation that the sidewalk is dry is presented as a reason to agree with the statement that it didn't rain last night. The argument also takes it to be implicitly understood that rain typically leaves sidewalks wet.

B. A *premise* is an idea that an argument explicitly or implicitly presents as a reason to accept another idea. An argument may include any number of premises.

The words and phrases below often immediately precede a stated premise:

after all	*for one thing*	*moreover*
because	*furthermore*	*seeing that*
for	*given that*	*since*
for the reason that	*in light of the fact that*	*whereas*

Example:

Our mayor should not support the proposal to expand the freeway, **because** the benefits of the expansion would not justify the cost. **Furthermore**, most voters oppose the expansion.

This is an example of an argument with two explicit premises. The word *because* introduces the first premise, that the benefits of the expansion would not justify the cost. The word *furthermore* introduces the second premise, that most voters oppose the expansion. Together, these premises argue that the mayor should not support the proposal.

C. A *conclusion* is an idea in support of which an argument presents one or more premises. When there is more than one conclusion in an argument, a *main conclusion* is a conclusion that is not presented to support any further conclusion, whereas an *intermediate conclusion* is a conclusion presented to support a further conclusion.

The words and phrases below often immediately precede a stated conclusion:

clearly	*it follows that*	*suggests that*
entails that	*proves*	*surely*
hence	*shows that*	*therefore*
implies that	*so*	*thus*

Example:

Julia just hiked fifteen kilometers, **so** she must have burned a lot of calories. **Surely** she's hungry now.

This is an example of an argument with a premise, an intermediate conclusion, and a main conclusion. The word *so* introduces the intermediate conclusion, that Julia must have burned a lot of calories. The word *surely* introduces the main conclusion, that Julia is hungry now. The premise that Julia just hiked fifteen kilometers is presented to support the intermediate conclusion, which in turn is presented to support the main conclusion.

In an argument, conclusions may be stated before, between, or after premises. There may be no indicator words to signal which statements are premises and which are conclusions. To identify the premises and conclusions in these cases, consider which statements the author is presenting as reasons to accept which other statements. The reasons presented are the premises, and the statements the author is trying to persuade readers to accept are the conclusions.

Example:

For healthy eating, Healthful Brand Donuts are the best donuts you can buy. Unlike any other donuts on the market, Healthful Brand Donuts contain plenty of fiber and natural nutrients.

In this argument, the author is obviously trying to persuade the reader that Healthful Brand Donuts are the best donuts to buy for healthy eating. Thus, the first sentence is the conclusion. The statement about Healthful Brand Donuts' ingredients is presented as a reason to accept that conclusion, so it is a premise. Since the author's intentions are clear, no indicator words are used.

All the practice questions that appear in this chapter are real questions from past GMAT exams and will test the concepts you have just reviewed. The full answer explanations follow the practice question(s) and outline the reasoning for why each answer choice is correct, or incorrect.

CR63800.03*

Practice Question 1

Thyrian lawmaker: Thyria's Cheese Importation Board inspects all cheese shipments to Thyria and rejects shipments not meeting specified standards. Yet only one percent is ever rejected. Therefore, since the health consequences and associated economic costs of not rejecting that one percent are negligible, whereas the board's operating costs are considerable, for economic reasons alone the board should be disbanded.

Consultant: I disagree. The threat of having their shipments rejected deters many cheese exporters from shipping substandard product.

The consultant responds to the lawmaker's argument by

(A)   rejecting the lawmaker's argument while proposing that the standards according to which the board inspects imported cheese should be raised

(B)   providing evidence that the lawmaker's argument has significantly overestimated the cost of maintaining the board

(C)   objecting to the lawmaker's introducing into the discussion factors that are not strictly economic

(D)   pointing out a benefit of maintaining the board which the lawmaker's argument has failed to consider

(E)   shifting the discussion from the argument at hand to an attack on the integrity of the cheese inspectors

CR32900.03

Practice Question 2

One summer, floods covered low-lying garlic fields situated in a region with a large mosquito population. Since mosquitoes lay their eggs in standing water, flooded fields would normally attract mosquitoes, yet no mosquitoes were found in the fields. Diallyl sulfide, a major component of garlic, is known to repel several species of insects, including mosquitoes, so it is likely that diallyl sulfide from the garlic repelled the mosquitoes.

Which of the following, if true, most strengthens the argument?

(A)   Diallyl sulfide is also found in onions but at concentrations lower than in garlic.

(B)   The mosquito population of the region as a whole was significantly smaller during the year in which the flooding took place than it had been in previous years.

(C)   By the end of the summer, most of the garlic plants in the flooded fields had been killed by waterborne fungi.

(D)   Many insect species not repelled by diallyl sulfide were found in the flooded garlic fields throughout the summer.

(E)   Mosquitoes are known to be susceptible to toxins in plants other than garlic, such as marigolds.

---

*These numbers correlate with the online test bank question number. See the GMAT™ Official Guide Verbal Review Question Index in the back of this book.

CR63800.03

Answer Explanation 1

Argument Construction

Situation   The Thyrian lawmaker argues that the Cheese Importation Board should be disbanded, because its operating costs are high and it rejects only a small percentage of the cheese it inspects. The consultant disagrees, pointing out that the board's inspections deter those who export cheese to Thyria from shipping substandard cheese.

Reasoning   *What strategy does the consultant use in the counterargument?* The consultant indicates to the lawmaker that there is a reason to retain the board that the lawmaker has not considered. The benefit the board provides is not that it identifies a great deal of substandard cheese and rejects it (thus keeping the public healthy), but that the possibility that their cheese could be found substandard is what keeps exporters from attempting to export low-quality cheese to Thyria.

A   The consultant does reject the lawmaker's argument, but the consultant does not propose higher standards. Indeed, in suggesting that the board should be retained, the consultant implies that the board's standards are appropriate.

B   The consultant does not provide any evidence related to the board's cost.

C   The only point the lawmaker raises that is not strictly economic is about the health consequences of disbanding the board, but the consultant does not address this point at all.

D   **Correct.** This statement properly identifies the strategy the consultant employs in his or her counterargument. The consultant points out that the board provides a significant benefit that the lawmaker did not consider.

E   The consultant does not attack the integrity of the cheese inspectors; to the contrary, the consultant says that their inspections deter the cheese exporters from shipping substandard cheese.

The correct answer is D.

CR32900.03

Answer Explanation 2

Argument Evaluation

Situation   When summer floods covered garlic fields in an area with many mosquitoes, no mosquitoes were found in the fields, even though flooded fields would normally attract mosquitoes to lay their eggs in the water. Diallyl sulfide, which is found in garlic, repels mosquitoes and some other insect species, and likely accounts for the lack of mosquitoes in the area.

Reasoning   *Given the facts cited, what would provide additional evidence that diallyl sulfide from the garlic made mosquitoes avoid the flooded fields?* The argument would be strengthened by any independent evidence suggesting that diallyl sulfide pervaded the flooded fields or excluding other factors that might explain the absence of mosquitoes in the fields.

A   This could strengthen the argument if mosquitoes also avoid flooded onion fields, but we do not know whether they do.

B   This would weaken the argument by suggesting that the general mosquito population decline, rather than the diallyl sulfide, could explain the absence of mosquitoes in the fields.

C   It is not clear how this would affect the amount of diallyl sulfide in the flooded fields, so this does not provide evidence that the diallyl sulfide repelled the mosquitoes.

D   **Correct.** This provides evidence that there was no factor other than diallyl sulfide that reduced insect populations in the flooded garlic fields.

E   If anything, this would weaken the argument, since it is at least possible that some of these toxins were present in the flooded fields.

The correct answer is D.

D. A *valid* argument is one whose conclusions follow from its premises. The premises and conclusions need not be true in order for an argument to be valid. An argument with false premises is valid as long as the conclusion *would* follow if the premises *were* true. A *sound* argument is a valid argument with true premises.

Examples:

i) Everyone who tries fried eggplant is guaranteed to love the taste. So if you try it, you'll love the taste too.

In example i), the premise is false if taken literally: in reality, not everyone who tries fried eggplant is guaranteed to love the taste. Thus, example i) is not a sound argument. Nonetheless, it is a valid argument, because if everyone who tried fried eggplant **were** guaranteed to love the taste, it would follow logically that you too would love the taste if *you* tried it.

ii) Some people who try fried eggplant dislike the taste. So if you try it, you'll probably dislike the taste too.

In example ii), the only premise is true: in reality, some people who try fried eggplant dislike the taste. Nonetheless, example ii) is an invalid argument, and thus is not sound. The mere fact that *some* people dislike the taste of fried eggplant doesn't entail that *you personally* will *probably* dislike the taste.

E. An *assumption* is an idea whose truth is taken for granted. An assumption may be a premise in an argument, an idea about a cause or an effect in a causal explanation, or any other type of unsupported idea in a descriptive passage. A conclusion is never an assumption—an argument presents reasons to agree with a conclusion rather than taking its truth for granted.

A passage may also rely on *implicit assumptions* that the author considers too obvious to state explicitly. Although unstated, such assumptions are needed to fill in gaps in the explicit material. An argument or explanation is weak and vulnerable to criticism if it relies on implausible or clearly false assumptions.

F. A *necessary assumption* of an argument is an idea that must be true in order for the argument's stated premises to adequately support one of the argument's conclusions. In other words, a necessary assumption is one that the argument requires in order to work.

Example:

Mario has booked a flight scheduled to arrive at 5:00 p.m.—which should allow him to get here around 6:30 p.m. So, by 7:00 p.m. we will be going out to dinner with Mario.

In this argument, one necessary assumption is that the plane Mario is booked on will arrive not significantly later than the scheduled time. A second necessary assumption is that Mario managed to catch his flight. Unless these and all of the argument's other necessary assumptions are true, the argument's stated premises would not adequately support the conclusion.

CR49110.03

Practice Question 3

The spacing of the four holes on a fragment of a bone flute excavated at a Neanderthal campsite is just what is required to play the third through sixth notes of the diatonic scale—the seven-note musical scale used in much of Western music since the Renaissance. Musicologists therefore hypothesize that the diatonic musical scale was developed and used thousands of years before it was adopted by Western musicians.

Which of the following, if true, most strongly supports the hypothesis?

(A)   Bone flutes were probably the only musical instrument made by Neanderthals.

(B)   No musical instrument that is known to have used a diatonic scale is of an earlier date than the flute found at the Neanderthal campsite.

(C)   The flute was made from a cave-bear bone and the campsite at which the flute fragment was excavated was in a cave that also contained skeletal remains of cave bears.

(D)   Flutes are the simplest wind instrument that can be constructed to allow playing a diatonic scale.

(E)   The cave-bear leg bone used to make the Neanderthal flute would have been long enough to make a flute capable of playing a complete diatonic scale.

CR49110.03

Answer Explanation 3

Argument Evaluation

Situation   The arrangement of the holes in a bone fragment from a Neanderthal campsite matches part of the scale used in Western music since the Renaissance. Musicologists hypothesize from this that the scale was developed thousands of years before Western musicians adopted it.

Reasoning   *Which of the options, if true, would provide the most support for the musicologists' hypothesis?* One way to approach this question is to ask yourself, "If this option were false, would the hypothesis be *less* likely to be true?" If the Neanderthal bone fragment could *not* have been part of a flute that encompassed *the entire* seven-note diatonic scale, then the bone fragment's existence would not provide strong support for the hypothesis.

A   To the extent that this is even relevant, it tends to weaken the hypothesis; it makes less likely the possibility that Neanderthals used other types of musical instruments employing the diatonic scale.

B   This also weakens the hypothesis because it states that there is no known evidence of a certain type that would support the hypothesis.

C   The fact that the cave-bear bone fragment that was apparently a flute came from a site where many other cave-bear skeletal remains were found has little bearing on the hypothesis, and in no way supports it.

D   This does not strengthen the hypothesis, for even if the option were false—even if a simpler instrument could be constructed that employed the diatonic scale—the existence of a flute employing the diatonic scale would provide no less support for the hypothesis.

E   **Correct.** This option most strongly supports the hypothesis.

The correct answer is E.

G. A *sufficient assumption* of an argument is an idea whose truth would ensure that the argument's main conclusion follows from the argument's stated premises.

> *Example:*
> The study of poetry is entirely without value, since poetry has no practical use.
>
> For this argument, one sufficient assumption would be that the study of what has no practical use is entirely without value. This assumption, together with the argument's stated premise, would sufficiently support the conclusion: if both the premise and the assumption are true, then the conclusion must also be true. Another sufficient assumption would be that the study of literature with no practical use is entirely without value, and poetry is a type of literature. Although these two distinct assumptions are each sufficient, neither one is necessary.

H. Arguments fall into several broad categories determined by the types of conclusions they support.

   i. A *prescriptive* argument supports a conclusion about what should or should not be done. Prescriptive arguments advocate adopting or rejecting policies, procedures, strategies, goals, laws, or ethical norms.

> *Example:*
> Our company's current staff is too small to handle our upcoming project. So, to ensure the project's success, the company should hire more employees.
>
> Another prescriptive argument can be found in the example in 3.2.1.B above, which concludes that the mayor should not support the proposed freeway expansion.

   ii. An *evaluative* argument supports a conclusion that something is good or bad, desirable or undesirable, without advocating any particular policy or course of action.

> *Example:*
> This early novel is clearly one of the greatest of all time. Not only did it pioneer brilliantly innovative narrative techniques, but it did so with exceptional grace, subtlety, and sophistication.

   iii. An *interpretive* argument supports a conclusion about the underlying significance of something. An interpretive argument may support or oppose an account of the meaning, importance, or implications of a set of observations, a theory, an artistic or literary work, or a historical event.

> *Example:*
> Many famous authors have commented emphatically on this early novel, either praising or condemning it. This suggests that the novel has had an enormous influence on later fiction.

iv. A *causal* argument supports a conclusion that one or more phenomena did or did not causally contribute to one or more effects. A causal argument may support or oppose an account of the causes, reasons, or motivations underlying an event, condition, decision, or outcome. For example, a causal argument may support or oppose an account of the influences underlying a literary or artistic style or movement.

> *Example:*
> Our houseplant started to thrive only when we moved it to a sunny window. So probably the reason it was sickly before then was that it wasn't getting enough sunlight.
>
> Another causal argument can be found in the example in 3.2.1.C above, which concludes that Julia must be hungry now.

v. A basic *factual* argument supports a factual conclusion that does not fit into any of the other categories explained above.

> *Example:*
> All dogs are mammals. Rover is a dog. Therefore, Rover is a mammal.

CR96370.03

Practice Question 4

The tulu, a popular ornamental plant, does not reproduce naturally, and is only bred and sold by specialized horticultural companies. Unfortunately, the tulu is easily devastated by a contagious fungal rot. The government ministry plans to reassure worried gardeners by requiring all tulu plants to be tested for fungal rot before being sold. However, infected plants less than 30 weeks old have generally not built up enough fungal rot in their systems to be detected reliably. And many tulu plants are sold before they are 24 weeks old.

Which of the following, if performed by the government ministry, could logically be expected to overcome the problem with their plan to test for the fungal rot?

(A) Releasing a general announcement that tulu plants less than 30 weeks old cannot be effectively tested for fungal rot

(B) Requiring all tulu plants less than 30 weeks old to be labeled as such

(C) Researching possible ways to test tulu plants less than 24 weeks old for fungal rot

(D) Ensuring that tulu plants are not sold before they are 30 weeks old

(E) Quarantining all tulu plants from horticultural companies at which any case of fungal rot has been detected until those tulu plants can be tested for fungal rot

CR96370.03

Answer Explanation 4

Evaluation of a Plan

Situation   There is a contagious fungal rot that devastates the tulu, a popular ornamental plant. To reassure worried gardeners, the government ministry plans to require that tulu plants be tested for the rot before being sold. However, many tulu plants are sold before they are 24 weeks old, yet fungal rot in plants less than 30 weeks old generally cannot be detected reliably.

Reasoning *What could the government ministry do to overcome the problem?* The problem arises from the fact that tulu plants are frequently sold before they are 24 weeks old, which is too soon for any fungal rot that is present to have built up enough in their root systems to be detected. Since the goal of the testing is to ensure that infected tulu plants are not sold, an obvious solution would be to make sure that no plants are sold before they are old enough for fungal rot to have built up to a detectable level. Thus, tulu plants should not be sold before they are 30 weeks old.

A   Releasing such an announcement would help overcome the problem if it guaranteed that no one would buy or sell tulu plants before the plants were 30 weeks old, but it is far from certain that it would guarantee this.

B   Similar to A, introducing such labeling would help overcome the problem if it guaranteed that no one would buy or sell tulu plants before the plants were 30 weeks old, but it is far from certain that it would guarantee this.

C   There is no guarantee that such research will be successful at reducing the age at which tulu plants can be reliably tested.

D   **Correct.** If the government *ensures* that no tulu plants less than 30 weeks of age are sold, then the specific problem mentioned in the passage would be overcome.

E   This will not help overcome the problem. Such a quarantine program might lead horticultural companies to start selling tulu plants *only* if they are less than 24 weeks old, thereby minimizing the chance of quarantine by minimizing the chance of detection.

The correct answer is D.

2. Explanations

A. A *causal explanation* asserts that one or more factors do or may causally contribute to one or more effects. A causal explanation is not necessarily an argument, and doesn't have to include any premises or conclusions. However, a causal explanation may be a premise or conclusion in an argument.

The words and phrases below often indicate a causal explanation:

as a result	due to	results in
because	leads to	that's why
causes	produces	thereby
contributes to	responsible for	thus

Note that some of these words can also be used to indicate premises or conclusions in arguments. In such cases you may need to determine whether the author is presenting reasons to accept a conclusion or is simply stating that one or more factors causally contribute to one or more effects. If the author is simply explaining what caused an effect, and is not trying to persuade the reader that the effect is real, then the passage is a causal explanation but not an argument.

Just as an argument may include premises, intermediate conclusions, and main conclusions, a causal explanation may assert that one or more causes produced one or more intermediate effects that in turn produced further effects.

Example:

Julia just hiked fifteen kilometers, **thereby** burning a lot of calories. **That's why** she's hungry now.

This is an example of a causal explanation asserting that a causal factor (Julia's fifteen-kilometer hike) produced an intermediate effect (Julia burning a lot of calories) that in turn produced a further effect (Julia being hungry now). The word *thereby* introduces the intermediate effect, and the phrase *that's why* introduces the final effect. This explanation assumes that you already know that Julia is hungry now; it does not present reasons to believe she is hungry, but rather explains why she is hungry, and therefore is not an argument.

CR03570.03

Practice Question 5

While many people think of genetic manipulation of food crops as being aimed at developing larger and larger plant varieties, some plant breeders have in fact concentrated on discovering or producing dwarf varieties, which are roughly half as tall as normal varieties.

Which of the following would, if true, most help to explain the strategy of the plant breeders referred to above?

(A) Plant varieties used as food by some are used as ornamentals by others.

(B) The wholesale prices of a given crop decrease as the supply of it increases.

(C) Crops once produced exclusively for human consumption are often now used for animal feed.

(D) Short plants are less vulnerable to strong wind and heavy rains.

(E) Nations with large industrial sectors tend to consume more processed grains.

CR03570.03

Answer Explanation 5

Evaluation of a Plan

Situation   Some plant breeders have concentrated on discovering or producing certain species of food crop plants to be roughly half as tall as normal varieties.

Reasoning   *Why would some plant breeders concentrate on discovering or producing smaller varieties of certain food crops?* Presumably these breeders would not seek smaller varieties of plant crops unless the smaller size conveyed some benefit. If short plants were less vulnerable to strong wind and heavy rains, they would be apt to be more productive, other things being equal. Plant breeders would have reason to try to discover or produce such more productive varieties.

A   This statement doesn't indicate whether those who use the plants as ornamentals desire shorter varieties.

B   At most this suggests that higher productivity is not as much of an advantage as it otherwise would be. But there is nothing in the passage that indicates that smaller varieties would be more productive than normal-sized plants.

C   No reason is given for thinking that smaller varieties of plants are more conducive to use for animal feed than are larger varieties.

D   Correct. This answer choice is correct because—unlike the other choices—it helps explain why smaller plant varieties could sometimes be preferable to larger varieties. A plant that is less vulnerable to wind and rain is apt to suffer less damage. This is a clear advantage that would motivate plant breeders to try to discover or produce smaller varieties.

E   This has no direct bearing on the question posed. Processed grains are not even mentioned in the passage, let alone linked to smaller plant varieties.

The correct answer is D.

B. An *observation* is a claim that some state of affairs has been observed or is otherwise directly known. In the example of a causal explanation above, the statements that Julia just hiked fifteen kilometers and that she is hungry now are observations. Assuming that her burning of calories is not directly known or observed, the statement that she burned a lot of calories is not an observation.

C. A *hypothesis* is a tentative factual idea whose truth is not known and not taken for granted. A hypothesis may serve as an argument's conclusion. Causal explanations are often hypotheses. A passage may discuss ***alternative hypotheses***, such as competing causal explanations for the same observation. In some cases, a passage may present pros and cons of two or more alternative hypotheses without arguing for any one of them as a conclusion.

Example:
A bush in our yard just died. The invasive insects we've seen around the yard lately might be responsible. Or the bush might not have gotten enough water. It's been a dry summer.

In this example, two alternative hypotheses are considered. The first hypothesis presents the observation that invasive insects have been in the yard as a possible causal explanation for the observed death of the bush. This hypothesis would require an implicit assumption that these insects are capable of injuring bushes of the species in question. The second hypothesis presents the observation that it's been a dry summer as an alternative causal explanation for the observed death of the bush. This hypothesis would require the assumption that the dry weather resulted in the bush not getting enough water. The passage presents observations in tentative support of each hypothesis but does not decisively argue for either of them as a conclusion.

This passage refers to Questions 6–9.

Line   Biologists have advanced two theories to explain why schooling of fish occurs in so many fish species. Because schooling is particularly widespread among species of small fish, both theories assume that schooling offers the advantage of some protection from predators.

(5)   Proponents of theory A dispute the assumption that a school of thousands of fish is highly visible. Experiments have shown that any fish can be seen, even in very clear water, only within a sphere of 200 meters in diameter. When fish are in a compact group, the spheres of visibility overlap. Thus the chance of a predator finding the school is only slightly greater than the chance of the predator finding a single fish swimming alone. Schooling is advantageous to the individual fish because a predator's chance of finding any particular fish swimming in the school is much smaller than its chance of finding at least one of the same group of fish if the fish were dispersed
(10)   throughout an area.

However, critics of theory A point out that some fish form schools even in areas where predators are abundant and thus little possibility of escaping detection exists. They argue that the school continues to be of value to its members even after detection. They advocate theory B, the "confusion effect," which can be explained in two different ways.

(15)   Sometimes, proponents argue, predators simply cannot decide which fish to attack. This indecision supposedly results from a predator's preference for striking prey that is distinct from the rest of the school in appearance. In many schools the fish are almost identical in appearance, making it difficult for a predator to select one. The second explanation for the "confusion effect" has to do with the sensory confusion caused by a large number of prey moving around the predator. Even if the predator makes the decision to attack a particular fish, the
(20)   movement of other prey in the school can be distracting. The predator's difficulty can be compared to that of a tennis player trying to hit a tennis ball when two are approaching simultaneously.

Questions 6–9 refer to the passage.

RC73100-01.03

Practice Question 6

According to the passage, theory B states that which of the following is a factor that enables a schooling fish to escape predators?

- (A)   The tendency of fish to form compact groups
- (B)   The movement of other fish within the school
- (C)   The inability of predators to detect schools
- (D)   The ability of fish to hide behind one another in a school
- (E)   The great speed with which a school can disperse

RC73100-03.03

Practice Question 7

According to the passage, both theory A and theory B have been developed to explain how

- (A)   fish hide from predators by forming schools
- (B)   forming schools functions to protect fish from predators
- (C)   schooling among fish differs from other protective behaviors
- (D)   small fish are able to make rapid decisions
- (E)   small fish are able to survive in an environment densely populated by large predators

RC73100-05.03

Practice Question 8

According to one explanation of the "confusion effect," a fish that swims in a school will have greater advantages for survival if it

- (A)   tends to be visible for no more than 200 meters
- (B)   stays near either the front or the rear of a school
- (C)   is part of a small school rather than a large school
- (D)   is very similar in appearance to the other fish in the school
- (E)   is medium-sized

RC73100-06.03

Practice Question 9

The author is primarily concerned with

- (A)   discussing different theories
- (B)   analyzing different techniques
- (C)   defending two hypotheses
- (D)   refuting established beliefs
- (E)   revealing new evidence

RC73100-01.03

Answer Explanation 6

According to the passage, theory B states that which of the following is a factor that enables a schooling fish to escape predators?

- (A)   The tendency of fish to form compact groups
- (B)   The movement of other fish within the school
- (C)   The inability of predators to detect schools
- (D)   The ability of fish to hide behind one another in a school
- (E)   The great speed with which a school can disperse

Supporting Idea

This question depends on understanding what the passage states about theory B, the "confusion effect." One element of theory B is that predators may experience sensory confusion created by large numbers of moving fish in a school.

A   The compactness of groups of schooling fish is an element of theory A, not theory B.

B   Correct. It is the movement of schooling fish around a predator that creates sensory confusion in the predator; this movement may distract the predator and help to protect individual fish in the school.

C   According to the passage's description of theory A, predators are actually slightly more likely to detect schools than they are to detect individual fish.

D   Theory B does not involve fish hiding behind one another, but rather moving around the predator.

E   The passage does not discuss the speed of dispersal of schools of fish.

The correct answer is B.

RC73100-03.03

Answer Explanation 7

According to the passage, both theory A and theory B have been developed to explain how

(A)   fish hide from predators by forming schools

(B)   forming schools functions to protect fish from predators

(C)   schooling among fish differs from other protective behaviors

(D)   small fish are able to make rapid decisions

(E)   small fish are able to survive in an environment densely populated by large predators

Supporting Idea

The passage states in its first paragraph that two theories were developed to explain why schooling occurs in so many fish species and that they both assume that schooling helps protect fish from predators.

A   While theory A involves an explanation of how schooling makes an individual fish less likely to be found by predators, theory B explains how schooling protects fish even when they are detected by predators.

B   Correct. Both theory A and theory B begin with the assumption that schooling provides protection from predators, and each theory offers a different explanation for how that protection occurs.

C   The passage does not discuss protective behaviors other than schooling.

D   The decision-making ability of predators, not schooling fish, is discussed in the passage; schooling is presented as an instinctive behavior.

E   The passage suggests that only theory B helps explain schooling behavior in environments where many predators, large or otherwise, are found, and that theory A explains schooling in areas where predators are not as abundant.

The correct answer is B.

RC73100-05.03

Answer Explanation 8

According to one explanation of the "confusion effect," a fish that swims in a school will have greater advantages for survival if it

- (A) tends to be visible for no more than 200 meters
- (B) stays near either the front or the rear of a school
- (C) is part of a small school rather than a large school
- (D) is very similar in appearance to the other fish in the school
- (E) is medium-sized

Inference

The "confusion effect" is discussed in the third and fourth paragraphs. The first explanation of the "confusion effect" proposes that because predators prefer to select distinctive prey, they find it difficult to select one fish from among many that look the same.

A   The 200-meter visibility of fish is part of the explanation for theory A, not theory B (the "confusion effect").

B   The location of an individual fish within a school is not discussed in the passage as being important to the "confusion effect."

C   The size of a school of fish is not discussed as an element of the "confusion effect."

D   Correct. Because predators, according to the "confusion effect," prefer to select prey that is distinct from the rest of the school, a fish that is similar in appearance to the other fish in its school would most likely enjoy a survival advantage.

E   The size of a fish relative to the other fish in its school would most likely contribute to its ability to survive: that is, if it resembled other fish in size, it would be safer, based on what the passage says about the "confusion effect." Furthermore, the passage gives no reason to think that merely being medium-sized would confer any advantage (unless the other fish were medium-sized as well).

The correct answer is D.

RC73100-06.03

Answer Explanation 9

The author is primarily concerned with

- (A) discussing different theories
- (B) analyzing different techniques
- (C) defending two hypotheses
- (D) refuting established beliefs
- (E) revealing new evidence

Main Idea

Determining the author's primary concern depends on understanding the focus of the passage as a whole. The author presents two theories that purport to account for why fish, particularly small fish, tend to school, and explains the arguments of proponents of each theory.

A   **Correct.** The author discusses two theories—identified as theory A and theory B—that account for the tendency of fish to school.

B   The author is not concerned with different techniques in the passage.

C   The two theories of why fish school could be referred to as hypotheses, but the author is not primarily concerned with defending them; rather, the passage explains how each attempts to account for the phenomenon in question.

D   The author presents, rather than refutes, beliefs about why fish tend to school.

E   The author reveals no evidence, new or otherwise, in the passage. The passage is a general discussion of scientific opinions based on existing evidence.

The correct answer is A.

3. Narratives and Descriptions

A. A *narrative* describes a chronological sequence of related events. A narrative is not in itself an argument or a causal explanation, but may contain one or more arguments or causal explanations, or be contained within them.

The words and phrases below often indicate narrative sequence:

after	*earlier*	*then*
afterwards	*later*	*thereafter*
before	*previously*	*until*
beforehand	*since*	*while*
during	*subsequently*	*when*

Example:
While Julia was hiking fifteen kilometers, she burned a lot of calories. **Afterwards**, she felt hungry.

This is an example of a narrative describing a chronological sequence of three events. The word *while* indicates that Julia's hike and her burning of calories happened at the same time. The word *afterwards* indicates that her hunger arose soon after the first two events. Although it is reasonable to assume that these events were causally related, the narrative doesn't actually say that they were. Thus, it is not an explicit causal explanation. And since the narrative simply reports the events without presenting any premises as reasons to accept any particular conclusion, it is not an argument either.

B. Not all passages are arguments, causal explanations, or narratives. Passages may also report on views, findings, innovations, places, societies, artistic works, devices, organisms, etc. without arguing for any conclusion, explaining any causal relationships, or narrating how any sequence of events unfolded over time.

C. Similarly, not all statements in a passage serve as premises, conclusions, observations to be explained, hypotheses, or reports of events. Some other roles that statements may play in passages include:

- Providing background information to help the reader understand the substance of the passage
- Describing details of something the passage is discussing
- Expressing the author's attitude toward material presented in the passage
- Providing examples to illustrate and clarify general statements
- Summarizing ideas that the passage is arguing against

3.3 Inductive Reasoning

1. Inductive Arguments

A. In an ***inductive argument,*** the premises are intended to support a conclusion but not to absolutely prove it. For example, the premises may provide evidence suggesting that the conclusion is likely to be true, without ruling out the possibility that the conclusion might nonetheless be false despite the evidence provided.

B. An inductive argument may be ***strengthened*** by providing further evidence or other reasons that directly support the argument's conclusion, or that make the argument's premises more compelling as reasons to accept its conclusion. Conversely, an inductive argument may be ***weakened*** or undermined by providing evidence or reasons that directly cast doubt on the argument's conclusion, or that make the argument's premises less compelling as reasons to accept the conclusion. Below we will consider examples of how various types of inductive arguments may be evaluated, strengthened, and weakened.

2. Generalizations and Predictions

A. An argument by ***generalization*** typically involves using one or more premises about a sample or subset of a population to support a conclusion about that population as a whole.

Example:

Of the eight apartments currently available for lease in this building, six are studio apartments. So probably about $\frac{3}{4}$ of all the apartments in the building are studio apartments.

In this example, the apartments currently available for lease in the building are a ***sample*** of the ***population*** of all the apartments in the building. Since six of the eight apartments currently available for lease are studio apartments, $\frac{3}{4}$ of the apartments in the sample are studio apartments.

This observation is used to argue by generalization that the population as a whole is probably similar to the sample; in other words, that probably about $\frac{3}{4}$ of all the apartments in the building are studio apartments.

B. A related type of argument by generalization uses premises about an entire population to support a conclusion about a subset of that population.

Example:

About $\frac{3}{4}$ of all the apartments in the building are studio apartments. So probably about $\frac{3}{4}$ of the apartments on the building's second floor are studio apartments.

In this example, a premise about the proportion of studio apartments among the entire population (all the apartments in the building) is used to support the conclusion that a similar proportion holds among a subset of the population (the apartments only on the second floor).

C. A *predictive* argument by generalization uses a premise about the sample of a population observed so far to support a conclusion about another sample of the population that has not yet been observed.

Example:

Of the eight apartments I have visited in this building so far, six have been studio apartments. So probably about six out of the next eight apartments I visit in the building will also be studio apartments.

In this example, the apartments the author has visited in the building are a sample consisting of only the apartments observed so far. The observation about the proportion of studio apartments in this sample is used to support a prediction that roughly the same proportion of studio apartments will be found among another sample, which consists of the next eight apartments in the building to be visited.

CR51800.03

Practice Question 10

In the United States, of the people who moved from one state to another when they retired, the percentage who retired to Florida has decreased by three percentage points over the past 10 years. Since many local businesses in Florida cater to retirees, these declines are likely to have a noticeably negative economic effect on these businesses and therefore on the economy of Florida.

Which of the following, if true, most seriously weakens the argument given?

(A) People who moved from one state to another when they retired moved a greater distance, on average, last year than such people did ten years ago.

(B) People were more likely to retire to North Carolina from another state last year than people were ten years ago.

(C) The number of people who moved from one state to another when they retired has increased significantly over the past ten years.

(D) The number of people who left Florida when they retired to live in another state was greater last year than it was ten years ago.

(E) Florida attracts more people who move from one state to another when they retire than does any other state.

CR51800.03

Answer Explanation 10

Argument Evaluation

Situation   Of those people who move to another state when they retire, the percentage moving to Florida has declined. This trend is apt to harm Florida's economy because many businesses there cater to retirees.

Reasoning   *Which of the options most weakens the argument?* The argument draws its conclusion from data about the *proportion* of emigrating retirees moving to Florida. Yet what matters more directly to the conclusion (and to Florida's economy) is the *absolute number* of retirees immigrating to Florida. That number could have remained constant, or even risen, if the absolute number of emigrating retirees itself increased while the proportion going to Florida decreased.

A   This has no obvious bearing on the argument one way or another. It makes it more likely, perhaps, that a person in a distant state will retire to Florida, but less likely that one in a neighboring state will do so.

B   This has no bearing on whether fewer people have been retiring to Florida over the last ten years.

C   Correct. This is the option that most seriously weakens the argument.

D   This makes it *more* likely that Florida's economy will be harmed because of decreasing numbers of retirees, but has no real bearing on the argument which concludes specifically that *declines in the proportion of emigrating retirees moving to Florida* will have a negative effect on the state's economy.

E   This is irrelevant. At issue is how the numbers of retirees in Florida from one year compare to the next, not how those numbers compare with numbers of retirees in other states.

The correct answer is C.

D. The strength of an argument by generalization depends largely on how similar the observed sample is to the overall population, or to the unobserved sample about which a prediction is made. If the sample is selected in a way that is likely to make it differ from the overall population in relevant respects, the argument is flawed in that it relies on a ***biased sample***.

> *Example:*
> In a telephone survey of our city's residents, about four out of every five respondents stated that they usually answer the phone when it rings. So probably about four out of every five residents of our city usually answer the phone when it rings.
>
> In this example, the sample consists of respondents to the telephone survey. People who usually answer the phone when it rings are more likely to respond to telephone surveys than are people who usually don't answer the phone. The way the sample was selected (via a telephone survey) makes it likely that a much greater proportion of respondents in the sample than of all the city's residents usually answer the phone when it rings. Therefore, the argument is flawed in that the sample is biased.

E. The strength of an argument generalizing from a sample also depends in part on how large the sample is. The larger the sample, the stronger the argument. This is partly because a smaller sample is statistically more likely to differ greatly from the broader population in its members' characteristics. An argument by generalization that relies on too small a sample to adequately justify the conclusion involves a ***hasty generalization***.

Example:
A coin came up heads five of the eight times Beth flipped it. This suggests that the coin she flipped is weighted so that it tends to come up heads more frequently than tails.

In this example, the sample consists of eight flips of the coin, and the population consists of all potential flips of the same coin. The sample is not clearly biased, because Beth's flips of the coin would not clearly be more likely to come up heads or tails than anyone else's flips of the same coin would. However, the sample is far too small to adequately justify the conclusion that the coin is weighted to favor heads. A coin flipped eight times is quite likely to come up heads more or fewer than exactly four times simply by chance, even if it is not weighted to favor one side. Therefore, this argument is flawed in that it involves a hasty generalization. If Beth and other people flipped the coin thousands or millions of times, and still observed that it comes up heads five out of every eight times, the argument would be stronger. No matter how many times the coin had been flipped to confirm this observed pattern, there would still remain at least some possibility that the coin was not weighted to favor heads and that the results had occurred purely by chance.

F. An argument by generalization is weaker when its conclusion is more precise, and stronger when its conclusion is vaguer, given the same premises. This is because a sample is unlikely to precisely match the population it's drawn from. A conclusion that allows for a broader range of potential mismatches between sample and population is more likely to be true, given the same evidence. An argument whose conclusion is too precise to be justified by the evidence presented is flawed in that it involves the ***fallacy of specificity***.

Example:
Biologists carefully caught, weighed, and released fifty frogs out of the hundreds in a local lake. These fifty frogs weighed an average of 32.86 grams apiece. Therefore, the frogs in the lake must also weigh an average of 32.86 grams apiece.

In this example, it is quite possible that the sample is biased, because frogs of certain types might have been easier for the biologists to catch. But even if we assume that the biologists avoided any sampling bias, it would be statistically unlikely that the average weight of the sampled frogs so precisely matched the average weight of all the frogs in the lake. Thus, the conclusion is unjustifiably precise, and the argument suffers from the fallacy of specificity. A much stronger argument might use the same evidence to support the conclusion that the frogs in the lake have an average weight of between 25 and 40 grams apiece. Since that conclusion would still be true even given a range of potential mismatches between the sample and the population, it is better justified by the same evidence.

3. Causal Reasoning

A. In causal arguments, premises about presumed causal relationships or correlations between phenomena are presented to support conclusions about causes and effects. Causal reasoning is intrinsically challenging, because causal relationships can't be directly observed, and there is no scientific or philosophical consensus about the nature of causality. To say that one phenomenon causally contributes to another generally implies that if the former phenomenon appears, the latter is more likely to subsequently appear. It also implies that the presence of the former phenomenon is part of a reasonable explanation for the appearance of the latter.

Example:
Bushes of the species in our yard tend to die after several weeks without water. Therefore, they must require water at least every few weeks to survive.

In this example, the premise is the observation that when one phenomenon appears (the bushes receive no water for several weeks), another phenomenon is more likely to subsequently occur (the bushes die). The conclusion is effectively that a period of several weeks without water causes bushes of that species to die.

B. A causal argument may also rely on a generally observed correlation as support for the conclusion that a particular instance of one phenomenon caused a particular instance of another.

Example:
A bush in our yard just died. There's been no rain this summer, and no one has been watering the yard. Bushes of the species in our yard tend to die after several weeks without water. Therefore, the bush probably died because it didn't get enough water.

In this example, a particular instance of one phenomenon (one bush of a specific species dying) is observed to follow a particular instance of another phenomenon (the bush went without any water for weeks). A generalization is then presented that instances of the former phenomenon (bushes of that species dying) generally tend to follow instances of the latter (bushes of that species not getting any water for weeks). These premises together support the conclusion that the lack of water caused the observed death of the particular bush in question.

C. Causal arguments may be weakened by observing other correlations that suggest alternative causal explanations that could be used in competing arguments. In order to evaluate the relative strengths of two alternative explanations, it is often helpful to find or experimentally create conditions in which one possible cause is present and the other is absent.

Example:

Causal Argument 1: Bushes of the species in our yard tend to die after several weeks without water. Therefore, they must require water at least every few weeks to survive.

Causal Argument 2: Bushes of this species grow only in a region in which dry weather always coincides with extreme heat. So the heat may be the main reason why these bushes tend to die after periods without water.

Experiment 1: Ensure some of the bushes receive water regularly during a period of extreme heat, and see how well they survive.

Experiment 2: Keep some of the bushes dry during cooler weather, and see how well they survive.

A finding that the bushes survive well in Experiment 1 but not in Experiment 2 would strengthen Argument 1 and weaken Argument 2.

Conversely, a finding that the bushes survive well in Experiment 2 but not in Experiment 1 would strengthen Argument 2 and weaken Argument 1.

A finding that the bushes consistently die in both experiments would strengthen both arguments, suggesting that either heat or drought alone will kill the bushes.

A finding that the bushes survive well in both experiments would weaken both arguments, suggesting that some factor other than drought or heat may be partially or entirely responsible for killing the bushes, or alternatively that both drought and heat must occur together in order to kill the bushes.

D. In setting up experiments to test causal hypotheses, it is important to avoid experimental conditions that might introduce or eliminate other potential causes that have not been considered.

Examples:

i) To run Experiment 1 mentioned above, a scientist planted some of the bushes in a tropical rainforest in which daily rainfall and extreme heat typically occur together.

ii) To run Experiment 2 mentioned above, a scientist planted some of the bushes under an awning where rain could not reach them in cooler weather.

Both versions of the two experiments are problematic because they introduce other causal variables. In example i), different soil conditions, insect populations, and humidity levels in the rainforest might make it harder or easier for the bushes to survive, independently of the heat and rainfall. In example ii), putting the bushes under an awning would likely reduce their exposure to sunlight, which might make it harder or easier for the bushes to survive regardless of the heat and rainfall. These flaws in experimental design would cast doubt on any argument that cited these versions of the experiments as evidence to strengthen or weaken Causal Argument 1 or Causal Argument 2.

Also note that testing a causal hypothesis through experimentation typically involves reasoning by generalization: a conclusion about a broad population is based on observations of the population sample in the experiment. Thus, causal reasoning based on experimentation is vulnerable to the same flaws previously discussed in 3.3.2 Generalizations and Predictions. A causal argument will be weak if it generalizes from a sample that is too small or selected in a biased way. Under these conditions, an apparent correlation is likely to arise merely by coincidence or due to extraneous factors, without indicating a real causal relationship.

E. Even when some kind of causal association between two phenomena clearly exists, it may be difficult to determine which phenomenon is the cause and which is the effect, or whether both phenomena are caused by a third, underlying phenomenon.

Example:
A certain type of earthworm is far more frequently found in the soil under healthy bushes of the species in our yard than in the soil under sickly bushes of that species.

Even if the earthworms' presence is clearly causally associated with the bushes' health, the causal relationship could be that:

i) the earthworms improve the bushes' health, or

ii) healthier bushes attract the earthworms, or

iii) particular soil conditions both improve the bushes' health and attract the earthworms.

More than one of these causal relationships, and others, may be true at the same time. To untangle the causal relationships, it would be helpful to conduct experiments or field observations to evaluate how healthy the bushes are in the same soil conditions without earthworms; how attracted the earthworms are to those soil conditions without the bushes; and whether the earthworms tend to appear around healthier bushes even in much different soil conditions.

F. Even reliable, consistent correlations between two phenomena may arise by sheer coincidence. To determine whether this is the case, it is helpful to test whether stopping one of the phenomena from occurring also results in the other ceasing to occur. Even when no such test is possible, it is also helpful to consider whether or not there is any plausible, specific way that one of the phenomena could cause the other.

Example:

For years, Juan has arrived at work at a hair salon every weekday at exactly 8 a.m. Five hundred miles to the north, over the same period, Ashley has arrived at work at a car dealership every weekday at exactly 8:01 a.m. Therefore, Juan's daily arrival time must causally determine when Ashley arrives at work.

In this example, even though for years Juan's arrival at work has been very consistently and reliably followed by Ashley's a moment later, the argument is absurdly weak because there does not seem to be any obvious way that Juan's arrival time could causally determine Ashley's arrival time. Nonetheless, it would be possible to test the hypothesis in the argument's conclusion by persuading Juan to change his arrival times in various ways, then seeing whether Ashley's arrival times also consistently changed in the same ways. Without a plausible reason for the two arrival times to be connected, quite a lot of evidence of this type would be required to reasonably overcome the suspicion that the observed correlation is purely coincidental. Alternatively, a discovery that Juan and Ashley knew each other and had reason to coordinate their work schedules might provide a plausible causal connection between their arrival times and greatly strengthen the argument.

This passage refers to Questions 11–14.

Line   Findings from several studies on corporate mergers and acquisitions during the 1970s and 1980s raise questions about why firms initiate and consummate such transactions. One study showed, for example, that acquiring firms were on average unable to maintain acquired firms' pre-merger levels of profitability. A second study concluded that post-acquisition gains to most acquiring firms were not adequate to cover the premiums paid to obtain
(5)   acquired firms. A third demonstrated that, following the announcement of a prospective merger, the stock of the prospective acquiring firm tends to increase in value much less than does that of the firm for which it bids. Yet mergers and acquisitions remain common, and bidders continue to assert that their objectives are economic ones. Acquisitions may well have the desirable effect of channeling a nation's resources efficiently from less to more efficient sectors of its economy, but the individual executives arranging these deals must see them as
(10)   advancing either their own or their companies' private economic interests. It seems that factors having little to do with corporate economic interests explain acquisitions. These factors may include the incentive compensation of executives, lack of monitoring by boards of directors, and managerial error in estimating the value of firms targeted for acquisition. Alternatively, the acquisition acts of bidders may derive from modeling: a manager does what other managers do.

Questions 11–14 refer to the passage.

RC00034-01

Practice Question 11

The primary purpose of the passage is to

(A)   review research demonstrating the benefits of corporate mergers and acquisitions and examine some of the drawbacks that acquisition behavior entails

(B)   contrast the effects of corporate mergers and acquisitions on acquiring firms and on firms that are acquired

(C)   report findings that raise questions about a reason for corporate mergers and acquisitions and suggest possible alternative reasons

(D)   explain changes in attitude on the part of acquiring firms toward corporate mergers and acquisitions

(E)   account for a recent decline in the rate of corporate mergers and acquisitions

RC00034-03
Practice Question 12

It can be inferred from the passage that the author would be most likely to agree with which of the following statements about corporate acquisitions?

(A)   Their known benefits to national economies explain their appeal to individual firms during the 1970s and 1980s.

(B)   Despite their adverse impact on some firms, they are the best way to channel resources from less to more productive sectors of a nation's economy.

(C)   They are as likely to occur because of poor monitoring by boards of directors as to be caused by incentive compensation for managers.

(D)   They will be less prevalent in the future, since their actual effects will gain wider recognition.

(E)   Factors other than economic benefit to the acquiring firm help to explain the frequency with which they occur.

RC00034-04
Practice Question 13

The author of the passage mentions the effect of acquisitions on national economies most probably in order to

(A)   provide an explanation for the mergers and acquisitions of the 1970s and 1980s overlooked by the findings discussed in the passage

(B)   suggest that national economic interests played an important role in the mergers and acquisitions of the 1970s and 1980s

(C)   support a noneconomic explanation for the mergers and acquisitions of the 1970s and 1980s that was cited earlier in the passage

(D)   cite and point out the inadequacy of one possible explanation for the prevalence of mergers and acquisitions during the 1970s and 1980s

(E)   explain how modeling affected the decisions made by managers involved in mergers and acquisitions during the 1970s and 1980s

RC00034-07
Practice Question 14

The author of the passage implies that which of the following is a possible partial explanation for acquisition behavior during the 1970s and 1980s?

(A)   Managers wished to imitate other managers primarily because they saw how financially beneficial other firms' acquisitions were.

(B)   Managers miscalculated the value of firms that were to be acquired.

(C)   Lack of consensus within boards of directors resulted in their imposing conflicting goals on managers.

(D)   Total compensation packages for managers increased during that period.

(E)   The value of bidding firms' stock increased significantly when prospective mergers were announced.

RC00034-01
Answer Explanation 11

The primary purpose of the passage is to

(A)   review research demonstrating the benefits of corporate mergers and acquisitions and examine some of the drawbacks that acquisition behavior entails

(B)   contrast the effects of corporate mergers and acquisitions on acquiring firms and on firms that are acquired

(C)   report findings that raise questions about a reason for corporate mergers and acquisitions and suggest possible alternative reasons

(D)   explain changes in attitude on the part of acquiring firms toward corporate mergers and acquisitions

(E)   account for a recent decline in the rate of corporate mergers and acquisitions

Main Idea

This question requires understanding what the passage as a whole is trying to do. The passage begins by citing three studies that demonstrate that when firms acquire other firms, there is not necessarily a worthwhile economic gain. The passage then cites economic interests as the reason given by firms when they acquire other firms but calls into question the veracity of this reasoning. The passage then goes on to speculate as to why mergers and acquisitions occur.

A   The research cited in the passage calls into question whether mergers and acquisitions are beneficial to firms.

B   The passage is not concerned with comparing the relative effects of mergers and acquisitions on the acquired and acquiring firms.

C   **Correct.** The passage surveys reports that question the reason given by firms when they acquire other firms and suggests other reasons for these acquisitions.

D   The passage does not indicate that there has been a change in the attitude of acquiring firms toward mergers and acquisitions.

E   The passage does not indicate that there has been a decline in the rate of mergers and acquisitions.

The correct answer is C.

RC00034-03

Answer Explanation 12

It can be inferred from the passage that the author would be most likely to agree with which of the following statements about corporate acquisitions?

(A)   Their known benefits to national economies explain their appeal to individual firms during the 1970s and 1980s.

(B)   Despite their adverse impact on some firms, they are the best way to channel resources from less to more productive sectors of a nation's economy.

(C)   They are as likely to occur because of poor monitoring by boards of directors as to be caused by incentive compensation for managers.

(D)   They will be less prevalent in the future, since their actual effects will gain wider recognition.

(E)   Factors other than economic benefit to the acquiring firm help to explain the frequency with which they occur.

Inference

This question requires understanding what view the author has about a particular issue. The three studies cited by the passage all suggest that mergers and acquisitions do not necessarily bring economic benefit to the acquiring firms. The author concludes therefore that *factors having little to do with corporate economic interests explain acquisitions* and then goes on to speculate as to what the reasons may actually be.

A   The passage indicates that while mergers and acquisitions may benefit the national economy, the appeal of mergers and acquisitions must be tied to companies' *private economic interests.*

B   The passage makes no judgment as to the best way for firms to channel resources from less to more efficient economic sectors.

C   The passage makes no comparison between the influence of poor monitoring by boards and that of executive incentives.

D   The passage makes no prediction as to future trends in the market for mergers and acquisitions.

E   **Correct.** The passage states that factors other than economic interests drive mergers and acquisitions.

The correct answer is E.

RC00034-04

Answer Explanation 13

The author of the passage mentions the effect of acquisitions on national economies most probably in order to

    (A)   provide an explanation for the mergers and acquisitions of the 1970s and 1980s overlooked by the findings discussed in the passage

    (B)   suggest that national economic interests played an important role in the mergers and acquisitions of the 1970s and 1980s

    (C)   support a noneconomic explanation for the mergers and acquisitions of the 1970s and 1980s that was cited earlier in the passage

    (D)   cite and point out the inadequacy of one possible explanation for the prevalence of mergers and acquisitions during the 1970s and 1980s

    (E)   explain how modeling affected the decisions made by managers involved in mergers and acquisitions during the 1970s and 1980s

Evaluation

This question requires understanding why a piece of information is included in the passage. After the passage cites the results of the three studies on mergers and acquisitions, which call into question the economic benefits of acquisitions, it indicates that firms nonetheless claim that their objectives are economic. The passage then states that while acquisitions *may well have* a desirable effect on national economies, the results of the studies suggest that factors other than economic interest must drive executives to arrange mergers and acquisitions.

A   The passage does not mention national economies as part of an explanation for the occurrence of mergers and acquisitions.

B   The passage suggests that the effect of acquisitions on national economies is not tied to any explanations for why acquisitions occur.

C   The effect of acquisitions on national economies is not mentioned in the passage as an explanation for why acquisitions occur.

D   **Correct.** The passage uses the mention of national economies as part of a larger point questioning the stated motivations behind firms' efforts to acquire other firms.

E   In the passage, modeling is unrelated to the idea that acquisitions may have a desirable effect on national economies.

The correct answer is D.

RC00034-07

Answer Explanation 14

The author of the passage implies that which of the following is a possible partial explanation for acquisition behavior during the 1970s and 1980s?

    (A)   Managers wished to imitate other managers primarily because they saw how financially beneficial other firms' acquisitions were.

    (B)   Managers miscalculated the value of firms that were to be acquired.

    (C)   Lack of consensus within boards of directors resulted in their imposing conflicting goals on managers.

    (D)   Total compensation packages for managers increased during that period.

    (E)   The value of bidding firms' stock increased significantly when prospective mergers were announced.

Inference

This question requires recognizing what can be inferred from the information in the passage. After providing the results of the studies of mergers and acquisitions, the author concludes that even though acquiring firms state that their objectives are economic, *factors having little to do with corporate economic interests explain acquisitions* (lines 10–11). Among alternative explanations, the author points to *managerial error in estimating the value of firms targeted for acquisition* (lines 12–13) as possibly contributing to acquisition behavior in the 1970s and 1980s.

A   While the passage indicates that managers may have modeled their behavior on other managers, it does not provide a reason for why this would be so.

B   Correct. The author states that one explanation for acquisition behavior may be that managers erred when they estimated the value of firms being acquired.

C   The author discusses a lack of monitoring by boards of directors but makes no mention of consensus within these boards.

D   The author does not discuss compensation packages for managers.

E   The passage does not state how significantly the value of the bidding firm's stock increased upon announcing a merger but only that it increased less in value than did the stock of the prospective firm being acquired.

The correct answer is B.

4. Analogies

A. In an argument by ***analogy***, at least two things are observed to be similar in certain respects. The argument then presents a claim about one of those two things as a reason to accept a similar claim about the other.

> *Example:*
> Laotian cuisine and Thai cuisine use many of the same ingredients and cooking techniques. Ahmed enjoys Thai cuisine. So if he tried Laotian cuisine, he would probably enjoy it too.
>
> In this example, Laotian cuisine and Thai cuisine are observed to be similar in the ingredients and cooking techniques they use. The argument then presents a claim about Thai cuisine: that Ahmed enjoys it. By analogy, the argument concludes that a similar claim is probably true of Laotian cuisine: Ahmed would enjoy it if he tried it.

B. For an argument by analogy to work properly, the observed similarities between the two things must be ***relevant*** to the question of whether those two things also share the further similarity indicated by the conclusion. The argument in the example above meets this standard. Since the ingredients and cooking techniques used in a particular cuisine generally influence whether a particular person would enjoy that cuisine, the observed similarities in ingredients and cooking techniques between Laotian and Thai cuisine are highly relevant to the question of how similar the two cuisines are likely to be with regard to how much Ahmed enjoys them. Alternatively, if the observed similarities are not very relevant to the conclusion, the argument is weak.

Example:
Laotian cuisine and Latvian cuisine both originated in nations whose English names start with the letter *L*. Ahmed enjoys Latvian cuisine. So if he tried Laotian cuisine, he would probably enjoy it too.

In this example, Laotian cuisine and Latvian cuisine are observed to be similar with respect to the English names of the nations in which they originated. Since the English spelling of a nation's name would be unlikely to influence how much a particular person enjoys that nation's cuisine, this observed similarity is irrelevant to the question of how similar Laotian and Latvian cuisine are likely to be with regard to how much Ahmed enjoys them. Thus, the analogy is absurd, and the argument is deeply flawed. To salvage the argument, it would be necessary to present a convincing reason why the observed similarities are relevant after all—for example, by presenting evidence that Ahmed is a very unusual person whose enjoyment of food is intensely affected by English spellings.

C. A reasonable argument by analogy may be strengthened by pointing out additional relevant similarities between the two things being compared, or weakened by pointing out relevant dissimilarities between them.

Example:
Beth and Alan are both children living on the same block in the Hazelfern School District. Beth attends Tubman Primary School. So probably Alan does too.

Pointing out that Beth and Alan are both in the same grade—a similarity that would make it even more likely that they attend the same school, might strengthen this moderately reasonable argument. On the other hand, the argument might be weakened by pointing out that Beth is eight years older than Alan—a dissimilarity suggesting that Alan may be too young to attend the same school Beth attends.

CR28310.03

Practice Question 15

Which of the following most logically completes the passage?

The figures in portraits by the Spanish painter El Greco (1541–1614) are systematically elongated. In El Greco's time, the intentional distortion of human figures was unprecedented in European painting. Consequently, some critics have suggested that El Greco had an astigmatism, a type of visual impairment, that resulted in people appearing to him in the distorted way that is characteristic of his paintings. However, this suggestion cannot be the explanation, because _____.

(A) several twentieth-century artists have consciously adopted from El Greco's paintings the systematic elongation of the human form

(B) some people do have elongated bodies somewhat like those depicted in El Greco's portraits

(C) if El Greco had an astigmatism, then, relative to how people looked to him, the elongated figures in his paintings would have appeared to him to be distorted

(D) even if El Greco had an astigmatism, there would have been no correction for it available in the period in which he lived

(E) there were non-European artists, even in El Greco's time, who included in their works human figures that were intentionally distorted

CR28310.03
Answer Explanation 15

Argument Evaluation

Situation Figures in portraits by the Spanish painter El Greco are elongated. Some critics infer that this was because El Greco suffered from an astigmatism that made people appear elongated to him. But this explanation cannot be correct.

Reasoning *Which option would most logically complete the argument?* We need something that provides the best reason for thinking that the explanation suggested by critics—astigmatism—cannot be right. The critics' explanation might seem to work because ordinarily an artist would try to paint an image of a person so that the image would have the same proportions as the perceived person. So if people seemed to El Greco to have longer arms and legs than they actually had, the arms and legs of the painted figures should appear to others to be longer than people's arms and legs normally are. This is how the explanation seems to make sense. But if astigmatism were the explanation, then the elongated images in his pictures should have appeared to El Greco to be too long: he would have perceived the images as longer than they actually are—and therefore as inaccurate representations of what he perceived. So astigmatism cannot be a sufficient explanation for the elongated figures in his paintings.

A Even if subsequent artists intentionally depicted human forms as more elongated than human figures actually are, and they did so to mimic El Greco's painted figures, that does not mean that El Greco's figures were intentionally elongated.

B Although this option provides another possible explanation for El Greco's elongated figures, it provides no evidence that the people El Greco painted had such elongated figures.

C **Correct**. El Greco would have perceived the images of people in his paintings as too long, relative to his perception of the people themselves. This means that even if El Greco did have astigmatism, that factor would not provide an answer to the question, Why did El Greco paint images that he knew were distorted?

D The absence of an ability to correct astigmatism in El Greco's day does not undermine the hypothesis that it was astigmatism that caused El Greco to paint elongated figures.

E Again, this suggests another possible explanation for the distortion—namely, that El Greco did it deliberately—but it does not provide any reason to think that this is the correct explanation (and that the critics' explanation is actually incorrect).

The correct answer is C.

3.4 Deductive Reasoning

1. Deductive Arguments

A. In a *deductive argument*, the premises are intended to absolutely prove the conclusion. In a valid deductive argument, if the premises are true, then the conclusion **must** also be true. In an argument presented as deductive, if there is any possibility of the premises being true while the conclusion is false, then the reasoning is flawed. However, a flawed deductive argument might work perfectly well as an inductive argument, provided that the author doesn't improperly present the premises as **proving** the conclusion.

2. Logical Operators

A. A *logical operator* expresses how the truth of one statement or idea is related to the truth of another. The basic types of logical operators are *negations*, *logical conjunctions*, *disjunctions*, and *implications*.

B. The *negation* of a statement is false because the statement itself is true, and vice versa. A negation is generally indicated by words and phrases such as *not, it is false that, it is not the case that, etc*.

Note that statements in ordinary speech and writing are often vague, ambiguous, context-sensitive, or subjective—they may be true in one sense and false in another, they may be only partly true, or their truth may be indeterminate. If a statement is true in a particular way or to a particular degree, the statement's negation is false in the same way and to the same degree.

Example:
The negation of the statement "The cat is on the mat" may be expressed as "The cat is not on the mat." "The cat is on the mat" is true because "The cat is not on the mat" is false, and vice versa— but only if both statements refer to the same cat and the same mat, in the same sense, and the same context. If the first statement is uttered while the cat is sleeping on the mat, but then the cat wakes up and leaves before the second sentence is uttered, then the context has changed, so the second utterance does not express the negation of the first. And if the cat is only partly on the mat when both statements are uttered, then the second statement as uttered is *partly* false to the degree that, and in the same sense that, the first is partly true.

C. The *logical conjunction* of two statements expresses the idea that both are true. The following words and terms often indicate a logical conjunction of two statements A and B:

A and B	*A even though B*	*not only A but also B*
Although A, B	*A. Furthermore, B.*	*A, whereas B*
A but B	*A, however B*	

In standard written English, the use of the conjunction indicators **and, furthermore**, and **not only . . . but also** usually implies that the A and B are relevant to each other or being mentioned for similar reasons—for example, that both are being presented as premises supporting the same conclusion. On the other hand, the conjunction indicators **although, but, even though, however**, and **whereas** convey the idea that there is some tension or conflict between A and B; for example, that it is surprising for both A and B to be true, or that A supports a conclusion that conflicts with a conclusion that B supports, or that A and B differ in some other unexpected way.

Examples:
i) Raul has worked for this company a long time, **and** he is searching for another job.

ii) **Although** Raul has worked for this company a long time, he is searching for another job.

Both the examples above state that Raul has worked for the company for a long time, and that he is searching for another job. But in example ii), the use of *although* may suggest that it is *surprising* that Raul is searching for another job, given that he has worked for the company a long time. In contrast, the use of *and* in example i) may suggest that it is *unsurprising* that Raul is searching for another job now that he has worked for the company a long time.

D. A *disjunction* indicates that either one of two statements is true. A disjunction of two statements *A* and *B* is usually expressed as *A or B, either A or B,* or *A unless B.*

An *inclusive disjunction* indicates that *A* and *B* might both be true, whereas an *exclusive disjunction* indicates that *A* and *B* are not both true. It is often unclear whether a disjunction expressed in English is meant to be inclusive or exclusive. For clarity, it may be helpful to write *A or B or both* to indicate an inclusive disjunction, or to write *A or B but not both* to indicate an exclusive disjunction.

Examples:

i) It will **either** rain **or** snow tomorrow.

ii) It will rain tomorrow **unless** it snows.

These examples both express the idea that at least one of the two statements "It will rain tomorrow" and "It will snow tomorrow" is true. In each case, it isn't entirely clear whether the author also means to imply that it won't ***both*** rain ***and*** snow tomorrow. The author could clarify by stating

iii) Tomorrow it will rain or snow, or both. (*inclusive disjunction*)

or iv) Tomorrow it will either rain or snow, but not both. (*exclusive disjunction*)

E. A *conditional* indicates that the truth of one statement would require or entail the truth of another—in other words, that the second statement could be properly inferred from the first. The following expressions all indicate the same conditional relationship between two statements *A* and *B*:

A would mean that B	B if A	A only if B
If A, then B	Not A unless B	B provided that A

Conditional statements of these forms don't imply that *A* is actually true, nor that *B* is. Thus, they don't present *A* as a reason to believe that *B*. So in a conditional statement, *A* is not a premise and *B* is not a conclusion. In other words, a conditional statement is not an argument. But a conditional statement ***if A then B*** does imply that assuming *A* as a premise, if appropriate, would allow one to correctly infer *B* as a conclusion.

Examples:

i) It will snow tonight **only if** the temperature falls below 5 degrees Celsius.

ii) It **won't** snow tonight **unless** the temperature falls below 5 degrees Celsius.

iii) **If** it snows tonight, it'll mean the temperature has fallen below 5 degrees Celsius.

These examples all express the idea that snow tonight would require temperatures below 5 degrees Celsius. They do not say that it actually will snow tonight, nor that temperatures actually will be below 5 degrees Celsius. But they do suggest, for example, that observing snow tonight would allow one to correctly infer that the temperature must be below 5 degrees Celsius.

Although conditionals are often used to express or suggest causal claims, their meaning is not necessarily causal. In the examples above, there is no implication that snow tonight would cause the temperature to fall below 5 degrees Celsius.

Also note that none of these examples say or imply that if the temperature falls below 5 degrees Celsius tonight, then it will necessarily snow. That is, a conditional of the form ***if A, then B*** doesn't necessarily imply that ***if B, then A.***

F. If two statements **A and B** are *logically equivalent*, then they are both true or false under the same conditions, and each can be correctly inferred from the other. In other words, if *A then B*, and if *B then A*. When precision is needed, this can be expressed by writing *A if and only if B*.

3. Reasoning with Logical Operators

A. Here is a list of some basic types of logically equivalent statements formed with various combinations of the logical operators. In this list, the word *not* is used to express negation, the word *and* is used to express logical conjunction, the word *or* is used to express inclusive disjunction, and the expression *if . . . then* is used to express implication.

Logical Equivalences with Logical Operators		
A and B	is logically equivalent to	*B and A*
not (A and B)	is logically equivalent to	*not-A or not-B*
A or B	is logically equivalent to	*B or A*
not (A or B)	is logically equivalent to	*not-A and not-B* (in other words, *neither A nor B*)
if A then B	is logically equivalent to	*if not-B then not-A*
if A then (B and C)	is logically equivalent to	*(if A then B) and (if A then C)*
if A then (B or C)	is logically equivalent to	*(if A then B) or (if A then C)*
if (A or B) then C	is logically equivalent to	*(if A then C) and (if B then C)*

B. When two statements are logically equivalent, either one can be used as a premise to support the other as a conclusion in a valid argument. So for any line in the list above, an argument in which a statement of the form on the left is used as a premise to support a statement of the form on the right is valid. So is an argument in which a statement of the form on the right is used as a premise to support a statement of the form on the left.

Examples:

The second line in the list above says that for any two statements *A* and *B*, the statement *not (A and B)* is logically equivalent to the statement *not-A or not-B*. This gives us two valid arguments:

i) *not (A and B), therefore not-A or not-B*

and ii) *not-A or not-B, therefore not (A and B)*

Let's consider a specific example in standard written English. The statement *Ashley and Tim don't both live in this neighborhood* is logically equivalent to *Either Ashley doesn't live in this neighborhood or Tim doesn't*. This yields two **valid** arguments:

iii) Ashley and Tim don't both live in this neighborhood. Therefore, either Ashley doesn't live in this neighborhood or Tim doesn't.

and iv) Either Ashley doesn't live in this neighborhood or Tim doesn't. Therefore, Ashley and Tim don't both live in this neighborhood.

C. Here is a list of several more forms of valid argument that use the logical operators, and several forms of invalid argument with which they are often confused.

Valid and Invalid Inferences with Logical Operators	
Valid: *A and B, therefore A*	**Invalid:** *A, therefore A and B*
Valid: *A, therefore A or B*	**Invalid:** *A or B, therefore A*
Valid: *not-A and not-B, therefore not (A and B)*	**Invalid:** *not (A and B), therefore not-A and not-B*
Valid: *not (A or B), therefore not-A or not-B*	**Invalid:** *not-A or not-B, therefore not (A or B)*
Valid: *if A, then B; and A; therefore B*	**Invalid:** *if A, then B; and B; therefore A*
Valid: *if A, then B; and not-B; therefore not-A*	**Invalid:** *if A, then B; and not-A; therefore not-B*

On the actual GMAT exam, you will sometimes need to judge whether or not an argument is valid.

Examples:
The third line in the previous table says that **not-A and not-B, therefore not (A and B)** is valid, whereas **not (A and B), therefore not-A and not-B** is invalid. So a simple example of a **valid** argument would be:

i) Ashley doesn't live in this neighborhood, and Tim doesn't either. Therefore, it's not true that Ashley and Tim both live in this neighborhood

Whereas a superficially similar but **invalid** argument would be:

ii) It's not true that Ashley and Tim both live in this neighborhood. Therefore, Ashley doesn't live in this neighborhood, and Tim doesn't either.

Similarly, the fifth line in the previous table says that **if A, then B; and A; therefore B** is valid, whereas **if A, then B; and B; therefore A** is invalid. So another **valid** argument would be:

iii) If Ashley lives in this neighborhood, so does Tim. And Ashley does live in this neighborhood. So Tim must too.

However, example iii) should not be confused with the similar **invalid** argument:

iv) If Ashley lives in this neighborhood, so does Tim. And Tim does live in this neighborhood. So Ashley must too.

CR88310.03

Practice Question 16

Museums that house Renaissance oil paintings typically store them in environments that are carefully kept within narrow margins of temperature and humidity to inhibit any deterioration. Laboratory tests have shown that the kind of oil paint used in these paintings actually adjusts to climatic changes quite well. If, as some museum directors believe, **paint is the most sensitive substance in these works**, then by relaxing the standards for temperature and humidity control, **museums can reduce energy costs without risking damage to these paintings**. Museums would be rash to relax those standards, however, since results of preliminary tests indicate that gesso, a compound routinely used by Renaissance artists to help paint adhere to the canvas, is unable to withstand significant variations in humidity.

In the argument above, the two portions in **boldface** play which of the following roles?

(A) The first is an objection that has been raised against the position taken by the argument; the second is the position taken by the argument.

(B) The first is the position taken by the argument; the second is the position that the argument calls into question.

(C) The first is a judgment that has been offered in support of the position that the argument calls into question; the second is a circumstance on which that judgment is, in part, based.

(D) The first is a judgment that has been offered in support of the position that the argument calls into question; the second is that position.

(E) The first is a claim that the argument calls into question; the second is the position taken by the argument.

CR88310.03

Answer Explanation 16

Argument Evaluation

Situation   Museums house Renaissance paintings under strictly controlled climatic conditions to prevent deterioration. This is costly. But the paint in these works actually adjusts well to climate changes. On the other hand, another compound routinely used in these paintings, gesso, does not react well to changes in humidity.

Reasoning   *What roles do the two boldfaced statements play in the argument?* The first statement is not asserted by the author of the argument, but rather attributed as a belief to some museum directors. What the argument itself asserts is that IF this belief is true THEN the second boldfaced statement is true. But the argument then goes on to offer evidence that the first statement is false and so concludes that museum directors would be ill-advised to assume that the second statement was true.

A   This option mistakenly claims that the argument adopts the second statement as its position, when in fact the argument calls this position into question.

B   Rather than adopting the first statement, the argument offers evidence that calls it into question.

C   This option contends that the first statement is a judgment that is based on the second; in fact the opposite is true.

D   **Correct.** This option properly identifies the roles the two portions in boldface play in the argument.

E   While the argument does call the first statement into question, it also calls the second statement into question as well.

The correct answer is D.

4. Necessity, Probability, and Possibility

A. A statement may be qualified with words or phrases expressing the likelihood that the statement is true. In the most basic cases, these words or phrases indicate that:

- The statement is *necessarily* true; that is, there is a 100 percent chance the statement is true; or

- The statement is *probably* true; that is, there is a substantial chance that the statement is true;

- The statement is *possibly* true; that is, the odds are greater than 0 percent but less than 100 percent that the statement is true.

Note that in ordinary English, saying that a claim is possibly true or probably true usually implies that the claim is not **necessarily** true.

B. The table below categorizes words and phrases often used to indicate various degrees of probability:

Words Indicating Necessity, Probability, and Possibility		
Necessity	Probability	Possibility
certainly	*probably*	*can*
clearly	*likely*	*could*
definitely	*more likely than not*	*may*
must		*maybe*
necessarily		*might*
surely		*perhaps*
		possibly

Note that in standard written English, the meanings of ***probably*** and ***likely*** are vague. In some contexts these terms might imply a high degree of probability, such as a 95 percent chance, whereas in other contexts they might be used to indicate a substantial chance below 50 percent. It is best not to assign any very precise meaning to these terms when you encounter them on the GMAT exam.

C. The table below lists several forms of valid argument involving necessity, probability, and possibility, and several forms of invalid argument with which they are often confused.

Valid and Invalid Inferences with Necessity, Probability, and Possibility	
Valid: *Probably A, therefore possibly A*	**Invalid:** *Possibly A, therefore probably A*
Valid: *Possibly (A and B), therefore possibly A and possibly B*	**Invalid:** *Possibly A and possibly B, therefore possibly (A and B)*
Valid: *Probably (A and B), therefore probably A and probably B*	**Invalid:** *Probably A and probably B, therefore probably (A and B)*
Valid: *Probably A or probably B, therefore probably (A or B)*	**Invalid:** *Probably (A or B), therefore probably A or probably B*
Valid: *Necessarily A or necessarily B, therefore necessarily (A or B)*	**Invalid:** *Necessarily (A or B), therefore necessarily A or necessarily B*

Examples:
The second line in the previous table says that ***possibly (A and B), therefore possibly A and possibly B*** is valid, whereas ***possibly A and possibly B, therefore possibly (A and B) is*** invalid. So a simple **valid** argument would be:

i) It's possible that Tim and Ashley both live in this house. So it's possible that Tim lives in this house, and it's also possible that Ashley does.

Whereas a superficially similar but **invalid** argument would be:

ii) It's possible that Tim lives in this house. It is also possible that Ashley lives in this house. So possibly both Tim and Ashley live in this house.

To see that argument ii) is invalid, suppose that you know for certain that the house has only one resident, but you don't know whether that resident is Tim, Ashley, or someone else. In that case the premises of argument ii) would be true, but its conclusion would be false. Thus, the conclusion can't be correctly inferred from the premises.

5. Quantifiers

A. A *quantifier* is a word or phrase that indicates proportion, number, or amount. In this section we will consider ordinary nonmathematical quantifiers used in the Verbal Reasoning section. Some basic examples of quantifiers are *all*, *most*, *some*, and *none*.

  i. A *universal quantifier* such as *all* indicates a reference to 100 percent of the individuals in a category or to the entirety of some collective.

  ii. A quantifier such as *most* indicates a reference to more than 50 percent of the individuals in a category. In standard written English, *most* sometimes implies *not all*, but not always—its meaning is somewhat vague. It is often helpful to write either *most but not all*, or else *most or all*, to indicate which meaning is intended.

  iii. An *existential quantifier* such as *some* indicates a reference to one or more individuals in a category or to at least a portion of some collective. In English it is often quite unclear whether *some* is being used to imply *not all*. For clarity it is often helpful to write *only some*, to indicate that *not all* is implied, or else *at least some*, to indicate the meaning *some or all*. When used with a plural noun, *some* may also imply *more than one*.

  iv. A quantifier such as *no* or *none of* indicates something is being denied about all the individuals in a category or about the entirety of some collective.

  v. Other common nonmathematical quantifiers have more nuanced meanings. For example, *a few* has the vague meaning of a relatively small number more than two. The upper limit of what counts as *a few* depends on the context: the expression *a few Europeans* might indicate a reference to many thousands of people (still a tiny part of Europe's overall population), whereas *a few residents in our building* would probably indicate a reference to only three or four people if the building had only fifteen residents.

CR13750.03

Practice Question 17

Codex Berinensis, a Florentine copy of an ancient Roman medical treatise, is undated but contains clues to when it was produced. Its first 80 pages are by a single copyist, but the remaining 20 pages are by three different copyists, which indicates some significant disruption. Since a letter in handwriting, identified as that of the fourth copyist, mentions a plague that killed many people in Florence in 1148, Codex Berinensis was probably produced in that year.

Which of the following, if true, most strongly supports the hypothesis that Codex Berinensis was produced in 1148 ?

(A) Other than Codex Berinensis, there are no known samples of the handwriting of the first three copyists.

(B) According to the account by the fourth copyist, the plague went on for 10 months.

(C) A scribe would be able to copy a page of text the size and style of Codex Berinensis in a day.

(D) There was only one outbreak of plague in Florence in the 1100s.

(E) The number of pages of Codex Berinensis produced by a single scribe becomes smaller with each successive change of copyist.

CR13750.03
Answer Explanation 17

Argument Evaluation

Situation   The Florentine copy of an ancient Roman work is undated but provides clues as to the time it was produced. The first 80 pages of Codex Berinensis are the work of one copyist. The fact that the last 20 pages are the work of a succession of three different copyists is an indication of serious turmoil at the time the copying was done. Since a letter in the fourth copyist's handwriting reveals that a plague killed many people there in 1148, Codex Berinensis was probably produced in that year.

Reasoning   *Which information supports the hypothesis dating the Codex to 1148?* Consider the basis of the hypothesis: the succession of copyists indicating the work was significantly disrupted, and the fourth copyist's letter indicating the plague of 1148 caused serious loss of life. From this, it is argued that the plague of 1148 was the reason for the multiple copyists and that the work can thus be dated to that year. What if there were multiple plagues?

In that case, Codex Berinensis could have been produced at another time. If, instead, only one plague occurred in the 1100s, the elimination of that possibility supports the hypothesis that the work was done in 1148.

A   Examples of the copyists' handwriting might help date Codex Berinensis; the absence of handwriting samples does not help support 1148 as the date.

B   The length of the plague, while it may account for the succession of copyists, does not help support the particular year the work was done.

C   The amount of work a copyist could achieve each day does not provide any information about the year the work appeared.

D   **Correct.** This statement properly identifies a circumstance that supports the hypothesis.

E   The productivity or tenure of the various copyists is irrelevant to establishing the date.

The correct answer is D.

B. The table below categorizes some of the basic English quantifier words by their meanings.

Basic English Quantifier Words			
"All" and similar quantifier words	**"Most" and similar quantifier words**	**"Some" and similar quantifier words**	**"No" and similar quantifier words**
all	*generally*	*a number*	*never*
always	*a majority*	*a portion*	*no*
any	*most*	*any*	*none*
both	*more than half*	*at least one*	*not any*
each	*usually*	*occasionally*	*not one*
every		*one or more*	*nowhere*
everywhere		*some*	
whenever		*sometimes*	
wherever		*somewhere*	

Note that the meaning of ***any*** varies greatly in different contexts. The sentence ***Any of the students would prefer chocolate ice cream*** means **Each** *of the students would prefer chocolate ice cream.* But confusingly, the sentence ***I don't know whether any of the students would prefer chocolate ice cream*** means ***I don't know whether*** **one or more** *of the students would prefer chocolate ice cream.*

C. In standard written English, using quantifiers in a declarative statement usually implies that there is at least one individual in each of the categories mentioned, and that any collective mentioned exists. However, this rule does not always apply in hypothetical statements, in conditionals, or with the quantifier *any*.

> *Examples:*
> i) **All** life forms native to planets other than Earth **are** carbon-based.
>
> ii) **Any** life forms native to planets other than Earth **would be** carbon-based.
>
> In statement i), the word *all* and the indicative verb form *are* suggests the opinion that there actually exist some life forms native to planets other than Earth. But in statement ii), the word *any* and the conditional verb form *would be* shows the author is carefully avoiding any implication about whether or not there are life forms native to planets other than Earth.

D. Superficially similar statements with two or more quantifiers can have very different meanings depending on word order and nuances of phrasing.

> *Examples:*
> i) There must be some beverage that is the favorite of every student in the class.
>
> ii) Each student in the class must have some favorite beverage.
>
> Statement i) suggests that there must be a *particular* beverage that is all the students' favorite. In other words, every student in the class must have *the same* favorite beverage. Statement ii) only suggests that each individual student must have one or another favorite beverage. In other words, the students in the class may have *different* favorite beverages from each other.

E. A *count noun* refers to a countable number of individuals, whereas a *mass noun* refers to a collective quantity rather than to individuals. Only count nouns can be plural; words used as mass nouns always have a singular form. English diction sometimes requires that you use a different quantifier with a count noun than with a similar mass noun. Sentence Correction questions may also test this skill.

> *Examples:*
> **Correct:** i) She drank **many** of the **sodas** in the refrigerator.
> **Correct:** ii) She drank **much** of the **soda** in the refrigerator.
> **Incorrect:** iii) She drank **many** of the **soda** in the refrigerator.
>
> In example i), *many* is used correctly with the count noun *sodas*, meaning *cans or bottles of soda*. Example ii) *much* is used correctly with the mass noun *soda*, which refers to the soda in the refrigerator collectively rather than to individual containers of soda. Example iii) is grammatically incorrect because it uses *many* with *soda* as a mass noun.

Except in certain technical mathematical contexts, the comparative quantifiers *less* and *least* are typically used with mass nouns for comparisons of amount or degree, whereas *fewer* and *fewest* are used with count nouns for comparisons of number.

Examples:
Correct: Fewer deliveries arrived today than yesterday.
Incorrect: Less deliveries arrived today than yesterday.

Since the plural form of *deliveries* clearly indicates it is a count noun, the appropriate comparison word is *fewer*, not *less*.

---

6. Reasoning with Quantifiers

A. Here is a list of a few types of logically equivalent statements formed with some of the basic quantifiers above. In this list, the letters *A* and *B* stand in for noun phrases, and the word *some* is used to mean *one or more*. For simplicity we use the plural in each statement, but this does not necessarily mean that a singular meaning is excluded. Similar equivalences hold when quantifiers are used with mass nouns.

Logical Equivalences with Quantifiers		
All As are Bs	is logically equivalent to	*No As are not Bs.*
Some As are Bs	is logically equivalent to	*Some Bs are As.*
No As are Bs	is logically equivalent to	*No Bs are As.*
Some As are not Bs	is logically equivalent to	*Not all As are Bs.*

Notice that ***All As are Bs*** is **not** equivalent to ***All Bs are As***, and that ***Some As are not Bs*** is **not** equivalent to ***Some Bs are not As***.

Examples:
i) The true statement ***All ostriches are birds*** is obviously not equivalent to the false statement ***All birds are ostriches***.

ii) The true statement ***Some birds are not ostriches*** is obviously not equivalent to the false statement ***Some ostriches are not birds***.

B. As explained previously, when two statements are logically equivalent, either one can be used as a premise to support the other as a conclusion in a valid argument. This principle applies to equivalences involving quantifiers just as it does to equivalences using logical operators.

C. A *syllogism* is a simple form of argument in which two premises containing quantifiers are used to support a conclusion that also contains quantifiers.

Here is a list of several forms of valid syllogism, and several forms of invalid syllogism with which they are sometimes confused. As explained previously, the letters *A, B,* and *C* stand in for noun phrases, and the word *some* is used to mean *one or more*.

Valid and Invalid Syllogisms
Valid: *All As are Bs. All Bs are Cs. So all As are Cs.*
—**Invalid:** *All As are Bs. All Bs are Cs. So all Cs are As.*
—**Invalid:** *All As are Bs. All Cs are Bs. So all As are Cs.*
—**Invalid:** *All Bs are As. All Bs are Cs. So all As are Cs.*
Valid: *Some As are Bs. All Bs are Cs. So some As are Cs.*
—**Invalid:** *All As are Bs. Some Bs are Cs. So some As are Cs.*
—**Invalid:** *Some As are Bs. Some Bs are Cs. So some As are Cs.*
Valid: *All As are Bs. No Bs are Cs. So no As are Cs.*
—**Invalid:** *No As are Bs. All Bs are Cs. So no As are Cs.*
—**Invalid:** *No As are Bs. No Bs are Cs. So all As are Cs.*
—**Invalid:** *No As are Bs. All Bs are Cs. So some As are not Cs.*

Examples:

The first line of the previous table states that the syllogism ***All As are Bs. All Bs are Cs. So all As are Cs*** is valid. A simple example of a **valid** syllogism following this pattern would be:

i) All the trees in the local park were planted by the town arborist. All the trees planted by that arborist have also been labeled by her. So all the trees in the local park must have been labeled by the arborist.

But a superficially similar but obviously **invalid** syllogism would follow the pattern in the second line of the table (***All As are Bs. All Bs are Cs. So all Cs are As***):

ii) All the trees in the local park were planted by the town arborist. All the trees the arborist has planted have also been labeled by her. So all the trees that have been labeled by the arborist must be in the local park.

To see that argument ii) is invalid, consider that even if both premises are true, the arborist might also have labeled trees outside the park (possibly including some trees she didn't plant).

Another **invalid** syllogism would follow the pattern in the third line of the table (***All As are Bs. All Cs are Bs. So all As are Cs***):

iii) All the trees in the local park were planted by the town arborist. All the trees the arborist has labeled are trees she planted. So all the trees in the local park must have been labeled by the arborist.

To see that argument iii) is invalid, consider that even if both premises are true, the arborist might not have labeled many of the trees she planted, including many or all of those in the park.

The pattern in the fourth line of the table (***All Bs are As. All Bs are Cs. So all As are Cs***) yields yet another **invalid** syllogism:

iv) All the trees the town arborist has planted are in the local park. All the trees planted by that arborist have also been labeled by her. So all the trees in the local park must have been labeled by the arborist.

To see that argument iv) is invalid, consider that even if both premises are true, the park might contain many trees that the arborist neither planted nor labeled.

D. Note that some of the quantifier words in the table "Basic English Quantifier Words" in section 3.4.5.B refer specifically to time or place. For example, *whenever* means *every time, usually* means *most times*, and *never* means *at no time*. Understanding these meanings may allow you to paraphrase these arguments into more standardized forms to check their validity.

Example:
Max **never** goes running when the sidewalks are icy. The sidewalks are **usually** icy on January mornings, so Max must not go running on most January mornings.

This example can be paraphrased as follows:

No times when Max goes running are times the sidewalks are icy. Most January mornings are times the sidewalks are icy. So most January mornings are not times when Max goes running.

Thus, this argument is a valid syllogism of the form *No As are Bs. Most Cs are Bs. So most Cs are not As.*

3.5 Grammar and Style

1. Subjects and Objects

A. A complete declarative sentence generally includes at least a *subject* (a noun, pronoun, or noun phrase) and a verb. Many verbs also require a second noun, pronoun, or noun phrase as the *direct object*. Some even require an additional component, which may be a noun, pronoun, or noun phrase, sometimes preceded by a preposition. If any one of these components is missing, the sentence is incomplete and is called a *sentence fragment*.

Examples:

i) **Complete Sentence:** The brown package arrived quickly.

Sentence fragment with subject missing: Arrived quickly.

Sentence fragment with verb missing: The brown package quickly.

In example i), the complete sentence includes a subject, ***the brown package***, the verb ***arrived***, and the adverb ***quickly***. The first sentence fragment is missing a subject. The second sentence fragment is missing a verb.

ii) **Complete Sentence:** I mailed the package yesterday.

Sentence Fragment with direct object missing: I mailed yesterday.

In example ii), the complete sentence includes the subject ***I***, the verb ***mailed***, the direct object ***the package***, and the adverb ***yesterday***. In standard written English, the verb ***to mail*** typically requires a direct object naming something that is mailed. Although the word ***yesterday*** can be a noun, yesterday is not something that can be mailed, so in this context ***yesterday*** is clearly being used as an adverb. Thus, the sentence fragment is missing the direct object the verb requires.

iii) **Complete Sentence:** He put the package on your desk.

Sentence Fragment with direct object missing: He put on your desk.

Sentence Fragment with indirect object missing: He put the package.

In example iii), the complete sentence includes the subject ***he***, the verb ***put***, the direct object ***the package***, and the prepositional phrase ***on your desk***, which contains the indirect object ***your desk***. The verb ***to put*** requires both a direct object naming something that is put somewhere and a phrase indicating where that thing is put. The first sentence fragment is missing the required direct object. The second sentence fragment is missing the required indirect object in a prepositional phrase. Note that this final sentence fragment could also be completed with an adverb of location such as ***right there*** or ***downstairs*** rather than with a prepositional phrase.

SC93410.03

Practice Question 18

In a review of 2,000 studies of human behavior that date back to the 1940s, two Swiss <u>psychologists, declaring that since most of the studies had failed to control for such variables as social class and family size,</u> none could be taken seriously.

(A) psychologists, declaring that since most of the studies had failed to control for such variables as social class and family size,

(B) psychologists, declaring that most of the studies failed in not controlling for such variables like social class and family size, and

(C) psychologists declared that since most of the studies, having failed to control for such variables as social class and family size,

(D) psychologists declared that since most of the studies fail in controlling for such variables like social class and family size,

(E) psychologists declared that since most of the studies had failed to control for variables such as social class and family size,

SC93410.03
Answer Explanation 18

Verb Form; Diction

The subject of the sentence, *two Swiss psychologists*, needs a main verb. The *ing* verb form *declaring* cannot, on its own, be the main verb of a correct English sentence. Furthermore, the clause that addresses the reason for not taking the studies seriously also needs a subject (*most of the studies*) and a verb (*had failed*).

A   The sentence needs a verb form that agrees in person and number with the subject, *two Swiss psychologists*, and that is in the appropriate tense.

B   In addition to the problem with *declaring*, explained above, in this version of the sentence the phrase *failed in not controlling for* is awkward and does not mean the same thing as *failed to control for*. Also, the expression *such X like Y* is incorrect in English; the correct usage is *such X as Y*.

C   The correct form for the sentence's main verb *declared* is used here, but *having failed* is a participial form and as such cannot be the main verb in the clause.

D   English has a rule of sequence of tenses: once a verb form is marked for past tense, the following verb forms that describe the same object or event have to be in the past tense as well. Thus, *fail* is the wrong verb form. The expression *such X like Y* is incorrect in English; the correct usage is *such X as Y*.

E   **Correct.** The subject *two Swiss psychologists* is followed by a verb in the past tense (*declared*); the dependent clause *since . . . family size* also has the correct verb form (*had failed*).

The correct answer is E.

> **B.** In some cases sentence fragments are grammatically acceptable.
>
> *Examples:*
> i) The greater the thread count, the higher the price.
>
> ii) Better a small nutritious meal than a large unwholesome one.
>
> iii) Here today, gone tomorrow.
>
> iv) No idea.
>
> Examples i) and ii) show grammatically standard ways of expressing comparisons without an explicit verb. Equivalent complete sentences would be:
>
> ***Whenever the thread count is greater, the price is higher*** and
>
> ***A small nutritious meal is better than a large unwholesome one.***
>
> Example iii) is a grammatically correct conventional saying with no subject and no verb. An equivalent complete sentence might be ***What is here today is gone tomorrow***.
>
> Example iv) would be a grammatically correct but informal reply to a question. In some contexts, an equivalent complete sentence might be ***I have no idea***.

C. The grammatical subject of a complete English sentence may be a placeholder pronoun that doesn't actually refer to anything. The two standard placeholder pronouns are *it* and *there*.

Examples:
i) **It** was raining yesterday.

ii) **There** are several reasons to prefer this theory to the proposed alternative.

In example i), the subject pronoun *it* does not refer to any actual entity that was raining. In example ii), the subject pronoun *there* does not refer to any place where the reasons are.

D. In a declarative sentence, the subject precedes the verb, and the direct and indirect objects follow the verb. But in some cases alternative word orders are also grammatically correct.

Examples:
i) "Tell me about it," said his uncle.

ii) In neither case could I find the needed information.

In example i), the direct object is the quotation **"Tell me about it."** The direct object precedes the verb **said**, which in turn precedes the subject **his uncle**. This word order is grammatically acceptable for direct quotations, especially in standard English writing.

Example ii) starts with a prepositional phrase **in neither case** that modifies the auxiliary verb **could**. The subject **I** is embedded between **could** and the main verb **find**. This word order is grammatically acceptable, especially in formal contexts.

E. Most pronouns take different forms as grammatical subjects than they take as direct and indirect objects. A common grammatical error is to use subject pronouns as objects, or vice versa. Although this is often acceptable in casual speech, it is considered ungrammatical in formal writing.

Examples:
Correct: **He** and Nina visited Paul and **me**.
Incorrect use of object pronoun as subject: Nina and **him** visited Paul and me.
Incorrect use of subject pronoun as object: He and Nina visited Paul and **I**.

In these sentences, the subject pronoun *he* is the correct one to use in the sentence's grammatical subject phrase **He and Nina**; the object form **him** is incorrect. And the object pronoun *me* is the correct one to use in the sentence's direct object phrase **Paul and me**; the subject form **I** is incorrect.

---

2. Number and Person

A. Standard written English makes few distinctions of number and person in verb forms, but most verbs change form with a third-person singular subject in the present tense. The verb *to be* also has distinct forms in the past tense and with the subject *I* in the present tense. The form a verb takes must be consistent with the number and person of the grammatical subject.

Examples:
Correct: Every one of the circuits **has** a separate switch.
Incorrect: Every one of the circuits **have** a separate switch.

In these sentences, the subject is the noun phrase *every one of the circuits*. It is singular, because every one of the circuits is being considered individually. Although *circuits* is plural and immediately precedes the verb, it is not the grammatical subject. Thus, the correct verb form is the singular form *has*, not the plural form *have*.

B. As a pronoun, *each* is singular. When *each* is used directly before a noun, the noun is singular. But *each* may also be used after a plural subject, with a plural verb form.

Examples:
i) **Each** has a separate switch.

ii) **Each circuit** has a separate switch.

iii) **The circuits each** have separate switches.

These three examples are all grammatically correct. In example i), the subject is the singular pronoun *each*. In example ii), the subject is the singular *each circuit*. In example iii), the subject is the plural *the circuits*, and *each* serves as an adverb.

Note that in examples i) and ii), the direct object a *separate switch* is also singular, whereas in example iii), the direct object *separate switches* is plural. This is appropriate because in examples i) and ii), each circuit and its switch are being considered separately, whereas in example iii), they are all being considered collectively. In example iii), the meaning is unclear whether each individual circuit has several separate switches, or whether the circuits have only one switch apiece. When precision is important, wordings like that in example iii) should be avoided.

C. In some cases, a term may take a plural verb form when used to refer to multiple individuals but a singular verb form when used to refer to a collective or quantity.

Examples:

i) Six dollars **were** withdrawn from the box, one at a time.

ii) Six dollars **is** a high price for that.

iii) The staff **are** working well together.

iv) The staff **is** larger than it used to be.

v) A number of the trees **are** now flowering.

vi) The number of trees now flowering **is** large.

These examples are all grammatically correct.

In example i), the subject *six dollars* is plural because it refers to six separate dollar bills.

In example ii), the subject *six dollars* is singular because it refers to a single amount of money.

In example iii), the subject *the staff* is plural because it refers to separate staff members working together.

In example iv), the subject *the staff* is singular because it refers to the staff as a single group that has become larger, rather than to individual staff members, who are not being described as having become larger.

In example v), the subject *a number of the trees* is plural because it refers to multiple trees, which are flowering, rather than to the number, which is not flowering.

In example vi), the subject *the number of trees* is singular because it refers to a number, which is large, rather than to the trees, which are not being described as large.

D. A pronoun often has an *antecedent*—a noun, a noun phrase, or another pronoun appearing elsewhere in the discourse. A pronoun and its antecedent share the same referent. When a pronoun has an antecedent, it should be clear what the antecedent is, and the pronoun should agree with the antecedent in person, number, and gender. Similarly, where a noun or noun phrase has the same referent as another noun or noun phrase, the two terms should agree in number.

Examples:
Correct: The agency regularly releases **reports**, but **they** have become less frequent this year.
Incorrect: The agency regularly releases reports, but **it** has become less frequent this year.
Incorrect: The agency is reporting regularly, but **they** have become less frequent this year.

In the correct example above, the plural pronoun *they* clearly refers to the plural antecedent *reports*.

In the first incorrect example, the grammatical antecedent for the singular pronoun *it* appears to be the singular *the agency*, but the resulting sentence makes no sense. Evidently the intended antecedent is supposed to be something like *the release of reports*. But because that phrase doesn't actually appear, the sentence is confusing.

In the second incorrect example, the plural *they* has no plural antecedent in the sentence. The noun *the agency* is clearly singular in this sentence, since it is used with the singular verb form *is*. Without a plural antecedent for *they*, the sentence is confusing and unclear.

SC06684

Practice Question 19

Faced with an estimated $2 billion budget gap, the city's mayor <u>proposed a nearly 17 percent reduction in the amount allocated the previous year to maintain the city's major cultural institutions and to subsidize</u> hundreds of local arts groups.

(A)   proposed a nearly 17 percent reduction in the amount allocated the previous year to maintain the city's major cultural institutions and to subsidize

(B)   proposed a reduction from the previous year of nearly 17 percent in the amount it was allocating to maintain the city's major cultural institutions and for subsidizing

(C)   proposed to reduce, by nearly 17 percent, the amount from the previous year that was allocated for the maintenance of the city's major cultural institutions and to subsidize

(D)   has proposed a reduction from the previous year of nearly 17 percent of the amount it was allocating for maintaining the city's major cultural institutions, and to subsidize

(E)   was proposing that the amount they were allocating be reduced by nearly 17 percent from the previous year for maintaining the city's major cultural institutions and for the subsidization

SC06684

Answer Explanation 19

Rhetorical Construction; Parallelism

The original sentence contains no errors. It uses the parallel construction *to maintain* and *to subsidize* to show clearly the two areas where the *17 percent reduction* in funds will be applied. In addition, the *17 percent reduction* is closely followed by *the amount allocated the previous year*, making it clear what is being reduced by 17 percent.

A   **Correct.** The sentence uses parallel construction and a well-placed modifier.

B   *To maintain* and *for subsidizing* are not parallel. The sentence is imprecise, and *it* does not have a clear antecedent.

C   *For the maintenance* and *to subsidize* are not parallel, and the sentence is wordy.

D   *For maintaining* and *to subsidize* are not parallel, *it* does not have a clear antecedent, and the sentence structure makes it unclear just what the writer is claiming.

E   *Maintaining* and *the subsidization* are not parallel, *they* does not have a clear antecedent, and the sentence structure makes it unclear just what the writer is claiming.

The correct answer is A.

3. Tense and Mood

A. The table below summarizes some of the main English tenses, with examples:

English Tenses		
Simple Present We <u>eat</u> dinner at 6 every evening.	**Simple Past** We <u>ate</u> dinner yesterday evening.	**Simple Future** We <u>will eat</u> dinner tomorrow evening.
Present Progressive We <u>are eating</u> dinner now.	**Past Progressive** We <u>were eating</u> dinner when you called.	**Future Progressive** We <u>will be eating</u> dinner when you arrive.
Present Perfect We <u>have eaten</u> dinner already this evening.	**Past Perfect** We <u>had eaten</u> dinner before you called.	**Future Perfect** We <u>will have eaten</u> dinner before you arrive.
Present Perfect Progressive We <u>have been eating</u> dinner for about ten minutes now.	**Past Perfect Progressive** We <u>had been eating</u> dinner for only ten minutes when dessert was served.	**Future Perfect Progressive** We <u>will have been eating</u> dinner for at least ten minutes by the time you arrive.

B. Standard written English generally uses the present progressive tense to describe events as currently occurring. The simple present tense is often reserved instead for describing events and conditions as occurring at indefinite or unspecified times, or as recurring. However, in compound sentences either the present progressive or the simple present may be used to describe events as hypothetical or occurring in the future.

Examples:
i) The dog **is barking** loudly.

ii) The dog **barks** loudly.

iii) If the dog **is barking** loudly, it will wake you up.

iv) If the dog **barks** loudly, it will wake you up.

These examples are all grammatically correct. In example i), the present progressive *is barking* indicates that the sentence is describing an event happening now, rather than the dog's general tendency to bark loudly. But in example ii), the simple present *barks* indicates that the sentence is describing the dog's general habit; the dog is inclined to bark loudly, but might not be doing so right at this moment. Examples iii) and iv) both describe hypothetical future events, but the use of the present progressive *is barking* in example iii) more clearly refers to prolonged barking, whereas the simple present *barks* in example iv) could refer to either prolonged barking or a single bark.

C. For a sentence with two or more verbs to make sense, the verbs' tenses must be aligned so that the timing of the events described is coherent. Progressive tenses are generally used to describe situations ongoing at a particular time, while perfect tenses are used to describe either situations that occurred up to a particular time or situations that occurred earlier but are still considered relevant to the time being discussed.

Examples:

i) **Correct:** I **enjoyed** my visit to Tianjin, a city whose history I **had researched** beforehand.
Incorrect: I **enjoyed** my visit to Tianjin, a city whose history I **have researched** beforehand.

In example i), the past perfect **had researched** is used correctly in describing a situation that occurred earlier than the main event described with the simple past **enjoyed**. In this context it is incorrect to use the present perfect **have researched**, because that would imply that the main event (the speaker's enjoying a stay in Tianjin) is occurring now—an implication contradicted by the use of the simple past **enjoyed**.

ii) **Correct:** When the researcher **begins** the next experiment, she **will be working** in a new laboratory.
Incorrect: When the researcher **begins** the next experiment, she **was working** in a new laboratory.

In example ii), the simple present **begins** is correctly used in a **when** clause to describe a future event. Therefore, the future progressive **will be working** is correctly used to describe a situation as ongoing at the time of that future event. However, it would make no sense to use the past progressive **was working** to describe a situation as ongoing at the time of that future event. The use of **was working** would signify a situation that was ongoing at the time of a past event.

SC02457

Practice Question 20

Being a United States citizen since 1988 and born in Calcutta in 1940, author Bharati Mukherjee has lived in England and Canada, and first came to the United States in 1961 to study at the Iowa Writers' Workshop.

- (A) Being a United States citizen since 1988 and born in Calcutta in 1940, author Bharati Mukherjee has
- (B) Having been a United States citizen since 1988, she was born in Calcutta in 1940; author Bharati Mukherjee
- (C) Born in Calcutta in 1940, author Bharati Mukherjee became a United States citizen in 1988; she has
- (D) Being born in Calcutta in 1940 and having been a United States citizen since 1988, author Bharati Mukherjee
- (E) Having been born in Calcutta in 1940 and being a United States citizen since 1988, author Bharati Mukherjee

SC02457

Answer Explanation 20

Verb Form; Rhetorical Construction

Being . . . since 1988 and born in Calcutta in 1940 is an awkward, wordy construction, which presents an unclear and potentially confusing chronological order. Since in the correct version of the sentence the original phrase (*being . . .*) has been made into a main clause, a semi-colon should separate it from the second main clause beginning *she has lived.*

A   The phrases are expressed in an illogical and potentially confusing sequence.

B   *Having been* suggests that the citizenship came chronologically before the birth. The pronoun *she* is the subject of the first clause; since the author's name is mentioned only after the semicolon, *she* has no clear referent.

C   **Correct.** In this sentence, the sequence of events is expressed logically, grammatically, and concisely in each independent clause.

D   The progressive verb forms *being born* and *having been* illogically suggest continuous action and fail to establish a logical time sequence. The sentence is wordy and awkward.

E   The progressive verb forms *having been born* and *being* illogically suggest continuous action and fail to establish a logical time sequence. The sentence is wordy and awkward.

The correct answer is C.

    D. All the verb forms considered above are in the *indicative mood*, which is generally used in statements describing actual or expected situations. In contrast, the *subjunctive mood* and the *conditional mood* are used in certain statements concerning orders, requests, wishes, and hypothetical or imaginary situations.

        i. The *present subjunctive* of a verb is simply the verb's bare infinitive without *to*. It is used in certain constructions to indicate an action being prescribed, required, requested, etc.

> *Examples:*
> **Correct:** He asked that they **try** the cake.
> **Incorrect:** He asked that they **tried** the cake.
>
> In these sentences, the present subjunctive *try* is the correct verb form to use when describing a requested action. The simple past *tried* is incorrect, even though *asked* is in the past tense.

        ii. The *past subjunctive* is generally identical in form to the simple past tense, except that in formal writing the past subjunctive of *to be* is always *were*, even with singular subjects. The past subjunctive is used in simple statements and in the antecedents of conditionals to indicate that the situation described is not real.

> *Examples:*
> **Correct:** I wish I **were** on vacation now.
> **Incorrect:** I wish I **am** on vacation now.
>
> In these sentences, *were* is the correct verb form to use in describing a wish for a vacation that is not actually happening. Although the wish is for a vacation in the present moment, the simple present *am* is incorrect because the sentence indicates the vacation is not presently occurring.

        iii. The *past perfect subjunctive* is identical in form to the past perfect and is used in simple statements and in the antecedents of conditionals to indicate that a situation was not real at some earlier time.

Examples:
Correct: I wish I **had gone** on vacation yesterday.
Incorrect: I wish I **went** on vacation yesterday.

In these sentences, the past perfect subjunctive *had gone* is the correct verb form to use in describing a wish for an imaginary past event to have occurred. The simple past tense *went* is incorrect because the sentence indicates the event did not actually occur.

iv. In conditional statements about unreal, imaginary situations, the past subjunctive or past perfect subjunctive should be used in the antecedent clause, while the verb in the consequent clause should be in the *conditional mood*. Like the past, present, and future tenses, the conditional mood comes in a simple form (*would eat*), a progressive form (*would be eating*), a perfect form (*would have eaten*), and a perfect progressive form (*would have been eating*). Conditional verb forms can also be formed with *could* and *should*.

Examples:
Correct: If I **were** on vacation now, I **would go** to the beach.
Incorrect: If I were on vacation now, I **am going** to the beach.
Incorrect: If I **would be** on vacation now, I would go to the beach.

In these conditional sentences describing an imaginary, unreal situation, the past subjunctive *were* is the correct verb form in the antecedent clause, and the conditional *would go* is the correct verb form in the consequent clause. When a conditional sentence describes an imaginary situation, it is incorrect to use a non-conditional verb form in the consequent clause or to use a conditional verb form in the antecedent clause.

E. Verb forms with *would, could,* and *should* can also be used in various contexts to describe actual, potential, or prescribed actions or situations.

Examples:
i) I **would like** to go on vacation next week.

ii) I really **could go** on vacation next week.

iii) I **should go** on vacation next week.

In these sentences the verb forms with *would, could,* and *should* are used to describe an actual desire in example i), an actual capacity in example ii), and a prescriptive judgment in example iii). In example i), the form *would like* is essentially a formal or polite substitute for the simple present *want*.

4. Modifiers

A. Adjectives modify nouns and noun phrases, whereas adverbs modify verbs, adjectives, other adverbs, and entire clauses. In standard written English, it is incorrect to use an adjective in place of an adverb or vice versa.

Examples:
Correct: She played the piano **really well**.
Incorrect in formal writing: She played the piano really **good**.
Incorrect in formal writing: She played the piano **real** well.

In the correct form of the sentence above, the adverb *well* modifies the verb *played*, and the adverb *really* modifies the adverb *well*. In formal writing, it is incorrect to use an adjective such as *good* to modify a verb or to use an adjective such as *real* to modify an adverb. However, both of the sentences labeled above as "incorrect in formal writing" would often be acceptable in casual speech.

B. Entire phrases may also modify nouns, verbs, and other parts of speech. Careful word ordering and phrasing is often needed to unambiguously indicate which sentence element a phrase is modifying. In most cases it is helpful to put the modifier close to the element it is intended to modify.

Examples:
Ambiguous Grammar: She saw a boy petting a dog **with her binoculars**.

Unambiguous Grammar: **Through her binoculars**, she saw a boy petting a dog.

Unambiguous Grammar: She saw a boy **who had her binoculars** and was petting a dog.

Unambiguous Grammar: She saw a boy **using her binoculars** to pet a dog.

Unambiguous Grammar: She saw a boy who was petting a dog **that had her binoculars**.

The sentence with ambiguous grammar is confusing because it is unclear whether the prepositional phrase *with her binoculars* is meant to modify *saw*, or *boy*, or *petting*, or *dog*. Rewording and reorganizing the sentence in any of the four grammatically unambiguous ways above clarifies which meaning is intended.

SC95430.03

Practice Question 21

Unlike the original National Museum of Science and Technology in Italy, where the models are encased in glass or operated only by staff members, the Virtual Leonardo Project, an online version of the museum, encourages visitors to "touch" each exhibit, which thereby activates the animated functions of the piece.

- (A) exhibit, which thereby activates
- (B) exhibit, in turn an activation of
- (C) exhibit, and it will activate
- (D) exhibit and thereby activate
- (E) exhibit which, as a result, activates

SC95430.03

Answer Explanation 21

Grammatical Construction; Logical Predication

The relative pronoun *which* requires an antecedent, and there is none provided in this sentence. It makes more sense to make the visitors the agents responsible for the action of both the verbs—*touch* and *activate*. Because *to* "*touch*" is an infinitive, the second verb form must be, as well, though the *to* may be implied.

A   *Which* has no antecedent in the sentence, so it is unclear what activated the display.

B   *In turn an activation* . . . seems to be the subject of a new clause, but it has no verb, so the sentence is incomplete.

C   There is no antecedent for *it* because *touch* is a verb.

D   **Correct.** The agent of the action is clearly indicated by the grammatical structure of the sentence; visitors are encouraged *to* "*touch*" . . . *and thereby (to) activate.*

E   *Which* has no antecedent in this sentence.

The correct answer is D.

> **C.** A dangling modifier is one that has been misplaced so that it grammatically modifies the wrong sentence element or no sentence element at all.

> *Examples:*
> **Correct:** i) Concerned that the snake might be poisonous, **the workers** decided to leave it untouched.
>
> **Incorrect:** ii) Concerned that it might be poisonous, **the snake** was left untouched by the workers.
>
> **Incorrect:** iii) Concerned that the snake might be poisonous, **the decision of the workers** was to leave it untouched.
>
> **Incorrect:** iv) Concerned that the snake might be poisonous, it was decided the workers would leave it untouched.
>
> In general, an adjective phrase at the beginning of a sentence modifies the following noun phrase, which is typically the sentence's grammatical subject. Thus, example i) above correctly expresses the intended meaning that the workers were concerned the snake might be poisonous. Example ii) incorrectly indicates that the snake was concerned, and example iii) incorrectly indicates that the decision was concerned. In example iv), there is no sentence element that could plausibly be modified by the phrase ***concerned that the snake might be poisonous***; the sentence's grammatical subject ***it*** is a dummy pronoun that doesn't refer to anything.

5. Clauses and Conjunctions

A. A *clause* is a part of a sentence containing at least a subject and a verb. Sentences may contain several types of clauses:

- An *independent clause* is one that could stand alone as a separate sentence with its meaning intact.

- A *subordinate clause* modifies an independent clause, usually by providing a time, place, or reason, but cannot stand on its own as a separate sentence with its meaning fully intact.

- A *relative clause* modifies a noun or verb in another clause. Often a relative clause starts with a relative pronoun such as *what, who, which,* or *that*, or a relative adverb such as *when, where,* or *why*, but in some cases these elements may be preceded by a preposition or omitted altogether.

- A *noun clause* looks like a relative clause, but serves as a noun in the sentence rather than as a modifier.

Examples:
i) They shipped the package last week, and it will arrive on time.

In example i), the two clauses *they shipped the package last week* and *it will arrive on time* are independent, because each can stand alone as a separate sentence with its meaning intact.

ii) **If they shipped the package last week**, it will arrive on time.

In example ii), the clause *if they shipped the package last week* is a subordinate clause. It cannot stand on its own, but rather states a condition under which the main clause *it will arrive on time* is true.

iii) The package **that they shipped last week** will arrive on time.

In example iii), the clause *that they shipped last week* is a relative clause modifying the subject of the main clause *The package will arrive on time*. The relative clause specifies which package will arrive on time. Omitting the relative pronoun *that* from this sentence would also be grammatically acceptable.

iv) I'm not sure **which package they shipped last week**.

In example iv), the noun clause *which package they shipped last week* does not modify any noun, but itself serves as the direct object of the sentence.

B. Appropriate punctuation or connectives must be used to separate clauses from other clauses or sentence components. Failure to do so may result in an ungrammatical ***run-on sentence***.

Examples:
Correct: i) The players decided to cancel the game; playing during the storm would have been unpleasant.

Correct: ii) The players decided to cancel the game **because** playing during the storm would have been unpleasant.

Correct: iii) The players decided to cancel the game, **which** would have been unpleasant to play during the storm.

Incorrect: iv) The players decided to cancel the game, playing during the storm would have been unpleasant.

Incorrect: v) The players decided to cancel the game would have been unpleasant to play during the storm.

Example i) correctly uses a semicolon to separate two independent clauses; example ii) correctly uses ***because*** to separate an independent clause from a subordinate clause; and example iii) correctly uses a comma and ***which*** to separate an independent clause from a relative clause. Example iv) is incorrect because it uses only a comma between two independent clauses, failing to separate them adequately. Example v) ungrammatically runs two clauses together into a monstrous hybrid clause in which the subject of ***would have been*** is unclear.

SC02605

Practice Question 22

As a result of record low temperatures, the water pipes on the third floor froze, <u>which caused the heads of the sprinkler system to burst, which released torrents of water</u> into offices on the second floor.

(A) which caused the heads of the sprinkler system to burst, which released torrents of water

(B) which caused the heads of the sprinkler system to burst and which released torrents of water

(C) which caused the heads of the sprinkler system to burst, torrents of water were then released

(D) causing the heads of the sprinkler system to burst, then releasing torrents of water

(E) causing the heads of the sprinkler system to burst and release torrents of water

SC02605
Answer Explanation 22

Logical Predication; Grammatical Construction

This sentence describes a causal sequence of events leading to flooded second-floor offices. One of the steps, sprinkler heads bursting, was presumably simultaneous with the release of torrents of water, so it is best to present these events as actions attached to the same subject (*heads of the sprinkler system*). The sentence as given attempts to explain the sequence in a chain of relative clauses, using the pronoun *which* to introduce successive steps. The precise reference of this relative pronoun is somewhat obscure—it appears to refer to the entire preceding clause—and the sequence separates the simultaneous bursting of heads and releasing of water into two temporally separate events.

A   The reference of the second *which* is obscure, and the sentence implausibly separates bursting heads and releasing of torrents into two temporally separate events.

B   Joining the relative pronouns with the conjunction *and* makes the freezing of the water pipes the subject of both *caused . . .* and *released . . .* Thus, it seems to indicate, somewhat implausibly, that the freezing of the pipes directly released torrents of water independently of its causing the sprinkler heads to burst.

C   The passive verb *were . . . released* obscures the causal sequence behind the releasing of torrents of water. The introduction of a new independent clause without a conjunction is ungrammatical and makes this version a run-on sentence.

D   As in (B), the structure of this version makes the freezing of the pipes the subject of both *causing . . .* and *releasing . . . .* The introduction of the sequential marker *then* divides the bursting of heads and releasing of torrents of water into two separate events in the sequence. It indicates, implausibly, that the pipes' freezing directly released torrents of water after it had also caused the sprinkler heads to burst.

E   **Correct.** The elimination of the relative pronouns clarifies the causal sequence of events, and the double infinitives *to burst* and (*to*) *release* underscores the simultaneity of these events.

The correct answer is E.

C.   *Grammatical conjunctions* connect sentence components and show the relationship between them. Grammatical conjunctions include not only words such as **and** that indicate logical conjunctions, but also words that indicate disjunctions, implications, premise-conclusion relationships, cause-effect relationships, relationships in time and space, and other types of relationship between sentence components. There are three types of conjunctions:

i.   *Coordinating conjunctions* connect at least two components of the same type, such as two clauses, two noun phrases, two verbs, two adjectives, or two adverbs. English coordinating conjunctions include **and, but, for, nor, or, so**, and **yet**. Of these, **for** and **so** are used as conjunctions only between clauses.

ii.   *Correlative conjunctions* consist of two words or phrases, each preceding one sentence component. Some common correlative conjunctions include **both/and, either/or, neither/nor**, and **not only/but also**. Most correlative conjunctions require that the two sentence components they connect be of the same grammatical type.

iii.   *Subordinating conjunctions* connect an independent clause to a subordinate clause. They generally indicate that the subordinate clause expresses the time, place, manner, or condition in which the statement in the independent clause holds. There are many subordinating conjunctions, including **as, because, if, once, though, unless, until, where, when, whether or not**, and **while**.

Examples:

i) I sat **and** relaxed in the easy chair.

ii) I **not only** sat **but also** relaxed in the easy chair.

iii) I relaxed **as** I sat in the easy chair.

All these examples are grammatically correct. In example i), the verbs *sat* and *relaxed* are joined by the coordinating conjunction *and*, while in example ii), the same two verbs are joined by the correlative conjunction *not only/but also*. In example iii), the subordinating conjunction *as* joins the independent clause *I relaxed* to the subordinate clause *I sat in the easy chair*. The subordinate clause indicates the situation in which the statement in the independent clause *I relaxed* holds.

Note that in each example, deleting the conjunction and either one of the components it connects leaves a grammatically correct sentence. For instance, in example i), deleting *sat and* would leave the grammatically correct sentence *I relaxed in the easy chair*. In contrast, *I sat and relaxing in the easy chair* would be grammatically incorrect, because deleting *sat and* from *I sat and relaxing in the easy chair* would leave the verbless sentence fragment *I relaxing in the easy chair*.

D. In many cases, using a conjunction to connect two components of different grammatical types is grammatically incorrect. This error frequently occurs with correlative conjunctions and in lists using coordinating conjunctions.

Examples:
Correct: i) I went to both **a park** and **the downtown library**.
Incorrect: ii) I went both **to a park** and **the downtown library**.

Correct: iii) I went to **a park**, **a movie theater**, and then **the downtown library**.
Incorrect: iv) I <u>went to</u> **a park**, **a movie theater**, and then went to **the downtown library**.

In example i), the correlative conjunction *both/and* is correctly used to connect two noun phrases: *a park* and *the downtown library*. In example ii), *both/and* incorrectly connects the prepositional phrase *to the park* to the noun phrase *the downtown library*. In example iii), the coordinating conjunction *and then* is used correctly to connect three noun phrases in a list: *a park*, *a movie theater*, and *the downtown library*. In example iv), *and then* is used incorrectly because at least two components in the list differ in grammatical type: *a movie theater* is a noun phrase, whereas *went to the downtown library* is a verb phrase. Given this grammatical error, it is unclear whether the first component in the list is supposed to be the noun phrase *a park* or the verb phrase *went to a park*.

SC74010.03
Practice Question 23

Tropical bats play important roles in the rain forest ecosystem, aiding in the dispersal of cashew, date, and fig seeds; <u>pollinating banana, breadfruit, and mango trees; and indirectly help produce</u> tequila by pollinating agave plants.

- (A) pollinating banana, breadfruit, and mango trees; and indirectly help produce
- (B) pollinating banana, breadfruit, and mango trees; and indirectly helping to produce
- (C) pollinating banana, breadfruit, and mango trees; and they indirectly help to produce
- (D) they pollinate banana, breadfruit, and mango trees; and indirectly help producing
- (E) they pollinate banana, breadfruit, and mango trees; indirectly helping the producing of

SC74010.03
Answer Explanation 23

Logical Predication; Parallelism

This sentence expresses a list of the roles tropical bats play in the rain forest ecosystem. Since these roles are enumerated in a list, and since the first member of the list is already provided, it is necessary to maintain the same structure for the rest of the members of the list in order to maintain parallelism and clarity. Note that semicolons separate the members of the list, leaving the commas to mark series of items within each member of the list.

A   In this version, the third member of the list does not maintain the *ing* verb form that the two previous members use.

B   Correct. This version correctly maintains the parallel structure (*aiding in . . .; pollinating . . .; and helping . . .*).

C   In this version, the third member of the list does not maintain the *ing* verb form of the two previous members of the list. In addition, this member of the list includes a subject (*they*) while the other members do not, again violating parallelism.

D   In order to maintain parallelism the verb that is the member of the list has to be in the *ing* form, not its complement. Thus, the *ing* has to be on the verb *help*, not on *produce*.

E   Although this version maintains parallelism throughout, the phrase *helping the producing* is an incorrect construction in English.

The correct answer is B.

6. Style

A. Sentences that are grammatically correct and unambiguous may nonetheless be poorly written in various ways. For example, they may contain more words than needed to convey the intended meaning, or be confusing and annoying to the reader. A few common errors of this type include redundancy, unnecessary use of noun phrases in place of verbs, and inappropriate use of passive voice or other convoluted verbal constructions.

Examples:

Correct: i) Bananas are almost always harvested green and allowed to ripen in transit or on supermarket shelves.

Incorrect: ii) **With regard to how bananas are harvested and allowed to ripen,** they are almost always harvested green and allowed to ripen in transit or on supermarket shelves.

Incorrect: iii) Bananas are almost always harvested green, and **the ripening of the bananas** is allowed in transit or on supermarket shelves.

Incorrect: iv) Bananas are almost always harvested green, and **it is allowed that they ripen** in transit or on supermarket shelves.

In example i), the wording is straightforward and concise. Example ii) incorrectly starts with a redundant announcement of the sentence's topic. The reader can easily see that the sentence is about how bananas are harvested and allowed to ripen without the phrase *with regard to how bananas are harvested and allowed to ripen*, so that phrase is a pointless distraction. In example iii), the noun phrase *the ripening of the bananas* is an unnecessarily wordy substitute for example i)'s simple infinitive *to ripen*. In example iv), the construction *it is allowed that they ripen* is an unnecessarily wordy substitute for example i)'s simple *allowed to ripen*.

The variety of common stylistic errors in standard English writing is too vast for this review chapter to survey adequately. To learn about more types of stylistic error, consult guides to writing styles. Keep in mind that opinions differ about what constitutes good writing style, and that different guidebooks may contradict each other in the stylistic practices they recommend. The GMAT exam does not test familiarity with specific and potentially controversial stylistic rules advocated by any single style guide.

SC92120.03

Practice Question 24

With corn, soybean, and wheat reserves being low enough so a poor harvest would send prices skyrocketing, grain futures brokers and their clients are especially interested in weather that could affect crops.

- (A)   being low enough so
- (B)   so low such that
- (C)   so low that
- (D)   that are low enough so
- (E)   that are so low such that

CR09351.03

Practice Question 25

To Josephine Baker, Paris was her home long before it was fashionable to be an expatriate, and she remained in France during the Second World War as a performer and an intelligence agent for the Resistance.

- (A)   To Josephine Baker, Paris was her home long before it was fashionable to be an expatriate,
- (B)   For Josephine Baker, long before it was fashionable to be an expatriate, Paris was her home,
- (C)   Josephine Baker made Paris her home long before to be an expatriate was fashionable,
- (D)   Long before it was fashionable to be an expatriate, Josephine Baker made Paris her home,
- (E)   Long before it was fashionable being an expatriate, Paris was home to Josephine Baker,

SC92120.03
Answer Explanation 24

Idiom; Rhetorical Construction

This sentence opens with a long participial phrase (*With . . . skyrocketing*) that describes conditions within which the action of the main clause (*grain futures brokers . . . crops*) occurs. The opening phrase compares one economic condition (grain reserve levels) with another (prices), using the idiomatic expression *so low that*. Some of the phrases used in expressing this kind of comparison are wordy and indirect (*being low enough so*). Thus, they are not standard in written English, even though they may be accepted in some informal speaking contexts.

A   This phrase is wordy and unidiomatic.

B   This phrase combines two idioms (*so . . . that* and *such that*) in a way that does not clearly make sense. It is wordy and redundant; both *so . . . that* and *such* signal comparison.

C   **Correct.** This wording is standard, clear, and direct.

D   The relative clause introduced by *that are* makes this phrase unnecessarily wordy and cumbersome; *enough* and *so* are redundant.

E   This version of the phrase is the most redundant of all—piling comparative terms one upon the other (*that are so* and *such*). The repetition obscures instead of develops meaning.

The correct answer is C.

CR09351.03
Answer Explanation 25

Rhetorical Construction; Parallelism

This compound sentence (consisting of two independent clauses joined by the coordinating conjunction *and*) would be most clearly expressed if Josephine Baker were the subject of the first clause since *she* is the subject of the second clause: *Josephine Baker made Paris her home* would clearly parallel *she remained in France*. The adverb clause *long . . . expatriate* is best placed before the main first clause.

A   *To Josephine Baker . . . her* is redundant and awkward; the subject of the first main clause is *Paris* rather than *Baker*.

B   *For Josephine Baker . . . her* is redundant and awkward; putting two introductory elements together before the main clause is awkward.

C   Inversion of the expected word order in *to be an expatriate was unfashionable* is awkward.

D   **Correct.** The clearest, most economical order for this sentence is to put the adverb clause first, and make *Baker* the subject of the first main clause, parallel to *she* in the second.

E   *Being* is awkward; *Baker* should be the subject of the first main clause, parallel to *she* in the second main clause.

The correct answer is D.

4.0   Reading Comprehension

4.0 Reading Comprehension

Reading Comprehension questions appear in the Verbal Reasoning section of the GMAT™. They refer to written passages consisting of generally between 200 to 350 words. The passages discuss topics in the social sciences, humanities, physical and biological sciences, and such business-related fields as marketing, economics, and human resource management. Each passage is accompanied by a short series of questions asking you to interpret the text, apply the information you gather from the reading, and make inferences (or informed assumptions) based on the reading. For these questions, you will see a split computer screen. The written passage will remain visible on the left side as each question associated with that passage appears, in turn, on the right side. You will see only one question at a time. However, the number of questions associated with each passage may vary.

As you move through the Reading Comprehension sample questions, try to determine a process that works best for you. You might begin by reading a passage carefully and thoroughly. Some test takers prefer to skim the passages the first time through, or even to read the first question before reading the passage. You may want to reread any sentences that present complicated ideas or that introduce terms new to you. Read each question and series of answers carefully. Make sure you understand exactly what the question is asking and what the answer choices are.

If you need to, you may reread any parts of the passage relevant to answering the question that you are currently viewing, but you will not be able to return to other questions after you have answered them and moved on. Some questions ask explicitly about particular portions of the passages. In some cases, the portion referred to is highlighted while the relevant question is displayed. In such cases, the question will explicitly refer to the highlighted part.

The following pages describe what Reading Comprehension questions are designed to measure, the directions that will precede the questions, and the various question types. This chapter also provides test-taking strategies, sample questions, and detailed explanations of all the questions. The explanations further illustrate how Reading Comprehension questions evaluate basic reading skills.

4.1 What Is Measured

GMAT Reading Comprehension questions measure your ability to understand, analyze, apply, and evaluate information and concepts presented in written form. All questions are to be answered on the basis of what is stated or implied in the reading material, and no specific prior knowledge of the material is required. Success in all types of GMAT questions—except those that are purely mathematical—requires strong reading skills. Thus, for some examinees, Critical Reasoning, Sentence Correction, and word-based Quantitative questions inevitably test reading comprehension in addition to the skills that they primarily target. But they do so only indirectly and only at the level of proficiency needed to demonstrate the skills that are directly targeted. By contrast, the Reading Comprehension questions are designed to focus directly on various components of Reading Comprehension and to measure different levels of skill in those components.

Generally speaking, reading comprehension skills are divided into two fundamental categories: *Identify Stated Idea* and *Identify Inferred Idea*.

- *Identify Stated Idea* refers to your ability to understand the passage as a whole and its constituent parts. To answer questions related to this skill category, you need not do anything further with the information. The skills required for *Identify Stated Idea* are typically prerequisites for those in the second category, *Identify Inferred Idea*, but questions targeting either of these fundamental skill types may be just as difficult as those targeting the other.

- *Identify Inferred Idea* refers to your ability to use information in a passage for purposes such as inferring additional information on the basis of what is given, applying the information to further contexts, critiquing the views expressed in the passage, and evaluating the ways in which the writing is structured.

More specifically, GMAT Reading Comprehension questions evaluate your ability to do the following:

- **Understand complex, sophisticated nontechnical writing.**
Effective reading involves understanding not only words and phrases in context but also the overall messages conveyed by the writer. Although the questions do not directly measure your vocabulary knowledge (they will not ask you to show that you know the standard meanings of terms), some of them may test your ability to interpret special meanings of terms as they are used in the reading passages.

- **Understand the purposes and functions of passage components, and the logical and rhetorical relationships among concepts and pieces of information.**
Questions that focus on this type of skill may ask you, for example, to determine how part of a passage relates to other parts, to identify the strong and weak points of an argument, or to evaluate the relative importance of arguments and ideas in a passage.

- **Draw inferences from facts and statements.**
With a little reflection, anyone who thoroughly comprehends a text should be able to determine what further information can be inferred from it. The inference questions will ask you to reach conclusions on the basis of factual statements, authors' claims and opinions, or other components of a reading passage.

- **Understand and follow the development of quantitative concepts in written material.**
Reading Comprehension questions do not measure mathematical knowledge. However, the passages sometimes contain quantitative information or opinions about such matters as percentages, proportions, trends, probabilities, or statistics, expressed in ways that should be understandable without technical mathematical training. You may be asked to interpret, evaluate, or apply such quantitative information, or to draw inferences from it. In some cases, you might need to use some very simple arithmetic.

There are six kinds of Reading Comprehension questions, each kind focusing on a different skill. But there is inevitably some peripheral overlap between the skills tested by one kind of question and those tested by others. For example, identifying a passage's main point often requires recognizing the logical or rhetorical structure of the text, while drawing inferences or applying information often requires accurately understanding of the passage's main and supporting ideas.

During the test, no labels will indicate which kind of Reading Comprehension question you are looking at, but each question's wording will clearly indicate what you need to do. Most of the Reading Comprehension question types will be represented among the several Reading Comprehension sets in your test, but you may not see all the types.

The Reading Comprehension questions fall into the following categories:

1. Main Idea

Each passage is a unified whole—that is, the individual sentences and paragraphs support and develop one central point and have a single unified purpose. Sometimes you will be told the central point in the passage itself, and sometimes you will need to determine the central point from the overall organization or development of the passage. A Main Idea question may ask you to

- recognize an accurate summary, restatement, or paraphrase of the main idea of a passage
- identify the author's primary purpose or objective in writing the passage
- assign a title that summarizes, briefly and pointedly, the main idea developed in the passage.

Main idea questions are usually easy to identify as such. They generally ask explicitly about the main idea or main purpose, using phrases such as:

> *Which of the following most accurately expresses the main idea of the passage?,*
> *The primary purpose of the passage as a whole is to ...,* or
> *In the passage, the author seeks primarily to ....*

Incorrect answer choices for these questions often take the form of ideas in the passage that are subsidiary or tangential to the main point, statements that are superficially similar to but demonstrably distinct from the main point, or statements that are simply outside the scope of the passage even though they may be conceptually related to it.

As you read a passage, you may find it helpful to consider the rhetorical strategy the author is using. For example, is the author primarily reporting facts, events, or other writers' views; arguing for a point of view; or commenting on others' views or on events or states of affairs? Identifying the rhetorical strategy is essential in answering Main Idea questions that ask about the passage's purpose, but can also help focus your thoughts for those that ask about a main idea as such. The two major rhetorical strategies in reading passages are argumentation and exposition, each involving different kinds of main-idea questions.

In passages primarily involving argumentation, the correct answer to a Main Idea question will typically be a paraphrase or description of the main conclusion of the passage's main argument. This conclusion is the main position the passage is intended to persuade readers to accept. The main conclusion is sometimes, but not always, stated explicitly in the passage. When it is not, the passage will make it clear to careful, perceptive readers what the author is arguing for. The correct answer choice may also briefly mention to the reasons given in support of the position. For example, the answer choice might begin with the words ***An analysis of recent findings supports the hypothesis that ....***

The answer to a Main Idea question about an expository passage can take various forms, depending on the author's purpose and focus. In general, the answer will summarize the most important overall idea or theme discussed throughout the passage, or the overall purpose of the passage. For example, the answer to a Main Idea question about a narrative passage may be either a concise one-sentence summary of the events described or a statement of the overall outcome of the events, depending on the author's focus. And the answer to a Main Idea question about the purpose of a descriptive passage might be a sentence fragment that begins with the words ***To describe the roles of ....***

2. Supporting Idea

These questions measure your ability to comprehend ideas directly expressed in a passage and differentiate them from ideas that are neither expressed nor implied in the passage. They also measure your ability to differentiate supporting ideas from the main idea and from ideas implied by the author but not explicitly stated.

Like Main Idea questions, Supporting Idea questions simply assess whether you understand the messages conveyed in the writing, without asking you to do anything further with the information. *Supporting* refers not only to ideas expressed as premises supporting a main conclusion, but also to other ideas other than the main idea. Since each GMAT Reading Comprehension passage has an overall main point or purpose, every part of the passage can be thought of as supporting that main point or purpose in some way, either directly or tangentially. Therefore, Supporting Idea questions may ask you to understand and identify anything (other than the main point) that is stated in the passage.

Correct answers to Supporting Idea questions almost never consist of verbatim quotations from the passage, so you will need to be able to recognize paraphrases or more abstract expressions of the passage material. Among the passage components you may be asked to understand and recognize are:

- a premise of an argument
- a tangential point such as an acknowledgment of a potential objection to the author's position
- an example given to illustrate a principle or generalization
- a counterexample intended to provide evidence against a principle or generalization
- a fact cited as background information relevant to the main idea or to a subsidiary idea
- a component of a complex explanation, description, or narration
- a brief statement of a position against which the author's reasoning is directed
- a descriptive detail used to support or elaborate on the main idea.

Whereas questions about the main idea ask you to determine the meaning of the passage as a whole, questions about supporting ideas ask you to determine the meanings of individual phrases, sentences, and paragraphs that contribute to the meaning of the passage as a whole. In many cases, these questions can be thought of as asking for the main point of one small part of the passage. Supporting Idea questions often contain key phrases such as:

According to the passage ...,
Which of the following does the author cite as ...,
The passage mentions which of the following ..., or
Which of the following does the author propose ....

Answering Supporting Idea questions requires remembering or quickly locating the relevant information in the passage. Occasionally, it may be possible to answer a question by quickly glancing to find the needed information without first fully reading through the passage, but as a general strategy, that could be risky and even time-consuming. Supporting Idea questions typically require a good understanding of the relationships among parts of the passage. In many cases, they will ask you to identify a piece of information that plays a specified role or is presented in a specified context. Thus, they may contain phrases such as:

Which of the following does the author offer as an objection to ...,
According to the passage, new businesses are more likely to fail if they ..., or
The passage compares the sea turtle's thermoregulation to ....

3. Inference

Inference questions ask about ideas that are not explicitly stated in a passage but are implied by the author or otherwise follow logically from the information in the passage. Unlike questions about supporting ideas, which ask about information directly expressed in a passage, inference questions ask about ideas or meanings that must be inferred from the information directly stated.

Authors often make their points in indirect ways, suggesting ideas without actually stating them. Inference questions measure your ability to understand an author's intended meaning in parts of a passage where the meaning is only suggested. They sometimes also measure your ability to understand further implications that clearly follow from the information in the passage, even if the author does not clearly intend them to be inferred. Therefore, when you read a passage, you should concentrate not only on the explicit meaning of the author's words, but also on the subtler meanings and unstated implications of those words. Inference questions do not ask about obscure or tenuous implications that are very remote from the passage; rather, they ask about things that any astute, observant reader should be able to infer from the passage after a little reflection.

You may be asked to draw inferences in order to identify:

- a likely cause of a phenomenon or situation described in the passage

- a likely effect of a phenomenon or situation described in the passage

- a specific instance or subset based on a generalization given in the passage.

For example, if the passage indicates that all reptiles have a certain property and also mentions that crocodiles are reptiles, you could infer that crocodiles have the property in question.

- a statement that the author (or someone referred to in the passage) likely considers true or false

- an evaluative position that the author (or someone referred to in the passage) likely holds.

For example, it may be possible to infer from the author's word choices that she or he disapproves of something discussed in the passage.

- the intended meaning of a word or phrase based on how that word or phrase is used in the passage. However, GMAT questions will not ask you to define a word used in the passage with a standard meaning that could be accurately guessed from background vocabulary knowledge.

In some cases, the inference you are asked to draw will follow from a single statement or series of statements in the passage. In other cases, it will require you to consider together two or more separate parts of the passage. The relevant parts may be close together or far apart, but they will always be significant aspects of the passage, not irrelevant or highly obscure details. The question may refer explicitly to one or more portions of the passage, or it may require you to locate or remember the relevant information.

Inference questions often contain phrases such as:

Which of the following statements about … is most strongly supported by the passage?,
It can be inferred from the passage that …,
If the claims made by the author about … are true, which of the following is most likely also true?,
The passage implies that …, or
The information in the passage suggests that ….

Some of the inferences might depend on commonly known and obviously true facts in addition to the information supplied by the passage. For example, if the passage says that an event happened during a snowstorm, you could reasonably infer that the weather was not hot at that time and place.

Incorrect answer choices for inference questions are often statements that appear superficially related to the passage but are not supported by the information in question. When the question asks what can be inferred from a specific part of the passage, you should be careful not to select an answer that follows from some other part of the passage but not from the part in question.

Incorrect answer choices are often true statements even though they are not supported by the information in the passage. Conversely, the correct answer could be a false statement implied by false information in the passage. For example, when the author explains why a theory is mistaken, you might be asked to infer that if the theory were true, such incorrect information would also have to be true.

Occasionally, it may not be possible to tell merely from a question's wording whether you are being asked to infer something or rather to recognize something directly expressed. For example, a question beginning *"In the passage, the author suggests …"* might be asking you to note that the author explicitly makes a certain suggestion in the passage. More typically, a question beginning *"The passage suggests …"* will be asking you to identify an idea the text implies but does not explicitly state. However, if you understand the passage and the relationships and implications of its parts, you will be able to find the correct answer without having to worry about how the test writers classified the question.

4. Application

Application questions measure your ability to discern relationships between situations or ideas presented in the passage and other situations or ideas beyond the direct scope of the passage. The most crucial skill involved in answering application questions is that of abstracting key features or principles from one context and applying them effectively to other contexts. This skill is often needed when working with scholarly, legal, professional, or business writings.

Application questions are often hypothetical or speculative, and therefore may contain words such as *would, could, might*, or *should*, or phrases such as *most clearly exemplifies, is most similar to*, or *is most likely ruled out by*. Some application questions pose analogies between passage topics and other topics.

Because application questions can be about the relationships of the passage to topics outside its scope, you should not expect to be able to eliminate any answer choice based on whether or not its topic appears in the passage. For instance, all the answer choices for an analogy question relating to a passage's explanation of a water-treatment process might refer to book-publishing processes.

Here are some major application types you may encounter on the exam:

A. *Analogies.* These could involve:

- a function or purpose similar to the function or purpose of something described in the passage.

A question might ask, for instance, ***In which of the following is the role played by a computer program most analogous to the role of the protein molecule in the pesticide discussed in the passage?***

- a method or procedure similar to one described in the passage but used in a different context
- a goal or purpose similar to the goal or purpose of something discussed in the passage.

For example, a protest demonstration's goal of changing one country's environmental policies would be more analogous to a politician's goal of changing another country's food safety regulations than to an employee's goal of finding a new job.

- a part–whole relationship similar to a part–whole relationship described in the passage.

This could be, for example, a relationship between an organism and its ecosystem, or between a book chapter and the book as a whole.

- a logical relationship similar to the relationship between parts of the passage or between elements of someone's reasoning described in the passage.

B. *Principles, policies, and procedures.* You may be asked to identify, for example:

- a rule or policy that if enforced could help bring about a goal presented in the passage
- a principle that is not explicitly formulated in the passage but underlies the author's reasoning
- a generalization supported by a range of specific instances referred to in the passage
- an action or situation violating or conforming to a rule or policy mentioned in the passage
- a potential solution to a problem discussed in the passage
- an alternative approach that could have the same effect as one discussed in the passage.

C. *Extensions of the author's rhetorical strategies.* These include such things as:

- an example effectively illustrating a point made by the author
- a prediction about how the author would likely respond to an objection to her or his position
- an additional topic that could be relevantly added to the discussion in the passage
- an idea the passage does not express but implies that the author would probably accept or reject.

D. *What-if scenarios.* You might need to identify, for example:

- a hypothetical extension of a trend or series of developments described in the passage
- how a researcher's conclusions would have been logically affected if some observed data had been different from the data reported in the passage

- how circumstances would likely have been different if developments described in the passage had not occurred

- how someone whose views are described in the passage would likely respond if that person read the passage.

5. Evaluation

Evaluation questions require you to analyze and evaluate a passage's organization and logic. They fall into two broad subcategories: analysis and critique.

Analysis-type evaluation questions require you to determine how parts of the passage work in relation to each other. These questions often ask about the author's purpose. Unlike main-idea questions about authors' purposes, they do not ask you to identify the entire passage's overall purpose, but rather the purposes of specific elements within the passage, and the relationships among those purposes. However, some evaluation questions may ask you to identify the logical structure of the passage or of a portion of the passage.

Critique-type evaluation questions require you to judge the strengths, weaknesses, relevance, or effectiveness of parts of the passage, as well as those parts' relationships to potential objections or justifications. These questions often involve some of the same types of reasoning encountered in Critical Reasoning questions. Reading Comprehension evaluation questions require neither technical knowledge of formal logic nor familiarity with specialized terms of logic or argumentation. You can answer these questions using the information in the passage and careful reasoning.

Evaluation questions often contain phrases such as:

The purpose of …,
… most accurately describes the structure of …,
… most strengthens …,
… would most justify …,
… is most vulnerable to the objection that …, or
Which … additional information would most help ….

Answer choices are often abstract and might not contain any words or concepts that appear in the passage. For example, a question that asks about a paragraph's function might have an answer choice such as: **It rejects a theory presented in the preceding paragraph and offers some criteria that an alternative theory would need to meet.**

Here are some major application types that you may encounter in the test:

A. *Analysis.* Answers to these questions might be, for example, statements about:

- how the passage as a whole is constructed.

In such cases, the answer will sometimes be expressed as an abstract summary of the elements that make up the passage.

- how a portion of the passage is constructed

- the purpose or function of one part of the passage.

For instance, does that part of the passage define a term, compare or contrast two ideas, present a new idea, or refute an idea?

- how one portion of the passage relates logically or rhetorically to surrounding parts
- how the author tries to persuade readers to accept his or her assertions
- a likely reason or motivation for a view the author expresses or attributes to someone else.

B. Critique. In these questions, you may be asked to identify, for example,

- an assumption involved in the author's reasoning or in someone else's reasoning discussed in the passage
- crucial gaps in the information provided in the passage
- a potential discovery that would help resolve an issue discussed in the passage
- a statement that, if true, would strengthen or weaken the author's reasoning or someone else's reasoning presented in the passage
- a potential counterexample to a general claim made in the passage.

6. Style and Tone

Effective reading often depends on recognizing and evaluating both the author's attitude toward a topic and the effect the author intends the writing to have on readers. These are often implicit in the passage's style and tone rather than stated explicitly.

Some questions focus directly and exclusively on the style or tone of the passage as a whole. They often involve phrases such as:

The overall tone of the passage can be most accurately described as …,
The passage, as a whole, functions primarily as a …, or
The author's approach to … can be most accurately described as ….

In the answer choices, you may be asked to select an adjective or adjective phrase that accurately describes the overall tone of the passage—for instance, *critical, questioning, objective, dismissive,* or *enthusiastic.* Answer choices may also be noun phrases such as *advocacy for a political position, a sarcastic portrayal of a historical trend,* or *a journalistic exploration of some attempts to solve a problem.* Or the answer choices may be more complex clauses or full sentences.

To answer questions about style and tone, you will typically have to consider the language of the passage or a large section of the passage as a whole. It takes more than one pointed, critical word to give an entire passage or section a critical tone. Sometimes, style and tone questions ask what audience the passage was probably intended for or what type of publication it would most appropriately appear in. To answer any question involving style and tone, you must ask yourself what attitudes or objectives a passage's words convey beyond their literal meanings.

You may sometimes need to consider style and tone in answering any type of Reading Comprehension question, even a question that does not explicitly ask about that aspect of the passage. Some question types are more likely than others to involve this type of consideration. An inference question, for example, may ask you to infer the author's attitude toward a topic. You may also need to consider the passage's tone in order to confidently identify the passage's main purpose. And some evaluation questions require you to recognize the rhetorical approach the author takes in a portion of the passage.

4.2 Test-Taking Strategies

1. **Do not expect to be completely familiar with material presented in the passages.**
   You may find some passages easier to understand than others, but all passages are designed to present a challenge. If you have some familiarity with the material presented in a passage, do not let this knowledge influence your choice of answers to the questions. Answer all questions on the basis of what is **stated or implied** in the passage itself.

2. **Analyze each passage carefully, because the questions require you to have a specific and detailed understanding of the passages.**
   You may find it easier to analyze a passage first before moving to the questions. Alternatively, you may prefer to skim the passage the first time and read more carefully once you understand the questions. You may even want to read the question before reading the passage. You should choose the method most suitable for you.

3. **Focus on key words and phrases, trying to maintain an overall sense of what is discussed in the passage.**

   Keep the following in mind:

   - Note how each fact relates to an idea or an argument
   - Note where the passage moves from one idea to the next
   - Distinguish the passage's main idea from its supporting ideas
   - Determine what conclusions are reached and why.

4. **Read the questions carefully, making sure you understand what is asked.**
   An answer choice that accurately restates information in the passage may be incorrect if it does not answer the question. Refer back to the passage for clarification if you need to.

5. **Read all the answer choices carefully.**
   Never assume that you have selected the best answer without first reading all the choices.

6. **Select the choice that answers the question best in terms of the information given in the passage.**
   Do not rely on outside knowledge of the material to help you answer the questions.

7. **Remember that comprehension—not speed—is the critical success factor on the Reading Comprehension section.**

4.3 Section Instructions

Go to www.mba.com/tutorial to view instructions for the section and get a feel for what the test center screens will look like on the actual GMAT exam.

4.4 Practice Questions

Each of the Reading Comprehension questions is based on the content of a passage. After reading the passage, answer all questions pertaining to it on the basis of what is stated or implied in the passage. For each question, select the best answer of the choices given. On the actual GMAT exam, you will see no more than four questions per passage.

Questions 1 to 36 - Difficulty: Easy

Line   Human beings, born with a drive to explore and experiment, thrive on learning. Unfortunately, corporations are oriented predominantly toward controlling employees, not fostering their learning.
(5) Ironically, this orientation creates the very conditions that predestine employees to mediocre performances. Over time, superior performance requires superior learning, because long-term corporate survival depends on continually exploring
(10) new business and organizational opportunities that can create new sources of growth.
     To survive in the future, corporations must become "learning organizations," enterprises that are constantly able to adapt and expand their
(15) capabilities. To accomplish this, corporations must change how they view employees. The traditional view that a single charismatic leader should set the corporation's direction and make key decisions is rooted in an individualistic worldview. In an
(20) increasingly interdependent world, such a view is no longer viable. In learning organizations, thinking and acting are integrated at all job levels. Corporate leadership is shared, and leaders become designers, teachers, and stewards, roles requiring
(25) new skills: the ability to build shared vision, to reveal and challenge prevailing mental models, and to foster broader, more integrated patterns of thinking. In short, leaders in learning organizations are responsible for building organizations in which
(30) employees are continually learning new skills and expanding their capabilities to shape their future.

Questions 1–4 refer to the passage.

*RC00184-01

1. According to the passage, traditional corporate leaders differ from leaders in learning organizations in that the former

(A) encourage employees to concentrate on developing a wide range of skills

(B) enable employees to recognize and confront dominant corporate models and to develop alternative models

(C) make important policy decisions alone and then require employees in the corporation to abide by those decisions

(D) instill confidence in employees because of their willingness to make risky decisions and accept their consequences

(E) are concerned with offering employees frequent advice and career guidance

RC00184-02

2. Which of the following best describes employee behavior encouraged within learning organizations, as such organizations are described in the passage?

(A) Carefully defining one's job description and taking care to avoid deviations from it

(B) Designing mentoring programs that train new employees to follow procedures that have been used for many years

(C) Concentrating one's efforts on mastering one aspect of a complicated task

(D) Studying an organizational problem, preparing a report, and submitting it to a corporate leader for approval

(E) Analyzing a problem related to productivity, making a decision about a solution, and implementing that solution

---

*These numbers correlate with the online test bank question number. See the GMAT™ Official Guide Verbal Review Question Index in the back of this book.

90

RC00184-03

3. According to the author of the passage, corporate leaders of the future should do which of the following?

(A) They should encourage employees to put long-term goals ahead of short-term profits.

(B) They should exercise more control over employees in order to constrain production costs.

(C) They should redefine incentives for employees' performance improvement.

(D) They should provide employees with opportunities to gain new skills and expand their capabilities.

(E) They should promote individual managers who are committed to established company policies.

RC00184-04

4. The primary purpose of the passage is to

(A) endorse a traditional corporate structure

(B) introduce a new approach to corporate leadership and evaluate criticisms of it

(C) explain competing theories about management practices and reconcile them

(D) contrast two typical corporate organizational structures

(E) propose an alternative to a common corporate approach

Line   Structural unemployment—the unemployment
that remains even at the peak of the economy's
upswings—is caused by an imbalance between the
types and locations of available employment on the
(5)   one hand and the qualifications and locations of
workers on the other hand. When such an imbalance
exists, both labor shortages and unemployment may
occur, despite a balance between supply and demand
for labor in the economy as a whole.
(10)   Because technological change is likely to displace
some workers, it is a major factor in producing
structural unemployment. While technological
advance almost invariably results in shifts in
demands for different types of workers, it does not
(15)   necessarily result in unemployment. Relatively small
or gradual changes in demand are likely to cause
little unemployment. In the individual firm or even in
the labor market as a whole, normal attrition may
be sufficient to reduce the size of the work force in
(20)   the affected occupations. Relatively large or rapid
changes, however, can cause serious problems.
Workers may lose their jobs and find themselves
without the skills necessary to obtain new jobs.
Whether this displacement leads to structural
(25)   unemployment depends on the amount of public and
private sector resources devoted to retraining and
placing those workers. Workers can be encouraged
to move where there are jobs, to reeducate or retrain
themselves, or to retire. In addition, other factors
(30)   affecting structural unemployment, such as capital
movement, can be controlled.
    Increased structural unemployment, should it occur,
makes it difficult for the economy to achieve desired low
rates of unemployment along with low rates of inflation.
(35)   If there is a growing pool of workers who lack the
necessary skills for the available jobs, increases in total
labor demand will rapidly generate shortages of qualified
workers. As the wages of those workers are bid up,
labor costs, and thus prices, rise. This phenomenon
(40)   may be an important factor in the rising trend, observed
for the past two decades, of unemployment combined
with inflation. Government policy has placed a priority on
reducing inflation, but these efforts have nevertheless
caused unemployment to increase.

Questions 5–10 refer to the passage.

RC00144-03

5.   All of the following are mentioned as ways of
controlling the magnitude of structural unemployment
EXCEPT

(A)   using public funds to create jobs

(B)   teaching new skills to displaced workers

(C)   allowing displaced workers to retire

(D)   controlling the movement of capital

(E)   encouraging workers to move to where jobs are
available

RC00144-04

6.   The passage suggests that a potential outcome of
higher structural unemployment is

(A)   increased public spending for social services

(B)   placement of workers in jobs for which they are
not qualified

(C)   higher wages for those workers who have skills
that are in demand

(D)   an increase in the length of time jobs remain
unfilled

(E)   a shift in the government's economic policy
priorities

RC00144-05

7. It can be inferred from the passage that even when there are unemployed workers, labor shortages are still likely to occur if

   (A) the inflation rate is unusually high

   (B) there is insufficient technological innovation

   (C) the level of structural unemployment is exceptionally low

   (D) the jobs available in certain places require skills that the labor force in those areas lacks

   (E) the workers in some industries are dissatisfied with the pay offered in those industries

RC00144-06

8. The passage suggests that the phenomenon of combined unemployment and inflation is

   (A) a socioeconomic problem that can only be addressed by government intervention

   (B) a socioeconomic problem that can be characteristic of periods of structural unemployment

   (C) an economic problem that results from government intervention in management-labor relations

   (D) an economic problem that results from imperfect applications of technology

   (E) an economic problem that can be eliminated by relatively small changes in the labor force

RC00144-07

9. The passage is primarily concerned with

   (A) clarifying the definition of a concept

   (B) proposing a way to eliminate an undesirable condition

   (C) discussing the sources and consequences of a problem

   (D) suggesting ways to alleviate the effects of a particular social policy

   (E) evaluating the steps that have been taken to correct an imbalance

RC00144-08

10. According to the passage, small downward shifts in the demand for labor will not usually cause unemployment because

   (A) such shifts are frequently accompanied by upswings in the economy

   (B) such shifts usually occur slowly

   (C) workers can be encouraged to move to where there are jobs

   (D) normal attrition is often sufficient to reduce the size of the work force

   (E) workers are usually flexible enough to learn new skills and switch to new jobs

Line   In 1971 researchers hoping to predict earthquakes in the short term by identifying precursory phenomena (those that occur a few days before large quakes but not otherwise) turned their attention to changes
(5)   in seismic waves that had been detected prior to earthquakes. An explanation for such changes was offered by "dilatancy theory," based on a well-known phenomenon observed in rocks in the laboratory: as stress builds, microfractures in rock close,
(10)   decreasing the rock's volume. But as stress continues to increase, the rock begins to crack and expand in volume, allowing groundwater to seep in, weakening the rock. According to this theory, such effects could lead to several precursory phenomena in
(15)   the field, including a change in the velocity of seismic waves, and an increase in small, nearby tremors.

Researchers initially reported success in identifying these possible precursors, but subsequent analyses of their data proved disheartening. Seismic waves
(20)   with unusual velocities were recorded before some earthquakes, but while the historical record confirms that most large earthquakes are preceded by minor tremors, these foreshocks indicate nothing about the magnitude of an impending quake and are
(25)   indistinguishable from other minor tremors that occur without large earthquakes.

In the 1980s, some researchers turned their efforts from short-term to long-term prediction. Noting that earthquakes tend to occur repeatedly in
(30)   certain regions, Lindh and Baker attempted to identify patterns of recurrence, or earthquake cycles, on which to base predictions. In a study of earthquake-prone sites along the San Andreas Fault, they determined that quakes occurred at intervals of approximately 22
(35)   years near one site and concluded that there was a 95 percent probability of an earthquake in that area by 1992. The earthquake did not occur within the time frame predicted, however.

Line   Evidence against the kind of regular
(40)   earthquake cycles that Lindh and Baker tried to establish has come from a relatively new field, paleoseismology. Paleoseismologists have unearthed and dated geological features such as fault scarps that were caused by
(45)   earthquakes thousands of years ago. They have determined that the average interval between ten earthquakes that took place at one site along the San Andreas Fault in the past two millennia was 132 years, but individual intervals ranged greatly,
(50)   from 44 to 332 years.

Questions 11–16 refer to the passage.

RC00113-01

11.   The passage is primarily concerned with

(A)   explaining why one method of earthquake prediction has proven more practicable than an alternative method

(B)   suggesting that accurate earthquake forecasting must combine elements of long-term and short-term prediction

(C)   challenging the usefulness of dilatancy theory for explaining the occurrence of precursory phenomena

(D)   discussing the deficiency of two methods by which researchers have attempted to predict the occurrence of earthquakes

(E)   describing the development of methods for establishing patterns in the occurrence of past earthquakes

RC00113-02

12. According to the passage, laboratory evidence concerning the effects of stress on rocks might help account for

   (A) differences in magnitude among earthquakes

   (B) certain phenomena that occur prior to earthquakes

   (C) variations in the intervals between earthquakes in a particular area

   (D) differences in the frequency with which earthquakes occur in various areas

   (E) the unreliability of short-term earthquake predictions

RC00113-03

13. It can be inferred from the passage that one problem with using precursory phenomena to predict earthquakes is that minor tremors

   (A) typically occur some distance from the sites of the large earthquakes that follow them

   (B) are directly linked to the mechanisms that cause earthquakes

   (C) are difficult to distinguish from major tremors

   (D) have proven difficult to measure accurately

   (E) are not always followed by large earthquakes

RC00113-04

14. According to the passage, some researchers based their research about long-term earthquake prediction on which of the following facts?

   (A) The historical record confirms that most earthquakes have been preceded by minor tremors.

   (B) The average interval between earthquakes in one region of the San Andreas Fault is 132 years.

   (C) Some regions tend to be the site of numerous earthquakes over the course of many years.

   (D) Changes in the volume of rock can occur as a result of building stress and can lead to the weakening of rock.

   (E) Paleoseismologists have been able to unearth and date geological features caused by past earthquakes.

RC00113-05

15. The passage suggests which of the following about the paleoseismologists' findings described in lines 42–50?

   (A) They suggest that the frequency with which earthquakes occurred at a particular site decreased significantly over the past two millennia.

   (B) They suggest that paleoseismologists may someday be able to make reasonably accurate long-term earthquake predictions.

   (C) They suggest that researchers may someday be able to determine which past occurrences of minor tremors were actually followed by large earthquakes.

   (D) They suggest that the recurrence of earthquakes in earthquake-prone sites is too irregular to serve as a basis for earthquake prediction.

   (E) They indicate that researchers attempting to develop long-term methods of earthquake prediction have overlooked important evidence concerning the causes of earthquakes.

RC00113-07

16. The author implies which of the following about the ability of the researchers mentioned in line 18 to predict earthquakes?

   (A) They can identify when an earthquake is likely to occur but not how large it will be.

   (B) They can identify the regions where earthquakes are likely to occur but not when they will occur.

   (C) They are unable to determine either the time or the place that earthquakes are likely to occur.

   (D) They are likely to be more accurate at short-term earthquake prediction than at long-term earthquake prediction.

   (E) They can determine the regions where earthquakes have occurred in the past but not the regions where they are likely to occur in the future.

Line   A key decision required of advertising managers is whether a "hard-sell" or "soft-sell" strategy is appropriate for a specific target market. The hard-sell approach involves the use of direct, forceful

(5)   claims regarding the benefits of the advertised brand over competitors' offerings. In contrast, the soft-sell approach involves the use of advertising claims that imply superiority more subtly.

         One positive aspect of the hard-sell approach is

(10)   its use of very simple and straightforward product claims presented as explicit conclusions, with little room for confusion regarding the advertiser's message. However, some consumers may resent being told what to believe and some may distrust

(15)   the message. Resentment and distrust often lead to counterargumentation and to boomerang effects where consumers come to believe conclusions diametrically opposed to conclusions endorsed in advertising claims. By contrast, the risk of

(20)   boomerang effects is greatly reduced with soft-sell approaches. One way to implement the soft-sell approach is to provide information that implies the main conclusions the advertiser wants the consumer to draw, but leave the conclusions

(25)   themselves unstated. Because consumers are invited to make up their own minds, implicit conclusions reduce the risk of resentment, distrust, and counterargumentation.

         Recent research on consumer memory and

(30)   judgment suggests another advantage of implicit conclusions. Beliefs or conclusions that are self-generated are more accessible from memory than beliefs from conclusions provided explicitly by other individuals, and thus have a greater impact on

(35)   judgment and decision making. Moreover, self-generated beliefs are often perceived as more accurate and valid than the beliefs of others, because other individuals may be perceived as less knowledgeable, or may be perceived as

(40)   manipulative or deliberately misleading.

Line   Despite these advantages, implicit conclusions may not always be more effective than explicit conclusions. One risk is that some consumers may fail to draw their own conclusions and thus miss the

(45)   point of the message. Inferential activity is likely only when consumers are motivated and able to engage in effortful cognitive processes. Another risk is that some consumers may draw conclusions other than the one intended. Even if inferential

(50)   activity is likely there is no guarantee that consumers will follow the path provided by the advertiser. Finally, a third risk is that consumers may infer the intended conclusion but question the validity of their inference.

Questions 17–23 refer to the passage.

RC00492-01

17. It can be inferred from the passage that one reason an advertiser might prefer a hard-sell approach to a soft-sell approach is that

(A)   the risks of boomerang effects are minimized when the conclusions an advertiser wants the consumer to draw are themselves left unstated

(B)   counterargumentation is likely from consumers who fail to draw their own conclusions regarding an advertising claim

(C)   inferential activity is likely to occur even if consumers perceive themselves to be more knowledgeable than the individuals presenting product claims

(D)   research on consumer memory suggests that the explicit conclusions provided by an advertiser using the hard-sell approach have a significant impact on decision making

(E)   the information presented by an advertiser using the soft-sell approach may imply different conclusions to different consumers

RC00492-02

18. Each of the following is mentioned in the passage as a characteristic of the hard-sell approach EXCEPT:

(A) Its overall message is readily grasped.

(B) It appeals to consumers' knowledge about the product.

(C) It makes explicit claims that the advertised brand is superior to other brands.

(D) It uses statements that are expressed very clearly.

(E) It makes claims in the form of direct conclusions.

RC00492-03

19. It can be inferred from the passage that advertisers could reduce one of the risks discussed in the last paragraph if they were able to provide

(A) motivation for consumers to think about the advertisement's message

(B) information that implies the advertiser's intended conclusion but leaves that conclusion unstated

(C) subtle evidence that the advertised product is superior to that of competitors

(D) information comparing the advertised product with its competitors

(E) opportunity for consumers to generate their own beliefs or conclusions

RC00492-04

20. The primary purpose of the passage is to

(A) point out the risks involved in the use of a particular advertising strategy

(B) make a case for the superiority of one advertising strategy over another

(C) illustrate the ways in which two advertising strategies may be implemented

(D) present the advantages and disadvantages of two advertising strategies

(E) contrast the types of target markets for which two advertising strategies are appropriate

RC00492-05

21. Which of the following best describes the function of the sentence in lines 25–28 in the context of the passage as a whole?

(A) It reiterates a distinction between two advertising strategies that is made in the first paragraph.

(B) It explains how a particular strategy avoids a drawback described earlier in the paragraph.

(C) It suggests that a risk described earlier in the paragraph is less serious than some researchers believe it to be.

(D) It outlines why the strategy described in the previous sentence involves certain risks for an advertiser.

(E) It introduces an argument that will be refuted in the following paragraph.

RC00492-06

22. It can be inferred from the passage that one situation in which the boomerang effect often occurs is when consumers

(A) have been exposed to forceful claims that are diametrically opposed to those in an advertiser's message

(B) have previous self-generated beliefs or conclusions that are readily accessible from memory

(C) are subjected to advertising messages that are targeted at specific markets to which those consumers do not belong

(D) are confused regarding the point of the advertiser's message

(E) come to view the advertiser's message with suspicion

RC00492-07

23. It can be inferred from the passage that the research mentioned in line 29 supports which of the following statements?

(A) Implicit conclusions are more likely to capture accurately the point of the advertiser's message than are explicit conclusions.

(B) Counterargumentation is less likely to occur if an individual's beliefs or conclusions are readily accessible from memory.

(C) The hard-sell approach results in conclusions that are more difficult for the consumer to recall than are conclusions resulting from the soft-sell approach.

(D) When the beliefs of others are presented as definite and forceful claims, they are perceived to be as accurate as self-generated beliefs.

(E) Despite the advantages of implicit conclusions, the hard-sell approach involves fewer risks for the advertiser than does the soft-sell approach.

Line   Suppose we were in a spaceship in free fall, where objects are weightless, and wanted to know a small solid object's mass. We could not simply balance that object against another of known weight, as we
(5)   would on Earth. The unknown mass could be determined, however, by placing the object on a spring scale and swinging the scale in a circle at the end of a string. The scale would measure the tension in the string, which would depend on both
(10)   the speed of revolution and the mass of the object. The tension would be greater, the greater the mass or the greater the speed of revolution. From the measured tension and speed of whirling, we could determine the object's mass.
(15)   Astronomers use an analogous procedure to "weigh" double-star systems. The speed with which the two stars in a double-star system circle one another depends on the gravitational force between them, which holds the system together. This
(20)   attractive force, analogous to the tension in the string, is proportional to the stars' combined mass, according to Newton's law of gravitation. By observing the time required for the stars to circle each other (the period) and measuring the distance
(25)   between them, we can deduce the restraining force, and hence the masses.

Questions 24–28 refer to the passage.

RC00222-01

24.   It can be inferred from the passage that the two procedures described in the passage have which of the following in common?

(A)   They have been applied in practice.

(B)   They rely on the use of a device that measures tension.

(C)   Their purpose is to determine an unknown mass.

(D)   They can only be applied to small solid objects.

(E)   They involve attraction between objects of similar mass.

RC00222-02

25.   According to the passage, the tension in the string mentioned in lines 8–9 is analogous to which of the following aspects of a double-star system?

(A)   The speed with which one star orbits the other

(B)   The gravitational attraction between the stars

(C)   The amount of time it takes for the stars to circle one another

(D)   The distance between the two stars

(E)   The combined mass of the two stars

RC00222-03

26.   Which of the following best describes the relationship between the first and the second paragraph of the passage?

(A)   The first paragraph provides an illustration useful for understanding a procedure described in the second paragraph.

(B)   The first paragraph describes a hypothetical situation whose plausibility is tested in the second paragraph.

(C)   The first paragraph evaluates the usefulness of a procedure whose application is described further in the second paragraph.

(D)   The second paragraph provides evidence to support a claim made in the first paragraph.

(E)   The second paragraph analyzes the practical implications of a methodology proposed in the first paragraph.

RC00222-04

27. The author of the passage mentions observations regarding the period of a double-star system as being useful for determining

(A) the distance between the two stars in the system

(B) the time it takes for each star to rotate on its axis

(C) the size of the orbit the system's two stars occupy

(D) the degree of gravitational attraction between the system's stars

(E) the speed at which the star system moves through space

RC00222-05.02

28. The primary purpose of the passage is to

(A) analyze a natural phenomenon in terms of its behavior under special conditions

(B) describe the steps by which a scientific measurement is carried out

(C) point out the conditions under which a scientific procedure is most useful

(D) contrast two different uses of a methodological approach in science

(E) explain a method by which scientists determine an unknown quantity

Line   Most pre-1990 literature on businesses' use of
information technology (IT)—defined as any form of
computer-based information system—focused on
spectacular IT successes and reflected a general
(5)   optimism concerning IT's potential as a resource
for creating competitive advantage. But toward the
end of the 1980s, some economists spoke of a
"productivity paradox": despite huge IT investments,
most notably in the service sectors, productivity
(10)   stagnated. In the retail industry, for example, in
which IT had been widely adopted during the 1980s,
productivity (average output per hour) rose at an
average annual rate of 1.1 percent between 1973 and
1989, compared with 2.4 percent in the preceding
(15)   25-year period. Proponents of IT argued that it takes
both time and a critical mass of investment for IT
to yield benefits, and some suggested that growth
figures for the 1990s proved these benefits were
finally being realized. They also argued that measures
(20)   of productivity ignore what would have happened
without investments in IT—productivity gains might
have been even lower. There were even claims that IT
had improved the performance of the service sector
significantly, although macroeconomic measures of
(25)   productivity did not reflect the improvement.
      But some observers questioned why, if IT had
conferred economic value, it did not produce
direct competitive advantages for individual firms.
Resource-based theory offers an answer, asserting
(30)   that, in general, firms gain competitive advantages
by accumulating resources that are economically
valuable, relatively scarce, and not easily replicated.
According to a recent study of retail firms, which
confirmed that IT has become pervasive and
(35)   relatively easy to acquire, IT by itself appeared to
have conferred little advantage. In fact, though little
evidence of any direct effect was found, the frequent
negative correlations between IT and performance
suggested that IT had probably weakened some
(40)   firms' competitive positions. However, firms' human
resources, in and of themselves, did explain improved
performance, and some firms gained IT-related
advantages by merging IT with complementary
resources, particularly human resources. The findings
(45)   support the notion, founded in resource-based theory,
that competitive advantages do not arise from easily
replicated resources, no matter how impressive or
economically valuable they may be, but from complex,
intangible resources.

Questions 29–36 refer to the passage.

RC38000-01.02

29.   The passage is primarily concerned with

(A)   describing a resource and indicating various
      methods used to study it

(B)   presenting a theory and offering an opposing
      point of view

(C)   providing an explanation for unexpected findings

(D)   demonstrating why a particular theory is unfounded

(E)   resolving a disagreement regarding the uses of a
      technology

RC38000-02.02

30.   The author of the passage discusses productivity in
      the retail industry in the first paragraph primarily in
      order to

(A)   suggest a way in which IT can be used to create
      a competitive advantage

(B)   provide an illustration of the "productivity
      paradox"

(C)   emphasize the practical value of the introduction
      of IT

(D)   cite an industry in which productivity did not
      stagnate during the 1980s

(E)   counter the argument that IT could potentially
      create competitive advantage

RC38000-03.02

31.   The passage suggests that proponents of resource-
      based theory would be likely to explain IT's inability to
      produce direct competitive advantages for individual
      firms by pointing out that

(A)   IT is not a resource that is difficult to obtain

(B)   IT is not an economically valuable resource

(C)   IT is a complex, intangible resource

(D)   economic progress has resulted from IT only in
      the service sector

(E)   changes brought about by IT cannot be detected
      by macroeconomic measures

RC38000-04.02

32. Which of the following best describes the content of the first paragraph?

    (A) It presents two explanations for the success of IT.

    (B) It provides evidence that decreases in productivity will continue.

    (C) It presents reasons for a decline in productivity.

    (D) It demonstrates the effect IT has had on productivity.

    (E) It contrasts views concerning the degree of IT's success.

RC38000-05.02

33. The passage suggests that the recent study of retail firms discussed in the second paragraph supports which of the following conclusions regarding a firm's competitive advantage?

    (A) Human resources alone are more likely to contribute to competitive advantage than is IT alone.

    (B) Human resources combined with IT are more likely than human resources alone to have a negative effect on competitive advantage.

    (C) Human resources combined with IT often have a negative effect on competitive advantage.

    (D) IT by itself is much more likely to have a positive effect than a negative effect on competitive advantage.

    (E) The positive effect of IT on competitive advantage increases with time.

RC38000-06.02

34. According to the passage, most pre-1990 literature on businesses' use of IT included which of the following?

    (A) Recommendations regarding effective ways to use IT to gain competitive advantage

    (B) Explanations of the advantages and disadvantages of adopting IT

    (C) Information about ways in which IT combined with human resources could be used to increase competitive advantage

    (D) A warning regarding the negative effect on competitive advantage that would occur if IT were not adopted

    (E) A belief in the likelihood of increased competitive advantage for firms using IT

RC38000-07.02

35. The author of the passage implies that toward the end of the 1980s, some economists described which of the following as a "productivity paradox" (see line 8)?

    (A) Investments in IT would not result in increases in productivity until the 1990s.

    (B) Investments in IT did not lead to expected gains in productivity.

    (C) Productivity in the retail industry rose less rapidly than did productivity in other industries.

    (D) The gains in productivity due to the introduction of IT were not reflected in macroeconomic measures of productivity.

    (E) Most gains in productivity occurred in the service sector and were therefore particularly difficult to measure.

RC38000-08.02

36. According to the passage, the recent study of retail firms discussed in the second paragraph (lines 33–63) best supports which of the following assessments of IT's potential?

    (A) Even when IT gives a firm a temporary competitive advantage, that firm is unlikely to continue to achieve productivity gains.

    (B) The competitive advantages conferred by a firm's introduction of IT are outweighed by IT's development costs.

    (C) A firm's introduction of IT is less likely to limit its ability to achieve productivity gains than to enhance that ability.

    (D) Although IT by itself is unlikely to give a firm a competitive advantage, IT combined with other resources may do so.

    (E) Although IT by itself is unlikely to give a firm a competitive advantage, a firm that does not employ IT cannot achieve a competitive advantage.

Line   The dry mountain ranges of the western United
        States contain rocks dating back 440 to 510 million
        years, to the Ordovician period, and teeming with
        evidence of tropical marine life. This rock record
(5)   provides clues about one of the most significant
        radiations (periods when existing life-forms gave rise
        to variations that would eventually evolve into entirely
        new species) in the history of marine invertebrates.
        During this radiation the number of marine biological
(10)   families increased greatly, and these families included
        species that would dominate the marine ecosystems
        of the area for the next 215 million years. Although
        the radiation spanned tens of millions of years,
        major changes in many species occurred during a
(15)   geologically short time span within the radiation and,
        furthermore, appear to have occurred worldwide,
        suggesting that external events were major factors
        in the radiation. In fact, there is evidence of major
        ecological and geological changes during this period:
(20)   the sea level dropped drastically and mountain ranges
        were formed. In this instance, rather than leading to
        large-scale extinctions, these kinds of environmental
        changes may have resulted in an enriched pattern of
        habitats and nutrients, which in turn gave rise to the
(25)   Ordovician radiation. However, the actual relationship
        between these environmental factors and the
        diversification of life-forms is not yet fully understood.

Questions 37 to 80 - Difficulty: **Medium**

Questions 37–39 refer to the passage.

RC00267-01
37. The passage is primarily concerned with

(A) evaluating the evidence of a major geologic
     period and determining its duration

(B) describing an evolutionary phenomenon and
     speculating about its cause

(C) explaining the mechanisms through which marine
     life-forms evolved during a particular period

(D) analyzing the impact on later life-forms of an
     important evolutionary development

(E) contrasting a period of evolutionary change with
     other such periods

RC00267-02
38. Which of the following can be inferred from the passage
     regarding the geologic changes that occurred during
     the Ordovician period?

(A) They were more drastic than those associated
     with other radiations.

(B) They may have created conditions favorable to
     the evolution of many new life-forms.

(C) They may have caused the extinction of many of
     the marine species living in shallow waters.

(D) They may have been a factor in the development
     of new species adapted to living both on land
     and in water.

(E) They hastened the formation of the extensive dry
     regions found in the western United States.

RC00267-03
39. Which of the following best describes the function of
     the last sentence of the passage?

(A) It points out that the events described in the
     passage may be atypical.

(B) It alludes to the fact that there is disagreement in
     the scientific community over the importance of
     the Ordovician radiation.

(C) It concludes that the evidence presented in the
     passage is insufficient to support the proposed
     hypothesis because it comes from a limited
     geographic area.

(D) It warns the reader against seeing a connection
     between the biological and geologic changes
     described in the passage.

(E) It alerts the reader that current knowledge
     cannot completely explain the relationship
     suggested by the evidence presented in the
     passage.

Line   Seventeenth-century philosopher John Locke stated that as much as 99 percent of the value of any useful product can be attributed to "the effects of labor." For Locke's intellectual heirs it was only a short step
(5)   to the "labor theory of value," whose formulators held that 100 percent of the value of any product is generated by labor (the human work needed to produce goods) and that therefore the employer who appropriates any part of the product's value as profit
(10)   is practicing theft.
       Although human effort is required to produce goods for the consumer market, effort is also invested in making capital goods (tools, machines, etc.), which are used to facilitate the production of consumer
(15)   goods. In modern economies about one-third of the total output of consumer goods is attributable to the use of capital goods. Approximately two-thirds of the income derived from this total output is paid out to workers as wages and salaries, the remaining
(20)   third serving as compensation to the owners of the capital goods. Moreover, part of this remaining third is received by workers who are shareholders, pension beneficiaries, and the like. The labor theory of value systematically disregards the productive contribution
(25)   of capital goods—a failing for which Locke must bear part of the blame.

Questions 40–45 refer to the passage.

RC00141-01

40.   The author of the passage is primarily concerned with

(A)   criticizing Locke's economic theories

(B)   discounting the contribution of labor in a modern economy

(C)   questioning the validity of the labor theory of value

(D)   arguing for a more equitable distribution of business profits

(E)   contending that employers are overcompensated for capital goods

RC00141-02

41.   According to the author of the passage, which of the following is true of the distribution of the income derived from the total output of consumer goods in a modern economy?

(A)   Workers receive a share of this income that is significantly smaller than the value of their labor as a contribution to total output.

(B)   Owners of capital goods receive a share of this income that is significantly greater than the contribution to total output attributable to the use of capital goods.

(C)   Owners of capital goods receive a share of this income that is no greater than the proportion of total output attributable to the use of capital goods.

(D)   Owners of capital goods are not fully compensated for their investment because they pay out most of their share of this income to workers as wages and benefits.

(E)   Workers receive a share of this income that is greater than the value of their labor because the labor theory of value overestimates their contribution to total output.

RC00141-04

42. Which of the following statements, if true, would most effectively counter the author's criticism of Locke at the end of the passage?

(A) Locke was unfamiliar with the labor theory of value as it was formulated by his intellectual heirs.

(B) In Locke's day, there was no possibility of ordinary workers becoming shareholders or pension beneficiaries.

(C) During Locke's lifetime, capital goods did not make a significant productive contribution to the economy.

(D) The precise statistical calculation of the productive contributions of labor and capital goods is not possible without computers.

(E) The terms "capital goods" and "consumer goods" were coined by modern economists and do not appear in Locke's writings.

RC00141-05

43. Which of the following best describes the organization of the passage?

(A) The author explores the origins of a theory and explains why the theory never gained widespread acceptance.

(B) The author introduces the premise of a theory, evaluates the premise by relating it to objective reality, then proposes a modification of the theory.

(C) After quoting a well-known authority, the author describes the evolution of a theory, then traces its modern form back to the original quotation.

(D) After citing a precursor of a theory, the author outlines and refutes the theory, then links its flaw to the precursor.

(E) After tracing the roots of a theory, the author attempts to undermine the theory by discrediting its originator.

RC00141-06

44. Which of the following arguments would a proponent of the labor theory of value, as it is presented in the first paragraph, be most likely to use in response to lines 23–25?

(A) The productive contributions of workers and capital goods cannot be compared because the productive life span of capital goods is longer than that of workers.

(B) The author's analysis of the distribution of income is misleading because only a small percentage of workers are also shareholders.

(C) Capital goods are valuable only insofar as they contribute directly to the production of consumer goods.

(D) The productive contribution of capital goods must be discounted because capital goods require maintenance.

(E) The productive contribution of capital goods must be attributed to labor because capital goods are themselves products of labor.

RC00141-07

45. The author of the passage implies which of the following regarding the formulators of the labor theory of value?

(A) They came from a working-class background.

(B) Their views were too radical to have popular appeal.

(C) At least one of them was a close contemporary of Locke.

(D) They were familiar with Locke's views on the relationship between labor and the value of products.

(E) They underestimated the importance of consumer goods in a modern economy.

Line Exactly when in the early modern era Native
Americans began exchanging animal furs with
Europeans for European-made goods is uncertain.
What is fairly certain, even though they left
(5) no written evidence of having done so, is that
the first Europeans to conduct such trade during
the modern period were fishing crews working the
waters around Newfoundland. Archaeologists had
noticed that sixteenth-century Native American
(10) sites were strewn with iron bolts and metal
pins. Only later, upon reading Nicolas Denys's
1672 account of seventeenth-century European
settlements in North America, did archaeologists
realize that sixteenth-century European fishing
(15) crews had dismantled and exchanged parts of their
ships for furs.

By the time Europeans sailing the Atlantic coast
of North America first documented the fur trade, it
was apparently well underway. The first to record
(20) such trade—the captain of a Portuguese vessel
sailing from Newfoundland in 1501—observed that a
Native American aboard the ship wore Venetian silver
earrings. Another early chronicler noted in 1524 that
Native Americans living along the coast of what is now
(25) New England had become selective about European
trade goods: they accepted only knives, fishhooks,
and sharp metal. By the time Cartier sailed the Saint
Lawrence River ten years later, Native Americans had
traded with Europeans for more than thirty years,
(30) perhaps half a century.

Questions 46–54 refer to the passage.

RC00204-01

46. The author of the passage draws conclusions about
the fur trade in North America from all of the following
sources EXCEPT

(A) Cartier's accounts of trading with Native
Americans

(B) a seventeenth-century account of European
settlements

(C) a sixteenth-century account written by a sailing
vessel captain

(D) archaeological observations of sixteenth-century
Native American sites

(E) a sixteenth-century account of Native Americans
in what is now New England

RC00204-02

47. The passage suggests that which of the following is
partially responsible for the difficulty in establishing
the precise date when the fur trade in North America
began?

(A) A lack of written accounts before that of Nicolas
Denys in 1672

(B) A lack of written documentation before 1501

(C) Ambiguities in the evidence from Native
American sources

(D) Uncertainty about Native American trade
networks

(E) Uncertainty about the origin of artifacts
supposedly traded by European fishing crews for
furs

RC00204-03

48. Which of the following, if true, most strengthens the
author's assertion in the first sentence of the second
paragraph?

(A) When Europeans retraced Cartier's voyage in
the first years of the seventeenth century, they
frequently traded with Native Americans.

(B) Furs from beavers, which were plentiful in North
America but nearly extinct in Europe, became
extremely fashionable in Europe in the final
decades of the sixteenth century.

(C) Firing arms were rarely found on sixteenth-
century Native American sites or on European
lists of trading goods since such arms required
frequent maintenance and repair.

(D) Europeans and Native Americans had established
trade protocols, such as body language assuring
one another of their peaceful intentions, that
antedate the earliest records of trade.

(E) During the first quarter of the sixteenth century,
an Italian explorer recorded seeing many Native
Americans with what appeared to be copper
beads, though they may have been made of
indigenous copper.

RC00204-04

49. Which of the following best describes the primary function of lines 11–16?

(A) It offers a reconsideration of a claim made in the preceding sentence.

(B) It reveals how archaeologists arrived at an interpretation of the evidence mentioned in the preceding sentence.

(C) It shows how scholars misinterpreted the significance of certain evidence mentioned in the preceding sentence.

(D) It identifies one of the first significant accounts of seventeenth-century European settlements in North America.

(E) It explains why Denys's account of seventeenth-century European settlements is thought to be significant.

RC00204-05

50. It can be inferred from the passage that the author would agree with which of the following statements about the fur trade between Native Americans and Europeans in the early modern era?

(A) This trade may have begun as early as the 1480s.

(B) This trade probably did not continue much beyond the 1530s.

(C) This trade was most likely at its peak in the mid-1520s.

(D) This trade probably did not begin prior to 1500.

(E) There is no written evidence of this trade prior to the seventeenth century.

RC00204-06

51. Which of the following can be inferred from the passage about the Native Americans mentioned in line 24?

(A) They had little use for decorative objects such as earrings.

(B) They became increasingly dependent on fishing between 1501 and 1524.

(C) By 1524, only certain groups of Europeans were willing to trade with them.

(D) The selectivity of their trading choices made it difficult for them to engage in widespread trade with Europeans.

(E) The selectivity of their trading choices indicates that they had been trading with Europeans for a significant period of time prior to 1524.

RC00204-07

52. The passage supports which of the following statements about sixteenth-century European fishing crews working the waters off Newfoundland?

(A) They wrote no accounts of their fishing voyages.

(B) They primarily sailed under the flag of Portugal.

(C) They exchanged ship parts with Native Americans for furs.

(D) They commonly traded jewelry with Native Americans for furs.

(E) They carried surplus metal implements to trade with Native Americans for furs.

RC00204-08

53. Which of the following can be inferred from the passage about evidence pertaining to the fur trade between Native Americans and Europeans in the early modern era?

(A) A lack of written evidence has made it difficult to establish which Europeans first participated in this trade.

(B) In general, the physical evidence pertaining to this trade has been more useful than the written evidence has been.

(C) There is more written evidence pertaining to this trade from the early part of the sixteenth century than from later in that century.

(D) The earliest written evidence pertaining to this trade dates from a time when the trade was already well established.

(E) Some important pieces of evidence pertaining to this trade, such as Denys's 1672 account, were long overlooked by archaeologists.

RC00204-09

54. The passage suggests which of the following about the sixteenth-century Native Americans who traded with Europeans on the coast of what is now called New England?

(A) By 1524 they had become accustomed to exchanging goods with Europeans.

(B) They were unfamiliar with metals before encountering Europeans.

(C) They had no practical uses for European goods other than metals and metal implements.

(D) By 1524 they had become disdainful of European traders because such traders had treated them unfairly in the past.

(E) By 1524 they demanded only the most prized European goods because they had come to realize how valuable furs were on European markets.

Line   Determining whether a given population of animals constitutes a distinct species can be difficult because no single accepted definition of the term exists. One approach, called the biological species
(5)   concept, bases the definition on reproductive compatibility. According to this view, a species is a group of animals that can mate with one another to produce fertile offspring but cannot mate successfully with members of a different
(10)   group. Yet this idea can be too restrictive. First, mating between groups labeled as different species (hybridization), as often occurs in the canine family, is quite common in nature. Second, sometimes the differences between two populations might not
(15)   prevent them from interbreeding, even though they are dissimilar in traits unrelated to reproduction; some biologists question whether such disparate groups should be considered a single species. A third problem with the biological species concept is
(20)   that investigators cannot always determine whether two groups that live in different places are capable of interbreeding.

    When the biological species concept is difficult to apply, some investigators use phenotype, an
(25)   organism's observable characteristics, instead. Two groups that have evolved separately are likely to display measurable differences in many of their traits, such as skull size or width of teeth. If the distribution of measurements from one group does
(30)   not overlap with those of another, the two groups might reasonably be considered distinct species.

Questions 55–58 refer to the passage.

RC00201-01

55. The passage is primarily concerned with

(A) describing the development of the biological species concept

(B) responding to a critique of reproductive compatibility as a criterion for defining a species

(C) considering two different approaches to identifying biological species

(D) pointing out the advantage of one method of distinguishing related species

(E) identifying an obstacle to the classification of biological species

RC00201-03

56. The author of the passage mentions "groups that live in different places" (line 21) most probably in order to

(A) point out a theoretical inconsistency in the biological species concept

(B) offer evidence in support of the biological species concept

(C) identify an obstacle to the application of the biological species concept

(D) note an instance in which phenotype classification is customarily used

(E) describe an alternative to the biological species concept

RC00201-04

57. With which of the following statements regarding the classification of individual species would the author most likely agree?

(A) Phenotype comparison may help to classify species when application of the biological species concept proves inconclusive.

(B) Because no standard definition exists for what constitutes a species, the classification of animal populations is inevitably an arbitrary process.

(C) The criteria used by biologists to classify species have not been based on adequate research.

(D) The existence of hybrids in wild animal species is the chief factor casting doubt on the usefulness of research into reproductive compatibility as a way of classifying species.

(E) Phenotype overlap should be used as the basic criterion for standardizing species classification.

RC00201-05

58. Which of the following best describes the function of lines 10–13?

(A) It elaborates the definition of the biological species concept given in a previous sentence.

(B) It develops a point about the biological species concept made in the previous sentence.

(C) It states the author's central point about the biological species concept.

(D) It identifies a central assumption underlying the biological species concept.

(E) It demonstrates why the biological species concept is invalid.

Line   Researchers studying how genes control animal behavior have had to deal with many uncertainties. In the first place, most behaviors are governed by more than one gene, and until recently geneticists
(5)   had no method for identifying the multiple genes involved. In addition, even when a single gene is found to control a behavior, researchers in different fields do not necessarily agree that it is a "behavioral gene." Neuroscientists, whose interest
(10)   in genetic research is to understand the nervous system (which generates behavior), define the term broadly. But ethologists—specialists in animal behavior—are interested in evolution, so they define the term narrowly. They insist that mutations
(15)   in a behavioral gene must alter a specific normal behavior and not merely make the organism ill, so that the genetically induced behavioral change will provide variation that natural selection can act upon, possibly leading to the evolution of a new species.
(20)   For example, in the fruit fly, researchers have identified the gene Shaker, mutations in which cause flies to shake violently under anesthesia. Since shaking is not healthy, ethologists do not consider Shaker a behavioral gene. In contrast, ethologists
(25)   do consider the gene period (per), which controls the fruit fly's circadian (24-hour) rhythm, a behavioral gene because flies with mutated per genes are healthy; they simply have different rhythms.

Questions 59–61 refer to the passage.

RC00322-01

59.   The primary purpose of the passage is to

(A)   summarize findings in an area of research

(B)   discuss different perspectives on a scientific question

(C)   outline the major questions in a scientific discipline

(D)   illustrate the usefulness of investigating a research topic

(E)   reconcile differences between two definitions of a term

RC00322-02

60.   The passage suggests that neuroscientists would most likely consider Shaker to be which of the following?

(A)   An example of a behavioral gene

(B)   One of multiple genes that control a single behavior

(C)   A gene that, when mutated, causes an alteration in a specific normal behavior without making the organism ill

(D)   A gene of interest to ethologists but of no interest to neuroscientists

(E)   A poor source of information about the nervous system

RC00322-05

61.   It can be inferred from the passage that which of the following, if true, would be most likely to influence ethologists' opinions about whether a particular gene in a species is a behavioral gene?

(A)   The gene is found only in that species.

(B)   The gene is extremely difficult to identify.

(C)   The only effect of mutations in the gene is to make the organism ill.

(D)   Neuroscientists consider the gene to be a behavioral gene.

(E)   Geneticists consider the gene to be a behavioral gene.

Line   For most species of animals, the number of individuals in the species is inversely proportional to the average body size for members of the species: the smaller the body size, the larger the number of individual animals.
(5)   The tamarin, a small South American monkey, breaks this rule. Of the ten primate species studied in Peru's Manu National Park, for example, the two species of tamarins, saddle-backed and emperor, are the eighth and ninth least abundant, respectively. Only the pygmy
(10)   marmoset, which is even smaller, is less abundant. The tamarin's scarcity is not easily explained; it cannot be dismissed as a consequence of diet, because tamarins feed on the same mixture of fruit, nectar, and small prey as do several of their more numerous larger
(15)   counterparts, including the two capuchins known as the squirrel monkey and the night monkey. Although the relative proportions of fruits consumed varies somewhat among species, it is hard to imagine that such subtle differences are crucial to understanding
(20)   the relative rarity of tamarins.
        To emphasize just how anomalously rare tamarins are, we can compare them to the other omnivorous primates in the community. In terms of numbers of individuals per square kilometer, they rank well below
(25)   the two capuchins, the squirrel monkey and the night monkey. And in terms of biomass, or the total weight of the individuals that occupy a unit area of habitat, each tamarin species is present at only one-twentieth the mass of brown capuchins or one-tenth that of
(30)   squirrel monkeys. To gain another perspective, consider the spatial requirements of tamarins. Tamarins are rigidly territorial, vigorously expelling any intruders that may stray within the sharply defined boundaries of their domains. Groups invest an
(35)   appreciable part of their time and energy in patrolling their territorial boundaries, announcing their presence to their neighbors with shrill, sweeping cries. Such concerted territoriality is rather exceptional among primates, though the gibbons and siamangs of Asia
(40)   show it, as do a few other New World species such as the titi and night monkeys. What is most surprising about tamarin territories is their size.

Line   Titi monkeys routinely live within territories of 6 to 8 hectares, and night monkeys seldom defend more
(45)   than 10 hectares, but tamarin groups routinely occupy areas of 30 to 120 hectares. Contrast this with the 1 to 2 hectares needed by the common North American gray squirrel, a nonterritorial mammal of about the same size. A group of tamarins uses about as much
(50)   space as a troop of brown capuchins, though the latter weighs 15 times as much. Thus, in addition to being rare, tamarins require an amount of space that seems completely out of proportion to their size.

Questions 62–68 refer to the passage.

RC22661-01.01

62.   The author indicates that tamarin territories are

(A)   surprisingly large

(B)   poorly situated

(C)   unusually abundant in food resources

(D)   incapable of supporting large troops of tamarins

(E)   larger in Peru than in other parts of South America

RC22661-02.01

63.   The author mentions the spatial requirements of the gray squirrel in order to

(A)   explain why they are so common

(B)   demonstrate the consequences of their nonterritoriality

(C)   emphasize the unusual territorial requirements of the tamarin

(D)   provide an example of a major difference between squirrels and monkeys

(E)   provide an example of an animal with requirements similar to those of the tamarin

RC22661-03.01

64.   The author regards the differences between the diets of the tamarins and several larger species as

(A)   generally explicable in terms of territory size

(B)   apparently too small to explain the rarity of tamarins

(C)   wholly predictable on the basis of differences in body size

(D)   a result of the rigid territoriality of tamarins

(E)   a significant factor in determining behavioral differences

RC22661-04.01

65. Which of the following would most probably be regarded by the author as anomalous?

(A) A large primate species that eats mostly plants

(B) A species of small mammals that is fiercely territorial

(C) Two species of small primates that share the same territories

(D) A species of small birds that is more abundant than many species of larger birds

(E) A species of small rodents that requires more living space per individual than most species of larger rodents

RC22661-05.01

66. The author most probably regards the tamarins studied in Manu National Park as

(A) an endangered species

(B) typical tamarins

(C) unusually docile

(D) the most unusual primates anywhere

(E) too small a sample to be significant

RC22661-06.01

67. Which of the following is NOT mentioned in the passage as a species whose groups display territoriality?

(A) Gibbons

(B) Siamangs

(C) Titi monkeys

(D) Squirrel monkeys

(E) Night monkeys

RC22661-07.01

68. The primary concern of the passage is to

(A) recommend a policy

(B) evaluate a theory

(C) describe an unusual condition

(D) explain the development of a hypothesis

(E) support one of several competing hypotheses

Line   According to many analysts, labor-management relations in the United States are undergoing a fundamental change: traditional adversarialism is giving way to a new cooperative relationship between the
(5)   two sides and even to concessions from labor. These analysts say the twin shocks of nonunion competition in this country and low-cost, high-quality imports from abroad are forcing unions to look more favorably at a variety of management demands: the need for
(10)   wage restraint and reduced benefits as well as the abolition of "rigid" work rules, seniority rights, and job classifications.

Sophisticated proponents of these new developments cast their observations in a prolabor
(15)   light. In return for their concessions, they point out, some unions have bargained for profit sharing, retraining rights, and job-security guarantees. Unions can also trade concessions for more say on the shop floor, where techniques such as quality circles and
(20)   quality-of-work-life programs promise workers greater control over their own jobs. Unions may even win a voice in investment and pricing strategy, plant location, and other major corporate policy decisions previously reserved to management.
(25)   Opponents of these concessions from labor argue that such concessions do not save jobs, but either prolong the agony of dying plants or finance the plant relocations that employers had intended anyway. Companies make investment decisions to fit their
(30)   strategic plans and their profit objectives, opponents point out, and labor costs are usually just a small factor in the equation. Moreover, unrestrained by either loyalty to their work force or political or legislative constraints on their mobility, the companies eventually
(35)   cut and run, concessions or no concessions.

Wage-related concessions have come under particular attack, since opponents believe that high union wages underlay much of the success of United States industry in this century. They point out that a
(40)   long-standing principle, shared by both management and labor, has been that workers should earn wages that give them the income they need to buy what they make. Moreover, high wages have given workers the buying power to propel the economy forward.

(45)   If proposals for pay cuts, two-tier wage systems, and subminimum wages for young workers continue to gain credence, opponents believe the U.S. social structure will move toward that of a less-developed nation: a small group of wealthy investors, a sizable
(50)   but still minority bloc of elite professionals and highly skilled employees, and a huge mass of marginal workers and unskilled laborers. Further, they argue that if unions willingly engage in concession bargaining on the false grounds that labor costs are the source
(55)   of a company's problems, unions will find themselves competing with Third World pay levels—a competition they cannot win.

Questions 69–75 refer to the passage.

RC32661-01.01

69.   It can be inferred from the passage that opponents of labor concessions would most likely describe many plant-relocation decisions made by United States companies as

(A)   capricious

(B)   self-serving

(C)   naive

(D)   impulsive

(E)   illogical

RC32661-02.01

70.   It can be inferred from the passage that, until recently, which of the following has been true of United States industry in the twentieth century?

(A)   Unions have consistently participated in major corporate policy decisions.

(B)   Maintaining adequate quality control in manufacturing processes has been a principal problem.

(C)   Union workers have been paid relatively high wages.

(D)   Two-tier wage systems have been the norm.

(E)   Goods produced have been priced beyond the means of most workers.

RC32661-03.01

71. The passage provides information to answer which of the following questions?

(A) What has caused unions to consider wage restraints and reduced benefits?

(B) Why do analysts study United States labor-management relations?

(C) How do job-security guarantees operate?

(D) Are investment and pricing strategies effective in combating imports?

(E) Do quality circles improve product performance and value?

RC32661-04.01

72. The passage is primarily concerned with the

(A) reasons for adversarialism between labor and management

(B) importance of cooperative labor-management relations

(C) consequences of labor concessions to management

(D) effects of foreign competition on the United States economy

(E) effects of nonunion competition on union bargaining strategies

RC32661-05.01

73. The sentence "If proposals for pay cuts . . . unskilled laborers" serves primarily to

(A) disprove a theory

(B) clarify an ambiguity

(C) reconcile opposing views

(D) present a hypothesis

(E) contradict accepted data

RC32661-06.01

74. It can be inferred from the passage that opponents of labor concessions believe that if concession bargaining continues, then

(A) plants will close instead of relocating

(B) young workers will need continued job retraining

(C) professional workers will outnumber marginal workers

(D) wealthy investors will invest in Third World countries instead of the United States

(E) the social structure of the United States will be negatively affected

RC32661-07.01

75. According to the author, "Sophisticated proponents" of concessions do which of the following?

(A) Support the traditional adversarialism characteristic of labor-management relations.

(B) Emphasize the benefits unions can gain by granting concessions.

(C) Focus on thorough analyses of current economic conditions.

(D) Present management's reasons for demanding concessions.

(E) Explain domestic economic developments in terms of worldwide trends.

Line   Historians who study European women of the Renaissance try to measure "independence," "options," and other indicators of the degree to which the expression of women's individuality was either
(5)   permitted or suppressed. Influenced by Western individualism, these historians define a peculiar form of personhood: an innately bounded unit, autonomous and standing apart from both nature and society. An anthropologist, however, would contend that a person
(10)   can be conceived in ways other than as an "individual." In many societies a person's identity is not intrinsically unique and self-contained but instead is defined within a complex web of social relationships.

     In her study of the fifteenth-century Florentine widow Alessandra Strozzi, a historian who specializes
(15)   in European women of the Renaissance attributes individual intention and authorship of actions to her subject. This historian assumes that Alessandra had goals and interests different from those of her sons,
(20)   yet much of the historian's own research reveals that Alessandra acted primarily as a champion of her sons' interests, taking their goals as her own. Thus Alessandra conforms more closely to the anthropologist's notion that personal motivation is
(25)   embedded in a social context. Indeed, one could argue that Alessandra did not distinguish her personhood from that of her sons. In Renaissance Europe the boundaries of the conceptual self were not always firm and closed and did not necessarily coincide with the
(30)   boundaries of the bodily self.

Questions 76–80 refer to the passage.

RC00097-02

76. According to the passage, much of the research on Alessandra Strozzi done by the historian mentioned in the second paragraph supports which of the following conclusions?

(A) Alessandra used her position as her sons' sole guardian to further interests different from those of her sons.

(B) Alessandra unwillingly sacrificed her own interests in favor of those of her sons.

(C) Alessandra's actions indicate that her motivations and intentions were those of an independent individual.

(D) Alessandra's social context encouraged her to take independent action.

(E) Alessandra regarded her sons' goals and interests as her own.

RC00097-03

77. In the first paragraph, the author of the passage mentions a contention that would be made by an anthropologist most likely in order to

(A) present a theory that will be undermined in the discussion of a historian's study later in the passage

(B) offer a perspective on the concept of personhood that can usefully be applied to the study of women in Renaissance Europe

(C) undermine the view that the individuality of European women of the Renaissance was largely suppressed

(D) argue that anthropologists have applied the Western concept of individualism in their research

(E) lay the groundwork for the conclusion that Alessandra's is a unique case among European women of the Renaissance whose lives have been studied by historians

RC00097-04
78. The passage suggests that the historians referred to in line 1 make which of the following assumptions about Renaissance Europe?

(A) That anthropologists overestimate the importance of the individual in Renaissance European society

(B) That in Renaissance Europe, women were typically allowed to express their individuality

(C) That European women of the Renaissance had the possibility of acting independently of the social context in which they lived

(D) That studying an individual such as Alessandra is the best way to draw general conclusions about the lives of women in Renaissance Europe

(E) That people in Renaissance Europe had greater personal autonomy than people do currently

RC00097-05
79. It can be inferred that the author of the passage believes which of the following about the study of Alessandra Strozzi done by the historian mentioned in the second paragraph?

(A) Alessandra was atypical of her time and was therefore an inappropriate choice for the subject of the historian's research.

(B) In order to bolster her thesis, the historian adopted the anthropological perspective on personhood.

(C) The historian argues that the boundaries of the conceptual self were not always firm and closed in Renaissance Europe.

(D) In her study, the historian reverts to a traditional approach that is out of step with the work of other historians of Renaissance Europe.

(E) The interpretation of Alessandra's actions that the historian puts forward is not supported by much of the historian's research.

RC00097-06
80. The passage suggests that the historian mentioned in the second paragraph would be most likely to agree with which of the following assertions regarding Alessandra Strozzi?

(A) Alessandra was able to act more independently than most women of her time because she was a widow.

(B) Alessandra was aware that her personal motivation was embedded in a social context.

(C) Alessandra had goals and interests similar to those of many other widows in her society.

(D) Alessandra is an example of a Renaissance woman who expressed her individuality through independent action.

(E) Alessandra was exceptional because she was able to effect changes in the social constraints placed upon women in her society.

Line In addition to conventional galaxies, the universe contains very dim galaxies that until recently went unnoticed by astronomers. Possibly as numerous as conventional galaxies, these galaxies have the
(5) same general shape and even the same approximate number of stars as a common type of conventional galaxy, the spiral, but tend to be much larger. Because these galaxies' mass is spread out over larger areas, they have far fewer stars per unit
(10) volume than do conventional galaxies. Apparently these low-surface-brightness galaxies, as they are called, take much longer than conventional galaxies to condense their primordial gas and convert it to stars—that is, they evolve much more slowly.
(15) These galaxies may constitute an answer to the long-standing puzzle of the missing baryonic mass in the universe. Baryons—subatomic particles that are generally protons or neutrons—are the source of stellar, and therefore galactic, luminosity, and so
(20) their numbers can be estimated based on how luminous galaxies are. However, the amount of helium in the universe, as measured by spectroscopy, suggests that there are far more baryons in the universe than estimates based on
(25) galactic luminosity indicate. Astronomers have long speculated that the missing baryonic mass might eventually be discovered in intergalactic space or as some large population of galaxies that are difficult to detect.

Questions 81 to 112 - Difficulty: **Hard**

Questions 81–87 refer to the passage.

RC00054-01

81. According to the passage, conventional spiral galaxies differ from low-surface-brightness galaxies in which of the following ways?

(A) They have fewer stars than do low-surface-brightness galaxies.
(B) They evolve more quickly than low-surface-brightness galaxies.
(C) They are more diffuse than low-surface-brightness galaxies.
(D) They contain less helium than do low-surface-brightness galaxies.
(E) They are larger than low-surface-brightness galaxies.

RC00054-02

82. It can be inferred from the passage that which of the following is an accurate physical description of typical low-surface-brightness galaxies?

(A) They are large spiral galaxies containing fewer stars than conventional galaxies.
(B) They are compact but very dim spiral galaxies.
(C) They are diffuse spiral galaxies that occupy a large volume of space.
(D) They are small, young spiral galaxies that contain a high proportion of primordial gas.
(E) They are large, dense spirals with low luminosity.

RC00054-03

83. It can be inferred from the passage that the "long-standing puzzle" refers to which of the following?

(A) The difference between the rate at which conventional galaxies evolve and the rate at which low-surface-brightness galaxies evolve
(B) The discrepancy between estimates of total baryonic mass derived from measuring helium and estimates based on measuring galactic luminosity
(C) The inconsistency between the observed amount of helium in the universe and the number of stars in typical low-surface-brightness galaxies
(D) Uncertainties regarding what proportion of baryonic mass is contained in intergalactic space and what proportion in conventional galaxies
(E) Difficulties involved in detecting very distant galaxies and in investigating their luminosity

RC00054-04

84. The author implies that low-surface-brightness galaxies could constitute an answer to the puzzle discussed in the second paragraph primarily because

(A) they contain baryonic mass that was not taken into account by researchers using galactic luminosity to estimate the number of baryons in the universe

(B) they, like conventional galaxies that contain many baryons, have evolved from massive, primordial gas clouds

(C) they may contain relatively more helium, and hence more baryons, than do galaxies whose helium content has been studied using spectroscopy

(D) they have recently been discovered to contain more baryonic mass than scientists had thought when low-surface-brightness galaxies were first observed

(E) they contain stars that are significantly more luminous than would have been predicted on the basis of initial studies of luminosity in low-surface-brightness galaxies

RC00054-05

85. The author mentions the fact that baryons are the source of stars' luminosity primarily in order to explain

(A) how astronomers determine that some galaxies contain fewer stars per unit volume than do others

(B) how astronomers are able to calculate the total luminosity of a galaxy

(C) why astronomers can use galactic luminosity to estimate baryonic mass

(D) why astronomers' estimates of baryonic mass based on galactic luminosity are more reliable than those based on spectroscopic studies of helium

(E) how astronomers know bright galaxies contain more baryons than do dim galaxies

RC00054-06

86. The author of the passage would be most likely to disagree with which of the following statements?

(A) Low-surface-brightness galaxies are more difficult to detect than are conventional galaxies.

(B) Low-surface-brightness galaxies are often spiral in shape.

(C) Astronomers have advanced plausible ideas about where missing baryonic mass might be found.

(D) Astronomers have devised a useful way of estimating the total baryonic mass in the universe.

(E) Astronomers have discovered a substantial amount of baryonic mass in intergalactic space.

RC00054-07

87. The primary purpose of the passage is to

(A) describe a phenomenon and consider its scientific significance

(B) contrast two phenomena and discuss a puzzling difference between them

(C) identify a newly discovered phenomenon and explain its origins

(D) compare two classes of objects and discuss the physical properties of each

(E) discuss a discovery and point out its inconsistency with existing theory

Line   The fact that superior service can generate a competitive advantage for a company does not mean that every attempt at improving service will create such an advantage. Investments in service,
(5)   like those in production and distribution, must be balanced against other types of investments on the basis of direct, tangible benefits such as cost reduction and increased revenues. If a company is already effectively on a par with its competitors
(10)   because it provides service that avoids a damaging reputation and keeps customers from leaving at an unacceptable rate, then investment in higher service levels may be wasted, since service is a deciding factor for customers only in extreme
(15)   situations.

    This truth was not apparent to managers of one regional bank, which failed to improve its competitive position despite its investment in reducing the time a customer had to wait for a
(20)   teller. The bank managers did not recognize the level of customer inertia in the consumer banking industry that arises from the inconvenience of switching banks. Nor did they analyze their service improvement to determine whether it would attract
(25)   new customers by producing a new standard of service that would excite customers or by proving difficult for competitors to copy. The only merit of the improvement was that it could easily be described to customers.

Questions 88–93 refer to the passage.

RC11238-01

88.   The primary purpose of the passage is to

(A)   contrast possible outcomes of a type of business investment

(B)   suggest more careful evaluation of a type of business investment

(C)   illustrate various ways in which a type of business investment could fail to enhance revenues

(D)   trace the general problems of a company to a certain type of business investment

(E)   criticize the way in which managers tend to analyze the costs and benefits of business investments

RC11238-02

89.   According to the passage, investments in service are comparable to investments in production and distribution in terms of the

(A)   tangibility of the benefits that they tend to confer

(B)   increased revenues that they ultimately produce

(C)   basis on which they need to be weighed

(D)   insufficient analysis that managers devote to them

(E)   degree of competitive advantage that they are likely to provide

RC11238-03

90.   The passage suggests which of the following about service provided by the regional bank prior to its investment in enhancing that service?

(A)   It enabled the bank to retain customers at an acceptable rate.

(B)   It threatened to weaken the bank's competitive position with respect to other regional banks.

(C)   It had already been improved after having caused damage to the bank's reputation in the past.

(D)   It was slightly superior to that of the bank's regional competitors.

(E)   It needed to be improved to attain parity with the service provided by competing banks.

RC11238-04

91. The passage suggests that bank managers failed to consider whether or not the service improvement mentioned in lines 18–20

   (A)   was too complicated to be easily described to prospective customers

   (B)   made a measurable change in the experiences of customers in the bank's offices

   (C)   could be sustained if the number of customers increased significantly

   (D)   was an innovation that competing banks could have imitated

   (E)   was adequate to bring the bank's general level of service to a level that was comparable with that of its competitors

RC11238-05

92. The discussion of the regional bank in the second paragraph serves which of the following functions within the passage as a whole?

   (A)   It describes an exceptional case in which investment in service actually failed to produce a competitive advantage.

   (B)   It illustrates the pitfalls of choosing to invest in service at a time when investment is needed more urgently in another area.

   (C)   It demonstrates the kind of analysis that managers apply when they choose one kind of service investment over another.

   (D)   It supports the argument that investments in certain aspects of service are more advantageous than investments in other aspects of service.

   (E)   It provides an example of the point about investment in service made in the first paragraph.

RC11238-06

93. The author uses the word "only" in line 27 most likely in order to

   (A)   highlight the oddity of the service improvement

   (B)   emphasize the relatively low value of the investment in service improvement

   (C)   distinguish the primary attribute of the service improvement from secondary attributes

   (D)   single out a certain merit of the service improvement from other merits

   (E)   point out the limited duration of the actual service improvement

Line   Antonia Castañeda has utilized scholarship from women's studies and Mexican-American history to examine nineteenth-century literary portrayals of Mexican women. As Castañeda notes, scholars of

(5)   women's history observe that in the United States, male novelists of the period—during which, according to these scholars, women's traditional economic role in home-based agriculture was threatened by the transition to a factory-based industrial economy—

(10)   define women solely in their domestic roles of wife and mother. Castañeda finds that during the same period that saw non-Hispanic women being economically displaced by industrialization, Hispanic law in territorial California protected the economic position of

(15)   "Californianas" (the Mexican women of the territory) by ensuring them property rights and inheritance rights equal to those of males.

For Castañeda, the laws explain a stereotypical plot created primarily by male, non-Hispanic novelists:

(20)   the story of an ambitious non-Hispanic merchant or trader desirous of marrying an elite Californiana. These novels' favorable portrayal of such women is noteworthy, since Mexican-American historians have concluded that unflattering literary depictions

(25)   of Mexicans were vital in rallying the United States public's support for the Mexican-American War (1846–1848). The importance of economic alliances forged through marriages with Californianas explains this apparent contradiction. Because of their real-

(30)   life economic significance, the Californianas were portrayed more favorably than were others of the same nationality.

Questions 94–97 refer to the passage.

RC00548-01.02

94. The primary purpose of the passage is to

(A)   trace historical influences on the depiction of Mexican Americans in the nineteenth century

(B)   explain how research in history has been affected by scholarship in women's studies

(C)   describe the historical origins of a literary stereotype

(D)   discuss ways in which minority writers have sought to critique a dominant culture through their writing

(E)   evaluate both sides in a scholarly debate about a prominent literary stereotype

RC00548-03

95. The "apparent contradiction" mentioned in line 29 refers to the discrepancy between the

(A)   legal status of Mexican women in territorial California and their status in the United States

(B)   unflattering depiction of Mexicans in novels and the actual public sentiment about the Mexican-American War

(C)   existence of many marriages between Californianas and non-Hispanic merchants and the strictures against them expressed in novels

(D)   literary depiction of elite Californianas and the literary depiction of other Mexican individuals

(E)   novelistic portrayals of elite Californianas' privileged lives and the actual circumstances of those lives

96. Which of the following could best serve as an example of the kind of fictional plot discussed by Antonia Castañeda?

    (A) A land speculator of English ancestry weds the daughter of a Mexican vineyard owner after the speculator has migrated to California to seek his fortune.

    (B) A Californian woman of Hispanic ancestry finds that her agricultural livelihood is threatened when her husband is forced to seek work in a textile mill.

    (C) A Mexican rancher who loses his land as a result of the Mexican-American War migrates to the northern United States and marries an immigrant schoolteacher.

    (D) A wealthy Californiana whose father has bequeathed her all his property contends with avaricious relatives for her inheritance.

    (E) A poor married couple emigrate from French Canada and gradually become wealthy as merchants in territorial California.

97. Which of the following, if true, would provide the most support for Castañeda's explanation of the "stereotypical plot" mentioned in the lines 18–19?

    (A) Non-Hispanic traders found business more profitable in California while it was a territory than when it became a state.

    (B) Very few marriages between Hispanic women and non-Hispanic men in nineteenth-century territorial California have actually been documented.

    (C) Records from the nineteenth century indicate that some large and valuable properties were owned by elite Californianas in their own right.

    (D) Unmarried non-Hispanic women in the nineteenth-century United States were sometimes able to control property in their own right.

    (E) Most of the property in nineteenth-century territorial California was controlled by Hispanic men.

Line   *This passage is excerpted from material published in 1997.*

Scientists have been puzzled by the seeming disparity between models of global warming based on
(5)   greenhouse gas emissions and actual climatological data. In short, the world is not warming up as much as these models have predicted. In the early 1990s, Pat Michaels sought to explain this disparity, suggesting that sulfate emissions in industrial areas had a cooling
(10)   effect, thus temporarily retarding global warming. Michaels later came to doubt this idea, however, pointing out that since most sulfate is emitted in the Northern Hemisphere, its cooling influence should be largely limited to that hemisphere. Yet, since 1987,
(15)   warming in the Southern Hemisphere, which had been relatively intense, has virtually ceased, while warming in the north has accelerated. Thus, Michaels not only doubted the idea of sulfate cooling, but came to feel that global warming models themselves may be
(20)   flawed.

Ben Santer disagrees. Santer contends that, in general, global warming occurs more slowly in the south because this hemisphere is dominated by oceans, which warm more slowly than the landmasses
(25)   that dominate the Northern Hemisphere. But, according to Santer, the situation remains complicated by sulfate cooling, which peaked in the north in the mid-twentieth century. It drastically slowed warming in the Northern Hemisphere, and warming in the
(30)   Southern Hemisphere raced ahead. Since 1987, Santer argues, the greenhouse effect has reasserted itself, and the north has taken the lead. Thus, Santer disputes Michaels's claim that model predictions and observed data differ fundamentally.

Questions 98–100 refer to the passage.

RC00533-03

98.   The passage suggests that, in the early 1990s, Michaels would have been most likely to agree with which of the following statements about the disparity mentioned in the lines 3–4?

(A)   This disparity is relatively less extreme in the Northern Hemisphere because of sulfate cooling.

(B)   This disparity is only a short-term phenomenon brought about by sulfate cooling.

(C)   This disparity is most significant in those parts of the world dominated by oceans.

(D)   The extent of this disparity is being masked by the temporary effect of sulfate cooling.

(E)   The disparity confirms that current models of global warming are correct.

RC00533-04

99.   According to the passage, Santer asserts which of the following about global warming?

(A)   It will become a more serious problem in the Southern Hemisphere than in the Northern Hemisphere in spite of the cooling influence of oceans in the south.

(B)   It is unlikely to be a serious problem in the future because of the pervasive effect of sulfate cooling.

(C)   It will proceed at the same general rate in the Northern and Southern Hemispheres once the temporary influence of sulfate cooling comes to an end.

(D)   Until the late 1980s, it was moderated in the Northern Hemisphere by the effect of sulfate cooling.

(E)   Largely because of the cooling influence of oceans, it has had no discernible impact on the Southern Hemisphere.

RC00533-05

100. The passage suggests that Santer and Michaels would be most likely to DISAGREE over which of the following issues?

(A) Whether climatological data invalidates global warming models

(B) Whether warming in the Northern Hemisphere has intensified since 1987

(C) Whether disparities between global warming models and climatological data can be detected

(D) Whether landmasses warm more rapidly than oceans

(E) Whether oceans have a significant effect on global climate patterns

Line   Micro-wear patterns found on the teeth of long-extinct specimens of the primate species australopithecine may provide evidence about their diets. For example, on the basis of tooth micro-wear

(5)   patterns, Walker dismisses Jolly's hypothesis that australopithecines ate hard seeds. He also disputes Szalay's suggestion that the heavy enamel of australopithecine teeth is an adaptation to bone crunching, since both seed cracking and bone

(10)   crunching produce distinctive micro-wear characteristics on teeth. His conclusion that australopithecines were frugivores (fruit eaters) is based upon his observation that the tooth micro-wear characteristics of east African

(15)   australopithecine specimens are indistinguishable from those of chimpanzees and orangutans, which are commonly assumed to be frugivorous primates.
     However, research on the diets of contemporary primates suggests that micro-wear

(20)   studies may have limited utility in determining the foods that are actually eaten. For example, insect eating, which can cause distinct micro-wear patterns, would not cause much tooth abrasion in modern baboons, who eat only soft-bodied insects

(25)   rather than hard-bodied insects. In addition, the diets of current omnivorous primates vary considerably depending on the environments that different groups within a primate species inhabit; if australopithecines were omnivores too, we might

(30)   expect to find considerable population variation in their tooth micro-wear patterns. Thus, Walker's description of possible australopithecine diets may need to be expanded to include a much more diverse diet.

Questions 101–108 refer to the passage.

RC00613-01

101. According to the passage, Walker and Szalay disagree on which of the following points?

(A)   The structure and composition of australopithecine teeth

(B)   The kinds of conclusions that can be drawn from the micro-wear patterns on australopithecine teeth

(C)   The idea that fruit was a part of the australopithecine diet

(D)   The extent to which seed cracking and bone crunching produce similar micro-wear patterns on teeth

(E)   The function of the heavy enamel on australopithecine teeth

RC00613-02

102. The passage suggests that Walker's research indicated which of the following about australopithecine teeth?

(A)   They had micro-wear characteristics indicating that fruit constituted only a small part of their diet.

(B)   They lacked micro-wear characteristics associated with seed eating and bone crunching.

(C)   They had micro-wear characteristics that differed in certain ways from the micro-wear patterns of chimpanzees and orangutans.

(D)   They had micro-wear characteristics suggesting that the diet of australopithecines varied from one region to another.

(E)   They lacked the micro-wear characteristics distinctive of modern frugivores.

RC00613-03

103. The passage suggests that which of the following would be true of studies of tooth micro-wear patterns conducted on modern baboons?

(A) They would inaccurately suggest that some baboons eat more soft-bodied than hard-bodied insects.

(B) They would suggest that insects constitute the largest part of some baboons' diets.

(C) They would reveal that there are no significant differences in tooth micro-wear patterns among baboon populations.

(D) They would inadequately reflect the extent to which some baboons consume certain types of insects.

(E) They would indicate that baboons in certain regions eat only soft-bodied insects, whereas baboons in other regions eat hard-bodied insects.

RC00613-04

104. The passage suggests which of the following about the micro-wear patterns found on the teeth of omnivorous primates?

(A) The patterns provide information about what kinds of foods are not eaten by the particular species of primate, but not about the foods actually eaten.

(B) The patterns of various primate species living in the same environment resemble one another.

(C) The patterns may not provide information about the extent to which a particular species' diet includes seeds.

(D) The patterns provide more information about these primates' diet than do the tooth micro-wear patterns of primates who are frugivores.

(E) The patterns may differ among groups within a species depending on the environment within which a particular group lives.

RC00613-05

105. It can be inferred from the passage that if studies of tooth micro-wear patterns were conducted on modern baboons, which of the following would most likely be true of the results obtained?

(A) There would be enough abrasion to allow a determination of whether baboons are frugivorous or insectivorous.

(B) The results would suggest that insects constitute the largest part of the baboons' diet.

(C) The results would reveal that there are no significant differences in tooth micro-wear patterns from one regional baboon population to another.

(D) The results would provide an accurate indication of the absence of some kinds of insects from the baboons' diet.

(E) The results would be unlikely to provide any indication of what inferences about the australopithecine diet can or cannot be drawn from micro-wear studies.

RC00613-08

106. It can be inferred from the passage that Walker's conclusion about the australopithecine diet would be called into question under which of the following circumstances?

(A) The tooth enamel of australopithecines is found to be much heavier than that of modern frugivorous primates.

(B) The micro-wear patterns of australopithecine teeth from regions other than east Africa are analyzed.

(C) Orangutans are found to have a much broader diet than is currently recognized.

(D) The environment of east Africa at the time australopithecines lived there is found to have been far more varied than is currently thought.

(E) The area in which the australopithecine specimens were found is discovered to have been very rich in soft-bodied insects during the period when australopithecines lived there.

RC00613-09.02
107. The passage is primarily concerned with

   (A) comparing two research methods for
        determining a species' dietary habits

   (B) describing and evaluating conjectures about a
        species' diet

   (C) contrasting several explanations for a species'
        dietary habits

   (D) discussing a new approach and advocating its
        use in particular situations

   (E) arguing that a particular research methodology
        does not contribute useful data

RC00613-10
108. The author of the passage mentions the diets of
     baboons and other living primates most likely in
     order to

   (A) provide evidence that refutes Walker's
        conclusions about the foods making up the diets
        of australopithecines

   (B) suggest that studies of tooth micro-wear
        patterns are primarily useful for determining the
        diets of living primates

   (C) suggest that australopithecines were probably
        omnivores rather than frugivores

   (D) illustrate some of the limitations of using
        tooth micro-wear patterns to draw definitive
        conclusions about a group's diet

   (E) suggest that tooth micro-wear patterns are
        caused by persistent, as opposed to occasional,
        consumption of particular foods

Line　In current historiography, the picture of a consistent, unequivocal decline in women's status with the advent of capitalism and industrialization is giving way to an analysis that not only emphasizes both change (whether
(5)　improvement or decline) and continuity but also accounts for geographical and occupational variation. The history of women's work in English farmhouse cheese making between 1800 and 1930 is a case in point. In her influential *Women Workers and the Industrial*
(10)　*Revolution* (1930), Pinchbeck argued that the agricultural revolution of the eighteenth and early nineteenth centuries, with its attendant specialization and enlarged scale of operation, curtailed women's participation in the business of cheese production. Earlier, she
(15)　maintained, women had concerned themselves with feeding cows, rearing calves, and even selling the cheese in local markets and fairs. Pinchbeck thought that the advent of specialization meant that women's work in cheese dairying was reduced simply to
(20)　processing the milk. "Dairymen" (a new social category) raised and fed cows and sold the cheese through factors, who were also men. With this narrowing of the scope of work, Pinchbeck believed, women lost business ability, independence, and initiative.
(25)　　Though Pinchbeck portrayed precapitalist, preindustrial conditions as superior to what followed, recent scholarship has seriously questioned the notion of a golden age for women in precapitalist society. For example, scholars note that women's control seldom
(30)　extended to the disposal of the proceeds of their work. In the case of cheese, the rise of factors may have compromised women's ability to market cheese at fairs. But merely selling the cheese did not necessarily imply access to the money: Davidoff cites
(35)　the case of an Essex man who appropriated all but a fraction of the money from his wife's cheese sales.
　　By focusing on somewhat peripheral operations, moreover, Pinchbeck missed a substantial element of continuity in women's participation: throughout the
(40)　period women did the central work of actually making cheese. Their persistence in English cheese dairying contrasts with women's early disappearance from arable agriculture in southeast England and from American cheese dairying. Comparing these
(45)　three divergent developments yields some reasons for the differences among them. English cheese-making women worked in a setting in which cultural values, agricultural conditions, and the nature of their work combined to support their continued
(50)　participation. In the other cases, one or more of these elements was lacking.

Questions 109–112 refer to the passage.

RC00512-01
109.　The primary purpose of the passage is to

(A)　present recently discovered evidence that supports a conventional interpretation of a historical period

(B)　describe how reinterpretations of available evidence have reinvigorated a once-discredited scholarly position

(C)　explain why some historians have tended to emphasize change rather than continuity in discussing a particular period

(D)　explore how changes in a particular occupation serve to counter the prevailing view of a historical period

(E)　examine a particular area of historical research in order to exemplify a general scholarly trend

RC00512-03
110.　Regarding English local markets and fairs, which of the following can be inferred from the passage?

(A)　Both before and after the agricultural revolution, the sellers of agricultural products at these venues were men.

(B)　Knowing who the active sellers were at these venues may not give a reliable indication of who controlled the revenue from the sales.

(C)　There were no parallel institutions at which American cheese makers could sell their own products.

(D)　Prior to the agricultural revolution, the sellers of agricultural products at these venues were generally the producers themselves.

(E)　Prior to the agricultural revolution, women sold not only cheese but also products of arable agriculture at these venues.

RC00512-05

111. The passage describes the work of Pinchbeck primarily in order to

    (A) demonstrate that some of the conclusions reached by recent historians were anticipated in earlier scholarship

    (B) provide an instance of the viewpoint that, according to the passage's author, is being superseded

    (C) illustrate the ways in which recent historians have built on the work of their predecessors

    (D) provide a point of reference for subsequent scholarship on women's work during the agricultural revolution

    (E) show the effect that the specialization introduced in the agricultural and industrial revolutions had on women's work

RC00512-07

112. It can be inferred from the passage that women did work in

    (A) American cheesemaking at some point prior to industrialization

    (B) arable agriculture in northern England both before and after the agricultural revolution

    (C) arable agriculture in southeast England after the agricultural revolution, in those locales in which cultural values supported their participation

    (D) the sale of cheese at local markets in England even after the agricultural revolution

    (E) some areas of American cheese dairying after industrialization

4.5 Answer Key

1.	C	24.	C	47.	B	70.	C	93.	B
2.	E	25.	B	48.	D	71.	A	94.	C
3.	D	26.	A	49.	B	72.	C	95.	D
4.	E	27.	D	50.	A	73.	D	96.	A
5.	A	28.	E	51.	E	74.	E	97.	C
6.	C	29.	C	52.	C	75.	B	98.	B
7.	D	30.	B	53.	D	76.	E	99.	D
8.	B	31.	A	54.	A	77.	B	100.	A
9.	C	32.	E	55.	C	78.	C	101.	E
10.	D	33.	A	56.	C	79.	E	102.	B
11.	D	34.	E	57.	A	80.	D	103.	D
12.	B	35.	B	58.	B	81.	B	104.	E
13.	E	36.	D	59.	B	82.	C	105.	D
14.	C	37.	B	60.	A	83.	B	106.	C
15.	D	38.	B	61.	C	84.	A	107.	B
16.	C	39.	E	62.	A	85.	C	108.	D
17.	E	40.	C	63.	C	86.	E	109.	E
18.	B	41.	C	64.	B	87.	A	110.	B
19.	A	42.	C	65.	E	88.	B	111.	B
20.	D	43.	D	66.	B	89.	C	112.	A
21.	B	44.	E	67.	D	90.	A		
22.	E	45.	D	68.	C	91.	D		
23.	C	46.	A	69.	B	92.	E		

4.6 Answer Explanations

The following discussion of Reading Comprehension is intended to familiarize you with the most efficient and effective approaches to the kinds of problems common to Reading Comprehension. The particular questions in this chapter are generally representative of the kinds of Reading Comprehension questions you will encounter on the GMAT exam. Remember that it is the problem solving strategy that is important, not the specific details of a particular question.

Questions 1 to 36 - Difficulty: Easy

Questions 1–4 refer to the passage on page 90.

*RC00184-01

1. According to the passage, traditional corporate leaders differ from leaders in learning organizations in that the former

    (A) encourage employees to concentrate on developing a wide range of skills

    (B) enable employees to recognize and confront dominant corporate models and to develop alternative models

    (C) make important policy decisions alone and then require employees in the corporation to abide by those decisions

    (D) instill confidence in employees because of their willingness to make risky decisions and accept their consequences

    (E) are concerned with offering employees frequent advice and career guidance

Supporting Idea

This question requires understanding of the contrast the passage draws between leaders of traditional corporations and leaders of learning organizations. According to the second paragraph, the former are traditionally charismatic leaders who set policy and make decisions, while the latter foster integrated thinking at all levels of the organization.

A   According to the passage, it is leaders in learning organizations, not traditional corporate leaders, who encourage the development of a wide range of skills.

B   Leaders in learning organizations are those who want their employees to challenge dominant models.

C   **Correct.** The second paragraph states that traditional corporate leaders are individualistic; they alone *set the corporation's direction and make key decisions.*

D   The passage does not address the question of whether traditional corporate leaders instill confidence in employees. In fact, the first paragraph suggests that they may not; rather, they might come across as objectionably controlling.

E   The passage suggests that advice and guidance are more likely to be offered by leaders of learning organizations than by leaders of traditional corporations.

The correct answer is C.

RC00184-02

2. Which of the following best describes employee behavior encouraged within learning organizations, as such organizations are described in the passage?

    (A) Carefully defining one's job description and taking care to avoid deviations from it

    (B) Designing mentoring programs that train new employees to follow procedures that have been used for many years

    (C) Concentrating one's efforts on mastering one aspect of a complicated task

    (D) Studying an organizational problem, preparing a report, and submitting it to a corporate leader for approval

    (E) Analyzing a problem related to productivity, making a decision about a solution, and implementing that solution

---

*These numbers correlate with the online test bank question number. See the GMAT™ Official Guide Verbal Review Question Index in the back of this book.

Application

The second paragraph of the passage indicates that employees of learning organizations are encouraged to think and act for themselves; they learn new skills and expand their capabilities.

A   Avoiding deviations from one's carefully defined job description would more likely be encouraged in a traditional corporation, as described in the first paragraph, than in a learning organization.

B   Any employee training that involves following long-standing procedures would more likely be encouraged in a traditional corporation than a learning organization.

C   According to the passage, mastering only one aspect of a task, no matter how complicated, would be insufficient in a learning organization, in which broad patterns of thinking are encouraged.

D   As described in the passage, the role of corporate leaders in learning organizations is not, characteristically, to approve employees' solutions to problems, but rather to enable and empower employees to implement solutions on their own.

E   **Correct.** Employees in learning organizations are expected to act on their own initiative; thus, they would be encouraged to analyze and solve problems on their own, implementing whatever solutions they devised.

The correct answer is E.

RC00184-03

3.   According to the author of the passage, corporate leaders of the future should do which of the following?

(A)   They should encourage employees to put long-term goals ahead of short-term profits.

(B)   They should exercise more control over employees in order to constrain production costs.

(C)   They should redefine incentives for employees' performance improvement.

(D)   They should provide employees with opportunities to gain new skills and expand their capabilities.

(E)   They should promote individual managers who are committed to established company policies.

Supporting Idea

This question focuses on what the author recommends in the passage for future corporate leaders. In the second paragraph, the author states that, among other things, corporate leaders need to be teachers to provide challenges to their employees and create an atmosphere where *employees are continually learning new skills and expanding their capabilities to shape their future.*

A   The passage does not directly discuss the issue of corporate goals and profitability in the long or short term.

B   The passage does not address the topic of production costs, and it suggests that its author would favor reducing, rather than increasing, corporate leaders' control over employees. The first paragraph states that leaders who attempt to control employees lead those employees to perform in mediocre fashion.

C   The passage does not discuss incentivizing employees' performance; rather, employees' performance will improve, the passage suggests, under different corporate leadership.

D   **Correct.** The final sentence of the passage states directly that leaders must build organizations in which employees can learn new skills and expand their capabilities.

E   The first paragraph indicates that clinging to established company policies is a strategy for the future that is likely to be unproductive.

The correct answer is D.

RC00184-04

4.   The primary purpose of the passage is to

(A)   endorse a traditional corporate structure

(B)   introduce a new approach to corporate leadership and evaluate criticisms of it

(C)   explain competing theories about management practices and reconcile them

(D)   contrast two typical corporate organizational structures

(E)   propose an alternative to a common corporate approach

Main Idea

This question depends on understanding the passage as a whole. The first paragraph explains the way in which corporations fail to facilitate how humans learn. The second paragraph suggests that corporations should change the way they view employees in order to promote learning, and it explains the positive outcomes that would result from that shift in thinking.

A   The first paragraph explains that the traditional corporate structure leads to mediocre performance; it does not endorse that structure.

B   The second paragraph introduces the concept of a *learning organization* and its attendant approach to corporate leadership. Rather than identifying any criticisms of that approach, the passage endorses it wholeheartedly.

C   The passage discusses the difference between the idea of a single charismatic leader and that of a shared corporate leadership, but it does not attempt to reconcile these two ideas.

D   The passage's main focus is on advocating a particular approach, not on merely contrasting it with another. Furthermore, it portrays only one of the approaches as typical. It suggests that the organizational structure that relies on a single charismatic leader is typical but that another approach, that in which leadership is shared, should instead become typical.

E   **Correct.** The passage identifies a common corporate approach, one based on controlling employees, and proposes that corporations should instead become *learning organizations*.

The correct answer is E.

Questions 5–10 refer to the passage on page 92.

RC00144-03

5.   All of the following are mentioned as ways of controlling the magnitude of structural unemployment EXCEPT

(A)   using public funds to create jobs

(B)   teaching new skills to displaced workers

(C)   allowing displaced workers to retire

(D)   controlling the movement of capital

(E)   encouraging workers to move to where jobs are available

Supporting Idea

This question addresses what the passage states directly about how the magnitude of structural unemployment can be controlled. The last few sentences of the second paragraph state several ways in which this control may be exerted.

A   **Correct.** The passage mentions using public sector resources, but it does not say that those resources could be used to create jobs.

B   The passage states that workers can be reeducated or retrained as a way of addressing structural unemployment.

C   Encouraging workers to retire is one of the options mentioned in the passage for controlling structural unemployment.

D   Capital movement is one of the factors affecting structural unemployment, and the passage states that controlling this movement can be used as a way of controlling structural unemployment.

E   The passage indicates that encouraging displaced workers to move where there are jobs is a way to help control structural unemployment.

The correct answer is A.

RC00144-04

6. The passage suggests that a potential outcome of higher structural unemployment is

(A) increased public spending for social services

(B) placement of workers in jobs for which they are not qualified

(C) higher wages for those workers who have skills that are in demand

(D) an increase in the length of time jobs remain unfilled

(E) a shift in the government's economic policy priorities

Supporting Idea

The third paragraph discusses a potential result of higher structural unemployment: if more workers lack skills that are in demand, there will be shortages of qualified workers. The wages of workers who do have the desired skills will thus rise.

A While higher structural unemployment might result in an increased demand for social services, such as job training and the like, the passage does not suggest that the government would in fact respond by spending more on such services.

B Nothing in the passage indicates that employers would hire workers who lack necessary skills—indeed, the lack of qualified workers is itself a cause of increased structural unemployment.

C **Correct.** The passage indicates that when growth in demand for workers with certain skills outpaces the growth in the number of workers who possess those skills, the wages of those workers are bid up, resulting in increased pay for the skilled workers.

D The passage does not discuss the length of time that jobs are likely to remain unfilled as structural unemployment increases. The amount of time jobs remain unfilled could remain the same, but the number or type of jobs that go unfilled may change.

E The passage suggests that certain types of public sector spending (presumably spending as a result of government policy) can help control the magnitude of structural

unemployment, but the passage does not indicate whether the government is in fact likely to change policy so as to try to control this magnitude. Furthermore, the passage states that government policy has placed a priority on reducing inflation. Yet there is no suggestion that the government is likely to shift away from this priority in the face of higher structural unemployment.

The correct answer is C.

RC00144-05

7. It can be inferred from the passage that even when there are unemployed workers, labor shortages are still likely to occur if

(A) the inflation rate is unusually high

(B) there is insufficient technological innovation

(C) the level of structural unemployment is exceptionally low

(D) the jobs available in certain places require skills that the labor force in those areas lacks

(E) the workers in some industries are dissatisfied with the pay offered in those industries

Inference

This question relies on the passage's characterization of structural unemployment—that there is a mismatch between the number of jobs available in a certain location and the number of workers in that location who possess the skills required for those jobs. Even if there is a sufficient number of workers in the area to fill the positions, if those workers had the requisite skills, labor shortages will occur if an insufficient number of those workers lack the required skills.

A The passage in the third paragraph explains that structural unemployment and inflation can coexist, but it does not suggest that a high rate of inflation will make labor shortages likely; rather, the passage indicates that structural unemployment may lead to inflation by pushing wages, and thus prices, higher.

B The passage indicates that greater technological innovation can produce structural unemployment, not that insufficient technological innovation can.

C   When there are unemployed workers, labor shortages would be unlikely to occur if the level of structural unemployment is low, because low structural unemployment would mean that no imbalance exists between available employment and workers with requisite skills. Thus, unemployed workers would likely be able to find jobs.

D   Correct. The labor shortages associated with structural unemployment can, according to the passage, be caused by a mismatch in a certain location between available jobs requiring particular skills and the number of workers possessing those skills.

E   The passage does not discuss what would happen if some industries' workers are dissatisfied with their pay. Presumably, though, even if those workers were to quit their jobs due to that dissatisfaction, unemployed workers may very well be happy to take those jobs (assuming they are not lacking the requisite skills). So the passage gives us no reason to think that labor shortages would be likely to occur—at least without a situation like that described in answer choice D.

The correct answer is D.

RC00144-06

8.   The passage suggests that the phenomenon of combined unemployment and inflation is

(A)   a socioeconomic problem that can only be addressed by government intervention

(B)   a socioeconomic problem that can be characteristic of periods of structural unemployment

(C)   an economic problem that results from government intervention in management-labor relations

(D)   an economic problem that results from imperfect applications of technology

(E)   an economic problem that can be eliminated by relatively small changes in the labor force

Supporting Idea

This question depends on understanding the phenomenon of combined unemployment and inflation, which is addressed in the third paragraph. That paragraph states that a trend associated with structural unemployment—that of rising labor costs and prices—is responsible for the phenomenon.

A   The third paragraph indicates that government policy has been unable, thus far, to remedy the problem of combined unemployment and inflation, and it gives no indication whether a nongovernmental solution is available.

B   Correct. Periods of structural unemployment have, according to the passage, featured both inflation and unemployment.

C   The passage does not discuss government intervention into management-labor relations.

D   Certain applications of technology may be responsible for increasing structural unemployment, but the passage provides no way to distinguish between imperfect and other such applications.

E   The passage discusses the phenomenon of combined unemployment and inflation only in relation to structural unemployment, which the passage suggests is likely to arise only in relation to large or rapid changes in demand for labor. Therefore, it seems unlikely that relatively small changes in the labor force can eliminate the phenomenon of combined unemployment and inflation.

The correct answer is B.

RC00144-07

9.   The passage is primarily concerned with

(A)   clarifying the definition of a concept

(B)   proposing a way to eliminate an undesirable condition

(C)   discussing the sources and consequences of a problem

(D)   suggesting ways to alleviate the effects of a particular social policy

(E)   evaluating the steps that have been taken to correct an imbalance

Main Idea

This question depends on understanding the passage as a whole in order to identify its primary concern. The first paragraph defines structural unemployment (which the passage, in its second paragraph, indicates is a *serious problem*). The second paragraph describes a major factor that can cause structural unemployment, as well as some steps that might be taken to alleviate it. Finally, the third paragraph identifies possible effects of structural unemployment, including wage and price inflation.

A   The first paragraph clarifies the definition of structural unemployment, but this definition is not the passage's primary concern.

B   The passage's second paragraph indicates some ways that an increase in structural unemployment can be mitigated, but nowhere does the passage suggest that the condition can be eliminated entirely.

C   **Correct.** The passage discusses the problem of structural unemployment, explaining how it can arise and what some of its consequences may be.

D   The passage does suggest some ways in which structural unemployment might be alleviated, but this kind of unemployment is not characterized as an effect of a social policy. Rather, it is a state of economic affairs.

E   The second paragraph identifies some steps that could be taken to correct a particular situation of worker displacement. It does not, however, evaluate those steps.

The correct answer is C.

RC00144-08

10. According to the passage, small downward shifts in the demand for labor will not usually cause unemployment because

(A)   such shifts are frequently accompanied by upswings in the economy

(B)   such shifts usually occur slowly

(C)   workers can be encouraged to move to where there are jobs

(D)   normal attrition is often sufficient to reduce the size of the work force

(E)   workers are usually flexible enough to learn new skills and switch to new jobs

Supporting Idea

This question requires noting that the second paragraph of the passage discusses small changes in demand for labor: their effect on unemployment is likely to be small because normal attrition can reduce the size of the work force accordingly.

A   The passage does not mention upswings in the economy in relation to small shifts in demand for labor. Furthermore, the passage indicates that structural unemployment can occur even at peaks of economic upswings, so presumably even if small downward shifts in the demand for labor are frequently accompanied by economic upswings, structural unemployment could still result.

B   The passage suggests that shifts in demand for workers that do not result in unemployment may be small *or* gradual. Nothing indicates that small changes are also necessarily gradual.

C   The second paragraph indicates that workers being encouraged to move to where there are jobs would be a reasonable response to large or rapid changes in demand for workers; it does not discuss such encouragement in relation to small shifts in demand.

D   **Correct.** The passage identifies normal attrition as a factor that can reduce the work force sufficiently to accommodate small reductions in the demand for labor in particular occupations.

E   Workers' ability to learn new skills is identified in the passage as a factor affecting whether structural unemployment will grow in response to large or rapid changes, not small changes, in the demand for workers in particular occupations.

The correct answer is D.

Questions 11–16 refer to the passage on page 94.

RC00113-01

11. The passage is primarily concerned with

(A) explaining why one method of earthquake prediction has proven more practicable than an alternative method

(B) suggesting that accurate earthquake forecasting must combine elements of long-term and short-term prediction

(C) challenging the usefulness of dilatancy theory for explaining the occurrence of precursory phenomena

(D) discussing the deficiency of two methods by which researchers have attempted to predict the occurrence of earthquakes

(E) describing the development of methods for establishing patterns in the occurrence of past earthquakes

Main Idea

To answer this question, focus on what the passage as a whole is trying to do. The first paragraph describes a method for predicting the occurrence of earthquakes, and the second paragraph explains problems with that method. The third paragraph describes a second method for predicting the occurrence of earthquakes, and the fourth paragraph explains problems with that method. Thus, the passage as a whole is primarily concerned with explaining the deficiencies of two methods for predicting the occurrence of earthquakes.

A The passage does not compare the practicability of the two methods.

B The passage does not discuss combining long-term and short-term methods.

C Only the first half of the passage discusses dilatancy theory; the second half discusses a different method for predicting the occurrence of earthquakes.

D **Correct.** The passage describes two methods for predicting the occurrence of earthquakes and explains the shortcomings of each method.

E Only the second half of the passage discusses patterns in the occurrence of past earthquakes; the first half discusses a different method for predicting the occurrence of earthquakes.

The correct answer is D.

RC00113-02

12. According to the passage, laboratory evidence concerning the effects of stress on rocks might help account for

(A) differences in magnitude among earthquakes

(B) certain phenomena that occur prior to earthquakes

(C) variations in the intervals between earthquakes in a particular area

(D) differences in the frequency with which earthquakes occur in various areas

(E) the unreliability of short-term earthquake predictions

Supporting Idea

This question asks for information explicitly stated in the passage. The first paragraph explains that rocks subjected to stress in the laboratory undergo multiple changes. According to *dilatancy theory*, such changes happening to rocks in the field could lead to earthquake precursors—phenomena that occur before large earthquakes.

A The passage explains how laboratory evidence might be used to predict the occurrence of large earthquakes, not to differentiate between earthquakes' magnitudes.

B **Correct.** According to dilatancy theory, the sort of changes that have been observed in laboratories to occur in rocks might lead to earthquake precursors in the field.

C Although the passage discusses variation in earthquake intervals, that evidence is based on historical records, not laboratory evidence.

D The passage does not refer in any way to differences in the frequency of earthquakes in various regions.

E   The unreliability of one method for making short-term earthquake predictions is implied by information gathered in the field, not by laboratory evidence.

The correct answer is B.

RC00113-03

13. It can be inferred from the passage that one problem with using precursory phenomena to predict earthquakes is that minor tremors

(A) typically occur some distance from the sites of the large earthquakes that follow them

(B) are directly linked to the mechanisms that cause earthquakes

(C) are difficult to distinguish from major tremors

(D) have proven difficult to measure accurately

(E) are not always followed by large earthquakes

Inference

This question asks what can be inferred from certain information in the passage. The second paragraph explains two problems with using minor tremors to predict earthquakes. First, minor tremors provide no information about how large an impending earthquake will be. Second, the minor tremors that occur prior to a large earthquake are indistinguishable from other minor tremors. Thus, it can be inferred that minor tremors sometimes occur when no large earthquake follows.

A   The passage does not mention the distance between minor tremors and ensuing earthquakes.

B   The passage implies that minor tremors sometimes occur without an ensuing earthquake, so the phenomena are most likely not directly linked.

C   The passage suggests no difficulty in distinguishing between minor tremors and major tremors.

D   The passage does not mention any difficulties in the measurement of minor tremors.

E   **Correct.** The passage indicates that minor tremors occurring prior to a large earthquake are indistinguishable from minor tremors that are not followed by large earthquakes. So the fact that minor tremors are not always followed by large earthquakes, together with the inability to distinguish between those that are and those that are not, poses a problem for any attempt to predict large earthquakes on the basis of this type of precursory phenomenon.

The correct answer is E.

RC00113-04

14. According to the passage, some researchers based their research about long-term earthquake prediction on which of the following facts?

(A) The historical record confirms that most earthquakes have been preceded by minor tremors.

(B) The average interval between earthquakes in one region of the San Andreas Fault is 132 years.

(C) Some regions tend to be the site of numerous earthquakes over the course of many years.

(D) Changes in the volume of rock can occur as a result of building stress and can lead to the weakening of rock.

(E) Paleoseismologists have been able to unearth and date geological features caused by past earthquakes.

Supporting Idea

This question asks for information explicitly provided in the passage. The question asks what the basis is for the research into long-term earthquake prediction described in the third paragraph. Based on the fact that numerous earthquakes occur in some regions over the course of many years, the researchers tried to identify regular earthquake intervals that would assist in making long-term predictions. Thus, the basis of their research is the occurrence of numerous earthquakes at particular sites.

A   The passage indicates that minor tremors are used by some scientists to make short-term earthquake predictions, not that they were the basis for research about long-term predictions.

B   This fact about the San Andreas Fault was used by paleoseismologists to show the inadequacy of the long-term prediction research, since actual earthquake intervals varied greatly from the average.

C   **Correct.** Since earthquakes occur repeatedly in certain regions, researchers tried to identify regular cycles in earthquake intervals.

D   The passage indicates that changes in rock volume have been used by some scientists to make short-term earthquake predictions, not that they were the basis for research about long-term predictions.

E   Paleoseismologists' research provided evidence against the existence of regular earthquake cycles used in making long-term predictions.

The correct answer is C.

RC00113-05

15. The passage suggests which of the following about the paleoseismologists' findings described in lines 42–50?

(A)   They suggest that the frequency with which earthquakes occurred at a particular site decreased significantly over the past two millennia.

(B)   They suggest that paleoseismologists may someday be able to make reasonably accurate long-term earthquake predictions.

(C)   They suggest that researchers may someday be able to determine which past occurrences of minor tremors were actually followed by large earthquakes.

(D)   They suggest that the recurrence of earthquakes in earthquake-prone sites is too irregular to serve as a basis for earthquake prediction.

(E)   They indicate that researchers attempting to develop long-term methods of earthquake prediction have overlooked important evidence concerning the causes of earthquakes.

Inference

This question asks about what can be inferred from a particular portion of the passage (lines 42–50). The third paragraph describes research that attempted to identify regular patterns of recurrence in earthquake-prone regions, to aid in long-term earthquake prediction. The fourth paragraph describes evidence discovered by paleoseismologists that undermines this idea that regular earthquake cycles exist. The paragraph indicates that in one region along the San Andreas Fault, the average interval between earthquakes was 132 years, but individual intervals varied widely—from 44 to 332 years. This information implies that earthquake intervals are too irregular to be used for accurate long-term earthquake prediction.

A   The evidence suggests that the earthquake intervals are irregular, not that they have become shorter over time.

B   The findings provide evidence against the use of regular earthquake cycles in long-term earthquake prediction.

C   The findings do not clearly pertain to minor tremors.

D   **Correct.** The great variation in intervals between earthquakes suggests that recurrence is too irregular to serve as the basis for long-term earthquake prediction.

E   The paleoseismologists studied evidence showing when earthquakes occurred. The passage does not suggest that the evidence has any implications regarding the causes of earthquakes.

The correct answer is D.

RC00113-07

16. The author implies which of the following about the ability of the researchers mentioned in line 18 to predict earthquakes?

(A)   They can identify when an earthquake is likely to occur but not how large it will be.

(B)   They can identify the regions where earthquakes are likely to occur but not when they will occur.

(C)   They are unable to determine either the time or the place that earthquakes are likely to occur.

(D)   They are likely to be more accurate at short-term earthquake prediction than at long-term earthquake prediction.

(E)   They can determine the regions where earthquakes have occurred in the past but not the regions where they are likely to occur in the future.

Supporting Idea

The question asks for information explicitly provided in the passage. The second paragraph indicates that researchers at first reported success in identifying earthquake precursors, but further analysis of the data undermined their theory. The passage then explains that atypical seismic waves were recorded before some earthquakes; this evidence at first seemed to support the researchers' theory, before further analysis proved the evidence inadequate.

A   Although earthquakes are caused by stress on rock, the passage does not indicate that this fact encouraged researchers to believe that precursors could be used to predict earthquakes.

B   This fact would undermine the theory that changes in seismic waves are precursory phenomena that can be used to predict earthquakes.

C   **Correct.** Seismic waves with unusual velocities occurring before earthquakes at first seemed to provide support for researchers' theory that earthquakes could be predicted by precursory phenomena.

D   Though earthquakes' recurrence in certain regions is mentioned as being important to researchers seeking to make long-term earthquake predictions, it is not mentioned as being relevant to researchers' theory that earthquakes can be predicted by precursory phenomena.

E   This is not mentioned as being relevant to scientists' belief that earthquakes could be predicted on the basis of precursory phenomena.

The correct answer is C.

Questions 17–23 refer to the passage on page 96.

RC00492-01

17.   It can be inferred from the passage that one reason an advertiser might prefer a hard-sell approach to a soft-sell approach is that

(A)   the risks of boomerang effects are minimized when the conclusions an advertiser wants the consumer to draw are themselves left unstated

(B)   counterargumentation is likely from consumers who fail to draw their own conclusions regarding an advertising claim

(C)   inferential activity is likely to occur even if consumers perceive themselves to be more knowledgeable than the individuals presenting product claims

(D)   research on consumer memory suggests that the explicit conclusions provided by an advertiser using the hard-sell approach have a significant impact on decision making

(E)   the information presented by an advertiser using the soft-sell approach may imply different conclusions to different consumers

Inference

This question relies on what the passage suggests about the difference between the hard-sell and soft-sell approaches—and why the hard-sell approach might be preferred. The hard-sell approach, according to the second paragraph, presents explicit conclusions. The soft-sell approach, on the other hand, does not explicitly state conclusions about products; instead, consumers make up their own minds.

A   While the passage makes clear that boomerang effects are minimized when conclusions are left unstated, this is an advantage of the soft-sell approach over the hard-sell approach.

B   According to the second paragraph, counterargumentation is a disadvantage, not an advantage, of the hard-sell approach. This is a reason not to prefer the hard sell.

C   The third paragraph suggests that in cases in which consumers may perceive themselves as more knowledgeable than individuals presenting product claims, the soft-sell approach offers an advantage over the hard-sell approach.

D   According to the third paragraph, self-generated conclusions that are associated with the soft-sell approach have a greater impact on decision making than explicit conclusions. The passage does not allude to any research on memory that would favor the hard-sell approach.

E   **Correct.** The fourth paragraph suggests that one problem with the soft-sell approach is that consumers could miss the point; they may not come to the conclusions that the advertiser would prefer. Thus an advertiser might prefer a hard-sell approach.

The correct answer is E.

RC00492-02

18. Each of the following is mentioned in the passage as a characteristic of the hard-sell approach EXCEPT:

(A)   Its overall message is readily grasped.

(B)   It appeals to consumers' knowledge about the product.

(C)   It makes explicit claims that the advertised brand is superior to other brands.

(D)   It uses statements that are expressed very clearly.

(E)   It makes claims in the form of direct conclusions.

Supporting Idea

This question asks about what is directly stated in the passage about the hard-sell approach. The first and second paragraphs provide the details about this approach, including that it uses *direct, forceful claims* about benefits of a brand over competitors' brands; its claims are simple and straightforward, in the form of explicit conclusions; and consumers are generally left with little room for confusion about the message.

A   The second paragraph states that there is little room for confusion about the message.

B   **Correct.** The extent of consumers' knowledge about the product is not mentioned in the passage.

C   The first paragraph indicates that in the hard-sell approach advertisers make direct claims regarding the benefits of the advertised brand over other offerings.

D   The first and second paragraphs say that hard-sell claims are direct, simple, and straightforward.

E   The second paragraph emphasizes that the hard-sell approach presents it claims in the form of explicit conclusions.

The correct answer is B.

RC00492-03

19. It can be inferred from the passage that advertisers could reduce one of the risks discussed in the last paragraph if they were able to provide

(A)   motivation for consumers to think about the advertisement's message

(B)   information that implies the advertiser's intended conclusion but leaves that conclusion unstated

(C)   subtle evidence that the advertised product is superior to that of competitors

(D)   information comparing the advertised product with its competitors

(E)   opportunity for consumers to generate their own beliefs or conclusions

Inference

This question requires understanding the risks discussed in the last paragraph of the passage. Those risks are, first, that consumers would not be motivated to think about the advertisement and thus would miss the message's point; second, that consumers may draw conclusions that the advertiser did not intend; and finally, that consumers could question the validity of the conclusions they reach, even if those conclusions are what advertisers intend.

A   **Correct.** Providing motivation for consumers to think about an advertisement's message would reduce the first risk discussed in the last paragraph: that consumers would fail to draw any conclusions because they would lack motivation to engage with advertisements.

B Providing *information that implies a conclusion but leaves it unstated* is the very definition of the soft-sell approach, and it is this approach that gives rise to the risks discussed in the last paragraph.

C Providing subtle evidence that a product is superior is most likely to give rise to all three of the risks identified in the last paragraph, in that its subtlety would leave consumers free to draw their own conclusions, to fail to draw those conclusions, or to question the validity of their own conclusions.

D A direct comparison of the advertised product with its competitors would run all the risks identified in the last paragraph: consumers might not find the comparison motivating; they could draw conclusions that the advertiser did not intend (e.g., that the competing products are superior); or they could question whatever conclusions they do draw.

E Giving consumers the opportunity *to generate their own beliefs or conclusions* is an intrinsic part of the soft-sell approach, which produces the risks discussed in the last paragraph.

The correct answer is A.

RC00492-04

20. The primary purpose of the passage is to

(A) point out the risks involved in the use of a particular advertising strategy

(B) make a case for the superiority of one advertising strategy over another

(C) illustrate the ways in which two advertising strategies may be implemented

(D) present the advantages and disadvantages of two advertising strategies

(E) contrast the types of target markets for which two advertising strategies are appropriate

Inference

Overall, the passage is concerned with two advertising strategies. The first paragraph introduces the strategies. The second paragraph explains how a particular aspect of one approach may be both positive and negative and how the second approach mitigates these problems. The third paragraph continues this discussion of mitigation, while the fourth paragraph points out that there are drawbacks to this approach, too. Thus, according to the passage, both strategies have positive and negative aspects.

A The passage is concerned not with one particular advertising strategy but with two, and it discusses benefits, as well as risks, involved with both strategies.

B The passage does not suggest that one strategy is superior to the other but rather that each has positive and negative aspects.

C The passage does not discuss how to implement either of the strategies it is concerned with; instead, it deals with how consumers are likely to respond once the implementation has already taken place.

D **Correct.** The passage is primarily concerned with showing that both of the strategies described have advantages and disadvantages.

E The passage provides some indirect grounds for inferring the target markets for which each advertising strategy might be appropriate, but it is not primarily concerned with contrasting those markets.

The correct answer is D.

RC00492-05

21. Which of the following best describes the function of the sentence in lines 25–28 in the context of the passage as a whole?

(A) It reiterates a distinction between two advertising strategies that is made in the first paragraph.

(B) It explains how a particular strategy avoids a drawback described earlier in the paragraph.

(C) It suggests that a risk described earlier in the paragraph is less serious than some researchers believe it to be.

(D) It outlines why the strategy described in the previous sentence involves certain risks for an advertiser.

(E) It introduces an argument that will be refuted in the following paragraph.

Evaluation

The sentence in lines 25–28 explains how the kinds of conclusions consumers are invited to draw based on the soft-sell approach reduce the risk that consumers will respond with *resentment, distrust, and counterargumentation*—that is, the possible *boomerang effect* identified earlier in the paragraph as a drawback of the hard-sell approach.

A The sentence does not reiterate the distinction between the hard- and soft-sell approaches; rather, it explains an advantage of the soft-sell approach.

B Correct. The sentence explains how the soft-sell approach avoids the problems that can arise from the hard-sell approach's explicitly stated conclusions.

C The sentence suggests that the risk of boomerang effects described earlier in the paragraph is serious but that a different approach can mitigate it.

D The sentence outlines why the strategy described in the previous sentence reduces advertisers' risks, not why it involves risks.

E At no point does the passage refute the idea that implicit conclusions reduce the risk of boomerang effects. It does say that there could be drawbacks to the soft-sell approach, but those drawbacks are related to the problem with implicit conclusions themselves and how people reach them. In addition, the *following paragraph* does not mention the drawbacks, only the advantages of implicit conclusions.

The correct answer is B.

22. It can be inferred from the passage that one situation in which the boomerang effect often occurs is when consumers

RC00492-06

(A) have been exposed to forceful claims that are diametrically opposed to those in an advertiser's message

(B) have previous self-generated beliefs or conclusions that are readily accessible from memory

(C) are subjected to advertising messages that are targeted at specific markets to which those consumers do not belong

(D) are confused regarding the point of the advertiser's message

(E) come to view the advertiser's message with suspicion

Inference

The passage discusses the boomerang effect in the second paragraph. This effect is defined as consumers deriving conclusions from advertising that are the opposite of those that advertisers intended to present, and it occurs when consumers resent and/or distrust what they are being told.

A The passage provides no grounds for inferring that consumers need to be exposed to opposing claims in order to believe such claims; they may reach opposing claims on their own.

B The passage indicates that the boomerang effect can be reduced by using a soft-sell approach, which can result in self-generated conclusions, but it provides no evidence about any possible effects of preexisting self-generated beliefs or conclusions on the boomerang effect.

C The passage does not address how consumers who are subjected to advertising messages not intended for them might respond.

D Confusion regarding the point of the advertiser's message is more likely to occur, the passage suggests, when advertisers use a soft-sell approach—but it is the hard-sell approach, not the soft-sell, that is likely to result in the boomerang effect.

E **Correct.** The second paragraph indicates that consumers who resent being told what to believe and come to distrust the advertiser's message—that is, those who view the message with suspicion—may experience a boomerang effect, believing the opposite of the conclusions offered.

The correct answer is E.

RC00492-07

23. It can be inferred from the passage that the research mentioned in line 29 supports which of the following statements?

(A) Implicit conclusions are more likely to capture accurately the point of the advertiser's message than are explicit conclusions.

(B) Counterargumentation is less likely to occur if an individual's beliefs or conclusions are readily accessible from memory.

(C) The hard-sell approach results in conclusions that are more difficult for the consumer to recall than are conclusions resulting from the soft-sell approach.

(D) When the beliefs of others are presented as definite and forceful claims, they are perceived to be as accurate as self-generated beliefs.

(E) Despite the advantages of implicit conclusions, the hard-sell approach involves fewer risks for the advertiser than does the soft-sell approach.

Inference

The research this item refers to—research on consumer memory and judgment—indicates that beliefs are more memorable when they are self-generated and so matter when making judgments and decisions. Further, self-generated beliefs seem more believable to those who have them than beliefs that come from elsewhere.

A The fourth paragraph indicates that implicit conclusions are more likely to fail to replicate the advertiser's message than explicit conclusions are.

B The research discussed in the passage does not address when counterargumentation is more or less likely to occur. Even though counterargumentation is a risk when consumers distrust the advertiser's message—as they may do when harder-to-recall explicit conclusions are given—it may be as much of a risk when consumers reach an implicit conclusion that is readily accessible from memory.

C **Correct.** The research indicates that it is easier for consumers to recall conclusions they have reached on their own—that is, the sorts of conclusions that are encouraged by the soft-sell approach—than conclusions that have been provided explicitly, as happens in the hard-sell approach.

D The research does not show that the forcefulness with which claims are presented increases perceptions of the accuracy of those claims. Indeed, it is most likely the opposite, as the forcefulness of others' claims may make them seem even less related to any conclusions the consumer might generate for him- or herself.

E The research suggests that it is the soft-sell, not the hard-sell, approach that has fewer risks. The fourth paragraph indicates that there could be some risks to the implicit conclusions that consumers draw, but this is not part of the research in question.

The correct answer is C.

Questions 24–28 refer to the passage on page 98.

RC00222-01

24. It can be inferred from the passage that the two procedures described in the passage have which of the following in common?

(A) They have been applied in practice.

(B) They rely on the use of a device that measures tension.

(C) Their purpose is to determine an unknown mass.

(D) They can only be applied to small solid objects.

(E) They involve attraction between objects of similar mass.

Inference

The procedures described in the passage are introduced by the suggestion in the first paragraph that someone in a spaceship who wanted to determine a solid object's mass could do so in a particular way. The second paragraph uses the word *weigh* in quotes to refer to a similar procedure for determining the mass of a double-star system.

A The language of the first paragraph is hypothetical: we *could* do particular things. Thus, there is no way to determine from the passage whether that procedure has been applied in practice.

B The first procedure relies on a spring scale, which measures tension, but the second procedure measures time and distance to determine restraining force.

C **Correct.** Both procedures determine mass: the first procedure can determine the mass of a small solid object on a spaceship in free fall, and the second can determine the mass of a double-star system.

D The first procedure would, according to the passage, be applied to a small solid object, but the second *weighs* double-star systems, which are clearly not small objects.

E The second procedure involves attraction between two stars, which could be of similar mass, in the same system, but the first procedure involves measuring tension in a string and speed of whirling, not attraction between objects.

The correct answer is C.

RC00222-02

25. According to the passage, the tension in the string mentioned in lines 8–9 is analogous to which of the following aspects of a double-star system?

(A) The speed with which one star orbits the other

(B) The gravitational attraction between the stars

(C) The amount of time it takes for the stars to circle one another

(D) The distance between the two stars

(E) The combined mass of the two stars

Supporting Idea

The second paragraph states that an *attractive force* is analogous to the tension in the string. This attractive force is identified in the previous sentence as the gravitational force between the two stars in a double-star system.

A The second paragraph states that the speed with which the stars circle each other depends on the gravitational force between them, but it is that force that is analogous to the tension in the string.

B **Correct.** The second paragraph clearly identifies the gravitational force between the two stars as the attractive force that is analogous to the tension in the spring scale's string.

C The amount of time it takes for the stars to circle one another is necessary for calculating the force that holds them together, but it is the force itself that is analogous to the string's tension.

D The distance between the stars must be measured if the attraction between them is to be determined, but the attraction, not the distance, is analogous to the string's tension.

E The combined mass of the two stars is what the procedure is designed to determine; it is analogous to the mass of the small solid object, as described in the first paragraph.

The correct answer is B.

RC00222-03

26. Which of the following best describes the relationship between the first and the second paragraph of the passage?

(A) The first paragraph provides an illustration useful for understanding a procedure described in the second paragraph.

(B) The first paragraph describes a hypothetical situation whose plausibility is tested in the second paragraph.

(C) The first paragraph evaluates the usefulness of a procedure whose application is described further in the second paragraph.

(D) The second paragraph provides evidence to support a claim made in the first paragraph.

(E) The second paragraph analyzes the practical implications of a methodology proposed in the first paragraph.

Evaluation

This question requires understanding that the second paragraph describes a somewhat difficult-to-understand procedure that the first paragraph illustrates in smaller, and simpler, terms.

A **Correct.** The first paragraph illustrates, hypothetically, a simple procedure for determining mass, and this illustration provides the grounds on which the passage explains the procedure of the second paragraph.

B The first paragraph describes a situation in hypothetical terms, but the second paragraph does not test that situation's plausibility. Instead, the second paragraph draws an analogy between the initial situation and another procedure.

C The first paragraph does not evaluate the usefulness of the procedure for determining a small solid object's mass while in a spaceship in freefall; it simply describes how that procedure would work.

D The second paragraph provides no evidence; it describes a procedure analogous to what is described in the first paragraph.

E The second paragraph does not discuss the practical implications of the first paragraph's methodology but rather a procedure that is analogous to the hypothetical situation of the first paragraph.

The correct answer is A.

RC00222-04

27. The author of the passage mentions observations regarding the period of a double-star system as being useful for determining

(A) the distance between the two stars in the system

(B) the time it takes for each star to rotate on its axis

(C) the size of the orbit the system's two stars occupy

(D) the degree of gravitational attraction between the system's stars

(E) the speed at which the star system moves through space

Supporting Idea

The author mentions the period of a double-star system in the final sentence of the second paragraph, defining it as the time required for stars to circle each other. Knowing this time, in combination with the distance between the stars, enables the determination of the restraining force between the stars.

A The final sentence of the second paragraph indicates that the period of a double-star system is measured independently of the distance between the two stars in the system.

B The passage is not concerned with how long it takes each star to rotate on its axis.

C The passage does not mention anyone's trying to determine the size of the orbit of a system's two stars. It does mention the related topic of distance between the stars but indicates that knowing such distance is required for measuring the stars' mass, not that it can be inferred from the period of the system.

D **Correct.** According to the passage, the restraining force, or gravitational attraction, between the two stars can be deduced based on the period and the distance between them.

E The passage does not mention the speed at which the star system moves through space.

The correct answer is D.

RC00222-05.02

28. The primary purpose of the passage is to

(A) analyze a natural phenomenon in terms of its behavior under special conditions

(B) describe the steps by which a scientific measurement is carried out

(C) point out the conditions under which a scientific procedure is most useful

(D) contrast two different uses of a methodological approach in science

(E) explain a method by which scientists determine an unknown quantity

Evaluation

What is the primary purpose of the passage? What we call the weight of an object is its weight as measured in Earth's gravitational field; that weight is a function of gravity and the mass of the object. How is the mass of an object determined in a weightless, zero-gravity environment? The first paragraph of the passage explains a method to determine this. The second paragraph explains an analogous method that astronomers use to measure the masses of stars in a double-star system.

A   Although the passage has portions containing analysis and references to characteristics of natural phenomena, these portions are merely subsidiary to explanations of measurement methods.

B   A description of steps in a measurement procedure occurs in the first paragraph, but this is merely preliminary to an explanation of how masses of stars in double-star systems can be measured. The passage mentions two aspects of the method used to measure the masses of double stars—measuring the period and measuring the distance—but it does not tell whether these are separate steps of the process, and it does not primarily focus on these as a main topic.

C   The passage describes some conditions under which a particular measurement method is valid, but that description is merely subsidiary to an explanation meant to show why the method is valid.

D   The structure of the passage is based on analogy rather than contrast.

E   **Correct.** The primary purpose of the passage is to explain, using analogy, methods for determining mass independently of Earth's gravity.

The correct answer is E.

Questions 29–36 refer to the passage on page 100.

RC38000-01.02

29.   The passage is primarily concerned with

(A)   describing a resource and indicating various methods used to study it

(B)   presenting a theory and offering an opposing point of view

(C)   providing an explanation for unexpected findings

(D)   demonstrating why a particular theory is unfounded

(E)   resolving a disagreement regarding the uses of a technology

Main Idea

What issue, problem, or puzzle is the passage primarily meant to address? The passage discusses whether—and if so why or under what conditions—adoption of information technology (IT) benefits businesses. The first paragraph provides background information by summarizing opinions and data concerning the extent to which businesses can benefit by adopting IT. It details pre-1990 findings showing that, contrary to some experts' expectations, overall productivity in business sectors that adopted IT did not improve. It summarizes contrasting attempts by proponents of IT to explain how, by different performance measures, IT may have actually yielded business benefits other than competitive advantage. The second paragraph discusses the puzzle that the passage primarily addresses: why, if IT had *conferred economic value*, the pre-1990 findings indicated that, contrary to expectations, IT failed to *produce direct competitive advantage for individual firms*. The passage invokes *resource-based theory* to help resolve this puzzle.

A   IT is accurately described as *a resource,* but the passage is not concerned at all with *describing* IT, except in its very brief parenthetical definition of IT. Neither is it directly concerned with methods used to study IT.

B   Opinions are presented in the passage. But the only perspective or point of view that is referred to and characterized as a *theory* is *resource-based theory*. A possible application of that theory is described, but neither that theory nor any other theory is *presented*.

C   **Correct.** As explained above, the passage is primarily concerned with explaining why findings based on pre-1990 data suggested that, contrary to expectations, adoption of IT failed to produce direct competitive advantage for many businesses.

D   The only *theory* referred to in the passage is *resource-based theory*, but the passage neither opposes nor attempts to refute that theory.

E   The first paragraph indicates that there was some disagreement as to the magnitude or nature of any business benefits possibly produced by IT. But the passage is not aimed at resolving any such disagreements; it is aimed, rather, at explaining why expectations regarding certain business benefits of IT were not fulfilled.

The correct answer is C.

RC38000-02.02

30. The author of the passage discusses productivity in the retail industry in the first paragraph primarily in order to

(A) suggest a way in which IT can be used to create a competitive advantage

(B) provide an illustration of the "productivity paradox"

(C) emphasize the practical value of the introduction of IT

(D) cite an industry in which productivity did not stagnate during the 1980s

(E) counter the argument that IT could potentially create competitive advantage

Evaluation

Why does the author, in the first paragraph of the passage, discuss productivity in the retail industry? In the first paragraph, the information concerning *productivity in the retail industry* is presented as an example that seemed to provide support for what some economists termed *the "productivity paradox."* The passage describes the paradox as follows: *despite huge IT investments, . . .*

productivity stagnated. As an example of this, pre-1990 data is cited for the retail industry, which had widely adopted IT; the data indicated that productivity increases had significantly slowed relative to the average for the 25 years preceding 1973.

A   The data in the first paragraph regarding productivity in the retail industry does not suggest that IT can be used to create a competitive advantage. In fact, the data presented could provide reason to doubt whether, in the retail sector, IT would fulfill expectations regarding its potential for creating competitive advantage.

B   **Correct.** As explained above, the primary purpose of the author's first paragraph of productivity in the retail industry is to illustrate the "productivity paradox."

C   This could not be the author's purpose in the discussion of productivity in the retail industry in the first paragraph, since that discussion casts doubt on whether IT would fulfill expectations regarding its potential for creating competitive advantage.

D   This cannot be the primary purpose of the discussion of productivity in the retail industry in the first paragraph. The data concerning the retail industry is cited as an instance supporting and illustrating the general point that when there were huge IT investments, especially *in the service sectors, productivity stagnated.*

E   The author's purpose in the discussion of productivity in the retail sector is not to *counter the argument that IT could potentially create competitive advantage.* In the first paragraph, the author neither argues for nor endorses the view that IT lacked potential to create competitive advantage.

The correct answer is B.

RC38000-03.02

31. The passage suggests that proponents of resource-based theory would be likely to explain IT's inability to produce direct competitive advantages for individual firms by pointing out that

(A) IT is not a resource that is difficult to obtain

(B) IT is not an economically valuable resource

(C) IT is a complex, intangible resource

(D) economic progress has resulted from IT only in the service sector

(E) changes brought about by IT cannot be detected by macroeconomic measures

Inference

How would a proponent of resource-based theory be likely to explain the pre-1990 failure of IT to produce direct competitive advantage for firms that adopted it? According to the passage, resource-based theory implies that *in general, firms gain competitive advantages by accumulating resources that are economically valuable, relatively scarce, and not easily replicated.* However, the passage cites a study indicating that IT had become *pervasive and relatively easy to acquire* but did not seem sufficient by itself to confer competitive advantage. Based on this information, a proponent of resource-based theory would likely claim that since IT proved to be *easily replicated*, one of the conditions stipulated by resource-based theory for gaining competitive advantage was violated.

A   Correct. According to the study mentioned in the second paragraph, IT was *relatively easy to acquire.* According to the conditions for gaining competitive advantage as attributed in the passage to resource-based theory, a proponent of resource-based theory would likely claim that the ease of acquiring IT could help explain why adoption of IT was not by itself sufficient for gaining competitive advantage.

B   The passage suggests neither that IT lacks economic value nor that resource-based theory assumes or implies that it does. Rather, resource-based theory suggests that the economic value of IT during the period discussed in the passage typically did not provide competitive advantages to any company that adopted it over others that did so.

C   Although IT may in some respects be both complex and intangible, the passage does not suggest that resource-based theory entails that resources need to be simple or tangible in order to confer competitive advantage.

D   This is not a view that the passage attributes, even by implication, to proponents of resource-based theory.

E   The first paragraph of the passage indicates that some IT advocates claimed that macroeconomic measures of productivity failed to reflect the economic benefits of IT. But the passage neither endorses this viewpoint nor attributes it to proponents of resource-based theory.

The correct answer is A.

RC38000-04.02

32. Which of the following best describes the content of the first paragraph?

(A) It presents two explanations for the success of IT.

(B) It provides evidence that decreases in productivity will continue.

(C) It presents reasons for a decline in productivity.

(D) It demonstrates the effect IT has had on productivity.

(E) It contrasts views concerning the degree of IT's success.

Evaluation

Among the choices given, which one best describes the content of the first paragraph of the passage? The first paragraph provides background information by summarizing opinions and data concerning the extent to which businesses benefited by adopting IT. It details pre-1990 findings showing that, contrary to some experts' expectations, overall productivity in business sectors that adopted IT did not significantly improve. It summarizes contrasting attempts by proponents of IT to explain how, judged by different performance measures, IT may have actually yielded business benefits other than competitive advantage.

A   The first paragraph provides information suggesting that IT did not provide the expected benefits. In other words, it casts doubt on whether IT succeeded.

B   The first paragraph considers neither past nor future decreases in productivity. (It does, however, describe past decreases in the rate of increase in productivity).

C   The first paragraph discusses certain pre-1990 decreases in the average rate of productivity growth, but it does not discuss declines in productivity.

D   The first paragraph suggests that IT may have had little or no effect in producing productivity growth. The passage does not claim that IT actually had an effect on productivity and does not demonstrate any way in which IT had such an effect.

E   **Correct.** The first paragraph describes differing views concerning whether IT may have met expectations in enhancing competitiveness or providing other economic benefits for business.

The correct answer is E.

RC38000-05.02

33.   The passage suggests that the recent study of retail firms discussed in the second paragraph supports which of the following conclusions regarding a firm's competitive advantage?

(A)   Human resources alone are more likely to contribute to competitive advantage than is IT alone.

(B)   Human resources combined with IT are more likely than human resources alone to have a negative effect on competitive advantage.

(C)   Human resources combined with IT often have a negative effect on competitive advantage.

(D)   IT by itself is much more likely to have a positive effect than a negative effect on competitive advantage.

(E)   The positive effect of IT on competitive advantage increases with time.

Inference

The second paragraph describes a study of retail firms. The study confirmed that IT, having

become relatively easy to acquire, by itself conferred little advantage. Negative correlations between IT and performance suggest that IT likely weakened some retail firms' competitive positions. Firms' human resources, however, did explain improved performance, both in and of themselves and when merged with IT.

A   **Correct.** As explained above, the study indicated that human resources in and of themselves led to improved performance, whereas there were negative correlations between IT and performance.

B   The passage indicates that some firms gained IT-related advantages when IT was merged with human resources. The passage gives no indication whether this—or human resources alone—ever has negative effects on performance.

C   The passage indicates that some firms gained IT-related advantages when IT was merged with human resources. The passage gives no indication whether this ever has negative effects on performance.

D   The passage states that the study found that IT by itself conferred little advantage, but the study found frequent negative correlations between IT and performance.

E   The first paragraph states that some people have argued that it takes time for IT to yield results, but the study discussed in the second paragraph provides no evidence to support this. The finding of the study that indicates that IT can yield results when merged with human resources says nothing about whether all the effects are immediate or whether they instead increase with time.

The correct answer is A.

RC38000-06.02

34.   According to the passage, most pre-1990 literature on businesses' use of IT included which of the following?

(A)   Recommendations regarding effective ways to use IT to gain competitive advantage

(B)   Explanations of the advantages and disadvantages of adopting IT

(C)   Information about ways in which IT combined with human resources could be used to increase competitive advantage

(D)   A warning regarding the negative effect on competitive advantage that would occur if IT were not adopted

(E)   A belief in the likelihood of increased competitive advantage for firms using IT

Supporting Idea

The passage begins by stating that most pre-1990 literature on businesses' use of IT was optimistic about IT's ability to create competitive advantage and focused on dramatic success stories.

A   The passage does not state that pre-1990 literature on businesses' use of IT made recommendations regarding ways IT could be used to gain competitive advantage.

B   The passage indicates that most pre-1990 literature on businesses' use of IT focused on the advantages IT was believed to confer. The passage does indicate that some literature at the end of the 1980s discussed some disadvantages of adopting IT; but the passage suggests that most of the literature of this period did not discuss any disadvantages.

C   The passage does not clearly indicate whether any pre-1990 literature discussed the results of combining human resources and IT. The study described as "recent" in the second paragraph does discuss such results, but the study was not pre-1990 and does not discuss any specific ways IT combined with human resources could be used to increase competitive advantage.

D   Pre-1990 literature on businesses' use of IT expressed optimism that IT could confer competitive advantage, but the passage does not mention whether this literature presented a warning about negative effects on performance if IT was not adopted.

E   **Correct.** The first paragraph of the passage states that most pre-1990 literature on businesses' use of IT was optimistic about IT's ability to create competitive advantage.

The correct answer is E.

RC38000-07.02

35.   The author of the passage implies that toward the end of the 1980s, some economists described which of the following as a "productivity paradox" (see line 8)?

(A)   Investments in IT would not result in increases in productivity until the 1990s.

(B)   Investments in IT did not lead to expected gains in productivity.

(C)   Productivity in the retail industry rose less rapidly than did productivity in other industries.

(D)   The gains in productivity due to the introduction of IT were not reflected in macroeconomic measures of productivity.

(E)   Most gains in productivity occurred in the service sector and were therefore particularly difficult to measure.

Inference

The passage indicates in the first paragraph that toward the end of the 1980s, economists noticed that productivity was not increasing, as it had been expected to do as a result of significant investments in IT. The economists referred to this as a *productivity paradox*.

A   Although the first paragraph does indicate that productivity growth did occur in the 1990s, this is not what is referred to by the term *productivity paradox*.

B   **Correct.** The passage begins by indicating that before 1990 there was general optimism that investments in IT would lead to competitive advantages. However, by the late 1980s some economists had identified a *productivity paradox*, noting that *despite huge IT investments . . . productivity stagnated*; that is, the IT investments had not resulted in the expected gains in productivity.

C   The passage does not indicate that productivity rose less rapidly in the retail industry than in other industries. It merely indicates that it rose less rapidly than had been expected and less rapidly than it did prior to large IT investments.

D   The *productivity paradox* refers to a lack of gains in productivity due to IT, not to a failure of macroeconomic measures to capture actual productivity gains.

E   The passage indicates that the service sector failed to show significant gains, and it makes no mention of any difficulty related to measuring productivity gains in the service sector.

The correct answer is B.

RC38000-08.02

36. According to the passage, the recent study of retail firms discussed in the second paragraph (lines 33–63) best supports which of the following assessments of IT's potential?

(A) Even when IT gives a firm a temporary competitive advantage, that firm is unlikely to continue to achieve productivity gains.

(B) The competitive advantages conferred by a firm's introduction of IT are outweighed by IT's development costs.

(C) A firm's introduction of IT is less likely to limit its ability to achieve productivity gains than to enhance that ability.

(D) Although IT by itself is unlikely to give a firm a competitive advantage, IT combined with other resources may do so.

(E) Although IT by itself is unlikely to give a firm a competitive advantage, a firm that does not employ IT cannot achieve a competitive advantage.

Supporting Idea

Answering this question correctly involves an understanding of what the second paragraph says about a particular study of retail firms, specifically, what that study has to say about IT's potential. The study confirmed that IT, having become relatively easy to acquire, by itself conferred little advantage. Negative correlations between IT and performance suggest that IT likely weakened some retail firms' competitive positions. On the other hand, the second paragraph states that *some firms gained IT-related advantages by merging IT with complementary resources.*

A   The study reveals that IT by itself does not give firms a competitive advantage, but that it does give some firms such an advantage when IT is merged with complementary resources. The study does not indicate that

any productivity gains that are achieved in this way are short lived.

B   The passage does not indicate whether any competitive advantages conferred by a firm's introduction of IT (for instance, those that arise when merged with other resources) are outweighed by IT's development costs.

C   The study indicates that a firm's introduction of IT is likely to limit its ability to achieve productivity when it is not merged with complementary resources, but that it can enhance that ability when it is merged with such resources. The passage does not indicate the relative likelihood of those outcomes.

D   Correct. The study as described in the passage's second paragraph states that *IT by itself conferred little advantage* but that *some firms gained IT-related advantages by merging IT with complementary resources.*

E   This statement correctly indicates that the study states that IT by itself is unlikely to give a firm a competitive advantage. However, the passage does not indicate that the study states that firms that do not employ IT are unable to achieve a competitive advantage.

The correct answer is D.

Questions 37 to 80 - Difficulty: **Medium**

Questions 37–39 refer to the passage on page 102.

RC00267-01

37. The passage is primarily concerned with

(A) evaluating the evidence of a major geologic period and determining its duration

(B) describing an evolutionary phenomenon and speculating about its cause

(C) explaining the mechanisms through which marine life-forms evolved during a particular period

(D) analyzing the impact on later life-forms of an important evolutionary development

(E) contrasting a period of evolutionary change with other such periods

Main Idea

This question asks for an assessment of what the passage as a whole is doing. The passage is mainly concerned with a possible link between certain geological and ecological changes that occurred during the Ordovician period and the Ordovician radiation (when existing marine invertebrate life-forms gave rise to new variations that would eventually lead to new species).

A   The passage is not particularly concerned with determining the length of the period in question.

B   **Correct.** The passage is mainly concerned with a possible link between the evolutionary phenomenon of the Ordovician radiation and certain environmental changes that may have resulted in an enriched pattern of habitats and nutrients that could have fostered that radiation.

C   The passage indicates that the particular mechanisms through which marine life-forms evolved are not well understood.

D   Although the passage indicates that the changes it discusses ultimately did lead to new life-forms, it does not analyze that relationship.

E   The passage does not discuss any period of evolutionary change besides the Ordovician radiation.

The correct answer is B.

RC00267-02

38. Which of the following can be inferred from the passage regarding the geologic changes that occurred during the Ordovician period?

(A)   They were more drastic than those associated with other radiations.

(B)   They may have created conditions favorable to the evolution of many new life-forms.

(C)   They may have caused the extinction of many of the marine species living in shallow waters.

(D)   They may have been a factor in the development of new species adapted to living both on land and in water.

(E)   They hastened the formation of the extensive dry regions found in the western United States.

Inference

The question asks what can be inferred from the passage's claims regarding the geologic changes that took place during the Ordovician period. The passage indicates that during this period the sea level dropped and mountain ranges were formed and that these changes, rather than leading to large-scale extinctions, may have created more favorable habitats providing greater nutrients, which would likely have been favorable to newly evolved life-forms.

A   The passage does not mention other radiations and does not compare the Ordovician geologic changes to geologic changes associated with other radiations.

B   **Correct.** The passage does suggest that certain geologic changes that occurred during the Ordovician period may have created conditions favorable to the new life-forms associated with the Ordovician radiation.

C   The passage does not indicate whether any marine species became extinct; in fact, it explicitly denies that the geologic changes led to any large-scale extinctions.

D   The passage does not indicate that any new species were adapted to living both on land and in water. It merely discusses marine life-forms.

E   Although these geologic changes did likely create newly dry areas in the western United States, it does not indicate that these areas are *extensive*.

The correct answer is B.

RC00267-03

39. Which of the following best describes the function of the last sentence of the passage?

(A)   It points out that the events described in the passage may be atypical.

(B)   It alludes to the fact that there is disagreement in the scientific community over the importance of the Ordovician radiation.

(C)   It concludes that the evidence presented in the passage is insufficient to support the proposed hypothesis because it comes from a limited geographic area.

(D)   It warns the reader against seeing a connection between the biological and geologic changes described in the passage.

(E)   It alerts the reader that current knowledge cannot completely explain the relationship suggested by the evidence presented in the passage.

Evaluation

The last sentence of the passage functions primarily to indicate that, though certain evidence from the geologic record suggests a possible cause of the Ordovician radiation, the current level of knowledge regarding the relationship between environmental factors and that radiation is not sufficient for a full understanding of that relationship.

A   Although there may be certain geologic or evolutionary aspects of the Ordovician period that are atypical, the final sentence of the passage does not address them.

B   Neither the final sentence nor the rest of the passage addresses any disagreements within the scientific community.

C   Although the final sentence of the passage does indicate that current understanding of the relationship between the environmental factors discussed and the Ordovician radiation is incomplete, it does not indicate that it is because the evidence comes from a limited geographic area that the evidence is insufficient.

D   The last sentence does not advise against seeing a connection between the biological and geologic changes discussed; it merely advises that such a connection is not yet fully understood.

E   **Correct.** The last sentence indicates to the reader that current knowledge is insufficient for fully explaining the relationships among the evidence provided in the passage regarding geologic, ecological, and evolutionary changes.

The correct answer is E.

Questions 40–45 refer to the passage on page 103.

RC00141-01

40.   The author of the passage is primarily concerned with

(A)   criticizing Locke's economic theories

(B)   discounting the contribution of labor in a modern economy

(C)   questioning the validity of the labor theory of value

(D)   arguing for a more equitable distribution of business profits

(E)   contending that employers are overcompensated for capital goods

Main Idea

This question depends on an understanding of the passage as a whole. The first paragraph describes the labor theory of value and the theory's historical origins in the philosophy of John Locke. The second paragraph provides some analysis of the theory and uses the analysis to support a critique.

A   The passages describes an historical connection between the labor theory of value and Locke's economic theories and suggests that the influence of Locke on the labor theory of value is one reason why, according to the author, the theory may be inadequate. This perhaps suggests an indirect criticism of Locke and his theories, via his influence on more recent theories. However, Locke's economic theories are not criticized directly and are not the focus of the passage.

B   Although the passage may suggest that a particular economic theory—the labor theory of value—may exaggerate the "contribution of labor in a modern economy" because the theory may neglect the importance of capital goods, the author does not suggest that the contribution of labor is unimportant.

C   **Correct.** The second paragraph—more than half of the passage—is almost entirely focused on critiquing the labor theory of value. The first paragraph, by introducing the theory and providing some historical context, can be seen as supporting the critique, by introducing the theory to readers who may not be familiar with it.

D   The passage offers no argument for or against a more equitable distribution of business profits.

E   The point at issue in this answer choice is similar to the point at issue in answer choice D, to do with what might be right or wrong, or more equitable, in matters concerning the distribution of money or "compensation." The passage makes no argument as to what might be right or wrong in this respect.

The correct answer is C.

RC00141-02

41.   According to the author of the passage, which of the following is true of the distribution of the income derived from the total output of consumer goods in a modern economy?

(A)   Workers receive a share of this income that is significantly smaller than the value of their labor as a contribution to total output.

(B)   Owners of capital goods receive a share of this income that is significantly greater than the contribution to total output attributable to the use of capital goods.

(C)   Owners of capital goods receive a share of this income that is no greater than the proportion of total output attributable to the use of capital goods.

(D)   Owners of capital goods are not fully compensated for their investment because they pay out most of their share of this income to workers as wages and benefits.

(E)   Workers receive a share of this income that is greater than the value of their labor because the labor theory of value overestimates their contribution to total output.

Supporting Idea

This question asks us to identify something that is true of the distribution of the income derived from all of the consumer goods that are produced in the modern economy.

A   The passage makes certain claims about the relative distribution of income between

workers and the owners of capital goods, with respect to the income derived from the total output of consumer goods. However, no clear comparison is made between the share thus received by workers and the "value" of their labor.

B   The passage states that roughly one-third of the total output of consumer goods is attributable to the use of capital goods and that the owners of capital receive one-third of the income from this total output. The shares of income are roughly the same.

C   **Correct.** As explained in answer choice B, the share of income to the owners of capital goods is roughly equal to the proportion of total output of consumer goods that can be attributed to the use of capital goods.

D   Although the passage mentions that some workers, because they are shareholders or pension beneficiaries, receive some of the income that "serves as compensation to the owners of capital goods," there is no indication that this is *most* of the share that serves as the compensation to these owners. Furthermore, the workers who are, say, shareholders, may be owners of capital themselves. Therefore, the income that these workers receive as shareholders may be no reduction at all to the income received by the owners of capital.

E   The passage does not suggest that workers receive a share of the income derived from the total output of consumer goods that is greater than the value of their labor. And it provides no explanation of such a phenomenon.

The correct answer is C.

RC00141-04

42.   Which of the following statements, if true, would most effectively counter the author's criticism of Locke at the end of the passage?

(A)   Locke was unfamiliar with the labor theory of value as it was formulated by his intellectual heirs.

(B)   In Locke's day, there was no possibility of ordinary workers becoming shareholders or pension beneficiaries.

(C)   During Locke's lifetime, capital goods did not make a significant productive contribution to the economy.

(D)   The precise statistical calculation of the productive contributions of labor and capital goods is not possible without computers.

(E)   The terms "capital goods" and "consumer goods" were coined by modern economists and do not appear in Locke's writings.

Application

The question asks us to identify the most effective counter to the criticism of Locke that he is at least somewhat responsible for the fact, according to the author of the passage, that the labor theory of value "systematically disregards" the contribution of capital goods to production.

A   The criticism of Locke in question has to do with his supposed responsibility for a supposed flaw in a certain theory, presumably because of his influence on later theorizers. That Locke was "unfamiliar" with this theory, which did not exist at the time of Locke, does not significantly mitigate Locke's (supposed) responsibility for the (supposed) flaw in the theory.

B   Once we see what the criticism of Locke is, to do with a claim that he is responsible for a "systematic disregard" of a certain theory of the productive contribution of capital goods, we can see that this answer choice is irrelevant.

C   **Correct.** Whatever the flaws in Locke's theories, it would seem wrong to hold him responsible for "neglecting" something—capital goods in this case—that was not a significant factor in his day. Given the fact (assuming that it is a fact) that capital goods were not a significant factor when Locke was alive, the responsibility for neglecting them (assuming that they have been neglected by economic theorists) may seem to rest with those who have neglected them after they have become a significant factor.

D   The precision of the calculation of the productive contributions of labor and capital goods—to the degree for which a computer would be necessary—is not a factor

anywhere in the passage, and it would not be relevant to the criticism of Locke.

E   That certain terms are used today that were not used in the past does not indicate that there were not other terms that were used to refer to the same thing. And the mere fact of the word we happen to use to refer to capital goods is not relevant to the criticism of Locke.

The correct answer is C.

RC00141-05

43.   Which of the following best describes the organization of the passage?

(A)   The author explores the origins of a theory and explains why the theory never gained widespread acceptance.

(B)   The author introduces the premise of a theory, evaluates the premise by relating it to objective reality, then proposes a modification of the theory.

(C)   After quoting a well-known authority, the author describes the evolution of a theory, then traces its modern form back to the original quotation.

(D)   After citing a precursor of a theory, the author outlines and refutes the theory, then links its flaw to the precursor.

(E)   After tracing the roots of a theory, the author attempts to undermine the theory by discrediting its originator.

Evaluation

The question asks us to identify the statement that most accurately describes the organization of the passage.

A   The author indeed explores an aspect of the origin of the labor theory of value, to do with the philosopher John Locke. However, the author neither claims that the theory never gained widespread acceptance nor tries to explain a supposed fact that the theory never gained widespread acceptance.

B   Although the author explains a fundamental aspect of a theory—the labor theory of value—and then may seem to evaluate this aspect by "relating it to objective reality," she or he does not propose a modification of the theory.

C The passage indeed quotes John Locke, who is well known and may be considered an authority on certain matters. However, Locke would not be considered an authority on the contents of the labor theory of value, which, the passage suggests, did not exist at the time of Locke. Furthermore, much of the passage is devoted to developing a criticism of the theory. A good characterization of the passage would need to at least mention this criticism.

D Correct. The author begins the passage by describing a theory of John Locke that is, according to the author, a precursor to the labor theory of value. Most of the second paragraph is devoted to a criticism of the theory, which the author ends by claiming that Locke is somewhat responsible for the supposed flaw.

E The criticism of the labor theory of value is based on certain purported claims, made by the theory, about the economy that, according to the author, do not agree with the theory. The criticism of John Locke is then based on this critique of the theory, and the claim that Locke is somewhat responsible for the flaw in the theory that the author claims to identify. Because the critique of the theory is thus not based on the critique of Locke, and thus not on something that would purportedly "discredit" him, this answer choice is clearly incorrect.

The correct answer is D.

RC00141-06

44. Which of the following arguments would a proponent of the labor theory of value, as it is presented in the first paragraph, be most likely to use in response to lines 23–25?

(A) The productive contributions of workers and capital goods cannot be compared because the productive life span of capital goods is longer than that of workers.

(B) The author's analysis of the distribution of income is misleading because only a small percentage of workers are also shareholders.

(C) Capital goods are valuable only insofar as they contribute directly to the production of consumer goods.

(D) The productive contribution of capital goods must be discounted because capital goods require maintenance.

(E) The productive contribution of capital goods must be attributed to labor because capital goods are themselves products of labor.

Application

The passage asks us to identify the most likely response of a proponent of the labor theory of value, as the theory is described in the passage, to lines 23–25. Because the statement in lines 23–25 is a criticism of the theory, it is reasonable to expect that a likely response of a proponent of the theory may be to defend the theory against this criticism.

A The labor theory of value, as described by the author, would suggest that the relative contributions of workers and capital goods can be compared. According to the theory (as described by the author), it is labor that makes the fundamental contribution—a clear comparison. So the statement that the relative contributions cannot be so compared would not defend the theory.

B Although this answer choice may offer a reasonable criticism of an aspect of the passage, it does not offer a criticism of the point that is made in lines 23–25.

C This answer choice may seem to describe how, according to the author, capital goods get their value. Restating this point of the author would not defend the labor theory of value against the author's arguments.

D This statement is consistent with the content of the passage; for example, the discount due to maintenance could already be figured into the calculations behind the author's claims as to the relative importance of capital goods and labor.

E Correct. If the productive contribution of capital goods is attributed to labor, then the author's claim, against the labor theory of value, that this productive contribution should not be attributed to labor, would be incorrect. The labor theory of value might therefore be justified when, according to lines 23–25, it "systematically disregards the productive contribution of capital goods."

The correct answer is E.

RC00141-07

45. The author of the passage implies which of the following regarding the formulators of the labor theory of value?

(A) They came from a working-class background.

(B) Their views were too radical to have popular appeal.

(C) At least one of them was a close contemporary of Locke.

(D) They were familiar with Locke's views on the relationship between labor and the value of products.

(E) They underestimated the importance of consumer goods in a modern economy.

Inference

The question asks us to identify an inference that can be made regarding the people who formulated the labor theory of value.

A   Although it is plausible that the formulators of the theory may have been sympathetic with the interests of people who may be described as working class, there is no indication that the author of the passage actually has a working-class background.

B   Although at least some proponents of the theory have been considered radical, there is nothing in the passage that indicates this, or indicates whether or not the theory had popular appeal.

C   The "short step," mentioned in the passage, from Locke's theory of value to the labor theory of value, could seem to indicate a short step in time, whereby at least one of the formulators of the theory would be a rough contemporary of Locke. However, this would be an incorrect reading. Rather than a "step" in time, the "short step" in the passage refers to a logical step, whereby it would be a "short step" from one theory to another that resembles it in fundamental respects.

D   **Correct.** The passage strongly suggests that the formulators of the labor theory of value were influenced by Locke's views in certain fundamental respects. This indicates that the

formulators would likely have been familiar with these views.

E   Although the author suggests that proponents of the labor theory of value may have significantly underestimated the importance of capital goods in the economy, no such suggestion is made about the importance of consumer goods.

The correct answer is D.

Questions 46–54 refer to the passage on page 105.

RC00204-01

46. The author of the passage draws conclusions about the fur trade in North America from all of the following sources EXCEPT

(A) Cartier's accounts of trading with Native Americans

(B) a seventeenth-century account of European settlements

(C) a sixteenth-century account written by a sailing vessel captain

(D) archaeological observations of sixteenth-century Native American sites

(E) a sixteenth-century account of Native Americans in what is now New England

Supporting Idea

This question asks about the sources mentioned by the author of the passage. Answering the question correctly requires determining which answer choice is NOT referred to in the passage as a source of evidence regarding the North American fur trade.

A   **Correct.** The passage mentions Cartier's voyage but does not refer to Cartier's accounts of his trading.

B   In the first paragraph, Nicolas Denys's 1672 account of European settlements provides evidence of fur trading by sixteenth-century European fishing crews.

C   In the second paragraph, a Portuguese captain's records provide evidence that the fur trade was going on for some time prior to his 1501 account.

D   In the first paragraph, archaeologists'
     observations of sixteenth-century Native
     American sites provide evidence of fur
     trading at that time.

E   In the second paragraph, a 1524 account
     provides evidence that Native Americans
     living in what is now New England had
     become selective about which European
     goods they would accept in trade for furs.

The correct answer is A.

RC00204-02

47. The passage suggests that which of the following is
     partially responsible for the difficulty in establishing
     the precise date when the fur trade in North America
     began?

     (A) A lack of written accounts before that of Nicolas
          Denys in 1672

     (B) A lack of written documentation before 1501

     (C) Ambiguities in the evidence from Native
          American sources

     (D) Uncertainty about Native American trade
          networks

     (E) Uncertainty about the origin of artifacts
          supposedly traded by European fishing crews for
          furs

Inference

The question asks about information implied by
the passage. The first paragraph points out the
difficulty of establishing exactly when the fur
trade between Native Americans and Europeans
began. The second paragraph explains that the
first written record of the fur trade (at least the
earliest known to scholars who study the history
of the trade) dates to 1501, but that trading was
already well established by that time. Thus, it can
be inferred that lack of written records prior to
1501 contributes to the difficulty in establishing
an exact date for the beginning of the fur trade.

A   Two written records of the fur trade prior
     to the account by Nicolas Denys are
     mentioned in the passage. The passage does
     not suggest that a lack of written records
     from before 1672 is a source of the difficulty
     in establishing the date.

B   **Correct.** The passage indicates that the fur
     trade was well established by the time of the
     documentation dating from 1501 but strongly
     suggests that there is no known earlier
     documentation regarding that trade, so a lack
     of records before that time contributes to the
     difficulty in establishing an exact date.

C   The only Native American sources
     mentioned in the passage are archaeological
     sites, and there is no indication of
     ambiguities at those sites.

D   Native American trade networks are not
     mentioned in the passage.

E   The passage mentions that fishing crews
     exchanged parts of their ships for furs and
     does not suggest any uncertainty about the
     origin of those artifacts.

The correct answer is B.

RC00204-03

48. Which of the following, if true, most strengthens the
     author's assertion in the first sentence of the second
     paragraph?

     (A) When Europeans retraced Cartier's voyage in
          the first years of the seventeenth century, they
          frequently traded with Native Americans.

     (B) Furs from beavers, which were plentiful in North
          America but nearly extinct in Europe, became
          extremely fashionable in Europe in the final
          decades of the sixteenth century.

     (C) Firing arms were rarely found on sixteenth-
          century Native American sites or on European
          lists of trading goods since such arms required
          frequent maintenance and repair.

     (D) Europeans and Native Americans had established
          trade protocols, such as body language assuring
          one another of their peaceful intentions, that
          antedate the earliest records of trade.

     (E) During the first quarter of the sixteenth century,
          an Italian explorer recorded seeing many Native
          Americans with what appeared to be copper
          beads, though they may have been made of
          indigenous copper.

Evaluation

The question depends on evaluating an assertion
made in the passage and determining which
additional evidence would most strengthen it.

The first sentence of the second paragraph claims that the fur trade was well established by the time Europeans sailing the Atlantic coast of America first documented it. The passage then indicates that the first written documentation of the trade dates to 1501. Thus, evidence showing that trade had been going on for some time before 1501 would strengthen (support) the assertion.

A   This evidence shows trade occurring in the first years of the seventeenth century, not prior to the first records from 1501.

B   This evidence shows trade occurring in the final decades of the sixteenth century, not prior to the first records from 1501.

C   This evidence does not indicate that trade took place prior to the first records from 1501.

D   Correct. Evidence that trade protocols had developed before the trade was first recorded in 1501 would strengthen support for the assertion that trade was taking place prior to the earliest documentation.

E   Because the copper beads may have been made by Native Americans rather than acquired through trade with other societies, this observation would not provide evidence that trade with Europeans took place prior to 1501.

The correct answer is D.

RC00204-04

49. Which of the following best describes the primary function of lines 11–16?

(A)   It offers a reconsideration of a claim made in the preceding sentence.

(B)   It reveals how archaeologists arrived at an interpretation of the evidence mentioned in the preceding sentence.

(C)   It shows how scholars misinterpreted the significance of certain evidence mentioned in the preceding sentence.

(D)   It identifies one of the first significant accounts of seventeenth-century European settlements in North America.

(E)   It explains why Denys's account of seventeenth-century European settlements is thought to be significant.

Evaluation

This question depends on understanding how the last sentence of the first paragraph functions in relation to the larger passage. The first paragraph explains that the earliest Europeans to trade with Native Americans were fishing crews near Newfoundland. The second-to-last sentence of the paragraph describes archaeological artifacts from Native American sites. The last sentence then explains that Nicolas Denys's 1672 account helped archaeologists realize that the artifacts were evidence of trade with fishing crews. Thus, the last sentence of the passage shows how archaeologists learned to interpret the evidence mentioned in the previous sentence.

A   The only claim made in the previous sentence is that archaeologists found a particular type of evidence. The final sentence of the paragraph does not suggest that this claim should be reconsidered.

B   Correct. After reading Denys's account, archaeologists were able to interpret the archaeological evidence mentioned in the previous sentence.

C   The passage suggests that archaeologists correctly interpreted the evidence, not misinterpreted it.

D   Denys's account is mentioned primarily to explain how archaeologists learned to interpret the archaeological evidence, not primarily to identify an important early account of settlements.

E   The passage does not discuss why Denys's account is significant, only that archaeologists used it to help understand the evidence mentioned in the previous sentence.

The correct answer is B.

RC00204-05

50. It can be inferred from the passage that the author would agree with which of the following statements about the fur trade between Native Americans and Europeans in the early modern era?

(A)   This trade may have begun as early as the 1480s.

(B)   This trade probably did not continue much beyond the 1530s.

(C) This trade was most likely at its peak in the mid-1520s.

(D) This trade probably did not begin prior to 1500.

(E) There is no written evidence of this trade prior to the seventeenth century.

Inference

The question requires determining which statement can most reasonably be inferred from the information in the passage. The passage argues that it is difficult to determine when the fur trade between Native Americans and Europeans began, since the earliest people to participate in that trade apparently left no written records. The second paragraph notes that at the time of the earliest known record in 1501, trade was already *well underway*. In the final two sentences of the passage, the author mentions an event that occurred in 1534 and then says that by that time the trade may have been going on for *perhaps half a century*.

A Correct. The next-to-last sentence of the passage cites evidence of fur trade between Native Americans and Europeans in 1524. In the final sentence of the passage, the author mentions an event that happened a decade after that date—thus in 1534—and expresses the opinion that the trade started *perhaps half a century* (fifty years) before that later date. Fifty years before 1534 would be 1484. This implies that the author accepts that the trade may have begun by the 1480s.

B The passage gives no indication that the author believes trade ended shortly after the 1530s.

C The passage does not discuss when the fur trade was at its peak.

D To the contrary, the passage argues that trade began well before 1501.

E The passage mentions written evidence of the trade from 1501 and 1524.

The correct answer is A.

RC00204-06

51. Which of the following can be inferred from the passage about the Native Americans mentioned in line 24?

(A) They had little use for decorative objects such as earrings.

(B) They became increasingly dependent on fishing between 1501 and 1524.

(C) By 1524, only certain groups of Europeans were willing to trade with them.

(D) The selectivity of their trading choices made it difficult for them to engage in widespread trade with Europeans.

(E) The selectivity of their trading choices indicates that they had been trading with Europeans for a significant period of time prior to 1524.

Inference

The question asks about information that can be inferred from the passage. The Native Americans mentioned in the 1524 chronicles accepted only certain kinds of European goods in trade. The passage indicates that these Native Americans *had become selective* about which goods they would accept, which implies that by 1524 they had been trading long enough to determine which European goods were most valuable to them.

A The passage does not imply that these Native Americans had no use for decorative objects, only that they did not desire to obtain such items through trade with Europeans.

B The passage does not suggest that the Native Americans' dependency on fishing changed over time.

C There is no indication that any groups of Europeans were unwilling to trade with these Native Americans.

D The passage notes that the Native Americans were selective in their trade choices but does not suggest that such selectivity made widespread trade difficult.

E Correct. The passage notes that by 1524, the Native Americans had become selective about which European goods they would accept, and the passage takes this to indicate that the trade with Europeans significantly predated 1524.

The correct answer is E.

52. The passage supports which of the following statements about sixteenth-century European fishing crews working the waters off Newfoundland?

(A) They wrote no accounts of their fishing voyages.

(B) They primarily sailed under the flag of Portugal.

(C) They exchanged ship parts with Native Americans for furs.

(D) They commonly traded jewelry with Native Americans for furs.

(E) They carried surplus metal implements to trade with Native Americans for furs.

Inference

The question asks which statement is supported by information provided in the passage. The first paragraph states that European fishing crews around Newfoundland were the first Europeans to trade goods for furs with Native Americans in the modern period. The last sentence of the paragraph states that archaeological evidence indicates the crews had dismantled their ships to trade ship parts for furs.

A The second sentence states that the crews left no written accounts of their trade with Native Americans, but it does not suggest that they left no written accounts of their voyages.

B The passage mentions one Portuguese vessel but does not suggest that the European crews who fished off Newfoundland were mostly on Portuguese vessels.

C **Correct.** The last sentence of the first paragraph supports the conclusion that the crews traded ship parts for furs.

D The passage mentions one instance of a Native American acquiring earrings from Europeans but does not suggest that trades for such goods were common.

E The passage indicates that fishing crews traded metal implements with Native Americans but does not suggest that they brought surplus implements for that purpose—and in fact mentions that sometimes traded metal articles had been parts of their own ships.

The correct answer is C.

53. Which of the following can be inferred from the passage about evidence pertaining to the fur trade between Native Americans and Europeans in the early modern era?

(A) A lack of written evidence has made it difficult to establish which Europeans first participated in this trade.

(B) In general, the physical evidence pertaining to this trade has been more useful than the written evidence has been.

(C) There is more written evidence pertaining to this trade from the early part of the sixteenth century than from later in that century.

(D) The earliest written evidence pertaining to this trade dates from a time when the trade was already well established.

(E) Some important pieces of evidence pertaining to this trade, such as Denys's 1672 account, were long overlooked by archaeologists.

Inference

This question asks about information that can be inferred from the passage. Any suggestion that Native Americans may have produced written evidence of the early-modern trade with Europeans is absent from the passage. The second paragraph states that by the time Europeans first documented the fur trade, it was already well underway. This statement, in the context of the passage, implies that the earliest written records of the trade date to a time after it was well established.

A The first paragraph indicates that the first Europeans to participate in the trade were quite certainly fishing crews near Newfoundland.

B The passage gives no indication that physical evidence of the trade has been more useful than written evidence.

C Although the passage does not cite written evidence from the late sixteenth century, the passage gives no reason to believe that less written evidence exists from that time.

D **Correct.** According to the passage, the fur trade was well underway when written evidence of the trade was first documented by Europeans. The passage contains no suggestion that there might have been earlier documentation of that trade by anybody other than Europeans.

E   The passage does not imply that archaeologists overlooked evidence for long periods of time.

The correct answer is D.

RC00204-09

54. The passage suggests which of the following about the sixteenth-century Native Americans who traded with Europeans on the coast of what is now called New England?

(A)   By 1524 they had become accustomed to exchanging goods with Europeans.

(B)   They were unfamiliar with metals before encountering Europeans.

(C)   They had no practical uses for European goods other than metals and metal implements.

(D)   By 1524 they had become disdainful of European traders because such traders had treated them unfairly in the past.

(E)   By 1524 they demanded only the most prized European goods because they had come to realize how valuable furs were on European markets.

Inference

The question asks about what is implied in the passage. The Native Americans trading with Europeans on the coast of what is now called New England are discussed in the 1524 chronicles mentioned in the second paragraph. The passage indicates that these Native Americans *had become selective* about which European goods they would accept in trade, which suggests they had become accustomed to trading with Europeans.

A   **Correct.** By the time the chronicle was written, the Native Americans were familiar enough with trade to be able to specify which European goods they would accept.

B   Although the Native Americans chose to trade furs for European metal goods, the passage does not imply they were unfamiliar with any metals prior to encountering Europeans.

C   The passage does not suggest why Native Americans preferred certain goods over others.

D   The passage does not attribute disdain for European traders to Native Americans.

E   There is no indication in the passage that Native Americans were aware of furs' value in European markets.

The correct answer is A.

Questions 55–58 refer to the passage on page 107.

RC00201-01

55. The passage is primarily concerned with

(A)   describing the development of the biological species concept

(B)   responding to a critique of reproductive compatibility as a criterion for defining a species

(C)   considering two different approaches to identifying biological species

(D)   pointing out the advantage of one method of distinguishing related species

(E)   identifying an obstacle to the classification of biological species

Main Idea

This question depends on understanding the passage as a whole. The passage begins by explaining that identifying a species can be difficult, because there are different ways of defining the term. The biological species concept is one approach, but it has problems. Phenotype is another approach that can be used when the biological species concept proves difficult.

A   The first paragraph defines the biological species concept and identifies some problems with its application, but it does not explain how that concept developed.

B   The passage presents some critiques of reproductive compatibility as a way of identifying a biological species; it does not concern itself with responding to those critiques.

C   **Correct.** The passage considers the biological species concept and the idea of phenotype as ways of identifying biological species.

D While the passage identifies two ways of distinguishing species and states that some investigators use one of those methods—the phenotype method—when the biological method is difficult to apply, the passage is not primarily concerned with pointing out that either one is better than the other.

E The passage does discuss certain obstacles to the classification of species. First, it points out that there is no single accepted definition of *distinct species*. Second, it points out obstacles related to one particular approach to the classification of species. However, the passage considers these obstacles in service of its primary concern, namely considering two different approaches to identifying biological species.

The correct answer is C.

RC00201-03
56. The author of the passage mentions "groups that live in different places" (line 21) most probably in order to

(A) point out a theoretical inconsistency in the biological species concept

(B) offer evidence in support of the biological species concept

(C) identify an obstacle to the application of the biological species concept

(D) note an instance in which phenotype classification is customarily used

(E) describe an alternative to the biological species concept

Evaluation

The author's mention of *groups that live in different places* comes at the end of the first paragraph, in the context of discussing a third problem with the biological species concept: that investigators may not know whether animals in such groups are able to interbreed.

A The author does not address theoretical inconsistencies in the biological species concept.

B The author mentions groups that live in different places in order to address a

problem with the biological species concept, not to support it.

C **Correct.** One obstacle to applying the biological species concept is that those attempting to distinguish among species may not be able to determine whether geographically separated groups of animals can interbreed.

D The passage does mention that some investigators use phenotype classification when the biological species concept is difficult to apply, but it does not mention specifically that a situation in which groups live in different places is an instance in which phenotype classification is customarily used.

E Animal groups that live in different places pose a problem for the application of the biological species concept, according to the author. The author does not mention these groups in order to describe an alternative to that concept.

The correct answer is C.

RC00201-04
57. With which of the following statements regarding the classification of individual species would the author most likely agree?

(A) Phenotype comparison may help to classify species when application of the biological species concept proves inconclusive.

(B) Because no standard definition exists for what constitutes a species, the classification of animal populations is inevitably an arbitrary process.

(C) The criteria used by biologists to classify species have not been based on adequate research.

(D) The existence of hybrids in wild animal species is the chief factor casting doubt on the usefulness of research into reproductive compatibility as a way of classifying species.

(E) Phenotype overlap should be used as the basic criterion for standardizing species classification.

Inference

This question depends on understanding the general points the author makes with regard to classification of individual species. The author explains that there is no single definition of species and then describes the biological species concept, which depends on reproductive compatibility. This approach has several problems, however, and the author goes on to say that phenotype may be used when the biological species concept is difficult to apply.

A **Correct.** The author states at the beginning of the second paragraph that some investigators use phenotype when they find it difficult to apply the biological species concept, and the passage provides no reason to believe that the author would disagree with the idea that phenotype comparison can be helpful in these situations.

B The author would most likely not agree that classification of animal populations is arbitrary. Investigators use clearly defined approaches, such as the biological species concept and phenotype classification, to make such classifications. That there may be problems with an approach does not make it arbitrary.

C The author states that the biological species concept can be too restrictive, but there is no suggestion that the author finds this approach, or phenotype classification, to be inadequately researched.

D The author mentions hybridization first as a factor casting doubt on the usefulness of the biological species concept, but nothing in the passage suggests that the author thinks that it is more significant than the other reasons offered for finding the biological species concept too restrictive.

E Phenotype overlap does not receive the author's endorsement as the best, or most basic, way of classifying species; instead, the author states merely that some investigators rely on this approach when they cannot apply the biological species concept.

The correct answer is A.

RC00201-05
58. Which of the following best describes the function of lines 10–13?

(A) It elaborates the definition of the biological species concept given in a previous sentence.

(B) It develops a point about the biological species concept made in the previous sentence.

(C) It states the author's central point about the biological species concept.

(D) It identifies a central assumption underlying the biological species concept.

(E) It demonstrates why the biological species concept is invalid.

Evaluation

The sentence in question discusses hybridization as a first factor complicating the applicability of the biological species concept. Thus its function is to help explain why, as the previous sentence states, that concept is too restrictive.

A The sentence in question brings up a problem with the biological species concept; it does not elaborate the definition of that concept.

B **Correct.** According to the sentence that precedes the sentence in question, the biological species concept can be too restrictive. The author offers three reasons to develop this point, and the first reason is given in the sentence in question.

C The sentence in question could be said to support the author's central point about the biological species concept—that it is one (flawed) way of determining whether a population is a species—but it does not state that central point.

D The sentence in question expresses a problem with the biological species concept, not a central assumption of it.

E The sentence in question serves to indicate a problem with the biological species concept, but it does not go so far as to demonstrate that it is invalid.

The correct answer is B.

Questions 59–61 refer to the passage on page 109.

RC00322-01

59. The primary purpose of the passage is to

(A) summarize findings in an area of research

(B) discuss different perspectives on a scientific question

(C) outline the major questions in a scientific discipline

(D) illustrate the usefulness of investigating a research topic

(E) reconcile differences between two definitions of a term

Main Idea

The passage discusses two problems confronting researchers studying the genetic bases of animal behavior: the complexity of the control of most behaviors by multiple genes, and divergence between research fields in what counts as a behavioral gene. The passage focuses mainly on the latter issue, discussing how ethologists define "behavioral gene" in a narrower manner than neuroscientists, who define the term broadly. To elucidate the ethologists' approach, two genes are discussed, one a behavioral gene, the other not.

A The passage primarily aims to explain how researchers in two different research areas define "behavioral gene." It does not try to summarize the research findings of either area.

B **Correct.** The primary purpose of the passage is to identify differing perspectives on the scientific question of how genes control animal behavior.

C The scientific disciplines of genetics, neuroscience, and ethology—all subdisciplines of biology—contain many different "major questions," and the passage does not try to outline the great variety of such questions in any one of those subdisciplines.

D The topic of the utility of doing research is not part of the passage discussion.

E An important purpose of the passage is to illustrate divergence among scientific fields in how a key term is defined, but the point is to show how the definitions differ rather than to "reconcile" the difference.

The correct answer is B.

RC00322-02

60. The passage suggests that neuroscientists would most likely consider Shaker to be which of the following?

(A) An example of a behavioral gene

(B) One of multiple genes that control a single behavior

(C) A gene that, when mutated, causes an alteration in a specific normal behavior without making the organism ill

(D) A gene of interest to ethologists but of no interest to neuroscientists

(E) A poor source of information about the nervous system

Application

The passage asserts that ethologists do not regard *Shaker* as a behavioral gene because it merely makes fruit flies exhibit unhealthy behavior (shaking under anesthesia). But neuroscientists, according to the passage, are mainly interested in how genes, via the nervous system, contribute to behavior. The passage suggests that neuroscientists, unlike ethologists, have no reservation about using the term *behavioral gene* to apply to any gene that contributes to behavior. The implication is that neuroscientists would probably regard *Shaker* as a behavioral gene.

A **Correct.** The passage suggests that neuroscientists would probably regard *Shaker* as a behavioral gene.

B The passage indicates that research shows *Shaker* is a sufficient cause, in fruit flies, of shaking under anesthesia. Although some organism might display a behavior controlled by *Shaker* in concert with other genes, the passage is silent on any such possibility.

C   The passage lacks information as to whether there is any alteration—one that neuroscientists would likely consider healthy—in a normal behavior if the alteration is caused by a mutation in *Shaker*.

D   The passage indicates that neuroscientists' interest in genetics is part of their effort to understand the nervous system. This seems to imply that neuroscientists might be interested in *Shaker*.

E   The passage is silent on how neuroscientists would evaluate the potential for *Shaker* to contribute to understanding of the nervous system.

The correct answer is A.

RC00322-05

61.   It can be inferred from the passage that which of the following, if true, would be most likely to influence ethologists' opinions about whether a particular gene in a species is a behavioral gene?

(A)   The gene is found only in that species.

(B)   The gene is extremely difficult to identify.

(C)   The only effect of mutations in the gene is to make the organism ill.

(D)   Neuroscientists consider the gene to be a behavioral gene.

(E)   Geneticists consider the gene to be a behavioral gene.

Application

The passage identifies two criteria that ethologists use in deciding whether a gene should count as a behavioral gene: a mutation in the gene alters a specific normal behavior and the mutation does not merely make the organism ill.

A   The passage is silent on whether either of two genes identified by ethologists in fruit flies are to be found only in fruit flies. The two criteria mentioned used by ethologists carry no implication as to whether any gene unique to a given species would count as a behavioral gene.

B   The difficulty of identifying a gene can obviously be due to many factors, such as limitations in existing scientific techniques, and the passage does not imply that such difficulty increases the likelihood that a gene would count as a behavioral gene for ethologists.

C   **Correct.** The passage implies that if this were found to be true, ethologists would regard it as sufficient reason for not counting the gene as a behavioral gene.

D   A central theme of the passage is that whether ethologists would count a gene as a behavioral gene is largely unaffected by whether neuroscientists do so, given the divergent perspectives of the scientists' respective disciplines.

E   The main contrast in the passage with respect to definitions of the term *behavioral gene* is between ethologists and neuroscientists, and no specific definitional criteria for this term are explicitly attributed to geneticists. However, there is a slight suggestion that since geneticists find that most behaviors are governed by multiple genes, geneticists might regard any gene involved in the governance of a behavior as a behavioral gene. This approach, however, would be unlikely to influence the opinions of ethologists concerning definition.

The correct answer is C.

Questions 62–68 refer to the passage on page 110.

RC22661-01.01

62.   The author indicates that tamarin territories are

(A)   surprisingly large

(B)   poorly situated

(C)   unusually abundant in food resources

(D)   incapable of supporting large troops of tamarins

(E)   larger in Peru than in other parts of South America

Supporting Idea

This question depends on understanding what the passage says about tamarin territories. In the second paragraph, the passage claims that the most surprising thing about tamarins is the size of their territories, and it indicates how large these territories are by comparing them to the territories of certain other animals.

A **Correct.** The passage indicates that the size of tamarins' territories—large in comparison to the territories of several other species—is surprising.

B The passage gives no indication as to whether tamarin territories are poorly situated.

C Although the passage does discuss the tamarin diet, it does not indicate how abundant in food sources tamarin territories are.

D The passage does indicate that relatively few tamarins live per square kilometer, but it does not claim that this is so because the territories are incapable of supporting a larger number of tamarins. In fact, there is some suggestion that the territories would seem to be capable of supporting more, which is one reason the size of the territories is so surprising.

E The passage does not compare the size of tamarin territories in Peru to tamarin territories elsewhere in South America.

The correct answer is A.

RC22661-02.01
63. The author mentions the spatial requirements of the gray squirrel in order to

(A) explain why they are so common

(B) demonstrate the consequences of their nonterritoriality

(C) emphasize the unusual territorial requirements of the tamarin

(D) provide an example of a major difference between squirrels and monkeys

(E) provide an example of an animal with requirements similar to those of the tamarin

Evaluation

The passage mentions the spatial requirements of the gray squirrel as part of its discussion of the surprising size of tamarin territories. Gray squirrel territories are mentioned for the specific purpose of highlighting how much more space tamarins require compared to another animal of roughly equal size.

A The passage does refer to "the common gray squirrel," but it does not explain why they are so common.

B The passage does not say anything about the consequences of the gray squirrel's nonterritoriality.

C **Correct.** The spatial requirements of gray squirrels are mentioned to highlight, by contrast, how expansive the spatial requirements of tamarins are.

D Although the passage mentions the spatial requirements of the gray squirrel to highlight how different the spatial requirements of one particular type of monkey, the tamarin, are from those of other animals, the passage does not mention the squirrels' spatial requirements to provide an example of a difference between squirrels and monkeys in general.

E The passage actually does the opposite of this—it mentions the gray squirrel's spatial requirements to provide an example of an animal with requirements vastly different from those of the tamarin.

The correct answer is C.

RC22661-03.01
64. The author regards the differences between the diets of the tamarins and several larger species as

(A) generally explicable in terms of territory size

(B) apparently too small to explain the rarity of tamarins

(C) wholly predictable on the basis of differences in body size

(D) a result of the rigid territoriality of tamarins

(E) a significant factor in determining behavioral differences

Supporting Idea

This question depends on recognizing that the passage rejects the idea that any differences between the diets of tamarins and those of certain larger animals are large enough to explain tamarins' relative rarity. The passage points out that these animals feed on the same fruits, nectar, and small prey, and claims that though the proportions of the fruits consumed varies somewhat, this variation is not sufficient to explain the tamarin's rarity.

A   The author does not seek to explain why these differences in diet—which the passage indicates are minimal—exist. Given that the author indicates that differences in territory size are large and differences in diet are small, it is unlikely, in any case, that the author would regard the former as explaining the latter.

B   **Correct.** The passage indicates that the differences in diet among these animals are too small to explain the rarity of tamarins.

C   The author does not give any indication that the differences in the diets of these animals are predictable based on differences in body size.

D   The author does indicate that tamarins are rather unusual among primates in their rigid territoriality, but there is no indication that this rigid territoriality explains the small differences in diet among tamarins and certain larger animals.

E   The author mentions differences in diet merely to rule out that these differences are large enough to explain tamarins' rarity; these differences are not mentioned as a factor in determining behavioral differences.

The correct answer is B.

RC22661-04.01

65. Which of the following would most probably be regarded by the author as anomalous?

(A)   A large primate species that eats mostly plants

(B)   A species of small mammals that is fiercely territorial

(C)   Two species of small primates that share the same territories

(D)   A species of small birds that is more abundant than many species of larger birds

(E)   A species of small rodents that requires more living space per individual than most species of larger rodents

Application

This question requires you to understand an underlying principle of the passage and to apply that principle to an instance that is not specifically discussed in the passage. The passage is concerned with how anomalous tamarins are: they are exceptions to the general rule that in general the number of animals in a species is proportional to the average body size of individuals within the species. The author also points out that tamarins are unusual in that the amount of space they require is out of proportion to their body size, suggesting the principle that an animal's spatial requirement is generally proportional to the animal's body size. And, though the passage is generally concerned with comparing tamarins to other primates, the author also compares tamarins' spatial requirements to those of gray squirrels, a type of rodent.

A   The author does not give any indication whether it would be anomalous for a species of large primates to eat mostly plants. The author does not present a general principle about the diets of primates, and says nothing specific about species of large primates.

B   Although the author indicates that the "rigid" territoriality of tamarins is "rather exceptional among primates," the author lists several other primate species that are also territorial. The author does not indicate whether such territoriality is rare among small mammals in general.

C   The author indicates that most primates do not have "such concerted territoriality" as tamarins do, suggesting that the author may not think that two other species of small primates sharing territories would be anomalous.

D   Given that the author indicates that generally the number of individuals within a species is inversely proportional to the average body size of the members of the species, the author would probably expect that a species of small birds would be more abundant than most species of larger birds and would not regard this as anomalous.

E   **Correct.** The author would generally expect that smaller animals would require less living space than larger animals.

The correct answer is E.

RC22661-05.01

66. The author most probably regards the tamarins studied in Manu National Park as

(A) an endangered species

(B) typical tamarins

(C) unusually docile

(D) the most unusual primates anywhere

(E) too small a sample to be significant

Inference

This question requires you to make an inference from what the author says about the tamarins studied in Manu National Park to a claim about how the author most likely regards these tamarins. The author considers certain information that has been gathered about the two tamarin species studied in the park, and on the basis of that, makes claims about tamarins in general (note that the author elsewhere in the passage simply refers to "tamarins" without qualification, i.e., without referring specifically to "the tamarins studied in Manu National Park"). This suggests that the author would regard the tamarins studied in the park as being typical of tamarins generally, at least in the ways discussed.

A   It is possible that the two tamarin species studied in the park are endangered, but apart from noting the surprisingly small number of individuals belonging to the species, there is no information that would suggest that they are endangered, and the mere fact that the number of members is relatively small compared to the number of members in other species is not sufficient to indicate that they are endangered, as that number could nonetheless be stable or even growing.

B   **Correct.** The author does not specifically mention anything that would indicate that these tamarins are atypical of tamarins in general, and appears to make inferences about tamarins in general on the basis of the two species studied in the park. The author would not be justified in making such inferences if the author believed that the tamarins observed in the park were not in fact typical.

C   The author does not give any indication that these species are unusually docile, and in fact suggests the opposite by indicating that tamarins vigorously expel any intruders from their territories.

D   The author does note some ways in which these tamarin species are unusual among primates, but does not indicate that they are "the most unusual primates anywhere." The author, in fact, indicates that in one of the ways that these species are unusual—their relative scarcity despite their small body size—another primate species, the pygmy marmoset, is even more unusual.

E   Because the author appears to make some inferences from information about the tamarins studied in the park to claims about tamarins in general, the author does not seem to regard the tamarins studied in the park as too small a sample to be significant.

The correct answer is B.

RC22661-06.01

67. Which of the following is NOT mentioned in the passage as a species whose groups display territoriality?

(A) Gibbons

(B) Siamangs

(C) Titi monkeys

(D) Squirrel monkeys

(E) Night monkeys

Inference

This question requires you, by process of elimination, to identify the species that is NOT explicitly mentioned as being a species displaying territoriality. Each of the species given in the answer choices is explicitly mentioned in the passage, and all but one of these species are explicitly described as displaying territoriality. In lines 38–41, the author states, "concerted territoriality [like that of tamarins] is rather exceptional among primates, though the gibbons and siamangs of Asia show it, as do a few other New World species such as the titi and night monkeys." So, clearly, gibbons, siamangs, titi monkeys, and night monkeys are each said to display territoriality. Squirrel monkeys, the remaining answer choice, are mentioned three different times in the passage (see lines 16, 25, 30), but never as displaying territoriality.

A   Gibbons are identified as displaying "concerted territoriality" (line 39).

B   Siamangs are identified as displaying "concerted territoriality" (line 39).

C   Titi monkeys are identified as displaying "concerted territoriality" (line 41).

D   Correct. Although squirrel monkeys are mentioned three times in the passage (lines 16, 25, and 30), in none of the instances are they mentioned as displaying territoriality.

E   Night monkeys are identified as displaying "concerted territoriality" (line 41).

The correct answer is D.

RC22661-07.01

68. The primary concern of the passage is to

(A)   recommend a policy

(B)   evaluate a theory

(C)   describe an unusual condition

(D)   explain the development of a hypothesis

(E)   support one of several competing hypotheses

Main Idea

Answering this question requires identifying an abstract description of the primary purpose of the passage. The passage focuses in different ways on an unusual condition, namely, the anomalous relationship between tamarins' relatively small average body size and the number of individuals in the species.

A   The passage is not concerned with recommending any policy.

B   The passage does not focus on any theory; it considers a phenomenon, but proposes no theory to explain that phenomenon.

C   Correct. The passage's primary concern is to describe an unusual phenomenon, namely, how tamarins "break the rule" that, in general, the number of individuals in a species is inversely proportional to the average body size of members of the species.

D   The passage is primarily concerned with a particular, unusual phenomenon, but it offers no hypothesis regarding it, nor does it discuss the development of any such hypothesis.

E   Although the passage gives passing consideration to some hypotheses, its primary concern is to note certain characteristics of tamarins. The passage does not primarily concern itself with any hypotheses.

The correct answer is C.

Questions 69–75 refer to the passage on page 112.

RC32661-01.01

69. It can be inferred from the passage that opponents of labor concessions would most likely describe many plant-relocation decisions made by United States companies as

(A)   capricious

(B)   self-serving

(C)   naive

(D)   impulsive

(E)   illogical

Evaluation

This question requires you to pick a word that the passage suggests opponents of labor concessions would apply to many plant-relocation decisions made by U.S. companies. The passage indicates that those who oppose labor concessions often do so on the grounds that companies will move their production overseas if it matches their perceived self-interest—regardless of any concessions labor has made in order to preserve jobs. According to the passage, opponents of labor concessions therefore tend to view such plant-relocation decisions as self-serving.

A   The passage does not attribute to opponents of labor concessions the view that corporate decisions are variable in a way that makes them unpredictable.

B   Correct. According to the passage, the opponents of labor concessions believe that companies make investment decisions that fit their strategic plans and profit objectives.

C   The passage suggests that the opponents may view plant managers' relocation decisions as based on realistic assessments of corporate interests.

D   The passage does not attribute to the opponents the view that companies make plant-relocation decisions on impulse; rather, it suggests that these opponents tend to see relocation decisions as based on analysis of how relocation would advance predetermined strategies and objectives.

E   According to the passage, the opponents see an inflexible logic governing such relocation decisions, which are based on an assessment of how best to serve companies' interests, as judged by reference to predetermined investment strategies and profit objectives.

The correct answer is B.

RC32661-02.01

70.   It can be inferred from the passage that, until recently, which of the following has been true of United States industry in the twentieth century?

(A)   Unions have consistently participated in major corporate policy decisions.

(B)   Maintaining adequate quality control in manufacturing processes has been a principal problem.

(C)   Union workers have been paid relatively high wages.

(D)   Two-tier wage systems have been the norm.

(E)   Goods produced have been priced beyond the means of most workers.

Inference

This question requires you to draw a conclusion about United States industry in the twentieth century from the information in the passage. The passage indicates that even opponents of labor concessions believe that union workers have traditionally been paid relatively high wages and that high wages underlay much of the success of industry in the United States in the twentieth century.

A   The passage suggests otherwise. It tells us that advocates of labor concessions believe it may eventually be possible for labor to participate in management decisions in a way that was not traditionally the case.

B   The passage mentions "quality circles" as a benefit that, according to some proponents of labor concessions, may eventually be gained in the context of having more say on the shop floor. But that does not imply that quality control in manufacturing has been a major problem.

C   Correct. The passage attributes a belief that this was so to opponents of labor concessions.

D   The passage tells us that opponents of labor concessions believe that proposals for two-tier wage systems could become a reality— which indicates that such systems have not been the norm.

E   According to the passage, opponents of labor concessions admit that wages have been relatively high for union workers and that labor and management have long been committed to the idea that workers should be able to afford to purchase the products they make.

The correct answer is C.

RC32661-03.01

71.   The passage provides information to answer which of the following questions?

(A)   What has caused unions to consider wage restraints and reduced benefits?

(B)   Why do analysts study United States labor-management relations?

(C) How do job-security guarantees operate?

(D) Are investment and pricing strategies effective in combating imports?

(E) Do quality circles improve product performance and value?

Evaluation

This question requires you to identify a question that the passage provides an answer to. In paragraph 1, the passage indicates some factors ("twin shocks") that have contributed to a change in the approach of labor unions to negotiations with management.

A **Correct.** The passage claims that competition from non-union companies and imports of low-priced high-quality products from abroad have induced labor unions to be more flexible in meeting the demands of management.

B The passage does not address this question either directly or indirectly.

C According to the passage, proponents of labor concessions claim that job-security guarantees can be negotiated if concessions are made, but the passage provides no further detail that would shed light on how such guarantees operate.

D The passage is silent on the effectiveness of investment and pricing strategies in combating imports.

E The passage mentions quality circles, but provides no information on their impact. Presumably, quality circles aim to improve quality, and such improvements would be pointless absent any payoff in "performance and value."

The correct answer is A.

RC32661-04.01

72. The passage is primarily concerned with the

(A) reasons for adversarialism between labor and management

(B) importance of cooperative labor-management relations

(C) consequences of labor concessions to management

(D) effects of foreign competition on the United States economy

(E) effects of nonunion competition on union bargaining strategies

Main Idea

This question asks us to identify the overall theme of the passage, i.e., the topic that motivates the discussion of various subtopics.

A The traditionally adversarial relationship between labor and management is mentioned in passing, but the reasons for that relationship are not probed.

B The passage details benefits that some labor unionists perceive in cooperative labor-management relations, but does not assess the importance of such relations.

C **Correct.** The passage explores this theme by looking at the new approach of some labor unions by discussing the pros and cons of labor concessions as perceived by proponents and opponents of such concessions.

D The passage alludes to these effects, but no sustained exploration of this topic is present in the passage.

E The passage alludes to these effects, but no sustained exploration of this topic is present in the passage.

The correct answer is C.

RC32661-05.01

73. The sentence "If proposals for pay cuts . . . unskilled laborers" serves primarily to

(A) disprove a theory

(B) clarify an ambiguity

(C) reconcile opposing views

(D) present a hypothesis

(E) contradict accepted data

Evaluation

This question asks you to determine the intended purpose of one of the passage's sentences. This sentence, found in the final paragraph, describes what opponents of labor concessions predict are possible consequences if labor unions agree to pay cuts, two-tier wage systems, or lower wages for newly hired workers. These hypothesized consequences can be summarized as a significant degradation in the overall material welfare of large sections of the population because of grossly unequal distribution of wealth and income such as exist in some less-developed societies.

A   The sentence describes what is perceived as something that could occur if labor unions were to make concessions resulting in reductions in wages. It is not framed as evidence to refute a theory, since it is merely a prediction of what could occur.

B   The sentence does not function in resolving an ambiguity; no ambiguity that the sentence could be meant to resolve is described or suggested.

C   The sentence does nothing to reconcile opposing views; it articulates a vision of a possible future that it attributes to those who oppose wage-reduction concessions by labor unions.

D   **Correct.** The sentence presents a hypothesis about the possible long-term consequences of labor-union concessions that would result in significantly lower wages.

E   Accepted data can be contradicted only by alternative datasets, but the sentence in question does not provide alternative data, only a prediction of what the future might bring for workers' material welfare if drastic wage reductions were to be conceded by labor unions.

The correct answer is D.

RC32661-06.01

74.   It can be inferred from the passage that opponents of labor concessions believe that if concession bargaining continues, then

(A)   plants will close instead of relocating

(B)   young workers will need continued job retraining

(C)   professional workers will outnumber marginal workers

(D)   wealthy investors will invest in Third World countries instead of the United States

(E)   the social structure of the United States will be negatively affected

Inference

This question concerns the beliefs of opponents of labor concessions, as those beliefs are represented in the passage. The passage attributes to those opponents the view that if the idea of reducing wages gains credence, the U.S. social structure will begin to decline and will eventually be on a par with the social structures of less-developed nations. Moreover, the passage represents the opponents as believing that if labor unions negotiate on the premise that high labor costs are causing a company's problems, eventually wages will be reduced drastically—potentially to Third World levels. In paragraph 1, the passage reports that analysts say that labor unions are currently forced to favorably consider management demands for "wage restraint" and concessions on benefits.

A   The passage indicates that the opponents believe companies relocate their plants whenever companies perceive this as in accord with their investment strategies and profit objectives.

B   A need for continued retraining of young workers is not a belief attributed by the passage to opponents of labor concessions.

C   The passage, in referring to "a huge mass of marginal workers," attributes a contrary view to opponents of labor concessions.

D   The passage does not attribute this view to opponents of labor concessions.

E   **Correct.** We learn from the passage that labor unions are engaged in concession bargaining, on topics that include wage restraint. The opponents of labor concessions believe, according to the passage, that eventually the result will be wage reductions, and the ultimate result will be degradation of the U.S. social structure, resulting in a social structure more like that of a less-developed nation.

The correct answer is E.

RC32661-07.01
75. According to the author, "Sophisticated proponents" of concessions do which of the following?

(A) Support the traditional adversarialism characteristic of labor-management relations.

(B) Emphasize the benefits unions can gain by granting concessions.

(C) Focus on thorough analyses of current economic conditions.

(D) Present management's reasons for demanding concessions.

(E) Explain domestic economic developments in terms of worldwide trends.

Supporting Idea

This question requires you to identify what the passage says "sophisticated proponents" of concessions do. According to the passage, these sophisticated proponents represent their concessions in a "prolabor light." They suggest that concessions by labor can bargain for profit sharing, retraining rights, and job-security guarantees—and can even bargain for "more say on the shop floor" and a voice in company strategy and decision making.

A According to the passage, analysts say that labor-management relations are increasingly cooperative rather than adversarial.

B Correct. As explained above, the proponents of labor concessions represent concessions in a prolabor light by detailing the types of labor gains that can come from such concessions.

C The proponents probably conduct such analyses, but no information about this is given in the passage.

D Sophisticated proponents may sometimes do this, but the passage emphasizes their focus on the opportunities for labor gains.

E Sophisticated proponents may sometimes do this, but the passage emphasizes their focus on the opportunities for labor gains.

The correct answer is B.

Questions 76–80 refer to the passage on page 114.

RC00097-02
76. According to the passage, much of the research on Alessandra Strozzi done by the historian mentioned in the second paragraph supports which of the following conclusions?

(A) Alessandra used her position as her sons' sole guardian to further interests different from those of her sons.

(B) Alessandra unwillingly sacrificed her own interests in favor of those of her sons.

(C) Alessandra's actions indicate that her motivations and intentions were those of an independent individual.

(D) Alessandra's social context encouraged her to take independent action.

(E) Alessandra regarded her sons' goals and interests as her own.

Supporting Idea

According to the passage, a historian of women in Renaissance Europe attributes to a Florentine widow Alessandra Strozzi "individual intention and authorship of actions" and argues that she had significant individual goals and interests other than those of her sons. But the passage states that much of the historian's research indicates otherwise.

A According to the passage, the historian's research provides much evidence that Alessandra Strozzi acted primarily to further her sons' interests.

B The passage does not cite any of the historian's research to suggest that Strozzi was an unwilling champion of her sons' interest.

C A theme of the passage is that the historian's research provides weak, if any, support for this claim.

D The historian's research is not invoked in the passage to support this. The passage suggests that such a claim is more compatible with an anthropologist's idea that identity is socially and culturally determined and not necessarily "independent," as various historians assume.

E   **Correct.** The passage states: "much of the historian's own research reveals that Alessandra acted primarily as a champion of her sons' interests, taking their goals as her own."

The correct answer is E.

RC00097-03

77.   In the first paragraph, the author of the passage mentions a contention that would be made by an anthropologist most likely in order to

(A)   present a theory that will be undermined in the discussion of a historian's study later in the passage

(B)   offer a perspective on the concept of personhood that can usefully be applied to the study of women in Renaissance Europe

(C)   undermine the view that the individuality of European women of the Renaissance was largely suppressed

(D)   argue that anthropologists have applied the Western concept of individualism in their research

(E)   lay the groundwork for the conclusion that Alessandra's is a unique case among European women of the Renaissance whose lives have been studied by historians

Evaluation

The passage asserts that an anthropologist would contend that "a person can be conceived in ways other than as an 'individual.'" Immediately preceding this assertion, the passage asserts that certain historians think of a person as "an innately bounded unit, autonomous and standing apart from both nature and society." The passage invokes anthropology to support the view that perhaps the findings of those historians regarding individualism among women in Renaissance Europe are biased.

A   Anthropology is invoked to provide a corrective to the findings of the historians mentioned—not to provide a critique of any anthropological theory.

B   **Correct.** The passage makes the case that the anthropological view may be more useful than the historian's in the study of women in Renaissance Europe.

C   The passage cites no claim by historians that individuality of women in Renaissance Europe was largely suppressed, and the passage presents no argument to critique or refute such a claim.

D   The passage makes no such claim about anthropologists, but does make a similar claim about certain historians.

E   The passage does not state or imply that Strozzi was atypical of women in Renaissance Europe that historians have studied, nor is the anthropological conception of personhood invoked to underpin any such view.

The correct answer is B.

RC00097-04

78.   The passage suggests that the historians referred to in line 1 make which of the following assumptions about Renaissance Europe?

(A)   That anthropologists overestimate the importance of the individual in Renaissance European society

(B)   That in Renaissance Europe, women were typically allowed to express their individuality

(C)   That European women of the Renaissance had the possibility of acting independently of the social context in which they lived

(D)   That studying an individual such as Alessandra is the best way to draw general conclusions about the lives of women in Renaissance Europe

(E)   That people in Renaissance Europe had greater personal autonomy than people do currently

Evaluation

The passage suggests that the historians, in their studies of women in Renaissance Europe, held a preconceived notion of personhood—a notion that implied at least the possibility of individual autonomous action unaffected by social context. By implication, the passage ascribes a similar preconception to the historian whose study of Strozzi is discussed.

A   No view concerning anthropologists or their work is attributed, even by implication, to the historians.

B   Even if the historians held a view regarding the scope of what women in Renaissance Europe were typically allowed to do, the passage does not attribute such a view to them.

C   **Correct.** The passage implies that the historians assumed it was at least sometimes possible for women in Renaissance Europe to act autonomously, unaffected by social context.

D   The passage does not indicate that the historians assumed study of a single individual was the best approach to study of women's lives in Renaissance Europe.

E   The passage neither explicitly nor implicitly claims that the historians assumed women had more personal autonomy in Renaissance Europe than women have currently.

The correct answer is C.

RC00097-05

79. It can be inferred that the author of the passage believes which of the following about the study of Alessandra Strozzi done by the historian mentioned in the second paragraph?

(A) Alessandra was atypical of her time and was therefore an inappropriate choice for the subject of the historian's research.

(B) In order to bolster her thesis, the historian adopted the anthropological perspective on personhood.

(C) The historian argues that the boundaries of the conceptual self were not always firm and closed in Renaissance Europe.

(D) In her study, the historian reverts to a traditional approach that is out of step with the work of other historians of Renaissance Europe.

(E) The interpretation of Alessandra's actions that the historian puts forward is not supported by much of the historian's research.

Inference

The passage tells us that the historian who studied Strozzi "attributes individual intention and authorship of actions" to her. But the passage author claims that much of the historian's own research supports the view that, contrary to the historian's interpretation, "Alessandra did not distinguish her personhood from that of her sons"—and therefore that her actions did not primarily express personal autonomy.

A   Nothing in the passage implies that this is true or that the passage author believes it was so.

B   The passage is in direct contradiction with this claim about the historian, and it strongly suggests that the author of the passage would reject this claim.

C   The passage author makes this point concerning "the boundaries of the conceptual self" as part of the critique of the historian's approach.

D   The passage author characterizes the historian's approach neither as traditional nor as nontraditional; nor does the passage author contrast the historian's approach with that of any other historian.

E   **Correct.** The passage author suggest that much of the historian's research provides support for an interpretation that is incompatible with the historian's own interpretation.

The correct answer is E.

RC00097-06

80. The passage suggests that the historian mentioned in the second paragraph would be most likely to agree with which of the following assertions regarding Alessandra Strozzi?

(A) Alessandra was able to act more independently than most women of her time because she was a widow.

(B) Alessandra was aware that her personal motivation was embedded in a social context.

(C) Alessandra had goals and interests similar to those of many other widows in her society.

(D) Alessandra is an example of a Renaissance woman who expressed her individuality through independent action.

(E) Alessandra was exceptional because she was able to effect changes in the social constraints placed upon women in her society.

Application

According to the passage, the historian whose study of Strozzi is discussed "attributes individual intention and authorship of actions" to her. The passage does not discuss whether, or how, the historian may have regarded Strozzi's widowhood as relevant to her exercise of autonomy; nor does the passage discuss the extent to which, if at all, the historian regarded Strozzi's actions, goals, or interests as typical of women in Renaissance Europe.

A   The passage provides no evidence as to whether the historian would agree with this.

B   The passage does not attribute to the historian, even implicitly, a view that Strozzi's personal motivation was primarily "embedded in a social context"; so the historian would likely believe that Strozzi herself did not see her personal motivation as so embedded.

C   The passage provides no evidence as to whether the historian would regard Strozzi's goals and interests as resembling those of other widows in her society.

D   Correct. The first sentence of the second paragraph indicates that the historian treats Strozzi as an example of a Renaissance woman who expressed her individuality through independent action.

E   The passage provides no evidence that the historian viewed Strozzi as exceptional in effecting any kind of social change.

The correct answer is D.

Questions 81 to 112 - Difficulty: **Hard**

Questions 81–87 refer to the passage on page 116.

RC00054-01

81.   According to the passage, conventional spiral galaxies differ from low-surface-brightness galaxies in which of the following ways?

(A)   They have fewer stars than do low-surface-brightness galaxies.

(B)   They evolve more quickly than low-surface-brightness galaxies.

(C)   They are more diffuse than low-surface-brightness galaxies.

(D)   They contain less helium than do low-surface-brightness galaxies.

(E)   They are larger than low-surface-brightness galaxies.

Supporting Idea

This question requires recognizing information that is provided in the passage. The first paragraph describes and compares two types of galaxies: conventional galaxies and dim, or low-surface-brightness, galaxies. It states that dim galaxies have the same approximate number of stars as a common type of conventional galaxy but tend to be larger and more diffuse because their mass is spread over wider areas (lines 4–10). The passage also indicates that dim galaxies take longer than conventional galaxies to convert their primordial gases into stars, meaning that dim galaxies evolve much more slowly than conventional galaxies (lines 10–14), which entails that conventional galaxies evolve more quickly than dim galaxies.

A   The passage states that dim galaxies have approximately the same numbers of stars as a common type of conventional galaxy.

B   Correct. The passage indicates that dim galaxies evolve much more slowly than conventional galaxies, which entails that conventional galaxies evolve more quickly.

C   The passage states that dim galaxies are more spread out, and therefore more diffuse, than conventional galaxies.

D   The passage does not mention the relative amounts of helium in the two types of galaxies under discussion.

E   The passage states that dim galaxies tend to be much larger than conventional galaxies.

The correct answer is B.

RC00054-02

82.   It can be inferred from the passage that which of the following is an accurate physical description of typical low-surface-brightness galaxies?

(A)   They are large spiral galaxies containing fewer stars than conventional galaxies.

(B)   They are compact but very dim spiral galaxies.

(C)   They are diffuse spiral galaxies that occupy a large volume of space.

(D)   They are small, young spiral galaxies that contain a high proportion of primordial gas.

(E)   They are large, dense spirals with low luminosity.

Inference

This question requires drawing an inference from information given in the passage. The first paragraph compares dim galaxies and conventional galaxies. Dim galaxies are described as having the same general shape (lines 4–5) as a common type of conventional galaxy, the spiral galaxy, suggesting that dim galaxies are, themselves, spiral shaped. The passage also indicates that, although both types of galaxies tend to have approximately the same number of stars, dim galaxies tend to be much larger and spread out over larger areas of space (lines 4–10) than conventional galaxies.

A   The passage states that the two types of galaxies have approximately the same number of stars.

B   The passage indicates that dim galaxies are relatively large and spread out.

C   **Correct.** The passage indicates that dim galaxies have the same general shape as spiral galaxies and that their mass is spread out over large areas of space.

D   The passage indicates that dim galaxies are relatively large and spread out.

E   The passage states that dim galaxies have few stars per unit of volume, suggesting that they are not dense but diffuse.

The correct answer is C.

RC00054-03

83.   It can be inferred from the passage that the "long-standing puzzle" refers to which of the following?

(A)   The difference between the rate at which conventional galaxies evolve and the rate at which low-surface-brightness galaxies evolve

(B)   The discrepancy between estimates of total baryonic mass derived from measuring helium and estimates based on measuring galactic luminosity

(C)   The inconsistency between the observed amount of helium in the universe and the number of stars in typical low-surface-brightness galaxies

(D)   Uncertainties regarding what proportion of baryonic mass is contained in intergalactic space and what proportion in conventional galaxies

(E)   Difficulties involved in detecting very distant galaxies and in investigating their luminosity

Inference

This question requires drawing an inference from information given in the passage. The second paragraph describes *the long-standing puzzle of the missing baryonic mass in the universe*. The passage states that baryons are the source of galactic luminosity, and so scientists can estimate the amount of baryonic mass in the universe by measuring the luminosity of galaxies (lines 17–21). The puzzle is that spectroscopic measures of helium in the universe suggest that the baryonic mass in the universe is much higher than measures of luminosity would indicate (21–25).

A   The differences between the rates of evolution of the two types of galaxies is not treated as being controversial in the passage.

B   **Correct.** The passage indicates that measurements using spectroscopy and measurements using luminosity result in puzzling differences in estimates of the universe's baryonic mass.

C   The passage does not suggest how helium might relate to the numbers of stars in dim galaxies.

D   The passage indicates that astronomers have speculated that the missing baryonic mass might be discovered in intergalactic space or hard-to-detect galaxies but does not suggest that these speculations are constituents of the long-standing puzzle.

E   The passage does not mention how the distance to galaxies affects scientists' ability to detect these galaxies.

The correct answer is B.

RC00054-04

84.   The author implies that low-surface-brightness galaxies could constitute an answer to the puzzle discussed in the second paragraph primarily because

(A)   they contain baryonic mass that was not taken into account by researchers using galactic luminosity to estimate the number of baryons in the universe

(B) they, like conventional galaxies that contain many baryons, have evolved from massive, primordial gas clouds

(C) they may contain relatively more helium, and hence more baryons, than do galaxies whose helium content has been studied using spectroscopy

(D) they have recently been discovered to contain more baryonic mass than scientists had thought when low-surface-brightness galaxies were first observed

(E) they contain stars that are significantly more luminous than would have been predicted on the basis of initial studies of luminosity in low-surface-brightness galaxies

Inference

This question requires drawing an inference from information given in the passage. The puzzle is that estimates of the baryonic mass of the universe based on luminosity are lower than those based on spectroscopy (lines 21–25). The passage states that astronomers did not notice dim galaxies until recently (lines 2–3) and that these galaxies may help account for the missing baryonic mass in the universe (lines 15–17). The passage also suggests that astronomers measure the luminosity of specific galaxies (lines 19–21). Thus it can be inferred that, prior to their being noticed by astronomers, the luminosity of these dim galaxies was not measured, and their baryonic mass was not taken into account in the estimates of luminosity that led to the long-standing puzzle.

A **Correct.** The passage states that the missing baryonic mass in the universe may be discovered in the dim galaxies that have only recently been noticed by astronomers.

B The passage does not suggest that dim and conventional galaxies both originating from primordial gas clouds help solve the long-standing puzzle of the missing baryonic mass in the universe.

C The passage does not suggest that dim galaxies might contain more helium than do conventional galaxies or that measures of baryonic mass using spectroscopy do not take some dim galaxies into account.

D The passage does not suggest that dim galaxies contain more baryonic mass than scientists originally believed upon discovering these galaxies.

E The passage suggests that scientists measured the luminosity of galaxies, not of individual stars.

The correct answer is A.

RC00054-05

85. The author mentions the fact that baryons are the source of stars' luminosity primarily in order to explain

(A) how astronomers determine that some galaxies contain fewer stars per unit volume than do others

(B) how astronomers are able to calculate the total luminosity of a galaxy

(C) why astronomers can use galactic luminosity to estimate baryonic mass

(D) why astronomers' estimates of baryonic mass based on galactic luminosity are more reliable than those based on spectroscopic studies of helium

(E) how astronomers know bright galaxies contain more baryons than do dim galaxies

Evaluation

This question requires understanding how one aspect of the passage relates to the reasoning in a larger portion of the passage. The second paragraph explains that scientists have been puzzled over missing baryonic mass in the universe as measured by luminosity (lines 21–25). Given that baryons are the source of luminosity in the galaxy (lines 17–19), astronomers can estimate the baryonic mass of a galaxy by measuring its luminosity.

A The passage discussion of baryons does not address the number of stars in individual galaxies.

B The passage discusses how the luminosity of galaxies can be used to estimate baryonic mass but does not address how total luminosity is measured.

C   **Correct.** The passage indicates that because baryons are the source of galactic luminosity, measuring luminosity can be used to estimate baryonic mass of galaxies.

D   The passage suggests that estimates based on luminosity may have been less accurate, not more accurate, than those based on spectroscopy.

E   The passage does not indicate that bright galaxies contain more baryons than do dim galaxies.

The correct answer is C.

RC00054-06
86.   The author of the passage would be most likely to disagree with which of the following statements?

(A)   Low-surface-brightness galaxies are more difficult to detect than are conventional galaxies.

(B)   Low-surface-brightness galaxies are often spiral in shape.

(C)   Astronomers have advanced plausible ideas about where missing baryonic mass might be found.

(D)   Astronomers have devised a useful way of estimating the total baryonic mass in the universe.

(E)   Astronomers have discovered a substantial amount of baryonic mass in intergalactic space.

Inference

This question involves identifying which answer choice potentially conflicts with the information the author has provided in the passage. The second paragraph indicates that astronomers' estimates of the baryonic mass of the universe is lower when measured using luminosity than it is when measured using spectroscopy (lines 21–25). The final sentence states that astronomers have speculated that the missing baryonic mass might be discovered in intergalactic space or in hard-to-detect galaxies (lines 25–29). Although the passage does indicate that the discovery of dim, low-surface-brightness galaxies might help account for the missing baryonic mass (lines 15–17), the passage provides no support for the possibility that baryonic mass has been discovered in intergalactic space.

A   The passage indicates that low-surface-brightness galaxies went unnoticed until recently, unlike conventional galaxies.

B   The passage indicates that low-surface-brightness galaxies have the same general shape as spiral galaxies.

C   The passage describes two possible explanations astronomers have given for the missing baryonic mass, one of which was made more plausible by the discovery of low-surface-brightness galaxies.

D   The passage indicates that astronomers have used spectroscopy to estimate baryonic mass and gives no reason to suspect that this method is not useful.

E   **Correct.** The passage does not indicate that astronomers have found any baryonic mass in intergalactic space.

The correct answer is E.

RC00054-07
87.   The primary purpose of the passage is to

(A)   describe a phenomenon and consider its scientific significance

(B)   contrast two phenomena and discuss a puzzling difference between them

(C)   identify a newly discovered phenomenon and explain its origins

(D)   compare two classes of objects and discuss the physical properties of each

(E)   discuss a discovery and point out its inconsistency with existing theory

Main Idea

This question requires understanding, in broad terms, the purpose of the passage as a whole. The first paragraph describes a phenomenon: the discovery of dim galaxies and some of their general attributes. The second paragraph describes how this discovery may help astronomers to solve a long-standing puzzle about the baryonic mass of the universe.

A **Correct.** The passage describes the phenomenon of dim galaxies and describes their significance in solving the long-standing puzzle of the missing baryonic mass in the universe.

B Although the passage discusses the puzzling difference between the two estimates of baryonic mass, this answer choice does not account for the broader topic of dim galaxies.

C While the passage identifies the newly discovered phenomenon of dim galaxies, it does not offer a significant explanation for these galaxies' origins.

D Although the passage compares dim and conventional galaxies in the first paragraph, this answer choice does not account for the important detail that dim galaxies may help solve a long-standing puzzle.

E The discovery of dim galaxies discussed in the passage is not said to be inconsistent with any existing scientific theory.

The correct answer is A.

Questions 88–93 refer to the passage on page 118.

RC11238-01

88. The primary purpose of the passage is to

(A) contrast possible outcomes of a type of business investment

(B) suggest more careful evaluation of a type of business investment

(C) illustrate various ways in which a type of business investment could fail to enhance revenues

(D) trace the general problems of a company to a certain type of business investment

(E) criticize the way in which managers tend to analyze the costs and benefits of business investments

Main Idea

Look at the passage as a whole to find the primary purpose. This passage uses an example, described in the second paragraph, to illustrate the principle of business practice explained in the first paragraph. The author begins by saying that efforts to improve service do not always result in a *competitive advantage* for a company. Thus, an investment in service must be carefully evaluated to determine if it will reduce costs or increase revenues (lines 4–8).

A Only one outcome, failure to gain a competitive advantage, is examined.

B **Correct.** Investments in service must be carefully evaluated for the returns they will bring.

C Only one way, an unnecessary investment in improved service, is discussed.

D The example of the bank is used only to illustrate a general business principle; the bank itself is not the focus of the passage.

E The passage criticizes the absence of such an analysis, not the way it is conducted.

The correct answer is B.

RC11238-02

89. According to the passage, investments in service are comparable to investments in production and distribution in terms of the

(A) tangibility of the benefits that they tend to confer

(B) increased revenues that they ultimately produce

(C) basis on which they need to be weighed

(D) insufficient analysis that managers devote to them

(E) degree of competitive advantage that they are likely to provide

Supporting Idea

The phrase *according to the passage* indicates that the question covers material that is explicitly stated in the passage. The answer to this question demands a careful reading of the second sentence (lines 4–8). Investments in service are like investments in production and distribution because they *must be balanced against other types of investments on the basis of direct, tangible benefits.*

Thus, these investments should be weighed on the same basis.

A   The author is not equating the tangible benefits the different kinds of investments reap but rather the basis on which decisions to make investments are made.

B   Revenues generated from investing in service are not said to be comparable to revenues generated from investing in production and distribution.

C   **Correct.** An evaluation of whether or not to make these investments must be made on the same basis.

D   How managers analyze investments in production and distribution is not discussed.

E   The competitive advantage of superior service is acknowledged, but not the degree of it; it is not mentioned at all in the context of production and distribution.

The correct answer is C.

RC11238-03

90.   The passage suggests which of the following about service provided by regional bank prior to its investment in enhancing that service?

(A)   It enabled the bank to retain customers at an acceptable rate.

(B)   It threatened to weaken the bank's competitive position with respect to other regional banks.

(C)   It had already been improved after having caused damage to the bank's reputation in the past.

(D)   It was slightly superior to that of the bank's regional competitors.

(E)   It needed to be improved to attain parity with the service provided by competing banks.

Inference

Because the question uses the word *suggests*, finding the answer depends on making an inference about service at the bank. The paragraph that discusses the bank begins with the transitional expression, *this truth*, which refers to the previous sentence (lines 8–15). The *truth* is that investing in improved service is a waste *if a company is already effectively on a par with its competitors because it provides service that avoids*

a damaging reputation and keeps customers from leaving at an unacceptable rate. Because of the way the author has linked this generalization to the description of the bank after investment, it is reasonable to infer that the hypothetical company's situation describes the bank prior to its investment in improved service.

A   **Correct.** The bank's service would have been good enough to avoid a damaging reputation and to retain customers at an acceptable rate.

B   The passage does not suggest that the bank's service was either poor or deficient to that of its competitors.

C   The passage implies that the bank's service avoided *a damaging reputation*.

D   The bank would have been *on a par with its competitors*, not superior to them.

E   The bank would have been *on a par with its competitors*, not inferior to them.

The correct answer is A.

RC11238-04

91.   The passage suggests that bank managers failed to consider whether or not the service improvement mentioned in lines 18–20

(A)   was too complicated to be easily described to prospective customers

(B)   made a measurable change in the experiences of customers in the bank's offices

(C)   could be sustained if the number of customers increased significantly

(D)   was an innovation that competing banks could have imitated

(E)   was adequate to bring the bank's general level of service to a level that was comparable with that of its competitors

Inference

The question's use of the word *suggests* means that the answer depends on making an inference. To answer this question, look at the entire second paragraph. Managers failed to think ahead. Would the service improvement attract new customers because other banks would find it difficult to copy? Or would the service improvement be easily imitated by competitors? The managers should have investigated this area before investing in improved service.

A   The passage states the improvement *could easily be described to customers* (lines 28–29).

B   No evidence in the passage shows that the managers failed to think about their customers' experience in the bank.

C   The passage does not imply that managers failed to consider an increase in clients.

D   **Correct.** The managers did not wonder if other banks would copy their service improvement.

E   Lines 8–12 imply that the bank enjoyed a comparable level of service before investing in service improvement.

The correct answer is D.

RC11238-05

92.   The discussion of the regional bank in the second paragraph serves which of the following functions within the passage as a whole?

(A)   It describes an exceptional case in which investment in service actually failed to produce a competitive advantage.

(B)   It illustrates the pitfalls of choosing to invest in service at a time when investment is needed more urgently in another area.

(C)   It demonstrates the kind of analysis that managers apply when they choose one kind of service investment over another.

(D)   It supports the argument that investments in certain aspects of service are more advantageous than investments in other aspects of service.

(E)   It provides an example of the point about investment in service made in the first paragraph.

Logical Structure

This question requires thinking about what the second paragraph contributes to the whole passage. The first paragraph makes a generalization about investing in improvements in service; in certain conditions, such improvements do not result in the *competitive*

advantage a company hopes for. The second paragraph offers the bank as an example of this generalization.

A   The first sentence of the passage explains that improving service does not necessarily bring a *competitive advantage*, so the bank is not exceptional.

B   The bank illustrates the pitfall of not evaluating a service improvement on the basis of tangible benefits; other areas of the bank are not mentioned.

C   The passage does not discuss how managers analyze and choose different service investments.

D   Investments in different aspects of service are not evaluated in the passage.

E   **Correct.** The bank is an example of the position stated in the first paragraph that investing in improved service can be a waste if the investment is not evaluated carefully.

The correct answer is E.

RC11238-06

93.   The author uses the word "only" in line 27 most likely in order to

(A)   highlight the oddity of the service improvement

(B)   emphasize the relatively low value of the investment in service improvement

(C)   distinguish the primary attribute of the service improvement from secondary attributes

(D)   single out a certain merit of the service improvement from other merits

(E)   point out the limited duration of the actual service improvement

Logical Structure

The question asks you to consider the logic of the author's word choice. The previous two sentences discuss why the service improvement was a wasted investment. In contrast, the final sentence turns to the sole advantage of the service improvement, which is trivial by comparison. The author uses *only* to modify *merit* in order to emphasize the minimal nature of this advantage.

A   The passage does not indicate that the service improvement is somehow strange or peculiar.

B   **Correct.** *Only* emphasizes the low value attached to the single benefit.

C   No attributes of the service improvement are mentioned.

D   *Only* signifies that there was one sole merit of the service improvement.

E   The duration of the benefit is not discussed in the passage.

The correct answer is B.

Questions 94–97 refer to the passage on page 120.

RC00548-01.02

94.   The primary purpose of the passage is to

(A)   trace historical influences on the depiction of Mexican Americans in the nineteenth century

(B)   explain how research in history has been affected by scholarship in women's studies

(C)   describe the historical origins of a literary stereotype

(D)   discuss ways in which minority writers have sought to critique a dominant culture through their writing

(E)   evaluate both sides in a scholarly debate about a prominent literary stereotype

Main Idea

Answering this question requires understanding, in general terms, the passage as a whole. The passage discusses Antonia Castañeda's scholarship concerning the historical economic conditions underlying the portrayal by male, non-Hispanic novelists writing in the United States of "Californianas," that is, Mexican women living in territorial California. Certain Hispanic laws in this territory protected these women's property and inheritance rights. These laws, Castañeda claims, explain a stereotypical plot, used by these novelists, depicting a non-Hispanic trader or merchant who wishes to marry an elite Californiana.

A   The passage is more narrowly focused than this answer choice indicates; it primarily investigates depictions of Californianas, Mexican women living in territorial California.

B   The passage primarily deals with how both women's studies and Mexican-American history can illuminate literary portrayals of Mexican women, and, in particular, Californianas. The passage does not provide a broad examination of how research in history has been affected by women's studies.

C   **Correct.** As explained above, the passage is focused on examining the historical origins of the stereotypical plot, employed by nineteenth-century non-Hispanic male novelists in the United States, in which a non-Hispanic male seeks to marry a Californiana.

D   The passage is focused on a plot used by nineteenth-century non-Hispanic male writers in the nineteenth century. There is no indication that these were minority writers.

E   The passage discusses only Castañeda's scholarship regarding this particular literary stereotype.

The correct answer is C.

RC00548-03

95.   The "apparent contradiction" mentioned in line 29 refers to the discrepancy between the

(A)   legal status of Mexican women in territorial California and their status in the United States

(B)   unflattering depiction of Mexicans in novels and the actual public sentiment about the Mexican-American War

(C)   existence of many marriages between Californianas and non-Hispanic merchants and the strictures against them expressed in novels

(D)   literary depiction of elite Californianas and the literary depiction of other Mexican individuals

(E)   novelistic portrayals of elite Californianas' privileged lives and the actual circumstances of those lives

Supporting Idea

The *apparent contradiction* in line 29 refers to the difference, noted in the previous sentence, between favorable literary portrayals of elite Californianas—that is, Mexican women of the California territory—on the one hand and novels' generally unflattering depictions of Mexicans on the other.

A The passage discusses the difference between the legal rights of Mexican women in the California territory and those of non-Hispanic women. The legal rights of Mexican women outside territorial California are not mentioned.

B The passage suggests that there is no contradiction between unflattering depictions of Mexicans in novels and public sentiment about the Mexican-American War: such depictions of Mexicans served to stir up sentiment in support of the war.

C According to the passage, novels expressed no strictures against marriages between Californianas and non-Hispanic merchants. Instead, the novels portrayed such marriages favorably.

D Correct. Non-Hispanic novelists glorified elite Californianas based on the importance of forging economic alliances with them, whereas novelists depicted other Mexicans in unflattering terms.

E The passage indicates that elite Californianas' lives were in fact privileged, at least in comparison to those of non-Hispanic women. It does not suggest that there was any contradiction between elite Californianas' lives and how those lives were portrayed in novels.

The correct answer is D.

RC00548-04

96. Which of the following could best serve as an example of the kind of fictional plot discussed by Antonia Castañeda?

(A) A land speculator of English ancestry weds the daughter of a Mexican vineyard owner after the speculator has migrated to California to seek his fortune.

(B) A Californian woman of Hispanic ancestry finds that her agricultural livelihood is threatened when her husband is forced to seek work in a textile mill.

(C) A Mexican rancher who loses his land as a result of the Mexican-American War migrates to the northern United States and marries an immigrant schoolteacher.

(D) A wealthy Californiana whose father has bequeathed her all his property contends with avaricious relatives for her inheritance.

(E) A poor married couple emigrate from French Canada and gradually become wealthy as merchants in territorial California.

Application

According to the passage, Castañeda focuses on a particular plot in which an elite Californiana is pursued by a non-Hispanic merchant or trader for the purpose of gaining economic advantage.

A Correct. The story of a non-Hispanic land speculator wedding a Californiana who is likely, based on the inheritance rights granted her by the Hispanic law in territorial California, to inherit her father's vineyard would precisely fit the plot that Castañeda discusses.

B This description fails to identify the ethnicity of the Californiana's husband and the reason he married her, so there is no way to determine whether the story would fit Castañeda's plot.

C Castañeda's plot involves a non-Hispanic male protagonist, so a Mexican rancher could not play the main male role in such a story.

D The presence of a wealthy Californiana who inherits property might make this story seem to be an example of the fictional plot that Castañeda discusses, but there is no mention of a non-Hispanic merchant or trader who seeks her hand in marriage.

E Simply taking place in territorial California would not make a story an appropriate example of the plot discussed by Castañeda.

The correct answer is A.

RC00548-05

97. Which of the following, if true, would provide the most support for Castañeda's explanation of the "stereotypical plot" mentioned in the lines 18–19?

(A) Non-Hispanic traders found business more profitable in California while it was a territory than when it became a state.

(B) Very few marriages between Hispanic women and non-Hispanic men in nineteenth-century territorial California have actually been documented.

(C) Records from the nineteenth century indicate that some large and valuable properties were owned by elite Californianas in their own right.

(D) Unmarried non-Hispanic women in the nineteenth-century United States were sometimes able to control property in their own right.

(E) Most of the property in nineteenth-century territorial California was controlled by Hispanic men.

Evaluation

Castañeda explains the *stereotypical plot* of a non-Hispanic merchant seeking to marry an elite Californiana based on economics: these women had property and inheritance rights equal to men. Novelists based their plots on the women's *real-life* economic power, which resulted in men's wishing to build economic alliances with them. Supporting this explanation requires supporting these economic ideas in some way.

A   The profitability of non-Hispanic traders' business is not an issue in Castañeda's explanation; thus the change described has no significant relevance to that explanation.

B   The lack of the type of documentation described, rather than providing support for Castañeda's explanation, signifies a deficit in documentary support for that explanation.

C   **Correct.** If elite Californianas did in fact own valuable properties, Castañeda's economic explanation gains force. The women did have the real economic significance upon which Castañeda suggests the novelists drew.

D   If it were true that some non-Hispanic women controlled property in this way,

Castañeda's explanation of Californianas' uniqueness would be somewhat undermined.

E   If most of the property in nineteenth-century territorial California was controlled by Hispanic men, that suggests that Californianas were less likely to possess the kind of economic power described in Castañeda's argument.

The correct answer is C.

Questions 98–100 refer to the passage on page 122.

RC00533-03

98. The passage suggests that, in the early 1990s, Michaels would have been most likely to agree with which of the following statements about the disparity mentioned in the lines 3–4?

(A) This disparity is relatively less extreme in the Northern Hemisphere because of sulfate cooling.

(B) This disparity is only a short-term phenomenon brought about by sulfate cooling.

(C) This disparity is most significant in those parts of the world dominated by oceans.

(D) The extent of this disparity is being masked by the temporary effect of sulfate cooling.

(E) The disparity confirms that current models of global warming are correct.

Inference

The disparity highlighted in this question is between global warming models and actual climate data—that is, that the models predicted warming that has not occurred. In the early 1990s, according to the passage, Michaels tried to explain this disparity by saying that industrial sulfate emissions had a cooling effect that slowed global warming briefly.

A   The passage does not indicate that Michaels came to distinguish between the Northern and Southern Hemispheres until he began to doubt his early 1990s explanation for the mentioned disparity.

B   **Correct.** Michaels claimed in the early 1990s that the disparity was temporary, and that it occurred due to the cooling effect of sulfate emissions.

C   Santer's contention, not Michaels's, is based on the effect of oceans on global warming.

D   In the early 1990s, Michaels used the idea of sulfate cooling to explain the observed disparity, not to suggest that the disparity itself was larger than observed.

E   In seeking to explain the disparity, Michaels seems to have assumed, in the early 1990s at least, that the models of global warming were correct. But he did not take the disparity as evidence of their correctness.

The correct answer is B.

RC00533-04

99.   According to the passage, Santer asserts which of the following about global warming?

(A)   It will become a more serious problem in the Southern Hemisphere than in the Northern Hemisphere in spite of the cooling influence of oceans in the south.

(B)   It is unlikely to be a serious problem in the future because of the pervasive effect of sulfate cooling.

(C)   It will proceed at the same general rate in the Northern and Southern Hemispheres once the temporary influence of sulfate cooling comes to an end.

(D)   Until the late 1980s, it was moderated in the Northern Hemisphere by the effect of sulfate cooling.

(E)   Largely because of the cooling influence of oceans, it has had no discernible impact on the Southern Hemisphere.

Supporting Idea

The second paragraph of the passage discusses Santer's take on global warming. He is concerned with the effect of oceans and of sulfate cooling on this process, and he argues that the rate of warming in the Southern and Northern Hemispheres has been differently affected by each of these. In general, oceans slow warming in the south, while sulfate cooling temporarily slowed warming in the north until the late 1980s.

A   According to the passage, Santer has argued that since 1987 the Northern Hemisphere has warmed more significantly than the Southern Hemisphere.

B   Santer maintains that sulfate cooling complicates our attempts to understand global warming. He notes, however, that sulfate cooling peaked in the Northern Hemisphere in the mid-1900s, and that that hemisphere's warming has increased considerably. So sulfate cooling's effect is not pervasive and has not mitigated the medium- and long-term problem of global warming.

C   Santer argues that, in the absence of sulfate cooling, global warming would occur more slowly in the Southern Hemisphere due to the greater ocean coverage there.

D   Correct. Santer says that sulfate cooling slowed warming in the Northern Hemisphere, but that in 1987, the influence of sulfate cooling was no longer significant.

E   Santer maintains that global warming happens more slowly in the Southern Hemisphere due to the greater ocean coverage there, not that it has no discernible impact there.

The correct answer is D.

RC00533-05

100.   The passage suggests that Santer and Michaels would be most likely to DISAGREE over which of the following issues?

(A)   Whether climatological data invalidates global warming models

(B)   Whether warming in the Northern Hemisphere has intensified since 1987

(C)   Whether disparities between global warming models and climatological data can be detected

(D)   Whether landmasses warm more rapidly than oceans

(E)   Whether oceans have a significant effect on global climate patterns

Inference

According to the end of the first paragraph, Michaels began to doubt that sulfate cooling had an effect on global warming, and, further, based on the fact that he could not find an answer for why climatological data did not line up with global warming models, he questioned the accuracy of those models. The second paragraph explains that Santer, in contrast, offered a more nuanced explanation for the effect of sulfate cooling, and that based on this explanation, he disputed the claim that climatological data were inconsistent with the models' predictions.

A **Correct.** Based on the passage, Santer and Michaels would clearly disagree about whether climatological data invalidate global warming models: Michaels came to question the models on the basis of those data, while Santer found the model predictions were in fact ultimately consistent with the observed data.

B Both Santer and Michaels accept the idea that warming in the north has accelerated since 1987.

C Santer and Michaels both offered reasons for why the seeming disparity between models and data occurred—thus they agreed that such disparities were in fact detected.

D According to the second paragraph, Santer holds that landmasses warm more rapidly than oceans. But the passage offers no indication that Michaels disagrees with this.

E Santer's argument is based in large part on the effect of oceans on global climate patterns, but nothing in the passage's discussion of Michaels's work indicates that Michaels would disagree that oceans have such an effect.

The correct answer is A.

Questions 101–108 refer to the passage on page 124.

RC00613-01

101. According to the passage, Walker and Szalay disagree on which of the following points?

(A) The structure and composition of australopithecine teeth

(B) The kinds of conclusions that can be drawn from the micro-wear patterns on australopithecine teeth

(C) The idea that fruit was a part of the australopithecine diet

(D) The extent to which seed cracking and bone crunching produce similar micro-wear patterns on teeth

(E) The function of the heavy enamel on australopithecine teeth

Supporting Idea

This question refers to the first paragraph, which states that Walker does not agree with Szalay's idea that *the heavy enamel of australopithecine teeth is an adaptation to bone crunching.*

A According to the passage, Walker and Szalay disagree about the function of heavy enamel on the teeth, not the structure and composition of the teeth.

B The passage does not indicate that Szalay has anything to say about the micro-wear patterns on the teeth.

C Walker does, according to the passage, believe that australopithecines ate fruit, but it gives no evidence about whether Szalay believes that they ate at least some fruit.

D According to the passage, Walker believes that seed cracking and bone crunching produce distinctive micro-wear patterns on teeth, but he does not necessarily believe that they are similar. The passage does not indicate Szalay's position on the difference between micro-wear patterns.

E **Correct.** The function of the heavy enamel on the teeth is the only idea about which the passage clearly indicates that Walker and Szalay disagree.

The correct answer is E.

RC00613-02

102. The passage suggests that Walker's research indicated which of the following about australopithecine teeth?

(A) They had micro-wear characteristics indicating that fruit constituted only a small part of their diet.

(B) They lacked micro-wear characteristics associated with seed eating and bone crunching.

(C) They had micro-wear characteristics that differed in certain ways from the micro-wear patterns of chimpanzees and orangutans.

(D) They had micro-wear characteristics suggesting that the diet of australopithecines varied from one region to another.

(E) They lacked the micro-wear characteristics distinctive of modern frugivores.

Inference

According to the passage, Walker's research focuses on micro-wear patterns on the teeth of australopithecines. He draws several conclusions on the basis of these patterns: first, that australopithecines did not eat hard seeds; next, that they did not crunch bones; and finally, that they ate fruit.

A The passage indicates that Walker's observation of micro-wear patterns led him to conclude that australopithecines ate mostly fruit, not that *fruit constituted only a small part of their diet.*

B Correct. The first paragraph explains that Walker concluded from micro-wear patterns that australopithecines did not eat hard seeds and did not crunch bones; thus, his research must have indicated that they lacked micro-wear characteristics associated with such activities.

C According to the passage, the opposite is true: based on the observation that their micro-wear patterns were indistinguishable from those of chimpanzees and orangutans, Walker concluded that australopithecines ate fruit.

D The second paragraph of the passage complicates Walker's view by suggesting that australopithecines' diet might have varied from one region to another, but the passage says nothing about Walker's research from which to infer that it indicated such variation.

E Chimpanzees and orangutans are assumed to be frugivores, according to the passage, and Walker's research indicated that australopithecine teeth had micro-wear characteristics identical to theirs.

The correct answer is B.

RC00613-03

103. The passage suggests that which of the following would be true of studies of tooth micro-wear patterns conducted on modern baboons?

(A) They would inaccurately suggest that some baboons eat more soft-bodied than hard-bodied insects.

(B) They would suggest that insects constitute the largest part of some baboons' diets.

(C) They would reveal that there are no significant differences in tooth micro-wear patterns among baboon populations.

(D) They would inadequately reflect the extent to which some baboons consume certain types of insects.

(E) They would indicate that baboons in certain regions eat only soft-bodied insects, whereas baboons in other regions eat hard-bodied insects.

Inference

The second paragraph states that modern baboons eat *only soft-bodied insects* and so would not exhibit tooth abrasion to indicate that they were insectivores. Thus, it would be difficult to determine exactly which soft-bodied insects they ate.

A The passage states that baboons eat only soft-bodied insects—so it is in fact accurate to suggest that all baboons eat more soft-bodied than hard-bodied insects.

B The passage says that baboons eat only soft-bodied insects. It also suggests that soft-bodied insects do not leave significant enough abrasions on baboons' teeth to provide evidence of this aspect of their diet. Therefore, the tooth-wear patterns would give little or no information regarding what proportion of the baboons' overall diet consists of insects.

C The passage does not provide grounds for inferring anything about the differences, or lack thereof, among baboon populations in terms of tooth micro-wear patterns.

D Correct. Because soft-bodied insects cause little tooth abrasion, micro-wear patterns would most likely not reflect the extent to which baboons consume soft-bodied insects.

E The passage states that baboons eat *only soft-bodied insects.* Nothing in the passage suggests that baboons in certain regions eat hard-bodied insects.

The correct answer is D.

RC00613-04

104. The passage suggests which of the following about the micro-wear patterns found on the teeth of omnivorous primates?

(A) The patterns provide information about what kinds of foods are not eaten by the particular species of primate, but not about the foods actually eaten.

(B) The patterns of various primate species living in the same environment resemble one another.

(C) The patterns may not provide information about the extent to which a particular species' diet includes seeds.

(D) The patterns provide more information about these primates' diet than do the tooth micro-wear patterns of primates who are frugivores.

(E) The patterns may differ among groups within a species depending on the environment within which a particular group lives.

Inference

This question focuses mainly on the end of the second paragraph, which states that *the diets of current omnivorous primates vary considerably depending on the environments* in which they live. It goes on to conclude that australopithecines, if they were omnivores, would similarly consume varied diets, depending on environment, and exhibit varied tooth micro-wear patterns as well. Thus, it is reasonable to conclude that any omnivorous primates living in different environments and consuming different diets would exhibit varied micro-wear patterns.

A The passage indicates that the absence of certain types of micro-wear patterns can provide evidence about what foods a species does not eat. It also says that among omnivorous primates, one might expect to find considerable population variation in their tooth micro-wear patterns. Wherever micro-wear patterns are present, they provide evidence about what kinds of foods are eaten.

B The passage suggests that various primate species living in the same environment might consume a variety of different diets, so there is no reason to conclude that their micro-wear patterns would resemble one another.

C The passage indicates that seed-eating produces distinctive micro-wear patterns, so the patterns, or lack thereof, on the teeth of any species would most likely provide information about the extent to which the species' diet includes seeds.

D The end of the first paragraph suggests that frugivores' micro-wear patterns are distinctive; the passage provides no reason to believe that omnivores' diets provide more information.

E **Correct.** According to the passage, omnivorous primates of a particular species may consume different diets depending on where they live. Thus, their micro-wear patterns may differ on this basis.

The correct answer is E.

RC00613-05

105. It can be inferred from the passage that if studies of tooth micro-wear patterns were conducted on modern baboons, which of the following would most likely be true of the results obtained?

(A) There would be enough abrasion to allow a determination of whether baboons are frugivorous or insectivorous.

(B) The results would suggest that insects constitute the largest part of the baboons' diet.

(C) The results would reveal that there are no significant differences in tooth micro-wear patterns from one regional baboon population to another.

(D) The results would provide an accurate indication of the absence of some kinds of insects from the baboons' diet.

(E) The results would be unlikely to provide any indication of what inferences about the australopithecine diet can or cannot be drawn from micro-wear studies.

Inference

The second paragraph states that modern baboons eat soft-bodied insects but not hard-bodied ones—and it is hard-bodied insects, the passage suggests, that would cause particular micro-wear patterns on teeth. So the patterns on modern baboons' teeth most likely do not exhibit the patterns indicating hard-bodied insect consumption.

A   The passage states that baboons' consumption of soft-bodied insects would not show up in the patterns on their teeth—so the abrasion would most likely not provide enough information for a determination of whether baboons are frugivorous or insectivorous.

B   Since soft-bodied insects do not abrade the teeth significantly, it would be difficult to determine, based on micro-wear patterns, the part such insects play in the baboons' diet. Furthermore, the passage does not suggest that micro-wear patterns can indicate the quantity of food an animal might have eaten.

C   There could be differences in tooth micro-wear patterns from one regional baboon population to another if they consumed anything in addition to soft-bodied insects.

D   Correct. Studying tooth micro-wear patterns on baboons' teeth would most likely show that their teeth do not exhibit patterns typical of creatures that consume hard-bodied insects.

E   The passage suggests that based on results from micro-wear patterns on modern baboons' teeth, one cannot infer from micro-wear studies whether australopithecines ate soft-bodied insects.

The correct answer is D.

RC00613-08

106. It can be inferred from the passage that Walker's conclusion about the australopithecine diet would be called into question under which of the following circumstances?

(A)   The tooth enamel of australopithecines is found to be much heavier than that of modern frugivorous primates.

(B)   The micro-wear patterns of australopithecine teeth from regions other than east Africa are analyzed.

(C)   Orangutans are found to have a much broader diet than is currently recognized.

(D)   The environment of east Africa at the time australopithecines lived there is found to have been far more varied than is currently thought.

(E)   The area in which the australopithecine specimens were found is discovered to have been very rich in soft-bodied insects during the period when australopithecines lived there.

Inference

The passage explains that Walker bases his conclusion about the frugivorous nature of the australopithecine diet on the fact that the micro-wear patterns on australopithecine teeth are indistinguishable from those of chimpanzees and orangutans, both of which are presumed to have frugivorous diets.

A   The passage indicates that Walker took into account the fact that australopithecines had relatively heavy tooth enamel and that he rejected the view that this heaviness was evidence against the hypothesis that they were frugivorous. For all we can tell from the information in the passage, the australopithecines' tooth enamel was already known to be much heavier than that of modern frugivorous primates.

B   It could be the case that analyzing the micro-wear patterns of australopithecine teeth from other regions would yield the same data as those from east Africa.

C   Correct. According to the passage, Walker bases the conclusion that australopithecines were frugivorous on the similarity between their micro-wear patterns and those of modern chimpanzees and orangutans. If orangutans were found to have a diet that included a greater range of non-fruit foods than is currently recognized, then the correspondence between their micro-wear patterns and australopithecines' micro-wear patterns would be consistent with the hypothesis that australopithecines' diet was broader as well.

D   Even if the environment of east Africa were more varied, that would not mean the australopithecines necessarily ate a more varied diet. Many species that live in very varied environments specialize narrowly on particular foods in those environments.

E   Just because many soft-bodied insects might have been available to australopithecines does not mean that australopithecines ate them.

The correct answer is C.

RC00613-09.02

107. The passage is primarily concerned with

(A)   comparing two research methods for determining a species' dietary habits

(B)   describing and evaluating conjectures about a species' diet

(C)   contrasting several explanations for a species' dietary habits

(D)   discussing a new approach and advocating its use in particular situations

(E)   arguing that a particular research methodology does not contribute useful data

Main Idea

Answering this question depends on identifying the main point of the passage and requires an understanding of the passage as a whole. The passage discusses Walker's dismissal of certain other researchers' hypotheses regarding the diet of the primate species australopithecine. Walker does so on the basis of tooth micro-wear patterns, which lead him to the hypothesis that australopithecines were fruit eaters. However, the passage goes on to point out limitations of the utility of micro-wear studies, and discusses certain considerations which suggest that the australopithecines may have had a more diverse diet.

A   The passage primarily focuses on using an analysis of micro-wear patterns to determine australopithecines' dietary habits, so it is not the case that the passage is primarily concerned with comparing two research methods.

B   **Correct.** The passage considers Walker's evidence against certain hypotheses regarding the australopithecine diet, as well as his evidence for his own hypothesis, and presents considerations that suggest an alternative hypothesis. Thus, the passage is

primarily concerned with describing and evaluating conjectures about the diet of a species—the australopithecines.

C   The passage is not so much concerned with contrasting explanations for a species' dietary habits as with describing and evaluating evidence for such explanations.

D   The passage gives no indication that the analysis of micro-wear patterns is a new approach.

E   The passage does not argue that micro-wear analysis fails to contribute useful data. It merely points out that such analysis has certain limitations.

The correct answer is B.

RC00613-10

108. The author of the passage mentions the diets of baboons and other living primates most likely in order to

(A)   provide evidence that refutes Walker's conclusions about the foods making up the diets of australopithecines

(B)   suggest that studies of tooth micro-wear patterns are primarily useful for determining the diets of living primates

(C)   suggest that australopithecines were probably omnivores rather than frugivores

(D)   illustrate some of the limitations of using tooth micro-wear patterns to draw definitive conclusions about a group's diet

(E)   suggest that tooth micro-wear patterns are caused by persistent, as opposed to occasional, consumption of particular foods

Evaluation

The passage discusses the diets of baboons and other living primates mainly in the second paragraph, which is concerned with explaining the limited utility of micro-wear studies.

A   The author raises some doubts about Walker's conclusions but does not go as far as to try to refute them outright. The author argues only that, as the final sentence of the passage states, they may need to be expanded.

B   The author discusses the diets of baboons and other living primates in relation to micro-wear research on extinct primates. Nothing in the discussion suggests that micro-wear studies would be more useful for determining the diets of living primates than for providing evidence regarding the diets of earlier primates or of other types of animals. Furthermore, the mention of baboon diets suggests that micro-wear studies may not be very useful for determining the diets of some living primates.

C   The author leaves open the question of whether australopithecines were omnivores or frugivores. The passage suggests that some australopithecines might have been omnivores, if australopithecines' diets varied according to the environments they inhabited. Walker's conclusion regarding east African australopithecines' being frugivores might still hold, however.

D   Correct. The author refers to baboons' diets and those of current omnivorous primates in order to suggest that there might be limitations to Walker's use of tooth micro-wear patterns to determine australopithecines' diet.

E   The passage does not make a distinction between persistent and occasional consumption of particular foods.

The correct answer is D.

Questions 109–112 refer to the passage on page 127.

RC00512-01

109. The primary purpose of the passage is to

(A) present recently discovered evidence that supports a conventional interpretation of a historical period

(B) describe how reinterpretations of available evidence have reinvigorated a once-discredited scholarly position

(C) explain why some historians have tended to emphasize change rather than continuity in discussing a particular period

(D) explore how changes in a particular occupation serve to counter the prevailing view of a historical period

(E) examine a particular area of historical research in order to exemplify a general scholarly trend

Main Idea

This question asks about the passage's main purpose. The first paragraph initially describes a way in which historiography is changing: the idea of a consistent, monolithic decline in women's status is being complicated by *recent research*. The rest of the passage uses the example of Pinchbeck's interpretation of women's work in English cheesemaking to show the limits of earlier ideas about women's status: Pinchbeck's work illustrates the idea of consistent decline, but recent scholarship has called that work into question.

A   The first paragraph suggests that Pinchbeck's work represents the conventional position that women's status declined consistently with the advent of capitalism; according to the passage, recent evidence undermines, rather than supports, that position.

B   According to the passage, reinterpretations of evidence have inspired new interpretations; they have not reinvigorated a discredited position.

C   The passage is concerned with noting both change and continuity, as stated in the first sentence.

D   In the passage, continuity, not change, in a particular occupation—English farmhouse cheesemaking—helps to counter the prevailing view.

E   Correct. The passage's main purpose is to examine women's work in English farmhouse cheesemaking so as to illustrate a trend in historiography of women's status under capitalism and industrialization.

The correct answer is E.

RC00512-03

110. Regarding English local markets and fairs, which of the following can be inferred from the passage?

(A) Both before and after the agricultural revolution, the sellers of agricultural products at these venues were men.

(B) Knowing who the active sellers were at these venues may not give a reliable indication of who controlled the revenue from the sales.

(C) There were no parallel institutions at which American cheese makers could sell their own products.

(D) Prior to the agricultural revolution, the sellers of agricultural products at these venues were generally the producers themselves.

(E) Prior to the agricultural revolution, women sold not only cheese but also products of arable agriculture at these venues.

Inference

The passage discusses English local markets and fairs in the first and second paragraphs: the first paragraph states that before the agricultural revolution, women had sold cheese in such venues but that after that, factors, who were men, sold the cheese. The second paragraph argues that even though English women in precapitalist, preindustrial times may have at one point sold cheese at fairs, evidence indicates that in at least one case, a man appropriated most of the money his wife made from her sales.

A The first paragraph states that prior to the agricultural revolution, women sold cheese at local markets and fairs.

B **Correct.** As the second paragraph indicates, women may have sold the cheese, but there is evidence to suggest that they did not necessarily control the revenue from its sale.

C The passage does not provide evidence regarding any institutions at which American cheese makers sold their products.

D While the passage indicates that the producers of English farmhouse cheese may have been the ones who sold that cheese at local markets and fairs, there is no evidence to suggest that this was necessarily the case for other agricultural products.

E The passage provides no information regarding whether women sold products of arable agriculture in any venue.

The correct answer is B.

RC00512-05

111. The passage describes the work of Pinchbeck primarily in order to

(A) demonstrate that some of the conclusions reached by recent historians were anticipated in earlier scholarship

(B) provide an instance of the viewpoint that, according to the passage's author, is being superseded

(C) illustrate the ways in which recent historians have built on the work of their predecessors

(D) provide a point of reference for subsequent scholarship on women's work during the agricultural revolution

(E) show the effect that the specialization introduced in the agricultural and industrial revolutions had on women's work

Evaluation

This question focuses on the function of Pinchbeck's work in the passage. Pinchbeck's study of women's work in cheese production is, according to the passage, an illustration of the view that women's status declined consistently with the advent of industrialization. That view, the author claims, is being challenged by current historiography.

A The passage indicates that the conclusions of Pinchbeck, who represents earlier scholarship, did not anticipate recent work, but rather that recent work argues against those conclusions.

B **Correct.** Pinchbeck's work illustrates earlier trends in historiography, trends that the author suggests are now giving way to newer ideas.

C The passage does not focus on any ways in which recent historians have built on Pinchbeck's work; instead, it discusses how they have argued against its conclusions.

D   Pinchbeck's work provides a point of reference only insofar as subsequent scholarship is arguing against it.

E   Pinchbeck makes the argument that specialization caused women's status to decline, but the passage is concerned with undermining this argument.

The correct answer is B.

RC00512-07

112.   It can be inferred from the passage that women did work in

(A)   American cheesemaking at some point prior to industrialization

(B)   arable agriculture in northern England both before and after the agricultural revolution

(C)   arable agriculture in southeast England after the agricultural revolution, in those locales in which cultural values supported their participation

(D)   the sale of cheese at local markets in England even after the agricultural revolution

(E)   some areas of American cheese dairying after industrialization

Inference

This question focuses mainly on the final paragraph of the passage, in which women's continued work in English cheese dairying is contrasted with what the passage calls their *disappearance from arable agriculture in southeast England and from American cheese dairying,* presumably during the period of industrialization. The correct answer will be a conclusion that can be drawn from this information.

A   **Correct.** That women "disappeared" from American cheese dairying during industrialization provides grounds for inferring that they did such dairying work at some point prior to industrialization.

B   The passage says that women disappeared from arable agriculture in southeast England, but it gives no information about their participation in arable agriculture in northern England.

C   The passage makes a blanket statement about women's *disappearance from arable agriculture in southeast England,* so there is no reason to infer that any locales supported women's participation in agriculture.

D   The first paragraph states that factors, who were men, sold cheese after the agricultural revolution.

E   The final paragraph explicitly states that women disappeared from American cheese dairying; thus, there is no basis for inferring that women worked in any areas of that field after industrialization.

The correct answer is A.

5.0   Critical Reasoning

5.0 Critical Reasoning

GMAT™ Critical Reasoning questions test the reasoning skills involved in:

- constructing an argument
- evaluating an argument, and
- formulating or evaluating a plan of action.

The questions are based on materials drawn from a variety of sources. Answering the questions does not require any familiarity with these materials' subject matter beyond what is generally known.

Critical Reasoning questions are based on passages typically less than 100 words in length. Unlike Reading Comprehension passages, each Critical Reasoning passage is associated with just one question. On the actual exam, you will see only one passage and question at a time.

While answering Critical Reasoning questions requires no specialized knowledge, you do need to be familiar with such basic logical terms as "premise," "conclusion," and "assumption." The practice Critical Reasoning questions in this chapter illustrate the variety of topics the test may cover, the kinds of questions it may ask, and the level of analysis it requires.

5.1 What Is Measured

Critical Reasoning questions provide one measure of your ability to deal with reasoning.

For purposes of the GMAT exam, any series of statements of which at least one is given as logical support for another can be considered an example of reasoning. Some examples include reasoning for the purpose of justifying belief in a statement, justifying some plan of action, or explaining why a certain phenomenon occurs.

Many Critical Reasoning passages contain or report reasoning. Others display no reasoning and simply present information. Every Critical Reasoning question, however, will require you to engage in reasoning based on its passage. You may, for example, be asked to draw a conclusion from the given information; i.e., to identify, among the answer choices, the one statement the information logically supports. Or you may be asked to identify the one statement that most plausibly explains why a phenomenon described in the passage occurred, or to evaluate whether a particular plan of action is likely to achieve its intended goal.

Many different skills are involved in analyzing and evaluating reasoning. In the GMAT™ Enhanced Score Report, these skills are divided into four fundamental categories: *Analysis, Construction, Critique,* and *Plan*.

- *Analysis* questions primarily test your skill in understanding a piece of logical reasoning as a whole and identifying the relationships among its constituent parts.

- *Construction* questions mainly test your skill in forming cogent arguments—for example, in determining what additional information can be inferred from given information, or what additional information would be needed for an argument to work.

- *Critique* questions test your skill in challenging the cogency of arguments, identifying their strengths and weaknesses, and determining how they could be improved.

- *Plan* questions overlap with both **Construction** and **Critique**. Unlike other Critical Reasoning questions, *Plan* questions are designed to test your skill in constructing and critiquing arguments about proposed courses of action.

The following table lists, in greater detail, the major skills that Critical Reasoning questions measure:

Question type	Skill	Examples
Analyzing reasoning structure	Identifying premises, conclusion, explanations, plan rationales, or background information in a passage containing reasoning	• *Ming uses which of the following techniques in responding to Wei?* • *Which of the following most accurately describes the functions of each boldfaced part of the passage?*
Drawing conclusions (inference)	Drawing a conclusion from given information	• *Which of the following is most strongly supported by the information provided?* • *Which of the following follows logically from the information provided?*
Identifying sufficient or required assumptions	Recognizing an assumption that can help fill a logical gap in a piece of reasoning	• *Which of the following is an assumption that Fang's reasoning requires?* • *The conclusion follows logically if which of the following is assumed?* • *The plan will fail unless which of the following occurs?*
Evaluating hypotheses	Identifying a hypothesis that most plausibly explains a phenomenon or event	• *Which of the following, if true, most helps explain the failure to achieve the plan's objective?* • *Which of the following is most likely to contribute to the occurrence of the phenomenon observed?* • *In order to evaluate the force of the archaeologists' evidence, it would be most useful to determine which of the following?*
Resolving apparent inconsistency	Reconciling two apparently conflicting assertions or states of affairs	• *Which of the following most helps to resolve the discrepancy between the reported level of rainfall and the occurrence of flooding in City X?*
Identifying information that strengthens or weakens reasoning	Identifying information that either provides additional support or undermines reasoning	• *Which of the following, if discovered, would cast the most doubt on the engineer's reasoning?* • *Which of the following, if true, would most strengthen the support for the physician's diagnosis?*

Question type	Skill	Examples
Recognizing and describing logical flaws	Identifying reasoning errors such as confusing correlation with causation or confusing a sufficient condition with a necessary one	• *Which of the following, if true, most strongly indicates a flaw in the reasoning?* • *The reasoning attributed to the executive is most vulnerable to which of the following criticisms?*
Identifying a point of disagreement	Precisely identifying the key issue on which two parties disagree, based on the statements they have made	• *Which of the following is the main point of disagreement between Mandeep and Saumya?*
Finding a solution to a practical problem	Recognizing an effective strategy for solving a practical problem	• *Which of the following would most help the polling specialists overcome the difficulty they encountered in surveying a sample of likely voters?*

5.2 Test-Taking Strategies

To answer Critical Reasoning questions, you must analyze and logically evaluate the passage on which each question is based, then select the answer choice that most appropriately answers the question. Carefully read the passage and the question asked about the passage, then read the five answer choices. If the correct answer is not immediately obvious to you, see whether you can eliminate some of the wrong answers. Reading the passage a second time may illuminate subtleties not evident on first reading.

1. **Decide whether you benefit most from reading the passage or the question first.**

   Some test-takers may want to read the passage very carefully first and then read the question. But it can be advantageous to read the question first. Doing so can orient you toward noticing the content or structural features of the passage that are relevant to answering the question. Working through the practice questions in this guide should help you get a good feel for the approach that suits you best.

   Be careful to respond to the precise question asked. For example, here are two questions that, in a hurried reading, could easily be confused:

   i) Which of the following is valued by **the most citizens** of Nation X?

   ii) Which of the following is **most valued** by the citizens of Nation X?

   Something valued by the most citizens of Nation X may not be the same as what is generally most valued by the citizens of Nation X. The most justified answer to i) could be *wealth* even if the most justified answer to ii) is *good community relations*.

2. **Determine whether the passage contains reasoning or merely provides information.**

   To determine whether the passage contains reasoning, consider whether one or more of the statements are intended to support the truth of any other statement provided, or to justify a plan of action, or to explain some phenomenon. To help determine this, look for certain sorts of words or phrases, sometimes called "inference indicators," that authors may provide when they are presenting a piece of reasoning. For instance, the word ***therefore*** is frequently used to indicate a conclusion, and the word ***because*** is frequently used to indicate a premise or reason. Here are other examples (the list is not exhaustive):

- Conclusion indicators: ***consequently, it follows that, so, hence***
- Premise indicators: ***since, as, for, as is shown by, follows from***

Some of these words have other uses; for example, ***since*** can signify time or can signify causation. Also, keep in mind that a passage may contain reasoning even if no such indicators are present. Ask yourself whether any of the statements support the truth of another statement, help explain a phenomenon described in the passage, or help support a plan proposed in the passage. Section 3.2 in the Verbal Review Chapter provides more information on how to identify reasoning in a passage.

3. **Identify the purpose and structure of any reasoning in a passage.**

   A good first step in analyzing passages that contain reasoning is to determine the purpose of the reasoning. Does the reasoning aim to provide logical support for a conclusion? If so, then identifying that conclusion will help. Or perhaps the reasoning aims to explain a phenomenon; i.e., to indicate what has caused the phenomenon to occur. If so, identifying the statement that predicts or hypothesizes the occurrence of the phenomenon will help. A third possibility is that the reasoning provides a rationale for a plan or policy. If so, identifying a statement that indicates the goal of the plan or policy will help.

   Once you have identified the reasoning's purpose, then you can identify the reasoning's structure (i.e., ***how*** the author makes the argument). Section 3.2.1 in the Verbal Review Chapter provides more information on how to analyze a passage's reasoning structure.

4. **To evaluate reasoning, try to imagine scenarios where the premises are true and the conclusion false.**

   Many Critical Reasoning questions will require you to evaluate the soundness of a passage's reasoning. To evaluate reasoning, you do not need to decide whether premises or conclusions are actually true. Determining actual truth is beyond the scope of the test: no test-taker could determine the truth or falsity of every assertion present in Critical Reasoning passages. Moreover, many Critical Reasoning passages refer to fictional scenarios. One technique often helpful in evaluating a piece of reasoning is to try to ***imagine*** a situation in which the premises would all be true but the conclusion false. If the conclusion would almost certainly be true provided the premises were all true, then the reasoning is typically strong. On the other hand, if the conclusion could likely be false, even provided that the premises were all true, then the reasoning is typically weak.

   This does not mean that considerations about the real world will not, at times, be helpful in evaluating reasoning. Consider the following:

   > Medical procedure A is as effective and cost-efficient as medical procedure B, but has fewer unwanted side-effects than B. Therefore, medical procedure A should be preferred over medical procedure B.

   In evaluating this reasoning, you can rely on the obvious consideration that, all else being equal, a procedure with fewer unwanted side-effects is preferable.

   Please refer to Sections 3.3 and 3.4 of Chapter 3 for more detailed information on how to evaluate the reasoning in various types of arguments.

5.3 Section Instructions

Go to www.mba.com/tutorial to view instructions for the section and get a feel for what the test center screens will look like on the actual GMAT exam.

5.4 Practice Questions

Each of the Critical Reasoning questions is based on a short argument, a set of statements, or a plan of action. For each question, select the best answer of the choices given.

Questions 113 to 154 - Difficulty: Easy

*CR14249

113. PhishCo runs a number of farms in the arid province of Nufa, depending largely on irrigation. Now, as part of a plan to efficiently increase the farms' total production, it plans to drill down to an aquifer containing warm, slightly salty water that will be used to raise fish in ponds. The water from the ponds will later be used to supplement piped-in irrigation water for PhishCo's vegetable fields, and the ponds and accompanying vegetation should help reduce the heat in the area of the farms.

Which of the following would, if true, most strongly suggest that the plan, if implemented, would increase the overall efficiency of PhishCo's farms?

(A) Most of the vegetation to be placed around the ponds is native to Nufa.

(B) Fish raised on PhishCo's farms are likely to be saleable in the nearest urban areas.

(C) Organic waste from fish in the pond water will help to fertilize fields where it is used for irrigation.

(D) The government of Nufa will help to arrange loan financing to partially cover the costs of drilling.

(E) Ponds will be located on low-lying land now partially occupied by grain crops.

CR12701.02

114. Stockholders have been critical of the Flyna Company, a major furniture retailer, because most of Flyna's furniture is manufactured in Country X from local wood, and illegal logging is widespread there. However, Flyna has set up a certification scheme for lumber mills. It has hired a staff of auditors and forestry professionals who review documentation of the wood supply of Country X's lumber mills to ensure its legal origin, make surprise visits to mills to verify documents, and certify mills as approved sources of legally obtained lumber. Flyna uses only lumber from certified mills. Thus, Flyna's claim that its Country X wood supply is obtained legally is justified.

Which of the following, if true, would most undermine the justification provided for Flyna's claim?

(A) Only about one-third of Flyna's inspectors were hired from outside the company.

(B) Country X's government recently reduced its subsidies for lumber production.

(C) Flyna has had to pay higher than expected salaries to attract qualified inspectors.

(D) The proportion of Country X's lumber mills inspected each year by Flyna's staff is about 10 percent, randomly selected.

(E) Illegal logging costs Country X's government a significant amount in lost revenue each year.

---

*These numbers correlate with the online test bank question number. See the GMAT™ Official Guide Verbal Review Question Index in the back of this book.

CR12721.02

115. The *XCT* automobile is considered less valuable than the *ZNK* automobile, because insurance companies pay less, on average, to replace a stolen *XCT* than a stolen *ZNK*. Surprisingly, the average amount insurance companies will pay to repair a car involved in a collision is typically higher for the *XCT* than for the *ZNK*. One insurance expert explained that repairs to *XCT* automobiles are especially labor-intensive, and labor is a significant factor in collision repair costs.

Which of the following, if true, most strongly supports the insurance expert's explanation?

(A) *ZNK* automobiles are involved in accidents more frequently than *XCT* automobiles.

(B) The cost of routine maintenance for the *ZNK* is about the same as for the *XCT*.

(C) There are more automobile mechanics who specialize in *XCT* repairs than in *ZNK* repairs.

(D) The ease of repair of *ZNK* automobiles is one factor that adds to their value.

(E) *XCT* automobiles are more likely to be stolen than *ZNK* automobiles.

CR07612

116. The sustained massive use of pesticides in farming has two effects that are especially pernicious. First, it often kills off the pests' natural enemies in the area. Second, it often unintentionally gives rise to insecticide-resistant pests, since those insects that survive a particular insecticide will be the ones most resistant to it, and they are the ones left to breed.

From the passage above, it can be properly inferred that the effectiveness of the sustained massive use of pesticides can be extended by doing which of the following, assuming that each is a realistic possibility?

(A) Using only chemically stable insecticides

(B) Periodically switching the type of insecticide used

(C) Gradually increasing the quantities of pesticides used

(D) Leaving a few fields fallow every year

(E) Breeding higher-yielding varieties of crop plants

CR00701

117. Which of the following, if true, most logically completes the argument below?

Manufacturers are now required to make all cigarette lighters child-resistant by equipping them with safety levers. But this change is unlikely to result in a significant reduction in the number of fires caused by children playing with lighters, because children given the opportunity can figure out how to work the safety levers and _____.

(A) the addition of the safety levers has made lighters more expensive than they were before the requirement was instituted

(B) adults are more likely to leave child-resistant lighters than non-child-resistant lighters in places that are accessible to children

(C) many of the fires started by young children are quickly detected and extinguished by their parents

(D) unlike child-resistant lighters, lighters that are not child-resistant can be operated by children as young as two years old

(E) approximately 5,000 fires per year have been attributed to children playing with lighters before the safety levers were required

CR04192

118. Which of the following most logically completes the passage?

A business analysis of the Appenian railroad system divided its long-distance passenger routes into two categories: rural routes and interurban routes. The analysis found that, unlike the interurban routes, few rural routes carried a high enough passenger volume to be profitable. Closing unprofitable rural routes, however, will not necessarily enhance the profitability of the whole system, since _____.

(A) a large part of the passenger volume on interurban routes is accounted for by passengers who begin or end their journeys on rural routes

(B) within the last two decades several of the least used rural routes have been closed and their passenger services have been replaced by buses

(C) the rural routes were all originally constructed at least one hundred years ago, whereas some of the interurban routes were constructed recently for new high-speed express trains

(D) not all of Appenia's large cities are equally well served by interurban railroad services

(E) the greatest passenger volume, relative to the routes' capacity, is not on either category of long-distance routes but is on suburban commuter routes

CR52441.01

119. In its search for new technologies for solar energy that can produce lower-cost electricity, Smith-Diatom is developing a new way to make dye-sensitive solar cells, in which photons strike light-sensitive dyes. The process uses diatoms, which are unicellular algae that have silicon shells with a complex structure. First, the organic material is removed, and then the shells are coated with a titanium dioxide film that acts as a semiconductor. The diatoms' structure results in more photon activity and thus more efficient production of electricity than with current dye-sensitized solar cells, which in turn lowers the cost.

Which of the following considerations would, if true, most strongly support the hypothesis that the plan, if implemented, will produce low-cost electricity from dye-sensitive solar cells?

(A) Diatoms are an important link in oceanic food chains and help cycle carbon dioxide from the atmosphere.

(B) The current cost of electricity produced by dye-sensitive solar cells is roughly three times that of non-solar electricity.

(C) Because diatoms occur naturally, no special engineering processes are needed to produce the basic dye-sensitive solar cell structures.

(D) Dye-sensitive solar cells work somewhat more efficiently in lower light than previous solar cell technologies.

(E) The production of dye-sensitive solar cells primarily uses materials that do not harm the environment.

CR03129

120. Although Ackerburg's subway system is currently operating at a deficit, the transit authority will lower subway fares next year. The authority projects that the lower fares will result in a ten percent increase in the number of subway riders. Since the additional income from the larger ridership will more than offset the decrease due to lower fares, the transit authority actually expects the fare reduction to reduce or eliminate the subway system's operating deficit for next year.

Which of the following, if true, provides the most support for the transit authority's expectation of reducing the subway system's operating deficit?

(A) Throughout the years that the subway system has operated, fares have never before been reduced.

(B) The planned fare reduction will not apply to students, who can already ride the subway for a reduced fare.

(C) Next year, the transit authority will have to undertake several large-scale track maintenance projects.

(D) The subway system can accommodate a ten percent increase in ridership without increasing the number of trains it runs each day.

(E) The current subway fares in Ackerburg are higher than subway fares in other cities in the region.

CR59590.02

121. At several locations on the northwest coast of North America are formations known as chevrons—wedge-shaped formations of mounded sediment—pointing toward the ocean. Most geologists take them to have been formed by erosion, but recently other scientists have proposed that they were thrown up from the ocean by massive waves triggered by meteor impacts in the Pacific Ocean.

Which of the following, if discovered, would most help in deciding which hypothesis is correct?

(A) Chevron-like structures which are not currently near glaciers, large rivers, or other bodies of water

(B) The presence, in chevrons, of deposits of ocean microfossils containing metals typically formed by meteor impacts

(C) Oral-history evidence for flooding that could have been caused by ocean waves

(D) The fact that exact data about the location and depth of any meteor impact craters on the Pacific seabed is lacking

(E) The fact that certain changes in the shape and location of maritime sand dunes have been produced by the action of wind and waves

CR20531.01

122. Sparrow Airlines is planning to reduce its costs by cleaning its planes' engines once a month, rather than the industry standard of every six months. With cleaner engines, Sparrow can postpone engine overhauls, which take planes out of service for up to 18 months. Furthermore, cleaning an engine reduces its fuel consumption by roughly 1.2 percent.

The airline's plan assumes that

(A) fuel prices are likely to rise in the near future and therefore cutting fuel consumption is an important goal

(B) the cost of monthly cleaning of an airplane's engines is not significantly greater in the long run than is the cost of an engine overhaul

(C) engine cleaning does not remove an airplane from service

(D) Sparrow Airlines has had greater problems with engine overhauls and fuel consumption than other airlines have

(E) cleaning engines once a month will give Sparrow Airlines a competitive advantage over other airlines

CR00828

123. Patrick usually provides child care for six children. Parents leave their children at Patrick's house in the morning and pick them up after work. At the end of each workweek, the parents pay Patrick at an hourly rate for the child care provided that week. The weekly income Patrick receives is usually adequate but not always uniform, particularly in the winter, when children are likely to get sick and be unpredictably absent.

Which of the following plans, if put into effect, has the best prospect of making Patrick's weekly income both uniform and adequate?

(A) Pool resources with a neighbor who provides child care under similar arrangements, so that the two of them cooperate in caring for twice as many children as Patrick currently does.

(B) Replace payment by actual hours of child care provided with a fixed weekly fee based upon the number of hours of child care that Patrick would typically be expected to provide.

(C) Hire a full-time helper and invest in facilities for providing child care to sick children.

(D) Increase the hourly rate to a level that would provide adequate income even in a week when half of the children Patrick usually cares for are absent.

(E) Increase the number of hours made available for child care each day, so that parents can leave their children in Patrick's care for a longer period each day at the current hourly rate.

CR10639

124. Editorial: Consumers in North America think that by drinking frozen concentrated orange juice, they are saving energy, because it takes fewer truckloads to transport it than it takes to transport an equivalent amount of not-from-concentrate juice. But they are mistaken, for the amount of energy required to concentrate the juice is far greater than the energy difference in the juices' transport.

Which of the following, if true, would provide the greatest additional support for the editorial's conclusion?

(A) Freezer trucks use substantially more energy per mile driven than do any other types of trucks.

(B) Frozen juice can be stored for several years, while not-from-concentrate juice lasts a much shorter time.

(C) Oranges grown in Brazil make up an increasing percentage of the fruit used in not-from-concentrate juice production.

(D) A serving of not-from-concentrate juice takes up to six times more space than a serving of frozen concentrated juice.

(E) Though frozen concentrated juice must be kept at a lower temperature, not-from-concentrate juice is far more sensitive to small temperature fluctuations.

CR07618

125. A computer equipped with signature-recognition software, which restricts access to a computer to those people whose signatures are on file, identifies a person's signature by analyzing not only the form of the signature but also such characteristics as pen pressure and signing speed. Even the most adept forgers cannot duplicate all of the characteristics the program analyzes.

Which of the following can be logically concluded from the passage above?

(A) The time it takes to record and analyze a signature makes the software impractical for everyday use.

(B) Computers equipped with the software will soon be installed in most banks.

(C) Nobody can gain access to a computer equipped with the software solely by virtue of skill at forging signatures.

(D) Signature-recognition software has taken many years to develop and perfect.

(E) In many cases even authorized users are denied legitimate access to computers equipped with the software.

CR02958

126. The rate at which a road wears depends on various factors, including climate, amount of traffic, and the size and weight of the vehicles using it. The only land transportation to Rittland's seaport is via a divided highway, one side carrying traffic to the seaport and one carrying traffic away from it. The side leading to the seaport has worn faster, even though each side has carried virtually the same amount of traffic, consisting mainly of large trucks.

Which of the following, if true, most helps to explain the difference in the rate of wear?

(A) The volume of traffic to and from Rittland's seaport has increased beyond the intended capacity of the highway that serves it.

(B) Wear on the highway that serves Rittland's seaport is considerably greater during the cold winter months.

(C) Wear on the side of the highway that leads to Rittland's seaport has encouraged people to take buses to the seaport rather than driving there in their own automobiles.

(D) A greater tonnage of goods is exported from Rittland's seaport than is imported through it.

(E) All of Rittland's automobiles are imported by ship.

CR75231.01

127. Ythex has developed a small diesel engine that produces 30 percent less particulate pollution than the engine made by its main rival, Onez, now widely used in Marania; Ythex's engine is well-suited for use in the thriving warehousing businesses in Marania, though it costs more than the Onez engine. The Maranian government plans to ban within the next two years the use of diesel engines with more than 80 percent of current diesel engine particulate emissions in Marania, and Onez will probably not be able to retool its engine to reduce emissions to reach this target. So if the ban is passed, the Ythex engine ought to sell well in Marania after that time.

Which of the following is an assumption on which the argument above depends?

(A) Marania's warehousing and transshipment business buys more diesel engines of any size than other types of engines.

(B) Ythex is likely to be able to reduce the cost of its small diesel engine within the next two years.

(C) The Maranian government is generally favorable to anti-pollution regulations.

(D) The government's ban on high levels of pollution caused by diesel engines, if passed, will not be difficult to enforce.

(E) The other manufacturers of small diesel engines in Marania, if there are any, have not produced an engine as popular and clean running as Ythex's new engine.

CR04073

128. In parts of South America, vitamin-A deficiency is a serious health problem, especially among children. In one region, agriculturists are attempting to improve nutrition by encouraging farmers to plant a new variety of sweet potato called SPK004 that is rich in beta-carotene, which the body converts into vitamin A. The plan has good chances of success, since sweet potato is a staple of the region's diet and agriculture, and the varieties currently grown contain little beta-carotene.

Which of the following, if true, most strongly supports the prediction that the plan will succeed?

(A) The growing conditions required by the varieties of sweet potato currently cultivated in the region are conditions in which SPK004 can flourish.

(B) The flesh of SPK004 differs from that of the currently cultivated sweet potatoes in color and texture, so traditional foods would look somewhat different when prepared from SPK004.

(C) There are no other varieties of sweet potato that are significantly richer in beta-carotene than SPK004 is.

(D) The varieties of sweet potato currently cultivated in the region contain some important nutrients that are lacking in SPK004.

(E) There are other vegetables currently grown in the region that contain more beta-carotene than the currently cultivated varieties of sweet potato do.

CR06018

129. Which of the following most logically completes the argument?

The last members of a now-extinct species of a European wild deer called the giant deer lived in Ireland about 16,000 years ago. Prehistoric cave paintings in France depict this animal as having a large hump on its back. Fossils of this animal, however, do not show any hump. Nevertheless, there is no reason to conclude that the cave paintings are therefore inaccurate in this regard, since _____.

(A) some prehistoric cave paintings in France also depict other animals as having a hump

(B) fossils of the giant deer are much more common in Ireland than in France

(C) animal humps are composed of fatty tissue, which does not fossilize

(D) the cave paintings of the giant deer were painted well before 16,000 years ago

(E) only one currently existing species of deer has any anatomical feature that even remotely resembles a hump

CR28931.01

130. Super Express Shipping Company has implemented a new distribution system that can get almost every package to its destination the day after it is sent. The company worries that this more efficient system will result in lower sales of its premium next-day delivery service, because its two-day service will usually arrive the following day anyway. The company plans to encourage sales of its next-day service by intentionally delaying delivery of its two-day packages so that they will not be delivered the following day, even if the package arrives at its destination city in time for next-day delivery.

The company's plan assumes that

(A) deliberate delay of packages will not affect the company's image in a way that significantly reduces its ability to attract and retain customers

(B) most people do not have a preference for either two-day or next-day delivery

(C) if the plan is not implemented, the company would lose more money in lost sales of overnight deliveries than it would save with its new efficient distribution system

(D) the overnight service is too expensive to be attractive to most customers currently

(E) competing companies' delivery services rarely deliver packages to their destination earlier than their promised time

CR04738

131. Cocoa grown organically on trees within the shade of the rain forest canopy commands a premium price. However, acquiring and maintaining the certification that allows the crop to be sold as organically grown is very time-consuming and laborious. Meanwhile, the price premium for the grower is about 30 percent, whereas cocoa trees grown in full sun using standard techniques can have twice the yield of organic, shade-grown trees. Financially, therefore, standard techniques are the better choice for the farmer.

Which of the following, if true, most seriously weakens the argument?

(A) Cocoa can be grown only in a climate that has the temperature and moisture characteristics of a tropical rain forest.

(B) Cocoa trees grown using standard techniques require costly applications of fertilizer and pesticides, unlike shade-grown trees.

(C) Although organically grown cocoa has long commanded a price premium over cocoa grown using standard techniques, its price has fluctuated considerably during that period.

(D) Cocoa is not the only cash crop that can be raised on plots that leave the rain forest canopy overhead essentially intact.

(E) Governments and international conservation organizations are working to streamline organic certification so as to relieve farmers of unnecessary work.

CR91131.02

132. Psychologists conducted an experiment in which half of the volunteers were asked to describe an unethical action they had performed, while the other half were asked to describe an ethical action they had performed. Some of the volunteers, chosen at random from each of the two groups, were encouraged to wash their hands afterward. Among those who described unethical actions, those who washed their hands were significantly less likely to volunteer for another, similar experiment than those who did not wash their hands. The researchers concluded that some of the subjects failed to volunteer again in part because of their having described an unethical action.

Which of the following would, if true, most help to support the researchers' conclusion?

(A) Among the volunteers who described ethical actions, those who washed their hands were significantly less likely to volunteer for another, similar experiment than those who did not wash their hands.

(B) The average likelihood of volunteering for another, similar experiment was higher among those who described ethical actions than among those who described unethical actions.

(C) Most of the volunteers who were encouraged to wash their hands did so.

(D) The volunteers in the study were not more disposed to washing their hands under normal circumstances than the general population was.

(E) Equal numbers of volunteers from both groups were encouraged to wash their hands.

CR07547

133. High levels of fertilizer and pesticides, needed when farmers try to produce high yields of the same crop year after year, pollute water supplies. Experts therefore urge farmers to diversify their crops and to rotate their plantings yearly.

To receive governmental price-support benefits for a crop, farmers must have produced that same crop for the past several years.

The statements above, if true, best support which of the following conclusions?

(A) The rules for governmental support of farm prices work against efforts to reduce water pollution.

(B) The only solution to the problem of water pollution from fertilizers and pesticides is to take farmland out of production.

(C) Farmers can continue to make a profit by rotating diverse crops, thus reducing costs for chemicals, but not by planting the same crop each year.

(D) New farming techniques will be developed to make it possible for farmers to reduce the application of fertilizers and pesticides.

(E) Governmental price supports for farm products are set at levels that are not high enough to allow farmers to get out of debt.

CR02270

134. Ten years ago the number of taxpayers in Greenspace County was slightly greater than the number of registered voters. The number of taxpayers has doubled over the last ten years, while the number of registered voters has increased, but at a lower rate than has the number of taxpayers.

Which of the following must be true in Greenspace County if the statements above are true?

(A) The number of taxpayers is now smaller than the number of registered voters.

(B) Everyone who is a registered voter is also a taxpayer.

(C) The proportion of registered voters to taxpayers has increased over the last ten years.

(D) The proportion of registered voters to taxpayers has decreased over the last ten years.

(E) The proportion of registered voters to taxpayers has remained unchanged over the last ten years.

CR01298

135. From 1900 until the 1930s, pellagra, a disease later discovered to result from a deficiency of the vitamin niacin, was common among poor cotton farmers in the United States whose diet consisted mostly of corn, the least costly food they could buy. Corn does not contain niacin in usable form. Curiously, during the Depression of the early 1930s, when cotton's price collapsed and cotton farmers' income declined, the incidence of pellagra among those farmers also declined.

Which of the following, if true, most helps to explain the decline in the incidence of pellagra?

(A) When growing a cash crop could not generate adequate income, poor farmers in the United States responded by planting their land with vegetables and fruits for their own consumption.

(B) People whose diets consist largely of corn often suffer from protein deficiency as well as niacin deficiency.

(C) Until the discovery of pellagra's link with niacin, it was widely believed that the disease was an infection that could be transmitted from person to person.

(D) Effective treatment for pellagra became available once its link with niacin was established.

(E) In parts of Mexico, where people subsisted on corn but pellagra was uncommon, corn was typically processed with alkaline substances, which make the niacin in the corn absorbable.

CR07589

136. The interview is an essential part of a successful hiring program because, with it, job applicants who have personalities that are unsuited to the requirements of the job will be eliminated from consideration.

The argument above logically depends on which of the following assumptions?

(A) A hiring program will be successful if it includes interviews.

(B) The interview is a more important part of a successful hiring program than is the development of a job description.

(C) Interviewers can accurately identify applicants whose personalities are unsuited to the requirements of the job.

(D) The only purpose of an interview is to evaluate whether job applicants' personalities are suited to the requirements of the job.

(E) The fit of job applicants' personalities to the requirements of the job was once the most important factor in making hiring decisions.

CR07785

137. Many leadership theories have provided evidence that leaders affect group success rather than the success of particular individuals. So it is irrelevant to analyze the effects of supervisor traits on the attitudes of individuals whom they supervise. Instead, assessment of leadership effectiveness should occur only at the group level.

Which of the following would it be most useful to establish in order to evaluate the argument?

(A) Whether supervisors' documentation of individual supervisees' attitudes toward them is usually accurate

(B) Whether it is possible to assess individual supervisees' attitudes toward their supervisors without thereby changing those attitudes

(C) Whether any of the leadership theories in question hold that leaders should assess other leaders' attitudes

(D) Whether some types of groups do not need supervision in order to be successful in their endeavors

(E) Whether individuals' attitudes toward supervisors affect group success

CR03535

138. A major health insurance company in Lagolia pays for special procedures prescribed by physicians only if the procedure is first approved as "medically necessary" by a company-appointed review panel. The rule is intended to save the company the money it might otherwise spend on medically unnecessary procedures. The company has recently announced that in order to reduce its costs, it will abandon this rule.

Which of the following, if true, provides the strongest justification for the company's decision?

(A) Patients often register dissatisfaction with physicians who prescribe nothing for their ailments.

(B) Physicians often prescribe special procedures that are helpful but not altogether necessary for the health of the patient.

(C) The review process is expensive and practically always results in approval of the prescribed procedure.

(D) The company's review process does not interfere with the prerogative of physicians, in cases where more than one effective procedure is available, to select the one they personally prefer.

(E) The number of members of the company-appointed review panel who review a given procedure depends on the cost of the procedure.

CR03826

139. Automobile ownership was rare in Sabresia as recently as 30 years ago, but with continuing growth of personal income there, automobile ownership has become steadily more common. Consequently, there are now far more automobiles on Sabresia's roads than there were 30 years ago, and the annual number of automobile accidents has increased significantly. Yet the annual number of deaths and injuries resulting from automobile accidents has not increased significantly.

Which of the following, if true, most helps to explain why deaths and injuries resulting from automobile accidents have not increased significantly?

(A) Virtually all of the improvements in Sabresia's roads that were required to accommodate increased traffic were completed more than ten years ago.

(B) With more and more people owning cars, the average number of passengers in a car on the road has dropped dramatically.

(C) The increases in traffic volume have been most dramatic on Sabresia's highways, where speeds are well above those of other roads.

(D) Because of a vigorous market in used cars, the average age of cars on the road has actually increased throughout the years of steady growth in automobile ownership.

(E) Automobile ownership is still much less common in Sabresia than it is in other countries.

CR01430

140. To evaluate a plan to save money on office-space expenditures by having its employees work at home, XYZ Company asked volunteers from its staff to try the arrangement for six months. During this period, the productivity of these employees was as high as or higher than before.

Which of the following, if true, would argue most strongly against deciding, on the basis of the trial results, to implement the company's plan?

(A) The employees who agreed to participate in the test of the plan were among the company's most self-motivated and independent workers.

(B) The savings that would accrue from reduced office-space expenditures alone would be sufficient to justify the arrangement for the company, apart from any productivity increases.

(C) Other companies that have achieved successful results from work-at-home plans have workforces that are substantially larger than that of XYZ.

(D) The volunteers who worked at home were able to communicate with other employees as necessary for performing the work.

(E) Minor changes in the way office work is organized at XYZ would yield increases in employee productivity similar to those achieved in the trial.

CR04180

141. A child learning to play the piano will not succeed unless the child has an instrument at home on which to practice. However, good-quality pianos, whether new or secondhand, are costly. Buying one is justified only if the child has the necessary talent and perseverance, which is precisely what one cannot know in advance. Consequently, parents should buy an inexpensive secondhand instrument at first and upgrade if and when the child's ability and inclination are proven.

Which of the following, if true, casts the most serious doubt on the course of action recommended for parents?

(A) Learners, particularly those with genuine musical talent, are apt to lose interest in the instrument if they have to play on a piano that fails to produce a pleasing sound.

(B) Reputable piano teachers do not accept children as pupils unless they know that the children can practice on a piano at home.

(C) Ideally, the piano on which a child practices at home should be located in a room away from family activities going on at the same time.

(D) Very young beginners often make remarkable progress at playing the piano at first, but then appear to stand still for a considerable period of time.

(E) In some parents, spending increasing amounts of money on having their children learn to play the piano produces increasing anxiety to hear immediate results.

CR05096

142. Nutritionists are advising people to eat more fish, since the omega-3 fatty acids in fish help combat many diseases. If everyone took this advice, however, there would not be enough fish in oceans, rivers, and lakes to supply the demand; the oceans are already being overfished. The obvious method to ease the pressure on wild fish populations is for people to increase their consumption of farmed fish.

Which of the following, if true, raises the most serious doubt concerning the prospects for success of the solution proposed above?

(A) Aquaculture, or fish farming, raises more fish in a given volume of water than are generally present in the wild.

(B) Some fish farming, particularly of shrimp and other shellfish, takes place in enclosures in the ocean.

(C) There are large expanses of ocean waters that do not contain enough nutrients to support substantial fish populations.

(D) The feed for farmed ocean fish is largely made from small wild-caught fish, including the young of many popular food species.

(E) Some of the species that are now farmed extensively were not commonly eaten when they were only available in the wild.

CR02851

143. Which of the following most logically completes the market forecaster's argument?

Market forecaster: The price of pecans is high when pecans are comparatively scarce but drops sharply when pecans are abundant. Thus, in high-yield years, growers often store part of their crop in refrigerated warehouses until after the next year's harvest, hoping for higher prices then. Because of bad weather, this year's pecan crop will be very small. Nevertheless, pecan prices this year will not be significantly higher than last year, since _____.

(A) the last time the pecan crop was as small as it was this year, the practice of holding back part of one year's crop had not yet become widely established

(B) last year's pecan harvest was the largest in the last 40 years

(C) pecan prices have remained relatively stable in recent years

(D) pecan yields for some farmers were as high this year as they had been last year

(E) the quality of this year's pecan crop is as high as the quality of any pecan crop in the previous five years

CR06331

144. It is often said that high rates of inflation tend to diminish people's incentive to save and invest. This view must be incorrect, however, because people generally saved and invested more of their income in the 1970's when inflation rates were high than they did in the 1980's when inflation rates were low.

Of the following, the best criticism of the argument above is that it overlooks the possibility that

(A) all people do not respond in the same way to a given economic stimulus

(B) certain factors operating in the 1980's but not in the 1970's diminished people's incentive to save and invest

(C) the population was larger in the 1980's than it was in the 1970's

(D) the proponents of the view cited would stand to gain if inflation rates become lower

(E) a factor that affects people's savings behavior in a certain way could affect people's investment behavior quite differently

CR02704
145. Which of the following most logically completes the argument below?

Within the earth's core, which is iron, pressure increases with depth. Because the temperature at which iron melts increases with pressure, the inner core is solid and the outer core is molten. Physicists can determine the melting temperature of iron at any given pressure and the pressure for any given depth in the earth. Therefore, the actual temperature at the boundary of the earth's outer and inner cores—the melting temperature of iron there—can be determined, since _____.

(A) the depth beneath the earth's surface of the boundary between the outer and inner cores is known

(B) some of the heat from the earth's core flows to the surface of the earth

(C) pressures within the earth's outer core are much greater than pressures above the outer core

(D) nowhere in the earth's core can the temperature be measured directly

(E) the temperatures within the earth's inner core are higher than in the outer core

CR03659
146. Which of the following most logically completes the reasoning?

Either food scarcity or excessive hunting can threaten a population of animals. If the group faces food scarcity, individuals in the group will reach reproductive maturity later than otherwise. If the group faces excessive hunting, individuals that reach reproductive maturity earlier will come to predominate. Therefore, it should be possible to determine whether prehistoric mastodons became extinct because of food scarcity or human hunting, since there are fossilized mastodon remains from both before and after mastodon populations declined, and _____.

(A) there are more fossilized mastodon remains from the period before mastodon populations began to decline than from after that period

(B) the average age at which mastodons from a given period reached reproductive maturity can be established from their fossilized remains

(C) it can be accurately estimated from fossilized remains when mastodons became extinct

(D) it is not known when humans first began hunting mastodons

(E) climate changes may have gradually reduced the food available to mastodons

CR02518

147. Many office buildings designed to prevent outside air from entering have been shown to have elevated levels of various toxic substances circulating through the air inside, a phenomenon known as sick building syndrome. Yet the air in other office buildings does not have elevated levels of these substances, even though those buildings are the same age as the "sick" buildings and have similar designs and ventilation systems.

Which of the following, if true, most helps to explain why not all office buildings designed to prevent outside air from entering have air that contains elevated levels of toxic substances?

(A) Certain adhesives and drying agents used in particular types of furniture, carpets, and paint contribute the bulk of the toxic substances that circulate in the air of office buildings.

(B) Most office buildings with sick building syndrome were built between 1950 and 1990.

(C) Among buildings designed to prevent outside air from entering, houses are no less likely than office buildings to have air that contains elevated levels of toxic substances.

(D) The toxic substances that are found in the air of "sick" office buildings are substances that are found in at least small quantities in nearly every building.

(E) Office buildings with windows that can readily be opened are unlikely to suffer from sick building syndrome.

CR08756

148. Newsletter: **A condominium generally offers more value for its cost than an individual house because of economies of scale.** The homeowners in a condominium association can collectively buy products and services that they could not afford on their own. And since a professional management company handles maintenance of common areas, **condominium owners spend less time and money on maintenance than individual homeowners do.**

The two portions in **boldface** play which of the following roles in the newsletter's argument?

(A) The first is the argument's main conclusion; the second is another conclusion supporting the first.

(B) The first is a premise, for which no evidence is provided; the second is the argument's only conclusion.

(C) The first is a conclusion supporting the second; the second is the argument's main conclusion.

(D) The first is the argument's only conclusion; the second is a premise, for which no evidence is provided.

(E) Both are premises, for which no evidence is provided, and both support the argument's only conclusion.

CR00780

149. Which of the following most logically completes the argument?

When officials in Tannersburg released their plan to widen the city's main roads, environmentalists protested that widened roads would attract more traffic and lead to increased air pollution. In response, city officials pointed out that today's pollution-control devices are at their most effective in vehicles traveling at higher speeds and that widening roads would increase the average speed of traffic. However, this effect can hardly be expected to offset the effect pointed out by environmentalists, since _____.

(A) increases in traffic volume generally produce decreases in the average speed of traffic unless roads are widened

(B) several of the roads that are slated for widening will have to be closed temporarily while construction is underway

(C) most of the air pollution generated by urban traffic comes from vehicles that do not have functioning pollution-control devices

(D) the newly widened roads will not have increased traffic volume if the roads that must be used to reach them are inadequate

(E) a vehicle traveling on a route that goes through Tannersburg will spend less time on Tannersburg's roads once the roads are widened

CR70661.01

150. Platinum is a relatively rare metal vital to a wide variety of industries. Xagor Corporation, a major producer of platinum, has its production plant in a country that will soon begin imposing an export tax on platinum sold and shipped to customers abroad. As a consequence, the price of platinum on the world market is bound to rise.

Which of the following, if true, tends to confirm the conclusion above?

(A) An inexpensive substitute for platinum has been developed and will be available to industry for the first time this month.

(B) The largest of the industries that depend on platinum reported a drop in sales last month.

(C) The producers of platinum in other countries taken together cannot supply enough platinum to meet worldwide demand.

(D) Xagor produced more platinum last month than in any previous month.

(E) New deposits of platinum have been found in the country in which Xagor has its production plant.

CR80661.01

151. From 1973 to 1986, growth in the United States economy was over 33 percent, while the percent growth in United States energy consumption was zero. The number of barrels of oil being saved per day by energy-efficiency improvements made since 1973 is now 13 million.

If the information above is correct, which of the following conclusions can properly be drawn on the basis of it?

(A) It is more difficult to find new sources of oil than to institute new energy-conservation measures.

(B) Oil imports cannot be reduced unless energy consumption does not grow at all.

(C) A reduction in the consumption of gasoline was the reason overall energy consumption remained steady.

(D) It is possible for an economy to grow without consuming additional energy.

(E) The development of nontraditional energy sources will make it possible for the United States economy to grow even faster.

CR01661.01

152. Although many customers do not make a sufficient effort to conserve water, water companies must also be held responsible for wasteful consumption. Their own policies, in fact, encourage excessive water use, and attempts at conservation will succeed only if the water companies change their practices.

Which of the following, if true, would most strongly support the view above?

(A) Most water companies reduce the cost per unit of water as the amount of water used by a customer increases.

(B) Most water companies keep detailed records of the quantity of water used by different customers.

(C) Most water companies severely curtail the use of water during periods of drought.

(D) Federal authorities limit the range of policies that can be enforced by the water companies.

(E) The price per unit of water charged by the water companies has risen steadily in the last 10 years.

CR11661.01

153. Despite legislation designed to stem the accumulation of plastic waste, the plastics industry continued to grow rapidly last year, as can be seen from the fact that sales of the resin that is the raw material for manufacturing plastics grew by 10 percent to $28 billion.

In assessing the support provided by the evidence cited above for the statement that the plastics industry continued to grow, in addition to the information above it would be most useful to know

(A) whether the resin has other uses besides the manufacture of plastics

(B) the dollar amount of resin sales the year before last

(C) the plastics industry's attitude toward the legislation concerning plastic waste

(D) whether sales of all goods and services in the economy as a whole were increasing last year

(E) what proportion of the plastics industry's output eventually contributes to the accumulation of plastic waste

CR41661.01

154. Studies of the political orientations of 1,055 college students revealed that the plurality of students in an eastern, big-city, private university was liberal, whereas in a state-supported, southern college, the plurality was conservative. Orientations were independent of the student's region of origin, and the trends were much more pronounced in seniors than in beginning students.

Which of the following hypotheses is best supported by the observations stated above?

(A) The political orientations of college students are more similar to the political orientations of their parents when the students start college than when the students are seniors.

(B) The political orientations of college seniors depend significantly on experiences they have had while in college.

(C) A college senior originally from the South is more likely to be politically conservative than is a college senior originally from the East.

(D) Whether their college is state-supported or private is the determining factor in college students' political orientations.

(E) College students tend to become more conservative politically as they become older and are confronted with pressures for financial success.

Questions 155 to 188 - Difficulty: Medium

CR90661.01

155. Donations of imported food will be distributed to children in famine-stricken countries in the form of free school meals. The process is efficient because the children are easy to reach at the schools and cooking facilities are often available on site.

Which of the following, if true, casts the most serious doubt on the efficiency of the proposed process?

(A) The emphasis on food will detract from the major function of the schools, which is to educate the children.

(B) A massive influx of donated food will tend to lower the price of food in the areas near the schools.

(C) Supplies of fuel needed for cooking at the schools arrive there only intermittently and in inadequate quantities.

(D) The reduction in farm surpluses in donor countries benefits the donor countries to a greater extent than the recipient countries are benefited by the donations.

(E) The donation of food tends to strengthen the standing of the political party that happens to be in power when the donation is made.

CR21661.01

156. *John:* You told me once that no United States citizen who supports union labor should buy an imported car. Yet you are buying an Alma. Since Alma is one of the biggest makers of imports, I infer that you no longer support unions.

Harry: I still support labor unions. Even though Alma is a foreign car company, the car I am buying, the Alma Deluxe, is designed, engineered, and manufactured in the United States.

Harry's method of defending his purchase of an Alma is to

(A) disown the principle he formerly held

(B) show that John's argument involves a false unstated assumption

(C) contradict John's conclusion without challenging John's reasoning in drawing that conclusion

(D) point out that one of the statements John makes in support of his argument is false

(E) claim that his is a special case in which the rule need not apply

CR31661.01

157. Public-sector (government-owned) companies are often unprofitable and a drain on the taxpayer. Such enterprises should be sold to the private sector, where competition will force them either to be efficient and profitable or else to close.

Which of the following, if true, identifies a flaw in the policy proposed above?

(A) The revenue gained from the sale of public-sector companies is likely to be negligible compared to the cost of maintaining them.

(B) By buying a public-sector company and then closing the company and selling its assets, a buyer can often make a profit.

(C) The services provided by many public-sector companies must be made available to citizens, even when a price that covers costs cannot be charged.

(D) Some unprofitable private-sector companies have become profitable after being taken over by the government to prevent their closing.

(E) The costs of environmental protection, contributions to social programs, and job-safety measures are the same in the public and private sectors.

CR91661.01

158. After receiving numerous complaints from residents about loud, highly amplified music played at local clubs, Middletown is considering a law that would prohibit clubs located in residential areas from employing musical groups that consist of more than three people.

The likelihood that the law would be effective in reducing noise would be most seriously diminished if which of the following were true?

(A) Groups that consist of more than three musicians are usually more expensive for clubs to hire than are groups that consist of fewer than three musicians.

(B) In towns that have passed similar laws, many clubs in residential areas have relocated to nonresidential areas.

(C) Most of the complaints about the music have come from people who do not regularly attend the clubs.

(D) Much of the music popular at the local clubs can be played only by groups of at least four musicians.

(E) Amplified music played by fewer than three musicians generally is as loud as amplified music played by more than three musicians.

CR02661.01

159. From enlargements that are commonly found on the ulna bones of the forearms of Ice Age human skeletons, anthropologists have drawn the conclusion that the Ice Age humans represented by those skeletons frequently hunted by throwing spears. The bone enlargements, the anthropologists believe, resulted from the stresses of habitual throwing.

Which of the following, if true, would be the LEAST appropriate to use as support for the conclusion drawn by the anthropologists?

(A) Humans typically favor one arm over the other when throwing, and most Ice Age human skeletons have enlargements on the ulna bone of only one arm.

(B) Such enlargements on the ulna bone do not appear on skeletons from other human cultures of the same time period whose diets are believed to have been mainly vegetarian.

(C) Cave paintings dating from approximately the same time period and located not far from where the skeletons were found show hunters carrying and throwing spears.

(D) Damaged bones in the skeletons show evidence of diseases that are believed to have afflicted most people living during the Ice Age.

(E) Twentieth-century athletes who use a throwing motion similar to that of a hunter throwing a spear often develop enlargements on the ulna bone similar to those detected on the Ice Age skeletons.

CR12661.01

160. The town council of North Tarrytown favored changing the name of the town to Sleepy Hollow. Council members argued that making the town's association with Washington Irving and his famous "legend" more obvious would increase tourism and result immediately in financial benefits for the town's inhabitants.

The council members' argument requires the assumption that

(A) most of the inhabitants would favor a change in the name of the town

(B) many inhabitants would be ready to supply tourists with information about Washington Irving and his "legend"

(C) the town can accomplish, at a very low cost per capita, the improvements in tourist facilities that an increase in tourism would require

(D) other towns in the region have changed their names to reflect historical associations and have, as a result, experienced a rise in tourism

(E) the immediate per capita cost to inhabitants of changing the name of the town would be less than the immediate per capita revenue they would receive from the change

CR06795

161. Premature babies who receive regular massages are more active than premature babies who do not. Even when all the babies drink the same amount of milk, the massaged babies gain more weight than do the unmassaged babies. This is puzzling because a more active person generally requires a greater food intake to maintain or gain weight.

Which of the following, if true, best reconciles the apparent discrepancy described above?

(A) Increased activity leads to increased levels of hunger, especially when food intake is not also increased.

(B) Massage increases premature babies' curiosity about their environment, and curiosity leads to increased activity.

(C) Increased activity causes the intestines of premature babies to mature more quickly, enabling the babies to digest and absorb more of the nutrients in the milk they drink.

(D) Massage does not increase the growth rate of babies over one year old, if the babies had not been previously massaged.

(E) Premature babies require a daily intake of nutrients that is significantly higher than that required by babies who were not born prematurely.

CR02865
162. In Australia, in years with below-average rainfall, less water goes into rivers and more water is extracted from rivers for drinking and irrigation. Consequently, in such years, water levels drop considerably and the rivers flow more slowly. Because algae grow better the more slowly the water in which they are growing moves, such years are generally beneficial to populations of algae. But, by contrast, populations of algae drop in periods of extreme drought.

Which of the following, if true, does most to explain the contrast?

(A) Algae grow better in ponds and lakes than in rivers.

(B) The more slowly water moves, the more conducive its temperature is to the growth of algae.

(C) Algae cannot survive in the absence of water.

(D) Algae must be filtered out of water before it can be used for drinking.

(E) The larger the population of algae in a body of water, the less sunlight reaches below the surface of the water.

CR00693
163. Which of the following, if true, most logically completes the politician's argument?

United States politician: Although the amount of United States goods shipped to Mexico doubled in the year after tariffs on trade between the two countries were reduced, it does not follow that the reduction in tariffs caused the sales of United States goods to companies and consumers in Mexico to double that year, because _____.

(A) many of the United States companies that produced goods that year had competitors based in Mexico that had long produced the same kind of goods

(B) most of the increase in goods shipped by United States companies to Mexico was in parts shipped to the companies' newly relocated subsidiaries for assembly and subsequent shipment back to the United States

(C) marketing goods to a previously unavailable group of consumers is most successful when advertising specifically targets those consumers, but developing such advertising often takes longer than a year

(D) the amount of Mexican goods shipped to the United States remained the same as it had been before the tariff reductions

(E) there was no significant change in the employment rate in either of the countries that year

CR06845

164. Budget constraints have made police officials consider reassigning a considerable number of officers from traffic enforcement to work on higher-priority, serious crimes. Reducing traffic enforcement for this reason would be counterproductive, however, in light of the tendency of criminals to use cars when engaged in the commission of serious crimes. An officer stopping a car for a traffic violation can make a search that turns up evidence of serious crime.

Which of the following, if true, most strengthens the argument given?

(A) An officer who stops a car containing evidence of the commission of a serious crime risks a violent confrontation, even if the vehicle was stopped only for a traffic violation.

(B) When the public becomes aware that traffic enforcement has lessened, it typically becomes lax in obeying traffic rules.

(C) Those willing to break the law to commit serious crimes are often in committing such crimes unwilling to observe what they regard as the lesser constraints of traffic law.

(D) The offenders committing serious crimes who would be caught because of traffic violations are not the same group of individuals as those who would be caught if the arresting officers were reassigned from traffic enforcement.

(E) The great majority of persons who are stopped by officers for traffic violations are not guilty of any serious crimes.

CR10106

165. Conventional wisdom suggests vaccinating elderly people first in flu season, because they are at greatest risk of dying if they contract the virus. This year's flu virus poses particular risk to elderly people and almost none at all to younger people, particularly children. Nevertheless, health professionals are recommending vaccinating children first against the virus rather than elderly people.

Which of the following, if true, provides the strongest reason for the health professionals' recommendation?

(A) Children are vulnerable to dangerous infections when their immune systems are severely weakened by other diseases.

(B) Children are particularly unconcerned with hygiene and therefore are the group most responsible for spreading the flu virus to others.

(C) The vaccinations received last year will confer no immunity to this year's flu virus.

(D) Children who catch one strain of the flu virus and then recover are likely to develop immunity to at least some strains with which they have not yet come in contact.

(E) Children are no more likely than adults to have immunity to a particular flu virus if they have never lived through a previous epidemic of the same virus.

CR01392

166. Pro-Tect Insurance Company has recently been paying out more on car-theft claims than it expected. Cars with special antitheft devices or alarm systems are much less likely to be stolen than are other cars. Consequently Pro-Tect, as part of an effort to reduce its annual payouts, will offer a discount to holders of car-theft policies if their cars have antitheft devices or alarm systems.

Which of the following, if true, provides the strongest indication that the plan is likely to achieve its goal?

(A) The decrease in the risk of car theft conferred by having a car alarm is greatest when only a few cars have such alarms.

(B) The number of policyholders who have filed a claim in the past year is higher for Pro-Tect than for other insurance companies.

(C) In one or two years, the discount that Pro-Tect is offering will amount to more than the cost of buying certain highly effective antitheft devices.

(D) Currently, Pro-Tect cannot legally raise the premiums it charges for a given amount of insurance against car theft.

(E) The amount Pro-Tect has been paying out on car-theft claims has been greater for some models of car than for others.

CR00783

167. While the total enrollment of public elementary and secondary schools in Sondland is one percent higher this academic year than last academic year, the number of teachers there increased by three percent. Thus, the Sondland Education Commission's prediction of a teacher shortage as early as next academic year is unfounded.

Which of the following, if true, most seriously weakens the claim that the prediction of a teacher shortage as early as next academic year is unfounded?

(A) Funding for public elementary schools in Sondland is expected to increase over the next ten years.

(B) Average salaries for Sondland's teachers increased at the rate of inflation from last academic year to this academic year.

(C) A new law has mandated that there be ten percent more teachers per pupil in Sondland's public schools next academic year than there were this academic year.

(D) In the past, increases in enrollments in public elementary and secondary schools in Sondland have generally been smaller than increases in the number of teachers.

(E) Because of reductions in funding, the number of students enrolling in teacher-training programs in Sondland is expected to decline beginning in the next academic year.

CR05590
168. Art restorers who have been studying the factors that cause Renaissance oil paintings to deteriorate physically when subject to climatic changes have found that the oil paint used in these paintings actually adjusts to these changes well. The restorers therefore hypothesize that it is a layer of material called gesso, which is under the paint, that causes the deterioration.

Which of the following, if true, most strongly supports the restorers' hypothesis?

(A) Renaissance oil paintings with a thin layer of gesso are less likely to show deterioration in response to climatic changes than those with a thicker layer.

(B) Renaissance oil paintings are often painted on wooden panels, which swell when humidity increases and contract when it declines.

(C) Oil paint expands and contracts readily in response to changes in temperature, but it absorbs little water and so is little affected by changes in humidity.

(D) An especially hard and nonabsorbent type of gesso was the raw material for moldings on the frames of Renaissance oil paintings.

(E) Gesso layers applied by Renaissance painters typically consisted of a coarse base layer onto which several increasingly fine-grained layers were applied.

CR10731
169. A newly discovered painting seems to be the work of one of two 17th-century artists, either the northern German Johannes Drechen or the Frenchman Louis Birelle, who sometimes painted in the same style as Drechen. Analysis of the carved picture frame, which has been identified as the painting's original 17th-century frame, showed that it is made of wood found widely in northern Germany at the time, but rare in the part of France where Birelle lived. This shows that the painting is most likely the work of Drechen.

Which of the following is an assumption that the argument requires?

(A) The frame was made from wood local to the region where the picture was painted.

(B) Drechen is unlikely to have ever visited the home region of Birelle in France.

(C) Sometimes a painting so closely resembles others of its era that no expert is able to confidently decide who painted it.

(D) The painter of the picture chose the frame for the picture.

(E) The carving style of the picture frame is not typical of any specific region of Europe.

CR09120

170. Archaeologists working in the Andes Mountains recently excavated a buried 4,000-year-old temple containing structures that align with a stone carving on a distant hill to indicate the direction of the rising sun at the summer solstice. Alignments in the temple were also found to point toward the position, at the summer solstice, of a constellation known in Andean culture as the Fox. Since the local mythology represents the fox as teaching people how to cultivate and irrigate plants, the ancient Andeans may have built the temple as a religious representation of the fox.

Which of the following is an assumption on which the argument is based?

(A) The constellation known as the Fox has the same position at the summer solstice as it did 4,000 years ago.

(B) In the region around the temple, the summer solstice marks the time for planting.

(C) The temple was protected from looters by dirt and debris built up over thousands of years.

(D) Other structural alignments at the temple point to further constellations with agricultural significance.

(E) The site containing the temple was occupied for a significant amount of time before abandonment.

CR05065

171. Meat from chickens contaminated with salmonella bacteria can cause serious food poisoning. Capsaicin, the chemical that gives chili peppers their hot flavor, has antibacterial properties. Chickens do not have taste receptors for capsaicin and will readily eat feed laced with capsaicin. When chickens were fed such feed and then exposed to salmonella bacteria, relatively few of them became contaminated with salmonella.

In deciding whether the feed would be useful in raising salmonella-free chicken for retail sale, it would be most helpful to determine which of the following?

(A) Whether feeding capsaicin to chickens affects the taste of their meat

(B) Whether eating capsaicin reduces the risk of salmonella poisoning for humans

(C) Whether chicken is more prone to salmonella contamination than other kinds of meat

(D) Whether appropriate cooking of chicken contaminated with salmonella can always prevent food poisoning

(E) Whether capsaicin can be obtained only from chili peppers

CRO4532
172. Which of the following most logically completes the argument below?

When mercury-vapor streetlights are used in areas inhabited by insect-eating bats, the bats feed almost exclusively around the lights, because the lights attract flying insects. In Greenville, the mercury-vapor streetlights are about to be replaced with energy-saving sodium streetlights, which do not attract insects. This change is likely to result in a drop in the population of insect-eating bats in Greenville, since

_____.

(A)　the bats do not begin to hunt until after sundown

(B)　the bats are unlikely to feed on insects that do not fly

(C)　the highway department will be able to replace mercury-vapor streetlights with sodium streetlights within a relatively short time and without disrupting the continuity of lighting at the locations of the streetlights

(D)　in the absence of local concentrations of the flying insects on which bats feed, the bats expend much more energy on hunting for food, requiring much larger quantities of insects to sustain each bat

(E)　bats use echolocation to catch insects and therefore gain no advantage from the fact that insects flying in the vicinity of streetlights are visible at night

CRO1353
173. Rats injected with morphine exhibit decreased activity of the immune system, the bodily system that fights off infections. These same rats exhibited heightened blood levels of corticosteroids, chemicals secreted by the adrenal glands. Since corticosteroids can interfere with immune-system activity, scientists hypothesized that the way morphine reduces immune responses in rats is by stimulating the adrenal glands to secrete additional corticosteroids into the bloodstream.

Which of the following experiments would yield the most useful results for evaluating the scientists' hypothesis?

(A)　Injecting morphine into rats that already have heightened blood levels of corticosteroids and then observing their new blood levels of corticosteroids

(B)　Testing the level of immune-system activity of rats, removing their adrenal glands, and then testing the rats' immune-system activity levels again

(C)　Injecting rats with corticosteroids and then observing how many of the rats contracted infections

(D)　Removing the adrenal glands of rats, injecting the rats with morphine, and then testing the level of the rats' immune-system responses

(E)　Injecting rats with a drug that stimulates immune-system activity and then observing the level of corticosteroids in their bloodstreams

CR06831

174. Curator: If our museum lends *Venus* to the Hart Institute for their show this spring, they will lend us their Rembrandt etchings for our print exhibition next fall. Having those etchings will increase attendance to the exhibition and hence increase revenue from our general admission fee.

Museum Administrator: But *Venus* is our biggest attraction. Moreover the Hart's show will run for twice as long as our exhibition. So on balance the number of patrons may decrease.

The point of the administrator's response to the curator is to question

(A) whether getting the Rembrandt etchings from the Hart Institute is likely to increase attendance at the print exhibition

(B) whether the Hart Institute's Rembrandt etchings will be appreciated by those patrons of the curator's museum for whom the museum's biggest attraction is *Venus*

(C) whether the number of patrons attracted by the Hart Institute's Rembrandt etchings will be larger than the number of patrons who do not come in the spring because *Venus* is on loan

(D) whether, if *Venus* is lent, the museum's revenue from general admission fees during the print exhibition will exceed its revenue from general admission fees during the Hart Institute's exhibition

(E) whether the Hart Institute or the curator's museum will have the greater financial gain from the proposed exchange of artworks

CR03697

175. Which of the following most logically completes the passage?

Leaf beetles damage willow trees by stripping away their leaves, but a combination of parasites and predators generally keeps populations of these beetles in check. Researchers have found that severe air pollution results in reduced predator populations. The parasites, by contrast, are not adversely affected by pollution; nevertheless, the researchers' discovery probably does explain why leaf beetles cause particularly severe damage to willows in areas with severe air pollution, since _____.

(A) neither the predators nor the parasites of leaf beetles themselves attack willow trees

(B) the parasites that attack leaf beetles actually tend to be more prevalent in areas with severe air pollution than they are elsewhere

(C) the damage caused by leaf beetles is usually not enough to kill a willow tree outright

(D) where air pollution is not especially severe, predators have much more impact on leaf-beetle populations than parasites do

(E) willows often grow in areas where air pollution is especially severe

CR05438

176. On May first, in order to reduce the number of overdue books, a children's library instituted a policy of forgiving fines and giving bookmarks to children returning all of their overdue books. On July first there were twice as many overdue books as there had been on May first, although a record number of books had been returned during the interim.

Which of the following, if true, most helps to explain the apparent inconsistency in the results of the library's policy?

(A) The librarians did not keep accurate records of how many children took advantage of the grace period, and some of the children returning overdue books did not return all of their overdue books.

(B) Although the grace period enticed some children to return all of their overdue books, it did not convince all of the children with overdue books to return all of their books.

(C) The bookmarks became popular among the children, so in order to collect the bookmarks, many children borrowed many more books than they usually did and kept them past their due date.

(D) The children were allowed to borrow a maximum of five books for a two-week period, and hence each child could keep a maximum of fifteen books beyond their due date within a two-month period.

(E) Although the library forgave overdue fines during the grace period, the amount previously charged the children was minimal; hence, the forgiveness of the fines did not provide enough incentive for them to return their overdue books.

CR00663

177. A certain species of desert lizard digs tunnels in which to lay its eggs. The eggs must incubate inside the tunnel for several weeks before hatching, and they fail to hatch if they are disturbed at any time during this incubation period. Yet these lizards guard their tunnels for only a few days after laying their eggs.

Which of the following, if true, most helps explain why there is no need for lizards to guard their tunnels for more than a few days?

(A) The eggs are at risk of being disturbed only during the brief egg-laying season when many lizards are digging in a relatively small area.

(B) The length of the incubation period varies somewhat from one tunnel to another.

(C) Each female lizard lays from 15 to 20 eggs, only about 10 of which hatch even if the eggs are not disturbed at any time during the incubation period.

(D) The temperature and humidity within the tunnels will not be suitable for the incubating eggs unless the tunnels are plugged with sand immediately after the eggs are laid.

(E) The only way to disturb the eggs of this lizard species is by opening up one of the tunnels in which they are laid.

CR00677

178. Most banks that issue credit cards charge interest rates on credit card debt that are ten percentage points higher than the rates those banks charge for ordinary consumer loans. These banks' representatives claim the difference is fully justified, since it simply covers the difference between the costs to these banks associated with credit card debt and those associated with consumer loans.

Which of the following, if true, most seriously calls into question the reasoning offered by the banks' representatives?

(A) Some lenders that are not banks offer consumer loans at interest rates that are even higher than most banks charge on credit card debt.

(B) Most car rental companies require that their customers provide signed credit card charge slips or security deposits.

(C) Two to three percent of the selling price of every item bought with a given credit card goes to the bank that issued that credit card.

(D) Most people need not use credit cards to buy everyday necessities, but could buy those necessities with cash or pay by check.

(E) People who pay their credit card bills in full each month usually pay no interest on the amounts they charge.

CR00726

179. Often patients with ankle fractures that are stable, and thus do not require surgery, are given follow-up x-rays because their orthopedists are concerned about possibly having misjudged the stability of the fracture. When a number of follow-up x-rays were reviewed, however, all the fractures that had initially been judged stable were found to have healed correctly. Therefore, it is a waste of money to order follow-up x-rays of ankle fractures initially judged stable.

Which of the following, if true, most strengthens the argument?

(A) Doctors who are general practitioners rather than orthopedists are less likely than orthopedists to judge the stability of an ankle fracture correctly.

(B) Many ankle injuries for which an initial x-ray is ordered are revealed by the x-ray not to involve any fracture of the ankle.

(C) X-rays of patients of many different orthopedists working in several hospitals were reviewed.

(D) The healing of ankle fractures that have been surgically repaired is always checked by means of a follow-up x-ray.

(E) Orthopedists routinely order follow-up x-rays for fractures of bones other than ankle bones.

CR05431

180. In setting environmental standards for industry and others to meet, it is inadvisable to require the best results that state-of-the-art technology can achieve. Current technology is able to detect and eliminate even extremely minute amounts of contaminants, but at a cost that is exorbitant relative to the improvement achieved. So it would be reasonable instead to set standards by taking into account all of the current and future risks involved.

The argument given concerning the reasonable way to set standards presupposes that

(A) industry currently meets the standards that have been set by environmental authorities

(B) there are effective ways to take into account all of the relevant risks posed by allowing different levels of contaminants

(C) the only contaminants worth measuring are generated by industry

(D) it is not costly to prevent large amounts of contaminants from entering the environment

(E) minute amounts of some contaminants can be poisonous

CR05750

181. The chemical adenosine is released by brain cells when those cells are active. Adenosine then binds to more and more sites on cells in certain areas of the brain, as the total amount released gradually increases during wakefulness. During sleep, the number of sites to which adenosine is bound decreases. Some researchers have hypothesized that it is the cumulative binding of adenosine to a large number of sites that causes the onset of sleep.

Which of the following, if true, provides the most support for the researchers' hypothesis?

(A) Even after long periods of sleep when adenosine is at its lowest concentration in the brain, the number of brain cells bound with adenosine remains very large.

(B) Caffeine, which has the effect of making people remain wakeful, is known to interfere with the binding of adenosine to sites on brain cells.

(C) Besides binding to sites in the brain, adenosine is known to be involved in biochemical reactions throughout the body.

(D) Some areas of the brain that are relatively inactive nonetheless release some adenosine.

(E) Stress resulting from a dangerous situation can preserve wakefulness even when brain levels of bound adenosine are high.

CR01101

182. A two-year study beginning in 1977 found that, among 85-year-old people, those whose immune systems were weakest were twice as likely to die within two years as others in the study. The cause of their deaths, however, was more often heart disease, against which the immune system does not protect, than cancer or infections, which are attacked by the immune system.

Which of the following, if true, would offer the best prospects for explaining deaths in which weakness of the immune system, though present, played no causal role?

(A) There were twice as many infections among those in the study with the weakest immune systems as among those with the strongest immune systems.

(B) The majority of those in the study with the strongest immune systems died from infection or cancer by 1987.

(C) Some of the drugs that had been used to treat the symptoms of heart disease had a side effect of weakening the immune system.

(D) Most of those in the study who survived beyond the two-year period had recovered from a serious infection sometime prior to 1978.

(E) Those in the study who survived into the 1980s had, in 1976, strengthened their immune systems through drug therapy.

CR13093

183. Most scholars agree that King Alfred (A.D. 849–899) personally translated a number of Latin texts into Old English. One historian contends that Alfred also personally penned his own law code, arguing that the numerous differences between the language of the law code and Alfred's translations of Latin texts are outweighed by the even more numerous similarities. Linguistic similarities, however, are what one expects in texts from the same language, the same time, and the same region. Apart from Alfred's surviving translations and law code, there are only two other extant works from the same dialect and milieu, so it is risky to assume here that linguistic similarities point to common authorship.

The passage above proceeds by

(A) providing examples that underscore another argument's conclusion

(B) questioning the plausibility of an assumption on which another argument depends

(C) showing that a principle if generally applied would have anomalous consequences

(D) showing that the premises of another argument are mutually inconsistent

(E) using argument by analogy to undermine a principle implicit in another argument

CR01355

184. Parland's alligator population has been declining in recent years, primarily because of hunting. Alligators prey heavily on a species of freshwater fish that is highly valued as food by Parlanders, who had hoped that the decline in the alligator population would lead to an increase in the numbers of these fish available for human consumption. Yet the population of this fish species has also declined, even though the annual number caught for human consumption has not increased.

Which of the following, if true, most helps to explain the decline in the population of the fish species?

(A) The decline in the alligator population has meant that fishers can work in some parts of lakes and rivers that were formerly too dangerous.

(B) Over the last few years, Parland's commercial fishing enterprises have increased the number of fishing boats they use.

(C) Many Parlanders who hunt alligators do so because of the high market price of alligator skins, not because of the threat alligators pose to the fish population.

(D) During Parland's dry season, holes dug by alligators remain filled with water long enough to provide a safe place for the eggs of this fish species to hatch.

(E) In several neighboring countries through which Parland's rivers also flow, alligators are at risk of extinction as a result of extensive hunting.

CR05418

185. A company plans to develop a prototype weeding machine that uses cutting blades with optical sensors and microprocessors that distinguish weeds from crop plants by differences in shade of color. The inventor of the machine claims that it will reduce labor costs by virtually eliminating the need for manual weeding.

Which of the following is a consideration in favor of the company's implementing its plan to develop the prototype?

(A) There is a considerable degree of variation in shade of color between weeds of different species.

(B) The shade of color of some plants tends to change appreciably over the course of their growing season.

(C) When crops are weeded manually, overall size and leaf shape are taken into account in distinguishing crop plants from weeds.

(D) Selection and genetic manipulation allow plants of virtually any species to be economically bred to have a distinctive shade of color without altering their other characteristics.

(E) Farm laborers who are responsible for the manual weeding of crops carry out other agricultural duties at times in the growing season when extensive weeding is not necessary.

CR05079

186. Aroca City currently funds its public schools through taxes on property. **In place of this system, the city plans to introduce a sales tax of 3 percent on all retail sales in the city.** Critics protest that 3 percent of current retail sales falls short of the amount raised for schools by property taxes. The critics are correct on this point. **Nevertheless, implementing the plan will probably not reduce the money going to Aroca's schools.** Several large retailers have selected Aroca City as the site for huge new stores, and these are certain to draw large numbers of shoppers from neighboring municipalities, where sales are taxed at rates of 6 percent and more. In consequence, retail sales in Aroca City are bound to increase substantially.

In the argument given, the two portions in **boldface** play which of the following roles?

(A) The first presents a plan that the argument concludes is unlikely to achieve its goal; the second expresses that conclusion.

(B) The first presents a plan that the argument concludes is unlikely to achieve its goal; the second presents evidence in support of that conclusion.

(C) The first presents a plan that the argument contends is the best available; the second is a conclusion drawn by the argument to justify that contention.

(D) The first presents a plan one of whose consequences is at issue in the argument; the second is the argument's conclusion about that consequence.

(E) The first presents a plan that the argument seeks to defend against a certain criticism; the second is that criticism.

CR06152

187. Which of the following most logically completes the argument?

A photograph of the night sky was taken with the camera shutter open for an extended period. The normal motion of stars across the sky caused the images of the stars in the photograph to appear as streaks. However, one bright spot was not streaked. Even if the spot were caused, as astronomers believe, by a celestial object, that object could still have been moving across the sky during the time the shutter was open, since _____.

(A) the spot was not the brightest object in the photograph

(B) the photograph contains many streaks that astronomers can identify as caused by noncelestial objects

(C) stars in the night sky do not appear to shift position relative to each other

(D) the spot could have been caused by an object that emitted a flash that lasted for only a fraction of the time that the camera shutter was open

(E) if the camera shutter had not been open for an extended period, it would have recorded substantially fewer celestial objects

CR09046

188. Economist: Paying extra for fair-trade coffee—coffee labeled with the Fairtrade logo—is intended to help poor farmers, because they receive a higher price for the fair-trade coffee they grow. But this practice may hurt more farmers in developing nations than it helps. By raising average prices for coffee, it encourages more coffee to be produced than consumers want to buy. This lowers prices for non-fair-trade coffee and thus lowers profits for non-fair-trade coffee farmers.

To evaluate the strength of the economist's argument, it would be most helpful to know which of the following?

(A) Whether there is a way of alleviating the impact of the increased average prices for coffee on non-fair-trade coffee farmers' profits

(B) What proportion of coffee farmers in developing nations produce fair-trade coffee

(C) Whether many coffee farmers in developing nations also derive income from other kinds of farming

(D) Whether consumers should pay extra for fair-trade coffee if doing so lowers profits for non-fair-trade coffee farmers

(E) How fair-trade coffee farmers in developing nations could be helped without lowering profits for non-fair-trade coffee farmers

Questions 189 to 233 - Difficulty: Hard

CR66900.02

189. Twenty-five years ago, 2,000 married people were asked to rank four categories—spouses, friends, jobs, and housework—according to the amount of time each category demanded. A recent follow-up survey indicates that a majority of those same people rank housework higher on the list now than they did twenty-five years ago. Yet most of the respondents also claim that housework has become less demanding of their time over the last twenty-five years.

Which of the following, if true, helps to explain the apparent discrepancy?

(A) Some of the people surveyed were married to other people in the survey.

(B) Many of the most time-consuming aspects of people's lives do not appear as categories on either survey.

(C) Most of those who responded to the follow-up survey have retired in the last twenty-five years.

(D) At the time of the follow-up survey, some of the people surveyed did no housework.

(E) Many of the respondents to the follow-up survey claim that they now spend much more time with their friends than they did twenty-five years ago.

CR59820.02

190. In order to achieve self-sufficiency in electricity production, **the Hasarian government proposes to construct eleven huge hydroelectric power plants**. Although this is a massive project, it is probably not massive enough to achieve the goal. It is true that **adding the projected output of the new hydroelectric plants to the output that Hasaria can achieve now would be enough to meet the forecast demand for electricity**. It will, however, take at least fifteen years to complete the project and by then the majority of Hasaria's current power plants will be too old to function at full capacity.

In the argument given, the two portions in **boldface** play which of the following roles?

(A) The first introduces a proposed course of action for which the argument provides support; the second gives evidence in support of that course of action.

(B) The first introduces a proposed course of action for which the argument provides support; the second gives a reason for not adopting a possible alternative course of action.

(C) The first introduces a plan that the argument evaluates; the second provides evidence that is used to support that plan against possible alternatives.

(D) The first introduces a proposed plan for achieving a certain goal; the second is a claim that has been used in support of the plan but that the argument maintains is inaccurate.

(E) The first introduces a proposed plan for achieving a certain goal; the second provides evidence that is used to support the argument's evaluation of that plan.

CR89820.02

191. In Cecropia, inspections of fishing boats that estimate the number of fish they are carrying are typically conducted upon their return to port. The high numbers so obtained have led the government to conclude that the coastal waters are being overfished. To allow commercial fishing stocks to recover, the government is considering introducing annual quotas on the number of fish that each fishing boat can catch. Compliance with the quotas would be determined by the established system of inspections.

Which of the following, if true, raises the most serious doubts about whether the government's proposed plan would succeed?

(A) Some commercial fishing boats in Cecropia are large enough to catch their entire annual quota in only a few months of fishing.

(B) The quotas would have to be reduced if more boats began fishing in Cecropia's coastal waters.

(C) Because fish prices will rise if the quotas go into effect, it is unlikely that the quotas will significantly change the number of boats fishing Cecropia's coastal waters.

(D) The procedure that inspectors use to estimate the number of fish a boat is carrying often results in a slight overcount.

(E) Quotas encourage fishers to bring only the most commercially valuable fish into port and to discard less valuable fish, most of them dead or dying.

CR55030.02

192. Consultant: **A significant number of complex repair jobs carried out by Ace Repairs have to be redone under the company's warranty, but when those repairs are redone they are invariably successful**. Since we have definitely established that **there is no systematic difference between the mechanics who are assigned to do the initial repairs and those who are assigned to redo unsatisfactory jobs**, it is clear that inadequacies in the initial repairs cannot be attributed to the mechanics' lack of competence. Rather, it is likely that complex repairs require a level of focused attention that the company's mechanics apply consistently only to repair jobs that have been inadequately done on the first try.

In the consultant's reasoning, the two portions in **boldface** play which of the following roles?

(A) The first is a claim that the consultant rejects as false; the second is evidence that forms the basis for that rejection.

(B) The first is part of an explanation that the consultant offers for a certain finding; the second is that finding.

(C) The first presents a pattern whose explanation is at issue in the reasoning; the second provides evidence to rule out one possible explanation of that pattern.

(D) The first presents a pattern whose explanation is at issue in the reasoning; the second is evidence that has been used to challenge the explanation presented by the consultant.

(E) The first is the position the consultant seeks to establish; the second is offered as evidence for that position.

CR08540.02

193. Half of Metroburg's operating budget comes from a payroll tax of 2 percent on salaries paid to people who work in the city. Recently a financial services company, one of Metroburg's largest private-sector employers, announced that it will be relocating just outside the city. All the company's employees, amounting to 1 percent of all people now employed in Metroburg, will be employed at the new location.

From the information given, which of the following can most properly be concluded?

(A) Unless other employers add a substantial number of jobs in Metroburg, the company's relocation is likely to result in a 1 percent reduction in the revenue for the city's operating budget.

(B) Although the company's relocation will have a negative effect on the city's tax revenue, the company's departure will not lead to any increase in the unemployment rate among city residents.

(C) One of the benefits that the company will realize from its relocation is a reduction in the taxes paid by itself and its employees.

(D) Revenue from the payroll tax will decline by 1 percent if there is no increase in jobs within the city to compensate, fully or partially, for the company's departure.

(E) The company's relocation will tend to increase the proportion of jobs in Metroburg that are in the public sector, unless it results in a contraction of the public-sector payroll.

CR62740.02

194. A library currently has only coin-operated photocopy machines, which cost 10 cents per copy. Library administrators are planning to refit most of those machines with card readers. The library will sell prepaid copy cards that allow users to make 50 copies at 9 cents per copy. Administrators believe that, despite the convenience of copy cards and their lower per-copy cost, the number of copies made in the library will be essentially unchanged after the refit.

On the assumption that administrators' assessment is correct, which of the following predictions about the effect of the refit is most strongly supported by the information given?

(A) Library patrons will only purchase a copy card on days when they need to make 50 or more copies.

(B) No library patrons will increase their usage of the library's photocopy machines once the refit has been made.

(C) If most of the copy cards sold in the library are used to their full capacity, the number of people using the library's photocopy machines over a given period will fall.

(D) Revenues from photocopying will decrease unless most library patrons choose to use the remaining coin-operated machines in preference to the card-reader equipped ones.

(E) Revenues from photocopying will increase if copy cards that are purchased are, on average, used to significantly less than 90 percent of their capacity.

CR09740.02

195. Harvester-ant colonies live for fifteen to twenty years, though individual worker ants live only a year. The way a colony behaves changes steadily in a predictable pattern as the colony grows older and larger. For the first few years, the foragers behave quite aggressively, searching out and vigorously defending new food sources, but once a colony has reached a certain size, its foragers become considerably less aggressive.

If the statements above are true, which of the following can most properly be concluded on the basis of them?

(A) As a result of pressure from neighbors, some colonies do not grow larger as they become older.

(B) Unpredictable changes in a colony's environment can cause changes in the tasks that the colony must perform if it is to continue to survive.

(C) The reason a mature colony goes out of existence is that younger, more aggressive colonies successfully outcompete it for food.

(D) The pattern of changing behavior that a colony displays does not arise from a change in the behavior of any individual worker ant or group of worker ants.

(E) A new colony comes into existence when a group of young, aggressive workers leaves a mature colony and sets up on its own.

CR29940.02

196. Trucking company owner: Theft of trucks containing valuable cargo is a serious problem. A new device produces radio signals that allow police to track stolen vehicles, and the recovery rate for stolen cargo in trucks equipped with the device is impressive. The device is too expensive to install in every truck, so we plan to install it in half of our trucks. Using those trucks for the most valuable cargo should largely eliminate losses from theft.

Which of the following, if true, most strongly supports the trucking company owner's expectation about the results of implementing the plan?

(A) For thieves, a cargo is valuable only if it is easy for them to dispose of profitably.

(B) Some insurance companies charge less to insure cargoes transported in trucks protected by the device.

(C) Most stolen trucks are eventually found, but unless a stolen truck is found very soon after it is taken, the likelihood that the trucking company will recover any of its cargo is very low.

(D) Thieves generally avoid trucks belonging to trucking companies that are known to have installed the device in a large proportion of their trucks.

(E) The manufacturer of the device offers a five-year warranty on each unit sold, a longer warranty than any that is offered on any competing antitheft device.

CR11050.02

197. To improve customer relations, several big retailers have recently launched "smile initiatives," requiring their employees to smile whenever they have contact with customers. These retailers generally have low employee morale, which is why they have to enforce smiling. However, studies show that customers can tell fake smiles from genuine smiles and that fake smiles prompt negative feelings in customers. So the smile initiatives are unlikely to achieve their goal.

The argument relies on which of the following as an assumption?

(A) The smile initiatives have achieved nearly complete success in getting employees to smile while they are around customers.

(B) Customers' feelings about fake smiles are no better than their feelings about the other facial expressions employees with low morale are likely to have.

(C) The feelings that employees generate in retail customers are a principal determinant of the amount of money customers will spend at a retailer.

(D) At the retailers who have launched the smile initiatives, none of the employees gave genuine smiles to customers before the initiatives were launched.

(E) Customers rarely, if ever, have a negative reaction to a genuine smile from a retail employee.

CR55190.02

198. Many economists hold that keeping taxes low helps to spur economic growth, and that low taxes thus lead to greater national prosperity. But Country X, which has unusually high taxes, has greater per-capita income than the neighboring Country Y, which has much lower taxes. Some politicians have concluded from this that high taxes do not hinder national prosperity.

The politicians' reasoning is most vulnerable to criticism on which of the following grounds?

(A) It overlooks the possibility that even if Country X reduced its taxes, it would not experience greater national prosperity in the long term.

(B) It confuses a claim that a factor does not hinder a given development with the claim that the same factor promotes that development.

(C) It fails to adequately address the possibility that Country X and Country Y differ in relevant respects other than taxation.

(D) It fails to take into account that the per-capita income of a country does not determine its rate of economic growth.

(E) It assumes that the economists' thesis must be correct despite a clear counterexample to that thesis.

CR11080.02

199. Urban rail systems have been proposed to alleviate traffic congestion, but results in many cities have been cited as evidence that this approach to traffic management is ineffective. For example, a U.S. city that opened three urban rail branches experienced a net decline of 3,100 urban rail commuters during a period when employment increased by 96,000. Officials who favor urban rail systems as a solution to traffic congestion have attempted to counter this argument by noting that commuting trips in that city represent just 20 percent of urban travel.

The response of the officials to the claim that urban rail systems are ineffective is most vulnerable to criticism on the grounds that it

(A) presents no evidence to show that the statistics are incorrect

(B) relies solely on general data about U.S. cities rather than data about the city in question

(C) fails to consider that commuting trips may cause significantly more than 20 percent of the traffic congestion

(D) fails to show that the decline in the number of urban rail commuters in one U.S. city is typical of U.S. cities generally

(E) provides no statistics on the use of urban rail systems by passengers other than commuters

CR63780.02

200. Mayor: The financial livelihood of our downtown businesses is in jeopardy. There are few available parking spaces close to the downtown shopping area, so if we are to spur economic growth in our city, we must build a large parking ramp no more than two blocks from downtown.

Which of the following, if true, most seriously weakens the mayor's reasoning?

(A) The city budget is not currently large enough to finance the construction of a new parking ramp.

(B) There are other more significant reasons for the financial woes of downtown businesses in addition to a lack of nearby parking spaces.

(C) Building a parking ramp as much as four blocks from downtown would be sufficient to greatly increase the number of shoppers to downtown businesses.

(D) Explosive growth is most often associated with large suburban shopping malls, not small businesses.

(E) Some additional parking spaces could be added to the downtown area without the construction of a parking ramp.

CR28001.02

201. Compact fluorescent light (CFL) bulbs are growing in market share as a replacement for the standard incandescent light bulb. However, an even newer technology is emerging: the light-emitting diode (LED) bulb. Like CFL bulbs, LED bulbs are energy efficient, and they can last around fifty thousand hours, about five times as long as most CFL bulbs. Yet, a single LED bulb costs much more than five CFL bulbs.

The information in the passage above most supports which of the following conclusions?

(A) LED bulbs are most likely to be used in locations where light bulbs would be difficult or costly to replace.

(B) CFL bulbs will need to come down further in price in order to compete with LED bulbs.

(C) LED bulbs are most likely to be used in locations where there is frequent accidental breakage of bulbs.

(D) CFL bulb designs are likely to advance to the point where they can last as long as LED bulbs.

(E) LED bulbs are likely to drop in price, to the point of being competitive with CFL bulbs.

CR01887

202. Tanco, a leather manufacturer, uses large quantities of common salt to preserve animal hides. New environmental regulations have significantly increased the cost of disposing of salt water that results from this use, and, in consequence, Tanco is considering a plan to use potassium chloride in place of common salt. Research has shown that Tanco could reprocess the by-product of potassium chloride use to yield a crop fertilizer, leaving a relatively small volume of waste for disposal.

In determining the impact on company profits of using potassium chloride in place of common salt, it would be important for Tanco to research all of the following EXCEPT:

(A) What difference, if any, is there between the cost of the common salt needed to preserve a given quantity of animal hides and the cost of the potassium chloride needed to preserve the same quantity of hides?

(B) To what extent is the equipment involved in preserving animal hides using common salt suitable for preserving animal hides using potassium chloride?

(C) What environmental regulations, if any, constrain the disposal of the waste generated in reprocessing the by-product of potassium chloride?

(D) How closely does leather that results when common salt is used to preserve hides resemble that which results when potassium chloride is used?

(E) Are the chemical properties that make potassium chloride an effective means for preserving animal hides the same as those that make common salt an effective means for doing so?

CR04999

203. Colorless diamonds can command high prices as gemstones. A type of less valuable diamonds can be treated to remove all color. Only sophisticated tests can distinguish such treated diamonds from naturally colorless ones. However, only 2 percent of diamonds mined are of the colored type that can be successfully treated, and many of those are of insufficient quality to make the treatment worthwhile. Surely, therefore, the vast majority of colorless diamonds sold by jewelers are naturally colorless.

A serious flaw in the reasoning of the argument is that

(A) comparisons between the price diamonds command as gemstones and their value for other uses are omitted

(B) information about the rarity of treated diamonds is not combined with information about the rarity of naturally colorless, gemstone diamonds

(C) the possibility that colored diamonds might be used as gemstones, even without having been treated, is ignored

(D) the currently available method for making colorless diamonds from colored ones is treated as though it were the only possible method for doing so

(E) the difficulty that a customer of a jeweler would have in distinguishing a naturally colorless diamond from a treated one is not taken into account

CR14448

204. The Sumpton town council recently voted to pay a prominent artist to create an abstract sculpture for the town square. Critics of this decision protested that town residents tend to dislike most abstract art, and any art in the town square should reflect their tastes. But a town council spokesperson dismissed this criticism, pointing out that other public abstract sculptures that the same sculptor has installed in other cities have been extremely popular with those cities' local residents.

The statements above most strongly suggest that the main point of disagreement between the critics and the spokesperson is whether

(A) it would have been reasonable to consult town residents on the decision

(B) most Sumpton residents will find the new sculpture to their taste

(C) abstract sculptures by the same sculptor have truly been popular in other cities

(D) a more traditional sculpture in the town square would be popular among local residents

(E) public art that the residents of Sumpton would find desirable would probably be found desirable by the residents of other cities

CR09085

205. Jay: Of course there are many good reasons to support the expansion of preventive medical care, but arguments claiming that it will lead to greater societal economic gains are misguided. Some of the greatest societal expenses arise from frequent urgent-care needs for people who have attained a long life due to preventive care.

Sunil: Your argument fails because you neglect economic gains outside the health care system: society suffers an economic loss when any of its productive members suffer preventable illnesses.

Sunil's response to Jay makes which of the following assumptions?

(A) Those who receive preventive care are not more likely to need urgent care than are those who do not receive preventive care.

(B) Jay intends the phrase "economic gains" to refer only to gains accruing to institutions within the health care system.

(C) Productive members of society are more likely than others to suffer preventable illnesses.

(D) The economic contributions of those who receive preventive medical care may outweigh the economic losses caused by preventive care.

(E) Jay is incorrect in stating that patients who receive preventive medical care are long-lived.

CR01766

206. Boreal owls range over a much larger area than do other owls of similar size. The reason for this behavior is probably that the small mammals on which owls feed are especially scarce in the forests where boreal owls live, and the relative scarcity of prey requires the owls to range more extensively to find sufficient food.

Which of the following, if true, most helps to confirm the explanation above?

(A) Some boreal owls range over an area eight times larger than the area over which any other owl of similar size ranges.

(B) Boreal owls range over larger areas in regions where food of the sort eaten by small mammals is sparse than they do in regions where such food is abundant.

(C) After their young hatch, boreal owls must hunt more often than before in order to feed both themselves and their newly hatched young.

(D) Sometimes individual boreal owls hunt near a single location for many weeks at a time and do not range farther than a few hundred yards.

(E) The boreal owl requires less food, relative to its weight, than is required by members of other owl species.

CR12567
207. Microbiologist: A lethal strain of salmonella recently showed up in a European country, causing an outbreak of illness that killed two people and infected twenty-seven others. Investigators blame the severity of the outbreak on the overuse of antibiotics, since the salmonella bacteria tested were shown to be drug-resistant. But this is unlikely because patients in the country where the outbreak occurred cannot obtain antibiotics to treat illness without a prescription, and the country's doctors prescribe antibiotics less readily than do doctors in any other European country.

Which of the following, if true, would most weaken the microbiologist's reasoning?

(A) Physicians in the country where the outbreak occurred have become hesitant to prescribe antibiotics since they are frequently in short supply.

(B) People in the country where the outbreak occurred often consume foods produced from animals that eat antibiotics-laden livestock feed.

(C) Use of antibiotics in two countries that neighbor the country where the outbreak occurred has risen over the past decade.

(D) Drug-resistant strains of salmonella have not been found in countries in which antibiotics are not generally available.

(E) Salmonella has been shown to spread easily along the distribution chains of certain vegetables, such as raw tomatoes.

CR37090.02
208. Economist: Construction moves faster in good weather than in bad, so mild winters in areas that usually experience harsh conditions can appear to create construction booms as builders complete projects that would otherwise have to wait. But forecasting one mild winter or even two for such areas generally does not lead to overall increases in construction during these periods, because construction loans are often obtained more than a year in advance, and because _____.

Which of the following, if true, most logically completes the economist's argument?

(A) construction workers often travel to warmer climates in the wintertime in search of work

(B) construction materials are often in short supply during construction booms

(C) many builders in these areas are likely to apply for construction loans at the same time

(D) it is frequently the case that forecasted weather trends do not actually occur

(E) mild winters are generally followed by spring and summer weather that promotes more rapid construction

CR03416

209. Historian: Newton developed mathematical concepts and techniques that are fundamental to modern calculus. Leibniz developed closely analogous concepts and techniques. It has traditionally been thought that these discoveries were independent. Researchers have, however, recently discovered notes of Leibniz's that discuss one of Newton's books on mathematics. Several scholars have argued that since **the book includes a presentation of Newton's calculus concepts and techniques,** and since the notes were written before Leibniz's own development of calculus concepts and techniques, it is virtually certain **that the traditional view is false.** A more cautious conclusion than this is called for, however. Leibniz's notes are limited to early sections of Newton's book, sections that precede the ones in which Newton's calculus concepts and techniques are presented.

In the historian's reasoning, the two portions in **boldface** play which of the following roles?

(A) The first is a claim that the historian rejects; the second is a position that that claim has been used to support.

(B) The first is evidence that has been used to support a conclusion about which the historian expresses reservations; the second is that conclusion.

(C) The first provides evidence in support of a position that the historian defends; the second is that position.

(D) The first and the second each provide evidence in support of a position that the historian defends.

(E) The first has been used in support of a position that the historian rejects; the second is a conclusion that the historian draws from that position.

CR03867

210. For over two centuries, no one had been able to make Damascus blades—blades with a distinctive serpentine surface pattern—but a contemporary sword maker may just have rediscovered how. Using iron with trace impurities that precisely matched those present in the iron used in historic Damascus blades, this contemporary sword maker seems to have finally hit on an intricate process by which he can produce a blade indistinguishable from a true Damascus blade.

Which of the following, if true, provides the strongest support for the hypothesis that trace impurities in the iron are essential for the production of Damascus blades?

(A) There are surface features of every Damascus blade—including the blades produced by the contemporary sword maker—that are unique to that blade.

(B) The iron with which the contemporary sword maker made Damascus blades came from a source of iron that was unknown two centuries ago.

(C) Almost all the tools used by the contemporary sword maker were updated versions of tools that were used by sword makers over two centuries ago.

(D) Production of Damascus blades by sword makers of the past ceased abruptly after those sword makers' original source of iron became exhausted.

(E) Although Damascus blades were renowned for maintaining a sharp edge, the blade made by the contemporary sword maker suggests that they may have maintained their edge less well than blades made using what is now the standard process for making blades.

CR01903

211. Images from ground-based telescopes are invariably distorted by the Earth's atmosphere. Orbiting space telescopes, however, operating above Earth's atmosphere, should provide superbly detailed images. Therefore, ground-based telescopes will soon become obsolete for advanced astronomical research purposes.

Which of the following statements, if true, would cast the most doubt on the conclusion drawn above?

(A) An orbiting space telescope due to be launched this year is far behind schedule and over budget, whereas the largest ground-based telescope was both within budget and on schedule.

(B) Ground-based telescopes located on mountain summits are not subject to the kinds of atmospheric distortion which, at low altitudes, make stars appear to twinkle.

(C) By careful choice of observatory location, it is possible for large-aperture telescopes to avoid most of the kind of wind turbulence that can distort image quality.

(D) When large-aperture telescopes are located at high altitudes near the equator, they permit the best Earth-based observations of the center of the Milky Way Galaxy, a prime target of astronomical research.

(E) Detailed spectral analyses, upon which astronomers rely for determining the chemical composition and evolutionary history of stars, require telescopes with more light-gathering capacity than space telescopes can provide.

CR07562

212. Generally scientists enter their field with the goal of doing important new research and accept as their colleagues those with similar motivation. Therefore, when any scientist wins renown as an expounder of science to general audiences, most other scientists conclude that this popularizer should no longer be regarded as a true colleague.

The explanation offered above for the low esteem in which scientific popularizers are held by research scientists assumes that

(A) serious scientific research is not a solitary activity, but relies on active cooperation among a group of colleagues

(B) research scientists tend not to regard as colleagues those scientists whose renown they envy

(C) a scientist can become a famous popularizer without having completed any important research

(D) research scientists believe that those who are well known as popularizers of science are not motivated to do important new research

(E) no important new research can be accessible to or accurately assessed by those who are not themselves scientists

CR07676

213. Urban planner: When a city loses population due to migration, property taxes in that city tend to rise. This is because there are then fewer residents paying to maintain an infrastructure that was designed to support more people. Rising property taxes, in turn, drive more residents away, compounding the problem. Since the city of Stonebridge is starting to lose population, the city government should therefore refrain from raising property taxes.

Which of the following, if true, would most weaken the urban planner's argument?

(A) If Stonebridge does not raise taxes on its residents to maintain its infrastructure, the city will become much less attractive to live in as that infrastructure decays.

(B) Stonebridge at present benefits from grants provided by the national government to help maintain certain parts of its infrastructure.

(C) If there is a small increase in property taxes in Stonebridge and a slightly larger proportion of total revenue than at present is allocated to infrastructure maintenance, the funding will be adequate for that purpose.

(D) Demographers project that the population of a region that includes Stonebridge will start to increase substantially within the next several years.

(E) The property taxes in Stonebridge are significantly lower than those in many larger cities.

CR01338

214. Which of the following most logically completes the argument?

Utrania was formerly a major petroleum exporter, but in recent decades economic stagnation and restrictive regulations inhibited investment in new oil fields. In consequence, Utranian oil exports dropped steadily as old fields became depleted. Utrania's currently improving economic situation, together with less-restrictive regulations, will undoubtedly result in the rapid development of new fields. However, it would be premature to conclude that the rapid development of new fields will result in higher oil exports, because

_____.

(A) the price of oil is expected to remain relatively stable over the next several years

(B) the improvement in the economic situation in Utrania is expected to result in a dramatic increase in the proportion of Utranians who own automobiles

(C) most of the investment in new oil fields in Utrania is expected to come from foreign sources

(D) new technology is available to recover oil from old oil fields formerly regarded as depleted

(E) many of the new oil fields in Utrania are likely to be as productive as those that were developed during the period when Utrania was a major oil exporter

CR09592

215. The use of growth-promoting antibiotics in hog farming can weaken their effectiveness in treating humans because such use can spread resistance to those antibiotics among microorganisms. But now the Smee Company, one of the largest pork marketers, may stop buying pork raised on feed containing these antibiotics. Smee has 60 percent of the pork market, and farmers who sell to Smee would certainly stop using antibiotics in order to avoid jeopardizing their sales. So if Smee makes this change, it will probably significantly slow the decline in antibiotics' effectiveness for humans.

Which of the following, if true, would most strengthen the argument above?

(A) Other major pork marketers will probably stop buying pork raised on feed containing growth-promoting antibiotics if Smee no longer buys such pork.

(B) The decline in hog growth due to discontinuation of antibiotics can be offset by improved hygiene.

(C) Authorities are promoting the use of antibiotics to which microorganisms have not yet developed resistance.

(D) A phaseout of use of antibiotics for hogs in one country reduced usage by over 50 percent over five years.

(E) If Smee stops buying pork raised with antibiotics, the firm's costs will probably increase.

CR10678

216. In an experiment, volunteers walked individually through a dark, abandoned theater. Half of the volunteers had been told that the theater was haunted and the other half that it was under renovation. The first half reported significantly more unusual experiences than the second did. The researchers concluded that reports of encounters with ghosts and other supernatural entities generally result from prior expectations of such experiences.

Which of the following, if true, would most seriously weaken the researchers' reasoning?

(A) None of the volunteers in the second half believed that the unusual experiences they reported were supernatural.

(B) All of the volunteers in the first half believed that the researchers' statement that the theater was haunted was a lie.

(C) Before being told about the theater, the volunteers within each group varied considerably in their prior beliefs about supernatural experiences.

(D) Each unusual experience reported by the volunteers had a cause that did not involve the supernatural.

(E) The researchers did not believe that the theater was haunted.

CR05665

217. In order to reduce dependence on imported oil, the government of Jalica has imposed minimum fuel-efficiency requirements on all new cars, beginning this year. The more fuel-efficient a car, the less pollution it produces per mile driven. As Jalicans replace their old cars with cars that meet the new requirements, annual pollution from car traffic is likely to decrease in Jalica.

Which of the following, if true, most seriously weakens the argument?

(A) In Jalica, domestically produced oil is more expensive than imported oil.

(B) The Jalican government did not intend the new fuel-efficiency requirement to be a pollution-reduction measure.

(C) Some pollution-control devices mandated in Jalica make cars less fuel-efficient than they would be without those devices.

(D) The new regulation requires no change in the chemical formulation of fuel for cars in Jalica.

(E) Jalicans who get cars that are more fuel-efficient tend to do more driving than before.

CR01173

218. Plantings of cotton bioengineered to produce its own insecticide against bollworms, a major cause of crop failure, sustained little bollworm damage until this year. This year the plantings are being seriously damaged by bollworms. Bollworms, however, are not necessarily developing resistance to the cotton's insecticide. Bollworms breed on corn, and last year more corn than usual was planted throughout cotton-growing regions. So it is likely that the cotton is simply being overwhelmed by corn-bred bollworms.

In evaluating the argument, which of the following would it be most useful to establish?

(A) Whether corn could be bioengineered to produce the insecticide

(B) Whether plantings of cotton that does not produce the insecticide are suffering unusually extensive damage from bollworms this year

(C) Whether other crops that have been bioengineered to produce their own insecticide successfully resist the pests against which the insecticide was to protect them

(D) Whether plantings of bioengineered cotton are frequently damaged by insect pests other than bollworms

(E) Whether there are insecticides that can be used against bollworms that have developed resistance to the insecticide produced by the bioengineered cotton

CR03331

219. Typically during thunderstorms most lightning strikes carry a negative electric charge; only a few carry a positive charge. Thunderstorms with unusually high proportions of positive-charge strikes tend to occur in smoky areas near forest fires. The fact that smoke carries positively charged smoke particles into the air above a fire suggests the hypothesis that the extra positive strikes occur because of the presence of such particles in the storm clouds.

Which of the following, if discovered to be true, most seriously undermines the hypothesis?

(A) Other kinds of rare lightning also occur with unusually high frequency in the vicinity of forest fires.

(B) The positive-charge strikes that occur near forest fires tend to be no more powerful than positive strikes normally are.

(C) A positive-charge strike is as likely to start a forest fire as a negative-charge strike is.

(D) Thunderstorms that occur in drifting clouds of smoke have extra positive-charge strikes weeks after the charge of the smoke particles has dissipated.

(E) The total number of lightning strikes during a thunderstorm is usually within the normal range in the vicinity of a forest fire.

CR01140

220. Many gardeners believe that the variety of clematis vine that is most popular among gardeners in North America is *jackmanii*. This belief is apparently correct since, of the one million clematis plants sold per year by the largest clematis nursery in North America, ten percent are *jackmanii*.

Which of the following is an assumption on which the argument depends?

(A) The nursery sells more than ten different varieties of clematis.

(B) The largest clematis nursery in North America sells nothing but clematis plants.

(C) Some of the *jackmanii* sold by the nursery are sold to gardeners outside North America.

(D) Most North American gardeners grow clematis in their gardens.

(E) For all nurseries in North America that specialize in clematis, at least ten percent of the clematis plants they sell are *jackmanii*.

CR06422

221. Since 1990 the percentage of bacterial sinus infections in Aqadestan that are resistant to the antibiotic perxicillin has increased substantially. Bacteria can quickly develop resistance to an antibiotic when it is prescribed indiscriminately or when patients fail to take it as prescribed. Since perxicillin has not been indiscriminately prescribed, health officials hypothesize that the increase in perxicillin-resistant sinus infections is largely due to patients' failure to take this medication as prescribed.

Which of the following, if true of Aqadestan, provides most support for the health officials' hypothesis?

(A) Resistance to several other commonly prescribed antibiotics has not increased since 1990 in Aqadestan.

(B) A large number of Aqadestanis never seek medical help when they have a sinus infection.

(C) When it first became available, perxicillin was much more effective in treating bacterial sinus infections than any other antibiotic used for such infections at the time.

(D) Many patients who take perxicillin experience severe side effects within the first few days of their prescribed regimen.

(E) Aqadestani health clinics provide antibiotics to their patients at cost.

CR07793

222. Psychologist: In a study, researchers gave 100 volunteers a psychological questionnaire designed to measure their self-esteem. The researchers then asked each volunteer to rate the strength of his or her own social skills. The volunteers with the highest levels of self-esteem consistently rated themselves as having much better social skills than did the volunteers with moderate levels. This suggests that attaining an exceptionally high level of self-esteem greatly improves one's social skills.

The psychologist's argument is most vulnerable to criticism on which of the following grounds?

(A) It fails to adequately address the possibility that many of the volunteers may not have understood what the psychological questionnaire was designed to measure.

(B) It takes for granted that the volunteers with the highest levels of self-esteem had better social skills than did the other volunteers, even before the former volunteers had attained their high levels of self-esteem.

(C) It overlooks the possibility that people with very high levels of self-esteem may tend to have a less accurate perception of the strength of their own social skills than do people with moderate levels of self-esteem.

(D) It relies on evidence from a group of volunteers that is too small to provide any support for any inferences regarding people in general.

(E) It overlooks the possibility that factors other than level of self-esteem may be of much greater importance in determining the strength of one's social skills.

CR06826

223. A product that represents a clear technological advance over competing products can generally command a high price. Because **technological advances tend to be quickly surpassed** and companies want to make large profits while they still can, **many companies charge the maximum possible price for such a product**. But large profits on the new product will give competitors a strong incentive to quickly match the new product's capabilities. Consequently, the strategy to maximize overall profit from a new product is to charge less than the greatest possible price.

In the argument above, the two portions in **boldface** play which of the following roles?

(A) The first is a consideration raised to argue that a certain strategy is counterproductive; the second presents that strategy.

(B) The first is a consideration raised to support the strategy that the argument recommends; the second presents that strategy.

(C) The first is a consideration raised to help explain the popularity of a certain strategy; the second presents that strategy.

(D) The first is an assumption, rejected by the argument, that has been used to justify a course of action; the second presents that course of action.

(E) The first is a consideration that has been used to justify adopting a certain strategy; the second presents the intended outcome of that strategy.

CR05554

224. Gortland has long been narrowly self-sufficient in both grain and meat. However, as per capita income in Gortland has risen toward the world average, per capita consumption of meat has also risen toward the world average, and it takes several pounds of grain to produce one pound of meat. Therefore, since per capita income continues to rise, whereas domestic grain production will not increase, Gortland will soon have to import either grain or meat or both.

Which of the following is an assumption on which the argument depends?

(A) The total acreage devoted to grain production in Gortland will not decrease substantially.

(B) The population of Gortland has remained relatively constant during the country's years of growing prosperity.

(C) The per capita consumption of meat in Gortland is roughly the same across all income levels.

(D) In Gortland, neither meat nor grain is subject to government price controls.

(E) People in Gortland who increase their consumption of meat will not radically decrease their consumption of grain.

CR05625

225. Political Advertisement:

Mayor Delmont's critics complain about the jobs that were lost in the city under Delmont's leadership. Yet the fact is that not only were more jobs created than were eliminated, but each year since Delmont took office the average pay for the new jobs created has been higher than that year's average pay for jobs citywide. So it stands to reason that throughout Delmont's tenure the average paycheck in this city has been getting steadily bigger.

Which of the following, if true, most seriously weakens the argument in the advertisement?

(A) The unemployment rate in the city is higher today than it was when Mayor Delmont took office.

(B) The average pay for jobs in the city was at a ten-year low when Mayor Delmont took office.

(C) Each year during Mayor Delmont's tenure, the average pay for jobs that were eliminated has been higher than the average pay for jobs citywide.

(D) Most of the jobs eliminated during Mayor Delmont's tenure were in declining industries.

(E) The average pay for jobs in the city is currently lower than it is for jobs in the suburbs surrounding the city.

CR04930

226. To prevent a newly built dam on the Chiff River from blocking the route of fish migrating to breeding grounds upstream, the dam includes a fish pass, a mechanism designed to allow fish through the dam. Before the construction of the dam and fish pass, several thousand fish a day swam upriver during spawning season. But in the first season after the project's completion, only 300 per day made the journey. Clearly, the fish pass is defective.

Which of the following, if true, most seriously weakens the argument?

(A) Fish that have migrated to the upstream breeding grounds do not return down the Chiff River again.

(B) On other rivers in the region, the construction of dams with fish passes has led to only small decreases in the number of fish migrating upstream.

(C) The construction of the dam stirred up potentially toxic river sediments that were carried downstream.

(D) Populations of migratory fish in the Chiff River have been declining slightly over the last 20 years.

(E) During spawning season, the dam releases sufficient water for migratory fish below the dam to swim upstream.

CR09969

227. Music critic: Fewer and fewer musicians are studying classical music, decreasing the likelihood that those with real aptitude for such music will be performing it. Audiences who hear these performances will not appreciate classical music's greatness and will thus decamp to other genres. So to maintain classical music's current meager popularity, we must encourage more young musicians to enter the field.

Which of the following, if true, most weakens the music critic's reasoning?

(A) Musicians who choose to study classical music do so because they believe they have an aptitude for the music.

(B) Classical music's current meager popularity is attributable to the profusion of other genres of music available to listeners.

(C) Most people who appreciate classical music come to do so through old recordings rather than live performances.

(D) It is possible to enjoy the music in a particular genre even when it is performed by musicians who are not ideally suited for that genre.

(E) The continued popularity of a given genre of music depends in part on the audiences being able to understand why that genre attained its original popularity.

CR67850.02

228. People with a college degree are more likely than others to search for a new job while they are employed. There are proportionately more people with college degrees among managers and other professionals than among service and clerical workers. Surprisingly, however, 2009 figures indicate that people employed as managers and other professionals were no more likely than people employed as service and clerical workers to have searched for a new job.

Which of the following, if true, most helps to resolve the apparent paradox?

(A) People generally do not take a new job that is offered to them while they are employed unless the new job pays better.

(B) Some service and clerical jobs pay more than some managerial and professional jobs.

(C) People who felt they were overqualified for their current positions were more likely than others to search for a new job.

(D) The percentage of employed people who were engaged in job searches declined from 2005 to 2009.

(E) In 2009 employees with no college degree who retired were more likely to be replaced by people with a college degree if they retired from a managerial or professional job than from a service or clerical job.

CR20190.02

229. To reduce traffic congestion, City X's transportation bureau plans to encourage people who work downtown to sign a form pledging to carpool or use public transportation for the next year. Everyone who signs the form will get a coupon for a free meal at any downtown restaurant.

For the transportation bureau's plan to succeed in reducing traffic congestion, which of the following must be true?

(A) Everyone who signs the pledge form will fully abide by the pledge for the next year.

(B) At least some people who work downtown prefer the restaurants downtown to those elsewhere.

(C) Most downtown traffic congestion in City X results from people who work downtown.

(D) The most effective way to reduce traffic congestion downtown would be to persuade more people who work there to carpool or use public transportation.

(E) At least some people who receive the coupon for a free meal will sometimes carpool or use public transportation during the next year.

CR05656

230. Commemorative plaques cast from brass are a characteristic art form of the Benin culture of West Africa. Some scholars, noting that the oldest surviving plaques date to the 1400s, hypothesize that brass-casting techniques were introduced by the Portuguese, who came to Benin in 1485 A.D. But Portuguese records of that expedition mention cast-brass jewelry sent to Benin's king from neighboring Ife. So it is unlikely that Benin's knowledge of brass casting derived from the Portuguese.

Which of the following, if true, most strengthens the argument?

(A) The Portuguese records do not indicate whether their expedition of 1485 included metalworkers.

(B) The Portuguese had no contact with Ife until the 1500s.

(C) In the 1400s the Portuguese did not use cast brass for commemorative plaques.

(D) As early as 1500 A.D., Benin artists were making brass plaques incorporating depictions of Europeans.

(E) Copper, which is required for making brass, can be found throughout Benin territory.

CR56601.02

231. When new laws imposing strict penalties for misleading corporate disclosures were passed, they were hailed as initiating an era of corporate openness. As an additional benefit, given the increased amount and accuracy of information disclosed under the new laws, it was assumed that analysts' predictions of corporate performance would become more accurate. Since the passage of the laws, however, the number of inaccurate analysts' predictions has not in fact decreased.

Which of the following would, if true, best explain the discrepancy outlined above?

(A) The new laws' definition of "misleading information" can be interpreted in more than one way.

(B) The new laws require corporations in all industries to release information at specific times of the year.

(C) Even before the new laws were passed, the information most corporations released was true.

(D) Analysts base their predictions on information they gather from many sources, not just corporate disclosures.

(E) The more pieces of information corporations release, the more difficult it becomes for anyone to organize them in a manageable way.

CR50611.02

232. Economist: Even with energy conservation efforts, current technologies cannot support both a reduction in carbon dioxide emissions and an expanding global economy. Attempts to restrain emissions without new technology will stifle economic growth. Therefore, increases in governmental spending on research into energy technology will be necessary if we wish to reduce carbon dioxide emissions without stifling economic growth.

Which of the following is an assumption the economist's argument requires?

(A) If research into energy technology does not lead to a reduction in carbon dioxide emissions, then economic growth will be stifled.

(B) Increased governmental spending on research into energy technology will be more likely to reduce carbon dioxide emissions without stifling growth than will nongovernmental spending.

(C) An expanding global economy may require at least some governmental spending on research into energy technology.

(D) Attempts to restrain carbon dioxide emissions without new technology could ultimately cost more than the failure to reduce those emissions would cost.

(E) Restraining carbon dioxide emissions without stifling economic growth would require both new energy technology and energy conservation efforts.

CR98001.02

233. Researchers have developed a technology that uses sound as a means of converting heat into electrical energy. Converters based on this technology can be manufactured small enough to be integrated into consumer electronics, where they will absorb significant quantities of heat. A group of engineers is now designing converters to be sold to laptop computer manufacturers, who are expected to use the electrical output of the converters to conserve battery power in their computers.

Which of the following would, if true, provide the strongest evidence that the engineers' plan will be commercially successful for their group?

(A) The sound that is used by the converters is generated by the converters themselves.

(B) Most laptop computer manufacturers today receive fewer complaints than in previous years regarding shortness of operating time on a single battery charge.

(C) The overheating of microprocessors in laptop computers presents a major technological challenge that manufacturers are prepared to meet at significant expense.

(D) Although battery technology has improved significantly, the average capacity of laptop computer batteries has not.

(E) Electrical power generated by the converters can be used to power the fans installed to cool computers' components.

5.5 Answer Key

113.	C	138.	C	163.	B	188.	B	213.	A
114.	D	139.	B	164.	C	189.	C	214.	B
115.	D	140.	A	165.	B	190.	E	215.	A
116.	B	141.	A	166.	C	191.	E	216.	B
117.	B	142.	D	167.	C	192.	C	217.	E
118.	A	143.	B	168.	A	193.	E	218.	B
119.	C	144.	B	169.	A	194.	E	219.	D
120.	D	145.	A	170.	A	195.	D	220.	A
121.	B	146.	B	171.	A	196.	D	221.	D
122.	B	147.	A	172.	D	197.	B	222.	C
123.	B	148.	A	173.	D	198.	C	223.	C
124.	A	149.	C	174.	C	199.	C	224.	E
125.	C	150.	C	175.	D	200.	C	225.	C
126.	D	151.	D	176.	C	201.	A	226.	C
127.	E	152.	A	177.	A	202.	E	227.	C
128.	A	153.	A	178.	C	203.	B	228.	C
129.	C	154.	B	179.	C	204.	B	229.	E
130.	A	155.	C	180.	B	205.	D	230.	B
131.	B	156.	B	181.	B	206.	B	231.	E
132.	B	157.	C	182.	C	207.	B	232.	B
133.	A	158.	E	183.	B	208.	D	233.	C
134.	D	159.	D	184.	D	209.	B		
135.	A	160.	E	185.	D	210.	D		
136.	C	161.	C	186.	D	211.	E		
137.	E	162.	C	187.	D	212.	D		

5.6 Answer Explanations

The following discussion is intended to familiarize you with the most efficient and effective approaches to Critical Reasoning questions. The particular questions in this chapter are generally representative of the kinds of Critical Reasoning questions you will encounter on the GMAT exam. Remember that it is the problem solving strategy that is important, not the specific details of a particular question.

Questions 113 to 154 - Difficulty: Easy

*CR14249
113. PhishCo runs a number of farms in the arid province of Nufa, depending largely on irrigation. Now, as part of a plan to efficiently increase the farms' total production, it plans to drill down to an aquifer containing warm, slightly salty water that will be used to raise fish in ponds. The water from the ponds will later be used to supplement piped-in irrigation water for PhishCo's vegetable fields, and the ponds and accompanying vegetation should help reduce the heat in the area of the farms.

Which of the following would, if true, most strongly suggest that the plan, if implemented, would increase the overall efficiency of PhishCo's farms?

(A) Most of the vegetation to be placed around the ponds is native to Nufa.

(B) Fish raised on PhishCo's farms are likely to be saleable in the nearest urban areas.

(C) Organic waste from fish in the pond water will help to fertilize fields where it is used for irrigation.

(D) The government of Nufa will help to arrange loan financing to partially cover the costs of drilling.

(E) Ponds will be located on low-lying land now partially occupied by grain crops.

Evaluation of a Plan

Situation   A company plans to increase the total efficiency of its farms in an arid region by drilling down to an aquifer whose water will be used to raise fish in ponds and to help irrigate the farms' vegetable fields. The ponds and accompanying vegetation should help reduce the heat around the farms.

Reasoning   *What would make it most likely that implementing the plan would increase the farms' overall efficiency?* The farms will become more efficient if the plan significantly increases their production for little or no added cost.

A   Vegetation native to an arid region may be no more likely to thrive around ponds than non-native vegetation would be, and in any case would not clearly increase the farms' total crop production or efficiency.

B   This makes it slightly more likely that the plan would increase the farms' profitability, not their efficiency or productivity.

C   **Correct.** Fertilizing the fields with the waste while irrigating the crops might significantly improve crop production. But it would cost little or nothing extra, since the waste would already be in the irrigation water. Thus, this feature of the plan would likely enhance the farms' efficiency by increasing their productivity for no significant extra cost.

D   This government assistance might slightly reduce the work the company has to do to procure a loan. But probably it would neither increase the farms' production nor reduce the overall expense of implementing the plan (including the expense incurred by the government).

E   If anything, this suggests that the plan might reduce the farms' efficiency by eliminating productive crop land.

The correct answer is C.

---

*These numbers correlate with the online test bank question number. See the GMAT™ Official Guide Verbal Review Question Index in the back of this book.

CR12701.02

114. Stockholders have been critical of the Flyna Company, a major furniture retailer, because most of Flyna's furniture is manufactured in Country X from local wood, and illegal logging is widespread there. However, Flyna has set up a certification scheme for lumber mills. It has hired a staff of auditors and forestry professionals who review documentation of the wood supply of Country X's lumber mills to ensure its legal origin, make surprise visits to mills to verify documents, and certify mills as approved sources of legally obtained lumber. Flyna uses only lumber from certified mills. Thus, Flyna's claim that its Country X wood supply is obtained legally is justified.

Which of the following, if true, would most undermine the justification provided for Flyna's claim?

(A) Only about one-third of Flyna's inspectors were hired from outside the company.

(B) Country X's government recently reduced its subsidies for lumber production.

(C) Flyna has had to pay higher than expected salaries to attract qualified inspectors.

(D) The proportion of Country X's lumber mills inspected each year by Flyna's staff is about 10 percent, randomly selected.

(E) Illegal logging costs Country X's government a significant amount in lost revenue each year.

Argument Evaluation

Situation   The Flyna Company sells furniture mostly made in Country X from local wood. Illegal logging is widespread in Country X. Flyna has set up a certification scheme for lumber mills. Specialized staff make surprise visits to Country X mills, inspect documentation to ensure that the wood supply has a legal origin, and certify mills as approved sources for legally obtained lumber. Flyna uses only lumber from certified mills. According to the argument, Flyna's claim that its wood supply is legally obtained is justified.

Reasoning   *What additional information would, if true, most undermine the justification for Flyna's claim that its Country X wood is legally obtained?* Clearly, much depends on the thoroughness of the certification scheme. For example, the staff auditing the mills would need to be qualified for the job and meticulous in meeting their responsibilities. The auditing visits would need to be frequent enough, and not predictable by mill management. Flyna would need to be genuinely committed to ensuring legality of wood sources; it would need to monitor its staff to ensure that they were doing their jobs effectively.

A   This suggests that Flyna could make good judgments as to the competence and trustworthiness of most of the inspectors hired to certify lumber mills.

B   This could provide a perverse incentive to loggers to violate legal restrictions on logging. However, this would not undercut Flyna's justification for its claim that its system ensures that all its lumber is legally sourced.

C   This has no bearing on whether Flyna's certification system will be effective in guaranteeing that Flyna's lumber is legally sourced. We are not told, for example, that Flyna has been unable to find enough qualified inspectors for the certification system to be effective.

D   **Correct.** This means that 90 percent of Country X's certified lumber mills are not inspected in any particular year. Moreover, since the selection of the 10 percent of lumber mills to be inspected in a given year is random, some lumber mills might go for much longer than ten years without inspection; during this period, many of those mills might fall below certification standards and even use lumber illegally obtained.

E   This indicates that a significant amount of illegal logging occurs in Country X; this suggests that it is possible that some illegally sourced wood could find its way to lumber mills that Flyna uses and has certified. But the information given here is not sufficiently specific to indicate that the Flyna certification system would fail to prevent the company's use of illegally sourced wood.

The correct answer is D.

CR12721.02
115. The *XCT* automobile is considered less valuable than the *ZNK* automobile, because insurance companies pay less, on average, to replace a stolen *XCT* than a stolen *ZNK*. Surprisingly, the average amount insurance companies will pay to repair a car involved in a collision is typically higher for the *XCT* than for the *ZNK*. One insurance expert explained that repairs to *XCT* automobiles are especially labor-intensive, and labor is a significant factor in collision repair costs.

Which of the following, if true, most strongly supports the insurance expert's explanation?

(A) *ZNK* automobiles are involved in accidents more frequently than *XCT* automobiles.

(B) The cost of routine maintenance for the *ZNK* is about the same as for the *XCT*.

(C) There are more automobile mechanics who specialize in *XCT* repairs than in *ZNK* repairs.

(D) The ease of repair of *ZNK* automobiles is one factor that adds to their value.

(E) *XCT* automobiles are more likely to be stolen than *ZNK* automobiles.

Argument Evaluation

Situation   Two automobile models *XCT* and *ZNK* are compared with respect to (1) what insurance companies pay on average to replace a stolen vehicle and (2) what insurance companies pay on average to repair a crashed vehicle. On (1), insurance companies pay less for XCTs than for *ZNK*s. On (2), insurance companies pay more for repairing *XCT*s than *ZNK*s. An insurance expert explains that repairs to XCTs are especially labor-intensive; this tends to raise the cost of repairs.

Reasoning   *Which piece of new information most strongly supports the expert's explanation for the fact that the replacement value is greater for the car that has lower repair costs?* We should look for information that supplements the explanation in a way that shows the coherence of the two facts given regarding insurance payments for the two cars.

A   The frequency of accidents is not directly relevant to the higher cost of collision repair for those *XCT*s that are involved in collisions.

B   This information is not directly relevant to the higher cost of collision repair for *XCT*s. It neither undermines nor supports the claim that *XCT* labor costs are higher per crashed vehicle and does not help support that claim as an explanation for the discrepancy in question.

C   This neither supports nor undermines the expert's explanation. If we had information concerning the supply of *XCT* mechanics and *ZNK* mechanics relative to the demand for each, we would have some evidence that could throw light on differences in labor costs.

D   **Correct.** *ZNK*s are more valuable because buyers know that total repair costs will be lower. This is reflected in the market value of *ZNK*s compared to that of *XCT*s. Replacing a stolen *XCT* costs insurance companies less than replacing a stolen *ZNK* because the lower market value of *XCT*s is related in the high cost of collision repair.

E   This is unlikely to lower the market value of *XCT*s. The market value of *XCT*s is the factor that determines how much it costs to replace a stolen *XCT*.

The correct answer is D.

CR07612

116. The sustained massive use of pesticides in farming has two effects that are especially pernicious. First, it often kills off the pests' natural enemies in the area. Second, it often unintentionally gives rise to insecticide-resistant pests, since those insects that survive a particular insecticide will be the ones most resistant to it, and they are the ones left to breed.

From the passage above, it can be properly inferred that the effectiveness of the sustained massive use of pesticides can be extended by doing which of the following, assuming that each is a realistic possibility?

(A) Using only chemically stable insecticides

(B) Periodically switching the type of insecticide used

(C) Gradually increasing the quantities of pesticides used

(D) Leaving a few fields fallow every year

(E) Breeding higher-yielding varieties of crop plants

Evaluation of a Plan

Situation Continued high-level pesticide use often kills off the targeted pests' natural enemies. In addition, the pests that survive the application of the pesticide may become resistant to it, and these pesticide-resistant pests will continue breeding.

Reasoning *What can be done to prolong the effectiveness of pesticide use?* It can be inferred that the ongoing use of a particular pesticide will not continue to be effective against the future generations of pests with an inherent resistance to that pesticide. What would be effective against these future generations? If farmers periodically change the particular pesticide they use, then pests resistant to one kind of pesticide might be killed by another. This would continue, with pests being killed off in cycles as the pesticides are changed. It is also possible that this rotation might allow some of the pests' natural enemies to survive, at least until the next cycle.

A   Not enough information about chemically stable insecticides is given to make a sound inference.

B   Correct. This statement properly identifies an action that could extend the effectiveness of pesticide use.

C   Gradually increasing the amount of the pesticides being used will not help the situation since the pests are already resistant to it.

D   Continued use of pesticides is assumed as part of the argument. Since pesticides would be unnecessary for fallow fields, this suggestion is irrelevant.

E   Breeding higher-yielding varieties of crops does nothing to extend the effectiveness of the use of pesticides.

The correct answer is B.

CR00701

117. Which of the following, if true, most logically completes the argument below?

Manufacturers are now required to make all cigarette lighters child-resistant by equipping them with safety levers. But this change is unlikely to result in a significant reduction in the number of fires caused by children playing with lighters, because children given the opportunity can figure out how to work the safety levers and _____.

(A) the addition of the safety levers has made lighters more expensive than they were before the requirement was instituted

(B) adults are more likely to leave child-resistant lighters than non-child-resistant lighters in places that are accessible to children

(C) many of the fires started by young children are quickly detected and extinguished by their parents

(D) unlike child-resistant lighters, lighters that are not child-resistant can be operated by children as young as two years old

(E) approximately 5,000 fires per year have been attributed to children playing with lighters before the safety levers were required.

Argument Construction

Situation   Manufacturers must equip all cigarette lighters with child-resistant safety levers, but children can figure out how to circumvent the safety levers and thereby often start fires.

Reasoning   *What point would most logically complete the argument?* What would make it likely that the number of fires caused by children playing with lighters would remain the same? In order for children to start fires using lighters equipped with safety levers, they must be given the opportunity to figure out how the safety levers work and then to use them. They must, that is, have access to the lighters.

A   If safety-lever-equipped lighters are more expensive than lighters that are not so equipped, fewer lighters might be sold. This would most likely afford children less access to lighters, thus giving them less opportunity to start fires with them.

B   **Correct.** This statement properly identifies a point that logically completes the argument: it explains why children are likely to have access to lighters equipped with safety levers.

C   The speed with which fires are extinguished does not have any bearing on the number of fires that are started.

D   This provides a reason to believe that the number of fires started by children will most likely decrease, rather than stay the same: fewer children will be able to operate the lighters, and thus fewer fires are likely to be started.

E   This information about how many fires were started by children before safety levers were required does not have any bearing on the question of how many fires are likely to be started by children now that the safety levers are required.

The correct answer is B.

CR04192
118. Which of the following most logically completes the passage?

A business analysis of the Appenian railroad system divided its long-distance passenger routes into two categories: rural routes and interurban routes. The analysis found that, unlike the interurban routes, few rural routes carried a high enough passenger volume to be profitable. Closing unprofitable rural routes, however, will not necessarily enhance the profitability of the whole system, since _____.

(A) a large part of the passenger volume on interurban routes is accounted for by passengers who begin or end their journeys on rural routes

(B) within the last two decades several of the least used rural routes have been closed and their passenger services have been replaced by buses

(C) the rural routes were all originally constructed at least one hundred years ago, whereas some of the interurban routes were constructed recently for new high-speed express trains

(D) not all of Appenia's large cities are equally well served by interurban railroad services

(E) the greatest passenger volume, relative to the routes' capacity, is not on either category of long-distance routes but is on suburban commuter routes

Argument Construction

Situation   In the Appenian railroad system, interurban routes generally carry enough passengers to be profitable, but few rural routes do.

Reasoning   *What would suggest that closing unprofitable rural routes would not enhance the railroad system's profitability?* Any evidence that closing the unprofitable rural routes would indirectly reduce the profitability of other components of the railroad system would support the conclusion that closing those rural routes will not enhance the system's profitability. Thus, a statement providing such evidence would logically complete the passage.

A   **Correct.** This suggests that closing the rural routes could discourage many passengers from traveling on the profitable interurban routes as well, thus reducing the profitability of the railroad system as a whole.

B   Even if some of the least used rural routes have already been closed, it remains true that most of the remaining rural routes are too little used to be profitable.

C   Closing very old routes would be at least as likely to enhance the railroad system's profitability as closing newer routes would be.

D   Even if there is better railroad service to some large cities than others, closing unprofitable rural routes could still enhance the system's profitability.

E   Even if suburban routes are the most heavily used and profitable, closing underused, unprofitable rural routes could still enhance the system's profitability.

The correct answer is A.

CR52441.01

119. In its search for new technologies for solar energy that can produce lower-cost electricity, Smith-Diatom is developing a new way to make dye-sensitive solar cells, in which photons strike light-sensitive dyes. The process uses diatoms, which are unicellular algae that have silicon shells with a complex structure. First, the organic material is removed, and then the shells are coated with a titanium dioxide film that acts as a semiconductor. The diatoms' structure results in more photon activity and thus more efficient production of electricity than with current dye-sensitized solar cells, which in turn lowers the cost.

Which of the following considerations would, if true, most strongly support the hypothesis that the plan, if implemented, will produce low-cost electricity from dye-sensitive solar cells?

(A) Diatoms are an important link in oceanic food chains and help cycle carbon dioxide from the atmosphere.

(B) The current cost of electricity produced by dye-sensitive solar cells is roughly three times that of non-solar electricity.

(C) Because diatoms occur naturally, no special engineering processes are needed to produce the basic dye-sensitive solar cell structures.

(D) Dye-sensitive solar cells work somewhat more efficiently in lower light than previous solar cell technologies.

(E) The production of dye-sensitive solar cells primarily uses materials that do not harm the environment.

Evaluation of a Plan

Situation Smith-Diatom is trying to develop a new way to make dye-sensitive solar cells in hopes of developing a means for using solar energy to produce lower-cost electricity. Their new technology will use diatoms, single-celled algae with silicon shells that have a complex structure. This structure results in increased photon activity, which results in more efficient and lower-cost energy production than current dye-sensitive solar cells do.

Reasoning *What statement would provide the strongest support for the claim that Smith-Diatom's plan would result in the production of lower-cost energy than can be attained from the current dye-sensitive solar cells?* One potential problem with Smith-Diatom's plan would be if the intended use of diatoms would be costly. Any statement that ruled out a potentially costly aspects of production, e.g., costly engineering processes, would provide support for the claim in question.

A Nothing in Smith-Diatom's plan is related to diatom's connection to oceanic food chains or to their role in cycling carbon dioxide from the atmosphere.

B That producing electricity by means of dye-sensitive solar cells is much more costly than other types of electricity production would help explain why Smith-Diatom wants to find a lower-cost means of producing solar energy, but it does not give us reason to think that Smith-Diatom's plan will be successful.

C **Correct.** If no special engineering processes are needed to carry out Smith-Diatom's plan, one potential costly aspect of solar-electricity production is ruled out, thereby providing some reason to think Smith-Diatom's goal of producing lower-cost electricity might be attainable.

D The fact that dye-sensitive solar cells work more efficiently in lower light than other solar cell technologies would help support the claim in question only if we knew that the cost of producing such cells is not prohibitive. Also, it could be the case that although dye-sensitive solar cells work more efficiently in lower light than other solar cell technologies, the other solar cell technologies might work much more efficiently in good lighting conditions.

E If the production of dye-sensitive solar cells does not harm the environment, that might be good reason to use such solar cells, but it is not relevant to determining whether Smith-Diatom's plan will be likely to attain its goal.

The correct answer is C.

CR03129

120. Although Ackerburg's subway system is currently operating at a deficit, the transit authority will lower subway fares next year. The authority projects that the lower fares will result in a ten percent increase in the number of subway riders. Since the additional income from the larger ridership will more than offset the decrease due to lower fares, the transit authority actually expects the fare reduction to reduce or eliminate the subway system's operating deficit for next year.

Which of the following, if true, provides the most support for the transit authority's expectation of reducing the subway system's operating deficit?

(A) Throughout the years that the subway system has operated, fares have never before been reduced.

(B) The planned fare reduction will not apply to students, who can already ride the subway for a reduced fare.

(C) Next year, the transit authority will have to undertake several large-scale track maintenance projects.

(D) The subway system can accommodate a ten percent increase in ridership without increasing the number of trains it runs each day.

(E) The current subway fares in Ackerburg are higher than subway fares in other cities in the region.

Argument Evaluation

Situation   Ackerburg's transit authority plans to lower subway fares, projecting that this will increase ridership by 10 percent and thereby reduce or eliminate the subway system's operating deficit.

Reasoning   *What evidence would support the expectation that lowering subway fares will reduce the operating deficit?* The passage says the additional income from the projected increase in ridership will more than offset the decrease due to the lowered fares. The claim that lowering fares will reduce the operating deficit could be supported either by additional evidence that lowering the fares will increase ridership at least as much as projected or by evidence that the plan will not increase overall operating expenses.

A   The fact that fares have never been reduced provides no evidence about what would happen if they were reduced.

B   This suggests that the planned fare reduction would not affect revenue from student riders, but it does not suggest how it would affect revenue from all other riders.

C   These maintenance projects will probably increase the operating deficit, making it less likely that the fare reduction will reduce or eliminate that deficit.

D   **Correct.** This indicates that the plan will not involve extra operating expenses for running trains and thus increases the likelihood that the plan will reduce the operating deficit.

E   Ackerburg may differ from other cities in the region in ways that make the higher fares optimal for Ackerburg's subway system.

The correct answer is D.

CR59590.02

121. At several locations on the northwest coast of North America are formations known as chevrons—wedge-shaped formations of mounded sediment—pointing toward the ocean. Most geologists take them to have been formed by erosion, but recently other scientists have proposed that they were thrown up from the ocean by massive waves triggered by meteor impacts in the Pacific Ocean.

Which of the following, if discovered, would most help in deciding which hypothesis is correct?

(A) Chevron-like structures which are not currently near glaciers, large rivers, or other bodies of water

(B) The presence, in chevrons, of deposits of ocean microfossils containing metals typically formed by meteor impacts

(C) Oral-history evidence for flooding that could have been caused by ocean waves

(D) The fact that exact data about the location and depth of any meteor impact craters on the Pacific seabed is lacking

(E) The fact that certain changes in the shape and location of maritime sand dunes have been produced by the action of wind and waves

Argument Evaluation

Situation   The northwest coast of North America has chevrons—large wedge-shaped mounds of sediment—pointing toward the ocean. Two explanations have been offered for these phenomena: (1) they were formed by erosion, according to most geologists; and (2) meteor impacts caused massive waves that threw the formations up from the Pacific Ocean.

Reasoning   *Which of the answer choices most helps to decide which explanation is correct?* If (2) is the true explanation, then one would expect evidence such as residues of ocean matter to be present in chevrons. If (1) is the true explanation, the chevrons would need to be analyzed to determine the sources of the eroded material, and the factors, such as wind or water, that produced the erosion.

A   This information neither confirms nor conclusively eliminates either explanation (1) or explanation (2). The scientists hypothesize is that these chevrons, at these locations on the coast, were caused by meteor impacts, not that geological structures with a similar shape are generally formed in that way. The scientists' reasoning is consistent with the hypothesis that different wedge-shaped geological structures are formed in many different ways.

B   **Correct.** The ocean microfossils containing metals typically found in meteors would indicate that the metals were found in fossils that originated in the ocean. This provides strong evidence that meteors landed in the ocean; the fact that the metals are now found in the chevrons strongly supports explanation (2).

C   The oral-history testimony concerning flooding by ocean waves provides weak evidence consistent with each of the two explanations. Erosion of rocks can deposit sediment, and ocean waves could form mounds of such sediment.

D   This information points out that some additional bits of evidence that might help confirm explanation (2) are currently lacking, but such evidence might be discovered later, and the impacts might have occurred so long ago that all evidence of their exact locations has been obliterated. The fact that such evidence happens to be lacking now does not significantly count for or against either of the proposed explanations.

E   This indicates that some types of sedimentary structures (such as sand dunes) can be shaped by ocean waves, but it gives no evidence of whether the chevrons might have originated as sand dunes. It also gives no indication of whether the dunes in question have a chevron shape or some other shape. So this does not provide information to significantly support either of the explanations.

The correct answer is B.

CR20531.01

122. Sparrow Airlines is planning to reduce its costs by cleaning its planes' engines once a month, rather than the industry standard of every six months. With cleaner engines, Sparrow can postpone engine overhauls, which take planes out of service for up to 18 months. Furthermore, cleaning an engine reduces its fuel consumption by roughly 1.2 percent.

The airline's plan assumes that

(A)   fuel prices are likely to rise in the near future and therefore cutting fuel consumption is an important goal

(B)   the cost of monthly cleaning of an airplane's engines is not significantly greater in the long run than is the cost of an engine overhaul

(C)   engine cleaning does not remove an airplane from service

(D)   Sparrow Airlines has had greater problems with engine overhauls and fuel consumption than other airlines have

(E)   cleaning engines once a month will give Sparrow Airlines a competitive advantage over other airlines

Evaluation of a Plan

Situation   Sparrow Airlines plans to clean the engines of its planes monthly rather than every six months. The goal is to reduce its costs.

Reasoning   *Which statement provides an assumption underlying the plan?* The plan will enable Sparrow to postpone engine overhauls, which put a plane out of service for up to 18 months. The monthly cleaning will reduce its fuel consumption by 1.2 percent. But suppose the long-run cost of monthly cleanings were greater than the cost of an engine overhaul, then the rationale for the airline's plan would fail.

A   Nothing in the information provided indicates that this is assumed in the plan.

B   **Correct.** The plan makes sense only if this is assumed. If the long-run total cost of monthly cleaning significantly exceeded the total cost of engine overhaul—which would include, in the long run, more frequent downtime of 18 months if the plan were not adopted—then it seems likely that the projected benefit of postponement of engine overhauls would not be compensated for by the 1.2 percent fuel-cost savings.

C   The plan does not have to assume this. Perhaps monthly engine cleaning requires only one day of down time.

D   This is perhaps a good reason for Sparrow to put in place the proposed cost-saving plan, but it is not an assumption that the plan requires for it to make sense.

E   The plan does not have to assume this, even if Sparrow's cost saving were to result in a competitive advantage. Sparrow's plan could equally be aimed at simply removing a competitive disadvantage. The issue of competition is not addressed in the given information.

The correct answer is B.

CR00828

123. Patrick usually provides child care for six children. Parents leave their children at Patrick's house in the morning and pick them up after work. At the end of each workweek, the parents pay Patrick at an hourly rate for the child care provided that week. The weekly income Patrick receives is usually adequate but not always uniform, particularly in the winter, when children are likely to get sick and be unpredictably absent.

Which of the following plans, if put into effect, has the best prospect of making Patrick's weekly income both uniform and adequate?

(A) Pool resources with a neighbor who provides child care under similar arrangements, so that the two of them cooperate in caring for twice as many children as Patrick currently does.

(B) Replace payment by actual hours of child care provided with a fixed weekly fee based upon the number of hours of child care that Patrick would typically be expected to provide.

(C) Hire a full-time helper and invest in facilities for providing child care to sick children.

(D) Increase the hourly rate to a level that would provide adequate income even in a week when half of the children Patrick usually cares for are absent.

(E) Increase the number of hours made available for child care each day, so that parents can leave their children in Patrick's care for a longer period each day at the current hourly rate.

Evaluation of a Plan

Situation   At the end of the workweek, Patrick is paid a certain amount for each hour of child care he has provided. Patrick usually receives adequate weekly income under this arrangement, but in the winter Patrick's income fluctuates, because children are unpredictably absent due to illness.

Reasoning   *Which plan would be most likely to meet the two goals of uniform weekly income and adequate weekly income?* Patrick must find a way to ensure that his weekly income is both adequate—that is, not reduced significantly from current levels—and uniform—that is, not subject to seasonal or other fluctuations. A successful plan would thus most likely be one that does not increase Patrick's costs. Further, the plan need not increase Patrick's weekly income; it must merely ensure that that income is more reliable. It should therefore also provide some way to mitigate the unexpected loss of income from children's absences.

A   This plan might raise Patrick's income slightly, because he and the neighbor might pay out less in costs if they pool their resources. But this plan would have no effect on the problem that unpredictable absences pose for Patrick's weekly income.

B   **Correct.** This statement properly identifies a plan that would most likely keep Patrick's income adequate (he would probably receive approximately the same amount of money per child as he does now) and uniform (he would receive the money regardless of whether a child was present or absent).

C   While this plan might somewhat mitigate the unpredictability in Patrick's income that results from sick children's absences—because parents would be less likely to keep sick children at home—it would increase Patrick's costs. Paying a helper and investing in different facilities would reduce Patrick's income and might thus result in that income being inadequate.

D   Under this plan, if we assume that parents did not balk at the increase in Patrick's hourly rate and find alternative child care, Patrick's income would most likely be adequate. But this plan would not help make Patrick's weekly income uniform. His income would continue to fluctuate when children are absent. Remember, there are two goals with regard to Patrick's income: adequacy and uniformity.

E   This plan might increase Patrick's income, in that he might be paid for more hours of child care each week. The goals here, however, are to make Patrick's weekly income both adequate and uniform, and this plan does not address the issue of uniformity.

The correct answer is B.

CR10639

124. Editorial: Consumers in North America think that by drinking frozen concentrated orange juice, they are saving energy, because it takes fewer truckloads to transport it than it takes to transport an equivalent amount of not-from-concentrate juice. But they are mistaken, for the amount of energy required to concentrate the juice is far greater than the energy difference in the juices' transport.

Which of the following, if true, would provide the greatest additional support for the editorial's conclusion?

(A)   Freezer trucks use substantially more energy per mile driven than do any other types of trucks.

(B)   Frozen juice can be stored for several years, while not-from-concentrate juice lasts a much shorter time.

(C)   Oranges grown in Brazil make up an increasing percentage of the fruit used in not-from-concentrate juice production.

(D)   A serving of not-from-concentrate juice takes up to six times more space than a serving of frozen concentrated juice.

(E)   Though frozen concentrated juice must be kept at a lower temperature, not-from-concentrate juice is far more sensitive to small temperature fluctuations.

Argument Evaluation

Situation   North American consumers think that drinking frozen concentrated orange juice saves energy because the concentrated juice can be transported in fewer truckloads than an equivalent amount of not-from-concentrate juice. But more energy is required to concentrate the juice than is saved by this reduction in the number of truckloads used for transportation.

Reasoning   *What additional evidence would most help to support the conclusion that drinking frozen concentrated orange juice rather than not-from-concentrate juice does not save energy?* Factors other than the concentration process and the number of truckloads used for transportation may also affect the amounts of energy used to provide the two types of juice. Evidence of any such factor that increases the amount of energy needed to provide frozen concentrated juice more than it increases the amount needed to provide the same amount of not-from-concentrate juice would help to support the editorial's conclusion.

A   **Correct.** This suggests that it takes much more energy per truckload to transport frozen concentrated juice than to transport not-from-concentrate juice, which is not frozen.

B   If anything, this suggests that a higher proportion of not-from-concentrate juice goes bad and is discarded rather than being drunk. This waste would increase the amount of energy used to provide each glass of not-from-concentrate juice that is drunk.

C   Since Brazil is far from North America, this suggests that the average amount of energy used to transport each serving of not-from-concentrate juice may be increasing.

D   Since both types of juice must be kept cold until ready to drink, this suggests that a much larger amount of space must be refrigerated to provide each serving of not-from-concentrate juice. That may mean that more energy needs to be used to keep each serving of not-from-concentrate juice cold.

E   It may take extra energy to keep the temperature of not-from-concentrate juice more constant. If it does, that would increase the amount of energy used to provide each serving of not-from-concentrate juice.

The correct answer is A.

CR07618

125. A computer equipped with signature-recognition software, which restricts access to a computer to those people whose signatures are on file, identifies a person's signature by analyzing not only the form of the signature but also such characteristics as pen pressure and signing speed. Even the most adept forgers cannot duplicate all of the characteristics the program analyzes.

Which of the following can be logically concluded from the passage above?

(A) The time it takes to record and analyze a signature makes the software impractical for everyday use.

(B) Computers equipped with the software will soon be installed in most banks.

(C) Nobody can gain access to a computer equipped with the software solely by virtue of skill at forging signatures.

(D) Signature-recognition software has taken many years to develop and perfect.

(E) In many cases even authorized users are denied legitimate access to computers equipped with the software.

Argument Construction

Situation Forgers cannot duplicate all the characteristics that signature-recognition software analyzes, including the form of a signature, pen pressure, and signing speed. Computers equipped with this software restrict access to those whose signatures are on file.

Reasoning *What conclusion can be reached about computers equipped with this software?* The passage states that the software detects more characteristics in a signature than the most accomplished forger can possibly reproduce. Thus, skill at forging signatures is not enough to allow someone to gain access to a computer equipped with the software.

A No information about the speed of the analysis is given, so no such conclusion can be drawn.

B Although the software would likely be of benefit to banks, we cannot conclude that it will be installed in most banks because the passage doesn't rule out, e.g., that the software may be too costly or that there may be proprietary constraints.

C **Correct.** This statement properly identifies a conclusion that can be drawn from the passage.

D Although it seems reasonable to think that the software took a long time to develop, nothing in the passage justifies the claim that it took years.

E Nothing in the passage rules out the possibility that the software functions so well that authorized users will never be denied legitimate access to computers equipped with the software.

The correct answer is C.

126. The rate at which a road wears depends on various factors, including climate, amount of traffic, and the size and weight of the vehicles using it. The only land transportation to Rittland's seaport is via a divided highway, one side carrying traffic to the seaport and one carrying traffic away from it. The side leading to the seaport has worn faster, even though each side has carried virtually the same amount of traffic, consisting mainly of large trucks.

Which of the following, if true, most helps to explain the difference in the rate of wear?

(A) The volume of traffic to and from Rittland's seaport has increased beyond the intended capacity of the highway that serves it.

(B) Wear on the highway that serves Rittland's seaport is considerably greater during the cold winter months.

(C) Wear on the side of the highway that leads to Rittland's seaport has encouraged people to take buses to the seaport rather than driving there in their own automobiles.

(D) A greater tonnage of goods is exported from Rittland's seaport than is imported through it.

(E) All of Rittland's automobiles are imported by ship.

Argument Construction

Situation   The side of a divided highway leading to a seaport has worn faster than the side leading away from the seaport. Both sides carry roughly the same amount of traffic, mainly consisting of large trucks.

Reasoning   *What could explain why the side of the highway leading to the seaport has worn faster than the other side?* We are told that climate, amount of traffic, and the size and weight of vehicles on a road affect how quickly the road wears. We are also told that the amounts of traffic on the two sides of the highway are almost identical. Probably the climate on the two sides is also almost identical. Thus, the most likely explanation for the different rates of wear is that the size or weight of the vehicles driving on the two sides differs significantly. So any factor that would make the vehicles' size or weight greater on the side leading to the seaport than on the other side could help explain the difference in wearing.

A   The increased traffic volume affects both sides of the highway, so it does not help explain why one side is wearing faster than the other.

B   The winter weather affects both sides of the highway, so it does not help explain why one side is wearing faster than the other.

C   The buses may contribute to wear on the side of the highway leading to the seaport, but not necessarily more than the car traffic they are replacing would (though the increased use of buses instead of cars may decrease the amount of traffic, buses would be heavier than cars and thus may result in an equal or greater amount of wear). Furthermore, the buses have to come back on the other side, probably carrying the returning travelers who have not left their cars at the airport.

D   Correct. This suggests that the many trucks visiting the seaport tend to be more heavily laden with goods when traveling on the side of the highway leading to the seaport than when returning on the other side. The resulting difference in the trucks' weight when traveling on the two sides could explain the different rates of wear.

E   These automobiles would be transported along the side of the highway leading from the seaport, but not along the side leading to it. This would likely create a pattern of wear opposite to the one observed.

The correct answer is D.

CR75231.01

127. Ythex has developed a small diesel engine that produces 30 percent less particulate pollution than the engine made by its main rival, Onez, now widely used in Marania; Ythex's engine is well-suited for use in the thriving warehousing businesses in Marania, although it costs more than the Onez engine. The Maranian government plans to ban within the next two years the use of diesel engines with more than 80 percent of current diesel engine particulate emissions in Marania, and Onez will probably not be able to retool its engine to reduce emissions to reach this target. So if the ban is passed, the Ythex engine ought to sell well in Marania after that time.

Which of the following is an assumption on which the argument above depends?

(A) Marania's warehousing and transshipment business buys more diesel engines of any size than other types of engines.

(B) Ythex is likely to be able to reduce the cost of its small diesel engine within the next two years.

(C) The Maranian government is generally favorable to anti-pollution regulations.

(D) The government's ban on high levels of pollution caused by diesel engines, if passed, will not be difficult to enforce.

(E) The other manufacturers of small diesel engines in Marania, if there are any, have not produced an engine as popular and clean-running as Ythex's new engine.

Argument Evaluation

Situation   Two companies, Ythex and Onez, produce diesel engines in Marania. Ythex has developed a small engine that produces less particulate pollution than the engine made by Onez, its main rival. The Maranian government will put a new maximum particulate-emission level in force within two years, but Onez will not be able to meet this target.

Reasoning   *What would have to be assumed for the argument to support the prediction that Ythex's engine will sell well in two years when the new maximum particulate level is introduced?* To answer this, one might ask, for example: Will the maximum level be efficiently enforced? Will Ythex have any rivals other than Onez that will compete in the low-pollution diesel market?

A   This tells us that there is a significant market for diesel engines, but this not an assumption that the reasoning depends on. The reasoning focuses only on the market for diesel engines and does not address the relative sizes of the market for diesel engines and that for non-diesel engines.

B   If this is true, it provides additional support for the conclusion that Ythex's engine will sell well in two years. However, it is not an assumption on which the reasoning relies.

C   This information is peripheral to the reasoning and not an assumption on which the reasoning relies. Adding it to the information given would not make the reasoning more logically compelling.

D   The ban might be quite difficult to enforce, but a more important issue is whether the ban will be effectively enforced (so the reasoning does have to assume that the ban would be at least somewhat effective). No assumption about the relative difficulty of enforcing the ban needs to be made for the reasoning to be logically compelling.

E   **Correct.** Are there one or more diesel engines from other companies that will be able to compete effectively with Ythex's engine when the ban is introduced? For the reasoning to be logically compelling, it needs to be assumed that the answer is no.

The correct answer is E.

CR04073

128. In parts of South America, vitamin-A deficiency is a serious health problem, especially among children. In one region, agriculturists are attempting to improve nutrition by encouraging farmers to plant a new variety of sweet potato called SPK004 that is rich in beta-carotene, which the body converts into vitamin A. The plan has good chances of success, since sweet potato is a staple of the region's diet and agriculture, and the varieties currently grown contain little beta-carotene.

Which of the following, if true, most strongly supports the prediction that the plan will succeed?

(A) The growing conditions required by the varieties of sweet potato currently cultivated in the region are conditions in which SPK004 can flourish.

(B) The flesh of SPK004 differs from that of the currently cultivated sweet potatoes in color and texture, so traditional foods would look somewhat different when prepared from SPK004.

(C) There are no other varieties of sweet potato that are significantly richer in beta-carotene than SPK004 is.

(D) The varieties of sweet potato currently cultivated in the region contain some important nutrients that are lacking in SPK004.

(E) There are other vegetables currently grown in the region that contain more beta-carotene than the currently cultivated varieties of sweet potato do.

Evaluation of a Plan

Situation   Agriculturists believe that if farmers in a particular South American region plant a new beta-carotene-rich variety of sweet potato, SPK004, the vitamin-A deficiency suffered in that region can be alleviated. Even though sweet potatoes are a staple of the region and the body can convert a sweet potato's beta-carotene into vitamin A, the varieties currently grown there contain little beta-carotene.

Reasoning   *What would most support the success of the plan to improve nutrition by encouraging farmers to plant SPK004?* What, that is, would make farmers respond positively to encouragement to plant SPK004? Farmers in the region would probably be inclined to substitute SPK004 for the varieties of sweet potato they currently grow if they could be assured that SPK004 would grow as well as those other varieties do. This would in turn most likely lead to SPK004 being substituted for current varieties of sweet potato in staple dishes, and thus to an improvement in nutrition in the region.

A   **Correct.** This statement properly identifies a factor that would support a prediction of the plan's success.

B   If dishes made with SPK004 look different than traditional sweet potato dishes in the region do, people might be less likely to eat those dishes; in such a situation, the plan's success would be less likely, rather than more likely.

C   It is SPK004's beta-carotene content relative to the beta-carotene content of the sweet potatoes currently grown in the region that is relevant here, so it does not matter if there are other varieties of sweet potato that are richer in beta-carotene than SPK004 is.

D   This suggests that switching from currently grown sweet potatoes to SPK004 could negatively affect nutrition in the region; this undermines, rather than supports, the prediction that the plan to improve nutrition will succeed.

E   These other vegetables, despite their beta-carotene content being higher than that of the currently cultivated varieties of sweet potato, are clearly not sufficient to prevent a vitamin-A deficiency in the region. This information does nothing to support the prediction that encouraging farmers to plant SPK004 will help to meet those beta-carotene needs.

The correct answer is A.

CR06018

129. Which of the following most logically completes the argument?

The last members of a now-extinct species of a European wild deer called the giant deer lived in Ireland about 16,000 years ago. Prehistoric cave paintings in France depict this animal as having a large hump on its back. Fossils of this animal, however, do not show any hump. Nevertheless, there is no reason to conclude that the cave paintings are therefore inaccurate in this regard, since _____.

(A) some prehistoric cave paintings in France also depict other animals as having a hump

(B) fossils of the giant deer are much more common in Ireland than in France

(C) animal humps are composed of fatty tissue, which does not fossilize

(D) the cave paintings of the giant deer were painted well before 16,000 years ago

(E) only one currently existing species of deer has any anatomical feature that even remotely resembles a hump

Argument Construction

Situation   Representations found in prehistoric cave paintings in France of the now-extinct giant deer species—the last members of which lived in Ireland about 16,000 years ago—depict the deer as having a hump on its back. Fossils of the deer, however, do not feature a hump.

Reasoning   *What point would most logically complete the argument? That is, what would show that the cave paintings are not inaccurate even though fossils of the giant deer show no hump?* How could it be the case that the paintings show a hump while the fossils do not? One way in which this could be so is if the humps are not part of the fossils—that is, if there is some reason why a hump would not be preserved with the rest of an animal's remains.

A   We do not know whether these other cave paintings accurately depict the animals as having humps, so this provides no reason to think that the depictions of giant deer are accurate.

B   Where giant deer fossils are found has no bearing on whether cave paintings of giant deer that show a hump on the animal's back are inaccurate. It could be that this suggests that the painters responsible for the representations would not be very familiar with the species; if this were so, it would give some reason to conclude that the representations *were* inaccurate.

C   **Correct.** This statement properly identifies a point that logically completes the argument. A hump would not be found as part of a giant deer's fossilized remains if the humps were fatty tissue that would not be fossilized.

D   That the cave paintings were painted well before 16,000 years ago shows that they were executed before the giant deer became extinct, but this does not help to explain the discrepancy between the paintings' depiction of a hump on the deer's back and the fossil record's lack of such a hump. It could be that even though the cave painters coexisted with the giant deer, they were not sufficiently familiar with them to depict them accurately.

E   That currently existing species of deer lack humps, or even that one species does have a feature resembling a hump, has little bearing on whether cave paintings in France accurately depict the giant deer as having a hump.

The correct answer is C.

CR28931.01

130. Super Express Shipping Company has implemented a new distribution system that can get almost every package to its destination the day after it is sent. The company worries that this more efficient system will result in lower sales of its premium next-day delivery service, because its two-day service will usually arrive the following day anyway. The company plans to encourage sales of its next-day service by intentionally delaying delivery of its two-day packages so that they will not be delivered the following day, even if the package arrives at its destination city in time for next-day delivery.

The company's plan assumes that

(A) deliberate delay of packages will not affect the company's image in a way that significantly reduces its ability to attract and retain customers

(B) most people do not have a preference for either two-day or next-day delivery

(C) if the plan is not implemented, the company would lose more money in lost sales of overnight deliveries than it would save with its new efficient distribution system

(D) the overnight service is too expensive to be attractive to most customers currently

(E) competing companies' delivery services rarely deliver packages to their destination earlier than their promised time

Evaluation of a Plan

Situation   Super Express, a shipping company, is concerned that a new level of efficiency in its delivery process, resulting in next-day delivery even with guaranteed two-day delivery, might sabotage the company's more expensive "premium" next-day delivery service. To promote the premium delivery service, the company plans to delay, for one day, two-day delivery packages that arrive one day early at a center near the customer and could be delivered that same day.

Reasoning   *What does the company's plan assume?* The company's rationale for its plan is that without the planned delay, its next-day premium service would lose revenue if potential customers realized that the less expensive two-day delivery service usually results in next-day delivery. So the plan must assume that the planned delivery day will not damage the company's image in a way that would cause significant loss of customers.

A   **Correct.** If it became public that the company was deliberately delaying packages, its brand and reputation would likely suffer major damage and its ability to promote its services—including its premium next-day delivery service—would probably be seriously impaired. Since presumably the company wants to retain existing customers and even attract new ones, its plan (including the rationale for it) would not make sense unless it were assumed that such catastrophic consequences would not result.

B   The given information indicates that the company believes that a sizeable number of customers would, in certain circumstances, prefer guaranteed next-day delivery and pay more for it.

C   Neither the plan nor its rationale is based on assuming that no other, equally good, plan could be devised to achieve the company's major objective and prevent the consequence of overall revenue loss.

D   The given information gives no indication that the company believes this is so, and nothing related to its plan implies otherwise.

E   Nothing is assumed in the company's plan about the frequency with which its competitors deliver packages to customers earlier than the promised delivery time.

The correct answer is A.

CR04738

131. Cocoa grown organically on trees within the shade of the rain forest canopy commands a premium price. However, acquiring and maintaining the certification that allows the crop to be sold as organically grown is very time-consuming and laborious. Meanwhile, the price premium for the grower is about 30 percent, whereas cocoa trees grown in full sun using standard techniques can have twice the yield of organic, shade-grown trees. Financially, therefore, standard techniques are the better choice for the farmer.

Which of the following, if true, most seriously weakens the argument?

(A) Cocoa can be grown only in a climate that has the temperature and moisture characteristics of a tropical rain forest.

(B) Cocoa trees grown using standard techniques require costly applications of fertilizer and pesticides, unlike shade-grown trees.

(C) Although organically grown cocoa has long commanded a price premium over cocoa grown using standard techniques, its price has fluctuated considerably during that period.

(D) Cocoa is not the only cash crop that can be raised on plots that leave the rain forest canopy overhead essentially intact.

(E) Governments and international conservation organizations are working to streamline organic certification so as to relieve farmers of unnecessary work.

Argument Evaluation

Situation Cocoa grown organically under the rain forest canopy can obtain a price premium of 30 percent for the grower. But the certification needed for the cocoa to be sold as organic is time-consuming and laborious. Since cocoa grown in full sun by standard (non-organic) techniques can have twice the yield, it is concluded that standard techniques are better financially for the farmer.

Reasoning *Among the pieces of information presented, which one, assuming it is accurate, would most weaken the argument if added to the given information?* Specific information about the costs associated with growing cocoa using standard techniques is lacking in the given information. For example, does use of the "standard techniques" entail lower or higher costs than use of organic techniques? If we had information that the costs are much higher, such information would tend to weaken the argument—unless we also knew that the much higher yields more than compensate for the much higher costs. If we had information that consumers are becoming increasingly concerned about chemical residues in cocoa, that information would also tend to weaken the argument.

A   If this is true, then the cocoa grown both in rain forest shade and in full sun satisfies the climate requirement.

B   **Correct.** This tells us that use of chemical pesticides and fertilizers entails very high costs for growers; moreover, such use of chemicals risks making the cocoa less attractive to consumers, ultimately impacting the grower's financial benefits.

C   If this were true only of the organic cocoa described in the given information, then it would tend to reinforce the argument rather than weaken it. If it were true of both kinds of cocoa, then it would neither strengthen nor weaken the argument.

D   This information has no obvious bearing on the question asked.

E   This information suggests that costs associated with growing organic cocoa may eventually decrease and the profits increase. But this does not weaken the argument as given, since its conclusion concerns what growing techniques are currently best for farmers.

The correct answer is B.

CR91131.02

132. Psychologists conducted an experiment in which half of the volunteers were asked to describe an unethical action they had performed, while the other half were asked to describe an ethical action they had performed. Some of the volunteers, chosen at random from each of the two groups, were encouraged to wash their hands afterward. Among those who described unethical actions, those who washed their hands were significantly less likely to volunteer for another, similar experiment than those who did not wash their hands. The researchers concluded that some of the subjects failed to volunteer again in part because of their having described an unethical action.

Which of the following would, if true, most help to support the researchers' conclusion?

(A)   Among the volunteers who described ethical actions, those who washed their hands were significantly less likely to volunteer for another, similar experiment than those who did not wash their hands.

(B)   The average likelihood of volunteering for another, similar experiment was higher among those who described ethical actions than among those who described unethical actions.

(C)   Most of the volunteers who were encouraged to wash their hands did so.

(D)   The volunteers in the study were not more disposed to washing their hands under normal circumstances than the general population was.

(E)   Equal numbers of volunteers from both groups were encouraged to wash their hands.

Argument Evaluation

Situation   In an experiment, volunteers in one group were asked to describe an unethical action they had performed; volunteers in another group were asked to describe an ethical action they had performed. Some of the volunteers, randomly selected from each group, were encouraged to wash their hands afterwards. Among those who had described unethical actions, those who washed their hands were significantly less likely to volunteer for another, similar experiment than were those who did not wash their hands. The researchers concluded that some of the volunteers declined to volunteer again because of their having described an unethical action.

Reasoning   *Which new information most strongly supports the researchers' conclusion?* The researchers offered an answer to the following question in their conclusion: What caused some subjects not to volunteer again for another, similar experiment? The researchers concluded that one causal factor was having described an unethical action. This conclusion is based only on data about those who had described their unethical actions; the data showed that the hand washers among them were less likely to volunteer again than were those who did not wash their hands. This data, by itself, seems to provide at best weak support for the researchers' conclusion. The hypothesis could be strengthened by data comparing those who had described their ethical actions with those who had described their unethical ones.

A   This information slightly weakens the researchers' conclusion in that it suggests that the decision not to volunteer for future experiments could have been due entirely to the hand washing rather than partly to the participants' having described unethical actions.

B   **Correct.** This information does not refer to hand washing but provides a comparison between those who described an ethical action and those who described an unethical one, with respect to the likelihood of their volunteering for another, similar experiment. The fact that those who described ethical actions were more likely than the others to volunteer for subsequent experiments provides some evidence that describing an unethical action could have been a factor, along with the hand washing, that caused the observed difference in the volunteering rate. This additional evidence is only prima facie, though; it would be weakened if we also knew that among those who described ethical actions, the hand washers were just as unlikely to volunteer again as were those who washed their hands after describing unethical actions.

C   This information about hand washing is largely irrelevant to the researchers' conclusion, which is focused on the hypothesis that having described an unethical action made some participants less likely to volunteer again. It provides only very slight, conjectural support in that it is inconsistent with a hypothesis that so few actually washed their hands that they constituted a statistically insignificant sample.

D   The researchers' conclusion is not about the general population, so the information in this answer choice could only be relevant if such a generalization were the goal.

E   Like answer choice C, this information about hand washing is largely irrelevant to the researchers' conclusion, which is focused on the hypothesis that having described an unethical action made some participants less likely to volunteer again. It provides only very slight, conjectural support in that it is inconsistent with a hypothesis that one or more of the groups being compared was too small to be statistically significant.

The correct answer is B.

CR07547

133. High levels of fertilizer and pesticides, needed when farmers try to produce high yields of the same crop year after year, pollute water supplies. Experts therefore urge farmers to diversify their crops and to rotate their plantings yearly.

To receive governmental price-support benefits for a crop, farmers must have produced that same crop for the past several years.

The statements above, if true, best support which of the following conclusions?

(A)   The rules for governmental support of farm prices work against efforts to reduce water pollution.

(B)   The only solution to the problem of water pollution from fertilizers and pesticides is to take farmland out of production.

(C)   Farmers can continue to make a profit by rotating diverse crops, thus reducing costs for chemicals, but not by planting the same crop each year.

(D)   New farming techniques will be developed to make it possible for farmers to reduce the application of fertilizers and pesticides.

(E)   Governmental price supports for farm products are set at levels that are not high enough to allow farmers to get out of debt.

Argument Construction

Situation   Farmers are urged to rotate crops annually because the chemicals they must use when continuing to produce the same crops pollute water supplies. On the other hand, farmers may receive federal price-support benefits only if they have been producing the same crop for the past several years.

Reasoning   *What conclusion can be drawn from this information?* Farmers wish to receive the price-support benefits offered by the government, so they grow the same crop for several years. In order to continue getting good yields, they use the high levels of chemicals necessary when the same crop is grown from year to year. The result is water pollution. The government's rules for price-support benefits work against the efforts to reduce water pollution.

A   **Correct.** This statement properly identifies the conclusion supported by the evidence.

B   The experts cited in the passage believe that the rotation of crops is the solution, not the removal of farmland from production.

C   The conclusion that farmers cannot make a profit by producing the same crop year after year is not justified by the information given in the premises. The information given suggests that this conclusion would actually be false, since these farmers would benefit by price-support measures for such a crop.

D No information in the passage supports a conclusion about farming techniques other than crop diversification and rotation, which are clearly existing farming techniques and not new or yet to be developed.

E This conclusion is unwarranted because there is no information in the two statements about the levels of the price supports and of the farmers' debts.

The correct answer is A.

CR02270

134. Ten years ago the number of taxpayers in Greenspace County was slightly greater than the number of registered voters. The number of taxpayers has doubled over the last ten years, while the number of registered voters has increased, but at a lower rate than has the number of taxpayers.

Which of the following must be true in Greenspace County if the statements above are true?

(A) The number of taxpayers is now smaller than the number of registered voters.

(B) Everyone who is a registered voter is also a taxpayer.

(C) The proportion of registered voters to taxpayers has increased over the last ten years.

(D) The proportion of registered voters to taxpayers has decreased over the last ten years.

(E) The proportion of registered voters to taxpayers has remained unchanged over the last ten years.

Argument Evaluation

Situation Ten years ago a county had slightly more taxpayers than registered voters. Since then the number of taxpayers has doubled, while the number of registered voters has increased less.

Reasoning *What can be deduced from the information about the changing numbers of taxpayers and registered voters?* There were already slightly more taxpayers than registered voters ten years ago, but since then the number of taxpayers has increased more than proportionately to the number of registered voters. It follows that there must still be more taxpayers than registered voters, that the absolute number of taxpayers must have increased more than the absolute number of registered voters has, and that the ratio of taxpayers to registered voters must have increased.

A Since there were already more taxpayers than registered voters ten years ago, and since the number of taxpayers has increased more than the number of registered voters, there must still be more taxpayers than registered voters.

B Although there are more taxpayers than registered voters overall, there could still be many individual registered voters who are not taxpayers.

C Since the number of taxpayers has doubled while the number of registered voters has less than doubled, the proportion of registered voters to taxpayers must have decreased, not increased as this answer choice claims.

D **Correct.** Since the number of taxpayers has doubled while the number of registered voters has less than doubled, the proportion of registered voters to taxpayers must have decreased.

E Since the number of taxpayers has doubled while the number of registered voters has less than doubled, the proportion of registered voters to taxpayers must have decreased, not remained unchanged.

The correct answer is D.

CR01298
135. From 1900 until the 1930s, pellagra, a disease later discovered to result from a deficiency of the vitamin niacin, was common among poor cotton farmers in the United States whose diet consisted mostly of corn, the least costly food they could buy. Corn does not contain niacin in usable form. Curiously, during the Depression of the early 1930s, when cotton's price collapsed and cotton farmers' income declined, the incidence of pellagra among those farmers also declined.

Which of the following, if true, most helps to explain the decline in the incidence of pellagra?

(A) When growing a cash crop could not generate adequate income, poor farmers in the United States responded by planting their land with vegetables and fruits for their own consumption.

(B) People whose diets consist largely of corn often suffer from protein deficiency as well as niacin deficiency.

(C) Until the discovery of pellagra's link with niacin, it was widely believed that the disease was an infection that could be transmitted from person to person.

(D) Effective treatment for pellagra became available once its link with niacin was established.

(E) In parts of Mexico, where people subsisted on corn but pellagra was uncommon, corn was typically processed with alkaline substances, which make the niacin in the corn absorbable.

Argument Construction

Situation The disease pellagra, which is due to a deficiency of the nutrient niacin, was common among poor cotton farmers in the United States during the early part of the 20th century, until the early 1930s. The diet of these farmers consisted mostly of the inexpensive grain corn, which lacked niacin in a form that can be absorbed by the body. However, when the cotton price collapsed during the Great Depression in the early 1930s, the incidence of pellagra decreased among these farmers.

Reasoning *What might explain the decline in incidence of pellagra among the cotton farmers during the Great Depression, despite the likelihood that the farmers would have experienced an increase in poverty?* It may seem "curious" that a disease associated with malnutrition and poverty would become less common during a severe economic downturn. Our task is to find something that would explain this curious fact.

A **Correct.** The passage suggests that the pellagra of the farmers was due to their diet of mostly corn, which they purchased. However, this answer choice indicates that, during the time that the farmers grew much of their own food during the Great Depression, the diet of the farmers changed significantly and had greater variety. This point, together with the fact that pellagra among the farmers decreased during this time, suggests that the decrease in pellagra among the farmers was due to their growing their own food.

B Although this answer choice mentions another aspect of nutritional deficiency due to narrowness of diet, the question to be addressed is about nutritional deficiency of niacin rather than of protein.

C The belief that pellagra was an infection transmitted from person to person would not explain why the incidence of pellagra decreased among the farmers during the Great Depression.

D This answer choice might explain the decrease in incidence of pellagra among the farmers if it was true that the link of pellagra with niacin deficiency was discovered before the decrease in incidence of pellagra among the farmers. Given the information provided, we don't know whether or not this is true.

E This answer choice might help to explain the decline in pellagra if it was the case that the cotton farmers started to eat corn that had been processed in the manner of the people in parts of Mexico. However, we have not been given a reason to suppose that the farmers ate corn that had been processed in this way.

The correct answer is A.

CR07589

136. The interview is an essential part of a successful hiring program because, with it, job applicants who have personalities that are unsuited to the requirements of the job will be eliminated from consideration.

The argument above logically depends on which of the following assumptions?

(A) A hiring program will be successful if it includes interviews.

(B) The interview is a more important part of a successful hiring program than is the development of a job description.

(C) Interviewers can accurately identify applicants whose personalities are unsuited to the requirements of the job.

(D) The only purpose of an interview is to evaluate whether job applicants' personalities are suited to the requirements of the job.

(E) The fit of job applicants' personalities to the requirements of the job was once the most important factor in making hiring decisions.

Argument Construction

Situation The interview is a necessary part of hiring because candidates with unsuitable personalities are eliminated from consideration.

Reasoning *What is being assumed in this argument?* The argument puts forth one reason that the interview is important: it eliminates candidates with unsuitable personalities. This presupposes that interviewers can, with a fair degree of accuracy, rule out those candidates whose personalities do not fit the needs of the job.

A The argument does not go so far as to say that interviews guarantee a successful hiring program.

B The argument does not prioritize the parts of a hiring program.

C **Correct.** This statement properly identifies the assumption underlying the argument.

D The argument gives one reason that the interview is important, but it does not say it is the *only* reason.

E This concerns past practices in hiring, and is irrelevant to the argument.

The correct answer is C.

CR07785

137. Many leadership theories have provided evidence that leaders affect group success rather than the success of particular individuals. So it is irrelevant to analyze the effects of supervisor traits on the attitudes of individuals whom they supervise. Instead, assessment of leadership effectiveness should occur only at the group level.

Which of the following would it be most useful to establish in order to evaluate the argument?

(A) Whether supervisors' documentation of individual supervisees' attitudes toward them is usually accurate

(B) Whether it is possible to assess individual supervisees' attitudes toward their supervisors without thereby changing those attitudes

(C) Whether any of the leadership theories in question hold that leaders should assess other leaders' attitudes

(D) Whether some types of groups do not need supervision in order to be successful in their endeavors

(E) Whether individuals' attitudes toward supervisors affect group success

Argument Evaluation

Situation   Many leadership theories have provided evidence that leaders affect the success of groups but not of individuals.

Reasoning   *What would be most helpful to know in order to evaluate how well the stated fact supports the conclusion that leadership effectiveness should be assessed only at the group level without considering supervisors' influence on the attitudes of the individuals they supervise?* Even if leaders do not affect the success of the individuals they lead, they might still affect those individuals' attitudes. And those attitudes in turn might affect group success. If so, the argument would be weak. So any evidence about the existence or strength of these possible effects in the relationship between supervisors and their supervisees would be helpful in evaluating the argument.

A   How accurately supervisors document their supervisees' attitudes is not clearly relevant to how much the supervisors affect those attitudes, nor to how much the attitudes affect group success.

B   Even if assessing supervisees' attitudes would in itself change those attitudes, the person doing the assessment might be able to predict this change and take it into account. Thus, considering individual supervisees' attitudes might still be worthwhile.

C   The argument is not about interactions among leaders, but rather about interactions between supervisors and supervisees.

D   The argument is not about groups without supervisors, or whether certain groups might be effective without a supervisor, but rather about how to assess the effectiveness of supervisors in groups that do have them.

E   **Correct.** As explained above, if individual supervisees' attitudes affect group success, the argument would be weak. And probably individual supervisees' attitudes toward their supervisors are influenced by those supervisors. So knowing whether individual attitudes toward supervisors affect group success would be helpful in evaluating the argument

The correct answer is E.

CR03535

138. A major health insurance company in Lagolia pays for special procedures prescribed by physicians only if the procedure is first approved as "medically necessary" by a company-appointed review panel. The rule is intended to save the company the money it might otherwise spend on medically unnecessary procedures. The company has recently announced that in order to reduce its costs, it will abandon this rule.

Which of the following, if true, provides the strongest justification for the company's decision?

(A) Patients often register dissatisfaction with physicians who prescribe nothing for their ailments.

(B) Physicians often prescribe special procedures that are helpful but not altogether necessary for the health of the patient.

(C) The review process is expensive and practically always results in approval of the prescribed procedure.

(D) The company's review process does not interfere with the prerogative of physicians, in cases where more than one effective procedure is available, to select the one they personally prefer.

(E) The number of members of the company-appointed review panel who review a given procedure depends on the cost of the procedure.

Evaluation of a Plan

Situation In order to cut costs, a major health insurance company is abandoning a rule stating that it will pay for special procedures only if the procedure is approved as medically necessary by a review panel.

Reasoning *What piece of information would most help to justify the company's decision?* For the company to save money, it would need to be in some way cutting its costs by abandoning the rule. Under what circumstances might the rule cost, rather than save, the company money? The panel itself might be expensive to convene, for example. Further, the cost savings achieved by the panel might be minimal if the panel did not deny significant numbers of procedures.

A This suggests that patients might be pressuring their physicians to prescribe certain unnecessary procedures for their ailments, which in turn suggests that the panel is reviewing these procedures and denying them. But if so, then the panel is probably saving the insurance company money, so abandoning the panel's review would not reduce the company's costs.

B This suggests that certain procedures that are being prescribed by physicians are not medically necessary, which in turn suggests that the panel reviewing these procedures may be denying them. If this is the case, then the panel is probably saving the insurance company a significant amount of money, so abandoning the panel's review may well increase rather than decrease the company's costs.

C **Correct.** This statement properly identifies information that would help to justify the company's decision.

D Even if the panel does not interfere with physicians' choices when more than one medically effective procedure is available, the panel may still be denying pay for many procedures that are not medically necessary. In such cases the panel may be saving the insurance company money, and abandoning the review process would not reduce the company's costs.

E This suggests that the more expensive the procedure under review, the more expensive the panel itself is. Even so, if the panel denies payment for very expensive procedures, it may nonetheless save the company significantly more than the company has to pay to convene the panel, so abandoning the review process would not reduce the company's costs.

The correct answer is C.

CR03826

139. Automobile ownership was rare in Sabresia as recently as 30 years ago, but with continuing growth of personal income there, automobile ownership has become steadily more common. Consequently, there are now far more automobiles on Sabresia's roads than there were 30 years ago, and the annual number of automobile accidents has increased significantly. Yet the annual number of deaths and injuries resulting from automobile accidents has not increased significantly.

Which of the following, if true, most helps to explain why deaths and injuries resulting from automobile accidents have not increased significantly?

(A) Virtually all of the improvements in Sabresia's roads that were required to accommodate increased traffic were completed more than ten years ago.

(B) With more and more people owning cars, the average number of passengers in a car on the road has dropped dramatically.

(C) The increases in traffic volume have been most dramatic on Sabresia's highways, where speeds are well above those of other roads.

(D) Because of a vigorous market in used cars, the average age of cars on the road has actually increased throughout the years of steady growth in automobile ownership.

(E) Automobile ownership is still much less common in Sabresia than it is in other countries.

Argument Construction

Situation Many more cars are on Sabresia's roads than 30 years ago; and there are also many more car accidents. Yet the annual number of deaths and injuries resulting from car accidents has not increased much, which is quite puzzling.

Reasoning *What factor could help explain the puzzling fact that the increase in car accidents was not reflected in a similar increase in deaths and injuries from car accidents?* One (but perhaps unlikely) possibility is that a significantly greater proportion of the recent annual number of car accidents consisted of merely minor accidents, unlike 30 years ago. Another possibility is that cars are currently much better engineered for driver and passenger safety than 30 years ago. Yet a third possibility is that the total number of people traveling by car—passengers and drivers—has not increased significantly despite the large increase in the number of cars. This would mean that the average occupancy of a car has greatly decreased; so, even though the number of car accidents has significantly increased, the average number of people per car involved in an accident would have decreased significantly. On average, this would mean significantly fewer deaths and injuries per accident.

A This throws little light on the central puzzle: why the current number of car accidents is significantly higher than 30 years ago, while the number of deaths and injuries in car accidents is not. The fact that there has been a significant increase in car accidents suggests that the roads were not made as safe as they could have been, and this just deepens the puzzle about the lack of a significant increase in deaths and injuries.

B **Correct.** This implies that the average number of passengers per car accident is significantly less, and this helps explain why the total number of deaths and injuries has not increased significantly.

C This information does not help explain the mismatch between increased accident numbers and relatively stable death-and-injury numbers. High-speed car accidents would likely have caused more fatalities, on average, than other car accidents; so, given that the increase in traffic volume has been greatest on Sabresia's high-speed roads, one would expect a significant increase in the number of accidents, and consequently in the number of deaths and injuries. But this expectation has not been fulfilled.

D   This does not help explain the surprisingly stable death-and-injury numbers in contrast with the significantly increased number of car accidents. The increase in average age of cars on the road might contribute to the increased number of accidents if older cars are more likely to be dangerously defective than newer ones.

E   The central puzzle already described involves no comparisons between Sabresia and other countries, so this information is irrelevant to explaining the puzzling discrepancy.

The correct answer is B.

CR01430

140. To evaluate a plan to save money on office-space expenditures by having its employees work at home, XYZ Company asked volunteers from its staff to try the arrangement for six months. During this period, the productivity of these employees was as high as or higher than before.

Which of the following, if true, would argue most strongly against deciding, on the basis of the trial results, to implement the company's plan?

(A)   The employees who agreed to participate in the test of the plan were among the company's most self-motivated and independent workers.

(B)   The savings that would accrue from reduced office-space expenditures alone would be sufficient to justify the arrangement for the company, apart from any productivity increases.

(C)   Other companies that have achieved successful results from work-at-home plans have workforces that are substantially larger than that of XYZ.

(D)   The volunteers who worked at home were able to communicate with other employees as necessary for performing the work.

(E)   Minor changes in the way office work is organized at XYZ would yield increases in employee productivity similar to those achieved in the trial.

Evaluation of a Plan

Situation   To save money on office space expenditures, a company considers having employees work at home. A six-month trial with employees who have volunteered to test the plan shows their productivity to be as high as or higher than before.

Reasoning   *Why would the trial results NOT provide a good reason to implement the plan?* Generalizing from a small sample to the group depends on having a sample that is representative. In this case, the employees who participated in the trial are not representative of all employees. The employees who volunteered for the trial may be the type of employees who would be most likely to work successfully at home. It would not be wise to base a generalization about all employees on this sample.

A   **Correct.** This statement properly identifies a flaw in the trial that is the basis for the plan.

B   This statement supports the implementation of the plan. Moreover, it is not based on the trial results, so it does not answer the question.

C   The passage gives no information about how company size might affect the implementation of the plan or the reliability of the trial results.

D   If anything, this would tend to support the plan.

E   The goal of the plan is to save money on office space, not to increase productivity, so an alternative plan to increase productivity is irrelevant.

The correct answer is A.

CR04180

141. A child learning to play the piano will not succeed unless the child has an instrument at home on which to practice. However, good-quality pianos, whether new or secondhand, are costly. Buying one is justified only if the child has the necessary talent and perseverance, which is precisely what one cannot know in advance. Consequently, parents should buy an inexpensive secondhand instrument at first and upgrade if and when the child's ability and inclination are proven.

Which of the following, if true, casts the most serious doubt on the course of action recommended for parents?

(A) Learners, particularly those with genuine musical talent, are apt to lose interest in the instrument if they have to play on a piano that fails to produce a pleasing sound.

(B) Reputable piano teachers do not accept children as pupils unless they know that the children can practice on a piano at home.

(C) Ideally, the piano on which a child practices at home should be located in a room away from family activities going on at the same time.

(D) Very young beginners often make remarkable progress at playing the piano at first, but then appear to stand still for a considerable period of time.

(E) In some parents, spending increasing amounts of money on having their children learn to play the piano produces increasing anxiety to hear immediate results.

Evaluation of a Plan

Situation   Children learning the piano need to have a piano on which to practice at home. Purchasing a high-quality piano is costly, and justified only if the child has talent and will persevere, which is hard to predict at an early stage. Parents should make do with a secondhand piano until the child's ability and inclination are proven.

Reasoning   *Which of the statements given would cast the most serious doubt on the recommendation given to parents?* Suppose that a child, because possessed of very high musical talent, is especially sensitive to imprecisions in tuning or imperfections of tone in a secondhand, less expensive piano (presumably Mozart would have been so!). This could, over time, make the child less interested in using the piano—especially if the child had the opportunity to hear music on far superior pianos. The result could be total loss of interest in learning to play the piano.

A   **Correct.** This, if true, would be a good reason to provide the child with the chance to practice regularly on a superior piano.

B   The issue is whether it would be best to provide the child with a superior piano at home, not whether it would be important to provide some piano at home.

C   This is irrelevant to the point at issue, which concerns how high a quality of piano should parents provide at home if they desire optimal development of the child's potential for piano musicianship.

D   Fluctuations in the pace of learning the piano are possible, but not relevant to the central question raised about the quality of the piano to be provided.

E   Investing so much in a piano, to the extent that doing so causes financial and psychological stress, might not be beneficial overall. However, if buying a new piano and buying a used piano are equally feasible financially for a given family, the question concerns which option would most achieve the objective of optimally developing the child's potential for piano musicianship.

The correct answer is A.

CR05096

142. Nutritionists are advising people to eat more fish, since the omega-3 fatty acids in fish help combat many diseases. If everyone took this advice, however, there would not be enough fish in oceans, rivers, and lakes to supply the demand; the oceans are already being overfished. The obvious method to ease the pressure on wild fish populations is for people to increase their consumption of farmed fish.

Which of the following, if true, raises the most serious doubt concerning the prospects for success of the solution proposed above?

(A) Aquaculture, or fish farming, raises more fish in a given volume of water than are generally present in the wild.

(B) Some fish farming, particularly of shrimp and other shellfish, takes place in enclosures in the ocean.

(C) There are large expanses of ocean waters that do not contain enough nutrients to support substantial fish populations.

(D) The feed for farmed ocean fish is largely made from small wild-caught fish, including the young of many popular food species.

(E) Some of the species that are now farmed extensively were not commonly eaten when they were only available in the wild.

Argument Evaluation

Situation Nutritionists advise people to eat fish for the omega-3 fatty acids, but there would not be enough fish to meet the demand if everyone followed this advice. Therefore, people should increase their consumption of farmed fish to ease pressure of wild fish populations.

Reasoning *What evidence would suggest that increasing consumption of farmed fish would not ease pressure on wild fish populations?* Any evidence suggesting that significantly increasing consumption of farmed fish would diminish the habitat or food available for wild fish would also suggest that increasing consumption of farmed fish would not ease pressure on wild fish populations.

A Probably the less space fish farming requires, the less pressure it creates on wild fish habitats and populations, other things being equal.

B Whether any fish farming takes place in enclosures in the ocean is not clearly relevant to whether it eases pressure on wild fish populations.

C Substantial fish populations may thrive in other large expanses of ocean water that contain more nutrients, and in rivers and lakes.

D **Correct.** This suggests that increasing consumption of farmed fish would require increased use of wild fish as feed for farmed fish and therefore would not ease pressure on wild fish populations.

E Even if some farmed fish are different species from the wild fish that are commonly eaten, increased consumption of the farmed fish could reduce demand for the wild fish and thereby ease pressure on wild fish populations.

The correct answer is D.

CR02851
143. Which of the following most logically completes the market forecaster's argument?

Market forecaster: The price of pecans is high when pecans are comparatively scarce but drops sharply when pecans are abundant. Thus, in high-yield years, growers often store part of their crop in refrigerated warehouses until after the next year's harvest, hoping for higher prices then. Because of bad weather, this year's pecan crop will be very small. Nevertheless, pecan prices this year will not be significantly higher than last year, since _____.

(A) the last time the pecan crop was as small as it was this year, the practice of holding back part of one year's crop had not yet become widely established

(B) last year's pecan harvest was the largest in the last 40 years

(C) pecan prices have remained relatively stable in recent years

(D) pecan yields for some farmers were as high this year as they had been last year

(E) the quality of this year's pecan crop is as high as the quality of any pecan crop in the previous five years

Argument Construction

Situation   The price of pecans fluctuates based on the fluctuations in market supplies. When pecan farmers have a large harvest, they tend to save some of the crop in refrigerated storage until the following year, hoping to get higher prices then. This year's crop will be very small. But prices are not predicted to be significantly higher than last year.

Reasoning   *What can most reasonably complete the argument by filling in the blank?* In other words, what would be the best reason for the prediction about this year's prices? This year's prices will be determined by the total market supply of pecans; this will include not only freshly harvested pecans but also pecans that were kept in storage from last year's harvest. Information about the relative size of last year's harvest could be partial evidence for a prediction about this year's prices.

A   What this tells us, in effect, is that previous experience with very poor harvests provide a poor guide about this year's total market supply, since the practice of refrigerated storage of pecans had not existed then.

B   **Correct.** This tells us that there was probably an unprecedented quantity of pecans in refrigerated storage from last year, so it is likely that the market supply of pecans this year will be relatively normal despite the poor harvest. This means that this year's prices will not be much higher than last year's; last year, the total pecan harvest was enormous and market supply probably relatively large.

C   This creates a general expectation of prices not being inordinately high this year, but since the harvest this year was "very small," such a general expectation could remain unfulfilled, absent countervailing factors.

D   This information is too vague to be useful. What percentage of farmers obtained satisfactory yields? Were these yields on farms that were by far the largest or the smallest?

E   The reasoning is silent on the issue of pecan quality, even though perceived quality could perhaps affect prices obtained. The additional information does not tell us that this year's quality is better than that found in recent harvests.

The correct answer is B.

CR06331

144. It is often said that high rates of inflation tend to diminish people's incentive to save and invest. This view must be incorrect, however, because people generally saved and invested more of their income in the 1970's when inflation rates were high than they did in the 1980's when inflation rates were low.

Of the following, the best criticism of the argument above is that it overlooks the possibility that

(A) all people do not respond in the same way to a given economic stimulus

(B) certain factors operating in the 1980's but not in the 1970's diminished people's incentive to save and invest

(C) the population was larger in the 1980's than it was in the 1970's

(D) the proponents of the view cited would stand to gain if inflation rates become lower

(E) a factor that affects people's savings behavior in a certain way could affect people's investment behavior quite differently

Argument Evaluation

Situation   People generally saved and invested more in the 1970's when inflation was high than in the 1980s when inflation was low, despite the fact that it is commonly believed that high inflation discourages savings and investment.

Reasoning   *Why does the observation about savings, investment, and inflation rates in the 1970's and 1980's not justify the conclusion that high inflation does not generally diminish people's incentive to save and invest?* The argument observes that over the course of two decades there was a positive rather than a negative correlation between inflation on the one hand and savings and investment on the other. It infers from this that high rates of inflation do not tend to diminish people's incentive to save and invest. Is this inference justified? Note that the claim that this argument is trying to discredit is not that high rates of inflation always diminished people's incentive to save and invest. Rather, the claim is merely that high rates of inflation tend to do this. The argument overlooks the possibility that during the two decades in question other factors may have caused a positive correlation to briefly appear even if in general the correlation is negative.

A   The argument is compatible with the hypothesis that some people respond to inflation by saving and investing more, while others do not.

B   **Correct.** If these other factors, unrelated to the inflation rate, that operated in the 1980's but not the 1970's, created an even greater disincentive to savings and investment than high inflation rates provide, then those trends do not provide evidence about the general relationship among savings, investment, and inflation.

C   The argument appears to concern savings and investment per capita, so total population size should be irrelevant. But increasing population would not explain declining total amounts of savings and investment, either.

D   If anything, the possibility that the proponents' ulterior motives distorted their reasoning would help to support the argument's conclusion that the proponents' view is incorrect.

E   The argument addresses this possibility by presenting evidence that inflation was positively correlated with both savings and investment during the 1970's and 1980's.

The correct answer is B.

CR02704

145. Which of the following most logically completes the argument below?

Within the earth's core, which is iron, pressure increases with depth. Because the temperature at which iron melts increases with pressure, the inner core is solid and the outer core is molten. Physicists can determine the melting temperature of iron at any given pressure and the pressure for any given depth in the earth. Therefore, the actual temperature at the boundary of the earth's outer and inner cores—the melting temperature of iron there—can be determined, since _____.

(A) the depth beneath the earth's surface of the boundary between the outer and inner cores is known

(B) some of the heat from the earth's core flows to the surface of the earth

(C) pressures within the earth's outer core are much greater than pressures above the outer core

(D) nowhere in the earth's core can the temperature be measured directly

(E) the temperatures within the earth's inner core are higher than in the outer core

Argument Construction

Situation   Pressure within the earth's iron core increases with depth. Because the melting temperature of iron increases with pressure, the inner core is solid and the outer core molten. Physicists can determine iron's melting temperature at any pressure and the pressure it is under at any depth.

Reasoning   *What further premise, combined with the information provided, would support the conclusion that physicists can determine the temperature at the boundary between the outer and inner cores?* Since physicists can determine iron's melting temperature at any pressure and the pressure it is under at any depth, they must be able to determine its melting temperature at any depth. The temperature at the boundary between the inner and outer cores must exactly equal the melting temperature there, since that is the boundary between the molten and solid parts of the core. To determine the temperature at the boundary, therefore, it would suffice to know the depth of the boundary.

A   **Correct.** If physicists know the depth of the boundary between the inner and outer cores, they can determine the temperature at the boundary.

B   The fact that *some heat* flows from the core to the surface is too vague to help in determining exact temperatures anywhere.

C   The difference in pressures between the outer core and the region above it is only vaguely described here and is not clearly relevant to the temperature at the boundary between the outer core and the inner core below it.

D   An absence of information would not be helpful in determining the temperature at the boundary between the outer and inner cores.

E   This information is not sufficiently specific to show that the temperature at the boundary between the outer and inner cores can be determined.

The correct answer is A.

CR03659

146. Which of the following most logically completes the reasoning?

Either food scarcity or excessive hunting can threaten a population of animals. If the group faces food scarcity, individuals in the group will reach reproductive maturity later than otherwise. If the group faces excessive hunting, individuals that reach reproductive maturity earlier will come to predominate. Therefore, it should be possible to determine whether prehistoric mastodons became extinct because of food scarcity or human hunting, since there are fossilized mastodon remains from both before and after mastodon populations declined, and _____.

(A) there are more fossilized mastodon remains from the period before mastodon populations began to decline than from after that period

(B) the average age at which mastodons from a given period reached reproductive maturity can be established from their fossilized remains

(C) it can be accurately estimated from fossilized remains when mastodons became extinct

(D) it is not known when humans first began hunting mastodons

(E) climate changes may have gradually reduced the food available to mastodons

Argument Construction

Situation   In a population of animals, food scarcity causes later reproductive maturity; if that population is hunted excessively, earlier-maturing animals will be more numerous in the population.

Reasoning   *What point would most logically complete the argument?* For the information given to be of use in determining what caused mastodons' extinction, mastodon fossils would need to indicate the age at which mastodons reached reproductive maturity, since that is what the argument suggests can indicate cause of extinction. If fossilized remains exist from before and after mastodon populations began to decline, and if the age at which those fossilized mastodons reached reproductive maturity can be determined, then we will have a good idea of what caused their extinction: if they reached reproductive maturity late, it was probably food scarcity, but if they matured earlier, it was most likely hunting.

A   This fact only helps indicate that there was a decline; it tells us nothing about what caused the decline.

B   **Correct.** This statement properly identifies a point that logically completes the argument: it explains how the fossilized mastodon remains could be used to help determine what caused mastodons' extinction.

C   The point at which mastodons became extinct is not part of this argument, which is concerned with the cause of their extinction. The only way in which this could be relevant to the issue at hand is if mastodons became extinct before humans took up hunting mastodons—but the argument includes no information on whether this was so.

D   Not knowing when humans began hunting mastodons would have no effect on the argument, which is concerned with how mastodon fossils, combined with knowledge about how food scarcity and hunting affect mastodon reproductive maturity, can help determine how mastodons became extinct.

E   This fact only shows that food scarcity *may* have led to mastodon's decline. It tells us nothing about whether fossilized remains can help determine whether it was food scarcity or human hunting that actually led to the decline.

The correct answer is B.

CRO2518

147. Many office buildings designed to prevent outside air from entering have been shown to have elevated levels of various toxic substances circulating through the air inside, a phenomenon known as sick building syndrome. Yet the air in other office buildings does not have elevated levels of these substances, even though those buildings are the same age as the "sick" buildings and have similar designs and ventilation systems.

Which of the following, if true, most helps to explain why not all office buildings designed to prevent outside air from entering have air that contains elevated levels of toxic substances?

(A) Certain adhesives and drying agents used in particular types of furniture, carpets, and paint contribute the bulk of the toxic substances that circulate in the air of office buildings.

(B) Most office buildings with sick building syndrome were built between 1950 and 1990.

(C) Among buildings designed to prevent outside air from entering, houses are no less likely than office buildings to have air that contains elevated levels of toxic substances.

(D) The toxic substances that are found in the air of "sick" office buildings are substances that are found in at least small quantities in nearly every building.

(E) Office buildings with windows that can readily be opened are unlikely to suffer from sick building syndrome.

Argument Evaluation

Situation Many office buildings designed to prevent outside air from entering have elevated levels of toxic substances in their interior air, but other such buildings similar in age, design, and ventilation do not.

Reasoning *What would help to explain the difference in air quality among buildings similar in age, design, and ventilation?* If office buildings are designed to prevent outside air from entering, toxic substances emitted into the interior air might not be ventilated out quickly, and thus might become more concentrated inside the building. But if such toxic substances are not emitted into a building's interior air in the first place, they will not become concentrated there, even if the building is poorly ventilated. So any factor that suggests why toxic substances are emitted into the interior air of some buildings but not others of similar age and design would help to explain the difference in the buildings' air quality.

A **Correct.** Some buildings may have these types of furniture, carpets, and paint, while other buildings similar in age, design, and ventilation do not.

B Since all these buildings were built during the same period, this does not help to explain the difference in air quality among buildings similar in age.

C The passage concerns air quality in office buildings only, not in houses.

D This does not help to explain why these toxic substances are more concentrated in some office buildings than in others.

E The passage concerns the differences in air quality only among office buildings that were designed to prevent outside air from entering.

The correct answer is A.

CR08756

148. Newsletter: **A condominium generally offers more value for its cost than an individual house because of economies of scale.** The homeowners in a condominium association can collectively buy products and services that they could not afford on their own. And since a professional management company handles maintenance of common areas, **condominium owners spend less time and money on maintenance than individual homeowners do.**

The two portions in **boldface** play which of the following roles in the newsletter's argument?

(A) The first is the argument's main conclusion; the second is another conclusion supporting the first.

(B) The first is a premise, for which no evidence is provided; the second is the argument's only conclusion.

(C) The first is a conclusion supporting the second; the second is the argument's main conclusion.

(D) The first is the argument's only conclusion; the second is a premise, for which no evidence is provided.

(E) Both are premises, for which no evidence is provided, and both support the argument's only conclusion.

Argument Construction

Situation Homeowners in a condominium association can buy products and services collectively. A management company handles maintenance of condominium common areas.

Reasoning *What roles are played in the argument by the statement that a condominium generally offers more value for its cost than a house because of economies of scale and by the statement that condominium owners spend less time and money on maintenance than owners of individual homes do?* In the passage, the first sentence (the first boldface statement) is a generalization. The second sentence provides an example of the economies of scale mentioned in the first sentence, so it helps support the first sentence as a conclusion. In the third sentence, the word *since* indicates that the first clause is a premise supporting the second clause (the second boldface statement) as a conclusion. That conclusion itself provides another example of the economies of scale mentioned in the first sentence, so it also helps support that first sentence as a conclusion.

A **Correct.** As explained above, the first boldface statement is supported by the rest of the statements in the argument, so it is the main conclusion. The second boldface statement supports the first, but is itself a conclusion supported by the *since* clause preceding it.

B The second and third sentences in the argument provide examples of economies of scale. These examples are evidence supporting the first boldface statement as a conclusion.

C Since the second boldface statement provides evidence of the economies of scale described by the first, it supports the first as a conclusion.

D The *since* clause immediately preceding the second boldface statement provides evidence that supports it, so the second boldface statement is a conclusion.

E Both the second and the third sentences of the argument support the first boldface statement as a conclusion. And the *since* clause immediately preceding the second boldface statement supports it as a conclusion.

The correct answer is A.

CR00780

149. Which of the following most logically completes the argument?

When officials in Tannersburg released their plan to widen the city's main roads, environmentalists protested that widened roads would attract more traffic and lead to increased air pollution. In response, city officials pointed out that today's pollution-control devices are at their most effective in vehicles traveling at higher speeds and that widening roads would increase the average speed of traffic. However, this effect can hardly be expected to offset the effect pointed out by environmentalists, since _____.

(A) increases in traffic volume generally produce decreases in the average speed of traffic unless roads are widened

(B) several of the roads that are slated for widening will have to be closed temporarily while construction is underway

(C) most of the air pollution generated by urban traffic comes from vehicles that do not have functioning pollution-control devices

(D) the newly widened roads will not have increased traffic volume if the roads that must be used to reach them are inadequate

(E) a vehicle traveling on a route that goes through Tannersburg will spend less time on Tannersburg's roads once the roads are widened

Argument Evaluation

Situation Environmentalists protested a plan to widen a city's main roads on the grounds that it would increase traffic and air pollution. City officials replied that widening the roads would increase average traffic speeds, which would improve the effectiveness of vehicles' pollution-control devices.

Reasoning *What would most support the conclusion that the improved effectiveness of the pollution-control devices would be insufficient to prevent the increased traffic from increasing air pollution?* The word *since* preceding the blank space at the end of the argument indicates that the space should be filled with a premise supporting the conclusion stated immediately before the *since*. To support this conclusion, we would need evidence that widening the roads and increasing traffic speeds would not improve the pollution-control devices' effectiveness enough to compensate for the amount of added air pollution generated by the additional traffic on the widened roads.

A It is unclear whether traffic volume would increase if the roads were not widened. But if it did, this would cast doubt on the conclusion by suggesting that a combination of higher traffic volume and lower speeds could make air pollution worse if the roads were not widened than if they were widened.

B The argument is about the long-term effects of widening the roads, not about the temporary effects of closing them during construction.

C **Correct.** If most vehicles in the area lack air-pollution devices altogether or have ones that do not work, then it is highly questionable whether the greater efficiency of the few functioning devices would be sufficient to compensate for the increase in air pollution that would result from increased traffic.

D If anything, this casts doubt on the conclusion by suggesting that widening the roads may not increase traffic volume or air pollution at all.

E If anything, this casts doubt on the conclusion by suggesting that widening the roads will decrease the amount of time each vehicle spends generating air pollution on those roads.

The correct answer is C.

CR70661.01

150. Platinum is a relatively rare metal vital to a wide variety of industries. Xagor Corporation, a major producer of platinum, has its production plant in a country that will soon begin imposing an export tax on platinum sold and shipped to customers abroad. As a consequence, the price of platinum on the world market is bound to rise.

Which of the following, if true, tends to confirm the conclusion above?

(A) An inexpensive substitute for platinum has been developed and will be available to industry for the first time this month.

(B) The largest of the industries that depend on platinum reported a drop in sales last month.

(C) The producers of platinum in other countries taken together cannot supply enough platinum to meet worldwide demand.

(D) Xagor produced more platinum last month than in any previous month.

(E) New deposits of platinum have been found in the country in which Xagor has its production plant.

Argument Evaluation

Situation Xagor Corporation produces platinum, a rare metal vital to many industries. Xagor's plant is in a country that will soon impose an export tax on platinum. The world market price of platinum is predicted to rise.

Reasoning *Which of the pieces of information given, if true, would most tend to confirm the prediction given?* The conclusion of the argument is a causal prediction: the world market price of platinum will increase because of the export tax on platinum. The argument tells us that a wide range of industries need platinum, so the introduction of taxes on exported platinum would likely make that platinum more expensive for the importing industries. This, in turn, would likely raise the world market price of platinum. But what if those industries could get all their platinum from countries that did not tax platinum exports? Then the world market price might not rise if exports from those countries could adequately fulfill market demand.

A This information tends to undermine the reasoning and does not confirm the conclusion. If a less expensive platinum-substitute were to be developed, the world market price of platinum would tend to decline.

B This information somewhat weakens support for the conclusion. It suggests that overall demand for platinum might decline, at least temporarily, which would tend to lower the world market price of platinum.

C **Correct.** This information strengthens the support for the conclusion. It indicates that some platinum subject to the export tax will almost certainly be exported and will cost importers more than before. This would tend to cause the world market price of platinum to rise, especially since platinum producers in other countries could remain competitive and still raise their prices.

D This information could indicate a possible upswing in platinum production, which could increase the total world supply of platinum. If the supply increased relative to world demand, the world market price of platinum could decrease, not increase as the argument's conclusion predicts.

E This information suggests a possible increase in the world market supply of platinum, which would tend to reduce the world market price, provided world demand for platinum did not also increase at least proportionately.

The correct answer is C.

CR80661.01

151. From 1973 to 1986, growth in the United States economy was over 33 percent, while the percent growth in United States energy consumption was zero. The number of barrels of oil being saved per day by energy-efficiency improvements made since 1973 is now 13 million.

If the information above is correct, which of the following conclusions can properly be drawn on the basis of it?

(A) It is more difficult to find new sources of oil than to institute new energy-conservation measures.

(B) Oil imports cannot be reduced unless energy consumption does not grow at all.

(C) A reduction in the consumption of gasoline was the reason overall energy consumption remained steady.

(D) It is possible for an economy to grow without consuming additional energy.

(E) The development of nontraditional energy sources will make it possible for the United States economy to grow even faster.

Argument Construction

Situation From 1973 to 1986, the United States economy grew over 33 percent while energy consumption did not grow. Energy improvements have made dramatic savings in annual oil consumption since 1973.

Reasoning *If the given information in the passage is true, which answer choice must be true based on that information?* To find that statement, look for the one that has the closest relevance to the information given. All of the answer choices refer to topics at least loosely associated with the topics discussed in the given information. But four of them introduce extraneous information, while just one relies solely on the given information, simply making explicit something implicit in that information.

A Nothing in the given information even implicitly depends on contrasting the relative difficulty of finding new oil with the difficulty of instituting new energy-conservation measures.

B Nothing in the given information refers, even implicitly, to oil imports, so this statement does not follow logically from the given information.

C This is new information that, if true, would help explain why there was zero percent growth in energy consumption in the period under discussion. But this new information could easily be false even if the given information is true. For instance, gasoline consumption could have held steady but the consumption of petroleum diesel or heating oil could have been reduced significantly.

D Correct. This statement must be true if the given information is accurate. If something of a given kind has occurred, then it must be possible for that kind of thing to occur. The given information cites an example of an economy that had 33 percent economic growth along with zero percent growth in energy consumption.

E The given information may be entirely accurate even if this claim is false. Even if this claim is true, the given information does not address, even implicitly, the development of nontraditional sources.

The correct answer is D.

CR01661.01

152. Although many customers do not make a sufficient effort to conserve water, water companies must also be held responsible for wasteful consumption. Their own policies, in fact, encourage excessive water use, and attempts at conservation will succeed only if the water companies change their practices.

Which of the following, if true, would most strongly support the view above?

(A) Most water companies reduce the cost per unit of water as the amount of water used by a customer increases.

(B) Most water companies keep detailed records of the quantity of water used by different customers.

(C) Most water companies severely curtail the use of water during periods of drought.

(D) Federal authorities limit the range of policies that can be enforced by the water companies.

(E) The price per unit of water charged by the water companies has risen steadily in the last 10 years.

Argument Evaluation

Situation   Water companies have policies that encourage excessive water use. Water conservation cannot succeed unless water companies change their practices.

Reasoning   *Which answer choice would indicate that water companies' policies and practices lead to wasteful water use?* If the companies have policies or practices that reduce customers' incentive to consume less water, then wasteful water consumption would be more likely to occur. Water companies would be contributing to wasteful water use and should be held accountable for that waste if water conservation is to succeed.

A   **Correct.** Water companies' charging customers less per additional unit of water consumed is likely to reduce customers' incentive to avoid wasteful water use. So water companies bear some responsibility for wasteful water use.

B   This shows that water companies have adequate data to indicate trends in customers' water consumption. But this does not, by itself, indicate that water companies incentivize wasteful consumption.

C   This indicates that water companies likely curtail wasteful water use during droughts, which somewhat weakens the argument.

D   This information is too nonspecific to allow us to judge whether the federal authorities' regulatory regime directly or indirectly contributes to wasteful water use.

E   If anything, this information tends to weaken the argument. Over a 10-year period, because most economies experience inflation, increases in the price per unit of water would naturally occur, absent special countervailing factors. But if the increases were large, they would, if anything, tend to reduce wasteful water use.

The correct answer is A.

CR11661.01
153. Despite legislation designed to stem the accumulation of plastic waste, the plastics industry continued to grow rapidly last year, as can be seen from the fact that sales of the resin that is the raw material for manufacturing plastics grew by 10 percent to $28 billion.

In assessing the support provided by the evidence cited above for the statement that the plastics industry continued to grow, in addition to the information above it would be most useful to know

(A) whether the resin has other uses besides the manufacture of plastics
(B) the dollar amount of resin sales the year before last
(C) the plastics industry's attitude toward the legislation concerning plastic waste
(D) whether sales of all goods and services in the economy as a whole were increasing last year
(E) what proportion of the plastics industry's output eventually contributes to the accumulation of plastic waste

Argument Evaluation

Situation There is legislation meant to slow the accumulation of plastic waste. Last year, however, the plastics industry continued to grow rapidly. Sales of the resin that is the raw material for plastics grew in monetary terms by 10 percent.

Reasoning *What additional information should we seek in order to evaluate the evidence offered for the conclusion that the plastics industry continued to grow rapidly last year?* The evidence offered is that sales of resin from which plastics can be made increased 10 percent over the preceding year. For example, we could inquire whether the resin is used exclusively for plastics manufacture. If this were found NOT to be so, then the evidence presented would be of little use in showing that the plastics industry grew rapidly last year.

A **Correct.** Knowing whether this is so is crucial for judging the evidential value of last year's growth in sales of resin.

B This information is implicit in the given information and is therefore not additional information.

C The central issue is whether the information about last year's resin sales is good evidence of the plastics industry growth. The question as to whether that industry favors curtailment of plastics pollution has little if any relevance to that issue.

D If the answer to this *whether*-question is yes, there was presumably some inflation in the currency, so the increase in nominal monetary value of resin sales may or may not reflect very strong evidence of growth in the plastics industry. If the answer to the question is no, the increase in resin sales could be evidence of growth but is not necessarily so. In either case, we would need further information, so either answer to the question would not be useful for assessing the evidence.

E Knowing the answer to this could be important, but it is irrelevant in determining the evidential value of the information about growth in resin sales last year.

The correct answer is A.

CR41661.01

154. Studies of the political orientations of 1,055 college students revealed that the plurality of students in an eastern, big-city, private university was liberal, whereas in a state-supported, southern college, the plurality was conservative. Orientations were independent of the student's region of origin, and the trends were much more pronounced in seniors than in beginning students.

Which of the following hypotheses is best supported by the observations stated above?

(A) The political orientations of college students are more similar to the political orientations of their parents when the students start college than when the students are seniors.

(B) The political orientations of college seniors depend significantly on experiences they have had while in college.

(C) A college senior originally from the South is more likely to be politically conservative than is a college senior originally from the East.

(D) Whether their college is state-supported or private is the determining factor in college students' political orientations.

(E) College students tend to become more conservative politically as they become older and are confronted with pressures for financial success.

Argument Evaluation

Situation   Studies of a total of 1,055 college students in an eastern big-city private university and in a state-supported southern college found that, in the sample, the political orientation of most students in the private college was liberal and that of most students in the southern college was conservative. Among the liberal students identified in the private college and among the conservative students identified in the state-supported college, significantly more were seniors than beginning students.

Reasoning   *What would best explain the trends observed in the college students' political orientations?* Five hypotheses to explain the trends are offered, and we are asked to identify the hypothesis that is most supported by the information already given about the studies. It should be noted that the information given is very limited, whereas the hypotheses offered involve quite broad generalizations, so whatever support is provided by the given information for any of these will at best be quite weak from a statistician's perspective. We should look for the hypothesis that makes the least ambitious claim and draws most closely on the given information.

A   The given information, without unjustified introduction of unstated assumptions, provides no insight into the political orientations of the students' parents.

B   **Correct.** Among the five hypotheses offered, this makes the least ambitious claim. Although its scope extends to college seniors in general (and in a statistical sense goes far beyond the evidence provided in the given information), it is the best supported of the five because it deviates least from the information we have. It is a good inference that the students' political re-orientation occurred as a result of the "experiences they have had while in college"—even if some of the truly mind-changing experiences were obtained in activities unrelated to their college life (e.g., speaking with fellow workers in a part-time restaurant job).

C   We are given no information about the students' places of origin. The passage states: "orientations were independent of the student's region of origin."

D   The given information provides no information regarding which among a multiplicity of conceivable influences contributed most strongly to the students' political orientations.

E   We are not told in the given information that the students were "confronted with pressures for financial success"—although it is a truism that they were becoming older in their progress toward graduation.

The correct answer is B.

Questions 155 to 188 - Difficulty: Medium

CR90661.01

155. Donations of imported food will be distributed to children in famine-stricken countries in the form of free school meals. The process is efficient because the children are easy to reach at the schools and cooking facilities are often available on site.

Which of the following, if true, casts the most serious doubt on the efficiency of the proposed process?

(A) The emphasis on food will detract from the major function of the schools, which is to educate the children.

(B) A massive influx of donated food will tend to lower the price of food in the areas near the schools.

(C) Supplies of fuel needed for cooking at the schools arrive there only intermittently and in inadequate quantities.

(D) The reduction in farm surpluses in donor countries benefits the donor countries to a greater extent than the recipient countries are benefited by the donations.

(E) The donation of food tends to strengthen the standing of the political party that happens to be in power when the donation is made.

Evaluation of a Plan

Situation   On grounds of efficiency, it has been proposed that food donated to famine-stricken countries be distributed free to children through the schools. Many of the country's children attend school. Many schools have cooking facilities. Distributing the food through the schools is thus an efficient way of providing nutrition, at least to the children.

Reasoning   *What would most cast doubt on the efficiency of the proposed distribution method?* The rationale offered for the method is twofold. First, many of the country's children attend school. Secondly, many schools have cooking facilities. Any additional information that weakens the significance of either of these two parts of the rationale would cast doubt on the efficiency of the proposed distribution process.

A   This information does not cast significant doubt on the rationale. Of course, providing nutrition might take some time that could otherwise be devoted to teaching and would in that sense perhaps "detract" from the schools' main mission. However, the focus of the given information is on the efficiency of food distribution through the schools, presumably as compared with other methods of distribution that would provide children with adequate nutrition. The trade-off involving some loss of teaching time may be rendered less significant by the fact that children lacking adequate nutrition cannot learn well.

B   This effect, if it occurred, could damage local markets but could also in the short term make locally grown food more available to those who need it. However, the point at issue is whether the rationale for distributing donated food through the schools to improve children's nutrition sufficiently indicates that this distribution method is efficient for that purpose.

C   **Correct.** This information indicates that one part of the rationale given for the efficiency of the distribution method should carry less weight. If the "cooking facilities" at the schools are often inoperable due to lack of fuel, then some of the food to be distributed (for example, staples such as corn, millet, rice, or sorghum) may not be consumable.

D   This information fails to address the central issue, which is the relative efficiency of the proposed distribution method for donated food, to improve children's nutrition.

E   This addresses a possible effect of any food donation and fails to focus on the central issue identified in the foregoing discussion.

The correct answer is C.

CR21661.01

156. *John:* You told me once that no United States citizen who supports union labor should buy an imported car. Yet you are buying an Alma. Since Alma is one of the biggest makers of imports, I infer that you no longer support unions.

Harry: I still support labor unions. Even though Alma is a foreign car company, the car I am buying, the Alma Deluxe, is designed, engineered, and manufactured in the United States.

Harry's method of defending his purchase of an Alma is to

(A) disown the principle he formerly held

(B) show that John's argument involves a false unstated assumption

(C) contradict John's conclusion without challenging John's reasoning in drawing that conclusion

(D) point out that one of the statements John makes in support of his argument is false

(E) claim that his is a special case in which the rule need not apply

Evaluation of a Plan

Situation   Harry has bought a car manufactured by Alma, a company among the largest makers of cars imported to the United States. From that fact John infers that Harry no longer holds a principle he formerly professed: that nobody who supports U.S. union labor should buy an imported car. Harry responds by clarifying that the Alma Deluxe he is buying is entirely a U.S. product.

Reasoning   *What method has Harry used to show that his purchasing an Alma is not inconsistent with his principles?* Harry does this by showing that John is incorrectly assuming that the car Harry is purchasing has been imported.

A   Harry does not disown the principle he formerly held; rather, he tries to show that his purchase is consistent with it.

B   **Correct.** John mistakenly assumes—without asserting—that the Alma that Harry is buying must be an imported car, and Harry indicates that this assumption is false.

C   Harry challenges John's conclusion but he also challenges John's reasoning, by indicating that it relies on a false unstated assumption.

D   John does not state the assumption that Harry indicates is false, but Harry recognizes that the assumption in question is unstated.

E   Harry does not claim this; he claims, rather, that the new Alma he is purchasing is not imported and so his purchase does not violate his principle concerning union labor.

The correct answer is B.

CR31661.01

157. Public-sector (government-owned) companies are often unprofitable and a drain on the taxpayer. Such enterprises should be sold to the private sector, where competition will force them either to be efficient and profitable or else to close.

Which of the following, if true, identifies a flaw in the policy proposed above?

(A) The revenue gained from the sale of public-sector companies is likely to be negligible compared to the cost of maintaining them.

(B) By buying a public-sector company and then closing the company and selling its assets, a buyer can often make a profit.

(C) The services provided by many public-sector companies must be made available to citizens, even when a price that covers costs cannot be charged.

(D) Some unprofitable private-sector companies have become profitable after being taken over by the government to prevent their closing.

(E) The costs of environmental protection, contributions to social programs, and job-safety measures are the same in the public and private sectors.

Evaluation of a Plan

Situation A policy position is advocated, i.e., that unprofitable public-sector companies that burden taxpayers should be sold to the private sector. As private-sector companies, they would either become efficient and profitable or go out of business.

Reasoning *In what way is the policy position flawed?* The rationale given for the policy is that unprofitable public-sector companies burden taxpayers and privatizing them would subject them to competition—which would force them either to become efficient and profitable or to go out of business. But one of the characteristics of some public-sector companies is that they must provide certain services in market segments where provision of the services cannot become profitable. For example, provision of transportation services in sparsely populated rural areas is likely to be unprofitable because utilization of the services is insufficient to cover the cost of those services at a price that the market can bear.

A   This information does not clearly indicate a flaw, since elimination of an exorbitant recurring cost by selling off, even at a very low price, an inefficient public company could be financially rational, even if not rational in other ways.

B   This scenario could result in the non-provision of services that should be provided in the public interest, but it represents an aberration relative to the privatization policy described and does not indicate an essential flaw in that policy.

C   **Correct.** This information indicates an essential flaw in the privatization policy described, since private companies are unlikely to provide services, even those needed by the public, in situations where provision of those services is unprofitable.

D   This information indicates that some government-controlled companies can be profitable even when those companies were not profitable when in the private sector. But this does not indicate a flaw in the reasoning concerning privatization.

E   This information offers no help in identifying a flaw in the argument. The types of costs listed are only some of the costs that companies incur and may not be the most significant cost factors in determining whether a company is profitable or not.

The correct answer is C.

CR91661.01

158. After receiving numerous complaints from residents about loud, highly amplified music played at local clubs, Middletown is considering a law that would prohibit clubs located in residential areas from employing musical groups that consist of more than three people.

The likelihood that the law would be effective in reducing noise would be most seriously diminished if which of the following were true?

(A) Groups that consist of more than three musicians are usually more expensive for clubs to hire than are groups that consist of fewer than three musicians.

(B) In towns that have passed similar laws, many clubs in residential areas have relocated to nonresidential areas.

(C) Most of the complaints about the music have come from people who do not regularly attend the clubs.

(D) Much of the music popular at the local clubs can be played only by groups of at least four musicians.

(E) Amplified music played by fewer than three musicians generally is as loud as amplified music played by more than three musicians.

Evaluation of a Plan

Situation   Middletown is considering a law to eliminate a nuisance that residents have complained about: loud, highly amplified music at local clubs. The proposed law would address this by prohibiting the clubs to have groups of more than three musicians playing at the club.

Reasoning   *Which statement, if true, would be the strongest indication that the proposed law would fail to reduce the noise that residents complained of?* The proposed limit on group size depends on the assumption that the music played by a group of three musicians or fewer would not be loud enough to bother Middletown's residents. If this assumption is false, for example if some of the smaller groups felt a need to use powerful amplification, the proposed law would be unlikely to be eliminate the nuisance by reducing the noise sufficiently.

A   We are given no information about whether Middletown, in framing its proposal, gave any consideration to the costs the clubs incur in hiring groups of various sizes. If the clubs' costs but not their revenues were to decrease by hiring smaller groups, they would likely obey the new law. However, this by itself would not indicate success for the noise abatement program.

B   If the Middletown clubs were to relocate to nonresidential areas as a result of the law, this would contribute to the law's effectiveness in alleviating the noise disturbance.

C   The proposal for the law is motivated by Middletown's need to respond to "numerous" resident complaints. If relatively few complaints come from residents who regularly attend the clubs, it may be because most of those residents either like loud music or are insensitive to it. But this has no bearing on whether the proposed law would be effective in addressing the noise level that bothers numerous other residents.

D   This could make the law less acceptable to the clubs or their patrons. If the law proved unacceptable, an unacceptable frequency of violation might result unless the law is well designed for effective enforcement. But perhaps the law will be well designed for effective enforcement. Nothing in the passage suggests otherwise.

E   **Correct.** This indicates that the size of a musical group generally has little impact on the volume of sound that the group produces. The proposed law is therefore likely to be ineffective in reducing the noise residents complained about.

The correct answer is E.

CR02661.01

159. From enlargements that are commonly found on the ulna bones of the forearms of Ice Age human skeletons, anthropologists have drawn the conclusion that the Ice Age humans represented by those skeletons frequently hunted by throwing spears. The bone enlargements, the anthropologists believe, resulted from the stresses of habitual throwing.

Which of the following, if true, would be the LEAST appropriate to use as support for the conclusion drawn by the anthropologists?

(A) Humans typically favor one arm over the other when throwing, and most Ice Age human skeletons have enlargements on the ulna bone of only one arm.

(B) Such enlargements on the ulna bone do not appear on skeletons from other human cultures of the same time period whose diets are believed to have been mainly vegetarian.

(C) Cave paintings dating from approximately the same time period and located not far from where the skeletons were found show hunters carrying and throwing spears.

(D) Damaged bones in the skeletons show evidence of diseases that are believed to have afflicted most people living during the Ice Age.

(E) Twentieth-century athletes who use a throwing motion similar to that of a hunter throwing a spear often develop enlargements on the ulna bone similar to those detected on the Ice Age skeletons.

Evaluation of a Plan

Situation The ulna-bone enlargements often found on forearms of skeletons of Ice Age humans have led anthropologists to conclude that those humans frequently hunted by throwing spears and that this practice caused the bone enlargement.

Reasoning *Which of the additional pieces of information offered provide the weakest (if any) support for the anthropologists' conclusion?* A premise of the anthropologists' reasoning is that many Ice Age humans developed enlarged ulna bones. Another premise is that the bone enlargements resulted from the stresses of habitual [spear] throwing. The anthropologists' conclusion is that those Ice Age humans frequently hunted by throwing spears. Several of the five additional pieces of information provide additional support for the anthropologists' conclusion.

A The information, if true, that the bone enlargement found on Ice Age skeletons is typically found on just one arm provides significant additional support for the argument's conclusion. Ice Age spear-throwing hunters would likely have been left-handed or right-handed and would have habitually used just one of their arms—either left or right—to throw spears.

B This information, if true, provides significant additional support for the anthropologists' conclusion. Ice Age humans with mainly vegetarian diets would have hunted, if at all, only infrequently—and so would not have been habitual spear-throwing hunters. We would expect, then, that if the anthropologists' conclusion is correct, enlarged ulna bones would not be found among the remains of such populations— and that is what the archaeological evidence indicates.

C This information, if true, provides compelling evidence that some Ice Age human populations hunted using spears, and so it provides significant additional support for the anthropologists' conclusion.

D Correct. This information, if true, tends to weaken the support for the anthropologists' conclusion. It vaguely suggests that diseases that were endemic in the Ice Age and caused bone damage might adequately explain the enlargement of ulna bones found in the archaeological evidence. If this were correct, then that bone enlargement could no longer be regarded as compelling evidence of spear-throwing.

E This information, if true, provides additional support for the anthropologists' conclusion. Twentieth-century athletes (perhaps javelin throwers, for example) use a throwing motion like that of spear throwers, and they often develop enlarged ulna bones like those found in the archaeological evidence.

The correct answer is D.

CR12661.01

160. The town council of North Tarrytown favored changing the name of the town to Sleepy Hollow. Council members argued that making the town's association with Washington Irving and his famous "legend" more obvious would increase tourism and result immediately in financial benefits for the town's inhabitants.

The council members' argument requires the assumption that

(A) most of the inhabitants would favor a change in the name of the town

(B) many inhabitants would be ready to supply tourists with information about Washington Irving and his "legend"

(C) the town can accomplish, at a very low cost per capita, the improvements in tourist facilities that an increase in tourism would require

(D) other towns in the region have changed their names to reflect historical associations and have, as a result, experienced a rise in tourism

(E) the immediate per capita cost to inhabitants of changing the name of the town would be less than the immediate per capita revenue they would receive from the change

Evaluation of a Plan

Situation   Members of the North Tarrytown town council argued for changing the town's name to Sleepy Hollow (the name of a fictitious place in stories by early nineteenth-century author Washington Irving). The goal was to increase tourism.

Reasoning   *What unstated assumption is required for the council members' argument to be logically compelling?* Their argument was that people who associate the name Sleepy Hollow with the author Washington Irving would come to visit the town because of that association. The resulting influx of tourists would provide additional spending that would "immediately" result in financial benefits for the town's inhabitants. There would not be such immediate benefits if the additional spending did not outweigh the costs of the name change.

A   This information about the popular acceptability of the name-change strategy could provide additional logical support for the proposal, but the information is not strictly required for the council members' reasoning to logically succeed.

B   If this occurred, it could benefit tourists and help enhance the town's reputation as a tourist venue, thus helping the name-change plan attain its goals. But an assumption that this would occur is not necessary for the logical success of the council members' reasoning.

C   This could make it more likely that the proposed name-change strategy would attain its financial goals. But the council members' reasoning does not have to assume that the relevant costs would be "very low."

D   This information, if true, would help dispel any doubts as to whether the proposed name change would attain its goals. But it is not information that is necessary for the council members' reasoning to logically succeed.

E   **Correct.** To be logically successful, the council members' reasoning requires that this be assumed. Part of the council members' reasoning is that the proposed name change would "result immediately in financial benefits for the town's inhabitants." This result will not occur unless the immediate costs associated with implementing the change are less than the revenue accruing to the town's inhabitants as a result. In the medium and long term, the name change could provide increased financial benefits to the town's inhabitants, but the council members' reasoning requires that those benefits flow immediately.

The correct answer is E.

CR06795

161. Premature babies who receive regular massages are more active than premature babies who do not. Even when all the babies drink the same amount of milk, the massaged babies gain more weight than do the unmassaged babies. This is puzzling because a more active person generally requires a greater food intake to maintain or gain weight.

Which of the following, if true, best reconciles the apparent discrepancy described above?

(A) Increased activity leads to increased levels of hunger, especially when food intake is not also increased.

(B) Massage increases premature babies' curiosity about their environment, and curiosity leads to increased activity.

(C) Increased activity causes the intestines of premature babies to mature more quickly, enabling the babies to digest and absorb more of the nutrients in the milk they drink.

(D) Massage does not increase the growth rate of babies over one year old, if the babies had not been previously massaged.

(E) Premature babies require a daily intake of nutrients that is significantly higher than that required by babies who were not born prematurely.

Argument Construction

Situation Premature babies who receive regular massages are more active and gain more weight than unmassaged premature babies do, even when they drink the same amount of milk.

Reasoning *What would help to explain how the massaged babies could be more active than the unmassaged babies and yet still gain more weight without consuming more milk?* If the massaged babies are burning more calories than unmassaged babies through their extra activity, but are not consuming more calories in the form of milk, then how are they gaining more weight than the unmassaged babies? Possible explanations could cite factors suggesting how the massaged babies might not actually burn more calories despite their greater activity; how they might consume or absorb more calories even without consuming more milk; or how they might gain more weight without extra calorie intake.

A Increased hunger without increased food intake would not help to explain why the massaged babies are gaining more weight.

B This only helps to explain why the massaged babies are more active, not why they are gaining more weight without consuming more milk.

C **Correct.** This suggests that the increased activity of the massaged babies could increase their calorie and nutrient intake from a given amount of milk, thereby explaining how they could gain extra weight without drinking more milk.

D This suggests that the apparent discrepancy is only present in premature babies under one year old, but it does not explain why that discrepancy exists.

E The passage does not compare premature babies to babies that were not born prematurely, but rather only compares premature babies that are massaged to premature babies that are not massaged.

The correct answer is C.

CR02865

162. In Australia, in years with below-average rainfall, less water goes into rivers and more water is extracted from rivers for drinking and irrigation. Consequently, in such years, water levels drop considerably and the rivers flow more slowly. Because algae grow better the more slowly the water in which they are growing moves, such years are generally beneficial to populations of algae. But, by contrast, populations of algae drop in periods of extreme drought.

Which of the following, if true, does most to explain the contrast?

(A) Algae grow better in ponds and lakes than in rivers.

(B) The more slowly water moves, the more conducive its temperature is to the growth of algae.

(C) Algae cannot survive in the absence of water.

(D) Algae must be filtered out of water before it can be used for drinking.

(E) The larger the population of algae in a body of water, the less sunlight reaches below the surface of the water.

Argument Construction

Situation   The quantity of water in Australian rivers greatly diminishes in years of below-average rainfall. When river levels become very low, the rivers flow more slowly. The low flow favors rapid algae growth. However, in periods of extreme drought, algae populations drop.

Reasoning   *What information would most help to explain the two contrasting trends in algae growth?* The information given indicates that algae proliferate when rivers flow slowly. When the water levels become extremely low, algae populations decrease. In periods of extreme drought, presumably some rivers retain little or no water.

A   This has no obvious relevance to explaining the contrast in the algae growth trends.

B   Nothing in the given information is explicit about the effects of water temperature and how that changes in rivers with changes in rainfall rates.

C   **Correct.** This information could help explain the decrease in algae populations during periods of extreme drought. It seems quite probable that during such periods, at least parts of some riverbeds would dry out.

D   This information does not help explain the contrasting trends in algae growth. Algae filtered out of river water to be used for drinking might not be returned to rivers, and this conceivably could affect algae populations. But it seems likely, based on the given information, that this would occur mainly during low-rainfall non-drought periods, when proliferation of algae has increased, so the impact on algae populations would probably be minimal.

E   This information is clearly irrelevant to the contrast that needs to be explained.

The correct answer is C.

CR00693
163. Which of the following, if true, most logically completes the politician's argument?

United States politician: Although the amount of United States goods shipped to Mexico doubled in the year after tariffs on trade between the two countries were reduced, it does not follow that the reduction in tariffs caused the sales of United States goods to companies and consumers in Mexico to double that year, because _____.

(A) many of the United States companies that produced goods that year had competitors based in Mexico that had long produced the same kind of goods

(B) most of the increase in goods shipped by United States companies to Mexico was in parts shipped to the companies' newly relocated subsidiaries for assembly and subsequent shipment back to the United States

(C) marketing goods to a previously unavailable group of consumers is most successful when advertising specifically targets those consumers, but developing such advertising often takes longer than a year

(D) the amount of Mexican goods shipped to the United States remained the same as it had been before the tariff reductions

(E) there was no significant change in the employment rate in either of the countries that year

Argument Construction

Situation   The politician suggests that tariffs on trade between Mexico and the United States were reduced during a certain year and notes that, in the year after that year, the amount of United States goods shipped to Mexico doubled. It may seem from this that the decrease in tariffs, because they may have reduced the prices of United States goods to Mexican companies and consumers, caused Mexican companies and consumers to double their purchases of United States goods in the year after the reduction in tariffs. This might explain the doubling of shipments of goods to Mexico. However, the politician argues that the decrease in tariffs did *not* cause the purchase of United States goods by Mexican companies and consumers to double.

Reasoning   *What possible facts would indicate that the decrease in tariffs may not have caused Mexican companies and consumers to double their purchases of United States goods?* The task in this question is to complete an argument that purports to show that a certain inference—that sales of United States goods to companies and consumers in Mexico increased as a result of the tariff decrease—does not follow logically from the fact that shipments of United States goods to Mexico doubled after the decrease in tariffs. Although it is not necessary to show that sales of United States goods to companies and consumers in Mexico did not double, any statement that would significantly decrease the strength of this inference may provide a reasonable answer to our question.

A   The argument that the politician is criticizing concerns a change in a certain year that purportedly caused another purported change in the next year. This answer choice, about longstanding relationships between United States and Mexican companies, does not address these changes.

B   **Correct.** If the statement in this answer choice is true, then we cannot, on the basis of an increase in shipments of goods to Mexico, infer that these goods were purchased by Mexican companies and consumers. The statement thus directly supports the politician's argument.

C   The argument that the politician is criticizing has to do with purported changes in purchasing behavior by Mexican companies and consumers, due to an increase in tariffs. This answer choice, being entirely concerned with the effectiveness of marketing and advertising, does not address the argument.

D   Although this answer choice may suggest that the change in tariffs did not cause a significant change in shipments of Mexican goods to the United States, it does not address the matter of shipments of United States goods to Mexico.

E   This answer choice addresses an aspect that would be of interest when examining the effects of the change in tariffs. But it does not address the purported change that is addressed by the politician's argument.

The correct answer is B.

CR06845

164. Budget constraints have made police officials consider reassigning a considerable number of officers from traffic enforcement to work on higher-priority, serious crimes. Reducing traffic enforcement for this reason would be counterproductive, however, in light of the tendency of criminals to use cars when engaged in the commission of serious crimes. An officer stopping a car for a traffic violation can make a search that turns up evidence of serious crime.

Which of the following, if true, most strengthens the argument given?

(A) An officer who stops a car containing evidence of the commission of a serious crime risks a violent confrontation, even if the vehicle was stopped only for a traffic violation.

(B) When the public becomes aware that traffic enforcement has lessened, it typically becomes lax in obeying traffic rules.

(C) Those willing to break the law to commit serious crimes are often in committing such crimes unwilling to observe what they regard as the lesser constraints of traffic law.

(D) The offenders committing serious crimes who would be caught because of traffic violations are not the same group of individuals as those who would be caught if the arresting officers were reassigned from traffic enforcement.

(E) The great majority of persons who are stopped by officers for traffic violations are not guilty of any serious crimes.

Argument Construction

Situation Budget constraints have made police officials consider reassigning many officers from traffic enforcement to work on serious crimes. But criminals often drive when committing serious crimes, and police who stop cars for traffic violations can find evidence of those crimes.

Reasoning *What additional information, when combined with the argument provided, would suggest that it would be counterproductive to reassign officers from traffic enforcement to work on serious crimes?* The argument implicitly reasons that because officers working on traffic enforcement can turn up evidence of serious crimes by searching cars that commit traffic violations, reassigning those officers would hinder police efforts to prevent serious crime, even if the officers were reassigned to work directly on serious crime. The argument could be strengthened by information suggesting that traffic enforcement may increase the probability that evidence relating to serious crimes will be discovered.

A   If anything, this risk of violence might discourage traffic enforcement officers from stopping and searching as many cars, thus reducing their effectiveness at preventing serious crimes.

B   This suggests that reassigning officers from traffic enforcement to work on serious crimes would increase the number of unpunished minor traffic violations, not the number of unpunished serious crimes.

C   **Correct.** This suggests that people committing serious crimes often commit traffic violations as well, increasing the likelihood that traffic enforcement officers will stop and search their cars and find evidence of those crimes.

D   The question at issue is not whether the same offenders would be caught if the officers were reassigned, but rather whether more or fewer offenders would be caught.

E   This weakens the argument by suggesting that most work by traffic enforcement officers is unrelated to preventing serious crimes.

The correct answer is C.

CR10106
165. Conventional wisdom suggests vaccinating elderly people first in flu season, because they are at greatest risk of dying if they contract the virus. This year's flu virus poses particular risk to elderly people and almost none at all to younger people, particularly children. Nevertheless, health professionals are recommending vaccinating children first against the virus rather than elderly people.

Which of the following, if true, provides the strongest reason for the health professionals' recommendation?

(A) Children are vulnerable to dangerous infections when their immune systems are severely weakened by other diseases.

(B) Children are particularly unconcerned with hygiene and therefore are the group most responsible for spreading the flu virus to others.

(C) The vaccinations received last year will confer no immunity to this year's flu virus.

(D) Children who catch one strain of the flu virus and then recover are likely to develop immunity to at least some strains with which they have not yet come in contact.

(E) Children are no more likely than adults to have immunity to a particular flu virus if they have never lived through a previous epidemic of the same virus.

Argument Construction

Situation   Although this year's flu virus poses particular risk to elderly people and almost no risk to children, health professionals are recommending vaccinating children before elderly people, contrary to what conventional wisdom recommends.

Reasoning   *What would help justify the health professionals' recommendation?* Since children will experience almost no risk from the virus, vaccinating them first for their own sake appears unnecessary. However, individuals at no personal risk from a virus can still transmit it to more-vulnerable individuals. If children are especially likely to transmit the virus, it could be reasonable to vaccinate them first in order to protect others, including elderly people, by preventing the virus from spreading.

A   This might be a reason to vaccinate certain children with severely weakened immune systems, if their weak immune systems would even respond effectively to the vaccine. However, it is not clearly a reason to vaccinate the vast majority of children.

B   **Correct.** This suggests that children are especially likely to transmit the virus even if it does not endanger them. So as explained above, it provides a good reason for the health professionals' recommendation.

C   This might be a good reason to vaccinate everyone, but it is not clearly a reason to vaccinate children before vaccinating elderly people.

D   If anything, this would suggest that there might be a reason not to vaccinate children against this year's strain at all: unvaccinated children who catch this year's strain, which the argument claims is relatively harmless to children, may develop immunity to more dangerous strains that might arise in the future.

E   The argument claims that this year's virus poses almost no risk to children. So even if they are not technically immune to it, it does not affect them significantly enough to justify vaccinating them before vaccinating elderly people.

The correct answer is B.

CR01392

166. Pro-Tect Insurance Company has recently been paying out more on car-theft claims than it expected. Cars with special antitheft devices or alarm systems are much less likely to be stolen than are other cars. Consequently Pro-Tect, as part of an effort to reduce its annual payouts, will offer a discount to holders of car-theft policies if their cars have antitheft devices or alarm systems.

Which of the following, if true, provides the strongest indication that the plan is likely to achieve its goal?

(A) The decrease in the risk of car theft conferred by having a car alarm is greatest when only a few cars have such alarms.

(B) The number of policyholders who have filed a claim in the past year is higher for Pro-Tect than for other insurance companies.

(C) In one or two years, the discount that Pro-Tect is offering will amount to more than the cost of buying certain highly effective antitheft devices.

(D) Currently, Pro-Tect cannot legally raise the premiums it charges for a given amount of insurance against car theft.

(E) The amount Pro-Tect has been paying out on car-theft claims has been greater for some models of car than for others.

Evaluation of a Plan

Situation An insurance company is paying more money on car-theft claims than anticipated. To reduce these payments, the company is planning to offer discounts to customers whose cars have antitheft devices or alarm systems, because such cars are less likely to be stolen.

Reasoning *What piece of information would indicate that the plan is likely to succeed?* Pro-Tect wishes to reduce its annual payouts, and one way for that to happen is for fewer cars insured by Pro-Tect to be stolen. To help accomplish this, Pro-Tect is offering discounts to policyholders whose cars are so equipped, because cars equipped with antitheft devices or alarm systems are less likely to be stolen than are cars without such devices. What would interfere with the success of Pro-Tect's plan? Car owners would probably resist investing in antitheft devices or alarm systems if the cost of such systems is higher than the discount they will receive. So if Pro-Tect sets the discount at a level that makes installing antitheft devices seem like a bargain to car owners, the plan will most likely succeed.

A Pro-Tect's plan is designed to increase the number of cars equipped with car alarms. If having more cars equipped with car alarms reduces those alarms' effectivity in preventing thefts, then Pro-Tect's plan is unlikely to achieve its goal.

B Pro-Tect's claims in relation to those of other insurance companies are not relevant to whether Pro-Tect's plan to reduce its own car-theft claims will achieve its goal.

C **Correct.** This statement suggests that Pro-Tect's plan will provide an effective incentive for car owners to install antitheft devices; this statement therefore properly identifies information that indicates the plan is likely to achieve its goal.

D Because Pro-Tect's plan does not involve raising the premiums it charges, restrictions on its ability to do so are irrelevant to whether that plan will achieve its goal.

E Pro-Tect's plan does not distinguish among different models of car, so this statement indicates nothing about whether the proposed plan will succeed.

The correct answer is C.

CR00783

167. While the total enrollment of public elementary and secondary schools in Sondland is one percent higher this academic year than last academic year, the number of teachers there increased by three percent. Thus, the Sondland Education Commission's prediction of a teacher shortage as early as next academic year is unfounded.

Which of the following, if true, most seriously weakens the claim that the prediction of a teacher shortage as early as next academic year is unfounded?

(A) Funding for public elementary schools in Sondland is expected to increase over the next ten years.

(B) Average salaries for Sondland's teachers increased at the rate of inflation from last academic year to this academic year.

(C) A new law has mandated that there be 10 percent more teachers per pupil in Sondland's public schools next academic year than there were this academic year.

(D) In the past, increases in enrollments in public elementary and secondary schools in Sondland have generally been smaller than increases in the number of teachers.

(E) Because of reductions in funding, the number of students enrolling in teacher-training programs in Sondland is expected to decline beginning in the next academic year.

Argument Evaluation

Situation In Sondland's public schools this academic year, the number of students is one percent higher and the number of teachers three percent higher than they were last academic year. For this reason, the Sondland Education Commission's prediction of a teacher shortage as early as next academic year is questionable.

Reasoning *What evidence would most weaken support for the claim that there will be no teacher shortage next academic year?* A teacher shortage will arise next academic year if the number of teachers needed will exceed the number of teachers employed. This will happen if the number of teachers needed increases without a sufficient increase in the number employed, or if the number employed decreases without a sufficient decrease in the number needed. Evidence that either or both of these changes will occur next academic year is evidence that the predicted shortage will occur, so any such evidence will weaken support for the claim that the prediction is unfounded.

A Increased funding will likely allow more teachers to be hired but will not necessarily increase the need for teachers, so it does not support the prediction of a teacher shortage (and indeed it very slightly undermines the prediction). Also, the funding is expected to increase over ten years, not necessarily next year. Furthermore, we are not told who expects this increase or why. Their expectation may be unjustifiable.

B A salary increase at the rate of inflation is equivalent to no change in the salary's actual value. The absence of a change in real salary in the past academic year does not by itself support any prediction of a change in the number of teachers needed or employed next academic year.

C **Correct.** The schools will need a lot more teachers next academic year to satisfy this mandate. It may be difficult for the schools to hire enough teachers in time. This provides at least some reason to predict that a teacher shortage will result.

D This means the number of students per teacher has been generally declining. It does not suggest that next academic year the number of teachers needed will increase, nor that the number employed will decrease.

E This does support the prediction that a shortage of trained teachers will arise eventually. But the declining number of students in teacher-training programs next academic year probably will not reduce the number of teachers available to teach during that same year.

The correct answer is C.

CR05590

168. Art restorers who have been studying the factors that cause Renaissance oil paintings to deteriorate physically when subject to climatic changes have found that the oil paint used in these paintings actually adjusts to these changes well. The restorers therefore hypothesize that it is a layer of material called gesso, which is under the paint, that causes the deterioration.

Which of the following, if true, most strongly supports the restorers' hypothesis?

(A) Renaissance oil paintings with a thin layer of gesso are less likely to show deterioration in response to climatic changes than those with a thicker layer.

(B) Renaissance oil paintings are often painted on wooden panels, which swell when humidity increases and contract when it declines.

(C) Oil paint expands and contracts readily in response to changes in temperature, but it absorbs little water and so is little affected by changes in humidity.

(D) An especially hard and nonabsorbent type of gesso was the raw material for moldings on the frames of Renaissance oil paintings.

(E) Gesso layers applied by Renaissance painters typically consisted of a coarse base layer onto which several increasingly fine-grained layers were applied.

Argument Evaluation

Situation   Renaissance paintings are subject to deterioration due to changes in climate, but their actual paint is not a factor in this deterioration. Instead, restorers hypothesize, it is gesso, the material under the paint, that causes problems for the paintings.

Reasoning   *What would most strongly support the hypothesis that gesso is causing the deterioration?* An indication that gesso is affected by climatic changes would be most helpful in supporting the hypothesis. What could show that gesso is affected in this way? If the extent of a painting's deterioration is directly related to the amount of gesso used under that painting, then the gesso clearly plays some part in that deterioration.

A   **Correct.** This statement properly identifies a point supporting the hypothesis.

B   This suggests that another factor—the wood of the panels—has a role in the paintings' deterioration. Thus it weakens the hypothesis that gesso causes the deterioration.

C   This merely reinforces given information, that the paint itself is not responsible for the paintings' deterioration.

D   Because this gives no information about any connection between this especially hard and nonabsorbent type of gesso and the type of gesso used under the paint in Renaissance paintings, the properties and usage of the former type of gesso are irrelevant to the question of whether gesso is responsible for the paintings' deterioration.

E   Because we are told nothing about whether this technique of gesso application increases or decreases the likelihood that gesso will be affected by climatic change, it does not support the restorers' hypothesis.

The correct answer is A.

CR10731

169. A newly discovered painting seems to be the work of one of two 17th-century artists, either the northern German Johannes Drechen or the Frenchman Louis Birelle, who sometimes painted in the same style as Drechen. Analysis of the carved picture frame, which has been identified as the painting's original 17th-century frame, showed that it is made of wood found widely in northern Germany at the time, but rare in the part of France where Birelle lived. This shows that the painting is most likely the work of Drechen.

Which of the following is an assumption that the argument requires?

(A) The frame was made from wood local to the region where the picture was painted.

(B) Drechen is unlikely to have ever visited the home region of Birelle in France.

(C) Sometimes a painting so closely resembles others of its era that no expert is able to confidently decide who painted it.

(D) The painter of the picture chose the frame for the picture.

(E) The carving style of the picture frame is not typical of any specific region of Europe.

Argument Construction

Situation   A 17th-century painting has been discovered that was either by Johannes Drechen from northern Germany or by French artist Louis Birelle. The painting's original picture frame is made of wood widely found in 17th-century northern Germany but rare in the French region where Birelle lived. So the painting was probably the work of Drechen.

Reasoning   *Which answer choice is an assumption required by the argument?* If the painting is correctly attributed to Drechen, then the wood that the frame was made from probably came from the region where Drechen lived and did his painting. The argument assumes that the specific wood used in the frame came from northern Germany rather than from some other place where that wood might have been found, and where (for all we know) Birelle might have visited.

A   **Correct.** Without an assumption equivalent to this, the argument would fail.

B   This is not a required assumption (unlike, for example, the following: Drechen did not give the picture frame to Birelle as a gift).

C   This is a truism but is not required to make the argument's conclusion well supported.

D   This does not need to be assumed; Drechen could, for example, have simply asked a local frame-maker to make a frame for his picture.

E   Neither the affirmation nor the denial of this statement is needed to underpin the argument.

The correct answer is A.

CR09120

170. Archaeologists working in the Andes Mountains recently excavated a buried 4,000-year-old temple containing structures that align with a stone carving on a distant hill to indicate the direction of the rising sun at the summer solstice. Alignments in the temple were also found to point toward the position, at the summer solstice, of a constellation known in Andean culture as the Fox. Since the local mythology represents the fox as teaching people how to cultivate and irrigate plants, the ancient Andeans may have built the temple as a religious representation of the fox.

Which of the following is an assumption on which the argument is based?

(A) The constellation known as the Fox has the same position at the summer solstice as it did 4,000 years ago.

(B) In the region around the temple, the summer solstice marks the time for planting.

(C) The temple was protected from looters by dirt and debris built up over thousands of years.

(D) Other structural alignments at the temple point to further constellations with agricultural significance.

(E) The site containing the temple was occupied for a significant amount of time before abandonment.

Argument Construction

Situation A recently excavated 4,000-year-old temple contains structures that point toward the positions at the summer solstice of both the rising sun and a constellation known in local culture as the Fox. Local mythology represents the fox as teaching people how to cultivate and irrigate plants.

Reasoning *What must be true in order for the argument's premises to suggest that the temple was built to religiously represent the fox?* The argument's premises are all observations about current conditions: the current alignment at the summer solstice of the temple relative to the sunrise and to the constellation known as the Fox, the current local name for a constellation, and current local mythology. To support the conclusion about the temple's original purpose, the argument has to assume that all these conditions may still be essentially the same as they were 4,000 years ago when the temple was built.

A **Correct.** If the constellation's position at the summer solstice relative to the temple is different from what it was 4,000 years ago, the temple must not have been aligned to point toward it when it was built. In that case, the argument's justification for associating the temple with that constellation and with the fox is undermined.

B This does not have to be assumed for the argument to succeed, though if true, it might strengthen the argument by providing additional evidence associating the temple with the mythological fox as a teacher of agriculture. But the argument could be just as strong if the solstice were instead associated with agricultural activities other than planting.

C Even if the temple was not protected from looters, the conditions described in the argument's premises may still be the same as they were 4,000 years ago.

D This is not assumed. Additional structural alignments pointing to different constellations associated with mythological beings other than the fox might weaken or even undermine the argument's justification for associating the temple with the fox specifically.

E The argument makes no assumption regarding how long the temple was occupied, or even regarding whether the temple was ever occupied.

The correct answer is A.

CR05065

171. Meat from chickens contaminated with salmonella bacteria can cause serious food poisoning. Capsaicin, the chemical that gives chili peppers their hot flavor, has antibacterial properties. Chickens do not have taste receptors for capsaicin and will readily eat feed laced with capsaicin. When chickens were fed such feed and then exposed to salmonella bacteria, relatively few of them became contaminated with salmonella.

In deciding whether the feed would be useful in raising salmonella-free chicken for retail sale, it would be most helpful to determine which of the following?

(A) Whether feeding capsaicin to chickens affects the taste of their meat

(B) Whether eating capsaicin reduces the risk of salmonella poisoning for humans

(C) Whether chicken is more prone to salmonella contamination than other kinds of meat

(D) Whether appropriate cooking of chicken contaminated with salmonella can always prevent food poisoning

(E) Whether capsaicin can be obtained only from chili peppers

Argument Evaluation

Situation   Chickens will readily eat feed laced with capsaicin, which appears to protect them from contamination with salmonella bacteria that can cause food poisoning.

Reasoning   *What information would help determine whether using the feed would be an effective strategy for raising salmonella-free chicken for retail sale?* In order for the strategy to be effective, it must be economically feasible for farmers to raise chickens using the feed, and there must be enough consumer demand for chickens raised this way. So any information about factors likely to affect either the economic feasibility of raising the chickens or consumer demand for them could be helpful in determining how useful the feed would be.

A   **Correct.** If chicken producers tried to market meat from capsaicin-fed chickens without knowing whether the taste is affected, they would risk alienating consumers. Of course, if they found that the taste is affected, they would then need to do further investigations to determine how consumers would likely respond to the difference. If consumers did not like the taste, this could negatively affect demand for the chickens. In that case, using the feed would not be an effective way to raise chickens for retail sale.

B   There are two ways this might be considered relevant. First, it might be thought that because capsaicin reduces the risk of salmonella poisoning in humans, it will also do so in chickens; but we already have good evidence of that in the argument. Second, it might be thought that, if the capsaicin does not produce chickens that are totally salmonella free, then if any capsaicin remains in the chickens, it will help prevent any humans who consume the chicken from getting salmonella poisoning. But the relevant issue is whether the capsaicin will make the chickens salmonella free, not whether humans will be protected whether the chickens are salmonella free or not.

C   The susceptibility of other types of meat to salmonella contamination would not affect the usefulness of the feed for preventing such contamination in chicken.

D   Presumably many people do not cook contaminated chicken appropriately, so consumers could still benefit from salmonella-free chicken whether or not appropriate cooking methods could prevent food poisoning.

E   Regardless of whether capsaicin can be obtained from other sources, chili peppers may be a perfectly viable source.

The correct answer is A.

CR04532

172. Which of the following most logically completes the argument below?

When mercury-vapor streetlights are used in areas inhabited by insect-eating bats, the bats feed almost exclusively around the lights, because the lights attract flying insects. In Greenville, the mercury-vapor streetlights are about to be replaced with energy-saving sodium streetlights, which do not attract insects. This change is likely to result in a drop in the population of insect-eating bats in Greenville, since _____.

(A) the bats do not begin to hunt until after sundown

(B) the bats are unlikely to feed on insects that do not fly

(C) the highway department will be able to replace mercury-vapor streetlights with sodium streetlights within a relatively short time and without disrupting the continuity of lighting at the locations of the streetlights

(D) in the absence of local concentrations of the flying insects on which bats feed, the bats expend much more energy on hunting for food, requiring much larger quantities of insects to sustain each bat

(E) bats use echolocation to catch insects and therefore gain no advantage from the fact that insects flying in the vicinity of streetlights are visible at night

Argument Construction

Situation   In areas with mercury-vapor streetlights, any insect-eating bats feed almost exclusively around the lights, which attract flying insects. In Greenville, mercury-vapor streetlights will soon be replaced with sodium streetlights that do not attract insects.

Reasoning   *What evidence would suggest that the change in streetlights will reduce Greenville's population of insect-eating bats?* Since the sodium streetlights will not attract flying insects, the bats will probably stop focusing their feeding around Greenville's streetlights after the lights are changed. A statement providing evidence that this will make it harder for the bats to get enough food to sustain themselves would support the conclusion that the change is likely to reduce Greenville's bat population and thus would logically complete the argument.

A   Insect-eating bats existed long before streetlights did, so they can probably find insects away from streetlights even if they hunt only after sundown.

B   Greenville will almost certainly still have flying insects for the bats to eat after the change, even if those insects no longer gather around the streetlights.

C   If anything, such a smooth transition would be less likely to disturb the bats and therefore less likely to reduce their population.

D   Correct. Since there will be no local concentrations of flying insects around Greenville streetlights after the change, the bats will most likely have more trouble getting enough to eat, and that their local population will therefore fall.

E   The advantage that the bats gain from mercury-vapor streetlights comes from the high concentration of insects. The fact that the bats get no additional advantage from the insects' visibility tells us nothing about what affect the change to a different type of light might have.

The correct answer is D.

CR01353

173. Rats injected with morphine exhibit decreased activity of the immune system, the bodily system that fights off infections. These same rats exhibited heightened blood levels of corticosteroids, chemicals secreted by the adrenal glands. Since corticosteroids can interfere with immune-system activity, scientists hypothesized that the way morphine reduces immune responses in rats is by stimulating the adrenal glands to secrete additional corticosteroids into the bloodstream.

Which of the following experiments would yield the most useful results for evaluating the scientists' hypothesis?

(A) Injecting morphine into rats that already have heightened blood levels of corticosteroids and then observing their new blood levels of corticosteroids

(B) Testing the level of immune-system activity of rats, removing their adrenal glands, and then testing the rats' immune-system activity levels again

(C) Injecting rats with corticosteroids and then observing how many of the rats contracted infections

(D) Removing the adrenal glands of rats, injecting the rats with morphine, and then testing the level of the rats' immune-system responses

(E) Injecting rats with a drug that stimulates immune-system activity and then observing the level of corticosteroids in their bloodstreams

Argument Evaluation

Situation Rats injected with morphine exhibit decreased immune-system activity and increased levels of corticosteroids, which are secreted by the adrenal glands and can interfere with immune-system activity.

Reasoning *What further experiment would help determine whether morphine reduces immune responses in rats by stimulating the adrenal glands to release more corticosteroids?* Contrary to the scientists' hypothesis, the experimental results might have occurred because the morphine injections directly reduced immune-system activity. Or the injections might have blocked some mechanism that reduces corticosteroid levels in the blood, even if the morphine did not stimulate the adrenal glands to produce more corticosteroids. To evaluate whether the scientists' hypothesis is more plausible than these rival hypotheses, it would be helpful to know whether similar experimental results would occur after morphine injections even if adrenal gland activity did not change.

A Morphine could stimulate the adrenal glands of rats with normal corticosteroid levels to produce more corticosteroids, whether or not it does so in rats whose corticosteroid levels are already heightened.

B Such an experiment would not involve morphine and thus would not help to determine how morphine affects immune-system activity in rats.

C Whether or not rats contract infections may not reliably indicate their levels of immune-system activity.

D Correct. If the immune system responses decreased after the morphine injections in this experiment, the hypothesis that it was by stimulation of the adrenal glands that morphine reduced immune-system activity would be undermined. But if no decrease in immune-system responses occurred, the hypothesis would be confirmed.

E Even if the mechanism by which a drug other than morphine increases immune-system activity were discovered, this discovery would not necessarily reveal the mechanism by which morphine reduces immune-system activity.

The correct answer is D.

CR06831

174. Curator: If our museum lends *Venus* to the Hart Institute for their show this spring, they will lend us their Rembrandt etchings for our print exhibition next fall. Having those etchings will increase attendance to the exhibition and hence increase revenue from our general admission fee.

Museum Administrator: But *Venus* is our biggest attraction. Moreover the Hart's show will run for twice as long as our exhibition. So on balance the number of patrons may decrease.

The point of the administrator's response to the curator is to question

(A) whether getting the Rembrandt etchings from the Hart Institute is likely to increase attendance at the print exhibition

(B) whether the Hart Institute's Rembrandt etchings will be appreciated by those patrons of the curator's museum for whom the museum's biggest attraction is *Venus*

(C) whether the number of patrons attracted by the Hart Institute's Rembrandt etchings will be larger than the number of patrons who do not come in the spring because *Venus* is on loan

(D) whether, if *Venus* is lent, the museum's revenue from general admission fees during the print exhibition will exceed its revenue from general admission fees during the Hart Institute's exhibition

(E) whether the Hart Institute or the curator's museum will have the greater financial gain from the proposed exchange of artworks

Argument Construction

Situation A curator and a museum administrator debate whether lending a particular artwork to the Hart Institute in exchange for a loan of some of the Hart Institute's artworks would increase or decrease attendance and revenue at the museum.

Reasoning *Which of the curator's explicit or implicit claims is the museum administrator questioning?* The administrator's statements that *Venus* is the museum's biggest attraction and that the Hart Institute's show will run twice as long as the museum's exhibition do not directly conflict with any statement or assumption made by the curator. However, the administrator's conclusion is that on balance the number of patrons at the museum may decrease if the curator's proposal is followed. This conclusion calls into question the curator's claim that the proposal will increase revenue from the general admission fee, since that claim presupposes that on balance the proposal will increase the number of visitors to the museum. (The context suggests that the administrator is using the term *patrons* to mean visitors rather than donors.)

A The administrator does not dispute that the Rembrandt etchings would probably increase attendance at the print exhibition but rather suggests that this increase would be exceeded by the loss of visitors to the museum while the Hart Institute borrows *Venus*.

B Neither the curator nor the administrator comments on whether the patrons attracted to the Rembrandt etchings would be the same people attracted to *Venus*.

C **Correct.** The curator implicitly infers that the former number will be larger than the latter, whereas the administrator questions this by asserting that the latter number may be larger than the former.

D The administrator does not question whether the revenue during the print exhibition will exceed the revenue during the Hart Institute's exhibition, but rather whether it will exceed the loss of revenue during the Hart Institute's exhibition.

E Neither the curator nor the administrator comments on whether the museum would gain more or less from the exchange than the Hart Institute would.

The correct answer is C.

CR03697

175. Which of the following most logically completes the passage?

Leaf beetles damage willow trees by stripping away their leaves, but a combination of parasites and predators generally keeps populations of these beetles in check. Researchers have found that severe air pollution results in reduced predator populations. The parasites, by contrast, are not adversely affected by pollution; nevertheless, the researchers' discovery probably does explain why leaf beetles cause particularly severe damage to willows in areas with severe air pollution, since _____.

(A) neither the predators nor the parasites of leaf beetles themselves attack willow trees

(B) the parasites that attack leaf beetles actually tend to be more prevalent in areas with severe air pollution than they are elsewhere

(C) the damage caused by leaf beetles is usually not enough to kill a willow tree outright

(D) where air pollution is not especially severe, predators have much more impact on leaf-beetle populations than parasites do

(E) willows often grow in areas where air pollution is especially severe

Argument Construction

Situation   Leaf beetles damage willow trees, but predators and parasites keep leaf beetle populations in check. Air pollution reduces populations of predators but not of parasites. Leaf beetles damage willows especially severely in areas with severe air pollution.

Reasoning   *What would support the conclusion that air pollution's effects on the predator populations (but not on the parasite populations) explains why leaf beetles damage willows the most in areas with severe air pollution?* The word *since* preceding the blank space at the end of the passage indicates that the space should be filled with a premise supporting the conclusion stated immediately before the *since*. To support this conclusion, it would help to have evidence that predators play a predominant role in keeping leaf beetle populations in check, and thus that the reduction of predator populations by air pollution could be sufficient to enable leaf beetle populations to grow and cause especially severe damage.

A   The fact that neither the predators nor the parasites directly contribute to harming the trees offers no reason to conclude that a difference in how they are affected by pollution would contribute to the harm that the beetles cause to the trees.

B   If the parasites are more prevalent in areas with severe air pollution, then they are more likely to keep leaf beetle populations in check in those areas, despite the reduced predator populations. Thus, the decline in predator populations would more likely be insufficient to explain why the leaf beetles cause more damage in those areas.

C   This observation is irrelevant to whether the decline in predator populations explains why leaf beetles damage willow trees more severely in areas with severe air pollution.

D   **Correct.** This indicates that predators play a predominant role in keeping leaf beetle populations in check, so, as explained above, it supports the argument's conclusion.

E   This is not clearly relevant to whether the decline in predator populations explains why leaf beetles damage willow trees more severely in areas with severe air pollution. The argument's conclusion could just as easily be true regardless of whether willows grow in such polluted areas frequently or infrequently.

The correct answer is D.

CR05438

176. On May first, in order to reduce the number of overdue books, a children's library instituted a policy of forgiving fines and giving bookmarks to children returning all of their overdue books. On July first there were twice as many overdue books as there had been on May first, although a record number of books had been returned during the interim.

Which of the following, if true, most helps to explain the apparent inconsistency in the results of the library's policy?

(A) The librarians did not keep accurate records of how many children took advantage of the grace period, and some of the children returning overdue books did not return all of their overdue books.

(B) Although the grace period enticed some children to return all of their overdue books, it did not convince all of the children with overdue books to return all of their books.

(C) The bookmarks became popular among the children, so in order to collect the bookmarks, many children borrowed many more books than they usually did and kept them past their due date.

(D) The children were allowed to borrow a maximum of five books for a two-week period, and hence each child could keep a maximum of fifteen books beyond their due date within a two-month period.

(E) Although the library forgave overdue fines during the grace period, the amount previously charged the children was minimal; hence, the forgiveness of the fines did not provide enough incentive for them to return their overdue books.

Argument Construction

Situation   After a library started forgiving fines and giving bookmarks to children who returned all their overdue books, the number of books returned greatly increased, but so did the number of overdue books.

Reasoning   *Why might the policy have simultaneously increased the number of overdue books and the number of books being returned?* In order to increase both these numbers, the policy must have resulted in more books being checked out, kept past their due dates, and then returned. But why would the policy have promoted that behavior? One possibility is that it rewarded the behavior. The policy involved giving children bookmarks as rewards for returning overdue books, while removing the fines that penalized the children for doing so. If the children liked the bookmarks, they might have tried to get more of them by deliberately checking books out in order to keep them past their due dates before returning them to get the bookmarks.

A   Failing to keep accurate records of the number of children would not clearly increase the number of books being returned. And the policy change did not apply to children who returned only some of their overdue books.

B   This suggests that the policy had limited effects, but does not help to explain why it had apparently inconsistent effects.

C   **Correct.** This explains how the policy gave the children a motive to check out and return more books while also allowing them to keep more of the books past the due dates.

D   This restriction would have limited the number of overdue books and thus would not help to explain why that number increased.

E   This suggests that the policy had little effect but does not help to explain why it had apparently inconsistent effects.

The correct answer is C.

CR00663

177. A certain species of desert lizard digs tunnels in which to lay its eggs. The eggs must incubate inside the tunnel for several weeks before hatching, and they fail to hatch if they are disturbed at any time during this incubation period. Yet these lizards guard their tunnels for only a few days after laying their eggs.

Which of the following, if true, most helps explain why there is no need for lizards to guard their tunnels for more than a few days?

(A) The eggs are at risk of being disturbed only during the brief egg-laying season when many lizards are digging in a relatively small area.

(B) The length of the incubation period varies somewhat from one tunnel to another.

(C) Each female lizard lays from 15 to 20 eggs, only about 10 of which hatch even if the eggs are not disturbed at any time during the incubation period.

(D) The temperature and humidity within the tunnels will not be suitable for the incubating eggs unless the tunnels are plugged with sand immediately after the eggs are laid.

(E) The only way to disturb the eggs of this lizard species is by opening up one of the tunnels in which they are laid.

Argument Construction

Situation Lizards of a certain species dig tunnels in which they lay their eggs. Although the eggs fail to hatch if disturbed during their several weeks of incubation, the lizards guard the tunnels for only a few days after laying the eggs.

Reasoning *What would help to explain why the lizards have to guard their tunnels for only a few days?* For the lizards to survive as a species, their behaviors must ensure that enough of their eggs hatch. Thus, they must successfully prevent enough of their eggs from being disturbed in the tunnels throughout the several weeks of incubation. If guarding the tunnels for only a few days accomplishes this, then some other factor must prevent the eggs from being disturbed during the remaining weeks. Evidence of any such factor would help to explain why the lizards do not have to guard the tunnels longer. For example, to protect the eggs without guarding them, the lizards might conceal the tunnel entrances after the first few days. Or animals likely to disturb the eggs might only be present for those first days, in which case there would be nothing for the lizards to guard against thereafter.

A **Correct.** This suggests that the only creatures likely to disturb the eggs are other lizards of the same species digging tunnels to lay their own eggs at around the same time. If so, each lizard can safely leave its eggs unguarded after a few days because all the other lizards will have finished digging.

B Even if the incubation period varies somewhat, the passage says it always lasts several weeks. So this does not explain why the lizards have to guard the tunnels for only a few days.

C If many eggs fail to hatch even when undisturbed, that is all the more reason for the lizards to protect the remaining eggs from disturbance throughout the incubation period so that at least some will hatch. So it does not explain why the lizards guard their tunnels only for a few days.

D Whether or not immediately plugging the tunnels with sand is enough to protect the eggs, this behavior does not explain why the lizards subsequently guard the tunnels for a few days and then leave for the rest of the incubation period.

E Even if it is impossible to disturb the eggs without opening the tunnels, that does not explain why the lizards guard the tunnels for a few days and then leave for the rest of the incubation period.

The correct answer is A.

CR00677

178. Most banks that issue credit cards charge interest rates on credit card debt that are ten percentage points higher than the rates those banks charge for ordinary consumer loans. These banks' representatives claim the difference is fully justified, since it simply covers the difference between the costs to these banks associated with credit card debt and those associated with consumer loans.

Which of the following, if true, most seriously calls into question the reasoning offered by the banks' representatives?

(A) Some lenders that are not banks offer consumer loans at interest rates that are even higher than most banks charge on credit card debt.

(B) Most car rental companies require that their customers provide signed credit card charge slips or security deposits.

(C) Two to three percent of the selling price of every item bought with a given credit card goes to the bank that issued that credit card.

(D) Most people need not use credit cards to buy everyday necessities, but could buy those necessities with cash or pay by check.

(E) People who pay their credit card bills in full each month usually pay no interest on the amounts they charge.

Argument Evaluation

Situation   Banks that issue credit cards tend to charge interest rates on the associated debt that are ten percentage points higher than the rates associated with "ordinary" consumer loans (consumer loans that are not associated with credit cards). Representatives of these banks have offered a justification of this practice, based on a claim that this difference in interest rates "simply covers the difference" in costs, to the banks, associated with these respective types of loans (loans associated with credit cards and consumer loans that are not associated with credit cards).

Reasoning   *What additional facts would indicate a flaw in the bank representatives' argument?* Given the description of the bank representatives' argument, we may assume that, by their estimation, the costs to banks associated with credit card debt are greater than the costs associated with other consumer loans. The representatives' argument, that the difference in interest rates "simply covers" this difference in costs, may then be seen as an argument that all of the extra money that the banks collect from the higher interest rates is *necessary* if the banks are to cover this difference in costs. If we can find a fact whereby the ten percentage point difference is not necessary to cover the difference in costs, then we may be able to "call into question" the bank representatives' argument.

A   The point of this response to the bank representatives' argument would seem to be that the relatively high interest rates on credit debt may be justified because certain other businesses charge even higher interest rates on consumer loans. Regardless of the merits of this response, it appears intended to *support* the argument of the representatives, whereas our task is to identify a fact that could be used to criticize the argument.

B   This purported fact does not address the argument concerning the interest rates on credit-card debt.

C   **Correct.** If two to three percent of the value of purchases made on credit cards goes to the issuing banks, then this money could be used to cover some of the difference in costs described by the bank representatives. The interest rates on credit cards could therefore be somewhat lower than they actually are, with the difference in costs nevertheless still fully covered. The difference in interest rates of ten percentage points may therefore not be necessary.

D   This point might be used in support of an argument that consumers have a genuine choice as to whether to use credit cards, and that they are therefore responsible for the higher rates of interest that they pay for credit-card debt. Such an argument would seem to *support* the position of bank representatives.

E   As with the point in answer choice D, this point might seem to suggest that consumers bear some of the responsibility for the higher interest rates they pay, thus perhaps mitigating the responsibility of the banks. The point might thus seem to *support* the position of the banks' representatives.

The correct answer is C.

CR00726

179. Often patients with ankle fractures that are stable, and thus do not require surgery, are given follow-up x-rays because their orthopedists are concerned about possibly having misjudged the stability of the fracture. When a number of follow-up x-rays were reviewed, however, all the fractures that had initially been judged stable were found to have healed correctly. Therefore, it is a waste of money to order follow-up x-rays of ankle fractures initially judged stable.

Which of the following, if true, most strengthens the argument?

(A) Doctors who are general practitioners rather than orthopedists are less likely than orthopedists to judge the stability of an ankle fracture correctly.

(B) Many ankle injuries for which an initial x-ray is ordered are revealed by the x-ray not to involve any fracture of the ankle.

(C) X-rays of patients of many different orthopedists working in several hospitals were reviewed.

(D) The healing of ankle fractures that have been surgically repaired is always checked by means of a follow-up x-ray.

(E) Orthopedists routinely order follow-up x-rays for fractures of bones other than ankle bones.

Argument Evaluation

Situation Often patients with ankle fractures that their orthopedists have judged not to require surgery are given follow-up x-rays to check whether the fracture healed correctly. An examination of a sample of those x-rays found that the ankle had, in each case, healed properly.

Reasoning *The question is which of the answer choices, if true, would most strengthen the argument.* The argument is based on data concerning follow-up x-rays, each of which revealed no problem with the orthopedist's initial judgment that the ankle fracture was stable (and would heal without surgery). This invites the question whether the follow-up x-rays are really needed. The argument concludes that they are a waste of money. But was the x-ray data truly representative of orthopedists generally? After all, some orthopedists—perhaps more experienced, better-trained, or employed at a facility with better staff or facilities—may be much better than others at judging ankle fractures. If we add the information that the data for the conclusion comes from many orthopedists working at many different hospitals, we have greater assurance that the x-ray data is representative, and the argument will be made much stronger.

A Neither the study nor the conclusion that is drawn from it concerns general practitioners, so this point is irrelevant.

B Naturally many ankle injuries do not involve fractures—x-rays may sometimes be used to determine this—but the argument concerns only cases where there have been ankle fractures.

C **Correct.** This shows that the sample of x-ray data examined was probably sufficiently representative of cases of ankle fracture judged to be stable by orthopedists.

D The argument does not concern cases of ankle fracture that have been surgically repaired.

E The argument concerns only x-rays of ankles. From the information given here, we cannot infer that orthopedists are generally wasteful in routinely ordering follow-up x-rays.

The correct answer is C.

CR05431
180. In setting environmental standards for industry and others to meet, it is inadvisable to require the best results that state-of-the-art technology can achieve. Current technology is able to detect and eliminate even extremely minute amounts of contaminants, but at a cost that is exorbitant relative to the improvement achieved. So it would be reasonable instead to set standards by taking into account all of the current and future risks involved.

The argument given concerning the reasonable way to set standards presupposes that

(A) industry currently meets the standards that have been set by environmental authorities

(B) there are effective ways to take into account all of the relevant risks posed by allowing different levels of contaminants

(C) the only contaminants worth measuring are generated by industry

(D) it is not costly to prevent large amounts of contaminants from entering the environment

(E) minute amounts of some contaminants can be poisonous

Argument Construction

Situation   State-of-the-art technology can detect and eliminate even tiny amounts of environmental contaminants, but at a cost that is exorbitant relative to its benefits.

Reasoning   *What must be true in order for the argument's premises to support its conclusion?* The argument is that environmental standards requiring the best results that state-of-the-art technology can provide are unreasonably expensive relative to their benefits, so it would be reasonable instead to set environmental standards that take into account all present and future risks from contaminants. In order for the premise to support the conclusion, the environmental standards based on present and future risks would have to be less expensive relative to their benefits than the *best results* environmental standards are. Furthermore, setting the *current and future risks* environmental standards cannot be reasonable unless it is feasible to assess present and future risks as those standards require.

A   The argument does not say which standards, if any, environmental authorities have set. In any case, such standards could be reasonable or unreasonable regardless of whether industry currently meets them.

B   **Correct.** If taking future risks into account were infeasible, then applying the *current and future risks* standards would also be infeasible. And setting those standards would be unreasonable if they could not feasibly be applied.

C   According to the stimulus, the proposed *current and future risks* standards would apply to industry *and others*. So those standards could be reasonable even if the unspecified *others* also generated contaminants worth measuring, and even if the standards required measuring those contaminants.

D   Even if it were costly to prevent large amounts of contaminants from entering the environment, the benefits of doing so to prevent present and future risks might outweigh the costs.

E   The *current and future risks* standards could take into account any poisoning risks posed by minute amounts of contaminants.

The correct answer is B.

CR05750

181. The chemical adenosine is released by brain cells when those cells are active. Adenosine then binds to more and more sites on cells in certain areas of the brain, as the total amount released gradually increases during wakefulness. During sleep, the number of sites to which adenosine is bound decreases. Some researchers have hypothesized that it is the cumulative binding of adenosine to a large number of sites that causes the onset of sleep.

Which of the following, if true, provides the most support for the researchers' hypothesis?

(A) Even after long periods of sleep when adenosine is at its lowest concentration in the brain, the number of brain cells bound with adenosine remains very large.

(B) Caffeine, which has the effect of making people remain wakeful, is known to interfere with the binding of adenosine to sites on brain cells.

(C) Besides binding to sites in the brain, adenosine is known to be involved in biochemical reactions throughout the body.

(D) Some areas of the brain that are relatively inactive nonetheless release some adenosine.

(E) Stress resulting from a dangerous situation can preserve wakefulness even when brain levels of bound adenosine are high.

Argument Evaluation

Situation Adenosine is released from brain cells that are active. The amount of adenosine released increases during wakefulness, and it binds to more and more sites on cells in certain brain locations. The number of sites to which it is bound decreases during sleep. Researchers have hypothesized that the cumulative binding of adenosine to many sites causes the onset of sleep.

Reasoning *Which answer choice most strongly supports the hypothesis?* If the hypothesis is correct, then some factor that impedes the binding of adenosine should be closely associated with wakefulness. Therefore, finding some such factor, and observing that it is accompanied by wakefulness when the factor operates, would tend to confirm the hypothesis.

A Without further, more specific information, this piece of information suffices neither to confirm nor to refute the hypothesis.

B **Correct.** A finding that caffeine, known to induce wakefulness, inhibits adenosine from binding to sites on brain cells helps confirm the hypothesis.

C This piece of information lacks a clear relevance to the hypothesized impact on sleep, and therefore does not help confirm the hypothesis.

D This information lacks a clear relevance to the hypothesized impact on sleep, and therefore does not help confirm the hypothesis.

E What this indicates is that stress may impede the hypothesized sleep-inducing effect of adenosine. It does not refute the hypothesis but does not confirm it either.

The correct answer is B.

CR01101

182. A two-year study beginning in 1977 found that, among 85-year-old people, those whose immune systems were weakest were twice as likely to die within two years as others in the study. The cause of their deaths, however, was more often heart disease, against which the immune system does not protect, than cancer or infections, which are attacked by the immune system.

Which of the following, if true, would offer the best prospects for explaining deaths in which weakness of the immune system, though present, played no causal role?

(A) There were twice as many infections among those in the study with the weakest immune systems as among those with the strongest immune systems.

(B) The majority of those in the study with the strongest immune systems died from infection or cancer by 1987.

(C) Some of the drugs that had been used to treat the symptoms of heart disease had a side effect of weakening the immune system.

(D) Most of those in the study who survived beyond the two-year period had recovered from a serious infection sometime prior to 1978.

(E) Those in the study who survived into the 1980s had, in 1976, strengthened their immune systems through drug therapy.

Argument Construction

Situation   This question presents a puzzling scenario and asks us to find a possible fact that could make the situation less puzzling. The scenario involves a study that was conducted a few decades ago on a certain group of older adults. Those with the weakest immune systems were much more likely to die within two years than were the other individuals in the study. However, among the individuals with the weakest immune systems, death was more often by heart disease, from which the immune system does not protect, than from cancer or infections, for which a strong immune system is protective.

Reasoning   *For the participants in the study with the weakest immune systems, what might best explain the deaths that were not due to weakness of the immune system?* We might expect that the people with the weakest immune systems would be more likely to die from diseases that a strong immune system would protect them from than from other diseases. An explanation of the deaths that were not due to weakness of the immune system would explain why this is not the case.

A   This point is irrelevant. The hypothesis that the participants in the study with the weakest immune systems had more infections than did the other participants does not explain why those participants died from conditions that were not infections.

B   Our question involves identifying a possible explanation for the deaths of the participants in the study with the weakest immune systems. This answer choice, about the deaths of those with strong immune systems, is thus irrelevant.

C   **Correct.** This answer choice suggests that those with heart disease—which would not have been due to weakness of the immune system—would have nevertheless had a weaker immune system due to the administration of certain drugs. Those with heart disease may for this reason have been among those with the weakest immune systems. If the individuals with weak immune systems due to treatment for heart disease formed a large-enough portion of the patients with the weakest immune systems, then we would have an explanation for why those with the weakest immune systems were more likely to die from heart disease than from infections or cancer.

D   This answer choice is not specific enough for us to use in the explanation we are looking for. For example, the "serious" infections in question may have occurred well before the 1977 study. Furthermore, there may appear to be no significant relationship between having had a serious infection and death from a condition that was not an infection.

E   This answer choice is also not specific enough to be a factor that might reasonably offer the explanation we are looking for. For example, given the information in this answer choice, it could have been the case that all of the participants had the drug therapy.

The correct answer is C.

CR13093

183. Most scholars agree that King Alfred (A.D. 849–899) personally translated a number of Latin texts into Old English. One historian contends that Alfred also personally penned his own law code, arguing that the numerous differences between the language of the law code and Alfred's translations of Latin texts are outweighed by the even more numerous similarities. Linguistic similarities, however, are what one expects in texts from the same language, the same time, and the same region. Apart from Alfred's surviving translations and law code, there are only two other extant works from the same dialect and milieu, so it is risky to assume here that linguistic similarities point to common authorship.

The passage above proceeds by

(A)   providing examples that underscore another argument's conclusion

(B)   questioning the plausibility of an assumption on which another argument depends

(C)   showing that a principle if generally applied would have anomalous consequences

(D)   showing that the premises of another argument are mutually inconsistent

(E)   using argument by analogy to undermine a principle implicit in another argument

Argument Evaluation

Situation   A historian argues that King Alfred must have written his own law code, since there are more similarities than differences between the language in the law code and that in Alfred's translations of Latin texts. Apart from Alfred's translations and law code, there are only two other extant works in the same dialect and from the same milieu.

Reasoning   *How does the reasoning in the passage proceed?* The first sentence presents a claim that is not disputed in the passage. The second sentence presents a historian's argument. Implicitly citing the undisputed claim in the passage's first sentence as evidence, the historian proposes an analogy between the law code and Alfred's translations, arguing on the basis of this analogy that Alfred wrote the law code. The third sentence of the passage casts doubt on this analogy, pointing out that it could plausibly apply to texts that Alfred did not write. The fourth sentence suggests that too few extant texts are available as evidence to rule out the possibility raised in the third sentence. Thus, the third and fourth sentences are intended to undermine the historian's argument.

A   As explained above, the passage is intended to undermine the conclusion of the historian's argument, not to *underscore* (emphasize) it.

B   **Correct.** The passage's third and fourth sentences question the plausibility of the historian's assumption that no one but Alfred would have been likely to write a text whose language has more similarities to than differences from the language in Alfred's translations.

C   Although there might well be anomalous consequences from generalizing the assumption on which the historian's argument relies, the passage does not mention or allude to any such consequences.

D   The passage does not mention, or suggest the existence of, any inconsistencies among the premises of the historian's argument.

E   Although the historian argues by analogy, the passage does not itself argue by analogy; it does not suggest any specific counteranalogy to undermine the historian's argument.

The correct answer is B.

CR01355

184. Parland's alligator population has been declining in recent years, primarily because of hunting. Alligators prey heavily on a species of freshwater fish that is highly valued as food by Parlanders, who had hoped that the decline in the alligator population would lead to an increase in the numbers of these fish available for human consumption. Yet the population of this fish species has also declined, even though the annual number caught for human consumption has not increased.

Which of the following, if true, most helps to explain the decline in the population of the fish species?

(A) The decline in the alligator population has meant that fishers can work in some parts of lakes and rivers that were formerly too dangerous.

(B) Over the last few years, Parland's commercial fishing enterprises have increased the number of fishing boats they use.

(C) Many Parlanders who hunt alligators do so because of the high market price of alligator skins, not because of the threat alligators pose to the fish population.

(D) During Parland's dry season, holes dug by alligators remain filled with water long enough to provide a safe place for the eggs of this fish species to hatch.

(E) In several neighboring countries through which Parland's rivers also flow, alligators are at risk of extinction as a result of extensive hunting.

Argument Construction

Situation   The alligators in a certain region prey heavily on a certain species of fish that is prized for human consumption. However, although in recent years hunting has reduced the population of alligators in the region, the population of the prized freshwater fish species has declined. The annual number caught for human consumption has not increased.

Reasoning   *What might explain the decline in the population of the prized fish species, despite both the decrease in population of another species that preys heavily on the prized fish and the lack of increase in fishing for the species for human consumption?* The population of the fish species declined, despite both the presence of a factor that we might be expected to produce an increase in the population of the species and the absence of a factor that we might ordinarily expect to explain the decrease. This situation may seem puzzling, and we may thus wish to find an explanation for it.

A   Given that fishers can work in parts of lakes and rivers that were formerly too dangerous to work in, we might expect fishing of the prized species to increase and thus expect the population of the species to decrease. Although this might explain a decrease in the population of the fish species if fishing for the species increased, we have been given reason to believe that fishing for the species *decreased*.

B   As with answer choice A, answer choice B suggests that fishing in the region may have increased and thus that fishing for the prized fish species for human consumption may have increased. This might explain the decrease in the population of the fish species if the statement were correct. However, we have been given that fishing for the prized fish species for human consumption has decreased.

C   The statement in this answer choice provides an explanation of why the alligator hunting has occurred. Given that the alligators prey on the fish, this might help to explain an increase in the population of the prized fish species, had such an increase occurred. However, we are given that the population of the fish species in the region has decreased.

D   **Correct.** Despite the fact that alligators prey on the prized fish species, this statement describes a way in which the fish species may be dependent on the alligators, in such a way that a decline in the population of the alligators could contribute to a decline in the fish species.

E   The statement in this answer choice serves to amplify a point that is given in the puzzling situation of a decline in the population of the fish species *despite* (among other factors) a decrease in the population of the alligators. It does not explain why a decline in the population of the alligator species may have contributed to a decline in the population of the fish species.

The correct answer is D.

CR05418
185. A company plans to develop a prototype weeding machine that uses cutting blades with optical sensors and microprocessors that distinguish weeds from crop plants by differences in shade of color. The inventor of the machine claims that it will reduce labor costs by virtually eliminating the need for manual weeding.

Which of the following is a consideration in favor of the company's implementing its plan to develop the prototype?

(A) There is a considerable degree of variation in shade of color between weeds of different species.

(B) The shade of color of some plants tends to change appreciably over the course of their growing season.

(C) When crops are weeded manually, overall size and leaf shape are taken into account in distinguishing crop plants from weeds.

(D) Selection and genetic manipulation allow plants of virtually any species to be economically bred to have a distinctive shade of color without altering their other characteristics.

(E) Farm laborers who are responsible for the manual weeding of crops carry out other agricultural duties at times in the growing season when extensive weeding is not necessary.

Evaluation of a Plan

Situation A company plans to develop an automated weeding machine that would distinguish weeds from crop plants by differences in shade of color. It is supposed to reduce labor costs by eliminating the need for manual weeding.

Reasoning *Which answer choice describes a consideration that would favor the company's plan?* The passage supports the plan by claiming that the machine would reduce labor costs by virtually eliminating weeding by hand. The correct answer choice will be one that adds to this support. Labor costs will be reduced only if the machine works well. The machine relies on shade of color to distinguish between weeds and crop plants. If crop plants can be bred to have distinctive color without sacrificing other qualities, it would be more likely that the machine could be used effectively.

A Greater variation among weed plants would make it more difficult for the machine to distinguish between weeds and crop plants, and this would make it less likely that the machine would be effective.

B This answer choice tends to disfavor the effectiveness of the machine. The more changeable the colors of the plants to be distinguished, the more complex the task of distinguishing between weeds and crop plants based on their color.

C This answer choice tends to disfavor the likely benefits of the machine because it indicates that manual weeding distinguishes weeds from crop plants by using criteria that the machine does not take into account. If the machine does not distinguish weeds from crop plants as accurately and reliably as manual weeding does, then the machine is less apt to make manual weeding unnecessary.

D **Correct.** Making crop plants easily distinguishable from weeds would facilitate the effective use of the weeding machine.

E This does not favor the company's implementing the plan to develop the machine. There would still be tasks other than weeding that would require hiring staff. Thus there would still be labor costs even if the need for manual weeding were eliminated.

The correct answer is D.

CR05079

186. Aroca City currently funds its public schools through taxes on property. **In place of this system, the city plans to introduce a sales tax of 3 percent on all retail sales in the city.** Critics protest that 3 percent of current retail sales falls short of the amount raised for schools by property taxes. The critics are correct on this point. **Nevertheless, implementing the plan will probably not reduce the money going to Aroca's schools.** Several large retailers have selected Aroca City as the site for huge new stores, and these are certain to draw large numbers of shoppers from neighboring municipalities, where sales are taxed at rates of 6 percent and more. In consequence, retail sales in Aroca City are bound to increase substantially.

In the argument given, the two portions in **boldface** play which of the following roles?

(A) The first presents a plan that the argument concludes is unlikely to achieve its goal; the second expresses that conclusion.

(B) The first presents a plan that the argument concludes is unlikely to achieve its goal; the second presents evidence in support of that conclusion.

(C) The first presents a plan that the argument contends is the best available; the second is a conclusion drawn by the argument to justify that contention.

(D) The first presents a plan one of whose consequences is at issue in the argument; the second is the argument's conclusion about that consequence.

(E) The first presents a plan that the argument seeks to defend against a certain criticism; the second is that criticism.

Argument Evaluation

Situation   Aroca City plans to switch the source of its public school funding from property taxes to a new local sales tax.

Reasoning   *What argumentative roles do the two portions in boldface play in the passage?* The first boldface portion simply describes the city's plan. The next two sentences in the passage describe an observation some critics have made in objecting to the plan and say that the observation is correct. But then the second boldface portion rejects the critics' implicit conclusion that the plan will reduce school funding. The final two sentences in the passage present reasons to accept the statement in the second boldface portion, so they are premises supporting it as a conclusion.

A   The argument concludes that the plan is unlikely to reduce funding for the schools. The passage does not mention the plan's goal, but presumably that goal is not to reduce school funding.

B   The second boldface portion presents the argument's conclusion, not evidence to support the conclusion. The passage does not mention the plan's goal, but presumably that goal is not to reduce school funding.

C   The passage does not say whether the plan is better than any other possible school funding plans.

D   **Correct.** The plan's likely effect on the amount of school funding is at issue in the argument, whose conclusion is that the plan probably will not reduce that funding.

E   The second boldface portion does not criticize the plan, but rather rejects a criticism of the plan by stating that the plan will probably not reduce school funding.

The correct answer is D.

CR06152
187. Which of the following most logically completes the argument?

A photograph of the night sky was taken with the camera shutter open for an extended period. The normal motion of stars across the sky caused the images of the stars in the photograph to appear as streaks. However, one bright spot was not streaked. Even if the spot were caused, as astronomers believe, by a celestial object, that object could still have been moving across the sky during the time the shutter was open, since _____.

(A) the spot was not the brightest object in the photograph

(B) the photograph contains many streaks that astronomers can identify as caused by noncelestial objects

(C) stars in the night sky do not appear to shift position relative to each other

(D) the spot could have been caused by an object that emitted a flash that lasted for only a fraction of the time that the camera shutter was open

(E) if the camera shutter had not been open for an extended period, it would have recorded substantially fewer celestial objects

Argument Construction

Situation   In a photograph of the night sky taken with the camera shutter open for an extended period, the images of stars appeared as streaks because of the stars' normal motion across the sky, but one bright spot was not streaked.

Reasoning   *What would most strongly suggest that a celestial object moving across the sky could have caused the spot?* An object moving across the sky that was bright throughout the time the camera shutter was open should have appeared as a streak in the photograph, just as the stars did. But if the moving object was bright for only a very brief moment, and thus not for an extended time while the camera shutter was open, the object's movement may not have been captured in the photograph, and thus would appear in the photograph as an unstreaked bright spot.

A   The argument is not about how bright the spot was compared to other objects in the photograph.

B   Streaks caused by noncelestial objects such as satellites or airplanes do not explain how only one of many celestial objects moving across the sky could have produced the unstreaked spot.

C   The passage indicates that the stars were shifting position relative to the camera, not relative to one another. In any case, this observation does not help to explain how a celestial object that may not have been a star but that was moving across the sky could have produced the unstreaked spot in the photograph.

D   Correct. As explained above, a moving celestial object that only produced a momentary flash of light would produce an unstreaked bright spot in the photograph.

E   This may be true, given that fewer celestial objects might have moved into the camera's range of view if the camera shutter had not been open as long. But it does not provide any evidence that a moving celestial object could have produced the unstreaked spot.

The correct answer is D.

CR09046

188. Economist: Paying extra for fair-trade coffee—coffee labeled with the Fairtrade logo—is intended to help poor farmers, because they receive a higher price for the fair-trade coffee they grow. But this practice may hurt more farmers in developing nations than it helps. By raising average prices for coffee, it encourages more coffee to be produced than consumers want to buy. This lowers prices for non-fair-trade coffee and thus lowers profits for non-fair-trade coffee farmers.

To evaluate the strength of the economist's argument, it would be most helpful to know which of the following?

(A) Whether there is a way of alleviating the impact of the increased average prices for coffee on non-fair-trade coffee farmers' profits

(B) What proportion of coffee farmers in developing nations produce fair-trade coffee

(C) Whether many coffee farmers in developing nations also derive income from other kinds of farming

(D) Whether consumers should pay extra for fair-trade coffee if doing so lowers profits for non-fair-trade coffee farmers

(E) How fair-trade coffee farmers in developing nations could be helped without lowering profits for non-fair-trade coffee farmers

Argument Evaluation

Situation   Poor farmers receive higher prices for fair-trade coffee. But paying extra for fair-trade coffee lowers prices for non-fair-trade coffee and thus lowers profits for non-fair-trade coffee farmers.

Reasoning   *What would be most helpful to know to evaluate how well the economist's observations support the conclusion that buying fair-trade coffee hurts more farmers in developing nations than it helps?* The economist suggests that buying fair-trade coffee benefits farmers who grow it because they receive higher prices, but that it hurts non-fair-trade coffee farmers by reducing their profits. So to know whether the practice hurts more farmers in developing nations than it helps, it would be helpful to know whether developing nations have more farmers who produce non-fair-trade coffee than produce fair-trade coffee.

A   Even if there were some potential way of alleviating the negative impact from buying fair-trade coffee on non-fair-trade coffee farmers, it still could be that the practice hurts more developing-nation farmers than it helps. Alleviating the negative impact does not entail that there is no negative impact.

B   **Correct.** If fewer than half of these farmers produce fair-trade coffee, then the economist's observations do suggest that buying fair-trade coffee hurts more coffee farmers in developing nations than it helps. But if more than half do, those observations suggest the contrary.

C   Although knowing this could be helpful in determining how intensely many farmers are economically affected by people buying fair-trade coffee, it is not helpful in determining whether more farmers are hurt than are helped.

D   The argument's conclusion is only about the economic impact of buying fair-trade coffee, not about how consumers should or should not respond to that impact.

E   Knowing how the fair-trade coffee farmers could potentially be helped without hurting the other coffee farmers is irrelevant to assessing whether the practice of buying fair-trade coffee hurts more developing-nation farmers than it helps.

The correct answer is B.

Questions 189 to 233 - Difficulty: **Hard**

CR66900.02

189. Twenty-five years ago, 2,000 married people were asked to rank four categories—spouses, friends, jobs, and housework—according to the amount of time each category demanded. A recent follow-up survey indicates that a majority of those same people rank housework higher on the list now than they did twenty-five years ago. Yet most of the respondents also claim that housework has become less demanding of their time over the last twenty-five years.

Which of the following, if true, helps to explain the apparent discrepancy?

(A) Some of the people surveyed were married to other people in the survey.

(B) Many of the most time-consuming aspects of people's lives do not appear as categories on either survey.

(C) Most of those who responded to the follow-up survey have retired in the last twenty-five years.

(D) At the time of the follow-up survey, some of the people surveyed did no housework.

(E) Many of the respondents to the follow-up survey claim that they now spend much more time with their friends than they did twenty-five years ago.

Argument Construction

Situation   Twenty-five years ago, 2,000 married people were asked in a survey to rank four categories—spouse, friends, jobs, and housework—with respect to the average amount of time demanded by activities in each category. In a recent survey, most of the same people were asked to rank those activities again. Many ranked housework higher than they had ranked it in the first survey. Yet most claimed that housework had become less demanding of their time over the past twenty-five years. In light of the higher ranking of housework, this claim is initially puzzling.

Reasoning   *Which answer choice provides the best explanation for the apparent inconsistency between the two findings cited from the recent survey?* A rise in the ranking of housework could occur either because the amount of time taken by housework increased or because the amount of time taken by one or more of the other categories declined over the twenty-five years. For example, suppose housework ranked fourth, i.e., lowest, in the first survey. If most of those surveyed had been fulltime employees twenty-five years ago, the category *jobs* would probably have ranked much higher than the category *housework*. But if those people were retired twenty-five years later, then the time demanded by jobs would be much less or even zero. Housework might then rank higher than jobs in the second survey even if it did not demand as many hours as it did previously.

A   The information that some people surveyed were spouses of others surveyed would not, by itself, indicate statistical error in the survey. Single people in the surveys would obviously have ranked the category *spouse* lower than did married people. We are given no information as to how many of those people who were single when first surveyed had since married. But even if we had such information, a rise in the ranking for the category *spouse* would not, without further information, explain the rise in the ranking for *housework*.

B   The surveys asked only for a ranking of activities in the four categories. Each ranking reflects the proportion of total time spent on those four categories, not including other kinds of activity.

C   **Correct.** Housework could move up in the ranking if the category *jobs*, for example, had drastically declined in the ranking below even housework. As explained above, this could occur if many or most of those surveyed had been employed fulltime twenty-five years ago but had retired in the meantime; this would be consistent with a rise in the ranking of housework as well as a reduction in the proportion of total time spent on housework.

D   This information is nonspecific about how many people did no housework. It is also nonspecific about how many of those who were surveyed ranked housework lowest or reported doing no housework. It does not help explain the apparent inconsistency in the overall survey results.

E   In the absence of further information about the ranking of the categories *housework* and *friends* in the two surveys, this new information does little to explain the apparent inconsistency. In fact, without some indication that many respondents do housework with their friends, this suggests that the ranking for the category *housework* should have declined if it changed at all.

The correct answer is C.

CR59820.02

190. In order to achieve self-sufficiency in electricity production, **the Hasarian government proposes to construct eleven huge hydroelectric power plants**. Although this is a massive project, it is probably not massive enough to achieve the goal. It is true that **adding the projected output of the new hydroelectric plants to the output that Hasaria can achieve now would be enough to meet the forecast demand for electricity**. It will, however, take at least fifteen years to complete the project and by then the majority of Hasaria's current power plants will be too old to function at full capacity.

In the argument given, the two portions in **boldface** play which of the following roles?

(A) The first introduces a proposed course of action for which the argument provides support; the second gives evidence in support of that course of action.

(B) The first introduces a proposed course of action for which the argument provides support; the second gives a reason for not adopting a possible alternative course of action.

(C) The first introduces a plan that the argument evaluates; the second provides evidence that is used to support that plan against possible alternatives.

(D) The first introduces a proposed plan for achieving a certain goal; the second is a claim that has been used in support of the plan but that the argument maintains is inaccurate.

(E) The first introduces a proposed plan for achieving a certain goal; the second provides evidence that is used to support the argument's evaluation of that plan.

Argument Construction

Situation   To achieve self-sufficiency in electricity production, the Hasarian government proposes to construct eleven large hydroelectric power plants. But the project might not be large enough to achieve its goal. It will take fifteen years to complete, but by then many of the existing power plants will not be able to function at full capacity.

Reasoning   *What logical roles in the argument do the boldfaced portions play?* The first reports the proposed plan. But it is argued that the plan might not achieve its goal. It is conceded that the amount of power projected to be generated by the new plants might be sufficient if added to the existing power generation capacity. But since it will take fifteen years to complete the project, some of the existing power generation capacity will no longer be fully available.

A   The first introduces a proposed plan. But the argument is critical of that proposal and indicates that the plan, if adopted, might ultimately NOT achieve its goal. The second does not give evidence in support of the plan.

B   The first introduces a proposed plan. The second does not give evidence against adopting an alternative course of action. No alternative plan is considered.

C   The first does introduce a plan that the argument evaluates, but the second does not provide evidence to support that plan against possible alternatives. No possible alternative plan is considered.

D   The first introduces a proposed plan for achieving a goal of energy self-sufficiency. The second gives a claim that the argument treats as accurate.

E   **Correct.** The first introduces a proposed plan for achieving a goal of energy self-sufficiency. The second provides support for the argument's evaluation of the plan. It provides information to indicate that the planned new energy generation capacity would provide energy self-sufficiency if existing generation capacity were added. However, the argument indicates a flaw in the plan: Hasaria's existing power plants will have significantly reduced generation capacity in fifteen years, the time it will take for the new plants to become operational.

The correct answer is E.

CR89820.02

191. In Cecropia, inspections of fishing boats that estimate the number of fish they are carrying are typically conducted upon their return to port. The high numbers so obtained have led the government to conclude that the coastal waters are being overfished. To allow commercial fishing stocks to recover, the government is considering introducing annual quotas on the number of fish that each fishing boat can catch. Compliance with the quotas would be determined by the established system of inspections.

Which of the following, if true, raises the most serious doubts about whether the government's proposed plan would succeed?

(A) Some commercial fishing boats in Cecropia are large enough to catch their entire annual quota in only a few months of fishing.

(B) The quotas would have to be reduced if more boats began fishing in Cecropia's coastal waters.

(C) Because fish prices will rise if the quotas go into effect, it is unlikely that the quotas will significantly change the number of boats fishing Cecropia's coastal waters.

(D) The procedure that inspectors use to estimate the number of fish a boat is carrying often results in a slight overcount.

(E) Quotas encourage fishers to bring only the most commercially valuable fish into port and to discard less valuable fish, most of them dead or dying.

Evaluation of a Plan

Situation   The government of Cecropia is considering introducing annual catch quotas for fishing boats in order to allow commercial fishing stocks in coastal waters to recover. The quotas would be enforced by inspectors who will estimate the number of fish brought into port by each boat.

Reasoning   *What new information raises the most serious doubts about whether the plan would succeed if it is implemented?* The quota restrictions could raise problems associated with enforcement, economic viability, and acceptance by those whose livelihood depends, directly or indirectly, on the fishing industry. The restrictions would be pointless and would not attain the goal of protecting fishing stocks unless they could be effectively enforced. Other issues would have to be resolved for the proposed quotas to pass into law.

A   For large commercial fishing boats, the quota system could pose difficulties. Large capital investment would likely be tied up in such boats, and such boats might have to supplement their catches by fishing in waters not controlled by any nation. But large boats could presumably do so.

B   We are given no information as to whether possible reduction of fishing quotas is envisaged in the government's proposed plan—or whether quota reduction would count as a different proposal superseding the one under discussion.

C   This is a consideration in favor of the proposal. It suggests that the proposed quota system would succeed and that the viability of commercial fishing boats and the livelihoods of fishers would not be negatively affected.

D   This information does not suggest that the quota system is likely to fail. If fish counts are adjusted using a reasonable margin of error and there are appeal procedures to resolve disputes about fish counts, such disputes, by themselves, would then be unlikely to cause the quota system to fail.

E   **Correct.** The information about the proposed quota system indicates that the fish catch of each boat is monitored only in port. Boats could circumvent the quota system by indiscriminately catching and letting die all available fish but discarding the least valuable fish out at sea before submitting to the inspections in port. The non-survival of this part of the catch could, over time, impair the recovery of the coastal fish populations.

The correct answer is E.

CR55030.02

192. Consultant: **A significant number of complex repair jobs carried out by Ace Repairs have to be redone under the company's warranty, but when those repairs are redone they are invariably successful.** Since we have definitely established that **there is no systematic difference between the mechanics who are assigned to do the initial repairs and those who are assigned to redo unsatisfactory jobs**, it is clear that inadequacies in the initial repairs cannot be attributed to the mechanics' lack of competence. Rather, it is likely that complex repairs require a level of focused attention that the company's mechanics apply consistently only to repair jobs that have been inadequately done on the first try.

In the consultant's reasoning, the two portions in **boldface** play which of the following roles?

(A) The first is a claim that the consultant rejects as false; the second is evidence that forms the basis for that rejection.

(B) The first is part of an explanation that the consultant offers for a certain finding; the second is that finding.

(C) The first presents a pattern whose explanation is at issue in the reasoning; the second provides evidence to rule out one possible explanation of that pattern.

(D) The first presents a pattern whose explanation is at issue in the reasoning; the second is evidence that has been used to challenge the explanation presented by the consultant.

(E) The first is the position the consultant seeks to establish; the second is offered as evidence for that position.

Argument Evaluation

Situation   The following information is attributed to a consultant. Some complex repair jobs done by Ace Repairs have to be redone under warranty and the repairs, when redone, are usually successful. But the mechanics who do the initial repairs and those who redo them are, overall, equally competent to do the repairs successfully.

Reasoning   *What role in the consultant's reasoning do the boldfaced statements play?* The first sentence describes a situation that is puzzling and needs explanation. One might be inclined to argue that the mechanics who redo the repairs are more competent that those who did the initial repairs. But the second boldfaced statement rebuts this explanation by telling us that it has been *definitely established* that there are no systematic differences in competence. The final sentence of the consultant's reasoning offers another explanation: that the redoing of a repair elicits from mechanics a higher level of focused attention than did the performance of the initial repair.

A   The first is an assertion made by the consultant concerning a puzzling phenomenon. It does not attribute a denial of any claim to the consultant; so the second does not provide a reason for a denial made by the consultant in the first boldfaced portion.

B   The first is not an explanation, or even part of one, for a finding, but rather, a description of a puzzling finding concerning a difference between success rates of initial repairs and those of repairs that are redone. The first, not the second, describes the finding itself.

C   **Correct.** The first is a statement of a puzzling fact that the consultant seems to have found and that needs explanation. The second provides evidence to exclude the hypothesis that the higher success rates in redoing repairs than in the initial doing of the repairs is explainable by reference to different levels of competence in the mechanics in each case.

D   The first is a statement of a puzzling fact that the consultant seems to believe needs explanation. Regarding the second, first note that the explanation that the consultant offers is to be found in the final sentence of the passage. The second boldfaced portion is part of the reasoning on which the consultant bases the explanation, not a claim that someone else has made in opposition to the consultant's explanation.

E   The first is an assertion by the consultant; the consultant presents it as established fact, not as a position that the consultant seeks to establish (i.e., provide evidence for). The second does not give evidence that helps establish the consultant's initial assertion.

The correct answer is C.

CR08540.02

193. Half of Metroburg's operating budget comes from a payroll tax of 2 percent on salaries paid to people who work in the city. Recently a financial services company, one of Metroburg's largest private-sector employers, announced that it will be relocating just outside the city. All the company's employees, amounting to 1 percent of all people now employed in Metroburg, will be employed at the new location.

From the information given, which of the following can most properly be concluded?

(A) Unless other employers add a substantial number of jobs in Metroburg, the company's relocation is likely to result in a 1 percent reduction in the revenue for the city's operating budget.

(B) Although the company's relocation will have a negative effect on the city's tax revenue, the company's departure will not lead to any increase in the unemployment rate among city residents.

(C) One of the benefits that the company will realize from its relocation is a reduction in the taxes paid by itself and its employees.

(D) Revenue from the payroll tax will decline by 1 percent if there is no increase in jobs within the city to compensate, fully or partially, for the company's departure.

(E) The company's relocation will tend to increase the proportion of jobs in Metroburg that are in the public sector, unless it results in a contraction of the public-sector payroll.

Argument Construction

Situation   Metroburg funds half of its operating budget with a 2 percent payroll tax for each person who works in the city. A large private-sector firm will soon relocate outside the city; all its current employees will be employed at the new location.

Reasoning   *Which answer choice is most strongly supported by the information provided?* The firm's employees comprise 1 percent of all employees working in Metroburg. But we have no information about the company's salaries; for all we can tell, they might be far higher or far lower than the Metroburg average. So we do not know what proportion of the city's total operating budget is funded by the taxes paid by the firm's employees.

A   As explained above, we do not know how much of the revenue for Metroburg's operating budget comes from the payroll taxes paid by the firm's employees.

B   We lack the information needed to predict what the downstream economic effects of the firm's departure will be. These effects could include an increase in the unemployment rate among city residents. We do not know whether all the firm's employees are city residents; perhaps none are. But it is conceivable that some of the spending now occurring in the city would migrate to the firm's new location; this loss of commercial business could presumably result in job losses and increased unemployment in the city, but there is little reason to suppose that it would do so.

C   We have no information to support this. The given information does not imply that the firm is relocating in order to avoid city taxes.

D   As explained, we do not know how much of the revenue for Metroburg's operating budget is currently funded by taxes on the firm's payroll.

E   **Correct.** The firm that will relocate is a private-sector employer, and its employees currently comprise 1 percent of the total workforce employed in Metroburg. As a city that collects taxes, Metroburg presumably has public-sector employees. The migration of jobs to a location outside the city will entail that the proportion of all those working in the city who are private-sector employees will decrease, and—all things being equal—this, in turn, will cause an increase in the proportion of all employees in the city that are public-sector employees. However, this consequence would not necessarily occur if the firm's relocation indirectly resulted in a sufficiently large reduction in the city's public-sector workforce.

The correct answer is E.

CR62740.02

194. A library currently has only coin-operated photocopy machines, which cost 10 cents per copy. Library administrators are planning to refit most of those machines with card readers. The library will sell prepaid copy cards that allow users to make 50 copies at 9 cents per copy. Administrators believe that, despite the convenience of copy cards and their lower per-copy cost, the number of copies made in the library will be essentially unchanged after the refit.

On the assumption that administrators' assessment is correct, which of the following predictions about the effect of the refit is most strongly supported by the information given?

(A) Library patrons will only purchase a copy card on days when they need to make 50 or more copies.

(B) No library patrons will increase their usage of the library's photocopy machines once the refit has been made.

(C) If most of the copy cards sold in the library are used to their full capacity, the number of people using the library's photocopy machines over a given period will fall.

(D) Revenues from photocopying will decrease unless most library patrons choose to use the remaining coin-operated machines in preference to the card-reader equipped ones.

(E) Revenues from photocopying will increase if copy cards that are purchased are, on average, used to significantly less than 90 percent of their capacity.

Evaluation of a Plan

Situation A library's photocopiers are coin-operated; a copy costs 10 cents. The library's management plans to refit most of the photocopiers to accept copy cards that allow 50 copies to be made at 9 cents each. The administrators believe that the refit will not result in fewer copies being made.

Reasoning *Assuming that the administrators are right, which of the five predictions about the effect of the refit is most strongly supported by the information provided?* Suppose that only one card were sold and only 45 copies were made with that card. Then the amount that the user paid per copy would be 10 cents. Whatever the number of cards sold, provided the number of copies made per card averages less than 45, then the average revenue per copy would be more than 10 cents. This would produce an increase in total revenue if the total number of photocopy uses were no less than in previous years. The greater the number of cards sold, the greater the increase in total revenues, provided that the usage per card averages less than 45 copies. The lower the average usage per card, the greater the increase in photocopy revenue. The information provided suggests that the number of cards sold will be considerable, given that *most of the machines* are being refitted with card readers (and may be usable only with card readers).

A The information provides no reason to suppose that library patrons would buy cards only for use on the same day they buy them. Furthermore, the claim that the number of copies made will not change suggests that this might be false; if, after the refit, patrons almost never make small numbers of copies and almost never make copies on impulse, one might expect a decrease in the number of copies made.

B This is not supported by the information provided. For example, some library patrons could increase their usage while others make a compensating reduction in their usage.

C If 51 percent of the cards sold *are used to their full capacity*, it could still be the case that average utilization per card would be substantially less than 50 copies. So it is possible that the total number of photocopy users would increase or remain constant over a given period even if there is no change in the number of copies made and most cards are used to their full capacity.

D The given information suggests otherwise. If some but not most library patrons choose to use the card-operated machines, revenues will increase if utilization per card averages less than 45 copies.

E **Correct.** Each card has a capacity of 50 copies, so 90 percent of that is 45 copies. If the total number of copies made in the library remains at least as great as before and utilization of each card averages less than 45, revenues will increase; the lower the average utilization, the greater the increase in revenue.

The correct answer is E.

CR09740.02

195. Harvester-ant colonies live for fifteen to twenty years, though individual worker ants live only a year. The way a colony behaves changes steadily in a predictable pattern as the colony grows older and larger. For the first few years, the foragers behave quite aggressively, searching out and vigorously defending new food sources, but once a colony has reached a certain size, its foragers become considerably less aggressive.

If the statements above are true, which of the following can most properly be concluded on the basis of them?

(A) As a result of pressure from neighbors, some colonies do not grow larger as they become older.

(B) Unpredictable changes in a colony's environment can cause changes in the tasks that the colony must perform if it is to continue to survive.

(C) The reason a mature colony goes out of existence is that younger, more aggressive colonies successfully outcompete it for food.

(D) The pattern of changing behavior that a colony displays does not arise from a change in the behavior of any individual worker ant or group of worker ants.

(E) A new colony comes into existence when a group of young, aggressive workers leaves a mature colony and sets up on its own.

Argument Construction

Situation   The given information contrasts the lifespan of harvester-ant colonies (twenty years) with that of individual foragers in the colonies (one year). When the colony is young and relatively small, its foragers aggressively seek and defend food resources. But when the colony grows older and reaches a certain size, its foragers become less aggressive.

Reasoning   *Which answer choice is most strongly supported by the given information?* Obviously, the survival of a colony can be jeopardized by encountering unusual environmental challenges. But the given information suggests that, provided no unusual threats to the colony's survival are encountered, a colony's life cycle is biologically determined by constraints of colony size and age. The behavior of the individual foragers is correlated with the age and size of the colony; how a forager behaves in a colony near its maximum limits of size and age is quite different from an individual forager's behavior in the colony's early years. The behaviors of individual foragers are highly coordinated; the patterns of behavior of the colony are not caused by individual behaviors of the worker ants.

A   Although this might be true, the given information suggests that the limits on colony size do not depend on competition from neighbors but are, rather, general constraints that are based in harvester-ant biology.

B   Although this is likely true, the given information does not address the issue of how colony dynamics might be affected by drastic and unusual environmental changes.

C   Obviously, the survival of a colony that fails over a period to secure the food resources it needs would be threatened. But the given information does not state or imply that such failures are generally due to more aggressive competition by ants in another colony. It suggests that, in general, a colony's demise is primarily dictated by the biological constraints on colony size and age.

D   **Correct.** As explained, the given information suggests that, provided no unusual threats to a colony's survival are encountered, its life cycle is biologically determined by constraints of colony size and age, not by the behavior of individual forager ants or groups of such ants. The given information suggests that the biological constraints on a colony's size and longevity also determine behaviors of individual worker ants, who live about one year.

E   Nothing in the given information suggests that worker ants are the founders of a harvester-ant colony.

The correct answer is D.

CR29940.02

196. Trucking company owner: Theft of trucks containing valuable cargo is a serious problem. A new device produces radio signals that allow police to track stolen vehicles, and the recovery rate for stolen cargo in trucks equipped with the device is impressive. The device is too expensive to install in every truck, so we plan to install it in half of our trucks. Using those trucks for the most valuable cargo should largely eliminate losses from theft.

Which of the following, if true, most strongly supports the trucking company owner's expectation about the results of implementing the plan?

(A) For thieves, a cargo is valuable only if it is easy for them to dispose of profitably.

(B) Some insurance companies charge less to insure cargoes transported in trucks protected by the device.

(C) Most stolen trucks are eventually found, but unless a stolen truck is found very soon after it is taken, the likelihood that the trucking company will recover any of its cargo is very low.

(D) Thieves generally avoid trucks belonging to trucking companies that are known to have installed the device in a large proportion of their trucks.

(E) The manufacturer of the device offers a five-year warranty on each unit sold, a longer warranty than any that is offered on any competing antitheft device.

Evaluation of a Plan

Situation   A new device that can be placed in trucks allows police to track stolen vehicles and quickly recover stolen cargo. A trucking company owner proposes to install the device in half of the company's trucks and use those trucks to haul the most valuable cargo. The owner suggests that doing this will largely eliminate losses from theft.

Reasoning   *What claim would most strongly suggest that trucking company owner's plan will meet the owner's expectations?* If thieves avoid stealing any trucks belonging to companies known to have installed the device in a large proportion of its vehicles, the company owner's expectations are likely to be met.

A   If thieves believe they can dispose of some of the company's cargo very quickly, before police can recover the cargo, thieves may find the cargo to be valuable enough for them to risk stealing from the company. Therefore, this does not strongly suggest that the owner's plan will meet expectations.

B   This suggests that insurance for the company will be less costly if the owner's plan is carried out. Most likely this is because insurance companies have found that thefts decline for trucks that have the device installed. It is nonetheless possible that even for trucks that have the device installed, there are still thefts, even if there are fewer of them. It is also possible that there will be no reduction in losses from thefts of cargo from the trucks that do not have the device installed.

C   This answer choice actually gives us some reason to think the truck owner's expectations about the results of the plan will not be met. Half of the trucks will not have the device installed. If the trucks are not found quickly after they are stolen, the likelihood that these trucks' cargo will be recovered is low, and there may be significant losses from theft.

D   **Correct.** If thieves find out that half of the company's trucks have the device installed, this answer choice suggests that the thieves may well avoid stealing any of the company's trucks.

E   This answer choice suggests that for five years the company will not have to pay to replace any of the devices installed in its trucks. But that tells us nothing about the likelihood that the owner's expectations will be met.

The correct answer is D.

CR11050.02

197. To improve customer relations, several big retailers have recently launched "smile initiatives," requiring their employees to smile whenever they have contact with customers. These retailers generally have low employee morale, which is why they have to enforce smiling. However, studies show that customers can tell fake smiles from genuine smiles and that fake smiles prompt negative feelings in customers. So the smile initiatives are unlikely to achieve their goal.

The argument relies on which of the following as an assumption?

(A) The smile initiatives have achieved nearly complete success in getting employees to smile while they are around customers.

(B) Customers' feelings about fake smiles are no better than their feelings about the other facial expressions employees with low morale are likely to have.

(C) The feelings that employees generate in retail customers are a principal determinant of the amount of money customers will spend at a retailer.

(D) At the retailers who have launched the smile initiatives, none of the employees gave genuine smiles to customers before the initiatives were launched.

(E) Customers rarely, if ever, have a negative reaction to a genuine smile from a retail employee.

Argument Construction

Situation   Several large retailers where employee morale is low are requiring their employees to smile when they interact with customers; these requirements are known as "smile initiatives." The author of the argument concludes that because fake smiles create negative feelings in customers, these initiatives are unlikely to achieve their goal of improving customer relations.

Reasoning   *What assumption is required by the argument?* Even if customers can tell fake smiles from real ones and have negative feelings about them, the fake smiles could nonetheless improve customer relations. How? Suppose customers' attitudes are less negative about the fake smiles than about other facial expressions that result from low morale. Therefore, the argument requires the assumption that customer feelings about fake smiles are no better than their feelings about other facial expressions resulting from low morale.

A   The argument does not require this assumption. The initiative could fail to achieve its goal simply by failing to get employees to smile.

B   **Correct.** As explained above, if customers' feelings about fake smiles are not as negative as their feelings about other facial expressions that result from low morale, the smile initiative might nonetheless help improve customer relations. As a result, the argument needs to assume that customers' feelings about fake smiles are no better than their feelings about these other facial expressions.

C   The argument does not need to assume that the feelings employees generate in customers are a principal determinant of the amount customers will spend. Such feelings merely must have some effect on customer relations.

D   The argument needs to assume that not all employees at these retailers will give customers genuine smiles as a result of the smile initiatives. The argument does not, however, need to make any assumption about how many employees gave customers genuine smiles before the initiatives (though, presumably, many did not).

E   If this claim were false, then the argument would be even stronger. Therefore, the argument does not need to assume this claim.

The correct answer is B.

CR55190.02

198. Many economists hold that keeping taxes low helps to spur economic growth, and that low taxes thus lead to greater national prosperity. But Country X, which has unusually high taxes, has greater per-capita income than the neighboring Country Y, which has much lower taxes. Some politicians have concluded from this that high taxes do not hinder national prosperity.

The politicians' reasoning is most vulnerable to criticism on which of the following grounds?

(A) It overlooks the possibility that even if Country X reduced its taxes, it would not experience greater national prosperity in the long term.

(B) It confuses a claim that a factor does not hinder a given development with the claim that the same factor promotes that development.

(C) It fails to adequately address the possibility that Country X and Country Y differ in relevant respects other than taxation.

(D) It fails to take into account that the per-capita income of a country does not determine its rate of economic growth.

(E) It assumes that the economists' thesis must be correct despite a clear counterexample to that thesis.

Argument Evaluation

Situation   Many economists hold that keeping taxes low helps increase economic growth and national prosperity. But a high-tax country, Country X, has greater per-capita income than Country Y, which has lower taxes. Some politicians have concluded from this that high taxes do not hinder national prosperity.

Reasoning   *What is a significant weakness in the politicians' reasoning?* Many factors besides level of taxation are likely to affect economic growth and national prosperity—factors such as having a highly skilled labor force, being rich in a valuable natural resource, and having effective and efficient government. So it is likely that more than one such factor is needed to sufficiently explain any country's level of economic growth or prosperity. A combination of such factors may be sufficient to outweigh any negative impact of high taxes on economic growth or national prosperity.

A   This possibility is quite consistent with the politicians' reasoning that higher taxes do not necessarily impede economic growth.

B   Nothing in the politicians' reasoning indicates that they believe that higher taxes contribute to economic growth or prosperity. They claim that higher taxes do not preclude economic growth and prosperity. Nothing suggests that the politicians conflate these two views in their reasoning.

C   **Correct.** Even though Country X, with unusually high taxes, has greater per-capita income than Country Y, which has much lower taxes, Country X's high-tax regime may contribute to making the country's per-capita income and national prosperity less than it would be with a low-tax regime. As explained earlier, many different factors can affect a country's national prosperity; some non-tax factors, absent in Country Y, may be boosting Country X's prosperity and compensating for some negative effects of its high-tax regime.

D   The politicians' reasoning suggests that high per-capita income may indicate, or result from, a high level of national prosperity or a favorable rate of economic growth. It need not—and does not—address the question of whether a country's per-capita income could decisively affect the country's rate of economic growth.

E   The politicians' reasoning indicates their disagreement with the economists' thesis; it cites as a counterexample to that thesis the fact that a high-tax country, Country X, has a higher per-capita income than a low-tax country, Country Y.

The correct answer is C.

CR11080.02

199. Urban rail systems have been proposed to alleviate traffic congestion, but results in many cities have been cited as evidence that this approach to traffic management is ineffective. For example, a U.S. city that opened three urban rail branches experienced a net decline of 3,100 urban rail commuters during a period when employment increased by 96,000. Officials who favor urban rail systems as a solution to traffic congestion have attempted to counter this argument by noting that commuting trips in that city represent just 20 percent of urban travel.

The response of the officials to the claim that urban rail systems are ineffective is most vulnerable to criticism on the grounds that it

(A) presents no evidence to show that the statistics are incorrect

(B) relies solely on general data about U.S. cities rather than data about the city in question

(C) fails to consider that commuting trips may cause significantly more than 20 percent of the traffic congestion

(D) fails to show that the decline in the number of urban rail commuters in one U.S. city is typical of U.S. cities generally

(E) provides no statistics on the use of urban rail systems by passengers other than commuters

Argument Evaluation

Situation Urban rail systems have been proposed to help solve traffic congestion in cities. But critics have cited data from many cities to argue that this approach is ineffective. In one U.S. city that increased its urban rail service, over 3,000 fewer commuters used rail when employment expanded by almost 100,000. But officials who favor urban rail have countered this example by claiming that commuters account for only 20 percent of urban travel in that city.

Reasoning *Which answer choice most undermines the officials' response to the claim that urban rail would be ineffective in relieving urban traffic congestion?* Theoretically, urban rail service should help reduce traffic congestion by encouraging people to travel by train instead of by car. However, there is purported evidence that this approach is ineffective: In at least one city, an increase in the availability of rail service correlated with a decrease in the number of commuters traveling by rail, even though the total number of commuters apparently increased. Some officials object that in that city, commuters account for only 20 percent of urban travel. The officials' point is presumably that even if there was a net decline in commuters using the rail system, there may have been an overall increase in the number of people who used rail instead of driving. However, the stated goal of building more rail systems is to reduce traffic congestion, not just to reduce the overall amount of urban car traffic. Even if commuting makes up only 20 percent of urban travel in the city in question, it might contribute disproportionately to traffic congestion, and if noncommuters typically use the rail system, commuting might even constitute most of the car traffic in the city. So a net movement of commuters from rail travel to car travel could be detrimental to the goal of alleviating traffic congestion even if a minority of urban travel is in the form of commuting.

A The point the officials make is not based on any assumption concerning the correctness of the statistics, nor do the officials appear to believe that the statistics are incorrect.

B In their response, the officials do not cite any general data about U.S. cities; their objection only addresses the use of data about a specific city.

C **Correct.** As explained above, the stated goal of building more rail systems is to reduce traffic congestion, not just to reduce the overall amount of urban car traffic. Even if commuting makes up only 20 percent of urban travel in the city in question, it might contribute disproportionately to traffic congestion, and if noncommuters typically use the rail system, commuting might even constitute most of the car traffic in the city. So a net movement of commuters from rail travel to car travel could be detrimental to the goal of alleviating traffic congestion even if a minority of urban travel is in the form of commuting.

D The officials' opponents appear to rely on the assumption that the decline in urban rail commuting in one U.S. city provides relevant evidence regarding the situation in other cities. However, the point that the officials make in response to that reasoning does not require that they show that the decline in urban rail commuting in one U.S. city is typical of U.S. cities.

E   Providing such statistics would at best be peripheral to the point that the officials make, which directly concerns urban rail utilization by urban commuters rather than by any other group of travelers.

The correct answer is C.

CR63780.02

200. Mayor: The financial livelihood of our downtown businesses is in jeopardy. There are few available parking spaces close to the downtown shopping area, so if we are to spur economic growth in our city, we must build a large parking ramp no more than two blocks from downtown.

Which of the following, if true, most seriously weakens the mayor's reasoning?

(A)   The city budget is not currently large enough to finance the construction of a new parking ramp.

(B)   There are other more significant reasons for the financial woes of downtown businesses in addition to a lack of nearby parking spaces.

(C)   Building a parking ramp as much as four blocks from downtown would be sufficient to greatly increase the number of shoppers to downtown businesses.

(D)   Explosive growth is most often associated with large suburban shopping malls, not small businesses.

(E)   Some additional parking spaces could be added to the downtown area without the construction of a parking ramp.

Evaluation of a Plan

Situation   A mayor argues that to help spur economic growth in the city and sustain business in the city's downtown, a large parking ramp should be constructed no more than two blocks from downtown to alleviate a parking shortage for business customers.

Reasoning   *Which answer choice provides the information that most seriously weakens the mayor's reasoning?* It is reasonable to assume that constructing a large parking ramp within two blocks of downtown will involve a large capital investment, made even larger by the high cost of land so near to downtown. If a ramp slightly farther from downtown could equally well serve downtown shoppers, and given that people are also likely to need nonresidential parking in another location, building a ramp in the specific location mentioned by the mayor would not be necessary. Note also that even if providing significantly more parking for business customers were necessary for the survival of downtown businesses, it might not be sufficient.

A   This information addresses a problem that would need to be overcome in order to have a parking ramp constructed. For example, taxes may need to be raised or a bond issued to fund the construction. It does not directly address the question whether the parking ramp would be necessary. If it were necessary but could not be financed, the result would be that the goal would not be met.

B   This information indicates that the construction of the parking ramp would likely not be sufficient to ensure the survival of downtown businesses and that other measures would also be needed. This does not weaken the mayor's argument that the ramp would be necessary.

C   **Correct.** If this were true, a parking ramp four blocks from downtown would suffice to solve the downtown parking shortage. Therefore, the construction of a ramp exactly two blocks from downtown would not be necessary.

D   This provides a superficial reason for wondering whether economic growth in the mayor's city could be spurred without the measure that the mayor advocates. However, the information provides no reason to suppose that this city has not already achieved all the growth that it can achieve from large suburban shopping malls. Furthermore, the contrast between large malls and small businesses is not clearly relevant; the downtown businesses whose livelihood the mayor wants to save may be large ones.

E   This information does not significantly weaken the mayor's proposal, since it does not tell us whether the additional parking spaces would suffice for meeting the mayor's goal to spur economic growth in the city.

The correct answer is C.

CR28001.02

201. Compact fluorescent light (CFL) bulbs are growing in market share as a replacement for the standard incandescent light bulb. However, an even newer technology is emerging: the light-emitting diode (LED) bulb. Like CFL bulbs, LED bulbs are energy efficient, and they can last around fifty thousand hours, about five times as long as most CFL bulbs. Yet, a single LED bulb costs much more than five CFL bulbs.

The information in the passage above most supports which of the following conclusions?

(A)   LED bulbs are most likely to be used in locations where light bulbs would be difficult or costly to replace.

(B)   CFL bulbs will need to come down further in price in order to compete with LED bulbs.

(C)   LED bulbs are most likely to be used in locations where there is frequent accidental breakage of bulbs.

(D)   CFL bulb designs are likely to advance to the point where they can last as long as LED bulbs.

(E)   LED bulbs are likely to drop in price, to the point of being competitive with CFL bulbs.

Argument Construction

Situation   Both compact fluorescent light (CFL) bulbs and light-emitting diode (LED) bulbs are energy-efficient bulbs. LED bulbs can last around 50,000 hours, about five times as long as CFL bulbs, though (at the time the passage was written) they cost more than five times as much as CFL bulbs.

Reasoning   *What claim is most strongly supported by the given information?* The information in the passage gives only one reason not to prefer LED bulbs over CFL bulbs—which last five times as long as CFL bulbs—namely, that LED bulbs are more than five times costlier. Because of the greater cost of LED bulbs, it might make economic sense simply to change CFL bulbs numerous times rather than to use the longer-lasting LED bulbs. If, however, there were any practical reason that outweighed that particular economic reason—perhaps the repeated replacement of CFL bulbs would be particularly problematic—then it might be wise to choose LED bulbs over CFL bulbs.

A   **Correct.** In locations where replacing bulbs is particularly difficult and even costly, it would probably make sense to use LED bulbs rather than CFL bulbs. Assuming, then, that both types of bulbs are otherwise acceptable and that their users are rational, LED bulbs would be most likely to be used in such locations.

B   The given information indicates that LED bulbs at the time the passage was written cost more than five times as much as CFL bulbs, but LED bulbs last only about five times as long as CFL bulbs. That suggests that CFL bulbs were competitive at that price.

C   If there is frequent accidental breakage of bulbs in a certain location, then it is likely that the advantage of LED bulbs mentioned in the passage would not hold in such locations.

D   Nothing in the passage suggests that CFL bulbs can be made to be longer lasting.

E   Nothing in the passage indicates whether there was any evidence, at the time the passage was written, that manufacturers of LED bulbs would be able to bring down the cost of producing such bulbs.

The correct answer is A.

CR01887

202. Tanco, a leather manufacturer, uses large quantities of common salt to preserve animal hides. New environmental regulations have significantly increased the cost of disposing of salt water that results from this use, and, in consequence, Tanco is considering a plan to use potassium chloride in place of common salt. Research has shown that Tanco could reprocess the by-product of potassium chloride use to yield a crop fertilizer, leaving a relatively small volume of waste for disposal.

In determining the impact on company profits of using potassium chloride in place of common salt, it would be important for Tanco to research all of the following EXCEPT:

(A) What difference, if any, is there between the cost of the common salt needed to preserve a given quantity of animal hides and the cost of the potassium chloride needed to preserve the same quantity of hides?

(B) To what extent is the equipment involved in preserving animal hides using common salt suitable for preserving animal hides using potassium chloride?

(C) What environmental regulations, if any, constrain the disposal of the waste generated in reprocessing the by-product of potassium chloride?

(D) How closely does leather that results when common salt is used to preserve hides resemble that which results when potassium chloride is used?

(E) Are the chemical properties that make potassium chloride an effective means for preserving animal hides the same as those that make common salt an effective means for doing so?

Evaluation of a Plan

Situation   New environmental regulations will increase the costs of disposing of the salt water that results from the use of large amounts of common salt in leather manufacturing. The manufacturer is considering switching from common salt to potassium chloride, because the by-product of the latter could be reprocessed to yield a crop fertilizer, with little waste left over to be disposed.

Reasoning   *In order to determine whether it would be profitable to switch from using common salt to using potassium chloride, which answer choice does the manufacturer NOT need to answer?* The chemical properties making potassium chloride an effective means of preserving animal hides might be quite different from those that make common salt effective, but there is no particular reason for thinking that this would impact the profitability of switching to potassium chloride. The relevant effects on the preserved hides might be the same even if the properties that brought about those effects were quite different. Thus, without more information than is provided in the passage, this question is irrelevant.

A   The savings in waste disposal costs that would be gained by switching to potassium chloride could be cancelled out if the cost of potassium chloride needed far exceeded that for common salt.

B   If switching to potassium chloride would force the manufacturer to replace the equipment it uses for preserving hides, then it might be less profitable to switch.

C   Even though there is said to be relatively little waste associated with using potassium chloride in the process, if the costs of this disposal are very high due to environmental regulations, it might be less profitable to switch.

D   If the leather that results from the use of potassium chloride looks substantially different from that which results when common salt has been used, then the leather might be less attractive to consumers, which would adversely affect the economics of switching to potassium chloride.

E   **Correct.** Note that the question as stated here presupposes that potassium chloride and salt are both effective means for preserving animal hides—so it does not raise any issue as to whether potassium chloride is adequately effective or as effective as salt (clearly, an issue of effectiveness *would* be relevant to profitability).

The correct answer is E.

CR04999

203. Colorless diamonds can command high prices as gemstones. A type of less valuable diamonds can be treated to remove all color. Only sophisticated tests can distinguish such treated diamonds from naturally colorless ones. However, only 2 percent of diamonds mined are of the colored type that can be successfully treated, and many of those are of insufficient quality to make the treatment worthwhile. Surely, therefore, the vast majority of colorless diamonds sold by jewelers are naturally colorless.

A serious flaw in the reasoning of the argument is that

(A) comparisons between the price diamonds command as gemstones and their value for other uses are omitted

(B) information about the rarity of treated diamonds is not combined with information about the rarity of naturally colorless, gemstone diamonds

(C) the possibility that colored diamonds might be used as gemstones, even without having been treated, is ignored

(D) the currently available method for making colorless diamonds from colored ones is treated as though it were the only possible method for doing so

(E) the difficulty that a customer of a jeweler would have in distinguishing a naturally colorless diamond from a treated one is not taken into account

Argument Evaluation

Situation Colored diamonds of a type that comprises 2 percent of all mined diamonds can be treated so that they are not easily distinguishable from more valuable, naturally colorless diamonds, but many are too low in quality for the treatment to be worthwhile.

Reasoning *Why do the argument's premises not justify the conclusion that the vast majority of colorless diamonds sold by jewelers are naturally colorless?* Since the type of colored diamonds that can be treated make up only 2 percent of all mined diamonds, and many diamonds of that type are too low in quality for treatment to be worthwhile, the vast majority of mined diamonds must not be treated to have their color removed. However, we are not told what proportion of all mined diamonds are naturally colorless. Naturally colorless diamonds may be far rarer even than the uncommon diamonds that have been treated to have their color removed. Thus, for all we can tell from the passage, it could well be that most colorless diamonds sold by jewelers have been treated to remove all color.

A Even if some types of diamonds command higher prices for uses other than as gemstones, the types discussed in the passage evidently command high enough prices as gemstones to be sold as such by jewelers.

B **Correct.** The argument does not work if naturally colorless diamonds are rarer than treated diamonds, as they may be for all we can tell from the information provided.

C The argument's conclusion is only that jewelers sell more naturally colorless diamonds than diamonds treated to be colorless. Whether jewelers sell any colored diamonds or other gemstones is irrelevant.

D The argument only concerns the types of colorless diamonds sold now, not the types that may be sold in the future if other treatment methods are discovered.

E The argument does suggest this difficulty but implies that even so there are too few treated diamonds available for jewelers to sell in place of naturally colorless ones.

The correct answer is B.

CR14448

204. The Sumpton town council recently voted to pay a prominent artist to create an abstract sculpture for the town square. Critics of this decision protested that town residents tend to dislike most abstract art, and any art in the town square should reflect their tastes. But a town council spokesperson dismissed this criticism, pointing out that other public abstract sculptures that the same sculptor has installed in other cities have been extremely popular with those cities' local residents.

The statements above most strongly suggest that the main point of disagreement between the critics and the spokesperson is whether

(A) it would have been reasonable to consult town residents on the decision

(B) most Sumpton residents will find the new sculpture to their taste

(C) abstract sculptures by the same sculptor have truly been popular in other cities

(D) a more traditional sculpture in the town square would be popular among local residents

(E) public art that the residents of Sumpton would find desirable would probably be found desirable by the residents of other cities

Argument Construction

Situation   After the Sumpton town council voted to pay a prominent sculptor to create an abstract sculpture for the town square, critics protested the decision. A town council spokesperson responded to the critics.

Reasoning   *What do the critics and the spokesperson mainly disagree about?* The critics argue that Sumpton residents dislike most abstract art and that art in the town square should reflect their taste. Since the critics are protesting the town council's decision, they are clearly inferring from the residents' general attitude toward abstract art that the residents will dislike the specific sculpture the prominent sculptor will create. The spokesperson replies by arguing that in other cities, sculptures by the same sculptor have been very popular with local residents. The spokesperson implicitly infers from this that the sculpture the prominent sculptor will create for Sumpton will be popular with Sumpton residents—and therefore that the critics are mistaken.

A   Neither the critics nor the spokesperson mentions consultation with the town residents on the decision.

B   **Correct.** As explained above, the critics raise points implicitly suggesting that the residents will dislike the sculpture, whereas the spokesperson responds with a point implicitly supporting the opposite conclusion.

C   The critics could concede that the sculptor's work has been popular in other cities, but nonetheless hold that Sumpton residents have different tastes from those of the other cities' residents.

D   The spokesperson gives no indication regarding the attitudes of Sumpton residents regarding traditional sculpture.

E   It may be that neither the critics nor the spokesperson holds this view. The spokesperson may hold that Sumpton residents are easier to please than residents of most other cities, whereas the critics may hold that Sumpton residents are far more traditional in their tastes than other cities' residents.

The correct answer is B.

CR09085

205. Jay: Of course there are many good reasons to support the expansion of preventive medical care, but arguments claiming that it will lead to greater societal economic gains are misguided. Some of the greatest societal expenses arise from frequent urgent-care needs for people who have attained a long life due to preventive care.

Sunil: Your argument fails because you neglect economic gains outside the health care system: society suffers an economic loss when any of its productive members suffer preventable illnesses.

Sunil's response to Jay makes which of the following assumptions?

(A) Those who receive preventive care are not more likely to need urgent care than are those who do not receive preventive care.

(B) Jay intends the phrase "economic gains" to refer only to gains accruing to institutions within the health care system.

(C) Productive members of society are more likely than others to suffer preventable illnesses.

(D) The economic contributions of those who receive preventive medical care may outweigh the economic losses caused by preventive care.

(E) Jay is incorrect in stating that patients who receive preventive medical care are long-lived.

Argument Construction

Situation   Some of the greatest societal expenses arise from frequent urgent-care needs for people who have reached old age thanks to preventive medical care. But society also suffers economic loss when any of its productive members suffer preventable illnesses.

Reasoning   *What is Sunil assuming in his argument that Jay's argument fails?* Jay implies that by helping people live longer, expanding preventive medical care may actually increase the amount of urgent medical care people need over the course of their lives, and that societal expenses for this additional urgent care may equal or exceed any societal economic benefits from expanding preventive care. Sunil responds by implying that expanding preventive care would allow society to avoid economic losses from lost productivity caused by preventable illnesses. In order for Sunil's argument to establish that Jay's argument fails, the potential economic benefits that Sunil implies would arise from expanded preventive care must be greater than the economic losses from the increased need for urgent care that Jay points out.

A   This is not an assumption that underpins Sunil's suggestion that the societal economic benefits from expanded preventive care may exceed any resulting economic losses from urgent care.

B   If Jay intends the phrase "economic gains" to refer only to gains within the health care system, then Sunil's point about economic gains outside the health care system is not even relevant to Jay's argument about economic gains within it.

C   Even if productive members of society are not more likely than others to suffer preventable illnesses, it still may be true, as Sunil suggests, that the economic benefits of preventing productive members of society from suffering those illnesses may outweigh the economic losses of doing so. In that case, Jay's argument could still fail in the way Sunil indicates.

D   **Correct.** Sunil must assume this in order to rebut Jay's argument. As explained above, if the economic contributions of those receiving preventive care definitely do not outweigh the economic losses caused by preventive care, then Sunil's implicit point that expanding preventive care would help to prevent the loss of such contributions is insufficient to rebut Jay's argument.

E   Whether Jay is correct or incorrect in this respect, Sunil may be correct that Jay's argument fails because Jay has neglected to consider how preventive care produces larger economic gains outside the health care system.

The correct answer is D.

CR01766

206. Boreal owls range over a much larger area than do other owls of similar size. The reason for this behavior is probably that the small mammals on which owls feed are especially scarce in the forests where boreal owls live, and the relative scarcity of prey requires the owls to range more extensively to find sufficient food.

Which of the following, if true, most helps to confirm the explanation above?

(A) Some boreal owls range over an area eight times larger than the area over which any other owl of similar size ranges.

(B) Boreal owls range over larger areas in regions where food of the sort eaten by small mammals is sparse than they do in regions where such food is abundant.

(C) After their young hatch, boreal owls must hunt more often than before in order to feed both themselves and their newly hatched young.

(D) Sometimes individual boreal owls hunt near a single location for many weeks at a time and do not range farther than a few hundred yards.

(E) The boreal owl requires less food, relative to its weight, than is required by members of other owl species.

Argument Evaluation

Situation   The small mammals on which owls prey are relatively scarce in the forests where boreal owls live. That is why boreal owls range more extensively than do other, similarly sized owls in search of food.

Reasoning   *Which answer choice, if true, would most help confirm the proposed explanation?* One way to confirm an explanation is by finding further information that one would expect to be true *if* the explanation is valid. If the explanation in the passage is valid, then one would expect that variations in the population density of available small-animal prey for boreal owls would be accompanied by variations in the ranges of the boreal owls. Naturally the population density of available small-animal prey is likely to be affected by how plentiful food is for those small animals.

A   The comparison between different groups of boreal owls is not relevant to the comparison between boreal owls and other owls.

B   **Correct.** This indicates that abundance of food for the boreal owls' small-animal prey in an area (and therefore abundance of small animals in that area) correlates with a smaller range for the boreal owls there. This strengthens the proposed explanation.

C   This answer choice concerns a correlation between owls' need for food and the frequency with which owls hunt, whereas the phenomenon described in the passage and the proposed explanation have to do with the range over which owls hunt.

D   If one were to assume that boreal owls never hunt near a single location for weeks, that would in no way undermine the proposed explanation.

E   If anything, this answer choice tends to undermine the proposed explanation, because it suggests the possibility that boreal owls need not make up for the relative scarcity of prey in their habitats by ranging over larger areas.

The correct answer is B.

CR12567

207. Microbiologist: A lethal strain of salmonella recently showed up in a European country, causing an outbreak of illness that killed two people and infected twenty-seven others. Investigators blame the severity of the outbreak on the overuse of antibiotics, since the salmonella bacteria tested were shown to be drug-resistant. But this is unlikely because patients in the country where the outbreak occurred cannot obtain antibiotics to treat illness without a prescription, and the country's doctors prescribe antibiotics less readily than do doctors in any other European country.

Which of the following, if true, would most weaken the microbiologist's reasoning?

(A) Physicians in the country where the outbreak occurred have become hesitant to prescribe antibiotics since they are frequently in short supply.

(B) People in the country where the outbreak occurred often consume foods produced from animals that eat antibiotics-laden livestock feed.

(C) Use of antibiotics in two countries that neighbor the country where the outbreak occurred has risen over the past decade.

(D) Drug-resistant strains of salmonella have not been found in countries in which antibiotics are not generally available.

(E) Salmonella has been shown to spread easily along the distribution chains of certain vegetables, such as raw tomatoes.

Argument Evaluation

Situation Antibiotic-resistant salmonella caused an outbreak of illness in a European country where patients need prescriptions to obtain antibiotics and where doctors dispense such prescriptions less readily than in other European countries.

Reasoning *What evidence would most strongly suggest that overuse of antibiotics was likely responsible for the outbreak, despite the cited facts?* The microbiologist reasons that because patients need prescriptions to obtain antibiotics in the country where the outbreak occurred, and the country's doctors dispense such prescriptions less readily than doctors in other European countries do, antibiotics are probably not being overused in the country—so antibiotic overuse was probably not responsible for the outbreak. Implicit in the microbiologist's reasoning is the assumption that overuse of antibiotics, if it had occurred, could probably have resulted only from overprescribing of antibiotics by physicians to treat illness in people in the country in question. Any evidence casting doubt on this complex assumption would suggest a weakness in the microbiologist's reasoning.

A   This strengthens the argument by providing additional evidence that antibiotics are not being overprescribed in the country.

B   **Correct.** This weakens the microbiologist's argument by indicating that an assumption implicit in the argument may be false: the salmonella outbreak could easily by explained by overuse of antibiotics in livestock feed (perhaps imported from other countries).

C   Even if antibiotic use has risen in the two neighboring countries, antibiotics still might be underused in both countries.

D   This suggests that antibiotic-resistant salmonella arises only in countries where antibiotics are used; even if this were true it would be quite compatible with the microbiologist's argument and does not weaken that argument.

E   This describes one mechanism by which salmonella can spread in a population; it says nothing about whether an outbreak of antibiotic-resistant strains of salmonella might have been caused by antibiotic overuse.

The correct answer is B.

CR37090.02
208. Economist: Construction moves faster in good weather than in bad, so mild winters in areas that usually experience harsh conditions can appear to create construction booms as builders complete projects that would otherwise have to wait. But forecasting one mild winter or even two for such areas generally does not lead to overall increases in construction during these periods, because construction loans are often obtained more than a year in advance, and because _____.

Which of the following, if true, most logically completes the economist's argument?

(A)   construction workers often travel to warmer climates in the wintertime in search of work

(B)   construction materials are often in short supply during construction booms

(C)   many builders in these areas are likely to apply for construction loans at the same time

(D)   it is frequently the case that forecasted weather trends do not actually occur

(E)   mild winters are generally followed by spring and summer weather that promotes more rapid construction

Argument Construction

Situation   According to an economist, construction booms can seem to occur when mild winters allow construction to proceed in places where harsh winters usually prevent it. But the economist suggests that the greater construction in mild winters than in harsh winters is not due to contractors prescheduling more construction during winters that are predicted to be mild. The economist says there are two reasons for this. One is that construction loans often need to be approved more than a year in advance.

Reasoning   *Which answer choice is logically most suited to be the second of the two reasons referred to by the economist?* The economist seeks to explain why a forecast of an unusually mild winter does not result in an overall increase in construction scheduled to take place in upcoming winters. One reason suggested is that loan approval—and presumably financial planning—for a construction project might often need to take place at least one year in advance. However, forecasts a year in advance that a mild winter will occur are quite likely to turn out to be wrong. The unreliability of such forecasts would make it unwise to intentionally schedule greater amounts of construction for winters that may or may not turn out to be mild.

A   If an adequate labor force were lacking for a project in a given area, that project might not proceed. However, as part of the planning of a project, construction firms would likely have an assurance that an adequate labor force would be available.

B   This suggests a slightly plausible hypothesis for why greater amounts of construction would not be scheduled for mild winters: if the construction firms have reason to believe that other companies will also have a motivation to schedule more construction at those times, they might all tacitly agree to distribute the projects more evenly across time to avoid shortages. However, it is also reasonable to suppose that shortages are a result of unforeseen boom conditions, not planned ones, and if the companies plan well in advance, they should be able to arrange for adequate supplies of materials.

C   A surge in loan applications might mean longer waits for loan approvals. Contrary to what the economist claims, the fact that *many builders* are planning projects tends to suggest that there could be a construction boom scheduled for winter. The economist aims to explain why forecasts of one or more mild winters in places where winters are usually harsh do not result in *overall increases in construction*.

D   Correct. The high likelihood that a forecast of a mild winter might turn out to be wrong is one reason for construction firms not to plan winter projects for areas where winters are usually harsh. This reason converges with the other reason provided: the forecast of a mild winter would have to occur up to one year in advance in order to obtain a loan approval in sufficient time to start construction.

E   This information does not contribute to explaining why prescheduled construction booms are unlikely during exceptionally mild winters where winters are usually harsh. If long-term winter-weather forecasts were reliable, this could be a reason why such construction booms might be planned for mild winters.

The correct answer is D.

CR03416

209. Historian: Newton developed mathematical concepts and techniques that are fundamental to modern calculus. Leibniz developed closely analogous concepts and techniques. It has traditionally been thought that these discoveries were independent. Researchers have, however, recently discovered notes of Leibniz's that discuss one of Newton's books on mathematics. Several scholars have argued that since **the book includes a presentation of Newton's calculus concepts and techniques,** and since the notes were written before Leibniz's own development of calculus concepts and techniques, it is virtually certain **that the traditional view is false.** A more cautious conclusion than this is called for, however. Leibniz's notes are limited to early sections of Newton's book, sections that precede the ones in which Newton's calculus concepts and techniques are presented.

In the historian's reasoning, the two portions in **boldface** play which of the following roles?

(A) The first is a claim that the historian rejects; the second is a position that that claim has been used to support.

(B) The first is evidence that has been used to support a conclusion about which the historian expresses reservations; the second is that conclusion.

(C) The first provides evidence in support of a position that the historian defends; the second is that position.

(D) The first and the second each provide evidence in support of a position that the historian defends.

(E) The first has been used in support of a position that the historian rejects; the second is a conclusion that the historian draws from that position.

Argument Construction

Situation A historian discusses a controversy about whether or not Leibniz developed calculus concepts and techniques independently of Newton.

Reasoning *What argumentative roles do the two portions in boldface play in the passage?* The first four sentences of the passage simply provide background information. Both boldface sections are within the fifth sentence, which reports an argument by *several scholars*. The key word *since* indicates that the first boldface section is a premise in the scholars' argument. A second premise preceded by another *since* follows in the next clause. The final clause of the fifth sentence reveals that the second boldface section is the conclusion of the scholars' argument. In the sixth sentence, the historian expresses misgivings about the scholars' conclusion, for reasons presented in the seventh and final sentence.

A The historian does not reject the claim that Newton's book includes a presentation of Newton's calculus concepts and techniques. Instead, the historian merely points out that Leibniz's notes do not cover those sections of Newton's book.

B **Correct.** The first boldface section is one of two premises in the scholars' argument, and the second boldface section is that argument's conclusion. In the following sentence the historian expresses reservations about that conclusion.

C The historian does not defend the scholars' conclusion but rather expresses misgivings about it.

D The second boldface section is the scholars' conclusion and does not present any evidence. Nor does it support the historian's position that a more cautious conclusion is called for.

E The second boldface section presents not the historian's conclusion but rather the scholars' conclusion, about which the historian expresses misgivings.

The correct answer is B.

CR03867

210. For over two centuries, no one had been able to make Damascus blades—blades with a distinctive serpentine surface pattern—but a contemporary sword maker may just have rediscovered how. Using iron with trace impurities that precisely matched those present in the iron used in historic Damascus blades, this contemporary sword maker seems to have finally hit on an intricate process by which he can produce a blade indistinguishable from a true Damascus blade.

Which of the following, if true, provides the strongest support for the hypothesis that trace impurities in the iron are essential for the production of Damascus blades?

(A) There are surface features of every Damascus blade—including the blades produced by the contemporary sword maker—that are unique to that blade.

(B) The iron with which the contemporary sword maker made Damascus blades came from a source of iron that was unknown two centuries ago.

(C) Almost all the tools used by the contemporary sword maker were updated versions of tools that were used by sword makers over two centuries ago.

(D) Production of Damascus blades by sword makers of the past ceased abruptly after those sword makers' original source of iron became exhausted.

(E) Although Damascus blades were renowned for maintaining a sharp edge, the blade made by the contemporary sword maker suggests that they may have maintained their edge less well than blades made using what is now the standard process for making blades.

Argument Evaluation

Situation   A sword maker may have recently rediscovered how to make Damascus blades using iron with trace impurities matching those in the iron from which historic Damascus blades were wrought.

Reasoning   *What evidence would suggest that the trace impurities are essential for producing Damascus blades?* The passage says the sword maker seems to have created blades indistinguishable from historic Damascus blades by using iron with the same trace impurities found in those blades. But that does not prove the trace impurities are essential to the process. Evidence suggesting that Damascus blades have never been made from iron without the trace impurities would support the hypothesis that the trace impurities are essential to their manufacture.

A   Damascus blades could vary in their surface features whether or not trace impurities are essential for their manufacture.

B   Whatever the source of the iron the contemporary sword maker used, it contains the same trace impurities as the iron historically used to make Damascus blades, which is what the hypothesis is about.

C   If anything, this might cast doubt on the hypothesis by suggesting that the special tools rather than the trace impurities could account for the distinctive features of Damascus blades.

D   Correct. This suggests that when the historic sword makers lost access to the special iron with its trace impurities, they could no longer make Damascus blades. Thus, it supports the hypothesis that the trace impurities are necessary for manufacturing Damascus blades.

E   Even if Damascus blades maintained their edges less well than most contemporary blades do, the trace impurities may not have been essential for manufacturing them.

The correct answer is D.

CR01903

211. Images from ground-based telescopes are invariably distorted by the Earth's atmosphere. Orbiting space telescopes, however, operating above Earth's atmosphere, should provide superbly detailed images. Therefore, ground-based telescopes will soon become obsolete for advanced astronomical research purposes.

Which of the following statements, if true, would cast the most doubt on the conclusion drawn above?

(A) An orbiting space telescope due to be launched this year is far behind schedule and over budget, whereas the largest ground-based telescope was both within budget and on schedule.

(B) Ground-based telescopes located on mountain summits are not subject to the kinds of atmospheric distortion which, at low altitudes, make stars appear to twinkle.

(C) By careful choice of observatory location, it is possible for large-aperture telescopes to avoid most of the kind of wind turbulence that can distort image quality.

(D) When large-aperture telescopes are located at high altitudes near the equator, they permit the best Earth-based observations of the center of the Milky Way Galaxy, a prime target of astronomical research.

(E) Detailed spectral analyses, upon which astronomers rely for determining the chemical composition and evolutionary history of stars, require telescopes with more light-gathering capacity than space telescopes can provide.

Argument Evaluation

Situation   Earth's atmosphere distorts images from ground-based telescopes, whereas space telescopes orbiting above the atmosphere should provide superbly detailed images.

Reasoning   *What evidence would undermine the claim that ground-based telescopes will soon become obsolete for advanced astronomical research?* The argument implicitly assumes that advanced astronomical research can be accomplished more effectively with the more detailed, less distorted images produced by space telescopes and that therefore almost all advanced astronomical research will soon be conducted with space telescopes. This reasoning would be undermined by evidence that ground-based telescopes have substantial advantages for advanced astronomical research despite their distorted images or by evidence that space telescopes will not soon become common or affordable enough to support most advanced astronomical research.

A   Even if this is true, there may be several orbiting space telescopes that will be, or have been, launched on schedule and within budget, so this answer choice does not cast doubt on the conclusion of the argument.

B   Ground-based telescopes on mountain summits are still subject to more atmospheric distortion than are space telescopes orbiting above the atmosphere.

C   Atmospheric distortion of telescopic images may result mainly from factors other than wind turbulence.

D   Even the best Earth-based observations of the center of the Milky Way Galaxy may be vastly inferior to space-based observations.

E   **Correct.** This indicates an inherent limitation of space-based telescopes: unlike Earth-based telescopes, they lack the light-gathering capacity that astronomers need to perform one of their primary tasks, i.e., detailed spectral analyses. So Earth-based telescopes are unlikely to soon become obsolete.

The correct answer is E.

CR07562

212. Generally scientists enter their field with the goal of doing important new research and accept as their colleagues those with similar motivation. Therefore, when any scientist wins renown as an expounder of science to general audiences, most other scientists conclude that this popularizer should no longer be regarded as a true colleague.

The explanation offered above for the low esteem in which scientific popularizers are held by research scientists assumes that

(A) serious scientific research is not a solitary activity, but relies on active cooperation among a group of colleagues

(B) research scientists tend not to regard as colleagues those scientists whose renown they envy

(C) a scientist can become a famous popularizer without having completed any important research

(D) research scientists believe that those who are well known as popularizers of science are not motivated to do important new research

(E) no important new research can be accessible to or accurately assessed by those who are not themselves scientists

Argument Construction

Situation   Research scientists desire to do important new research and treat as colleagues just those who have a similar desire. When a scientist becomes popular among a general audience for explaining principles of science, other scientists have less esteem for this popularizer, no longer regarding such a scientist as a serious colleague.

Reasoning   *What assumption do research scientists make about scientists who become popularizers?* The community of scientists shares a common goal: to do important new research. What would cause this community to disapprove of a popularizer and to cease to regard the popularizer as a colleague? It must be because many scientists believe that becoming a popularizer is incompatible with desiring to do important new research.

A   Many scientists make this assumption, of course—but it is not an assumption on which the explanation specifically depends. The explanation concerns the scientists' motivation, not their style of doing research.

B   This statement gives another reason that scientists may reject a popularizer, but because it is not the reason implied in the passage, it is not assumed.

C   Even if this is true, it does not address the core issue of the argument: what scientists believe about the *motivation* of popularizers.

D   **Correct.** This statement properly identifies an assumption on which the explanation for scientists' rejection of popularizers depends.

E   The passage is not concerned with whether nonscientists can understand new research, but rather with the beliefs and motivations of scientists who reject popularizers as colleagues.

The correct answer is D.

CR07676

213. Urban planner: When a city loses population due to migration, property taxes in that city tend to rise. This is because there are then fewer residents paying to maintain an infrastructure that was designed to support more people. Rising property taxes, in turn, drive more residents away, compounding the problem. Since the city of Stonebridge is starting to lose population, the city government should therefore refrain from raising property taxes.

Which of the following, if true, would most weaken the urban planner's argument?

(A) If Stonebridge does not raise taxes on its residents to maintain its infrastructure, the city will become much less attractive to live in as that infrastructure decays.

(B) Stonebridge at present benefits from grants provided by the national government to help maintain certain parts of its infrastructure.

(C) If there is a small increase in property taxes in Stonebridge and a slightly larger proportion of total revenue than at present is allocated to infrastructure maintenance, the funding will be adequate for that purpose.

(D) Demographers project that the population of a region that includes Stonebridge will start to increase substantially within the next several years.

(E) The property taxes in Stonebridge are significantly lower than those in many larger cities.

Argument Evaluation

Situation   When a city loses population due to migration, fewer residents remain to pay to maintain the city's infrastructure, so property taxes tend to rise. These rising property taxes then drive even more residents away. The city of Stonebridge is starting to lose population, so Stonebridge's government should not raise property taxes.

Reasoning   *What would weaken the urban planner's justification for concluding that Stonebridge's government should refrain from raising property taxes?* The urban planner implicitly reasons that raising property taxes in Stonebridge in order to maintain the city's infrastructure would make the city lose even more residents, leaving even fewer paying to maintain the infrastructure, and that this would worsen the funding problem the tax increase would have been intended to solve. The urban planner's argument would be weakened by any evidence that raising property taxes in Stonebridge would not drive residents away or that refraining from raising property taxes would cause the same problems as raising them would cause, or worse.

A   **Correct.** This suggests that refraining from raising property taxes could drive more residents out of Stonebridge than raising them would, and thus would not help the city avoid the problem the urban planner describes.

B   This does slightly weaken the argument because the grants may still be provided to maintain certain parts of the infrastructure, even if increased property taxes drive more residents away. But losing more residents could still make it harder to raise enough funds to maintain the rest of the city's infrastructure, as the urban planner argues.

C   Even if this approach would address the immediate maintenance funding problem, the small increase in property taxes could still drive more residents away, forcing additional future tax increases on those who remain, just as the urban planner suggests.

D   This does slightly weaken the argument, but the residents who will move to the region might still avoid moving to Stonebridge if the property taxes there are too high, and those who live in Stonebridge might still move to other cities in the region.

E   Residents fleeing Stonebridge because of high property taxes would likely avoid moving to the many larger cities with even higher property taxes, but they might be happy to move to many other places with low property taxes.

The correct answer is A.

CR01338

214. Which of the following most logically completes the argument?

Utrania was formerly a major petroleum exporter, but in recent decades economic stagnation and restrictive regulations inhibited investment in new oil fields. In consequence, Utranian oil exports dropped steadily as old fields became depleted. Utrania's currently improving economic situation, together with less-restrictive regulations, will undoubtedly result in the rapid development of new fields. However, it would be premature to conclude that the rapid development of new fields will result in higher oil exports, because _____.

(A) the price of oil is expected to remain relatively stable over the next several years

(B) the improvement in the economic situation in Utrania is expected to result in a dramatic increase in the proportion of Utranians who own automobiles

(C) most of the investment in new oil fields in Utrania is expected to come from foreign sources

(D) new technology is available to recover oil from old oil fields formerly regarded as depleted

(E) many of the new oil fields in Utrania are likely to be as productive as those that were developed during the period when Utrania was a major oil exporter

Argument Construction

Situation A country that had been a major oil exporter has seen its exports decline in recent decades due to economic stagnation, a failure to invest in new fields, and the steady depletion of its old fields. But looser regulations and an improving economy will bring rapid development of new oil fields in the country.

Reasoning *Which answer choice would most logically complete the argument?* The passage describes the conditions that led to Utrania's no longer being a major oil exporter: a lack of investment in new oil fields due to a stagnant economy and restrictive regulations. The passage then says that due to changed regulatory and economic conditions, there will now be rapid development of new oil fields. Nonetheless, this might not bring about an increase in Utrania's oil exports. To logically complete the argument, one must explain how oil exports might not increase even when the condition that led to decreased oil exports has been removed. Suppose there were an increase in domestic oil consumption. A dramatic increase in the rate of car ownership in Utrania could reasonably be expected to significantly increase domestic oil consumption, which could eat up the added oil production from the new fields.

A This answer choice is incorrect. There is no reason why stable oil prices should prevent Utrania's oil exports from increasing.

B **Correct.** An increase in car ownership would increase Utrania's oil consumption—and this supports the claim that oil exports might not increase.

C If anything, this suggests that oil exports should increase. So it would not be a good choice for completion of the argument.

D The advent of new technology allowing oil to be extracted from fields previously thought to be depleted would mean that there is even more reason to think that Utrania's oil exports will increase.

E This does not help to explain why exports would not increase. On the contrary, it suggests that the new fields will lead to increased exports.

The correct answer is B.

CR09592

215. The use of growth-promoting antibiotics in hog farming can weaken their effectiveness in treating humans because such use can spread resistance to those antibiotics among microorganisms. But now the Smee Company, one of the largest pork marketers, may stop buying pork raised on feed containing these antibiotics. Smee has 60 percent of the pork market, and farmers who sell to Smee would certainly stop using antibiotics in order to avoid jeopardizing their sales. So if Smee makes this change, it will probably significantly slow the decline in antibiotics' effectiveness for humans.

Which of the following, if true, would most strengthen the argument above?

(A) Other major pork marketers will probably stop buying pork raised on feed containing growth-promoting antibiotics if Smee no longer buys such pork.

(B) The decline in hog growth due to discontinuation of antibiotics can be offset by improved hygiene.

(C) Authorities are promoting the use of antibiotics to which microorganisms have not yet developed resistance.

(D) A phaseout of use of antibiotics for hogs in one country reduced usage by over 50 percent over five years.

(E) If Smee stops buying pork raised with antibiotics, the firm's costs will probably increase.

Argument Evaluation

Situation   Using growth-promoting antibiotics in hog farming can produce widespread resistance to antibiotics among microorganisms, thereby making the antibiotics less effective in treating humans. The Smee Company, a pork marketer with 60 percent of the pork market, may stop buying pork raised on feed containing these antibiotics.

Reasoning   *What additional evidence would most help to support the conclusion that if Smee makes the change, it will significantly slow the decline in antibiotics' effectiveness for humans?* We are already informed that if Smee makes the change, it will eliminate the use of antibiotics in hog feed by farmers supplying at least 60 percent of the pork market. The argument would be strengthened by evidence that Smee's decision would indirectly cause use of the antibiotics to stop more broadly, for example in hog farms supplying significantly more than 60 percent of the total amount of pork marketed.

A   **Correct.** This suggests that if Smee makes the change, hog farmers supplying other major pork marketers will also have to stop using antibiotics in hog feed, making the change more widespread and thus probably more effective.

B   Even if the decline in hog growth from discontinuing the antibiotics cannot be offset, many hog farmers will still have to stop using the antibiotics as a result of Smee's decision. On the other hand, even if the decline can be offset with improved hygiene, that change might be too expensive or difficult to be worth its benefits for most hog farmers.

C   Whatever new antibiotics authorities are promoting, microorganisms may soon develop resistance to them as well. Smee may or may not refuse to buy pork raised on feed containing these new antibiotics.

D   This is evidence that Smee's decision may significantly reduce antibiotic use in hogs, but it provides no evidence of how this reduction may affect antibiotics' effectiveness for humans.

E   If anything, this provides reason to suspect that Smee will not stick with the change for long after the costs increase, so it weakens rather than strengthens the argument that the change will significantly slow the decline in antibiotics' effectiveness.

The correct answer is A.

CR10678

216. In an experiment, volunteers walked individually through a dark, abandoned theater. Half of the volunteers had been told that the theater was haunted and the other half that it was under renovation. The first half reported significantly more unusual experiences than the second did. The researchers concluded that reports of encounters with ghosts and other supernatural entities generally result from prior expectations of such experiences.

Which of the following, if true, would most seriously weaken the researchers' reasoning?

(A) None of the volunteers in the second half believed that the unusual experiences they reported were supernatural.

(B) All of the volunteers in the first half believed that the researchers' statement that the theater was haunted was a lie.

(C) Before being told about the theater, the volunteers within each group varied considerably in their prior beliefs about supernatural experiences.

(D) Each unusual experience reported by the volunteers had a cause that did not involve the supernatural.

(E) The researchers did not believe that the theater was haunted.

Argument Evaluation

Situation   Volunteers in an experiment walked through a dark, abandoned theater. Those who had been told the theater was haunted reported more unusual experiences than those who had been told it was under renovation.

Reasoning   *What evidence would most strongly suggest that the experimental results do not indicate that reports of supernatural encounters result from prior expectations of such experiences?* The researcher assumes that the half of the volunteers who had been told the theater was haunted were more inclined to expect supernatural experiences in the theater than were the other half of the volunteers. Based on this assumption and the greater incidence of reports of unusual experiences among the first half of the volunteers, the researcher concludes that prior expectation of supernatural experiences makes people more likely to report such experiences. The researchers' reasoning would be weakened by evidence that the volunteers did not actually have the expectations the researchers assumed them to have, or by evidence that any such expectations did not influence their reports.

A   This strengthens the argument by indicating that the volunteers whom the researchers did not lead to expect supernatural experiences reported no such experiences.

B   **Correct.** If none of the volunteers believed the researchers' claim that the theater was haunted, then the implicit assumption that several of those volunteers expected supernatural experiences in the theater is flawed, and so the inference that their prior expectations probably account for their reports of supernatural experiences is flawed.

C   This is compatible with the researchers' inference and does not undermine it. Even if the volunteers' initial beliefs about supernatural experiences varied, the researchers' claims about the theater might have strongly influenced how many volunteers in each group expected to have such experiences in the theater specifically.

D   The researchers argue that the volunteers' prior expectations account for all the reports of unusual experiences, and this is compatible with there being no genuine supernatural occurrences in the theater.

E   Whatever the researchers personally believed about the theater, they might still have successfully influenced the volunteers' beliefs about it.

The correct answer is B.

CR05665
217. In order to reduce dependence on imported oil, the government of Jalica has imposed minimum fuel-efficiency requirements on all new cars, beginning this year. The more fuel-efficient a car, the less pollution it produces per mile driven. As Jalicans replace their old cars with cars that meet the new requirements, annual pollution from car traffic is likely to decrease in Jalica.

Which of the following, if true, most seriously weakens the argument?

(A) In Jalica, domestically produced oil is more expensive than imported oil.

(B) The Jalican government did not intend the new fuel-efficiency requirement to be a pollution-reduction measure.

(C) Some pollution-control devices mandated in Jalica make cars less fuel-efficient than they would be without those devices.

(D) The new regulation requires no change in the chemical formulation of fuel for cars in Jalica.

(E) Jalicans who get cars that are more fuel-efficient tend to do more driving than before.

Argument Evaluation

Situation The Jalican government is requiring all new cars to meet minimum fuel-efficiency requirements starting this year. Cars that are more fuel efficient produce less pollution per mile driven.

Reasoning *What evidence would suggest that annual pollution from car traffic will not decrease in Jalica, despite the new policy?* Air pollution from car traffic is unlikely to decrease if the new standards will result in more cars on the road or more miles driven per car; or if air pollution from car traffic in Jalica is increasing because of unrelated factors such as growing numbers of Jalicans who can afford cars, construction of more roads, etc. Evidence that any of these factors is present would cast doubt on the argument's conclusion and thus weaken the argument.

A The question at issue is not whether the new policy will reduce dependence on imported oil as the government intends, but rather whether it will reduce air pollution from car traffic.

B A government policy may have consequences that the government did not intend it to have.

C Even if these pollution-control devices make cars less fuel efficient, the new fuel-efficiency standards may still improve cars' average fuel efficiency and thereby reduce air pollution.

D Even if the fuel is unchanged, the new fuel-efficiency standards may still result in cars using less fuel and may thereby reduce air pollution.

E **Correct.** If the new fuel-efficient cars are driven more miles per year than older cars are, they may produce as much or more pollution per year than older cars do even though they produce less pollution per mile driven.

The correct answer is E.

CR01173

218. Plantings of cotton bioengineered to produce its own insecticide against bollworms, a major cause of crop failure, sustained little bollworm damage until this year. This year the plantings are being seriously damaged by bollworms. Bollworms, however, are not necessarily developing resistance to the cotton's insecticide. Bollworms breed on corn, and last year more corn than usual was planted throughout cotton-growing regions. So it is likely that the cotton is simply being overwhelmed by corn-bred bollworms.

In evaluating the argument, which of the following would it be most useful to establish?

(A) Whether corn could be bioengineered to produce the insecticide

(B) Whether plantings of cotton that does not produce the insecticide are suffering unusually extensive damage from bollworms this year

(C) Whether other crops that have been bioengineered to produce their own insecticide successfully resist the pests against which the insecticide was to protect them

(D) Whether plantings of bioengineered cotton are frequently damaged by insect pests other than bollworms

(E) Whether there are insecticides that can be used against bollworms that have developed resistance to the insecticide produced by the bioengineered cotton

Argument Evaluation

Situation Although plantings of cotton bioengineered to produce an insecticide to combat bollworms were little damaged by the pests in previous years, they are being severely damaged this year. Since the bollworms breed on corn, and there has been more corn planted this year in cotton-growing areas, the cotton is probably being overwhelmed by the corn-bred bollworms.

Reasoning *In evaluating the argument, which question would it be most useful to have answered?* The argument states that the bioengineered cotton crop failures this year (1) have likely been due to the increased corn plantings and (2) not due to the pests having developed a resistance to the insecticide. This also implies (3) that the failures are not due to some third factor.

It would be useful to know how the bioengineered cotton is faring in comparison to the rest of this year's cotton crop. If the bioengineered cotton is faring better against the bollworms, that fact would support the argument because it would suggest that the insecticide is still combating bollworms. If, on the other hand, the bioengineered cotton is being more severely ravaged by bollworms than is other cotton, that suggests that there is some third cause that is primarily at fault.

A This would probably be useful information to those trying to alleviate the bollworm problem in bioengineered cotton. But whether such corn could be developed has no bearing on what is causing the bioengineered cotton to be damaged by bollworms this year.

B **Correct.** If bollworm damage on non-bioengineered cotton is worse than usual this year, then bollworm infestation in general is simply worse than usual, so pesticide resistance does not need to be invoked to explain the bollworm attacks on the bioengineered cotton.

C Even if other crops that have been bioengineered to resist pests have not successfully resisted them, that fact would not mean that the same is true of this cotton. Furthermore, the facts already suggest that the bioengineered cotton has resisted bollworms.

D Whether other types of pests often damage bioengineered cotton has no bearing on why bollworms are damaging this type of cotton more this year than in the past.

E This, too, might be useful information to those trying to alleviate the bollworm problem in bioengineered cotton, but it is not particularly useful in evaluating the argument. Even if there are pesticides that could be used against bollworms that have developed resistance to the insecticide of the bioengineered cotton, that does not mean that such pesticides are being used this year.

The correct answer is B.

CR03331

219. Typically during thunderstorms most lightning strikes carry a negative electric charge; only a few carry a positive charge. Thunderstorms with unusually high proportions of positive-charge strikes tend to occur in smoky areas near forest fires. The fact that smoke carries positively charged smoke particles into the air above a fire suggests the hypothesis that the extra positive strikes occur because of the presence of such particles in the storm clouds.

Which of the following, if discovered to be true, most seriously undermines the hypothesis?

(A) Other kinds of rare lightning also occur with unusually high frequency in the vicinity of forest fires.

(B) The positive-charge strikes that occur near forest fires tend to be no more powerful than positive strikes normally are.

(C) A positive-charge strike is as likely to start a forest fire as a negative-charge strike is.

(D) Thunderstorms that occur in drifting clouds of smoke have extra positive-charge strikes weeks after the charge of the smoke particles has dissipated.

(E) The total number of lightning strikes during a thunderstorm is usually within the normal range in the vicinity of a forest fire.

Argument Evaluation

Situation Thunderstorms with unusually high proportions of positive-charge lightning strikes tend to occur in smoky areas near forest fires. Smoke carries positively charged particles into the air above fires, suggesting that smoke particles in storm clouds are responsible for the higher proportion of positive strikes.

Reasoning *What would cast doubt on the hypothesis that the extra positive-charge lightning strikes in thunderstorms near forest fires result from positively charged smoke particles carried into the storm clouds?* The hypothesis would be weakened by evidence that the positively charged smoke particles do not enter the storm clouds in the first place, or that they do not retain their charge in the clouds long enough to produce an effect, or that their positive charge cannot affect the charges of the storm's lightning strikes in any case, or that some other factor tends to make the lightning strikes above these storms positively charged.

A It could be that positively charged smoke particles cause these other kinds of rare lightning, too, so this does not seriously undermine the hypothesis.

B The hypothesis is not about the power of the positive-charge lightning strikes, only about why a high proportion of them occur in thunderstorms near forest fires.

C The hypothesis is about why positive-charge strikes tend to occur in smoky areas near forest fires that have already started before the strikes occur. Furthermore, an equal likelihood of positive-charge and negative-charge strikes starting fires cannot explain a correlation between fires and positive-charge strikes specifically.

D **Correct.** This means that even when drifting clouds of smoke persist for weeks after a fire, when the charge of their particles has already dissipated, the smoke somehow still makes the strikes positively charged in any thunderstorms arising within it. If so, some factor other than positively charged smoke particles must affect the strikes' charge.

E This information does not undermine the hypothesis. The hypothesis does not concern the possibility that there might be more lightning strikes in the vicinity of forest fires; rather it concerns the proportion of all such lightning strikes that are positively charged.

The correct answer is D.

CR01140

220. Many gardeners believe that the variety of clematis vine that is most popular among gardeners in North America is *jackmanii*. This belief is apparently correct since, of the one million clematis plants sold per year by the largest clematis nursery in North America, ten percent are *jackmanii*.

Which of the following is an assumption on which the argument depends?

(A)   The nursery sells more than ten different varieties of clematis.

(B)   The largest clematis nursery in North America sells nothing but clematis plants.

(C)   Some of the *jackmanii* sold by the nursery are sold to gardeners outside North America.

(D)   Most North American gardeners grow clematis in their gardens.

(E)   For all nurseries in North America that specialize in clematis, at least ten percent of the clematis plants they sell are *jackmanii*.

Argument Construction

Situation   Of the clematis plants sold by the largest clematis nursery in North America, 10 percent are *jackmanii*, which many gardeners believe to be the most popular variety of clematis in North America.

Reasoning   *What must be true in order for the fact that 10 percent of the clematis sold at the nursery are* jackmanii *to provide evidence that jackmanii is the most popular variety of clematis in North America?* The argument assumes that sales of different varieties of clematis at the nursery reflect the relative levels of popularity of those varieties among North American gardeners. It also assumes that *jackmanii* is the best-selling clematis variety at the nursery, an assumption which requires that less than 10 percent of the nursery's clematis sales are of any one variety other than *jackmanii*.

A   **Correct.** Suppose the nursery sold ten or fewer varieties of clematis. Then at least one variety other than *jackmanii* would have to account for at least 10 percent of the nursery's clematis sales, so *jackmanii* would not be the best-selling clematis variety at the nursery as the argument assumes.

B   The argument only concerns how popular *jackmanii* is relative to other varieties of clematis, not relative to any plants other than clematis that the nursery may sell.

C   If anything, this would weaken the argument by suggesting that the nursery's *jackmanii* sales might reflect *jackmanii*'s popularity outside North America more than its popularity within North America.

D   This would indicate that clematis is a popular plant among North American gardeners, not that *jackmanii* is the most popular variety of clematis.

E   Even if *jackmanii* accounts for less than 10 percent of clematis sales at a few individual nurseries, it may still account for 10 percent or more of North American clematis sales overall.

The correct answer is A.

CR06422
221. Since 1990 the percentage of bacterial sinus infections in Aqadestan that are resistant to the antibiotic perxicillin has increased substantially. Bacteria can quickly develop resistance to an antibiotic when it is prescribed indiscriminately or when patients fail to take it as prescribed. Since perxicillin has not been indiscriminately prescribed, health officials hypothesize that the increase in perxicillin-resistant sinus infections is largely due to patients' failure to take this medication as prescribed.

Which of the following, if true of Aqadestan, provides most support for the health officials' hypothesis?

(A) Resistance to several other commonly prescribed antibiotics has not increased since 1990 in Aqadestan.

(B) A large number of Aqadestanis never seek medical help when they have a sinus infection.

(C) When it first became available, perxicillin was much more effective in treating bacterial sinus infections than any other antibiotic used for such infections at the time.

(D) Many patients who take perxicillin experience severe side effects within the first few days of their prescribed regimen.

(E) Aqadestani health clinics provide antibiotics to their patients at cost.

Argument Construction

Situation   In Aqadestan the percentage of bacterial sinus infections resistant to the antibiotic perxicillin has been increasing even though perxicillin has not been indiscriminately prescribed.

Reasoning   *What evidence most strongly suggests that the main reason perxicillin-resistant sinus infections are becoming more common is that patients are failing to take perxicillin as prescribed?* Any evidence suggesting that patients have in fact been failing to take perxicillin as prescribed would support the hypothesis, as would any evidence casting doubt on other possible explanations for the increasing proportion of perxicillin-resistant sinus infections.

A   This suggests that some factor specific to perxicillin is increasing bacterial resistance to it, but that could be true whether or not the factor is patients' failure to take perxicillin as prescribed.

B   If anything, this weakens the argument by suggesting that most people with sinus infections are never prescribed perxicillin, and that therefore relatively few people are getting prescriptions and then failing to follow them.

C   The relative effectiveness of perxicillin when it first became available does not suggest that the reason it is now becoming less effective is that many patients are failing to take it as prescribed.

D   **Correct.** These side effects would discourage patients from taking perxicillin as prescribed, so their existence provides evidence that many patients are not taking it as prescribed.

E   If the clinics do not charge extra for perxicillin, that would make it more affordable and hence easier for many patients to take as prescribed.

The correct answer is D.

CR07793

222. Psychologist: In a study, researchers gave 100 volunteers a psychological questionnaire designed to measure their self-esteem. The researchers then asked each volunteer to rate the strength of his or her own social skills. The volunteers with the highest levels of self-esteem consistently rated themselves as having much better social skills than did the volunteers with moderate levels. This suggests that attaining an exceptionally high level of self-esteem greatly improves one's social skills.

The psychologist's argument is most vulnerable to criticism on which of the following grounds?

(A) It fails to adequately address the possibility that many of the volunteers may not have understood what the psychological questionnaire was designed to measure.

(B) It takes for granted that the volunteers with the highest levels of self-esteem had better social skills than did the other volunteers, even before the former volunteers had attained their high levels of self-esteem.

(C) It overlooks the possibility that people with very high levels of self-esteem may tend to have a less accurate perception of the strength of their own social skills than do people with moderate levels of self-esteem.

(D) It relies on evidence from a group of volunteers that is too small to provide any support for any inferences regarding people in general.

(E) It overlooks the possibility that factors other than level of self-esteem may be of much greater importance in determining the strength of one's social skills.

Argument Evaluation

Situation   In a psychological study of 100 volunteers, those found to have the highest self-esteem consistently rated themselves as having much better social skills than did those found to have moderate self-esteem.

Reasoning   *What is wrong with the psychologist citing the study's results to justify the conclusion that exceptionally high self-esteem greatly improves social skills?* The psychologist reasons that the study shows a correlation between very high self-esteem and how highly one rates one's social skills, and that this correlation in turn suggests that very high self-esteem improves social skills. This argument is vulnerable to at least two criticisms: First, the argument assumes that the volunteers' ratings of their own social skills are generally accurate. But very high self-esteem might in many cases result from a tendency to overestimate oneself and one's skills, including one's social skills. Second, the argument fails to address the possibility that good social skills promote high self-esteem rather than vice versa, as well as the possibility that some third factor (such as a sunny disposition or fortunate circumstances) promotes both high self-esteem and good social skills.

A   An experiment's subjects do not have to understand the experiment's design in order for the experimental results to be accurate.

B   To the contrary, the argument concludes that the volunteers with the highest self-esteem attained their enhanced social skills as a result of attaining such high self-esteem.

C   **Correct.** As explained above, very high self-esteem may often result from a tendency to overestimate oneself in general, and thus to overestimate one's social skills.

D   A group of 100 volunteers is large enough for an experiment to provide at least a little support for at least some inferences regarding people in general.

E   As explained above, the argument overlooks the possibility that some third factor may play a significant role in determining the strength of one's social skills. But even if some factor other than self-esteem is more important in determining the strength of social skills, that would still be compatible with very high self-esteem being of some importance in improving one's social skills.

The correct answer is C.

CR06826

223. A product that represents a clear technological advance over competing products can generally command a high price. Because **technological advances tend to be quickly surpassed** and companies want to make large profits while they still can, **many companies charge the maximum possible price for such a product**. But large profits on the new product will give competitors a strong incentive to quickly match the new product's capabilities. Consequently, the strategy to maximize overall profit from a new product is to charge less than the greatest possible price.

In the argument above, the two portions in **boldface** play which of the following roles?

(A) The first is a consideration raised to argue that a certain strategy is counterproductive; the second presents that strategy.

(B) The first is a consideration raised to support the strategy that the argument recommends; the second presents that strategy.

(C) The first is a consideration raised to help explain the popularity of a certain strategy; the second presents that strategy.

(D) The first is an assumption, rejected by the argument, that has been used to justify a course of action; the second presents that course of action.

(E) The first is a consideration that has been used to justify adopting a certain strategy; the second presents the intended outcome of that strategy.

Argument Construction

Situation   Often, when a company comes out with an innovative product, it will price the product as high as it can to maximize profits before the competitors quickly catch up. But this is not a good strategy because the very high price of the new product only encourages competitors to match the technological advance more quickly.

Reasoning   *Which answer choice best describes the roles that the boldface portions play in the argument?* This type of item concerns only the argument's structure—the way it is intended to work, not the quality of the argument or what might strengthen or weaken the argument. So even if a boldface portion could be used by the argument in a certain way, all that matters is its actual intended role. The fact that *technological advances tend to be quickly surpassed* serves to partly explain why *many companies charge the maximum possible price for such a product*. In other words, the first boldface portion helps explain the popularity of the strategy presented in the second boldface portion. The conclusion of the argument, however, is that the strategy exemplified in this latter boldface portion is unwise, so the argument as a whole opposes that strategy.

A   Although the first boldface portion could be used as part of an argument that the strategy presented in the second boldface portion is counterproductive, that is not how it is used here. Rather, it immediately follows the word *because* and serves to explain the occurrence of what is described in the second boldface portion.

B   This is clearly wrong because the second boldface portion presents the strategy that the argument opposes.

C   **Correct.** It is the only answer choice that is consistent with the analysis of the reasoning presented above.

D   The first boldface portion is not an assumption rejected by the argument; rather, it is affirmed in the argument.

E   The argument does not expressly claim that the first boldface portion has been used to justify the strategy of setting the price as high as possible, although it implies that this is part of the justification that those adopting the strategy would give. More clearly, the second boldface portion does not describe the intended outcome of the strategy, but rather the means of bringing about that intended outcome (maximizing profits, by means of high prices).

The correct answer is C.

CR05554

224. Gortland has long been narrowly self-sufficient in both grain and meat. However, as per capita income in Gortland has risen toward the world average, per capita consumption of meat has also risen toward the world average, and it takes several pounds of grain to produce one pound of meat. Therefore, since per capita income continues to rise, whereas domestic grain production will not increase, Gortland will soon have to import either grain or meat or both.

Which of the following is an assumption on which the argument depends?

(A) The total acreage devoted to grain production in Gortland will not decrease substantially.

(B) The population of Gortland has remained relatively constant during the country's years of growing prosperity.

(C) The per capita consumption of meat in Gortland is roughly the same across all income levels.

(D) In Gortland, neither meat nor grain is subject to government price controls.

(E) People in Gortland who increase their consumption of meat will not radically decrease their consumption of grain.

Argument Construction

Situation   A country previously self-sufficient in grain and meat will soon have to import one or the other or both because its consumption of meat has risen as per capita income has risen. It takes several pounds of grain to produce one pound of meat.

Reasoning   *What conditions must be true for the conclusion to be true?* Meat consumption is rising. What about grain consumption? A sharp reduction in the amount of grain directly consumed by meat eaters could compensate for increased meat consumption, making the conclusion false. If people did radically decrease their grain consumption, it might not be necessary to import grain or meat. Since the argument concludes that the imports are necessary, it assumes that direct consumption of grain by those who begin to eat meat will not plunge.

A   The argument makes no assumptions about the acreage devoted to grain; it assumes only that the demand for grain will rise.

B   The argument is based on rising per capita income, not population levels.

C   The argument involves only meat consumption in general, not its distribution by income level.

D   Since the argument does not refer to price controls, it cannot depend on an assumption about them.

E   **Correct.** This statement properly identifies the assumption that those who begin to eat meat do not then greatly decrease their direct consumption of grains.

The correct answer is E.

CR05625

225. Political Advertisement:

Mayor Delmont's critics complain about the jobs that were lost in the city under Delmont's leadership. Yet the fact is that not only were more jobs created than were eliminated, but each year since Delmont took office the average pay for the new jobs created has been higher than that year's average pay for jobs citywide. So it stands to reason that throughout Delmont's tenure the average paycheck in this city has been getting steadily bigger.

Which of the following, if true, most seriously weakens the argument in the advertisement?

(A) The unemployment rate in the city is higher today than it was when Mayor Delmont took office.

(B) The average pay for jobs in the city was at a ten-year low when Mayor Delmont took office.

(C) Each year during Mayor Delmont's tenure, the average pay for jobs that were eliminated has been higher than the average pay for jobs citywide.

(D) Most of the jobs eliminated during Mayor Delmont's tenure were in declining industries.

(E) The average pay for jobs in the city is currently lower than it is for jobs in the suburbs surrounding the city.

Argument Evaluation

Situation Every year since Mayor Delmont took office, average pay for new jobs has exceeded average pay for jobs citywide. So, the average paycheck in the city has been increasing since Delmont took office.

Reasoning *Which answer choice, if true, would most seriously weaken the argument?* If average pay for new jobs continually exceeds that for jobs generally, new jobs pay better (on average) than old jobs that still exist. But suppose the following occurred. Every year all of the highest paying jobs are eliminated and replaced with somewhat lower-paying jobs that still pay more than the average job. The result would be that every year the average pay for a new job would be greater than that for existing jobs, but the average pay for all jobs would nonetheless decrease. Thus, if every year during the mayor's tenure the jobs that were eliminated paid better on average than jobs citywide, that would seriously weaken the argument: the conclusion could be false even if the information on which it is based is true.

A The percentage of people in the city who have a job has no direct bearing on whether the average pay for jobs citywide is increasing or decreasing.

B Whether the average pay was low when the mayor took office in comparison to the ten preceding years is immaterial to the comparison addressed in the argument's conclusion.

C **Correct.** This information weakens the argument because it opens up the possibility that the jobs eliminated had higher average pay than the jobs created during Mayor Delmont's tenure. This in turn would mean that the average pay was not increasing during Mayor Delmont's tenure.

D This, too, has no bearing on the argument, because we have no information about the average pay for jobs in those declining industries.

E This is also irrelevant. No comparison is made (or implied) in the argument between jobs in the city and jobs in the suburbs.

The correct answer is C.

CR04930

226. To prevent a newly built dam on the Chiff River from blocking the route of fish migrating to breeding grounds upstream, the dam includes a fish pass, a mechanism designed to allow fish through the dam. Before the construction of the dam and fish pass, several thousand fish a day swam upriver during spawning season. But in the first season after the project's completion, only 300 per day made the journey. Clearly, the fish pass is defective.

Which of the following, if true, most seriously weakens the argument?

(A) Fish that have migrated to the upstream breeding grounds do not return down the Chiff River again.

(B) On other rivers in the region, the construction of dams with fish passes has led to only small decreases in the number of fish migrating upstream.

(C) The construction of the dam stirred up potentially toxic river sediments that were carried downstream.

(D) Populations of migratory fish in the Chiff River have been declining slightly over the last 20 years.

(E) During spawning season, the dam releases sufficient water for migratory fish below the dam to swim upstream.

Argument Evaluation

Situation   A new dam includes a mechanism called a fish pass designed to allow fish to migrate upstream past the dam to their breeding grounds. The number of migrating fish fell from several thousand per day before the dam was built to three hundred per day in the first season after it was built, indicating—according to the argument—that the fish pass is defective.

Reasoning   *What evidence would suggest that the fish pass is not defective?* The argument implicitly reasons that a defective fish pass would make it difficult for the fish to migrate, which would explain why the number of migrating fish fell when the dam was completed. Any evidence suggesting an alternative explanation for the reduced number of migrating fish, such as an environmental change that occurred when the dam was built, would cast doubt on the argument's reasoning.

A   A defective fish pass could prevent most of the fish from migrating upstream regardless of whether those that succeed ever return downstream.

B   This would suggest that dams with properly functioning fish passes do not greatly reduce the number of migrating fish, so it would provide further evidence that the fish pass in this particular dam is defective.

C   **Correct.** This suggests that the toxic sediments may have poisoned the fish and reduced their population. A smaller fish population could be sufficient to explain the reduced number of fish migrating, which casts doubt on the argument's assumption that the explanation for their declining numbers involves the fish pass.

D   A slight and gradual ongoing decline in migratory fish populations would not explain an abrupt and extreme decline right after the dam was built.

E   This supports the argument's proposed explanation for the declining fish population by ruling out the alternative explanation that the dam does not release enough water for the fish to migrate.

The correct answer is C.

CR09969

227. Music critic: Fewer and fewer musicians are studying classical music, decreasing the likelihood that those with real aptitude for such music will be performing it. Audiences who hear these performances will not appreciate classical music's greatness and will thus decamp to other genres. So to maintain classical music's current meager popularity, we must encourage more young musicians to enter the field.

Which of the following, if true, most weakens the music critic's reasoning?

(A) Musicians who choose to study classical music do so because they believe they have an aptitude for the music.

(B) Classical music's current meager popularity is attributable to the profusion of other genres of music available to listeners.

(C) Most people who appreciate classical music come to do so through old recordings rather than live performances.

(D) It is possible to enjoy the music in a particular genre even when it is performed by musicians who are not ideally suited for that genre.

(E) The continued popularity of a given genre of music depends in part on the audience's being able to understand why that genre attained its original popularity.

Argument Evaluation

Situation   Fewer musicians are studying classical music. This reduces the likelihood that those performing the music will have real aptitude for it, which in turn reduces audience's appreciation of classical music performances.

Reasoning   *What evidence would cast the most doubt on the support provided for the conclusion that encouraging more young musicians to study classical music is necessary in order to maintain the genre's meager popularity?* The music critic's argument is that because fewer talented classical musicians are performing, audiences hearing their performances will fail to appreciate the genre, and thus will abandon it. The critic reasons that to solve this problem, it will be necessary to encourage more young musicians to study classical music so that audiences will eventually be exposed to more talented classical performers and decide the genre is worthwhile after all. The argument would be weakened, for example, by evidence that hearing unremarkable live performances does not really drive many people away from classical music, or that the number of audience members hearing great performances does not depend much on the number of talented performers, or that encouraging young musicians to study classical music is either ineffective or not the only effective way to increase the number of talented classical performers.

A   This does not weaken the critic's reasoning. However much confidence musicians studying classical music have in their own talent, a decline in the total number of classical musicians will probably result in a decline in the number of truly talented classical musicians, just as the critic assumes.

B   The critic is only proposing a way to at least maintain classical music's current meager popularity, which might be accomplished even if the profusion of other genres prevents classical music's popularity from increasing.

C   **Correct.** This suggests that classical music's meager popularity could at least be maintained by encouraging people to listen to great old recordings of classical music rather than by increasing the supply of great live performances.

D   This does weaken the argument slightly. But even if a few audience members manage to enjoy mediocre classical music performances, they might still be more strongly drawn to other genres with more talented performers.

E   Listeners exposed to more impressive live performances of classical music by talented performers would probably better understand why classical music was once popular than would listeners exposed only to mediocre classical performances.

The correct answer is C.

CR67850.02

228. People with a college degree are more likely than others to search for a new job while they are employed. There are proportionately more people with college degrees among managers and other professionals than among service and clerical workers. Surprisingly, however, 2009 figures indicate that people employed as managers and other professionals were no more likely than people employed as service and clerical workers to have searched for a new job.

Which of the following, if true, most helps to resolve the apparent paradox?

(A) People generally do not take a new job that is offered to them while they are employed unless the new job pays better.

(B) Some service and clerical jobs pay more than some managerial and professional jobs.

(C) People who felt they were overqualified for their current positions were more likely than others to search for a new job.

(D) The percentage of employed people who were engaged in job searches declined from 2005 to 2009.

(E) In 2009 employees with no college degree who retired were more likely to be replaced by people with a college degree if they retired from a managerial or professional job than from a service or clerical job.

Argument Construction

Situation   College graduates are more likely than others to search for another job while they are employed. A greater percentage of managers and other professionals are college graduates than of service and clerical workers. In 2009, however, managers and other professionals were no more likely than service and clerical workers to have searched for another job while employed.

Reasoning   *What additional piece of information would most help resolve the apparent paradox described?* The apparent paradox concerns a 2009 phenomenon that initially seems at odds with a general pattern in job-search behavior. However, the phenomenon seems less puzzling when one considers the following. Depending on the current state of the employment market, some college graduates may choose to take a job as a service or clerical worker, seeing it as a way of paying their expenses while aiming to transition to a job more suited to their medium- and long-term career aspirations.

A   This information provides one answer to the question, why do people choose to accept or decline a particular job? However, this has no clear relevance to the apparent paradox we are asked to resolve; the paradox concerns the proportions of people in different kinds of jobs who search for a new job even while employed.

B   This information is too vague to contribute to resolving the apparent paradox. It is little more than a truism that, given certain labor supply and demand conditions, pay rates for different jobs vary.

C   **Correct.** College graduates in clerical jobs might feel that they had more advanced skills than their jobs demanded. College graduates in managerial or professional jobs would be less likely to have a similar feeling.

D   This information regarding a decline in job searches from 2005 to 2009 has no clear relevance to the apparent paradox we are asked to resolve. For example, we are not told that this decline occurred predominantly among managerial or professional workers.

E   This information suggests that the supply of college graduates was larger in 2009 than it had been some decades before. If the supply were large enough in 2009, it could be the case that some college graduates accepted service or clerical jobs that, decades previously, would not have been filled by college graduates. But we lack enough specific information for this answer choice to help resolve the apparent paradox.

The correct answer is C.

CR20190.02

229. To reduce traffic congestion, City X's transportation bureau plans to encourage people who work downtown to sign a form pledging to carpool or use public transportation for the next year. Everyone who signs the form will get a coupon for a free meal at any downtown restaurant.

For the transportation bureau's plan to succeed in reducing traffic congestion, which of the following must be true?

(A) Everyone who signs the pledge form will fully abide by the pledge for the next year.

(B) At least some people who work downtown prefer the restaurants downtown to those elsewhere.

(C) Most downtown traffic congestion in City X results from people who work downtown.

(D) The most effective way to reduce traffic congestion downtown would be to persuade more people who work there to carpool or use public transportation.

(E) At least some people who receive the coupon for a free meal will sometimes carpool or use public transportation during the next year.

Evaluation of a Plan

Situation In City X, the transportation bureau's plan to reduce traffic congestion involves giving every downtown worker who signs a form pledging to carpool or use public transportation next year a coupon for a free meal at any downtown restaurant.

Reasoning *What claim must be true for the transportation bureau's plan to reduce traffic congestion to succeed?* Obviously, if people sign the pledge just so they can get a coupon for a free meal, and if no one who signs the pledge actually carpools or uses public transportation, then the plan will not succeed. Therefore, for the plan to be successful, at least some of the people who receive the coupon must at least occasionally carpool or use public transportation during the next year.

A If this were true, it would certainly help the plan succeed. But the question asks what *must* be true for the plan to succeed, and it is not necessary that anyone fully abide by the plan. The plan could well succeed, for instance, if no one fully abided by the pledge but a large number of people only partially abided by the pledge.

B This is not necessary. Even if everyone prefers restaurants outside the downtown area, they may still want a free meal at a downtown restaurant.

C It could be that a majority of the downtown traffic congestion in City X results not from people who work downtown, but from people who shop downtown or live downtown but work elsewhere. The plan could still work as long as there was a sufficient reduction in the congestion caused by the downtown workers.

D The plan could work even if it is not the most effective way to reduce traffic congestion. If there is a more effective way to reduce traffic congestion, then it might be advisable to implement that plan instead of, or in addition to, this one. But second-best plans, for instance, can be successful.

E **Correct.** Certainly, this is not sufficient for the plan to succeed; compliance would probably need to be well above the minimal level. But, as explained above, this is necessary for the plan to succeed. Suppose someone objected to the idea that this must be true for the plan to succeed by saying that, even if no one who received the coupon carpooled or used public transportation, congestion could still be reduced if enough *other* people carpooled or used public transportation. That is true, but in that case, it would not be the *plan* that succeeded. The goal would be accomplished, but it would have been accomplished without the plan itself being successful at accomplishing it.

The correct answer is E.

CR05656

230. Commemorative plaques cast from brass are a characteristic art form of the Benin culture of West Africa. Some scholars, noting that the oldest surviving plaques date to the 1400s, hypothesize that brass-casting techniques were introduced by the Portuguese, who came to Benin in 1485 A.D. But Portuguese records of that expedition mention cast-brass jewelry sent to Benin's king from neighboring Ife. So it is unlikely that Benin's knowledge of brass casting derived from the Portuguese.

Which of the following, if true, most strengthens the argument?

(A) The Portuguese records do not indicate whether their expedition of 1485 included metalworkers.

(B) The Portuguese had no contact with Ife until the 1500s.

(C) In the 1400s the Portuguese did not use cast brass for commemorative plaques.

(D) As early as 1500 A.D., Benin artists were making brass plaques incorporating depictions of Europeans.

(E) Copper, which is required for making brass, can be found throughout Benin territory.

Argument Construction

Situation | The oldest surviving cast-brass plaques from the Benin culture date to the 1400s. Records of a Portuguese expedition to Benin in 1485 mention cast-brass jewelry sent to Benin's king from neighboring Ife.

Reasoning | *What additional evidence, when combined with the argument's premises, would most help support the conclusion that Benin's knowledge of brass casting did not derive from the Portuguese?* The argument is that since the expedition records indicate that cast-brass jewelry from Ife was already known in Benin when the Portuguese first came there, Benin's knowledge of brass casting probably did not derive from the Portuguese. This argument assumes that receiving the brass-cast jewelry from Ife could have transmitted knowledge of brass casting to Benin, and also that knowledge of brass casting in Ife did not itself derive from the Portuguese. Any evidence supporting either of these assumptions would strengthen the argument.

A | This is compatible with a Portuguese origin for brass-casting in Benin. The expedition might well have included metalworkers even if the records do not mention whether it did. Furthermore, other Portuguese expeditions with metalworkers might have quickly followed the initial expedition.

B | **Correct.** If the Portuguese had no contact with Ife before 1500, then Ife's earlier knowledge of brass casting did not derive directly from the Portuguese. This increases the likelihood that knowledge of brass-casting in Benin did not derive from the Portuguese, even if it derived from Ife.

C | This is compatible with a Portuguese origin for brass-casting in Benin. Even if the Portuguese did not use cast brass for commemorative plaques, they could have used it for jewelry or other items they brought to Benin or manufactured there, and thus they could have transmitted the knowledge to the Benin culture.

D | This leaves open the possibility that the Benin culture learned about brass casting from the Portuguese in 1485 and started using it to produce plaques of this type by 1500.

E | Even if copper has always been common in the Benin territory, brass-casting techniques could have been introduced by the Portuguese.

The correct answer is B.

CR56601.02

231. When new laws imposing strict penalties for misleading corporate disclosures were passed, they were hailed as initiating an era of corporate openness. As an additional benefit, given the increased amount and accuracy of information disclosed under the new laws, it was assumed that analysts' predictions of corporate performance would become more accurate. Since the passage of the laws, however, the number of inaccurate analysts' predictions has not in fact decreased.

Which of the following would, if true, best explain the discrepancy outlined above?

(A) The new laws' definition of "misleading information" can be interpreted in more than one way.

(B) The new laws require corporations in all industries to release information at specific times of the year.

(C) Even before the new laws were passed, the information most corporations released was true.

(D) Analysts base their predictions on information they gather from many sources, not just corporate disclosures.

(E) The more pieces of information corporations release, the more difficult it becomes for anyone to organize them in a manageable way.

Evaluation of a Plan

Situation It was assumed that new laws, implemented to increase the amount and accuracy of information released by corporations, would increase the accuracy of analysts' predictions about corporate performance. This outcome has not occurred, however.

Reasoning *What claim would best explain the new laws' failure to reduce the number of inaccurate analysts' predictions?* The new laws were intended to increase both the accuracy and the amount of information. If the amount of information increased to such a level that analysts became overwhelmed by it, this could help explain the laws' failure to reduce the number of inaccurate predictions.

A Even if the new laws' definition of "misleading information" can be interpreted in multiple ways, it could be that the accuracy of corporate information has increased. This fact alone does little if anything to explain the discrepancy.

B The fact that all industries are required to release information at specific times of the year is not helpful in explaining why the number of inaccurate analysts' predictions has not declined. Presumably analysts would wait for the information to be released to make predictions.

C This might help somewhat in explaining the failure to bring about the desired outcome. It would do so by ruling out one scenario that would make the outcome more likely to occur: If past predictions had been inaccurate because they were based on false information, it would seem likely that the law would reduce the number of inaccurate predictions. But even if most of the information corporations released in the past was true, one would still expect some improvement in the accuracy of predictions if the information became universally accurate, and there was more of it available.

D The fact that analysts base their predictions about corporate performance on information gathered from many sources in addition to corporate disclosures does not explain why, if corporate disclosures improved, there would not be at least some improvement in the accuracy of predictions about corporate performance.

E **Correct.** If the amount of information corporations release becomes so great that organizing it in a manageable way becomes difficult or impossible, then it could become more difficult to interpret and understand. This could interfere with analysts' ability to make accurate predictions about performance, even if the information provided is 100 percent accurate.

The correct answer is E.

CR50611.02
232. Economist: Even with energy conservation efforts, current technologies cannot support both a reduction in carbon dioxide emissions and an expanding global economy. Attempts to restrain emissions without new technology will stifle economic growth. Therefore, increases in governmental spending on research into energy technology will be necessary if we wish to reduce carbon dioxide emissions without stifling economic growth.

Which of the following is an assumption the economist's argument requires?

(A) If research into energy technology does not lead to a reduction in carbon dioxide emissions, then economic growth will be stifled.

(B) Increased governmental spending on research into energy technology will be more likely to reduce carbon dioxide emissions without stifling growth than will nongovernmental spending.

(C) An expanding global economy may require at least some governmental spending on research into energy technology.

(D) Attempts to restrain carbon dioxide emissions without new technology could ultimately cost more than the failure to reduce those emissions would cost.

(E) Restraining carbon dioxide emissions without stifling economic growth would require both new energy technology and energy conservation efforts.

Evaluation of a Plan

Situation An economist argues that without new technology, attempts to restrain carbon dioxide emissions will stifle economic growth. The economist concludes from this that if such emissions are to be reduced without stifling economic growth, there must be increases in governmental spending on research into energy technology.

Reasoning *What assumption is required by the economist's argument?* An obvious question to the economist's argument is why an increase in *governmental* spending is required. Could nongovernmental spending alone not be at least as effective? If it could be, then the economist's conclusion would not follow. Therefore, for the economist's argument to be a good one, it would need to be true that nongovernmental spending alone would not be as effective for the intended purpose as increased governmental spending would be.

A   Nothing in the argument requires the assumption that only a reduction in carbon dioxide emissions can stifle economic growth. The argument is perfectly compatible, for instance, with the assumption that economic growth would be stifled if there were significant climate change—perhaps leading to severe crop shortages—as a result of increased carbon dioxide emissions.

B   **Correct.** As explained above, a natural response to the economist's argument is to ask, "Why can we not just use nongovernmental spending to come up with new technologies that will allow us to restrain carbon dioxide emissions without stifling economic growth?" Without an answer to that question, the economist's argument cannot be a good one. If answer choice B were true, it would bridge the logical gap by providing a reason that increased governmental spending—and not just nongovernmental spending—would be needed.

C   This does not have to be assumed. True, the argument assumes that *if* we try to reduce carbon dioxide emissions without increased governmental spending on research into energy technology, then the economy will be stifled. But the argument is compatible with the occurrence of economic growth despite a lack of governmental spending on research into energy technology, as long as carbon dioxide emissions are not reduced.

D   The argument does not require this assumption. As explained in answer choice A, the argument is compatible with the idea that the economy could be stifled by climate change that results from a failure to reduce carbon emissions. This could result in great economic cost.

E   The argument does not indicate that new energy technology alone cannot be sufficient for restraining carbon dioxide emissions without stifling economic growth.

The correct answer is B.

CR98001.02

233. Researchers have developed a technology that uses sound as a means of converting heat into electrical energy. Converters based on this technology can be manufactured small enough to be integrated into consumer electronics, where they will absorb significant quantities of heat. A group of engineers is now designing converters to be sold to laptop computer manufacturers, who are expected to use the electrical output of the converters to conserve battery power in their computers.

Which of the following would, if true, provide the strongest evidence that the engineers' plan will be commercially successful for their group?

(A) The sound that is used by the converters is generated by the converters themselves.

(B) Most laptop computer manufacturers today receive fewer complaints than in previous years regarding shortness of operating time on a single battery charge.

(C) The overheating of microprocessors in laptop computers presents a major technological challenge that manufacturers are prepared to meet at significant expense.

(D) Although battery technology has improved significantly, the average capacity of laptop computer batteries has not.

(E) Electrical power generated by the converters can be used to power the fans installed to cool computers' components.

Evaluation of a Plan

Situation   A group of engineers is designing converters that absorb heat and then use sound to convert it into electrical energy. The engineers hope to sell the converters to laptop manufacturers for the purpose of using the electrical output of the converters to conserve battery power.

Reasoning   *Which claim provides the strongest evidence that the engineers' plan will be commercially successful?* A claim that reveals that there would be demand among laptop manufacturers for the converters would provide such evidence. If these manufacturers currently face a major challenge that they would be willing to meet at significant expense, they would provide a demand for this product if it could be shown to work well.

A   Whether the sound is generated by the converters or by something else would be irrelevant to whether the plan would be commercially successful, unless the sound production required a significant amount of electrical energy. If it did require a significant amount of electrical energy, this would tend to weaken the hypothesis that the plan would succeed.

B   This suggests that laptop manufacturers may not feel a great need to use these converters to conserve battery power.

C   **Correct.** If laptop manufacturers are prepared to meet the challenge of the overheating of microprocessors at significant expense, in a way that provides an additional benefit such as conserving battery power, they could very well be a receptive market for these converters.

D   This would not provide strong evidence that the plan will be commercially successful unless we had further evidence that laptop manufacturers see it as a challenge that they would be willing to meet at significant expense.

E   Presumably, the electricity generated by the converter should be able to contribute toward satisfying any of the energy needs of the computer. The passage provides no reason to think that the cooling fans are special in this regard. The converters generate electrical energy by absorbing heat so, in principle, there might even be circumstances in which the use described in this answer choice could undermine the converters' functionality.

The correct answer is C.

6.0   Sentence Correction

6.0 Sentence Correction

Each GMAT™ Sentence Correction question presents a statement in which words are underlined. The question asks you to select the best expression of the idea or relationship described in the underlined section from the answer options. The first answer choice always repeats the original phrasing, whereas the other four provide alternatives. In some cases, the original phrasing is the best choice. In other cases, the underlined section has obvious or subtle errors that require correction. These questions require you to be familiar with the stylistic conventions and grammatical rules of standard written English and to demonstrate your ability to improve incorrect or ineffective expressions. Sentence Correction questions may include English-language idioms, which are standard constructions not derived from the most basic rules of grammar and vocabulary, but questions about idioms are not intended to measure any specialized knowledge of colloquialisms or regionalisms.

You should begin each question by reading the sentence carefully. Note whether there are any obvious grammatical errors as you read the underlined portion. Then read the five answer choices carefully. If there is a subtle error you did not recognize the first time you read the sentence, it may become apparent after you have read the answer choices. If the error is still unclear, see whether you can eliminate some of the answers as being incorrect. Remember that in some cases, the original selection may be the best answer.

6.1 Some Comments About How It Works

Sentence Correction questions require a good understanding of how the conventions of standard written English can be used for effective communication. However, that understanding does not have to come from extensive explicit training in grammar and usage or from knowledge of specialized linguistic terminology. Many people may have the needed insights without being able to explain them in technical terms. Analogously, without knowing the scientific name of baker's yeast or the chemistry of the Maillard reaction, a talented baker or food critic may be able to tell whether a loaf of bread was properly prepared. This is not to say that explicit training in grammar and usage is unhelpful. As an adjunct to experience in critical reading and writing, it can be a useful way to develop insights into good written communication. It is good to be cautious, though; books and websites offering advice about how to write may occasionally stipulate outmoded or idiosyncratic rules not generally followed in effective professional writing.

The problems posed in Sentence Correction take a different approach from those in the other Verbal Reasoning sections, and fall within a different domain. But like the questions in those sections, they test skills of critical reasoning, problem solving, and reading comprehension. Sentence Correction tasks can be aptly thought of as requiring detective work. A key part of this work consists in understanding the differences among formulations the answer choices offer and in seeing that some do not make sense when they are plugged into the larger sentence. In this way, the Sentence Correction questions pose some of the most refined and closely targeted reading comprehension tasks in the GMAT exam. To see why certain wordings do not work, you will need to use critical analysis, forming hypotheses about what the writer is trying to express and being ready to revise the hypotheses as you read through the answer choices.

The more difficult questions are not essentially designed to test for knowledge of rules or facts that are harder to learn or that require more technical training. Difficulty often stems from complexity and subtlety among the interconnected parts of the sentence and involves critical application of principles that all astute users of English should understand. Sentence Correction tasks are puzzles of a sort, but they are not arbitrarily contrived. Typically, the incorrect answer choices represent flaws that even an experienced writer might introduce by temporarily losing track of a sentence's structure or by accidentally moving a piece of text to an unsuitable position.

Sometimes you may be able to think of a wording that works better than any of the options presented, but the task is to find the most effective of the wording choices offered. In writing, there are almost always tradeoffs. For example, conciseness is sometimes the enemy of adequate precision and specificity. Certain types of redundancy can be annoying and can make the writer seem inept, but other types of repetition and paraphrasing can improve readability and comprehension. Language serves many purposes, not all of which are cooperative or directly informative. In sincere, straightforwardly informative writing—although not in all advertising, entertainment, and poetry—one should minimize ambiguity, yet in the end every sentence is at least somewhat open to multiple interpretations. Because one can never absolutely eliminate the risk of unintended interpretations, Sentence Correction answers should minimize that risk relative to the context, setting, and ordinary assumptions about the intent of the writer. It is safe to assume that any GMAT Sentence Correction sentence you encounter will be intended to sincerely inform, instruct, or inquire, rather than to parody bad writing, confuse the reader, or provoke laughter, outrage, or derision.

You will not be expected to take sides in contentious controversies about grammar, usage, or style or to apply rules widely regarded as highly pedantic or outdated. A few of these are mentioned in the discussions of the specific categories that follow.

6.2 The Eight Sentence Correction Categories

Sentence Correction questions are classified into eight grammar and usage categories. Each incorrect answer choice contains a flaw in at least one of these categories, and some span two or more categories. Each test contains questions representing a wide range of different types of problems. In the answer explanations in section 6.9, the categories shown in each question's heading are the most salient, but many questions contain problems in other categories as well. Although these eight categories represent the full range of Sentence Correction questions, the discussions about each category below are not exhaustive and are not intended as a comprehensive guide to English grammar and usage. For each category, the discussion aims to provide a general understanding of the kinds of reasoning that may be involved in solving Sentence Correction problems of that type. For more information about English grammar and style, please refer to section 3.5 of Chapter 3.

1. Agreement

Effective verbal communication requires clarity about how a sentence's elements relate to one another. The conventions of agreement help maintain such clarity; constructions that violate these conventions can be confusing or even nonsensical. There are two types of agreement: subject-verb agreement and agreement of terms that have the same referent.

A. *Subject-verb agreement:* Singular subjects take singular verbs, whereas plural subjects take plural verbs.

B. *Agreement between terms that have the same referent:* A pronoun that stands for another element in the discourse—a noun, a noun phrase, or another pronoun—must agree with its antecedent in person, number, and gender.

For details about and examples of these two types of agreement, see section 3.5.2 of Chapter 3.

Almost all educated users of English have internalized the conventions of agreement, yet we all occasionally make grammatical mistakes involving agreement because we lose track of the structure of our wording. Keep in mind that as you evaluate different wording choices, context is vitally important.

Examples:

i) We can see immediately that an entire clause consisting of the words *you is working* would be incorrect. On the other hand, that same sequence of words is correct in the following sentence:

> The team member who used to assist **you is working** on a different project now.

Seeing this depends on recognizing that the subject of *is* is not *you* but rather the entire noun phrase preceding the verb. This recognition may be either intuitive or based on explicit analysis.

ii) Similarly, no one would seriously claim that the plural *they* should stand for the singular noun *proposal*, but one might more easily overlook the failure of agreement in the following sentence:

> From among the six submitted proposals, they chose number four, believing that **they** could be more easily implemented than the other five.

Many readers may see the problem quickly, but in doing so they are noting some complex features of the sentence structure. Grammatically, *they* could refer to the six proposals or to those who chose from among them, but neither of those tentative interpretations makes sense. The choosers are not the sorts of things that could be implemented, and the comparative phrase *than the other five* rules out the hypothesis that the antecedent of *they* is the plural *six submitted proposals*. Changing *they* to *it* resolves the discrepancy by providing a pronoun that clearly has the singular noun phrase *number four* as its antecedent. Here the reasoning overlaps with that involved in the category of logical predication discussed in section 3.2.5 below.

Some complicating factors to consider:

When analyzing potential agreement issues in Sentence Correction, keep in mind that not all cases conform obviously and straightforwardly to the basic rules of agreement reviewed in section 3.5 of Chapter 3. Here are a few special considerations not reviewed in that section.

A. *Plurals that appear singular:* Fluent English speakers are aware that for some words the plural is the same as the singular (*sheep* and *deer*, for example). But there are subtle cases, as when a formally singular noun referring to a group or culture is construed as plural. No simple rule governs the use of such terms; one can say, for example, *the British are or the Inuit are but not the German are or the Cuban are. Police* is plural, but many similar group words, such as *navy*, are typically construed as singular.

B. *Plurals construed as singular:* Some formally plural nouns, such as news, are construed as singular in normal usage. A title with a plural form (such as *The Grapes of Wrath*) takes a singular verb if it refers to a single work, and some names of organizations or political entities may be construed as singular even though they have a plural form. For example, the phrase *the Cayman Islands* may be singular when referring to the country as a political entity but plural when referring to the islands as multiple pieces of land.

C. *Singular verbs that could appear plural:* For most English verbs (with the notable exception of *to be*), the infinitive is the same as the present plural, and the present subjunctive for all persons is the same as the infinitive. Furthermore, the singular past subjunctive is the same as the plural. Thus, there is a risk that at first glance a correct verb form used with a singular subject may appear plural.

Examples:

i) "The researcher suspend further testing" and "I were you" would be incorrect as complete sentences, but in the following sentences they are in the subjunctive mood and are correct:

> We considered it imperative that **the researcher suspend further testing.**
> I wouldn't do that if **I were you.**

ii) As a complete sentence, "The mayor attend the hearings" would be incorrect, but in the following sentence it is correct because the verb form ***attend*** is an infinitive preceded by the auxiliary verb ***will:***

> In none of these cases will either the councilor or **the mayor attend the hearings.**

Some issues that are not tested:

The following are a few examples of issues outside the scope of the agreement-related Sentence Correction questions:

A. Especially in informal discourse, the plural pronoun ***they*** and related forms ***them, their,*** and ***theirs*** are sometimes used as nonspecific, genderless ways of referring to a singular person. Consider, for example, "Somebody left **their** notebook on the conference room table."

The reasoning surrounding such usage and the alternatives (***he, she, she or he, she/he***) is complex and evolving. You should not expect to see questions that require you to judge which usage is preferable.

B. Although you should be able to recognize commonly used irregular plurals or special classes of plurals (such as ***phenomena, cacti, genera***), you will not be asked to correct an improper plural spelling. For example, you will not be asked to correct ***the genuses are*** to the ***genera are.***

C. You will also not be expected to know whether certain highly technical terms or local organization names take singular or plural verbs and pronouns unless the context makes it clear whether they are singular or plural. For example, those who are very familiar with the Centers for Disease Control (a U.S. government organization) will know that it is normally referred to in the singular, but others would not be able to determine this merely from seeing the name.

2. Diction

Sentences that are structurally well formed can still be confusing, or can make the writer seem inept, if the words are not chosen appropriately and effectively. Effective diction involves using the right part of speech and observing other conventions regarding which words to use in which contexts. Word choices involving agreement and verb form may also be thought of partly as matters of diction, but they are treated separately under the Agreement and Verb Form headings. The diction issues you may encounter in Sentence Correction questions are too many and varied to list here. Many such issues are discussed and examples provided in Chapter 3. Here are a few salient categories often encountered in diction-related Sentence Correction questions:

A. *Parts of speech:* Even accomplished writers sometimes accidentally use an inappropriate part of speech, such as an adjective where an adverb is needed or a preposition where a conjunction is needed.

> *Example:*
> **Correct:** I could **easily** tell that the cat was friendly.
> **Incorrect:** I could **easy** tell that the cat was friendly.

B. *Pronoun cases:* Pronouns should be in the right case. A writer might compromise clarity by using a subject form of a pronoun as an object or vice versa or a reflexive pronoun in a nonreflexive context.

C. *Counting and quantifying:* Although the conventions for quantification of mass nouns and count nouns have some subtle complexities, keep in mind the general rule that mass nouns are quantified by an amount, whereas count nouns are quantified by numbers or by words (such as *many*) that indicate multiple units.

> *Example:*
> **Correct:** **Fewer** deliveries arrived today than yesterday.
> **Incorrect:** **Less** deliveries arrived today than yesterday.

D. *Prepositions:* Subtle differences of relationship are often expressed by different prepositions that function similarly to one another. Consider, for example, *in/into/within, to/toward, on/onto/above, through/throughout, beside/besides, beside/along/against,* and *on/over/above.*

> *Examples:*
> i) **Correct:** We were standing **beside** the river.
> **Incorrect:** We were standing **besides** the river.
>
> The incorrect version above can also be thought of as displaying a problem of logical predication in that it appears to say illogically that the river was also standing.
>
> ii) **Correct:** The editor was sitting **in** his office all afternoon.
> **Incorrect:** The editor was sitting **into** his office all afternoon.
>
> The preposition *into* indicates motion from outside a location to within that location. Since it is unlikely that sitting would be a motion from outside an office to within an office over the course of an entire afternoon, *into* is the wrong preposition to use in this context.

Word choices that are inherently very simple and obvious can become a little more difficult in complex settings, and a Sentence Correction answer choice that appears appropriate on its own may not work when plugged into the larger sentence.

Examples:

i) In isolation, ***distributed throughout*** is recognizable as a standard phrase, but in the following sentence it does not make sense:

> The computers were **distributed throughout** the generosity of a group of donors.

Replacing ***throughout*** with ***through*** solves the problem. The issue here is a matter not only of diction but also of logical predication: the wording causes the sentence to make an illogical claim about the computers.

ii) Similarly, the phrase ***we were confident*** is fine as a freestanding clause, but it is nonsense in the following context:

> The lawyer who consulted with **we were confident** that we could negotiate a settlement.

This displays combined problems of diction (***with we***), agreement (the plural ***were*** with the singular subject ***lawyer***), and grammatical construction.

iii) The phrase ***us was confident*** sounds strange out of context, but substituting ***us was*** for the offending part of the sentence solves the problem:

> The lawyer who consulted with **us was confident** that we could negotiate a settlement.

Some complicating factors to consider:

The following are only a few examples of the types of subtleties and complexities that may be involved in deciding what words are appropriate:

A. ***Potentially misleading grammatical constructions:*** In some contexts, a verb might superficially appear to require an adverb when in fact an adjective is appropriate. For example, it is correct to say "The surface feels rough" rather than "The surface feels roughly." And "The animal does not smell well" means something very different from "The animal does not smell good." Both can be correct depending on what the writer wants to convey.

B. Words ending in *-ing* that are derived from verbs (such as ***going, assessing,*** and ***hurting***) can be either gerunds or participles. Generally, in carefully crafted formal writing, a pronoun or noun that modifies a gerund will be possessive. However, in some similar constructions the *-ing* word is intended as a participle with the noun or pronoun as its subject.

Examples:

i) **Correct:** The schedule depends on **our** receiving the materials on time.
Incorrect in formal writing: The schedule depends on **us** receiving the materials on time.
ii) **Correctly expresses one meaning:** I was concerned about **my friend's lying on the ground.**
iii) **Correctly expresses a different meaning:** I was concerned about **my friend lying on the ground.**

In ii) the object noun phrase is headed by the gerund ***lying***, indicating that the concern is about the situation the friend was in. But in iii), ***lying*** is a participle modifying the noun ***friend***, indicating that the concern is explicitly about the friend rather than the situation.

C. *Words with multiple functions:* In English, almost any noun can function as an adjective. Nouns that also function as verbs are well known (as in **chaired the meeting** or **tabled the motion**), but words that are not normally used as verbs can also be pressed into special service as verbs on an ad hoc basis. One could say, for example, "She plans to **greenhouse** her tender plants when the weather turns cold." Some words regularly function as both adjectives and adverbs. One can say, for example, both "This is a **hard** job" and "We are working <u>hard</u>." Likewise, *fast* is used correctly as both adjective and adverb in the following sentence: "This is not usually a <u>fast</u> train, but it is moving **fast** at this moment."

D. *Considerations in applying between and among: Among* is generally not appropriate for relationships that involve only two entities. It is standard to say *the distance between my house and yours*, not *the distance among my house and yours.* For relationships involving more than two entities, *among* is usually needed instead of between, but there are exceptions. *Between* is sometimes the more accurate preposition to use where the relationship holds, independently, between each member of the group and another individual member. Thus, for example, it would be appropriate to say, "In planning your trip <u>among</u> the five destinations, consider the distances **between** cities."

Some issues that are not tested:

The following are a few examples of issues outside the scope of the diction-related Sentence Correction questions:

A. *Which/that:* Some American publishers have adopted the convention that *which*, used as a relative pronoun, should always be nonrestrictive and should be replaced with *that* in restrictive contexts (as in "Laws **which** have been repealed are no longer enforced" versus "Laws **that** have been repealed are no longer enforced"). You should not expect to see questions for which the deciding factor is merely whether the writer adheres to this convention.

B. *Object words with* to be: Some usage advisors prescribe the use of nominative (subject) pronouns in both the subject position and the object position with the verb *to be.* According to this convention, "If I were **her**, I would be happy to accept the job" is incorrect; it should be "If I were **she**, I would be happy to accept the job." In some contexts, this latter form of expression could seem annoyingly stilted and pedantic, and thus could violate other standards of effective expression. You should not expect to see questions for which the deciding factor is merely whether the writer adheres to this convention.

C. *Slang, archaic diction, and words that are distinctively regional or limited to certain subsets of English:* You will not be expected, for example, to correct *thou* or *you-all* to *you*, to understand that *skint* could be paraphrased as *lacking resources*, to judge whether *mickle* is a synonym of *muckle* or whether either of these should be paraphrased with *large*, or to understand that *give* (a test) in some usages is synonymous with *take* (a test) in others.

D. *Variant forms and spellings:* You will not be asked to choose between variant forms that have the same function and meaning. Some examples of such variant pairs are: *whilst/while, toward/towards, until/till*, and *outward/outwards.*

3. Grammatical Construction

Many issues of agreement, verb form, parallelism, diction, and idiom can be described as matters of grammar, but those categories by no means cover the full range of grammar-related tasks in Sentence Correction. The Grammatical Construction category concerns issues of grammar not treated elsewhere in this classification scheme. For the most part, these are matters of syntax—the ways a sentence's elements are arranged. Effective communication depends on shared understandings between the writer and reader about how the relative positions of words and phrases help convey meaning. A series of words and punctuation marks that does not follow predictable conventions of syntax can be puzzling, annoying, or even incomprehensible. In section 3.5 of Chapter 3, grammatical issues are reviewed extensively and many examples provided. Here are a few major issues often encountered in Sentence Correction questions related to grammatical construction:

A. *Complete structure:* In English, a well-formed sentence or independent clause generally needs both a subject and a predicate that contains a main verb.

B. *Clear and correct linkages and punctuation:* A sentence's elements need to be linked to and separated from one another with standard punctuation and, when appropriate, with links such as conjunctions and relative pronouns.

C. *Proper ordering of words and phrases:* A sentence whose components are ordered in ways incompatible with the conventions of standard English can be confusing and can make the writer appear unfamiliar with the language.

To see how a Sentence Correction answer choice affects a sentence's grammatical construction, you may need to analyze the relationship between widely separated parts.

Examples:

i) **Incorrect: If you clean** the filter before it becomes so clogged that it impedes the flow can prevent costly repairs in the long run.
Correct: Cleaning the filter before it becomes so clogged that it impedes the flow can prevent costly repairs in the long run.

It is important to see that the main verb phrase in these sentences is ***can prevent***; the intervening verbs are embedded in the clause modifying ***clean the filter***. In the incorrect version, the opening phrase ***if you clean*** is not grammatically structured to function as a subject. But in the correct version that phrase is replaced with ***cleaning***, which allows the noun phrase ***cleaning the filter*** to serve correctly as the sentence's subject. This sentence correction task involves both grammatical construction and verb form (discussed later under that heading).

ii) **Incorrect:** The headphones that were provided with the audio player **that although she bought them last year, they never worked.**
Correct: The headphones that were provided with the audio player **she bought last year never worked.**

The phrase ***she bought last year never worked*** would be ungrammatical in isolation, but if substituted for the underlined phrase in the incorrect version, it makes the sentence grammatically correct. The crucial relationship here is between the opening words (***the headphones***) and the final phrase of the sentence.

Some complicating factors to consider:

In informal contexts and in many formal contexts where economy of words and smoothness of flow are key considerations, certain sentence elements may be omitted when the writer's intent is entirely clear without them. For example, *that* is often omitted at the start of a relative clause, as in "The film I saw last night was boring" or "I was afraid they might be angry." It is also often acceptable to omit infinitive verbs to avoid awkward repetition, leaving the preposition *to* dangling, as in "I reviewed the report even though I didn't want to."

Some issues that are not tested:

The following two issues are outside the scope of Sentence Correction questions related to grammatical construction.

A. *Fragments that function as complete sentences in special contexts:* A group of words with no subject or verb can sometimes stand as a well-formed sentence. For example, "No" can be a complete sentence in answer to a stated or hypothetical question, as can "The one on the left." Similarly, a clause beginning with a conjunction and not followed by any other clause can sometimes be an acceptable sentence, as, for example, "Because the delivery was late." Exclamations such as "Not again!" are also complete and well formed in special contexts. You should not expect to see a Sentence Correction question that appears likely to be drawn from a context in which it is intended to function in any of these ways or as a headline, title, or line of poetry.

B. *Punctuation as editorial style:* You will need to judge issues of punctuation only insofar as they involve standard conventions that make a difference for the sentence's meaning and coherence. Beyond the basic grammatical principles, some punctuation conventions vary by region or academic discipline, are matters of pure style, or are determined by publishers or editors for their own purposes. You will not need to judge, for example, whether a comma should be inside or outside a closing quotation mark, whether emphasis should be indicated by italics, or whether an apostrophe should be inserted before the s in a plural non-word such as *IOUs/IOU's* or *1980s/1980's*.

4. Idiom

Idioms are standard forms of expression that consist of ordinary words but whose uses cannot be inferred from the meanings of their component parts or the basic conventions of grammar and usage. There is ultimately no logical reason why English speakers say *on average* rather than *at average* or *depending on* rather than *depending from*. This is simply how we do things. Thus, knowing idiomatic constructions is rather like knowing vocabulary words. Accidentally using the wrong combination of words in an idiomatic construction or structuring a phrase in an unidiomatic way can make it difficult for readers to discern the writer's intended meaning. Here are a few major categories of idiomatic wording issues that you may encounter in Sentence Correction questions:

A. *Prepositions with abstract concepts:* For abstract concepts, there is no top, bottom, inside, or outside, yet with terms denoting such concepts we often use the same prepositions that denote spatial relationships between concrete objects. There are some patterns, but for the most part knowing which preposition to use with which abstract noun or verb depends on familiarity. The idiomatic pairings of prepositions with abstract concepts are far too many and varied to list here. A few illustrations are: *in* love, different *from*, *in* a while, *on* guard, *at* work.

Examples:

i) **Correct: With** regard **to** your party invitation, I may not be able to go, because I will be **on** call at the clinic that evening.

Incorrect: On regard **with** your party invitation, I may not be able to go, because I will be **in** call at the clinic that evening.

ii) **Correct:** The cost of the repairs will depend **on** what clever solutions the contractors come **up with**.

Incorrect: The cost of the repairs will depend **from** what clever solutions the contractors come **out through**.

B. *Correlatives:* Certain standard correlative structures provide economical ways of expressing relationships between concepts. For example, it can be more efficient to say "Neither she nor he is going" than to say "He is not going, and she is also not going." However, if such structures are not skillfully handled in accordance with standard conventions, they can be puzzling and misleading.

Examples:

i) **Correct:** Neither the pomegranates **nor** the melons have arrived yet from the vendor.

Incorrect: Neither the pomegranates have arrived yet **neither** the melons from the vendor.

ii) **Correct:** She was almost **as** sure that if we installed this system it would fail **as** that we would need some such system.

Incorrect: She was almost **as** sure that if we installed this system it would fail **than** that we would need some such system.

C. *Verb phrases:* Many combinations of verbs with adverbs and/or prepositions have conventional meanings that do not follow directly from the meanings of their component parts. These include such phrases as *give up, give up on, come through with, come up, come up with, come down with, do without, have at, get over, get on with, go through, go through with,* and *get through with.* Similarly, there are many idiomatic combinations of verbs and objects, such as *have had it, make waves, make one's mark,* and *put one's finger on.*

Example:

Correct: When they checked the patient's temperature, it **turned out** that he was **running a fever**.

Incorrect: When they checked the patient's temperature, it **veered off** that he was **doing a fever**.

D. *Pronouns with no reference:* As discussed in section 3.5, English requires stated subjects in most sentences with active verb forms. Where there is no real subject, one uses specific referentless placeholder pronouns: *it* and *there*.

E. *Compound modifiers:* Some adverbs and adjectives are idiomatically built out of multiple words. A few examples are: *all in all, by and by, by and large, on the whole, through and through, on the up and up,* and *on the other hand* (which is sometimes, but not always, correlated with *on the one hand*).

Examples:
i) **Correct:** She listened to the radio **off and on** throughout the day.
Incorrect: She listened to the radio **off but again on** throughout the day.

ii) **Correct:** You wondered whether anyone would mention you at the meeting; in fact, two people **did so**.
Incorrect: You wondered whether anyone would mention you at the meeting; in fact, two people **did thus and so**.

Idiom-related questions do not always involve identifying malformed idioms. Sometimes the crucial insight may involve determining which of multiple idiomatic meanings is intended, or whether a phrase should be treated as an idiom or not.

Example:
Incorrect: She asked for information **on purpose** of the order I had submitted.
The meaning of the sentence above is unclear. However, a plausible hypothesis is that the writer meant to say *information on the purpose*, with *on* serving as an informal equivalent of *regarding*. On that reading, the apparent use of the idiom *on purpose* results from an accidental juxtaposition of the two words. Substituting a phrase such as *regarding the* for *on* can turn this into a meaningful, well-formed sentence:
Correct: She asked for information **regarding the purpose** of the order I had submitted.

Some complicating factors to consider:

Here are just a few of the many subtleties that one may encounter in judging whether idiomatic usages are correct and effective:

A. Similar phrases often have very different idiomatic uses and meanings; consider, for example, *come through with, come down with,* and *come up with.*

B. Some idiomatic preposition-plus-noun phrases have alternate forms. For example, it is correct to say either *with regard to* or *in regard to.*

C. Many idiomatic phrases have multiple meanings, which are not always similar. For example, *come out with* in some contexts means *express* and in others means *publish* or *begin marketing.*

D. For many idiomatic expressions, there are special exceptions to the standard forms.

Example:
Phrases of the form *not only . . . but* are standardly completed with *also,* but there are special cases in which *also* is unnecessary or misleading.
Correct: Surprisingly, the endangered species was found **not only** at the valley's lowest elevations **but** throughout the entire valley.
Incorrect: Surprisingly, the endangered species was found **not only** at the valley's lowest elevations **but also** throughout the entire valley.

If the lowest elevations referred to are in the valley, *but also* would misleadingly seem to indicate that the entire valley was a separate category rather than a more general category encompassing the lower elevations.

E. Words that form standard pairs, such as *neither* and *nor*, often have other meanings and uses as well. In some contexts, *neither* or *nor* might appear at first glance to need the other term. However, *neither* often occurs as an adjective (as in "**Neither book** has been opened"), a pronoun (as in "**Neither of them** has been opened"), or a freestanding clause negator (as in "My supervisor is not fond of filing reports, but **neither am I**"). Similarly, *nor* can occur without *neither* (as in "None of the strata in the escarpment were fractured in the earthquake, **nor** were any of the exposed formations displaced").

Some issues that are not tested:

GMAT Sentence Correction questions neither assess nor presuppose knowledge of obsolete forms of idiomatic expression, highly specialized technical jargon, distinctive dialect constructions, or slang idioms that have not become standard forms of expression.

5. Logical Predication

Logical predication is the modification of one sentence element by another. Accidentally modifying the wrong sentence element may create unintended meanings even in a grammatically correct sentence. Issues of logical predication intersect with all the other categories discussed here and are involved in many of the Sentence Correction questions. Here are a few ways they may occur. See Chapter 3 for more details and examples.

A. *Position and scope of modifiers:* Modifiers should be positioned so that it is clear what word or words they are meant to modify. If modifiers are not positioned clearly, they can cause illogical references or comparisons, or otherwise distort the meaning of the sentence.

> *Example:*
> **Correct:** I put the cake **that I baked** by the door.
> **Incorrect:** I put the cake by the door **that I baked**.

B. *Pronoun-antecedent relationships:* A misplaced pronoun can bind to the wrong noun, pronoun, or noun phrase and thus create an unintended meaning.

> *Example:*
> **Correct:** After **it** has reviewed the report from the consultants, **the company** may consider changing the logo.
> **Incorrect:** After **it** has reviewed the report from the consultants, **changing the logo** may be considered by the company.

C. *Compatibility of concepts:* Careless wording can cause a predicate to say something inconsistent with the nature of the subject and vice versa.

Examples:

i) **Correct:** **The three types of wildlife** most often seen in the park **are sparrows, mallards, and squirrels**, in that order.

Incorrect: **The type of wildlife** most often seen in the park **is the sparrow, the mallard, and the squirrel**, in that order.

ii) **Correct:** Stock prices **rose** abruptly today **to an all-time high**.

Incorrect: Stock prices **dropped** abruptly today **to an all-time high**.

D. *Ellipses and extraneous elements:* Omission of a crucial word or phrase or inclusion of an extraneous element can shift the subject to an unintended element while leaving the sentence grammatically well formed. Accidents of this sort can also make an unintended noun or pronoun the subject or object of a verb.

Examples:

i) **Correct:** Work on the stadium renovations is temporarily **at a standstill**.

Incorrect: Work on the stadium renovations is temporarily **a standstill**.

In the incorrect version of i), the omission of *at* causes the sentence to claim illogically that the work itself is a standstill.

ii) **Correct:** **The car was traveling** slowly along the highway.

Incorrect: **The car's speed was traveling** slowly along the highway.

In the incorrect version of ii), the redundant reference to speed makes the sentence say, absurdly, that the speed rather than the car was traveling along the highway.

E. *Reversed relationships:* An unintended meaning can result from accidentally or misguidedly reversing a relationship between sentence elements.

Examples:

i) **Correct:** Last week's unusually high sales of electric fans can almost certainly be **blamed on** the unseasonably hot weather.

Incorrect: Last week's unusually high sales of electric fans can almost certainly be **blamed for** the unseasonably hot weather.

Example i) also involves idiomatic usage of prepositions (discussed under the Idiom category above).

ii) **Correct:** **Forecasters said the cold front** will move through the region tomorrow.

Incorrect: **Forecasters, said the cold front**, will move through the region tomorrow.

F. *Ambiguous words and phrases:* Writers should be cautious in using words or phrases that have multiple standard meanings. Often the context makes it clear which meaning is intended, but sometimes it does not. Paraphrasing to rule out unwanted meanings can sometimes require adding words or increasing a sentence's structural complexity.

Examples:

i) **Incorrect:** She has studied Greek and speaks it **as well as** Gujarati.
Correct: She has studied Greek and speaks it **in addition to** Gujarati.
Correct: She has studied Greek and speaks it **as well as she speaks** Gujarati.

As well as is an entirely acceptable equivalent of *and also* or *in addition to*, but it can be an unfortunate choice of words for a context in which *well* makes perfect sense as an evaluative judgment. The second correct version of i) captures this alternate, evaluative meaning.

ii) **Incorrect:** Although visitors **may not** enter the loading docks, they occasionally **may** wander past the area.
Correct: Although visitors **might not** enter the loading docks, they occasionally **might** wander past the area.
Correct: Although visitors **are not allowed to** enter the loading docks, they occasionally **are allowed to** wander past the area.

Here again, there is no firm basis for deciding which way the incorrect version is intended. Both occurrences of *may* could mean either *are permitted to* or *might*.

Few incorrect answers in actual Sentence Correction questions will be as easy to dismiss as the most obvious of these illustrative examples. Most Logical Predication questions will require careful analysis of the relationships between the answer choice and the nonunderlined portions of the sentence. Be alert for all types of problematic relationships among sentence parts, not just for stereotypical dangling modifiers.

Some complicating factors to consider:

Given that all Sentence Correction questions are presented out of context, there may be no basis for certainty about which of several possible interpretations the writer intended to convey. You will not be given multiple equally good versions of a sentence and asked to guess which one accurately represents the writer's true intention. In principle, almost any illogically constructed sentence could be intended to convey a bizarre meaning. One could hypothesize that the writer of the first incorrect example under *Reversed relationships* really did intend to say that the fan sales somehow caused the hot weather. Even on that hypothesis, the most reasonable judgment for Sentence Correction purposes would be that the sentence is poorly constructed. A careful writer who wants to convey a straightforward message should make it clear that the unusual meaning is the intended one instead of leading the reader to believe that she or he is ineptly trying to convey the more plausible meaning.

Some issues that are not tested:

Occasionally, you may find a poorly worded version of a sentence amusing. However, you should not expect to see Sentence Correction sentences that can be interpreted as jokes. Among the answer choices, there will always be a serious way of resolving ambiguities and illogical meanings.

6. Parallelism

Words or phrases that have similar roles in a sentence should be treated in ways that make the similarity clear. This often requires ensuring that parallel clauses have parallel structure, that verbs having the same function are in the same form, and that elements within the scope of a modifier all relate to the modifier in the same way. Here are some major categories in which parallelism can be an issue:

A. *Elements of a series:* Where the elements of a series all have the same role or function, they often should be in parallel form.

> *Example:*
> **Correct:** She tackled the problem calmly, **efficiently**, and **analytically**.
> **Incorrect:** She tackled the problem calmly, **by being efficient in tackling it**, and **was analytic**.
>
> In this example, the nonparallel version of the sentence is also awkward and wordy. Problems of these types are further discussed under the category of rhetorical construction.

B. *Correlations and comparisons:* As explained in section 3.5.5.D of Chapter 3, the sides of a correlative structure often need parallel treatment to make the relationship clear and accurate.

C. *Issues of scope and repetition of elements:* To determine what elements of a sentence should be made parallel to each other, it is sometimes necessary to determine how much of the wording should fall within the scope of a verb, preposition, or modifier. The scope may determine which elements need to be in parallel form and whether certain elements need to be repeated. Issues of this type overlap with those discussed previously.

> *Examples:*
> i) **Correct:** He mended the torn fabric **with a needle and thread**.
> **Incorrect:** He mended the torn fabric **with a needle and with thread**.
>
> Assuming that the needle and thread were used together as a unit, the incorrect version's repetition of *with* misrepresents the relationship, suggesting that the needle was used separately from the thread.
>
> Contrast this with example ii) below, in which the incorrect version inappropriately combines one action that used the needle with a separate action that used the thread:
>
> ii) **Correct:** He **punched holes** in the decoration **with a needle** and **tied it** to the lamp **with thread**.
> **Incorrect:** He **punched holes in and tied** the decoration to the lamp **with a needle and thread**.
>
> In example iii) below, the preposition *on* functions so differently in the two phrases that it makes no sense to subsume both the fire and the list under a single occurrence of the preposition. Therefore, we need the repetition of *was on*.
>
> ii) **Correct:** The house **that was on fire was on the list** of historically significant buildings.
> **Incorrect:** The house **was on fire and the list** of historically significant buildings.

D. *Corresponding series:* Where the elements of one series are supposed to correspond to those of another series, the order of elements in each series should parallel the order of elements in the other. This parallelism can help prevent confusion about how the two series relate to each other without using cumbersome repetition.

> *Example:*
> **Correct:** Our **first, second, and third meetings** last week were **on Tuesday, Wednesday, and Thursday respectively**.
> **Incorrect:** Of our **first, second, and third meetings** last week, **one was on Thursday and on Tuesday and Wednesday the others occurred**.

E. *Grammatical considerations:* Some requirements of parallelism, including some of those illustrated above, are also requirements of grammatical construction.

> *Example:*
> **Correct:** **The shipping delays** and **the two-day closure** have caused a backlog of orders.
> **Incorrect:** **The shipping was delayed** and **the two-day closure** have caused a backlog of orders.
>
> To function properly as subjects of *have caused*, both of the stated causes need to be in the form of noun phrases.

Some complicating factors to consider:

Problems of idiomatic structure and of logical predication sometimes involve parallelism as well. The following sentence displays all three:

> Not only the CEO, and also the executive vice president's proposed policies, have been distributed to the relevant people in middle management.

In presenting a faulty parallelism between the *not only* term and the *and also* term, the sentence appears illogically to claim that the CEO has been distributed. It also falls short of the clarity that could be achieved with a more standard *not only . . . but also* structure.

Agreement, as discussed previously, represents a special kind of parallelism. For example, where a singular noun and a pronoun refer to the same thing, the two terms should be parallel in both being singular, and when a verb has a plural subject, the two should be parallel in both being plural. However, in the Sentence Correction classification scheme, agreement is treated as a distinct category. Thus, agreement-related answer explanations in section 6.9 will not automatically carry the parallelism label as well.

Some issues that are not tested:

Sentence Correction questions do not require decisions about purely aesthetic or decorative types of parallelism. For example, you will not be asked to decide whether a rhymed pair such as *highways and byways* would be preferable to another phrase that is equivalent in meaning and function.

7. Rhetorical Construction

A sentence that is grammatically and idiomatically correct and conforms to good standards of parallelism and logical predication may still be unclear or annoying or may appear ineptly written. Rhetorical construction problems arise in many ways, including the following.

A. *Economy of wording:* Superfluous words, unneeded punctuation, pointless redundancies, or convoluted structures that do not enhance precision and adequacy of detail can make a sentence confusing or simply annoying.

> *Example:*
> **Correct:** We will carefully review your memo and let you know whether we are interested in the solutions you propose.
> **Incorrect:** We will "review"—i.e., carefully scrutinize—your memo submitted, letting you know, vis-à-vis the memo's contained proposal details, whether there is interest, on our part, or not, in those.

B. *Precision and adequacy of detail:* Wording that is too vague, sparse, indeterminate, or incomplete can fail to effectively communicate the intended message. Precision often requires including details and qualifying phrases. How much specificity and qualification are required depends on the communication's purpose. Scientific and legal contexts, for example, often require far more precision than do casual communications between friends.

> *Example:*
> **Correct:** The contractor shall deliver the completed materials, as defined in Section 5 of this agreement, no later than the thirtieth calendar day after the date on which the signed and ratified contract is distributed to the contracting parties.
> **Incorrect:** The contractor shall finish taking the actions for relevant agreement sections within a month of contract distribution and related events.
>
> The latter version of this sentence is poorly constructed and very vague. The acceptability of the former version depends on the wording's adequacy for the intended purpose.

C. *Active and passive voice:* Passive voice is a means of bringing a verb's object into the subject position. It can sometimes be more straightforward and economical than active voice where the verb's subject in the active voice is unknown or irrelevant. However, passive-voice constructions are often objectionably vague, awkward, or indirect.

Examples:

i) **Correct:** **We had** lunch in the hotel and then **spent** the afternoon **looking at** paintings and sculptures in the museum.
Incorrect: Lunch **was had** in the hotel **by us** before the afternoon **was spent** in the museum where paintings and sculptures **were looked at**.

In the correct version of i), the sentence's subject *we* is known and relevant, and only needs to be stated once to serve as the subject of both verbs and of the gerund. Thus, the use of passive voice in the incorrect version is needlessly vague and convoluted.

ii) **Correct:** The fruits **are left** to dry for two weeks and then collected, sorted, and packaged for shipment.
Incorrect: **Relevant people leave** the fruits to dry for two weeks, and then **people, devices, and systems collect, sort, and package** them for **someone or something to ship**.

In the incorrect version of ii), the active voice requires specifying vague or unimportant grammatical subjects, making the sentence much wordier than the correct version, which appropriately uses the passive voice.

D. *Other types of awkwardness and inelegance:* Problems of rhetorical construction take many different forms, some of which do not fall neatly into standard categories.

Examples:

i) **Correct:** As expected, she did the job very well.
Incorrect: Expectedly, the goodness of her doing the job was considerable.

ii) **Correct:** She hoped that humans would be able to explore some of the planets in other solar systems.
Incorrect: Her hope was for other solar systems' planets' possible human exploration.

Some complicating factors to consider:

Because rhetorical construction is one of the points tested in Sentence Correction, some people might be tempted to guess that shorter answer choices are a safer bet than longer ones. Wordiness is a stereotypical feature of some inelegant writing, and teachers and writing coaches often emphasize conciseness as a goal. On the other hand, some might guess that a longer version or one with more qualifiers and caveats is more likely correct. No such guessing strategy is justified. Sentence Correction questions are designed to represent a wide range of issues. Highly professional expert question writers and test assemblers would be unlikely to create predictable patterns that could be exploited in guessing. There is simply no substitute for careful analysis and understanding of the content of each question and answer choice.

Some issues that are not tested:

Sentence Correction questions do not require judgments about rhetorical appropriateness that depend on knowledge of highly technical or specialized vocabulary or syntax. Similarly, you should not expect to see questions for which the deciding factor is merely whether the writer uses jargon or buzzwords. For example, you would not be asked to determine whether *contact* might be preferable to *reach out to*—or whether *sunsetting* might be an effective substitute for *phasing out*—in a sentence such as: "I will reach out to various stakeholders to leverage decisions about the timeframe for phasing out the product."

8. Verb Form

Verbs should be in the right tenses and moods and should have the right relationships to other verbs. Uses of infinitives and participles should follow standard conventions so that the intended meanings are clear. For an extended discussion and examples of appropriate uses of verb tenses and moods, see section 3.5.3 of Chapter 3. Some of the problems posed in Sentence Correction questions involve choices among verb tenses, but many are concerned with other verb-form issues. Here are some categories in which verb-form problems may occur:

A. *Temporal relationships:* Because Sentence Correction questions are presented without any context, it is sometimes impossible to tell when they were written or whether the events they refer to were in the past, present, or future from the writer's point of view. Therefore, to the extent that verb tenses are at issue, they are often a matter of internal coherence of the parts of the sentence.

Example:
Correct: Chili peppers **belong** to the Solanaceae family of flowering plants.
Incorrect: Chili peppers **are belonging** to the Solanaceae family of flowering plants.

The present progressive form ***are belonging*** is used unidiomatically in the incorrect version. That form indicates that the event or condition referred to is ongoing at the time of writing and may not continue. The simple present form ***belong*** is coherent with the permanence and timelessness of the stated fact.

B. *Conditionals and subjunctives:* As explained in section 3.5.3.D of Chapter 3, conditional verb forms referring to conjectural or counterfactual events are typically created with the auxiliary *would. Would* constructions often require the antecedent (the *if* clause) to be in subjunctive form. Subjunctives have other purposes as well, such as expressing wishes and requests.

C. *Auxiliary verbs:* English uses auxiliary verbs for many purposes, some of which are mentioned in the discussions of temporal relationships and conditionals in section 3.5.3 of Chapter 3. For effective communication, the use of auxiliary verbs should conform to standard conventions.

Examples:
i) **Correct: Does** the professor **teach** that course often?
Incorrect: Teaches the professor that course often?

In contemporary English, interrogative forms of most verbs are created using appropriate forms of the auxiliary verb ***to do.*** The simple inversion of subject and verb seen in the incorrect version of i) is an obsolete form.

ii) **Correct:** The new book might turn out **to be** a best seller.
Incorrect: The new book might turn out **will be** a best seller.

The auxiliary verbal phrase ***might turn out*** is correctly used with infinitive verb forms such as ***to be***, not with simple future forms such as ***will be***.

D. *Treatment of participles, gerunds, and infinitives:* Present participles (such as *finding* and *taking*) are used with the verb *to be* to express progressive verb forms (*is finding, had been taking*). They also function as modifiers in phrases such as *he bought the book, hoping he would like it* and as nouns in phrases such as *his buying the book was unexpected.* When used as nouns, present participles are known as gerunds.

Past participles (such as *found* and *taken*) are used with the verb *to have* to express perfect verb forms (*has found, will have taken*). They also function as adjectives in phrases such as *the book published last year* and *the withered plant.*

The infinitive form is used for verbs that are modified by other verbs. With some modifying verbs, the infinitive must be preceded by *to.* With other verbs (certain modal and auxiliary verbs) it must not. With yet others (such as *help, go,* and *need*) it can be used either with or without *to.* Infinitives can be treated as nouns, serving as subjects or objects of verbs, as in *to laugh at one's own mistakes can be therapeutic.*

Examples:
i) **Correct: Being** widely disliked, the software went unused.
Incorrect: Been widely disliked, the software went unused.

In i), the present participle *being* can correctly head a modifying phrase, but the past participle *been* cannot.

ii) **Correct:** My colleague went **to find** another microphone.
Incorrect: My colleague went **find** another microphone.

Although such expressions as *go find* and *go get* are standard, they are unidiomatic in affirmative past tenses, which require the preposition *to* with the infinitive (*went to find*).

Some complicating factors to consider:

English verb forms and surrounding idiomatic wording conventions have many peculiarities and nuances. The following are reminders of just a few such complications.

A. Keep in mind that the subtleties of how English tenses are used cannot always be inferred from the names of the tenses. For example, in some other European languages, actions that are currently occurring are indicated by the simple present tense. But English typically uses the present progressive form for that purpose, as in "The dog is barking" or "The car is running." The simple present tense in English is typically reserved instead for events and conditions that occur at indefinite or unspecified times or that recur, as in "Dogs bark for various reasons" or "The car runs on unleaded fuel."

B. *Going to (do or happen)* is a standard way of expressing the future tense, but unlike in French for example, there is no parallel form *coming from (doing or happening).* To indicate that an action was recently completed, English uses the idiom *has/have/had just,* as in "I had just finished composing the email."

C. The preposition *to* has many different uses in combination with verbs. These differences can sometimes lead to ambiguous constructions and potential confusion. Stereotypically, *to* before a verb is thought of as an infinitive marker, but it can also indicate purpose or intention. Thus, for example, "I need your truck to haul the boxes" is indeterminate between two meanings. More precise expressions of these could be "I need your truck so that I can haul the boxes" and "It is essential for me that your truck haul the boxes." The latter may seem very formal but could be appropriate where precision is needed. *To* with a verb can also be prescriptive, as in "The borrower is to pay a fine if the materials are not returned by the due date," or simply predictive, as in "The visitors are to arrive soon." It can even be used in expressing a past tense in a construction such *as was never to see him again* or *was the last one to leave the building.*

D. *Shall* also has multiple meanings. As a simple future-tense indicator, it is an alternative to *will* for first-person verbs ("I shall tell you about it tomorrow"). However, it can also be used prescriptively, similarly to *must,* as in "The borrower shall pay a fine if the materials are not returned by the due date."

Some issues that are not tested:

You may hear that some usage advisors object to placing anything between *to* and an infinitive verb, as in *to finally reach the destination.* You should not expect to see Sentence Correction questions for which the deciding factor is merely whether the writer follows this advice. However, you might encounter a sentence that is awkward and unclear because too many words—or words that would go better elsewhere—are crammed in between the preposition and the verb. This occurs in the following sentence:

I try to remember **to scrupulously every day before I leave work log off** my computer.

This sentence has an issue of general unclarity and inelegance falling under the heading of rhetorical construction, and not a mere case of a split infinitive.

6.3 Study Suggestions

There are two basic ways you can study for Sentence Correction questions:

1. **Read material that reflects standard usage.**
   One way to gain familiarity with the basic conventions of standard written English is simply to read. Suitable material will usually be found in good magazines and nonfiction books, editorials in outstanding newspapers, and the collections of essays used by many college and university writing courses.

2. **Review basic rules of grammar and practice with writing exercises.**
   Begin by reviewing the grammar rules laid out in this chapter. Then, if you have school assignments (such as essays and research papers) that have been carefully evaluated for grammatical errors, it may be helpful to review the comments and corrections.

6.4 What Is Measured

Sentence Correction questions test three broad aspects of language proficiency:

- **Correct expression**

  A correct sentence is grammatically and structurally sound. It conforms to all the rules of standard written English, including noun-verb agreement, noun-pronoun agreement, pronoun consistency, pronoun case, and verb tense sequence. A correct sentence will not have dangling, misplaced, or improperly formed modifiers; unidiomatic or inconsistent expressions; or faults in parallel construction.

- **Effective expression**

  An effective sentence expresses an idea or relationship clearly and concisely as well as grammatically. This does not mean the choice with the fewest and simplest words is necessarily the best answer. It means there are no superfluous words or needlessly complicated expressions in the best choice.

- **Proper diction**

  An effective sentence also uses proper diction. In evaluating the diction of a sentence, you must be able to recognize whether the words are well chosen, accurate, and suitable for the context.

In the GMAT™ Enhanced Score Report, the Sentence Correction skills are divided into two fundamental categories, *Grammar* and *Communication*.

The skills classified as *Grammar* are represented primarily by the Agreement, Diction, Grammatical Construction, and Verb Form question types and by some aspects of the Idiom and Parallelism questions. *Grammar* tasks primarily give you an opportunity to show your skill in judging whether a sentence structure conforms to the basic conventions of standard English syntax and word use.

The skills classified as *Communication* are represented primarily by the Logical Predication and Rhetorical Construction question types and by some aspects of the Idiom and Parallelism questions. *Communication* tasks given you an opportunity to show your skill in judging whether a sentence effectively and reasonably communicates a coherent message.

6.5 Test-Taking Strategies

1. **Read the entire sentence carefully.**

    Try to understand the specific idea or relationship that the sentence should express.

2. **Evaluate the underlined passage for errors and possible corrections before reading the answer choices.**

    This strategy will help you discriminate among the answer choices. Remember, in some cases the underlined section of the sentence is correct.

3. **Read each answer choice carefully.**

    The first answer choice always repeats the underlined portion of the original sentence. Choose this answer if you think that the sentence is best as originally written, but do so **only after** examining all the other choices.

4. **Try to determine how to correct what you consider to be wrong with the original sentence.**

    Some of the answer choices may change things that are not wrong, whereas others may not change everything that is wrong.

5. **Make sure that you evaluate the sentence and the choices thoroughly.**

    Pay attention to general clarity, grammatical and idiomatic usage, economy and precision of language, and appropriateness of diction.

6. **Read the whole sentence, substituting the choice that you prefer for the underlined passage.**

    An answer choice may be wrong because it does not fit grammatically or structurally with the rest of the sentence. Remember that some sentences will require no correction. When the given sentence requires no correction, choose the first answer choice.

6.6 Section Instructions

Go to www.mba.com/tutorial to view instructions for the section and get a feel for what the test center screens will look like on the actual GMAT exam.

6.7 Practice Questions

Each of the Sentence Correction questions presents a sentence, part of or all of which is underlined. Beneath the sentence you will find five ways of phrasing the underlined part. The first of these repeats the original; the other four are different. Follow the requirements of standard written English to choose your answer, paying attention to grammar, word choice, and sentence construction. Select the answer that produces the most effective sentence; your answer should make the sentence clear, exact, and free of grammatical error. It should also minimize awkwardness, ambiguity, and redundancy.

Questions 234 to 268 - Difficulty: **Easy**

*SC01545

234. With respect to most species of animals, they are evenly divided in right- or left-handedness, unlike humans.

   (A) With respect to most species of animals, they are evenly divided in right- or left-handedness, unlike humans.

   (B) With respect to right- or left-handedness, most species of animals are evenly divided, unlike in humans.

   (C) Unlike humans, most species of animals are evenly divided with respect to right- or left-handedness.

   (D) Unlike in humans, most species of animals with respect to right- or left-handedness are evenly divided.

   (E) Unlike humans, with respect to right- or left-handedness, in most species of animals it is evenly divided.

SC07435

235. Using digital enhancements of skull fragments from five prehistoric hominids dating to more than 350,000 years ago, anthropologists argue that these human ancestors probably had hearing similar to that of people today.

   (A) anthropologists argue that these human ancestors

   (B) anthropologists argue, so these human ancestors

   (C) anthropologists argue, these human ancestors

   (D) these human ancestors, anthropologists argue,

   (E) these human ancestors are argued by anthropologists to have

SC14890

236. The interior minister explained that one of the village planning proposal's best characteristics was their not detracting from the project's overall benefit by being a burden on the development budget.

   (A) one of the village planning proposal's best characteristics was their not detracting

   (B) one of the village's planning proposal's best characteristics were its not taking

   (C) one of the best characteristics of the village's planning proposal was that it did not detract

   (D) a best characteristic of the village planning proposal was, it did not take

   (E) among the village planning proposal's best characteristics, one was, it did not detract

SC02940

237. Like ants, termites have an elaborate social structure in which a few individuals reproduce and the rest are serving the colony by tending juveniles, gathering food, building the nest, or they battle intruders.

   (A) are serving the colony by tending juveniles, gathering food, building the nest, or they battle

   (B) are serving the colony in that they tend juveniles, gather food, build the nest, or battle

   (C) serve the colony, tending juveniles, gathering food, building the nest, or by battling

   (D) serve the colony by tending juveniles, gathering food, by building the nest, or by battling

   (E) serve the colony by tending juveniles, gathering food, building the nest, or battling

---

*These numbers correlate with the online test bank question number. See the GMAT™ Official Guide Verbal Review Question Index in the back of this book.

402

238. Global warming is said to be responsible for extreme weather changes, <u>which, like the heavy rains that caused more than $2 billion in damages and led to flooding throughout the state of California,</u> and the heat wave in the northeastern and midwestern United States, which was also the cause of a great amount of damage and destruction.

    (A) which, like the heavy rains that caused more than $2 billion in damages and led to flooding throughout the state of California,

    (B) which, like the heavy rains that throughout the state of California caused more than $2 billion in damages and led to flooding,

    (C) like the heavy flooding that, because of rains throughout the state of California, caused more than $2 billion in damages,

    (D) such as the heavy flooding that led to rains throughout the state of California causing more than $2 billion in damages,

    (E) such as the heavy rains that led to flooding throughout the state of California, causing more than $2 billion in damages,

239. Hundreds of species of fish generate and discharge electric currents, in bursts or as steady electric fields around their bodies, using their power <u>either to find and attack prey, to defend themselves, or also for communicating and navigating.</u>

    (A) either to find and attack prey, to defend themselves, or also for communicating and navigating

    (B) either for finding and attacking prey, defend themselves, or for communication and navigation

    (C) to find and attack prey, for defense, or communication and navigation

    (D) for finding and attacking prey, to defend themselves, or also for communication and navigation

    (E) to find and attack prey, to defend themselves, or to communicate and navigate

240. Native to South America, <u>when peanuts were introduced to Africa by Portuguese explorers early in the sixteenth century they were quickly adopted into Africa's agriculture, probably because of being</u> so similar to the Bambarra groundnut, a popular indigenous plant.

    (A) when peanuts were introduced to Africa by Portuguese explorers early in the sixteenth century they were quickly adopted into Africa's agriculture, probably because of being

    (B) peanuts having been introduced to Africa by Portuguese explorers early in the sixteenth century and quickly adopted into Africa's agriculture, probably because of being

    (C) peanuts were introduced to Africa by Portuguese explorers early in the sixteenth century and were quickly adopted into Africa's agriculture, probably because they were

    (D) peanuts, introduced to Africa by Portuguese explorers early in the sixteenth century and quickly adopted into Africa's agriculture, probably because they were

    (E) peanuts, introduced to Africa by Portuguese explorers early in the sixteenth century and having been quickly adopted into Africa's agriculture, probably because they were

241. <u>It stood twelve feet tall, weighed nine thousand pounds, and wielded seven-inch claws, and *Megatherium americanum*, a giant ground sloth,</u> may have been the largest hunting mammal ever to walk the Earth.

    (A) It stood twelve feet tall, weighed nine thousand pounds, and wielded seven-inch claws, and *Megatherium americanum*, a giant ground sloth,

    (B) It stood twelve feet tall, weighing nine thousand pounds, and wielding seven-inch claws, *Megatherium americanum* was a giant ground sloth and

    (C) The giant ground sloth *Megatherium americanum*, having stood twelve feet tall, weighing nine thousand pounds, and wielding seven-inch claws, it

    (D) Standing twelve feet tall, weighing nine thousand pounds, and wielding seven-inch claws, *Megatherium americanum*, a giant ground sloth,

    (E) Standing twelve feet tall, weighing nine thousand pounds, it wielded seven-inch claws, and the giant ground sloth *Megatherium americanum*

SC04083

242. <u>Studying skeletons unearthed near Rome, DNA evidence was recovered by scientists, who were able to deduce from this</u> that an epidemic of malaria struck in the empire's waning days.

(A) Studying skeletons unearthed near Rome, DNA evidence was recovered by scientists, who were able to deduce from this

(B) In studying skeletons unearthed near Rome, DNA evidence was recovered by scientists, who were able to deduce from this

(C) Scientists recovered DNA evidence from studying skeletons unearthed near Rome, being able to deduce from this

(D) Skeletons unearthed near Rome allowed scientists to recover DNA evidence, and they were able to deduce from it

(E) Scientists studying skeletons unearthed near Rome recovered DNA evidence from which they were able to deduce

SC01594

243. Butterflies come in more than 17,000 species, <u>displaying a wing pattern unique to each one.</u>

(A) displaying a wing pattern unique to each one

(B) displaying a unique wing pattern in each

(C) each uniquely displaying a wing pattern

(D) each of which displays a unique wing pattern

(E) each of which uniquely displays a wing pattern

SC04652

244. A March 2000 Census Bureau survey showed that Mexico accounted for more than a quarter of all foreign-born residents of the United States, <u>the largest share for any country to contribute</u> since 1890, when about 30 percent of the country's foreign-born population was from Germany.

(A) the largest share for any country to contribute

(B) the largest share that any country has contributed

(C) which makes it the largest share for any country to contribute

(D) having the largest share to be contributed by any country

(E) having the largest share to have been contributed by any country

SC01579

245. Recently declassified information from military satellites in orbit thousands of miles above the Earth <u>show the planet continually bombarded by</u> large meteoroids that explode with the power of atomic bomb blasts.

(A) show the planet continually bombarded by

(B) show continual bombarding of the planet by

(C) show a continual bombardment of the planet from

(D) shows continually that the planet is bombarded from

(E) shows that the planet is continually bombarded by

SC04026

246. Child development specialists believe <u>that, in confining babies much of the time to strollers, high chairs, playpens, and walkers, muscle development can be inhibited.</u>

(A) that, in confining babies much of the time to strollers, high chairs, playpens, and walkers, muscle development can be inhibited

(B) that, in their confinement much of the time to strollers, high chairs, playpens, and walkers, muscle development can be inhibited in babies

(C) that confining babies much of the time to strollers, high chairs, playpens, and walkers can inhibit muscle development

(D) that babies, if confined much of the time to strollers, high chairs, playpens, and walkers can inhibit muscle development

(E) that strollers, high chairs, playpens, and walkers can, if babies are confined to them much of the time, result in muscle development being inhibited

SC01482

247. Together with Key Largo National Marine Sanctuary, the John Pennekamp Coral Reef State Park, the first underwater park in the United States, <u>provide 165 square nautical miles of marine life for underwater explorers, which includes</u> more than 500 species of fish and 55 varieties of coral.

(A) provide 165 square nautical miles of marine life for underwater explorers, which includes

(B) provide for underwater explorers 165 square nautical miles of marine life, which include

(C) provide 165 square nautical miles of marine life for underwater explorers and includes

(D) provides 165 square nautical miles of marine life for underwater explorers and including

(E) provides underwater explorers with 165 square nautical miles of marine life, including

SC01481

248. While Hollywood makes films primarily for entertainment, the motion picture <u>was not first developed to entertain, but it was</u> to allow detailed analysis of animal motion.

    (A)   was not first developed to entertain, but it was
    (B)   was developed not first to entertain, but it was
    (C)   was first developed not to entertain, but
    (D)   did not first develop for entertainment, but
    (E)   did not first develop for entertainment, but it was

SC01069

249. The personal income tax did not become permanent in the United States until the First World War; before that time <u>the federal government was dependent on tariffs to be their main source of revenue.</u>

    (A)   the federal government was dependent on tariffs to be their main source of revenue
    (B)   the federal government had depended on tariffs as its main source of revenue
    (C)   tariffs were what the federal government was dependent on to be its main source of revenue
    (D)   the main source of revenue for the federal government was dependent on tariffs
    (E)   for their main source of revenue, tariffs were depended on by the federal government

SC02628

250. In 1776 Adam Smith wrote that it is young people <u>who have</u> "the contempt of risk and the presumptuous hope of success" needed to found new businesses.

    (A)   who have
    (B)   with
    (C)   having
    (D)   who are those with
    (E)   who are the ones to have

SC04198

251. <u>Palladium prices have soared, with Russia restricting exports and because automakers have started using</u> it to make the huge engines in sport utility vehicles and other light trucks.

    (A)   Palladium prices have soared, with Russia restricting exports and because automakers have started using
    (B)   Palladium prices have soared, with Russia restricting exports, in addition to automakers that have started to use
    (C)   Prices for palladium have soared as Russia has restricted exports and automakers have started using
    (D)   Prices for palladium have soared as Russia has been restricting exports, in addition to automakers starting to use
    (E)   Prices for palladium have soared because Russia is restricting exports, as well as automakers that have started using

SC01543

252. Variability in individual physical traits <u>both are determined through genetic factors, environmental factors, and interaction between</u> these factors.

    (A)   both are determined through genetic factors, environmental factors, and interaction between
    (B)   are both determined by genetic factors, environmental factors, as well as interaction among
    (C)   both is determined by genetic factors, environmental factors, and interaction between
    (D)   is determined through genetic factors, environmental factors, as well as interaction among
    (E)   is determined by genetic factors, environmental factors, and interaction between

SC06613

253. In his *Uses of Enchantment* (1976), <u>it was psychologist Bruno Bettelheim's assertion that the apparently cruel and arbitrary nature of many fairy tales actually are</u> an instructive reflection of a child's natural and necessary "killing off" of successive phases in his or her own development.

(A) it was psychologist Bruno Bettelheim's assertion that the apparently cruel and arbitrary nature of many fairy tales actually are

(B) it was the assertion of psychologist Bruno Bettelheim that what is apparently the cruel and arbitrary nature of many fairy tales actually is

(C) psychologist Bruno Bettelheim's assertion that what is apparently the cruel and arbitrary nature of many fairy tales actually is

(D) psychologist Bruno Bettelheim asserted that the apparently cruel and arbitrary nature of many fairy tales actually are

(E) psychologist Bruno Bettelheim asserted that the apparently cruel and arbitrary nature of many fairy tales is actually

SC06012

254. After weeks of uncertainty about the course the country would pursue to stabilize its troubled economy, officials reached a revised agreement with the International Monetary Fund, pledging <u>the enforcement of substantially greater budget discipline as that which was originally promised and to keep inflation below ten percent.</u>

(A) the enforcement of substantially greater budget discipline as that which was originally promised and to keep inflation below ten percent

(B) the enforcement of substantially greater budget discipline than originally promised and keeping inflation below the ten percent figure

(C) to enforce substantially greater budget discipline than originally promised and to keep inflation below ten percent

(D) to enforce substantially greater budget discipline than that which was originally promised and keeping inflation less than the ten percent figure

(E) to enforce substantially greater budget discipline as that which was originally promised and to keep inflation less than ten percent

SC01596

255. <u>A new satellite sweeping over the poles at altitudes of up to 32,000 miles is called POLAR, giving scientists their best look yet at the magnetosphere, the region of space under the invisible influence of Earth's magnetic field.</u>

(A) A new satellite sweeping over the poles at altitudes of up to 32,000 miles is called POLAR, giving scientists their best look yet at the magnetosphere, the region of space under the invisible influence of Earth's magnetic field.

(B) A new satellite called POLAR that is giving scientists their best look yet at the magnetosphere, the region of space under the invisible influence of Earth's magnetic field, sweeping over the poles at altitudes of up to 32,000 miles.

(C) Scientists are getting their best look yet at the magnetosphere, the region of space under the invisible influence of Earth's magnetic field, from a new satellite sweeping over the poles at altitudes of up to 32,000 miles called POLAR.

(D) Sweeping over the poles at altitudes of up to 32,000 miles, a new satellite called POLAR is giving scientists their best look yet at the magnetosphere, the region of space under the invisible influence of Earth's magnetic field.

(E) Sweeping over the poles at altitudes of up to 32,000 miles, scientists' best look yet at the magnetosphere, the region of space under the invisible influence of Earth's magnetic field, is coming from a new satellite called POLAR.

SC05787

256. The treasury market dropped in response to a decrease in the value of the dollar and to continued concern <u>that the economy might be growing as fast as</u> to accelerate inflation and drive interest rates higher.

(A) that the economy might be growing as fast as

(B) that the economy might be growing fast enough

(C) with the economy's possibly growing so fast as

(D) with the possibility of the economy growing fast enough so as

(E) with the possibility of the economy possibly growing fast enough

SC03724

257. Despite a growing population, in 1998 the United States used 38 billion fewer gallons of water a day when comparing it to the period of all-time highest consumption almost 20 years earlier.

   (A) day when comparing it to the period of all-time highest consumption almost 20 years earlier

   (B) day than it did during the period of all-time highest consumption almost 20 years earlier

   (C) day than were used almost 20 years earlier, which had been the all-time high consumption

   (D) day, compared to almost 20 years earlier, that having been the all-time high consumption

   (E) day, which is in comparison to the period of all-time highest consumption almost 20 years earlier

SC01600

258. A federal advisory panel proposes expanding a national computerized file to permit law-enforcement agencies to track people under criminal investigation but have not yet been charged.

   (A) under criminal investigation but

   (B) under criminal investigation, but who

   (C) under criminal investigation, but they

   (D) who are under criminal investigation, but they

   (E) who are under criminal investigation but

SC03779

259. Analysts believe that whereas bad decisions by elected leaders can certainly hurt the economy, no administration can really be said to control or manage all of the complex and interrelated forces that determine the nation's economic strength.

   (A) no administration can really be said to control

   (B) no administration can be said that it really controls

   (C) that no administration can really be said to control

   (D) that no administration can really be said that it controls

   (E) that it cannot be said that any administration really controls

SC03146

260. Nearly unrivaled in their biological diversity, coral reefs provide a host of benefits that includes the supply of protein for people, protecting shorelines, and they contain biochemical sources for new life-saving medicines.

   (A) coral reefs provide a host of benefits that includes the supply of protein for people, protecting shorelines,

   (B) coral reefs provide a host of benefits: they supply people with protein, they protect the shorelines,

   (C) coral reefs provide a host of benefits that include supplying protein for people, as well as shoreline protection,

   (D) a coral reef provides a host of benefits; they supply protein for people, the protecting of shorelines,

   (E) a coral reef provides a host of benefits, including protein for people, protecting shorelines,

SC12367

261. Literacy opened up entire realms of verifiable knowledge to ordinary men and women having been previously considered incapable of discerning truth for themselves.

   (A) having been previously considered incapable of discerning truth for themselves

   (B) who had previously been considered incapable of discerning truth for themselves

   (C) previously considered incapable of discerning truth for himself or herself

   (D) of whom it had previously been considered they were incapable of discerning truth for themselves

   (E) who had previously been considered incapable of discerning truth for himself or herself

SC01915

262. In early Mesopotamian civilization, castor oil served not only as a laxative, but also a skin-softening lotion and it was a construction lubricant for sliding giant stone blocks over wooden rollers.

   (A) not only as a laxative, but also a skin-softening lotion and it was a construction

   (B) as not only a laxative, but also a skin-softening lotion, and it was a construction

   (C) not only as a laxative but also as a skin-softening lotion and as a construction

   (D) as not only a laxative but as a skin-softening lotion and in construction, as a

   (E) not only as a laxative, but a skin-softening lotion and in construction, a

SC06935

263. An analysis of tree bark all over the globe shows that chemical insecticides have often spread thousands of miles from where they were originally used.

    (A) that chemical insecticides have often spread thousands of miles from where they were originally used

    (B) that chemical insecticides have spread, often thousands of miles from their original use

    (C) chemical insecticides, having often spread thousands of miles from where they were used originally

    (D) chemical insecticides, often spreading thousands of miles from where their original use

    (E) chemical insecticides, often spreading thousands of miles from where they were originally used

SC02241

264. According to the Economic Development Corporation of Los Angeles County, if one were to count the Los Angeles metropolitan area as a separate nation, it would have the world's eleventh largest gross national product, that is bigger than that of Australia, Mexico, or the Netherlands.

    (A) if one were to count the Los Angeles metropolitan area as a separate nation, it would have the world's eleventh largest gross national product, that is

    (B) if the Los Angeles metropolitan area is counted as a separate nation, it has the world's eleventh largest gross national product, that being

    (C) if the Los Angeles metropolitan area were a separate nation, it would have the world's eleventh largest gross national product,

    (D) were the Los Angeles metropolitan area a separate nation, it will have the world's eleventh largest gross national product, which is

    (E) when the Los Angeles metropolitan area is counted as a separate nation, it has the world's eleventh largest gross national product, thus

SC51661.01

265. Some sociologists claim to have found a direct link from the appearance of news stories about violence to the rate of homicide.

    (A) from the appearance of news stories about violence to

    (B) between the appearance of news stories about violence to

    (C) between the appearance of news stories about violence and

    (D) with the appearance of news stories about violence to

    (E) with the appearance of news stories about violence and

SC61661.01

266. Government statistics on the size of foreign investment in real estate are inconclusive because neither federal nor state laws require disclosure of foreign ownership, and the Commerce Department, in its public tallies, does not categorize the owners.

    (A) are inconclusive because neither federal nor state laws require

    (B) are inconclusive because neither the federal nor state laws requires

    (C) are inconclusive because neither federal laws or state laws require

    (D) is inconclusive because neither the federal or state laws requires

    (E) is inconclusive because neither federal laws nor state laws require

SC81661.01

267. In the United States one of the earliest challengers of the economic principle of free trade was Alexander Hamilton, who in 1791 advocated government policies that would encourage indigenous manufacturing and to protect it from competition from British exports.

    (A) and to protect it

    (B) but protecting it

    (C) while protecting it

    (D) for protecting them

    (E) to protect them

SC94920.02

268. Some business experts think that allowing employees to buy their employer's stock for a set price, no matter how high the stock rises, will give the employees a powerful incentive to work together, making a company more prosperous, which will thus increase the return to shareholders.

   (A) to work together, making a company more prosperous, which will thus

   (B) to work together to make a company more prosperous and will thus

   (C) for working together, making a company more prosperous, and thus they

   (D) for working together to make a company more prosperous, and thus it will

   (E) for working together and making a company more prosperous, which will thus

Questions 269 to 303 - Difficulty: **Medium**

SC71661.01

269. Desertification, a process in which the biological productivity of the land is sharply degraded by human abuse and natural phenomena, helped cause the famines that have killed hundreds of thousands in recent years.

   (A) a process in which the biological productivity of the land is sharply degraded by human abuse and natural phenomena

   (B) a process of the biological productivity of the land being sharply degraded by human abuse and natural phenomena

   (C) a process of human abuse and natural phenomena that sharply degrade the biological productivity of the land

   (D) which is the process of human abuse and natural phenomena sharply degrading the land's biological productivity

   (E) which is the process of human abuse and natural phenomena that sharply degrade the land's biological productivity

SC42661.01

270. Open to the public and operated like conventional hotels, condominium hotels permit buyers to acquire a specific room or suite, as well as a proportionate interest in the rest of the establishment.

   (A) condominium hotels permit buyers to acquire a specific room or suite, as well as

   (B) buyers are permitted to acquire a specific room or suite in a condominium hotel, as well as

   (C) a specific room or suite in condominium hotels may be acquired by buyers, as well as acquiring

   (D) condominium hotels permit buyers to acquire a specific room or suite, as well as acquiring

   (E) it is permitted for buyers to acquire a specific room or suite in a condominium hotel, as well as the acquisition of

SC52661.01

271. The methods proposed for reducing the amount of interest to be paid are not able to be used successfully without creating a problem of insufficient cash flow in the future.

   (A) are not able to be used successfully without creating a problem of insufficient cash flow in the future

   (B) are not able successfully to be used without creating a problem in the future of insufficient cash flow

   (C) cannot successfully be used without creating a future problem of insufficient cash flow

   (D) cannot be used without succeeding in creating a problem in the future of insufficient cash flow

   (E) cannot be used without succeeding in creating a future problem of insufficient cash flow

SC62661.01

272. Despite the Puritan sumptuary laws prohibiting the wearing of bright or elaborate clothing, if you had either a liberal education or an annual income of two hundred pounds one was permitted to display their material prosperity in public.

(A) if you had either a liberal education or an annual income of two hundred pounds one was permitted to display their material prosperity in public

(B) if one had either a liberal education or annual income of two hundred pounds one was permitted the public display of their material prosperity

(C) having either a liberal education or annual income of two hundred pounds would allow one to publicly display their material prosperity

(D) those with either a liberal education or an annual income of two hundred pounds were allowed to display their material prosperity in public

(E) those having either a liberal education or annual income of two hundred pounds were permitted their public display of material prosperity

SC72661.01

273. Like Darwin and his fruitful voyage on the *Beagle*, Banks's trip with Captain Cook on the *Endeavour* inspired and shaped his remarkable career in natural science.

(A) Like Darwin and his fruitful voyage on the *Beagle*, Banks's trip with Captain Cook on the *Endeavour* inspired and shaped his remarkable career in natural science.

(B) Just as Darwin had a fruitful voyage on the *Beagle*, Banks's trip with Captain Cook on the *Endeavour* inspired and shaped a remarkable career as a natural scientist.

(C) Like Darwin's fruitful voyage on the *Beagle*, Banks's trip with Captain Cook on the *Endeavour* inspired and shaped a remarkable career in natural science.

(D) Just as Darwin's fruitful voyage on the *Beagle*, Banks sailed with Captain Cook on the *Endeavour*, inspiring and shaping his remarkable career as a natural scientist.

(E) Like Darwin's fruitful voyage on the *Beagle*, Banks sailed with Captain Cook on the *Endeavour*, which inspired and shaped a remarkable career in natural science.

SC82661.01

274. When more and more factories move out of the cities each year, manufacturing jobs, historically the first step into the job market for the urban poor, have become fewer and fewer.

(A) When more and more factories move out of the cities each year, manufacturing jobs, historically the first step into the job market for the urban poor, have become fewer and fewer.

(B) At the time that more and more factories move out of the cities each year, manufacturing jobs, historically the first step into the job market for the urban poor, become less and less.

(C) When more and more factories move out of the cities each year, then manufacturing jobs, historically the first step into the urban poor's job market, become less and less.

(D) Since more and more factories have moved out of the cities each year, manufacturing jobs, historically the first step into the urban poor's job market, have become less and less.

(E) As more and more factories move out of the cities each year, manufacturing jobs, historically the first step into the job market for the urban poor, become fewer and fewer.

SC92661.01

275. The thousands of volcanic islands and coral atolls of the South Seas have a total population of about four million, but the paucity of natural resources does not permit such economic development that would be needed by them to support more population.

(A) does not permit such economic development that would be needed by them to support more population

(B) does not permit economic development such as is needed for supporting a larger number

(C) does not permit the economic development needed to support a larger population

(D) do not permit the economic development needed to support a larger population

(E) do not permit needed economic development for supporting a larger number of people

SC03661.01

276. In contrast with a dark surface and its tendency toward heat absorption, a large expanse of snow and ice reflects incoming radiation into space.

(A) In contrast with a dark surface and its tendency toward heat absorption

(B) Contrasted with a dark surface's tendency to absorb heat

(C) Since it is in contrast to a dark surface and its tendency to absorb heat

(D) Contrasted to the tendency of a dark surface to absorb heat

(E) In contrast to a dark surface, which tends to absorb heat

SC37620.01

277. The greatest road system built in the Americas prior to the arrival of Christopher Columbus was the Incan highway, which, over 2,500 miles long and extending from northern Ecuador through Peru to southern Chile.

(A) Columbus was the Incan highway, which, over 2,500 miles long and extending

(B) Columbus was the Incan highway, over 2,500 miles in length, which had extended

(C) Columbus, the Incan highway, which was over 2,500 miles in length and extended

(D) Columbus, the Incan highway, being over 2,500 miles in length, was extended

(E) Columbus, the Incan highway was over 2,500 miles long, extending

SC99250.01

278. Due to poaching and increased cultivation in their native habitats, researchers have determined that there are fewer than 100 Arabian leopards left in the wild, and thus the leopards are many times as rare as China's giant pandas.

(A) Due to poaching and increased cultivation in their native habitats, researchers have determined that there are fewer than 100 Arabian leopards left in the wild, and thus the leopards are many times as rare as

(B) Due to poaching and increased cultivation in their native habitats, there are fewer than 100 Arabian leopards left in the wild, researchers have determined, making them many times more rare than

(C) There are fewer than 100 Arabian leopards left in the wild due to poaching and increased cultivation in their native habitats, researchers have determined, which makes the leopards many times more rare compared to

(D) Researchers have determined that, because of poaching and increased cultivation in their native habitats, there are fewer than 100 Arabian leopards left in the wild, thus making them many more times as rare as

(E) Researchers have determined that, because of poaching and increased cultivation in their native habitats, there are fewer than 100 Arabian leopards left in the wild, and thus the leopards are many times more rare than

SC04215

279. Developed by Pennsylvania's Palatine Germans about 1750, Conestoga wagons, with high wheels capable of crossing rutted roads, muddy flats, and the nonroads of the prairie and they had a floor curved upward on either end so as to prevent cargo from shifting on steep grades.

(A) wagons, with high wheels capable of crossing rutted roads, muddy flats, and the nonroads of the prairie and they had a floor curved upward on either end so as to prevent

(B) wagons, with high wheels capable of crossing rutted roads, muddy flats, and the nonroads of the prairie, and with a floor that was curved upward at both ends to prevent

(C) wagons, which had high wheels capable of crossing rutted roads, muddy flats, and the nonroads of the prairie, and floors curved upward on their ends so that they prevented

(D) wagons had high wheels capable of crossing rutted roads, muddy flats, and the nonroads of the prairie, and a floor that was curved upward at both ends to prevent

(E) wagons had high wheels capable of crossing rutted roads, muddy flats, and the nonroads of the prairie and floors curving upward at their ends so that it prevented

SC60440.01

280. The current economic downturn has significantly reduced advertising income both for business journals as well as general consumer magazines, especially if focusing on technology.

(A) has significantly reduced advertising income both for business journals as well as general consumer magazines, especially if focusing

(B) has significantly reduced advertising income both for business journals and for general consumer magazines, especially those focusing

(C) significantly reduced advertising income for both business journals and for general consumer magazines, especially when focused

(D) reduced both business journals' and general consumer magazines' advertising income significantly, especially if focused

(E) reduced advertising income significantly for both business journals, as well as for general consumer magazines, especially those focusing

SC01002

281. The reason many people consider the Mediterranean island to be ungovernable is because that the inhabitants long ago learned to distrust and neutralize all written laws.

(A) is because that the inhabitants long ago learned to distrust and neutralize

(B) is the inhabitants long ago learned distrusting and neutralizing

(C) was because of the inhabitants long ago learning to distrust and to be neutralizing

(D) is that the inhabitants long ago learned to distrust and to neutralize

(E) was on account of the inhabitants long ago learning to distrust and neutralize

SC28801.01

282. Though there is some overlap with the two concepts market economy and laissez faire, several important differences between them must be borne in mind.

(A) with the two concepts market economy and laissez faire, several important differences between them must be borne in mind

(B) between the two concepts market economy and laissez faire, several important differences must be borne in mind

(C) spanning the two concepts market economy and laissez faire, one must bear several important differences between them in mind

(D) among the two concepts of market economy and laissez faire, there are several important differences among them that must be borne in mind

(E) with the two concepts of market economy and laissez faire, one must bear in mind several important differences

SC71061.01

283. <u>Because of the erratic pattern of sales increases this year, retailers and analysts hesitate to predict</u> five-year trends in retail sales during the months that have historically been the most profitable.

(A) Because of the erratic pattern of sales increases this year, retailers and analysts hesitate to predict

(B) With the erratic pattern of this year's sales increases, retailers and analysts are hesitant in predicting

(C) This year, due to the erratic pattern of increasing sales, there is some hesitation among retailers and analysts in predicting

(D) The erratic pattern of sales increases have made retailers and analysts hesitate this year to predict

(E) This year's erratic pattern of increasing sales have made retailers and analysts hesitate to predict

SC89941.01

284. <u>Proceeding without a definite plan for upcoming labor negotiations, like the firm had agreed to last year, it would surely have proven to be a disaster</u> in the face of the skilled and resolute opposition involved this time.

(A) Proceeding without a definite plan for upcoming labor negotiations, like the firm had agreed to last year, it would surely have proven to be a disaster

(B) Proceeding without a definite plan for upcoming labor negotiations, as the firm agreed last year to do, would surely have proven to be a disaster

(C) Going ahead without the presence of a definite plan for upcoming labor negotiations, like the firm had agreed last year to do, would surely have proven disastrous

(D) To proceed without the presence of a definite plan for upcoming labor negotiations, as the firm had agreed to last year, would surely have proven disastrous

(E) Going ahead without their having a definite plan for upcoming labor negotiations, as they agreed to last year, it would surely have proven to be a disaster for the firm

SC03916

285. <u>Because the collagen fibers in skin line up in the direction of tension, surgical cuts made along these so-called Langer's lines sever fewer</u> fibers and is less likely to leave an unsightly scar.

(A) Because the collagen fibers in skin line up in the direction of tension, surgical cuts made along these so-called Langer's lines sever fewer

(B) Because the collagen fibers in skin line up in the direction of tension, a surgical cut having been made along these so-called Langer's lines severs less

(C) Because the collagen fibers in skin line up in the direction of tension, a surgical cut made along these so-called Langer's lines severs fewer

(D) With the collagen fibers in skin lining up in the direction of tension, surgical cuts made along these so-called Langer's lines sever less

(E) With the collagen fibers in skin lining up in the direction of tension, a surgical cut made along these so-called Langer's lines sever fewer

SC01639

286. The completion in 1925 of the Holland Tunnel, <u>linking Manhattan with New Jersey's highways, which permitted 2,000 cars to pass through each tube every hour and</u> was hailed as the decade's $48 million engineering masterpiece.

(A) Tunnel, linking Manhattan with New Jersey's highways, which permitted 2,000 cars to pass through each tube every hour and

(B) Tunnel, linking Manhattan with New Jersey's highways and permitting 2,000 cars to pass through each tube every hour, it

(C) Tunnel, linking Manhattan with New Jersey's highways and permitting 2,000 cars to pass through each tube every hour,

(D) Tunnel linked Manhattan with New Jersey's highways, which permitted 2,000 cars to pass through each tube every hour and

(E) Tunnel linked Manhattan with New Jersey's highways, permitting 2,000 cars to pass through each tube every hour,

SC03315

287. The World Wildlife Fund has declared that global warming, a phenomenon that most scientists agree is caused by human beings' burning of fossil fuels, will create havoc among migratory birds by harming their habitats as a result of altering the environment.

(A) by harming their habitats as a result of altering the environment

(B) by altering the environment to the extent of it harming their habitats

(C) by altering the environment in ways harmful to their habitats

(D) from the fact that their habitats will be harmed by the environment being altered

(E) from the fact that the environment will be altered and this will harm their habitats

SC05244

288. Tropical bats play an important role in the rain forest ecosystem, aiding in the dispersal of cashew, date, and fig seeds; pollinating banana, breadfruit, and mango trees; and indirectly help the producing of tequila by pollinating agave plants.

(A) pollinating banana, breadfruit, and mango trees; and indirectly help the producing of

(B) pollinating banana, breadfruit, and mango trees; and indirectly helping to produce

(C) pollinating banana, breadfruit, and mango trees; and they indirectly help to produce

(D) they pollinate banana, breadfruit, and mango trees; and indirectly help producing

(E) they pollinate banana, breadfruit, and mango trees; indirectly helping the producing of

SC04346

289. A recent court decision has qualified a 1998 ruling that workers cannot be laid off if they have been given reason to believe that their jobs will be safe, provided that their performance remains satisfactory.

(A) if they have been given reason to believe that their jobs will

(B) if they are given reason for believing that their jobs would still

(C) having been given reason for believing that their jobs would

(D) having been given reason to believe their jobs to

(E) given reason to believe that their jobs will still

SC04874

290. Of all the record companies involved in early jazz, the three most prominent were Columbia, Victor, and OKeh.

(A) Of all the record companies involved in early jazz, the three most prominent were Columbia, Victor, and OKeh.

(B) Three most prominent record companies of all the ones that were involved in early jazz were Columbia, Victor, and OKeh.

(C) Columbia, Victor, and OKeh were, of all the record companies involved in early jazz, the three of them that were most prominent.

(D) Columbia, Victor, and OKeh were three most prominent of all the record companies involved in early jazz.

(E) Out of all the record companies that were involved in early jazz, three of them that were the most prominent were Columbia, Victor, and OKeh.

SC01451

291. Since 1992, in an attempt to build up the Atlantic salmon population in each of the seven rivers in which salmon still spawn, state officials in Maine have stocked them with fry raised in hatcheries from eggs produced by wild fish found in that particular river.

(A) them

(B) the river

(C) the rivers

(D) each river

(E) that river

SC02382

292. On the tournament roster are listed several tennis students, most all of which play as good as their instructors.

(A) most all of which play as good

(B) most all of whom play as good

(C) almost all of which play as well

(D) almost all of whom play as good

(E) almost all of whom play as well

SC07143
293. In 1974 a large area of the surface of Mercury was photographed from varying distances, <u>which revealed a degree of cratering similar to that of the Moon's.</u>

   (A)   which revealed a degree of cratering similar to that of the Moon's

   (B)   to reveal a degree of cratering similar to the Moon

   (C)   revealing a degree of cratering similar to that of the Moon

   (D)   and revealed cratering similar in degree to the Moon

   (E)   that revealed cratering similar in degree to that of the Moon

SC46270.02
294. The survival of a rare New Zealand species of mistletoe that produces spectacular sprays of scarlet flowers <u>is threatened both because their leaves are extremely tasty to a voracious opossum species and also because their</u> flowers are pollinated by two species of birds whose populations are in decline.

   (A)   is threatened both because their leaves are extremely tasty to a voracious opossum species and also because their

   (B)   is threatened both because its leaves are extremely tasty to a voracious opossum species and because its

   (C)   is threatened both because its leaves are extremely tasty to a voracious opossum species and also its

   (D)   are threatened both because its leaves are extremely tasty to a voracious opossum species and its

   (E)   are threatened both because their leaves are extremely tasty to a voracious opossum species and because their

SC05894
295. <u>The computer company reported strong second-quarter earnings that surpassed Wall Street's estimates and announced the first in a series of price cuts intended to increase sales further.</u>

   (A)   The computer company reported strong second-quarter earnings that surpassed Wall Street's estimates and announced the first in a series of price cuts intended to increase sales further.

   (B)   The report of the computer company showed strong second-quarter earnings, surpassing Wall Street's estimates, and they announced the first in a series of price cuts that they intend to increase sales further.

   (C)   Surpassing Wall Street's estimates, the report of the computer company showed strong second-quarter earnings, and, for the purpose of increasing sales further, they announced the first in a series of price cuts.

   (D)   The computer company reported strong second-quarter earnings, surpassing Wall Street's estimates, and announcing the first in a series of price cuts for the purpose of further increasing sales.

   (E)   The computer company, surpassing Wall Street's estimates, reported strong second-quarter earnings, while announcing that to increase sales further there would be the first in a series of price cuts.

SC01562
296. Long overshadowed by the Maya and Aztec civilizations, <u>historians are now exploring the more ancient Olmec culture for the legacy it had for succeeding Mesoamerican societies.</u>

   (A)   historians are now exploring the more ancient Olmec culture for the legacy it had for succeeding Mesoamerican societies

   (B)   historians' exploration is now of the more ancient Olmec culture's legacy to the Mesoamerican societies succeeding them

   (C)   the legacy of the more ancient Olmec culture to the Mesoamerican societies that succeeded them is what historians are now exploring

   (D)   the more ancient Olmec culture is now being explored by historians for its legacy to succeeding Mesoamerican societies

   (E)   the Olmec culture is more ancient and had a legacy to succeeding Mesoamerican societies that historians are now exploring

SC02370
297. The bank holds $3 billion in loans that are seriously delinquent or in such trouble that <u>they do not expect payments when</u> due.

   (A)   they do not expect payments when

   (B)   it does not expect payments when it is

   (C)   it does not expect payments to be made when they are

   (D)   payments are not to be expected to be paid when

   (E)   payments are not expected to be paid when they will be

SC01435
298. <u>A researcher claims that a tornado of a given size and strength is likely to cause more deaths, both proportionately and in absolute numbers, in the southeastern region of the United States than in the northeastern.</u>

   (A)   A researcher claims that a tornado of a given size and strength is likely to cause more deaths, both proportionately and in absolute numbers, in the southeastern region of the United States than in the northeastern.

   (B)   A researcher claims that a tornado, if of a given size and strength, is likely both proportionately and in absolute numbers to cause more deaths in the southeastern region of the United States than in the northeastern.

   (C)   A researcher claims that, with a tornado of a given size and strength, it is likely to cause more death, both proportionately and in absolute numbers, in the southeastern rather than in the northeastern region of the United States.

   (D)   If a tornado is of a given size and strength, a researcher claims, it is more likely, both proportionately and in absolute numbers, to cause death if it is in the southeastern region of the United States rather than in the northeastern region.

   (E)   Both proportionately and in absolute numbers, a researcher claims that a tornado of a given size and strength is likely to cause more deaths in the southeastern region of the United States rather than in the northeastern.

SC04603
299. Heirloom tomatoes, grown from seeds saved from the previous year, only look less appetizing than their round and red supermarket <u>cousins, often green and striped, or have plenty of bumps and bruises, but are</u> more flavorful.

   (A)   cousins, often green and striped, or have plenty of bumps and bruises, but are

   (B)   cousins, often green and striped, or with plenty of bumps and bruises, although

   (C)   cousins, often green and striped, or they have plenty of bumps and bruises, although they are

   (D)   cousins; they are often green and striped, or with plenty of bumps and bruises, although

   (E)   cousins; they are often green and striped, or have plenty of bumps and bruises, but they are

SC05381
300. In the textbook publishing business, the second quarter is historically weak, because revenues are <u>low and marketing expenses are high as companies prepare</u> for the coming school year.

   (A)   low and marketing expenses are high as companies prepare

   (B)   low and their marketing expenses are high as they prepare

   (C)   low with higher marketing expenses in preparation

   (D)   low, while marketing expenses are higher to prepare

   (E)   low, while their marketing expenses are higher in preparation

SC01485
301. Because of the sharp increases in the price of gold and silver, the value of Monica Taylor's portfolio rose <u>as her daughter-in-law's dropped.</u>

   (A)   as her daughter-in-law's dropped

   (B)   while her daughter-in-law's has dropped

   (C)   as there was a drop in her daughter-in-law's

   (D)   while that of her daughter-in-law's dropped

   (E)   as it dropped for her daughter-in-law's

SC02791

302. Ms. Chambers is among the forecasters who predict that the rate of addition to arable lands will drop while <u>those of loss rise.</u>

   (A)   those of loss rise

   (B)   it rises for loss

   (C)   those of losses rise

   (D)   the rate of loss rises

   (E)   there are rises for the rate of loss

SC00987

303. In keeping with her commitment to her Christian faith, Sojourner Truth demonstrated as a public speaker <u>a dedication both to the nonviolent abolition of slavery as well as for women to be emancipated.</u>

   (A)   a dedication both to the nonviolent abolition of slavery as well as for women to be emancipated

   (B)   her being dedicated to both the nonviolent abolishing of slavery as well as for women's emancipation

   (C)   a dedication to both the nonviolent abolition of slavery and the emancipation of women

   (D)   that she was dedicated both to abolishing slavery nonviolently and to emancipate women

   (E)   her dedication both to the nonviolent abolition of slavery and emancipation of women

Questions 304 to 348 - Difficulty: **Hard**

SC01972

304. <u>Less than 400 Sumatran rhinos survive on the Malay peninsula and on the islands of Sumatra and Borneo, and they occupy a small fraction of the species' former range.</u>

   (A)   Less than 400 Sumatran rhinos survive on the Malay peninsula and on the islands of Sumatra and Borneo, and they occupy a small fraction of the species' former range.

   (B)   Less than 400 Sumatran rhinos, surviving on the Malay peninsula and on the islands of Sumatra and Borneo, occupy a small fraction of the species' former range.

   (C)   Occupying a small fraction of the species' former range, the Malay peninsula and the islands of Sumatra and Borneo are where fewer than 400 Sumatran rhinos survive.

   (D)   Occupying a small fraction of the species' former range, fewer than 400 Sumatran rhinos survive on the Malay peninsula and on the islands of Sumatra and Borneo.

   (E)   Surviving on the Malay peninsula and on the islands of Sumatra and Borneo, less than 400 Sumatran rhinos occupy a small fraction of the species' former range.

SC11068

305. Certain pesticides can become ineffective if used repeatedly in the same place; one reason is suggested by the finding that there are much larger populations of pesticide-degrading microbes in soils with a relatively long history of pesticide use than in soils that are free of such chemicals.

(A) Certain pesticides can become ineffective if used repeatedly in the same place; one reason is suggested by the finding that there are much larger populations of pesticide-degrading microbes in soils with a relatively long history of pesticide use than in soils that are free of such chemicals.

(B) If used repeatedly in the same place, one reason that certain pesticides can become ineffective is suggested by the finding that there are much larger populations of pesticide-degrading microbes in soils with a relatively long history of pesticide use than in soils that are free of such chemicals.

(C) If used repeatedly in the same place, one reason certain pesticides can become ineffective is suggested by the finding that much larger populations of pesticide-degrading microbes are found in soils with a relatively long history of pesticide use than those that are free of such chemicals.

(D) The finding that there are much larger populations of pesticide-degrading microbes in soils with a relatively long history of pesticide use than in soils that are free of such chemicals is suggestive of one reason, if used repeatedly in the same place, certain pesticides can become ineffective.

(E) The finding of much larger populations of pesticide-degrading microbes in soils with a relatively long history of pesticide use than in those that are free of such chemicals suggests one reason certain pesticides can become ineffective if used repeatedly in the same place.

SC11854

306. While some academicians believe that business ethics should be integrated into every business course, others say that students will take ethics seriously only if it would be taught as a separately required course.

(A) only if it would be taught as a separately required course

(B) only if it is taught as a separate, required course

(C) if it is taught only as a course required separately

(D) if it was taught only as a separate and required course

(E) if it would only be taught as a required course, separately

SC08272

307. Whether they will scale back their orders to pre-2003 levels or stop doing business with us altogether depends on whether the changes that their management has proposed will be fully implemented.

(A) Whether they will scale back their orders to pre-2003 levels or stop doing business with us altogether depends on whether the changes that their management has proposed will be fully implemented.

(B) Whether they scale back their orders to pre-2003 levels or whether they discontinue their business with us altogether depends on the changes their management has proposed, if fully implemented or not.

(C) Their either scaling back their orders in the future to pre-2003 levels, or their outright termination of business with us, depends on their management's proposed changes being fully implemented or not.

(D) Whether they will scale back their orders to pre-2003 levels or stop doing business with us altogether depends if the changes that their management has proposed become fully implemented.

(E) They will either scale back their orders to pre-2003 levels, or they will stop doing business with us altogether dependent on whether the changes their management has proposed will be fully implemented, or not.

SC00975
308. <u>Until 1868 and Disraeli, Great Britain had no prime ministers not coming</u> from a landed family.

   (A) Until 1868 and Disraeli, Great Britain had no prime ministers not coming

   (B) Until 1868 and Disraeli, Great Britain had had no prime ministers who have not come

   (C) Until Disraeli in 1868, there were no prime ministers in Great Britain who have not come

   (D) It was not until 1868 that Great Britain had a prime minister—Disraeli—who did not come

   (E) It was only in 1868 and Disraeli that Great Britain had one of its prime ministers not coming

SC02011
309. Around 1900, fishermen in the Chesapeake Bay area landed more than seventeen million pounds of shad in a single year, but by 1920, overfishing and the proliferation of milldams and culverts <u>that have blocked shad migrations up their spawning streams had reduced landings to less</u> than four million pounds.

   (A) that have blocked shad migrations up their spawning streams had reduced landings to less

   (B) that blocked shad from migrating up their spawning streams had reduced landings to less

   (C) that blocked shad from migrating up their spawning streams reduced landings to a lower amount

   (D) having blocked shad from migrating up their spawning streams reduced landings to less

   (E) having blocked shad migrations up their spawning streams had reduced landings to an amount lower

SC04492
310. By offering lower prices and a menu of personal communications options, such as caller identification and voice mail, the new telecommunications company <u>has not only captured customers from other phone companies but also forced them</u> to offer competitive prices.

   (A) has not only captured customers from other phone companies but also forced them

   (B) has not only captured customers from other phone companies, but it also forced them

   (C) has not only captured customers from other phone companies but also forced these companies

   (D) not only has captured customers from other phone companies but also these companies have been forced

   (E) not only captured customers from other phone companies, but it also has forced them

SC06132
311. After suffering $2 billion in losses and 25,000 layoffs, the nation's semiconductor industry, which makes chips that run everything from <u>computers and spy satellites to dishwashers, appears to have</u> made a long-awaited recovery.

   (A) computers and spy satellites to dishwashers, appears to have

   (B) computers, spy satellites, and dishwashers, appears having

   (C) computers, spy satellites, and dishwashers, appears that it has

   (D) computers and spy satellites to dishwashers, appears that it has

   (E) computers and spy satellites as well as dishwashers, appears to have

SC04588
312. <u>Over a range of frequencies from 100 to 5,000 hertz, monkeys and marmosets have a hearing sensitivity remarkably similar to humans,</u> above which the sensitivity begins to differ.

   (A) Over a range of frequencies from 100 to 5,000 hertz, monkeys and marmosets have a hearing sensitivity remarkably similar to humans

   (B) Compared to humans, the hearing sensitivity of monkeys and marmosets are remarkably similar over a range of frequencies from 100 to 5,000 hertz

   (C) Compared to humans over a range of frequencies from 100 to 5,000 hertz, the hearing sensitivity of monkeys and marmosets is remarkably similar

   (D) The hearing sensitivity of monkeys and marmosets, when compared to humans over a range of frequencies from 100 to 5,000 hertz, is remarkably similar

   (E) The hearing sensitivity of monkeys, marmosets, and humans is remarkably similar over a range of frequencies from 100 to 5,000 hertz

SC03998

313. The computer company has announced that it will purchase the color-printing division of a rival company for $950 million, which is part of a deal that will make it the largest manufacturer in the office color-printing market.

   (A)   million, which is part of a deal that will make

   (B)   million, a part of a deal that makes

   (C)   million, a part of a deal making

   (D)   million as a part of a deal to make

   (E)   million as part of a deal that will make

SC03289

314. Kudzu, an Asian vine that has grown rampantly in the southern United States since introducing it in the 1920s to thwart soil erosion, has overrun many houses and countless acres of roadside.

   (A)   that has grown rampantly in the southern United States since introducing it in the 1920s to thwart

   (B)   that has grown rampantly in the southern United States, since it was introduced in the 1920s for thwarting

   (C)   that has grown rampant in the southern United States since it was introduced in the 1920s to thwart

   (D)   growing rampant in the southern United States since introducing it in the 1920s for thwarting

   (E)   growing rampantly in the southern United States, since it was introduced in the 1920s to thwart

SC01712

315. Unable to build nests or care for their young, a female cowbird lays up to 40 eggs a year in the nests of other birds, including warblers, vireos, flycatchers, and thrushes.

   (A)   a female cowbird lays up to 40 eggs a year in the nests of other birds, including

   (B)   a female cowbird will use the nests of other birds to lay up to 40 eggs a year, including those of

   (C)   female cowbirds use the nests of other birds to lay up to 40 eggs a year, including those of

   (D)   female cowbirds lay up to 40 eggs a year in the nests of other birds, including

   (E)   up to 40 eggs a year are laid by female cowbirds in the nests of other birds, including

SC01954

316. Bluegrass musician Bill Monroe, whose repertory, views on musical collaboration, and vocal style were influential on generations of bluegrass artists, was also an inspiration to many musicians, that included Elvis Presley and Jerry Garcia, whose music differed significantly from his own.

   (A)   were influential on generations of bluegrass artists, was also an inspiration to many musicians, that included Elvis Presley and Jerry Garcia, whose music differed significantly from

   (B)   influenced generations of bluegrass artists, also inspired many musicians, including Elvis Presley and Jerry Garcia, whose music differed significantly from

   (C)   was influential to generations of bluegrass artists, was also inspirational to many musicians, that included Elvis Presley and Jerry Garcia, whose music was different significantly in comparison to

   (D)   was influential to generations of bluegrass artists, also inspired many musicians, who included Elvis Presley and Jerry Garcia, the music of whom differed significantly when compared to

   (E)   were an influence on generations of bluegrass artists, was also an inspiration to many musicians, including Elvis Presley and Jerry Garcia, whose music was significantly different from that of

SC12645

317. In many of the world's regions, increasing pressure on water resources has resulted <u>both from expanding development, changes in climate, and from pollution, so that the future supply in some of the more arid areas is a concern going forward</u>.

(A) both from expanding development, changes in climate, and from pollution, so that the future supply in some of the more arid areas is a concern going forward

(B) both from expanding development or changes in climate, and pollution, so that future supplies in some of the more arid areas are a concern

(C) from expanding development, changes in climate, and also from pollution, so that the future supply in some of the more arid areas is a matter of concern going forward

(D) from expanding development, changes in climate, and pollution, so that future supplies in some of the more arid areas are a concern

(E) from expansion of development, changes in climate, and from pollution, so that supplies in some of the more arid areas are a future concern

SC01747

318. The computer company's present troubles are a result of technological stagnation, marketing missteps, and managerial blunders <u>so that several attempts to revise corporate strategies have failed to correct it</u>.

(A) so that several attempts to revise corporate strategies have failed to correct it

(B) so that several attempts at revising corporate strategies have failed to correct

(C) in that several attempts at revising corporate strategies have failed to correct them

(D) that several attempts to revise corporate strategies have failed to correct

(E) that several attempts at revising corporate strategies have failed to correct them

SC11880

319. The root systems of most flowering perennials either become too crowded, <u>which results in loss in vigor, and spread</u> too far outward, producing a bare center.

(A) which results in loss in vigor, and spread

(B) resulting in loss in vigor, or spreading

(C) with the result of loss of vigor, or spreading

(D) resulting in loss of vigor, or spread

(E) with a resulting loss of vigor, and spread

SC11910

320. In theory, international civil servants at the United Nations are prohibited from continuing to draw salaries from their own governments; in practice, however, some governments merely substitute living allowances <u>for their employees' paychecks, assigned by them</u> to the United Nations.

(A) for their employees' paychecks, assigned by them

(B) for the paychecks of their employees who have been assigned

(C) for the paychecks of their employees, having been assigned

(D) in place of their employees' paychecks, for those of them assigned

(E) in place of the paychecks of their employees to have been assigned by them

SC05216

321. Industry analysts said that the recent rise in fuel prices may be an early signal <u>of the possibility of gasoline and heating oil prices staying higher than usually through</u> the end of the year.

(A) of the possibility of gasoline and heating oil prices staying higher than usually through

(B) of the possibility that gasoline and heating oil prices could stay higher than usual throughout

(C) of prices of gasoline and heating oil possibly staying higher than usually through

(D) that prices of gasoline and heating oil could stay higher than they usually are throughout

(E) that prices of gasoline and heating oil will stay higher than usual through

SC07141

322. The Anasazi settlements at Chaco Canyon were built on a spectacular scale, with more than 75 carefully engineered structures, of up to 600 rooms each, were connected by a complex regional system of roads.

   (A) scale, with more than 75 carefully engineered structures, of up to 600 rooms each, were

   (B) scale, with more than 75 carefully engineered structures, of up to 600 rooms each,

   (C) scale of more than 75 carefully engineered structures of up to 600 rooms, each that had been

   (D) scale of more than 75 carefully engineered structures of up to 600 rooms and with each

   (E) scale of more than 75 carefully engineered structures of up to 600 rooms, each had been

SC07066

323. Even though the overall consumer price index did not change in April, indicating the absence of any general inflation or deflation, prices in several categories of merchandise have fallen over the last several months.

   (A) April, indicating the absence of any general inflation or deflation, prices in several categories of merchandise have fallen

   (B) April, indicating that any general inflation or deflation were absent, prices in several categories of merchandise fell

   (C) April and indicated that absence of any general inflation or deflation, prices in several categories of merchandise fell

   (D) April, having indicated the absence of any general inflation or deflation, prices in several categories of merchandise fell

   (E) April, which indicated that any general inflation or deflation were absent, prices in several categories of merchandise have fallen

SC12460

324. Despite Japan's relative isolation from world trade at the time, the prolonged peace during the Tokugawa shogunate produced an almost explosive expansion of commerce.

   (A) Japan's relative isolation from world trade at the time, the prolonged peace during the Tokugawa shogunate

   (B) the relative isolation of Japan from world trade at the time and the Tokugawa shogunate's prolonged peace, it

   (C) being relatively isolated from world trade at the time, the prolonged peace during Japan's Tokugawa shogunate

   (D) Japan's relative isolation from world trade at the time during the Tokugawa shogunate, prolonged peace

   (E) its relative isolation from world trade then, prolonged peace in Japan during the Tokugawa shogunate

SC02333

325. Government officials announced that restrictions on the use of water would continue because no appreciative increase in the level of the river resulted from the intermittent showers that had fallen throughout the area the day before.

   (A) restrictions on the use of water would continue because no appreciative increase in the level of the river

   (B) restricting the use of water would continue because there had not been any appreciative increase in the river's level that

   (C) the use of water would continue to be restricted because not any appreciable increase in the river's level had

   (D) restrictions on the use of water would continue because no appreciable increase in the level of the river had

   (E) using water would continue being restricted because not any appreciable increase in the level of the river

SC04732

326. According to United States census data, <u>while there was about one-third of mothers with young children working outside the home in 1975, in 2000, almost two-thirds of those mothers were employed outside the home.</u>

   (A)   while there was about one-third of mothers with young children working outside the home in 1975, in 2000, almost two-thirds of those mothers were employed outside the home

   (B)   there were about one-third of mothers with young children who worked outside the home in 1975; in 2000, almost two-thirds of those mothers were employed outside the home

   (C)   in 1975 about one-third of mothers with young children worked outside the home; in 2000, almost two-thirds of such mothers were employed outside the home

   (D)   even though in 1975 there were about one-third of mothers with young children who worked outside the home, almost two-thirds of such mothers were employed outside the home in 2000

   (E)   with about one-third of mothers with young children working outside the home in 1975, almost two-thirds of such mothers were employed outside the home in 2000

SC04672

327. <u>Clouds are formed from the evaporation of the oceans' water that is warmed by the sun and rises high into the atmosphere, condensing in tiny droplets on minute particles of dust.</u>

   (A)   Clouds are formed from the evaporation of the oceans' water that is warmed by the sun and rises high into the atmosphere, condensing in tiny droplets on minute particles of dust.

   (B)   Clouds form by the sun's warmth evaporating the water in the oceans, which rises high into the atmosphere, condensing in tiny droplets on minute particles of dust.

   (C)   Warmed by the sun, ocean water evaporates, rises high into the atmosphere, and condenses in tiny droplets on minute particles of dust to form clouds.

   (D)   The water in the oceans evaporates, warmed by the sun, rises high into the atmosphere, and condenses in tiny droplets on minute particles of dust, which forms clouds.

   (E)   Ocean water, warmed by the sun, evaporates and rises high into the atmosphere, which then condenses in tiny droplets on minute particles of dust to form as clouds.

SC02664

328. Schistosomiasis, a disease caused by a parasitic worm, is prevalent in hot, humid climates, and it has become more widespread as irrigation projects have enlarged the habitat of <u>the freshwater snails that are the parasite's hosts for part of its life cycle.</u>

   (A)   the freshwater snails that are the parasite's hosts for part of its life cycle

   (B)   the freshwater snails that are the parasite's hosts in part of their life cycle

   (C)   freshwater snails which become the parasite's hosts for part of its life cycles

   (D)   freshwater snails which become the hosts of the parasite during the parasite's life cycles

   (E)   parasite's hosts, freshwater snails which become their hosts during their life cycles

SC07754

329. Sor Juana Inés de la Cruz was making the case for women's equality long before the cause had a name: Born in the mid-seventeenth century in San Miguel Nepantla, Mexico, <u>the convent was the perfect environment for Sor Juana to pursue intellectual pursuits, achieving</u> renown as a mathematician, poet, philosopher, and playwright.

   (A)   the convent was the perfect environment for Sor Juana to pursue intellectual pursuits, achieving

   (B)   Sor Juana found the convent provided the perfect environment for intellectual pursuits, and she went on to achieve

   (C)   the convent provided the perfect environment for intellectual pursuits for Sor Juana; going on to achieve

   (D)   Sor Juana found the convent provided the perfect environment for intellectual pursuits; achieving

   (E)   the convent was, Sor Juana found, the perfect environment for intellectual pursuits, and she went on to achieve

SC14406

330. By devising an instrument made from a rod, wire, and lead balls, and employing uncommonly precise measurements, in 1797–1798 Henry Cavendish's apparatus enabled him to arrive at an astonishingly accurate figure for the weight of the earth.

(A) By devising an instrument made from a rod, wire, and lead balls, and employing uncommonly precise measurements, in 1797–1798 Henry Cavendish's apparatus enabled him

(B) In 1797–1798, by devising an instrument made from a rod, wire, and lead balls, and employing uncommonly precise measurements, Henry Cavendish's apparatus enabled him

(C) Henry Cavendish devised an instrument made from a rod, wire, and lead balls, and employed uncommonly precise measurements, and in 1797–1798 was able

(D) Having devised an instrument from a rod, wire, and lead balls, and employment of uncommonly precise measurements, Henry Cavendish in 1797–1798 was able

(E) By devising an instrument made from a rod, wire, and lead balls, and employing uncommonly precise measurements, Henry Cavendish was able in 1797–1798

SC08285

331. The growth projected for these storms in different computerized weather models varies widely.

(A) projected for these storms in different computerized weather models varies widely

(B) for these storms is projected in different computerized models of weather to vary widely

(C) of these storms, projected in different computerized weather models, vary widely

(D) projected for these storms, which vary widely in different computerized weather models

(E) that varies widely for these storms are projected in different computerized weather models

SC02131

332. By using a process called echolocation to analyze the echoes of the high-pitched sounds they produce, bats can determine not only the distance to an object, but they also can determine its shape and size and the direction in which it is moving.

(A) can determine not only the distance to an object, but they also can determine

(B) not only can determine the distance to an object but also

(C) can determine not only the distance to an object but also

(D) not only can determine its distance from an object but also

(E) can determine not only their distance from an object, but they can also determine

SC06205

333. Carbon dioxide, which traps heat in the atmosphere and helps regulate the planet's surface temperature, is constantly being exchanged between the atmosphere on the one hand and the oceans and terrestrial plants on the other.

(A) exchanged between the atmosphere on the one hand and the oceans and terrestrial plants on the other

(B) exchanged, on the one hand, between the atmosphere and the oceans and terrestrial plants, on the other

(C) exchanged between, on the one hand, the atmosphere, with the oceans and terrestrial plants, on the other

(D) exchanged, on the one hand, among the oceans and terrestrial plants, and the atmosphere, on the other

(E) exchanged among the oceans and terrestrial plants on the one hand and the atmosphere on the other

SC01990

334. Floating in the waters of the equatorial Pacific, an array of buoys collects and transmits data on long-term interactions between the ocean and the atmosphere, interactions that affect global climate.

(A) atmosphere, interactions that affect

(B) atmosphere, with interactions affecting

(C) atmosphere that affects

(D) atmosphere that is affecting

(E) atmosphere as affects

SC04344

335. Sixty-five million years ago, according to some scientists, an asteroid bigger than Mount Everest slammed into North America, which, causing plant and animal extinctions, marks the end of the geologic era known as the Cretaceous Period.

    (A)   which, causing plant and animal extinctions, marks

    (B)   which caused the plant and animal extinctions and marks

    (C)   and causing plant and animal extinctions that mark

    (D)   an event that caused plant and animal extinctions, which marks

    (E)   an event that caused the plant and animal extinctions that mark

SC02338

336. Although the first pulsar, or rapidly spinning collapsed star, to be sighted was in the summer of 1967 by graduate student Jocelyn Bell, it had not been announced until February 1968.

    (A)   Although the first pulsar, or rapidly spinning collapsed star, to be sighted was in the summer of 1967 by graduate student Jocelyn Bell, it had not been announced until February 1968.

    (B)   Although not announced until February 1968, in the summer of 1967 graduate student Jocelyn Bell observed the first pulsar, or rapidly spinning collapsed star, to be sighted.

    (C)   Although observed by graduate student Jocelyn Bell in the summer of 1967, the discovery of the first sighted pulsar, or rapidly spinning collapsed star, had not been announced before February 1968.

    (D)   The first pulsar, or rapidly spinning collapsed star, to be sighted was observed in the summer of 1967 by graduate student Jocelyn Bell, but the discovery was not announced until February 1968.

    (E)   The first sighted pulsar, or rapidly spinning collapsed star, was not announced until February 1968, while it was observed in the summer of 1967 by graduate student Jocelyn Bell.

SC02766

337. Sound can travel through water for enormous distances, prevented from dissipating its acoustic energy as a result of boundaries in the ocean created by water layers of different temperatures and densities.

    (A)   prevented from dissipating its acoustic energy as a result of

    (B)   prevented from having its acoustic energy dissipated by

    (C)   its acoustic energy prevented from dissipating by

    (D)   its acoustic energy prevented from being dissipated as a result of

    (E)   preventing its acoustic energy from dissipating by

SC10996

338. Last year, land values in most parts of the pinelands rose almost so fast, and in some parts even faster than what they did outside the pinelands.

    (A)   so fast, and in some parts even faster than what they did

    (B)   so fast, and in some parts even faster than, those

    (C)   as fast, and in some parts even faster than, those

    (D)   as fast as, and in some parts even faster than, those

    (E)   as fast as, and in some parts even faster than what they did

SC03010

339. The North American moose's long legs enable it to move quickly through the woods, stepping easily over downed trees, but predators pursuing it must leap or go around them.

(A) moose's long legs enable it to move quickly through the woods, stepping easily over downed trees, but predators pursuing it must leap or go around them

(B) moose's long legs enable it to move quickly through the woods, stepping easily over downed trees while predators pursuing them must leap or go around

(C) moose's long legs enable it to move quickly through the woods and to step easily over downed trees, but predators pursuing them must leap over or go around them

(D) moose has long legs, enabling it to move quickly through the woods and to step easily over downed trees while predators pursuing them must leap or go around

(E) moose has long legs that enable it to move quickly through the woods, stepping easily over downed trees while predators pursuing it must leap over or go around them

SC07885

340. Early administrative decisions in China's Ming Dynasty eventually caused a drastic fall in tax revenues, a reduction in military preparedness, the collapse of the currency system, and failed to make sufficient investment in vital transportation infrastructure.

(A) the collapse of the currency system, and failed

(B) the collapse of the currency system, and failing

(C) and the collapse of the currency system, also failed

(D) the collapse of the currency system, as well as failing

(E) and the collapse of the currency system, as well as a failure

SC11017

341. Seismologists studying the earthquake that struck northern California in October 1989 are still investigating some of its mysteries: the unexpected power of the seismic waves, the upward thrust that threw one man straight into the air, and the strange electromagnetic signals detected hours before the temblor.

(A) the upward thrust that threw one man straight into the air, and the strange electromagnetic signals detected hours before the temblor

(B) the upward thrust that threw one man straight into the air, and strange electromagnetic signals were detected hours before the temblor

(C) the upward thrust threw one man straight into the air, and hours before the temblor strange electromagnetic signals were detected

(D) one man was thrown straight into the air by the upward thrust, and hours before the temblor strange electromagnetic signals were detected

(E) one man who was thrown straight into the air by the upward thrust, and strange electromagnetic signals that were detected hours before the temblor

SC10878

342. The type of behavior exhibited when an animal recognizes itself in a mirror comes within the domain of "theory of mind," thus is best studied as part of the field of animal cognition.

(A) of "theory of mind," thus is best

(B) "theory of mind," and so is best to be

(C) of a "theory of mind," thus it is best

(D) of "theory of mind" and thus is best

(E) of the "theory of mind," and so it is best to be

SC11054

343. Unlike the United States, where farmers can usually depend on rain or snow all year long, the rains in most parts of Sri Lanka are concentrated in the monsoon months, June to September, and the skies are generally clear for the rest of the year.

    (A) Unlike the United States, where farmers can usually depend on rain or snow all year long, the rains in most parts of Sri Lanka

    (B) Unlike the United States farmers who can usually depend on rain or snow all year long, the rains in most parts of Sri Lanka

    (C) Unlike those of the United States, where farmers can usually depend on rain or snow all year long, most parts of Sri Lanka's rains

    (D) In comparison with the United States, whose farmers can usually depend on rain or snow all year long, the rains in most parts of Sri Lanka

    (E) In the United States, farmers can usually depend on rain or snow all year long, but in most parts of Sri Lanka, the rains

SC01564

344. In preparation for the prediction of a major earthquake that will hit the state, a satellite-based computer network is being built by the California Office of Emergency Services for identifying earthquake damage and to pinpoint the most affected areas within two hours of the event.

    (A) In preparation for the prediction of a major earthquake that will hit the state, a satellite-based computer network is being built by the California Office of Emergency Services for identifying

    (B) In preparing for the prediction that a major earthquake will hit the state, the California Office of Emergency Services is building a satellite-based computer network that will identify

    (C) In preparing for a major earthquake that is predicted to hit the state, the California Office of Emergency Services is building a satellite-based computer network to identify

    (D) To prepare for the prediction of a major earthquake hitting the state, a satellite-based computer network is being built by the California Office of Emergency Services to identify

    (E) To prepare for a major earthquake that is predicted to hit the state, the California Office of Emergency Services is building a satellite-based computer network that will identify

SC06727

345. Once numbering in the millions worldwide, it is estimated that the wolf has declined to 200,000 in 57 countries, some 11,000 of them to be found in the lower 48 United States and Alaska.

    (A) it is estimated that the wolf has declined to 200,000 in 57 countries, some

    (B) the wolf is estimated to have declined to 200,000 in 57 countries, with approximately

    (C) the wolf has declined to an estimate of 200,000 in 57 countries, some

    (D) wolves have declined to an estimate of 200,000 in 57 countries, with approximately

    (E) wolves have declined to an estimated 200,000 in 57 countries, some

SC11926

346. As business grows more complex, students majoring in specialized areas like those of finance and marketing have been becoming increasingly successful in the job market.

    (A) majoring in specialized areas like those of finance and marketing have been becoming increasingly

    (B) who major in such specialized areas as finance and marketing are becoming more and more

    (C) who majored in specialized areas such as those of finance and marketing are being increasingly

    (D) who major in specialized areas like those of finance and marketing have been becoming more and more

    (E) having majored in such specialized areas as finance and marketing are being increasingly

SC04682

347. Created in 1945 to reduce poverty and stabilize foreign currency markets, the World Bank and the International Monetary Fund have, according to some critics, continually struggled to meet the expectations of their major shareholders—a group comprising many of the world's rich nations—but neglected their intended beneficiaries in the developing world.

  (A) continually struggled to meet the expectations of their major shareholders—a group comprising many of the world's rich nations—but neglected

  (B) continually struggled as they try to meet the expectations of their major shareholders—a group comprising many of the world's rich nations—while neglecting that of

  (C) continually struggled to meet their major shareholders' expectations—a group comprising many of the world's rich nations—but neglected that of

  (D) had to struggle continually in trying to meet the expectations of their major shareholders—a group comprising many of the world's rich nations—while neglecting that of

  (E) struggled continually in trying to meet their major shareholders' expectations—a group comprising many of the world's rich nations—and neglecting

SC11934

348. Unlike auto insurance, the frequency of claims does not affect the premiums for personal property coverage, but if the insurance company is able to prove excessive loss due to owner negligence, it may decline to renew the policy.

  (A) Unlike auto insurance, the frequency of claims does not affect the premiums for personal property coverage,

  (B) Unlike with auto insurance, the frequency of claims do not affect the premiums for personal property coverage,

  (C) Unlike the frequency of claims for auto insurance, the premiums for personal property coverage are not affected by the frequency of claims,

  (D) Unlike the premiums for auto insurance, the premiums for personal property coverage are not affected by the frequency of claims,

  (E) Unlike with the premiums for auto insurance, the premiums for personal property coverage is not affected by the frequency of claims,

6.8 Answer Key

234.	C	257.	B	280.	B	303.	C	326.	C
235.	A	258.	E	281.	D	304.	D	327.	C
236.	C	259.	A	282.	B	305.	A	328.	A
237.	E	260.	B	283.	A	306.	B	329.	B
238.	E	261.	B	284.	B	307.	A	330.	E
239.	E	262.	C	285.	C	308.	D	331.	A
240.	C	263.	A	286.	C	309.	B	332.	C
241.	D	264.	C	287.	C	310.	C	333.	A
242.	E	265.	C	288.	B	311.	A	334.	A
243.	D	266.	A	289.	A	312.	E	335.	E
244.	B	267.	C	290.	A	313.	E	336.	D
245.	E	268.	B	291.	D	314.	C	337.	C
246.	C	269.	A	292.	E	315.	D	338.	D
247.	E	270.	A	293.	C	316.	B	339.	E
248.	C	271.	C	294.	B	317.	D	340.	E
249.	B	272.	D	295.	A	318.	D	341.	A
250.	A	273.	C	296.	D	319.	D	342.	D
251.	C	274.	E	297.	C	320.	B	343.	E
252.	E	275.	C	298.	A	321.	E	344.	C
253.	E	276.	E	299.	E	322.	B	345.	E
254.	C	277.	E	300.	A	323.	A	346.	B
255.	D	278.	E	301.	D	324.	A	347.	A
256.	B	279.	D	302.	D	325.	D	348.	D

6.9 Answer Explanations

The following discussion of Sentence Correction is intended to familiarize you with the most efficient and effective approaches to these kinds of questions. The particular questions in this chapter are generally representative of the kinds of Sentence Correction questions you will encounter on the GMAT™ exam.

Questions 234 to 268 - Difficulty: **Easy**

*SC01545

234. <u>With respect to most species of animals, they are evenly divided in right- or left-handedness, unlike humans.</u>

   (A)   With respect to most species of animals, they are evenly divided in right- or left-handedness, unlike humans.

   (B)   With respect to right- or left-handedness, most species of animals are evenly divided, unlike in humans.

   (C)   Unlike humans, most species of animals are evenly divided with respect to right- or left-handedness.

   (D)   Unlike in humans, most species of animals with respect to right- or left-handedness are evenly divided.

   (E)   Unlike humans, with respect to right- or left-handedness, in most species of animals it is evenly divided.

Rhetorical Construction; Parallel Construction

The sentence contrasts humans with other species with respect to the distribution of left-handedness and right-handedness. Issues include use of the correct prepositions and the correct placement of component phrases such as *unlike humans*.

A   This is wordy because the phrase beginning *with respect to* is redundant, given the pronoun *they*, which refers to *most species of animals*. Placing the phrase *unlike humans* at the end of the sentence tends to blunt the force of the comparison between humans and other animals.

B   The *in* preceding *humans* makes the sentence incorrect. Because the intended contrast is between humans and most species of animals, the reference to humans would be better placed closer to the phrase *most species of animals*.

C   **Correct.** The start of the sentence immediately highlights the contrast between humans and most animal species. The adverbial phrase *with respect to right- or left-handedness* is placed adjacent to the verbal phrase that it modifies (*are evenly divided*).

D   The *in* preceding *humans* makes the sentence incorrect. Placing the adverbial phrase *with respect to right- or left-handedness* immediately following *animals* is confusing; it would be better placed immediately following the verbal phrase that it modifies (*are evenly divided*).

E   To make the intended contrast clear, the reference to humans should be adjacent to (and parallel to) the reference to most species of animals. But the use of *in* in one case but not in the other makes the references nonparallel. For clarity, the adverbial phrase *with respect to right- or left-handedness* should follow the verbal phrase that it modifies (*are evenly divided*).

The correct answer is C.

SC07435

235. Using digital enhancements of skull fragments from five prehistoric hominids dating to more than 350,000 years ago, <u>anthropologists argue that these human ancestors</u> probably had hearing similar to that of people today.

   (A)   anthropologists argue that these human ancestors

   (B)   anthropologists argue, so these human ancestors

   (C)   anthropologists argue, these human ancestors

   (D)   these human ancestors, anthropologists argue,

   (E)   these human ancestors are argued by anthropologists to have

*These numbers correlate with the online test bank question number. See the GMAT™ Official Guide Verbal Review Question Index in the back of this book.

430

Logical Predication; Diction

The verb *argue* here, because it expresses the idea of arguing for a position or theory, should be followed directly by a clause introduced by *that*, without a pause. Verb forms ending with –*ing* with understood subjects, like the one beginning this sentence, must have their subject supplied elsewhere—preferably by the subject of the main clause.

A **Correct.** *Argue* is followed immediately by a *that* clause, and the subject of *using* is supplied by *anthropologists*.

B *Argue* is not directly followed by a *that* clause; moreover, by continuing with *so ...*, the sentence does not coherently express the intended idea.

C *Argue* is not directly followed by a *that* clause.

D The subject of the main clause, *these human ancestors*, will illogically be taken as the subject of *using*.

E The subject of the main clause, *these human ancestors*, will illogically be taken as the subject of *using*.

The correct answer is A.

SC14890

236. The interior minister explained that <u>one of the village planning proposal's best characteristics was their not detracting</u> from the project's overall benefit by being a burden on the development budget.

(A) one of the village planning proposal's best characteristics was their not detracting

(B) one of the village's planning proposal's best characteristics were its not taking

(C) one of the best characteristics of the village's planning proposal was that it did not detract

(D) a best characteristic of the village planning proposal was, it did not take

(E) among the village planning proposal's best characteristics, one was, it did not detract

Agreement; Rhetorical Construction

The noun phrase beginning with *one* is singular, as is one of its constituent parts, *the village planning proposal*, so any pronouns for which it is the antecedent should be singular; furthermore, any verb for which the noun phrase beginning with *one ...* is the subject should be in the singular. The verb *detract* is more appropriate to the thought being expressed than *take*.

A The plural pronoun *their* has a singular noun phrase as its antecedent, namely, *the village planning proposal*. (It is illogical to take the antecedent of *their* to be *best characteristics*.)

B The plural verb *were* does not agree with the singular subject. Also, the verb *taking* should be replaced by the verb *detracting*.

C **Correct.** The verb is correctly in the singular form.

D *A best characteristic* is awkward; the idea is better phrased as *one of the best characteristics*. Also the verb *take* should be replaced by the verb *detract*.

E Instead of the awkward sequence *one was, it did not*, a better choice would be *was that it did not*.

The correct answer is C.

SC02940

237. Like ants, termites have an elaborate social structure in which a few individuals reproduce and the rest <u>are serving the colony by tending juveniles, gathering food, building the nest, or they battle</u> intruders.

(A) are serving the colony by tending juveniles, gathering food, building the nest, or they battle

(B) are serving the colony in that they tend juveniles, gather food, build the nest, or battle

(C) serve the colony, tending juveniles, gathering food, building the nest, or by battling

(D) serve the colony by tending juveniles, gathering food, by building the nest, or by battling

(E) serve the colony by tending juveniles, gathering food, building the nest, or battling

Parallelism; Rhetorical Construction

The sentence most effectively uses parallel structure to contrast two types of termites in the social structure of termite colonies: those who reproduce, and those who serve the colony in a number of ways. The progressive verb form *are serving* should be changed to simple present tense *serve* to parallel *reproduce*. In the final list of responsibilities, parallelism demands that all assume the gerund form as objects of the preposition: *by tending … gathering … building … or battling*.

A   The progressive verb form *are serving* is inappropriate for this general claim about termite behavior. It should parallel the previous verb *reproduce*. It is unnecessary to introduce a new clause *or they battle intruders*, because *battling* is another way some termites serve the colony and should therefore be expressed as another object of the preposition *by*.

B   *In that they* is an awkward and wordy construction—a poor substitute for *by* in this context.

C   The preposition *by* clarifies *how* the termites serve their colony and should govern all of the task descriptions, not just the final one.

D   There is no need to repeat the preposition *by*, because all tasks can be described in a series of parallel objects of the same preposition. To violate parallel structure by omitting the preposition before one gerund but repeating it for the rest confuses the reader.

E   **Correct.** The sentence uses proper parallel structure and is clear and concise.

The correct answer is E.

SC01519

238. Global warming is said to be responsible for extreme weather changes, <u>which, like the heavy rains that caused more than $2 billion in damages and led to flooding throughout the state of California,</u> and the heat wave in the northeastern and midwestern United States, which was also the cause of a great amount of damage and destruction.

(A)   which, like the heavy rains that caused more than $2 billion in damages and led to flooding throughout the state of California,

(B)   which, like the heavy rains that throughout the state of California caused more than $2 billion in damages and led to flooding,

(C)   like the heavy flooding that, because of rains throughout the state of California, caused more than $2 billion in damages,

(D)   such as the heavy flooding that led to rains throughout the state of California causing more than $2 billion in damages,

(E)   such as the heavy rains that led to flooding throughout the state of California, causing more than $2 billion in damages,

Grammatical Construction: Logical Predication

This sentence introduces the claim that global warming is considered to be the cause of extreme weather changes and then illustrates these changes with two examples introduced by the phrase *such as*. The correct causal sequence of events in the first example is heavy rain, which caused *significant damage and flooding*. The relative pronoun *which*, referring to *changes*, is lacking a verb to complete the relative clause.

A   The relative pronoun, *which*, is without a verb. The phrase *which, like the heavy rains* incorrectly suggests that the *extreme weather* is something different from the *heavy rains* and the *heat wave*, and that each of these three phenomena separately caused damage and destruction.

B   Like answer choice A, the relative pronoun has no verb to complete the phrase, and the sequence of events in the first example positions costly destruction and flooding as two separate or unrelated results of the rain.

C   The causal sequence in the first example is confusing, suggesting, somewhat implausibly, that heavy flooding occurred on its own but caused damage only because of the rain.

D   The sequential logic of the first example is confused—indicating, implausibly, that flooding caused heavy rain and that the rain, but not the flooding, caused more than $2 billion in damages.

E   Correct. This version of the sentence correctly uses the phrase *such as* to introduce the two examples of extreme weather changes, and it correctly identifies the sequence of events in the first example.

The correct answer is E.

SC02548

239.   Hundreds of species of fish generate and discharge electric currents, in bursts or as steady electric fields around their bodies, using their power either to find and attack prey, to defend themselves, or also for communicating and navigating.

   (A)   either to find and attack prey, to defend themselves, or also for communicating and navigating

   (B)   either for finding and attacking prey, defend themselves, or for communication and navigation

   (C)   to find and attack prey, for defense, or communication and navigation

   (D)   for finding and attacking prey, to defend themselves, or also for communication and navigation

   (E)   to find and attack prey, to defend themselves, or to communicate and navigate

Idiom; Verb Form

The sentence explains that fish discharge electric currents for several purposes, which are most efficiently and effectively described in a parallel structure: *to find and attack*, *to defend*, *or to communicate and navigate*. The use of *either* is inappropriate in this sentence because more than two uses of electric currents are listed; idiomatic usage requires *either* to be followed by *or* to identify alternatives, not by *also*.

A   *Either* inappropriately introduces a list of more than two alternatives, and it should not be followed by *or also*; parallelism requires that *for communicating and navigating* be changed to *to communicate and navigate*.

B   *Defend* is not parallel with the list of gerunds, leaving the reader to wonder how to make sense of *defend themselves*.

C   The lack of parallelism obscures the relationships among the items in the series; it is especially confusing to list an infinitive phrase (*to find …*), an object of a preposition (*for defense*), and nouns with no grammatical connection to the verb phrase (*communication and navigation*).

D   This answer choice also violates parallelism by mixing an infinitive with objects of the preposition *for*. *Or also* is an unidiomatic, contradictory expression.

E   Correct. The different ways in which the various species of fish use their electric power are correctly expressed in a series of parallel infinitives.

The correct answer is E.

SC05367

240.   Native to South America, when peanuts were introduced to Africa by Portuguese explorers early in the sixteenth century they were quickly adopted into Africa's agriculture, probably because of being so similar to the Bambarra groundnut, a popular indigenous plant.

   (A)   when peanuts were introduced to Africa by Portuguese explorers early in the sixteenth century they were quickly adopted into Africa's agriculture, probably because of being

   (B)   peanuts having been introduced to Africa by Portuguese explorers early in the sixteenth century and quickly adopted into Africa's agriculture, probably because of being

   (C)   peanuts were introduced to Africa by Portuguese explorers early in the sixteenth century and were quickly adopted into Africa's agriculture, probably because they were

   (D)   peanuts, introduced to Africa by Portuguese explorers early in the sixteenth century and quickly adopted into Africa's agriculture, probably because they were

   (E)   peanuts, introduced to Africa by Portuguese explorers early in the sixteenth century and having been quickly adopted into Africa's agriculture, probably because they were

Grammatical Construction; Logical Predication

The opening adjectival phrase *Native to South America* must be followed immediately by the noun it modifies: *peanuts*. The sentence makes two main points about peanuts—they were introduced to Africa and they were quickly adopted there. The most efficient way to make these points is to make *peanuts* the subject of two main verbs: *were introduced* and *were … adopted*.

A   *When* incorrectly intervenes between the opening adjectival phrase and the noun it modifies, and it is also unnecessary because *early in the sixteenth century* explains when. *Because of being* is wordy and indirect.

B   This version of the sentence has no main verb, since *having been introduced* and *quickly adopted* both introduce adjectival phrases.

C   Correct. The sentence is properly structured and grammatically correct.

D   This version of the sentence has no main verb because *introduced* and *adopted* both function as adjectives.

E   This version of the sentence has no main verb because *introduced* and *having been … adopted* function as adjectives.

The correct answer is C.

SC03552

241. It stood twelve feet tall, weighed nine thousand pounds, and wielded seven-inch claws, and *Megatherium americanum, a giant ground sloth,* may have been the largest hunting mammal ever to walk the Earth.

(A)   It stood twelve feet tall, weighed nine thousand pounds, and wielded seven-inch claws, and *Megatherium americanum, a giant ground sloth,*

(B)   It stood twelve feet tall, weighing nine thousand pounds, and wielding seven-inch claws, *Megatherium americanum* was a giant ground sloth and

(C)   The giant ground sloth *Megatherium americanum,* having stood twelve feet tall, weighing nine thousand pounds, and wielding seven-inch claws, it

(D)   Standing twelve feet tall, weighing nine thousand pounds, and wielding seven-inch claws, *Megatherium americanum, a giant ground sloth,*

(E)   Standing twelve feet tall, weighing nine thousand pounds, it wielded seven-inch claws, and the giant ground sloth *Megatherium americanum*

Grammatical Construction; Parallelism

The point of the sentence is to describe several features of *Megatherium americanum,* to identify this creature as a giant ground sloth, and to speculate about its status as the largest hunting mammal in Earth's history. *Megatherium americanum* is therefore the sole subject of the sentence. When its features are presented as parallel adjective phrases and its common identification is presented as an appositive, a single main verb *may have been* is all that is required to complete the sentence. When the conjunction *and* constructs a compound sentence, the subjects *it* and *ground sloth* or *Megatherium americanum* appear to name separate entities.

A   The compound sentence structure suggests that *it* and *Megatherium americanum* are two separate entities, making it unclear what, if anything, the pronoun refers to.

B   Like answer choice A, *it* and *Megatherium americanum* appear to name different entities. This a run-on sentence; the comma after *claws* is not sufficient to join the two main clauses in a single sentence. The series describing the sloth is also nonparallel.

C   The present-perfect tense of the first participial phrase in the series (*having stood*) is not parallel with the (timeless) present tense of the other two participials. The introduction of the main subject *it* leaves *ground sloth* without a verb.

D   Correct. The series of present-tense participial phrases describes the main subject, *Megatherium americanum,* which is clarified by the common name expressed as an appositive.

E   The identity of *it* is ambiguous, and the second subject of the compound sentence *giant ground sloth* appears to name something other than *it.* This makes the sentence ungrammatical.

The correct answer is D.

SCO4083

242. Studying skeletons unearthed near Rome, DNA evidence was recovered by scientists, who were able to deduce from this that an epidemic of malaria struck in the empire's waning days.

(A) Studying skeletons unearthed near Rome, DNA evidence was recovered by scientists, who were able to deduce from this

(B) In studying skeletons unearthed near Rome, DNA evidence was recovered by scientists, who were able to deduce from this

(C) Scientists recovered DNA evidence from studying skeletons unearthed near Rome, being able to deduce from this

(D) Skeletons unearthed near Rome allowed scientists to recover DNA evidence, and they were able to deduce from it

(E) Scientists studying skeletons unearthed near Rome recovered DNA evidence from which they were able to deduce

Logical Predication; Rhetorical Construction

The sentence explains that scientists recovered DNA evidence from skeletons, revealing evidence of malaria. As the sentence is written, the participial phrase *studying skeletons* is misplaced; grammatically it modifies the subject of the main clause, thus illogically indicating that the *evidence* studied the skeletons.

A The participial phrase *studying skeletons* illogically modifies *evidence*.

B The participial phrase *studying skeletons* illogically modifies *evidence*.

C The sentence incorrectly states that DNA evidence was recovered from *studying skeletons* rather than from the skeletons; the phrase *being able to deduce from this* is awkward and wordy.

D The construction *skeletons … allowed scientists* gives the action of the sentence to the skeletons rather than the scientists; the antecedent of the pronoun *they* is ambiguous, possibly referring either to *scientists* or to *skeletons*.

E **Correct.** *Scientists* is the subject of the main clause, and *studying skeletons* correctly modifies *scientists*.

The correct answer is E.

SCO1594

243. Butterflies come in more than 17,000 species, displaying a wing pattern unique to each one.

(A) displaying a wing pattern unique to each one

(B) displaying a unique wing pattern in each

(C) each uniquely displaying a wing pattern

(D) each of which displays a unique wing pattern

(E) each of which uniquely displays a wing pattern

Diction; Logical Predication

As well as noting the surprisingly large number of butterfly species, the sentence probably seeks to make the point that no two species have the same wing pattern. Which of the suggested ways of conveying this information is clearest and unambiguous?

A In a conversational context, the thought underlying this version would probably be successfully understood by most listeners. However, the participle *displaying* modifies *butterflies*, not *species*. Thus the sentence as written seems to say, illogically, that each butterfly displays a wing pattern unique to each one.

B The phrase *in each* is illogical: what cannot have been intended in the given sentence is that all 17,000 species display a single wing pattern.

C This produces nonsense: all butterflies presumably display some wing pattern; it is not clear, however, what it could mean to "uniquely" display a wing pattern.

D **Correct.** In the given phrase, the *which* refers to *17,000 species;* it conveys exactly the same information as the following sentence: *Each of 17,000 species displays a unique wing pattern.* Both convey the information that no two of the species have the same wing pattern.

E It is not clear what it could mean to "uniquely" display a wing pattern.

The correct answer is D.

SC04652

244. A March 2000 Census Bureau survey showed that Mexico accounted for more than a quarter of all foreign-born residents of the United States, <u>the largest share for any country to contribute</u> since 1890, when about 30 percent of the country's foreign-born population was from Germany.

(A) the largest share for any country to contribute

(B) the largest share that any country has contributed

(C) which makes it the largest share for any country to contribute

(D) having the largest share to be contributed by any country

(E) having the largest share to have been contributed by any country

Logical Predication; Rhetorical Construction

This sentence claims that the 2000 Census showed that at the time Mexico's contribution to the foreign-born population of United States residents exceeded that of any other country since 1890. It makes the comparison in an appositive that modifies *more than a quarter of all foreign-born residents of the United States*.

A   The phrase *for any country to contribute* makes the sentence wordy and indirect.

B   **Correct.** This form of the appositive is the most efficient way to express the comparison. Depending on when the sentence was written and what the writer intended to express, the verb form could be either *had contributed* or *has contributed*. The use of *has contributed* implies that, from the perspective of the sentence, the comparison between German-born U.S. residents and those from other countries still holds true.

C   The antecedents of the relative pronoun *which* and the pronoun *it* are ambiguous. Along with the prepositional phrase, the pronouns contribute wordiness and indirection.

D   This construction is awkward, wordy, and indirect, and the use of the present tense of the infinitive is inappropriate.

E   This construction is awkward, wordy, and indirect.

The correct answer is B.

SC01579

245. Recently declassified information from military satellites in orbit thousands of miles above the Earth <u>show the planet continually bombarded by</u> large meteoroids that explode with the power of atomic bomb blasts.

(A) show the planet continually bombarded by

(B) show continual bombarding of the planet by

(C) show a continual bombardment of the planet from

(D) shows continually that the planet is bombarded from

(E) shows that the planet is continually bombarded by

Agreement; Idiom

The sentence indicates that information shows the planet to be continually bombarded by meteors. However, the plural verb *show* incorrectly corresponds to the word *satellites* in the prepositional phrase *from military satellites*, rather than to the singular subject *information*. The correct combination of subject and verb is *information shows*.

A   The singular subject *information* does not agree with the plural verb *show*.

B   The singular subject *information* does not agree with the plural verb *show*. The verbal noun *bombarding* (rather than *bombardment*) is awkward and unnecessary.

C   The singular subject *information* does not agree with the plural verb *show*. *Bombardment from* is an unidiomatic way of expressing the intended relationship. This construction appears to indicate, illogically, that someone or something located on the large, exploding meteoroids is sending the bombardment to Earth.

D   *Continually* should modify *bombarded*, not *shows*. *Bombardment from* is an unidiomatic way of expressing the intended relationship. This construction appears to indicate, illogically, that someone or something located on the large, exploding meteoroids is sending the bombardment to Earth.

E   **Correct.** The singular subject *information* agrees with the singular verb *shows*.

The correct answer is E.

SC04026

246. Child development specialists believe <u>that, in confining babies much of the time to strollers, high chairs, playpens, and walkers, muscle development can be inhibited.</u>

(A) that, in confining babies much of the time to strollers, high chairs, playpens, and walkers, muscle development can be inhibited

(B) that, in their confinement much of the time to strollers, high chairs, playpens, and walkers, muscle development can be inhibited in babies

(C) that confining babies much of the time to strollers, high chairs, playpens, and walkers can inhibit muscle development

(D) that babies, if confined much of the time to strollers, high chairs, playpens, and walkers can inhibit muscle development

(E) that strollers, high chairs, playpens, and walkers can, if babies are confined to them much of the time, result in muscle development being inhibited

Logical Predication; Rhetorical Construction

The point of the sentence is that confining babies can inhibit muscle development. As it is written, however, *muscle development* is the subject of the sentence, and the sentence appears to be saying that muscle development confines babies much of the time. Furthermore, the passive construction *can be inhibited* could even be seen as illogically suggesting that inhibiting development is the purpose of confinement. The sentence can be expressed more clearly and concisely by making *confining* the subject of the verb *can inhibit*: *confining babies … can inhibit muscle development.*

A The intended meaning of the sentence is obscured. The sentence appears to indicate that muscle development confines babies much of the time, which surely is not what is intended.

B The antecedent of *their* should be *babies*, but given that *babies* comes far after the pronoun, the reader is liable to take the antecedent of *their* to be *child development specialists.*

C **Correct.** The sentence clearly and concisely indicates that *confining babies … can inhibit muscle development.*

D The word *babies* is the subject of the verb *can inhibit*, suggesting incorrectly that babies inhibit their own or someone else's muscle development.

E This sentence uses an awkward and wordy construction to indicate that the sites of confinement *can result in muscle development being inhibited*, when in fact the confinement itself is the cause.

The correct answer is C.

SC01482

247. Together with Key Largo National Marine Sanctuary, the John Pennekamp Coral Reef State Park, the first underwater park in the United States, <u>provide 165 square nautical miles of marine life for underwater explorers, which includes</u> more than 500 species of fish and 55 varieties of coral.

(A) provide 165 square nautical miles of marine life for underwater explorers, which includes

(B) provide for underwater explorers 165 square nautical miles of marine life, which include

(C) provide 165 square nautical miles of marine life for underwater explorers and includes

(D) provides 165 square nautical miles of marine life for underwater explorers and including

(E) provides underwater explorers with 165 square nautical miles of marine life, including

Agreement; Grammatical Construction

The sentence mentions two marine sites, but the grammatical subject of the sentence refers to only one of them, so the use of the plural verb *provide* is incorrect. The antecedent of *which* is unclear; for example, it cannot be *explorers*, since the singular verb *includes* indicates that its subject *which* must also be singular. Thus, the antecedent must be the singular noun phrase *marine life*. However, the sentence would be clearer and less awkward if this antecedent were placed closer to *which*.

A This cannot be correct, given the problems explained above.

B   The plural *provide* is incorrect. The plural verb *include* indicates that one of the preceding noun phrases, e.g., *165 square nautical miles*, or *underwater explorers*, should be the antecedent, but neither of these readings would convey a coherent meaning.

C   The plural *provide* is incorrect, as the subject is singular (*Key Largo Marine Sanctuary* is not part of the subject). Stating that the park (as opposed to the marine life) "includes" 500 species does not seem to capture the intended meaning.

D   The portion that precedes *and* here is correct; however, *and including* creates a grammatically incorrect sentence fragment.

E   **Correct.** The use of a participial phrase introduced by *including* avoids the need to use a relative clause introduced by *which*, but serves the same function as would a relative clause with antecedent *marine life*.

The correct answer is E.

SC01481

248. While Hollywood makes films primarily for entertainment, the motion picture was not first developed to entertain, but it was to allow detailed analysis of animal motion.

(A)   was not first developed to entertain, but it was

(B)   was developed not first to entertain, but it was

(C)   was first developed not to entertain, but

(D)   did not first develop for entertainment, but

(E)   did not first develop for entertainment, but it was

Grammatical Construction; Parallelism

The sentence expresses, in an awkward and unclear manner, the thought that the initial development of the motion picture was for science rather than for entertainment. One flaw in the given sentence concerns the placement of *not*; another flaw is that the pronoun *it* has no clear antecedent (its antecedent does not seem to be *the motion picture*, for example).

A   The placement of *not* suggests that it is intended to negate a verbal phrase *was first developed*, but this makes no sense in context. As explained, the pronoun *it* lacks a clear antecedent.

B   As explained, the pronoun *it* lacks a clear antecedent. Only if *first* meant "primarily" could the phrase *not first to entertain* make some sense in context.

C   **Correct.** This accurately conveys the claim that the intended purpose of the motion picture when it was first developed was not entertainment but something else, i.e., scientific observation. The parallelism between *to entertain* and *to allow* removes unnecessary wordiness.

D   The placement of *not* is inappropriate, given the intended meaning. The parallelism mentioned earlier is missing here.

E   The word *not* seems, misleadingly, to negate the verb *first developed*, which would fail to convey the intended sense of the given sentence. The antecedent of *it* is unclear. The parallelism explained earlier is missing here.

The correct answer is C.

SC01069

249. The personal income tax did not become permanent in the United States until the First World War; before that time the federal government was dependent on tariffs to be their main source of revenue.

(A)   the federal government was dependent on tariffs to be their main source of revenue

(B)   the federal government had depended on tariffs as its main source of revenue

(C)   tariffs were what the federal government was dependent on to be its main source of revenue

(D)   the main source of revenue for the federal government was dependent on tariffs

(E)   for their main source of revenue, tariffs were depended on by the federal government

Agreement; Logical Predication

The First World War is designated as past tense in the opening clause of this sentence. The relationship between that time and whatever happened earlier can be most clearly indicated by using the past-perfect tense for the earlier events.

[*T*]*he federal government* is a singular subject of the second clause, so a singular pronoun, *its* rather than *their*, must refer to it. The phrase *was dependent on* causes unnecessary wordiness, as does the passive construction in answer choice E.

A   The plural pronoun *their* inappropriately refers to the singular noun *government*.

B   **Correct.** The pronoun *its* agrees with the singular subject *government*, and the past perfect, active verb *had depended* refers clearly to government activity prior to the First World War.

C   This version of the sentence is wordy because of the inverted word order that makes the subject of the second clause an object of the preposition *on*.

D   This version of the sentence nonsensically makes *source* the subject of the verb *was* [dependent on].

E   The plural possessive pronoun *their* does not agree with its singular antecedent *government*. In fact, because of the placement of *tariffs* immediately after the opening prepositional phrase, *their* seems at first to refer to *tariffs*, which is illogical. The passive verb form *were depended on* is wordy and indirect.

The correct answer is B.

SC02628

250. In 1776 Adam Smith wrote that it is young people <u>who have</u> "the contempt of risk and the presumptuous hope of success" needed to found new businesses.

(A)   who have

(B)   with

(C)   having

(D)   who are those with

(E)   who are the ones to have

Grammatical Construction; Rhetorical Construction

This sentence identifies which people have the attitudes needed to be successful entrepreneurs, according to the economist Adam Smith. The main clause *it is young people* is followed by a relative clause that modifies *young people* and

defines the attributes important to their ability to found businesses: caring little about risk and being extremely optimistic about succeeding. The use of the idiomatic construction *it is … who* is a way of placing primary emphasis on the question that Smith addressed with the quoted words.

A   **Correct.** The relative clause beginning *who have* grammatically and concisely identifies the relevant attitudes that *young people* have.

B   In this version, the relative clause modifying *young people* is replaced with a prepositional phrase, introduced by *with*. This clause appears to modify *young people* restrictively. Thus, the sentence simply identifies a subcategory of young people (those with *the contempt of risk* …) and does not clearly explain which *people* have the attitudes that Smith identifies.

C   Replacing the relative clause with a participial phrase introduced by *having* makes the sentence incomplete, since the point of the sentence is to explain which people *have* the attitudes that Smith identifies.

D   Inserting the phrase *are those with* makes the sentence awkward and wordy.

E   The word group *are the ones to have* is less concise than the simple verb *have* and fails to convey the meaning that is clearly intended.

The correct answer is A.

SC04198

251. <u>Palladium prices have soared, with Russia restricting exports and because automakers have started using it</u> to make the huge engines in sport utility vehicles and other light trucks.

(A)   Palladium prices have soared, with Russia restricting exports and because automakers have started using

(B)   Palladium prices have soared, with Russia restricting exports, in addition to automakers that have started to use

(C)   Prices for palladium have soared as Russia has restricted exports and automakers have started using

(D)   Prices for palladium have soared as Russia has been restricting exports, in addition to automakers starting to use

(E)   Prices for palladium have soared because Russia is restricting exports, as well as automakers that have started using

Parallelism; Rhetorical Construction

The sentence indicates that a rapid increase in palladium prices is related to a restriction in Russian exports and to the fact that automakers have started using palladium to make engines. It makes sense to see the increase in palladium prices as being a result of the other two factors, and the sentence should clearly suggest this link. Furthermore, the grammatical construction of the sentence should display parallelism. For instance, if the phrase *Russia restricting exports* is used, then the parallel phrase *automakers having started* should be used so as to create a parallel construction. On the other hand, if the clause *Russia has restricted exports* is used, then the clause *automakers have started* should be paired with it to create a parallel structure.

A   The use of the word *with* before *Russia restricting exports* does not clearly indicate the causal link between this restriction and the price increases. Furthermore, *with Russia restricting exports* is not appropriately parallel with *because automakers have started using*.

B   The use of the word *with* before *Russia restricting exports* does not clearly indicate the causal link between this restriction and the price increases. Also, *with Russia restricting exports* is not appropriately grammatically parallel with *automakers that have started to use*.

C   **Correct.** The use of the word *as* suggests a possible causal link between the price increases and the combination of Russia's restriction of exports and automakers' use of palladium in the manufacture of engines. The sentence also displays an appropriate grammatical parallelism among *Prices for palladium have soared*, *Russia has restricted exports*, and *automakers have started using*.

D   There is not an appropriate grammatical parallelism between *Russia has been restricting exports* and *automakers starting to use*.

E   There is not an appropriate grammatical parallelism between *Russia is restricting exports* and *automakers that have started using*.

The correct answer is C.

SC01543

252.   Variability in individual physical traits <u>both are determined through genetic factors, environmental factors, and interaction between</u> these factors.

(A)   both are determined through genetic factors, environmental factors, and interaction between

(B)   are both determined by genetic factors, environmental factors, as well as interaction among

(C)   both is determined by genetic factors, environmental factors, and interaction between

(D)   is determined through genetic factors, environmental factors, as well as interaction among

(E)   is determined by genetic factors, environmental factors, and interaction between

Agreement; Grammatical Construction

In discussing the factors that produce variations in individuals' physical traits, the sentence uses the structure *both … and …* unnecessarily and incorrectly: this structure can coordinate exactly two elements of a sentence, whereas here, three elements (genetic factors, environmental factors, and interaction between them) are named. The preposition *by* is more idiomatic than *through* with *determined*. The subject of the sentence is the noun phrase *variability in … traits*, so the verb of which it is subject must be singular, whereas *are* is plural. The preposition *among* (unlike *between*) is normally used to indicate some relationship involving more than two elements.

A   This has multiple problems, as explained above. Replacing *both are determined through* with the phrase *is determined by* would greatly improve the overall structure of the given sentence.

B   The verb *are* is plural but should be singular, since its subject is singular. The word *both* should be omitted. Introducing *as well as* into the sentence without certain other changes is not an improvement; the phrase is not substitutable for *and* without further changes elsewhere in the sentence.

C   The word *both* in this case raises the expectation that exactly two elements would be coordinated, but this does not occur here.

D   The preposition *through* is unidiomatic with *determined*. The phrase *as well as* cannot be used in the same way as *and* can (in this case, to coordinate three elements in a series).

E   **Correct.** The singular verb *is* has *variability* as its subject. Three elements in a series are coordinated, using two commas plus *and*. The preposition *between* is correctly used to refer to a relationship involving two sets of factors.

The correct answer is E.

SC06613

253. In his *Uses of Enchantment* (1976), it was psychologist Bruno Bettelheim's assertion that the apparently cruel and arbitrary nature of many fairy tales actually are an instructive reflection of a child's natural and necessary "killing off" of successive phases in his or her own development.

(A)   it was psychologist Bruno Bettelheim's assertion that the apparently cruel and arbitrary nature of many fairy tales actually are

(B)   it was the assertion of psychologist Bruno Bettelheim that what is apparently the cruel and arbitrary nature of many fairy tales actually is

(C)   psychologist Bruno Bettelheim's assertion that what is apparently the cruel and arbitrary nature of many fairy tales actually is

(D)   psychologist Bruno Bettelheim asserted that the apparently cruel and arbitrary nature of many fairy tales actually are

(E)   psychologist Bruno Bettelheim asserted that the apparently cruel and arbitrary nature of many fairy tales is actually

Agreement; Rhetorical Construction

The sentence attributes to psychologist Bruno Bettelheim a particular view regarding the nature of fairy tales. The construction *it was psychologist Bruno Bettelheim's assertion that* lacks the clarity and directness of the more active construction *Bruno Bettelheim asserted that*. The subject of the subordinate clause containing *nature of many fairy tales actually are* is the singular noun *nature*, not the plural noun in the prepositional phrase *of fairy tales*. Thus, the verb of that clause should be *is*, not *are*.

A   *It was psychologist Bruno Bettelheim's assertion that* is wordy and awkward. Presumably this phrase is intended to be equivalent to *Bettelheim asserted that* (just as *it is my opinion that* is another way of saying *I believe that*). However, given the surrounding structure of the sentence, *it* appears to refer to some unnamed entity or condition that occurs in Bettelheim's book, and the entire sequence *was … development* appears to be predicated of the subject *it*. The plural verb *are* does not agree with the singular subject *nature*.

B   *It was psychologist Bruno Bettelheim's assertion that* is wordy and awkward. Presumably this phrase is intended to be equivalent to *Bettelheim asserted that* (just as *it is my opinion that* is another way of saying *I believe that*). However, given the surrounding structure of the sentence, *it* appears to refer to some unnamed entity or condition that occurs in Bettelheim's book, and the entire sequence *was … development* appears to be predicated of the subject *it*. The plural verb *are* does not agree with the singular subject *nature*.

C   According to the most plausible parsing of the sentence, everything that follows *asserted that* is intended to express Bettelheim's assertion. On that interpretation, though, the sentence is ungrammatical; the subject of the main clause, *assertion*, is not paired with a verb. If the verb *is* were paired with the subject *assertion*, the sentence would be nonsensical.

D   The plural verb *are* does not agree with the singular subject *nature*.

E   **Correct**. The construction *Bruno Bettelheim asserted* gives vigor to the main clause, and the singular verb *is* agrees with the subject *nature* in the subordinate clause.

The correct answer is E.

SC06012

254.   After weeks of uncertainty about the course the country would pursue to stabilize its troubled economy, officials reached a revised agreement with the International Monetary Fund, pledging <u>the enforcement of substantially greater budget discipline as that which was originally promised and to keep inflation below ten percent.</u>

(A)   the enforcement of substantially greater budget discipline as that which was originally promised and to keep inflation below ten percent

(B)   the enforcement of substantially greater budget discipline than originally promised and keeping inflation below the ten percent figure

(C)   to enforce substantially greater budget discipline than originally promised and to keep inflation below ten percent

(D)   to enforce substantially greater budget discipline than that which was originally promised and keeping inflation less than the ten percent figure

(E)   to enforce substantially greater budget discipline as that which was originally promised and to keep inflation less than ten percent

Logical Predication; Parallelism

This sentence explains the two-part strategy an unnamed country agreed to pursue in order to stabilize its economy. Nominalization (*the enforcement of ...*) and an incorrect form of comparison (*as that which was ...*) in the account of the first strategy causes excessive wordiness and indirection and makes the account of the first strategy nonparallel with the account of the second strategy. To reduce wordiness and achieve parallelism, both strategies pledged by the country should be presented in infinitive form (*to enforce ... and to keep ...*). The sentence also needs to employ the correct comparative form *greater discipline than ...*.

A   The two strategies (*the enforcement of* and *keeping*) are not presented in parallel form; the nominalized presentation of the first

strategy is wordy and indirect, and the comparative form is incorrect.

B   The two strategies (*the enforcement of* and *keeping*) are not presented in parallel form.

C   **Correct**. The comparative form is correct, and the two strategies are presented in parallel form, as infinitives completing the verb *pledged*.

D   The two strategies are not presented in parallel form, and the comparative form is unnecessarily wordy.

E   The comparative form is incorrect and wordy.

The correct answer is C.

SC01596

255.   <u>A new satellite sweeping over the poles at altitudes of up to 32,000 miles is called POLAR, giving scientists their best look yet at the magnetosphere, the region of space under the invisible influence of Earth's magnetic field.</u>

(A)   A new satellite sweeping over the poles at altitudes of up to 32,000 miles is called POLAR, giving scientists their best look yet at the magnetosphere, the region of space under the invisible influence of Earth's magnetic field.

(B)   A new satellite called POLAR that is giving scientists their best look yet at the magnetosphere, the region of space under the invisible influence of Earth's magnetic field, sweeping over the poles at altitudes of up to 32,000 miles.

(C)   Scientists are getting their best look yet at the magnetosphere, the region of space under the invisible influence of Earth's magnetic field, from a new satellite sweeping over the poles at altitudes of up to 32,000 miles called POLAR.

(D)   Sweeping over the poles at altitudes of up to 32,000 miles, a new satellite called POLAR is giving scientists their best look yet at the magnetosphere, the region of space under the invisible influence of Earth's magnetic field.

(E)   Sweeping over the poles at altitudes of up to 32,000 miles, scientists' best look yet at the magnetosphere, the region of space under the invisible influence of Earth's magnetic field, is coming from a new satellite called POLAR.

Logical Predication; Grammatical Construction

The point of the sentence is that a *new satellite* is *giving scientists their best look yet at the magnetosphere*. As the sentence is written, the participial phrase *giving scientists … magnetosphere* illogically modifies the preceding clause *A new … is called POLAR*, suggesting illogically that the naming of the satellite is what provides scientists with a look at the magnetosphere. The sentence can be constructed more clearly with *satellite* as the subject of the main clause and *is giving* as its verb.

A The participial phrase *giving scientists … magnetosphere* illogically modifies the whole preceding clause, rather than *satellite*.

B The subject *satellite* has no corresponding verb that would create an independent clause; the word *that* introduces a subordinate clause, and the overall result is merely a sentence fragment.

C The modifier *called POLAR* is awkwardly placed too far away from the word *satellite*, which it is intended to modify; in its current incorrect position, it appears to modify *altitudes*.

D **Correct.** The sentence is constructed clearly with *satellite* and *is giving* as the subject and verb of the main clause, and the modifiers are placed appropriately near the words they are meant to modify.

E *Sweeping* incorrectly modifies *look*, and the main subject *look* is awkwardly paired with the verb *is coming from*.

The correct answer is D.

SC05787

256. The treasury market dropped in response to a decrease in the value of the dollar and to continued concern that the economy might be growing as fast as to accelerate inflation and drive interest rates higher.

(A) that the economy might be growing as fast as

(B) that the economy might be growing fast enough

(C) with the economy's possibly growing so fast as

(D) with the possibility of the economy growing fast enough so as

(E) with the possibility of the economy possibly growing fast enough

Idiom; Rhetorical Construction

This sentence expresses a possible condition related to the relative speed of the economy's growth. The possible condition is expressed succinctly through the modal verb *might* in the subordinate clause *that the economy might be growing*. However, the correct idiom for expressing the relative speed is *fast enough to* precipitate negative economic consequences—not *as fast as*.

A *As fast as* is not the correct idiom.

B **Correct.** The possible condition is expressed succinctly using the modal verb *might*, and idioms are used correctly.

C *Concern with* is not the correct idiom; the phrases *economy's possibly growing* and *so fast as to* are wordy and awkward.

D *Concern with* is not the correct idiom; the phrase *possibility of the economy growing fast enough so as to* is wordy and awkward.

E *Concern with* is not the correct idiom; *possibility* and *possibly* are unnecessarily and awkwardly repetitive.

The correct answer is B.

SC03724

257. Despite a growing population, in 1998 the United States used 38 billion fewer gallons of water a day when comparing it to the period of all-time highest consumption almost 20 years earlier.

(A) day when comparing it to the period of all-time highest consumption almost 20 years earlier

(B) day than it did during the period of all-time highest consumption almost 20 years earlier

(C) day than were used almost 20 years earlier, which had been the all-time high consumption

(D) day, compared to almost 20 years earlier, that having been the all-time high consumption

(E) day, which is in comparison to the period of all-time highest consumption almost 20 years earlier

Rhetorical Construction; Logical Predication

When making a direct comparison (in this case, with *fewer*), the standard way to express the object of comparison is with *than*. Here, the sentence uses *fewer … when comparing it to*, which not only is unidiomatic, but also creates an illogical predication: *United States* is the only possible subject for the verb *comparing* (surely the sentence doesn't mean to say the United States used 38 billion fewer gallons at the time it was making some comparison!). Also, what is the antecedent of *it* here? Grammatically, there is no clear candidate.

A   Instead of using *fewer … than*, this version uses the unidiomatic *fewer … when comparing it to*, which also introduces a logical predication problem.

B   **Correct.** *Fewer than* is correct, and this version of the sentence has no logical predication problems.

C   This has a logical predication problem: because the relative clause beginning with *which* immediately follows *almost 20 years earlier*, it seems that the time period is being described as having been *the all-time high consumption*.

D   *Fewer than* is preferable to *fewer … compared to*; also, there is a logical predication problem: because the phrase beginning with *that* immediately follows *almost 20 years earlier*, it seems that the time period is being described as having been *the all-time high consumption*.

E   This is awkwardly and confusingly worded. Rather than comparing the United States' water usage in 1998 to its water usage nearly 20 years earlier, this appears illogically to compare the United States' water usage in 1998 to a period of time, namely *the period of all-time highest consumption almost 20 years earlier*.

The correct answer is B.

SC01600
258. A federal advisory panel proposes expanding a national computerized file to permit law-enforcement agencies to track people under criminal investigation but have not yet been charged.

(A)   under criminal investigation but

(B)   under criminal investigation, but who

(C)   under criminal investigation, but they

(D)   who are under criminal investigation, but they

(E)   who are under criminal investigation but

Parallelism; Grammatical Construction

The sentence describes a proposal to allow law-enforcement agencies to track people who have not been charged with a crime but are under investigation. However, the description of the group is flawed, in that the two defining properties—not having been charged; being under investigation—are not expressed in a parallel form: the verb *have been charged* lacks a grammatically correct subject.

A   The adjectival phrase *under criminal investigation*, modifying *people*, is nonparallel to *have not yet been charged*; the latter is a mere sentence fragment.

B   The required parallelism is lacking here. The word *but* introduces a sentence fragment.

C   The required parallelism is lacking here: we have an adjectival phrase, and the coordinate conjunction *but* introducing what appears to be an independent clause. It is unclear what the antecedent of the pronoun *they* is.

D   The required parallelism is lacking here: we have a relative clause, followed by the coordinate conjunction *but* introducing what appears to be an independent clause. It is structurally unclear what the antecedent of the pronoun *they* is.

E   **Correct.** The relative pronoun *who* has *people* as its antecedent and introduces a complex relative clause containing two parallel verbal phrases correctly coordinated with the conjunction *but*.

The correct answer is E.

SC03779

259. Analysts believe that whereas bad decisions by elected leaders can certainly hurt the economy, <u>no administration can really be said to control</u> or manage all of the complex and interrelated forces that determine the nation's economic strength.

(A) no administration can really be said to control

(B) no administration can be said that it really controls

(C) that no administration can really be said to control

(D) that no administration can really be said that it controls

(E) that it cannot be said that any administration really controls

Grammatical Construction; Verb Form

The point of this sentence is to explain analysts' common two-part belief about the limited power of elected officials to control a national economy. It presents this belief as the direct object in the main clause, [a]nalysts believe, and introduces it with the subordinating conjunction *that*, which governs both the positive dependent clause (*decisions … can hurt*) introduced by *whereas*, and the subsequent negative independent clause (*no administration can … be said to control …*). The additional appearances of *that* in some of the versions of the sentence are ungrammatical.

A **Correct.** Introduced by the subordinating conjunction *that*, the complex clause succinctly contrasts leaders' powers to hurt the economy with their inability to control all economic forces.

B The idiom *can be said to* would be appropriate, but *no administration can be said that it* is ungrammatical.

C The repetition of *that* is ungrammatical, since both clauses are governed by the initial appearance of *that* after [a]nalysts believe.

D This version of the sentence combines the mistakes explained in answer choices B and C.

E The repetition of *that* is ungrammatical, since both clauses are governed by the first appearance of *that*. The appearance of *it* makes the sentence unnecessarily wordy and convoluted.

The correct answer is A.

SC03146

260. Nearly unrivaled in their biological diversity, <u>coral reefs provide a host of benefits that includes the supply of protein for people, protecting shorelines, and</u> they contain biochemical sources for new life-saving medicines.

(A) coral reefs provide a host of benefits that includes the supply of protein for people, protecting shorelines,

(B) coral reefs provide a host of benefits: they supply people with protein, they protect the shorelines,

(C) coral reefs provide a host of benefits that include supplying protein for people, as well as shoreline protection,

(D) a coral reef provides a host of benefits; they supply protein for people, the protecting of shorelines,

(E) a coral reef provides a host of benefits, including protein for people, protecting shorelines,

Parallelism; Agreement

When listing several items (here, benefits of coral reefs), they should be expressed in a parallel way, such as by using all noun phrases or all full clauses. Also, pronoun subjects in one clause that refer to the subject of a preceding clause should agree in number.

A The three items after *includes* are not parallel (*the supply; protecting shorelines; they contain*).

B **Correct.** The three items after *benefits* are parallel (*they supply; they protect; they contain*). The subject of the next clause (*they*) is correctly plural given that its antecedent is *coral reefs.*

C The three items after *include* are not parallel: *supplying, shoreline protection, they contain.*

D The three items after *benefits* are not parallel (*they supply; the protecting of; they contain*), and in the next clause they is the incorrect pronoun given that the antecedent here is the singular *a coral reef*.

E   The three items after *benefits* are not parallel (*protein; protecting; they contain*), and in the next clause *they* is the incorrect pronoun given that the antecedent here is the singular *a coral reef*.

The correct answer is B.

SC12367

261. Literacy opened up entire realms of verifiable knowledge to ordinary men and women <u>having been previously considered incapable of discerning truth for themselves</u>.

(A)   having been previously considered incapable of discerning truth for themselves

(B)   who had previously been considered incapable of discerning truth for themselves

(C)   previously considered incapable of discerning truth for himself or herself

(D)   of whom it had previously been considered they were incapable of discerning truth for themselves

(E)   who had previously been considered incapable of discerning truth for himself or herself

Rhetorical Construction; Agreement

The phrase beginning with *having been* modifies the noun phrase *ordinary men and women*. In cases like this, it is best to use a full relative clause, starting with *that* or a relative pronoun such as *which* or *who*, instead of a clause with the *-ing* form of the verb. Also, *themselves* is the correct form of a reflexive pronoun to refer back to the plural noun phrase *ordinary men and women*.

A   A phrase starting with the *-ing* verb form, instead of with *that* or *who*, is awkward in this context.

B   **Correct.** A relative clause correctly beginning with *who* is used, and *themselves* is the correct form for the reflexive pronoun.

C   *Himself or herself* is not the correct form for the plural reflexive pronoun.

D   Though the relative and reflexive pronouns are grammatically correct, the relative clause

(the clause that starts with *of whom*) is unnecessarily long and complex.

E   *Himself or herself* is not the correct form for the plural reflexive pronoun.

The correct answer is B.

SC01915

262. In early Mesopotamian civilization, castor oil served <u>not only as a laxative, but also a skin-softening lotion and it was a construction</u> lubricant for sliding giant stone blocks over wooden rollers.

(A)   not only as a laxative, but also a skin-softening lotion and it was a construction

(B)   as not only a laxative, but also a skin-softening lotion, and it was a construction

(C)   not only as a laxative but also as a skin-softening lotion and as a construction

(D)   as not only a laxative but as a skin-softening lotion and in construction, as a

(E)   not only as a laxative, but a skin-softening lotion and in construction, a

Parallelism; Rhetorical Construction

The sentence indicates three uses for castor oil. The first two are correctly joined using the correlative conjunction *not only, but also*. However, the three uses are not listed in parallel grammatical form. The sentence would be better with three adverb phrases beginning with *as*: *as a laxative, as a skin-softening lotion,* and *as a construction lubricant*.

A   The three uses for castor oil are not listed in parallel grammatical form since the first is an adverb phrase, the second is a noun phrase, and the third is an independent clause, which is ungrammatically conjoined to the preceding part of the sentence without an intervening comma.

B   The three uses for castor oil are not listed in parallel grammatical form since the first two are noun phrases and the third is an independent clause.

C **Correct.** The three uses for castor oil are listed as parallel adverb phrases, and the correlative conjunction *not only, but also* is constructed correctly.

D The three uses for castor oil are not listed in parallel grammatical form. The placing of *not only* after *as* is incorrect; the phrase *in construction* is also incorrectly placed.

E The word *as* is missing from the second and third elements of the correlative conjunction, so the three uses for castor oil are not listed correctly in parallel grammatical form.

The correct answer is C.

SC06935

263. An analysis of tree bark all over the globe shows <u>that chemical insecticides have often spread thousands of miles from where they were originally used.</u>

(A) that chemical insecticides have often spread thousands of miles from where they were originally used

(B) that chemical insecticides have spread, often thousands of miles from their original use

(C) chemical insecticides, having often spread thousands of miles from where they were used originally

(D) chemical insecticides, often spreading thousands of miles from where their original use

(E) chemical insecticides, often spreading thousands of miles from where they were originally used

Grammatical Construction; Diction

To express the intended meaning, *shows* can be followed by a clause beginning with *that*. Another option would be to use the special clause type *show* + noun phrase + *ing* verb form, such as *show chemical insecticides spreading many miles*—but there should be no pause in the middle of a construction of this latter type. If there is such a pause, then *chemical insecticides* becomes the direct object of *show*, and the following verb-*ing* phrase is an awkward attempt at a modifier of this object. Note also that if something spreads, it spreads from a place or an entity; other ways of expressing this idea in the answer choices are awkward or illogical. Verbs without overt subjects (such as *spreading* here) normally are to be understood as having the same subject as the main clause.

A **Correct.** *Show* is correctly followed by a *that* clause, and a place is correctly identified (*from where*) as the source of the spread.

B *Show* is followed by a *that* clause, but insecticides are illogically said to have spread from a use, rather than from a place.

C *Show* can sometimes take a direct object (here, *chemical insecticides*). However, the construction used here makes *analysis* the subject of *having*. Thus it appears to say, illogically, that the analysis shows that the analysis itself has spread from where the insecticides were used.

D *Show* can sometimes take a direct object (here, *chemical insecticides*). However, the construction used here makes *analysis* the subject of *spreading*. Thus, it appears to say, illogically, that the analysis shows that the analysis itself often spreads from where the insecticides were used. Also, *where their original use* is grammatically incorrect (*where they were originally used* is a correct alternative).

E *Show* can sometimes take a direct object (here, *chemical insecticides*). However, the construction used here makes *analysis* the subject of *spreading*. Thus, it appears to say, illogically, that the analysis shows that the analysis itself often spreads from where the insecticides were used.

The correct answer is A.

SC02241

264. According to the Economic Development Corporation of Los Angeles County, <u>if one were to count the Los Angeles metropolitan area as a separate nation, it would have the world's eleventh largest gross national product, that is</u> bigger than that of Australia, Mexico, or the Netherlands.

(A) if one were to count the Los Angeles metropolitan area as a separate nation, it would have the world's eleventh largest gross national product, that is

(B) if the Los Angeles metropolitan area is counted as a separate nation, it has the world's eleventh largest gross national product, that being

(C) if the Los Angeles metropolitan area were a separate nation, it would have the world's eleventh largest gross national product,

(D)   were the Los Angeles metropolitan area a separate nation, it will have the world's eleventh largest gross national product, which is

(E)   when the Los Angeles metropolitan area is counted as a separate nation, it has the world's eleventh largest gross national product, thus

Diction; Verb Form

The point of this sentence is to explain the implications of a contrary-to-fact state of affairs (Los Angeles metropolitan area as a nation). The subjunctive verb form is needed (*were ... would have*). To attribute this proposed state of affairs to the calculations of an anonymous agent (*one*) causes unnecessary wordiness. The implication of the hypothetical situation is that the Los Angeles area would have the eleventh-largest gross national product (GNP) in the world, a GNP that is further described as larger than the GNP of any of three nations named. This descriptive information is most efficiently presented as a terminal adjective phrase.

A   By introducing the subject *one*, the opening clause becomes unnecessarily wordy and indirect. The relative clause at the end of the sentence causes additional wordiness. The present indicative verb form *is* in the phrase *that is bigger than ...* is inconsistent with the conditional context established earlier in the sentence (*were ... would*). Since Los Angeles is not a nation, its *national* product is purely hypothetical and contrary to fact.

B   Because the *if* clause introduces a situation that is contrary to fact, the verbs *is counted* and *has* should be subjunctive and conditional, respectively (*were counted* and *would have*). The relative pronoun phrase *that being* is awkward, wordy, and repetitive.

C   **Correct.** The subjunctive mood of the verbs is appropriate to the contrary-to-fact situation being described, and the terminal adjective phrase without an introductory relative pronoun is an appropriate way of making the comparison among GNPs.

D   Although the opening subjunctive verb is appropriate, it must be followed by a conditional verb in the main clause; the relative clause at the end of the sentence,

beginning with *which is*, is indirect and wordy. Like answer choice A, *is* is not the most appropriate verb form to express a counterfactual condition.

E   The verbs *is counted ... has* are incorrect for describing a contrary-to-fact situation. Beginning the final adjective phrase with the word *thus* makes the relationship of the phrase to the rest of the sentence unclear.

The correct answer is C.

SC51661.01

265.   Some sociologists claim to have found a direct link from the appearance of news stories about violence to the rate of homicide.

(A)   from the appearance of news stories about violence to

(B)   between the appearance of news stories about violence to

(C)   between the appearance of news stories about violence and

(D)   with the appearance of news stories about violence to

(E)   with the appearance of news stories about violence and

Idiom; Logical Predication

The sentence's use of the form *a direct link from X to Y* is unidiomatic; the correct idiom would be of the form *a direct link between X and Y*. Because of the inappropriate use of *from*, the sentence initially sets up the expectation that the claim the sociologists make is that they became aware of a direct link from the appearance of news stories about violence.

A   The sentence uses the unidiomatic form *a direct link from X to Y.*

B   The sentence uses the unidiomatic form *a direct link between X to Y.*

C   **Correct.** The sentence uses the correct idiomatic form *direct link between X and Y.*

D   The sentence uses the unidiomatic form *a direct link with X to Y.*

E   The sentence uses the unidiomatic form *a direct link with X and Y.*

The correct answer is C.

SC61661.01

266. Government statistics on the size of foreign investment in real estate are <u>inconclusive because neither federal nor state laws require</u> disclosure of foreign ownership, and the Commerce Department, in its public tallies, does not categorize the owners.

(A) are inconclusive because neither federal nor state laws require

(B) are inconclusive because neither the federal nor state laws requires

(C) are inconclusive because neither federal laws or state laws require

(D) is inconclusive because neither the federal or state laws requires

(E) is inconclusive because neither federal laws nor state laws require

Idiom; Agreement

The sentence uses the correct idiomatic form *neither X nor Y*. Also, *statistics* is plural, so *are* is correct; similarly, *laws* is plural so *require* is correct.

A **Correct.** The sentence uses the correct idiomatic form *neither X nor Y*; *are* and *require* correctly match their subjects in number, *statistics* and *laws*, respectively.

B The sentence uses the idiomatic form *neither X nor Y*, but lacks parallelism in that it matches *the federal* and *state*; it should either match *federal* with *state* or *the federal* with *the state*. Also, because *laws* is plural, the verb should be *require*, not *requires*.

C The sentence uses the unidiomatic form *neither X or Y*.

D The sentence uses the unidiomatic form *neither X or Y*; it also lacks parallelism in that it matches *the federal* and *state*; it should either match *federal* with *state* or *the federal* with *the state*. Also, because *statistics* is plural, the verb should be *are*, not *is*, and because *laws* is plural, the verb should be *require*, not *requires*.

E Because *statistics* is plural, the verb should be *are*, not *is*.

The correct answer is A.

SC81661.01

267. In the United States one of the earliest challengers of the economic principle of free trade was Alexander Hamilton, who in 1791 advocated government policies that would encourage indigenous manufacturing <u>and to protect it</u> from competition from British exports.

(A) and to protect it

(B) but protecting it

(C) while protecting it

(D) for protecting them

(E) to protect them

Verb Form; Agreement; Parallelism

The point of the sentence is that Alexander Hamilton challenged free trade by advocating government policies that would encourage indigenous manufacturing and, at the same time, protect this manufacturing from competition from British exports. Some of the answer choices use the plural pronoun *them*, but the antecedent of the pronoun is *manufacturing*, which is singular, so the singular pronoun *it* should be used. As given, the sentence correctly uses the singular pronoun *it*, but, because the sentence's predicate is a compound predicate, in which two verb phrases are conjoined by the word *and*, the same verb form should be used, which is not the case here.

A Because the predicate is compound, with verb phrases conjoined by *and*, the verb forms should be the same; thus, *to protect* is incorrect. The pronoun *it* is correct, however, as its antecedent is *manufacturing*.

B Because the predicate is compound, with verb phrases conjoined by *but*, the verb forms should be the same; thus, *to protect* is incorrect. The pronoun *it* is correct, however, as its antecedent is *manufacturing*.

C **Correct.** The sentence is well expressed. The pronoun *it* is correct as its antecedent is *manufacturing*, and the use of the participle phrase *while protecting it from competition from British imports* (the subject, *indigenous manufacturing*, is given earlier and need not be repeated) appropriately conveys the idea that Hamilton advocated policies that protected the manufacturing at the same time as they encouraged its development.

D   The use of *them* is incorrect. Since it is plural the antecedent cannot be the singular *indigenous manufacturing*, though that would appear to be the intended antecedent (the idea underlying the sentence is that Hamilton, in a challenge to the principle of free trade, sought both to encourage and protect indigenous manufacturing). To take either of the plural nouns *government policies* or *earliest challengers* as the antecedent renders the sentence illogical, as does the use of the preposition *for*. Although it might make sense to think that encouraging indigenous manufacturing would protect the United States, *United States*, like *manufacturing*, is singular, and so cannot serve as the antecedent of *them*.

E   As with answer choice D, there is no plural noun that is a logically plausible antecedent for the plural pronoun *them*.

The correct answer is C.

SC94920.02

268. Some business experts think that allowing employees to buy their employer's stock for a set price, no matter how high the stock rises, will give the employees a powerful incentive to work together, making a company more prosperous, which will thus increase the return to shareholders.

(A)   to work together, making a company more prosperous, which will thus

(B)   to work together to make a company more prosperous and will thus

(C)   for working together, making a company more prosperous, and thus they

(D)   for working together to make a company more prosperous, and thus it will

(E)   for working together and making a company more prosperous, which will thus

Logical Predication; Rhetorical Construction

The sentence describes the thinking of *some business experts* concerning a recommended policy. Those experts claim that allowing employees to purchase their company's stock at a set price (even if its market value is much higher at the time of purchase) would incentivize employees to work together. They further claim that this would increase shareholder returns. One weakness of the sentence concerns the phrase *making a company more prosperous*. The sentence structure seems to indicate that *allowing their employees to buy* . . . will merely give employees an incentive to work together (something they probably do already out of necessity) and that by providing such an incentive, the policy will make a company more prosperous. But it is difficult to see why a policy that merely encourages employees to work together would make the company more prosperous. The sentence would be more clear if [*to make*] *the company more prosperous* were part of what the employees have an incentive to do. The structure also makes the intended referent of *which* somewhat unclear.

A   As explained above, the structure of the sentence makes its meaning unclear and potentially puzzling.

B   **Correct.** This version makes the sentence clearer. It expresses purpose using the adverbial infinitive phrase *to make a company more prosperous*, modifying *to work together*. The noun phrase *allowing . . . rises* that is the subject of the verb *will give* carries over to the parallel verb *will . . . increase;* the two verb phrases are correctly conjoined by *and*.

C   The phrase *for working together* is not idiomatic with *incentive; incentive to work together* is more standard and more effectively expresses the relationship between the incentive and the goal. As explained above, the occurrence of the phrase *making a company more prosperous* between commas makes the sentence potentially misleading and puzzling. Finally, it is unclear what the pronoun *they* refers to. The fact that *they* is the subject of the present tense verb *increase* suggests that *they* refers to *business experts*, which is also the subject of the present tense verb *think*, but this gives a nonsensical reading.

D   The prepositional phrase *for working together* is not idiomatic with *incentive*. It is somewhat unclear what the pronoun *it* refers to; it could refer to *allowing . . . rises*, to *a power incentive*, or to *a company*.

E   The prepositional phrase *for working together and . . . prosperous* is not idiomatic with *incentive*. Also, it is unclear what the antecedent of *which* is.

The correct answer is B.

Questions 269 to 303 - Difficulty: **Medium**

SC71661.01

269. Desertification, <u>a process in which the biological productivity of the land is sharply degraded by human abuse and natural phenomena</u>, helped cause the famines that have killed hundreds of thousands in recent years.

(A) a process in which the biological productivity of the land is sharply degraded by human abuse and natural phenomena

(B) a process of the biological productivity of the land being sharply degraded by human abuse and natural phenomena

(C) a process of human abuse and natural phenomena that sharply degrade the biological productivity of the land

(D) which is the process of human abuse and natural phenomena sharply degrading the land's biological productivity

(E) which is the process of human abuse and natural phenomena that sharply degrade the land's biological productivity

Rhetorical Construction; Agreement; Logical Predication

The purpose of the underlined phrase is to clarify what *desertification* is. The sentence's description of it as *a process in which the biological diversity of the land is sharply degraded by human abuse and natural phenomena* clearly expresses the intended meaning.

A   **Correct.** The sentence as worded is clear and to the point.

B   By saying that *desertification* is *a process of the biological productivity of the land . . .*, this version is potentially ambiguous because it is unclear which noun (*process, productivity, land*) the participial phrase *being . . . phenomena* modifies.

C   As is the case in answer choice B, this does not clearly indicate that *desertification* simply is a process that consists in the sharp

degradation of the biological productivity of the land by human abuse and natural phenomena. Furthermore, because *natural phenomena* is plural, there is an ambiguity: it is unclear whether the subject of the verb *degrade* is both *human abuse* and *natural phenomena*, or simply *natural phenomena*. Also, *process* at least arguably should be the antecedent of the relative pronoun *that*, in which case the verb should be *degrades*.

D   It is unclear whether *degrading* modifies both *human abuse* and *natural phenomena* or only *natural phenomena*.

E   Because *natural phenomena* is plural, there is an ambiguity: it is unclear whether the subject *that* of the verb *degrade* has *human abuse and natural phenomena* as antecedent, or simply *natural phenomena*. Also, *process* arguably should be the antecedent, in which case the verb should be *degrades*.

The correct answer is A.

SC42661.01

270. Open to the public and operated like conventional hotels, <u>condominium hotels permit buyers to acquire a specific room or suite, as well as</u> a proportionate interest in the rest of the establishment.

(A) condominium hotels permit buyers to acquire a specific room or suite, as well as

(B) buyers are permitted to acquire a specific room or suite in a condominium hotel, as well as

(C) a specific room or suite in condominium hotels may be acquired by buyers, as well as acquiring

(D) condominium hotels permit buyers to acquire a specific room or suite, as well as acquiring

(E) it is permitted for buyers to acquire a specific room or suite in a condominium hotel, as well as the acquisition of

Logical Predication; Verb Form

The sentence as worded is the best choice. Clearly, the sentence is intended to characterize *condominium hotels* as being *open to the public and operated like conventional hotels*, yet some of the incorrect answer choices illogically predicate the opening description of *buyers* or *a specific room or suite*. Furthermore, some of the incorrect answer choices are either ungrammatical or awkwardly worded (in some cases through unnecessary use of a passive-voice verb form), or they illogically indicate that *a specific room or suite*, rather than *buyers*, may be acquiring *a proportional interest in the rest of the establishment* of *a specific room or suite*.

A   **Correct.** The opening description correctly modifies *condominium hotels,* and the rest of the sentence is well formed.

B   The opening description should modify *condominium hotels*, not *buyers*, as it does here.

C   The opening description should modify *condominium hotels*, not *a specific room or suite in condominium hotels*, as it does here. Also, clearly it is the *buyers* who may acquire *a proportionate interest in the rest of the establishment*. As worded here, the sentence seems to say that a specific room or suite in a condominium hotel may be acquiring a proportional interest in the rest of the establishment, which is absurd.

D   The use of the present participle, *acquiring,* is ungrammatical; the infinitive, *to acquire,* should have been used.

E   The opening description should modify *condominium hotel*; here it modifies *it*. Also, as worded, the sentence says *it is permitted for buyers to acquire … the acquisition of a proportionate interest in the rest of the establishment*, which is awkward and redundant.

The correct answer is A.

SC52661.01

271. The methods proposed for reducing the amount of interest to be paid <u>are not able to be used successfully without creating a problem of insufficient cash flow in the future</u>.

(A)   are not able to be used successfully without creating a problem of insufficient cash flow in the future

(B)   are not able successfully to be used without creating a problem in the future of insufficient cash flow

(C)   cannot successfully be used without creating a future problem of insufficient cash flow

(D)   cannot be used without succeeding in creating a problem in the future of insufficient cash flow

(E)   cannot be used without succeeding in creating a future problem of insufficient cash flow

Diction; Rhetorical Construction

The wording is unnecessarily awkward. Also, "able" suggests agency, which is not appropriate with the subject *methods*. The phrase *cannot be used* would be preferable to *are not able to be used*.

A   The wording is awkward, as explained.

B   The wording is awkward, as explained above and because of the phrase *in the future of insufficient cash flow*.

C   **Correct.** This version uses the preferable *cannot successfully be used* and is otherwise clearly and concisely worded.

D   *Cannot be used without succeeding in creating a problem* is badly worded. Surely the point of the sentence is that the methods cannot be used successfully without creating a future problem of insufficient cash flow; as worded, this version seems to suggest that successfully creating a cash flow problem is a prerequisite for being able to use the methods. Also, *in the future of insufficient cash flow* is awkward.

E   As explained above, this version seems to suggest that successfully creating a cash flow problem is a prerequisite for being able to use the methods.

The correct answer is C.

SC62661.01

272. Despite the Puritan sumptuary laws prohibiting the wearing of bright or elaborate clothing, <u>if you had either a liberal education or an annual income of two hundred pounds one was permitted to display their material prosperity in public</u>.

(A)   if you had either a liberal education or an annual income of two hundred pounds one was permitted to display their material prosperity in public

(B)   if one had either a liberal education or annual income of two hundred pounds one was permitted the public display of their material prosperity

(C)   having either a liberal education or annual income of two hundred pounds would allow one to publicly display their material prosperity

(D)   those with either a liberal education or an annual income of two hundred pounds were allowed to display their material prosperity in public

(E)   those having either a liberal education or annual income of two hundred pounds were permitted their public display of material prosperity

Diction; Agreement; Rhetorical Construction

The use of *you* is strange, because the sentence is discussing a set of laws that were in place long before the time of the reader. Also, the sentence shifts from *you* to *one*. *One* would be preferable throughout, given that the sentence concerns laws in place long ago. Finally, the use of *their* does not agree in number with *one*. Although in some contexts it is acceptable to use *their* as a singular possessive adjective, it should not be used along with *one* (*one's* would be preferable), and its use in this sentence creates an ambiguity: is its antecedent intended to be *one* or is its antecedent intended to be the plural noun *laws*?

A   This version fails for the reasons explained above.

B   The use of *their* is incorrect; in this instance, it can simply be deleted.

C   The use of *their* is incorrect.

D   Correct. The use of *those* is preferable to *you*. *Their* is acceptable here because *those* is plural.

E   The force of *their* is unclear. It could, for example, convey a presumption that the people designated by the subject *those … pounds* would all actually display material prosperity, rather than merely be permitted to do so.

The correct answer is D.

SC72661.01

273.   Like Darwin and his fruitful voyage on the *Beagle*, Banks's trip with Captain Cook on the *Endeavour* inspired and shaped his remarkable career in natural science.

(A)   Like Darwin and his fruitful voyage on the *Beagle*, Banks's trip with Captain Cook on the *Endeavour*

inspired and shaped his remarkable career in natural science.

(B)   Just as Darwin had a fruitful voyage on the *Beagle*, Banks's trip with Captain Cook on the *Endeavour* inspired and shaped a remarkable career as a natural scientist.

(C)   Like Darwin's fruitful voyage on the *Beagle*, Banks's trip with Captain Cook on the *Endeavour* inspired and shaped a remarkable career in natural science.

(D)   Just as Darwin's fruitful voyage on the *Beagle*, Banks sailed with Captain Cook on the *Endeavour*, inspiring and shaping his remarkable career as a natural scientist.

(E)   Like Darwin's fruitful voyage on the *Beagle*, Banks sailed with Captain Cook on the *Endeavour*, which inspired and shaped a remarkable career in natural science.

Parallelism; Diction; Rhetorical Construction; Logical Predication

Absent relevant context or detailed knowledge about the relevant history, the given sentence seems open to more than one interpretation. Such ambiguity indicates a rhetorical-construction failure. On one interpretation, the given sentence seems aimed at comparing Banks's sea voyage and Darwin's with respect to the influence those voyages had on scientific careers—but the given sentence and its alternatives vary in how successfully this comparison is executed. For example, the comparison in the given sentence is presented loosely and somewhat illogically: Bank's trip is compared with "Darwin and his fruitful voyage." In some variants, *just as* is used instead of *like*. These uses of *just as* fail to make clear the comparison intended. The word *like* is a preposition that is normally followed by a noun, noun phrase, or pronoun that it governs; *just as* is normally used as a conjunction, introducing a subordinate clause. Failure to take this distinction into account is a diction error.

A   This is ambiguous and for that reason fails rhetorically. The comparison between Banks's trip and "Darwin and his fruitful voyage" is drawn loosely and somewhat illogically.

B   The comparison articulated here is between two disparate facts: Darwin had a fruitful voyage, and Banks's trip inspired and shaped a scientific career. The expected parallelism between two sea voyages is absent. The conjunction *just as* is used idiomatically, however.

C   **Correct.** This version articulates the comparison more clearly than any of the other versions. It conveys that Banks's voyage resembled Darwin's voyage in one respect: each inspired and shaped a scientific career. The preposition *like* is used to indicate the resemblance.

D   The phrase *just as* is normally used as a conjunction, introducing a subordinate clause; here the clause, made explicit, is: *Just as Darwin's fruitful voyage on the* Beagle *[did]*. The verb *did* is implicit. However, this reading creates a nonsensical parallelism that, taken strictly, represents Darwin's fruitful voyage as having sailed with Captain Cook—a logical-predication issue. A separate point is that the participial phrase *inspiring ... scientist,* which modifies *Banks,* represents Banks as inspiring his own scientific career—probably not the intended meaning.

E   The phrase *like ...* Beagle is a prepositional phrase and is nonparallel with the main clause *Banks sailed ...* Endeavor. This failure of parallelism impairs the expression of the intended comparison, which is between Darwin's voyage and Banks's. The structure of the sentence also involves a logical-predication error in that it indicates (absurdly) a similarity between a person (Banks) and Darwin's voyage.

The correct answer is C.

SC82661.01

274. When more and more factories move out of the cities each year, manufacturing jobs, historically the first step into the job market for the urban poor, have become fewer and fewer.

(A)   When more and more factories move out of the cities each year, manufacturing jobs, historically the first step into the job market for the urban poor, have become fewer and fewer.

(B)   At the time that more and more factories move out of the cities each year, manufacturing jobs, historically the first step into the job market for the urban poor, become less and less.

(C)   When more and more factories move out of the cities each year, then manufacturing jobs, historically the first step into the urban poor's job market, become less and less.

(D)   Since more and more factories have moved out of the cities each year, manufacturing jobs, historically the first step into the urban poor's job market, have become less and less.

(E)   As more and more factories move out of the cities each year, manufacturing jobs, historically the first step into the job market for the urban poor, become fewer and fewer.

Verb Form; Diction

The verb tenses of the sentence should match. *When more and more factories move out* dictates that the verb predicated of *manufacturing jobs* should be *become,* not *have become.* For *have become* to be correct, the sentence would need to begin with *When more and more factories have moved out.* Some of the answer choices incorrectly have *less and less;* because manufacturing jobs are countable, *fewer and fewer* is correct (as it is in the underlined portion of the sentence).

A   *Have become* is incorrect. The tense should match that in *when more and more factories move out;* thus, *become* would be correct.

B   This version of the sentence is unnecessarily wordy (e.g., *at the time that*) and incorrectly uses *less and less* rather than *fewer and fewer.*

C   This version of the sentence incorrectly uses *less and less* rather than *fewer and fewer.* The use of *then* after the first comma is unnecessary and unidiomatic.

D   This version of the sentence incorrectly uses *less and less* rather than *fewer and fewer.*

E   **Correct.** The verb *become* has the same tense as the phrasal verb *move out* and *fewer and fewer* is correct.

The correct answer is E.

SC92661.01

275. The thousands of volcanic islands and coral atolls of the South Seas have a total population of about four million, but the paucity of natural resources <u>does not permit such economic development that would be needed by them to support more population</u>.

(A) does not permit such economic development that would be needed by them to support more population

(B) does not permit economic development such as is needed for supporting a larger number

(C) does not permit the economic development needed to support a larger population

(D) do not permit the economic development needed to support a larger population

(E) do not permit needed economic development for supporting a larger number of people

Diction; Agreement; Rhetorical Construction

The use of *that* in *does not permit such economic development that would be needed* is incorrect. *That* should be replaced with *as*. However, even if this correction were made, the sentence would still be poorly worded. The antecedent of *them* (*volcanic islands and coral atolls*) is too far separated from the pronoun, and the use of the passive voice (*would be needed by them*) lacks the clarity and rhetorical force the active voice would have provided (*they would need*). That said, it would be preferable to avoid the *such … as* form entirely. *Does not permit the economic development needed to support a larger population* conveys the same idea more succinctly.

A The sentence has the problems explained above.

B *Such as is needed* is awkward; *a larger number* is unclear.

C **Correct.** This version clearly and concisely conveys the intended idea.

D The subject of the verb is *paucity*, which is singular; thus, *do* is incorrect and should be replaced with *does*.

E The subject of the verb is *paucity*, which is singular; thus, *do* is incorrect and should be replaced with *does*; also, *needed economic development for supporting a larger number of people* is awkward.

The correct answer is C.

SC03661.01

276. <u>In contrast with a dark surface and its tendency toward heat absorption</u>, a large expanse of snow and ice reflects incoming radiation into space.

(A) In contrast with a dark surface and its tendency toward heat absorption

(B) Contrasted with a dark surface's tendency to absorb heat

(C) Since it is in contrast to a dark surface and its tendency to absorb heat

(D) Contrasted to the tendency of a dark surface to absorb heat

(E) In contrast to a dark surface, which tends to absorb heat

Idiom; Parallelism

When *contrast* follows *in*, *contrast* functions as a noun; the appropriate preposition to use after *contrast* when it functions as a noun is *to*; *with* is the preferred preposition to use after *contrast* only when *contrast* functions as a verb. Thus, the sentence's use of *in contrast with* is incorrect. Also, the logical contrast would be between *a dark surface* and *a large expanse of snow and ice*, not between both *a dark surface and its tendency toward heat absorption* and *a large expanse of snow*.

A *In contrast with* is not idiomatic; the correct preposition to use when *contrast* functions as a noun is *to*. Also, the logical contrast to make would be between *a dark surface* and *a large expanse of snow and ice*, not between both *a dark surface and its tendency toward heat absorption* and *a large expanse of snow*.

B The appropriate contrast is between *a dark surface* and *a large expanse of snow and ice*, not, as it is here, between *a dark surface's tendency to absorb heat* and *a large expanse of snow and ice*.

C   Because of its use of *since*, this version illogically states that the reason a large expanse of snow and ice reflects incoming radiation into space is that it is in contrast to a dark surface and its tendency to absorb heat.

D   The preferred preposition to use with *contrasted* (and with *contrast* whenever it is used as a verb rather than as a noun) is *with*, not *to*, which is used here. Also, *a large expanse of snow and ice* is illogically contrasted with *the tendency of a dark surface to absorb heat.*

E   **Correct.** *In contrast to* is the correct idiom; *a large expanse of snow and ice* is logically contrasted with *a dark surface.*

The correct answer is E.

SC37620.01

277. The greatest road system built in the Americas prior to the arrival of Christopher Columbus was the Incan highway, which, over 2,500 miles long and extending from northern Ecuador through Peru to southern Chile.

(A)   Columbus was the Incan highway, which, over 2,500 miles long and extending

(B)   Columbus was the Incan highway, over 2,500 miles in length, which had extended

(C)   Columbus, the Incan highway, which was over 2,500 miles in length and extended

(D)   Columbus, the Incan highway, being over 2,500 miles in length, was extended

(E)   Columbus, the Incan highway was over 2,500 miles long, extending

Grammatical Construction; Verb Form

The sentence begins with a long noun phrase *the greatest … Columbus,* a description that we are told refers to the Incan highway. The sentence also aims to tell us the length of this highway and what regions it passed through. One issue in the sentence concerns correct sentence formation. A related issue concerns the appropriate verb form to be used.

A   The formation of the relative clause introduced by *which* is faulty, mainly because of its present-participle verb form *extending.* A relative clause giving a correct completion

of the sentence would have been *which was over 2,500 miles long and extended … Chile.*

B   This has two flaws present in the phrase *which had extended.* The relative pronoun *which* could be read as having the immediately preceding noun *length,* rather than *highway,* as its antecedent. Also, the complex verb form *had extended,* which normally refers to a time preceding a past time mentioned in the sentence, is incorrect here; the simple past *extended* is needed.

C   The passage, if completed with this wording, would lack a main verb and therefore would not be a sentence, as opposed to a very long noun phrase followed by a relative clause.

D   A glaring flaw here is use of the passive verb form *was extended* instead of the active and intransitive verb form *extended.* This conveys an unintended meaning, i.e., that the highway was initially 2,500 miles long but was later made even longer. Another flaw is the unnecessary and awkward use of the participle *being.*

E   **Correct.** Completing the passage with this wording gives a sentence with *the Incan highway* as its subject. The noun phrase *the greatest … Columbus* provides a description of the Incan highway. The participial phrase beginning with *extending* modifies the sentence subject, thereby providing a further description of the highway.

The correct answer is E.

SC99250.01

278. Due to poaching and increased cultivation in their native habitats, researchers have determined that there are fewer than 100 Arabian leopards left in the wild, and thus the leopards are many times as rare as China's giant pandas.

(A)   Due to poaching and increased cultivation in their native habitats, researchers have determined that there are fewer than 100 Arabian leopards left in the wild, and thus the leopards are many times as rare as

(B)   Due to poaching and increased cultivation in their native habitats, there are fewer than 100 Arabian leopards left in the wild, researchers have determined, making them many times more rare than

(C) There are fewer than 100 Arabian leopards left in the wild due to poaching and increased cultivation in their native habitats, researchers have determined, which makes the leopards many times more rare compared to

(D) Researchers have determined that, because of poaching and increased cultivation in their native habitats, there are fewer than 100 Arabian leopards left in the wild, thus making them many more times as rare as

(E) Researchers have determined that, because of poaching and increased cultivation in their native habitats, there are fewer than 100 Arabian leopards left in the wild, and thus the leopards are many times more rare than

Grammatical Construction; Diction

The sentence contains three errors. The adverbial phrase *due to … habitats* is so positioned as to appear to modify the verb *have determined*—thus making the possessive adjective *their* seem, incorrectly, to refer to *researchers*. The comparison indicated by *many times as rare as* is intended to indicate that one group is rarer than another, a meaning properly conveyed by a comparative adjective—either *rarer* or *more rare*—plus *than*.

A This fails to give a correct sentence, for the reasons explained above.

B This wording is awkward in part because of the placement of *researchers have determined*. It also contains a subtle error in failing to indicate clearly that the researchers ascertained not only the reduction in the number of leopards but also the causes of this reduction.

C The phrasing is ambiguous and awkward. The reason the remaining leopards are "left in the wild" is surely not due to poaching or increased cultivation; the determinations made by the researchers have surely not made the leopards rarer—and one can assume that the writer of the passage did not intend to state otherwise. Another point: the comparison indicated by *more rare* would normally be completed by use of *than*, not *compared to*.

D The phrase *many more times as rare as* is not the correct way to indicate that the Arabian

leopards are much more rare than giant pandas. Also, the participial phrase *making them* can be read as an awkwardly placed modifier of the sentence subject *researchers*, which would convey the nonsensical idea that the researchers made the leopards rarer.

E **Correct.** This version is the only one that avoids all the errors explained above.

The correct answer is E.

SC04215

279. Developed by Pennsylvania's Palatine Germans about 1750, Conestoga wagons, with high wheels capable of crossing rutted roads, muddy flats, and the nonroads of the prairie and they had a floor curved upward on either end so as to prevent cargo from shifting on steep grades.

(A) wagons, with high wheels capable of crossing rutted roads, muddy flats, and the nonroads of the prairie and they had a floor curved upward on either end so as to prevent

(B) wagons, with high wheels capable of crossing rutted roads, muddy flats, and the nonroads of the prairie, and with a floor that was curved upward at both ends to prevent

(C) wagons, which had high wheels capable of crossing rutted roads, muddy flats, and the nonroads of the prairie, and floors curved upward on their ends so that they prevented

(D) wagons had high wheels capable of crossing rutted roads, muddy flats, and the nonroads of the prairie, and a floor that was curved upward at both ends to prevent

(E) wagons had high wheels capable of crossing rutted roads, muddy flats, and the nonroads of the prairie and floors curving upward at their ends so that it prevented

Logical Predication; Parallelism; Grammatical Construction

The main subject of this sentence is *Conestoga wagons* and the main verb is *had*. The opening participial phrase describes the origin of the wagons, and the rest of the sentence describes the features they possessed. These features must be presented in parallel form as objects of the verb *had*. The sentence first presented is a fragment; the prepositional phrase *with …* leaves the subject *Conestoga wagons* without a verb. When the verb *had* finally appears, a new subject *they* has been unnecessarily introduced.

A   The subject *wagons* is without a verb. The introduction of a new subject *they* is unnecessary. Given the absence of *had* after *wagons* and of a comma after *prairie*, it is also ungrammatical.

B   This version of the sentence has no main verb for the subject *wagons*.

C   As in answer choices A and B, this version of the sentence fails to provide a main verb for the subject *wagons*.

D   Correct. The main verb *had* completes the subject *wagons* and accommodates the two direct objects, *wheels* and *a floor*. The comma after *prairie* helps to clarify that *floors* is a direct object of *had*, parallel with *high wheels*.

E   The referent for *it* is ambiguous.

The correct answer is D.

SC60440.01

280. The current economic downturn has significantly reduced advertising income both for business journals as well as general consumer magazines, especially if focusing on technology.

(A)   has significantly reduced advertising income both for business journals as well as general consumer magazines, especially if focusing

(B)   has significantly reduced advertising income both for business journals and for general consumer magazines, especially those focusing

(C)   significantly reduced advertising income for both business journals and for general consumer magazines, especially when focused

(D)   reduced both business journals' and general consumer magazines' advertising income significantly, especially if focused

(E)   reduced advertising income significantly for both business journals, as well as for general consumer magazines, especially those focusing

Idiom; Grammatical Construction; Parallelism

The sentence contains errors related to the use of *both* to signal coordination of two elements of the sentence. The correct idiom is *both … and*; the phrase *as well as* is not interchangeable with *and*. Moreover, the elements meant to be coordinated are prepositional phrases, the first one being *for business journals*—but the preposition *for* is incorrectly omitted in the second element to be coordinated, a failure of required parallelism. The structure of the sentence suggests that the phrase *especially if focusing on technology* modifies the subject of the sentence, *the current economic downturn*. However, this is not the intended meaning. What is intended is a reference to a subclass of magazines (those that focus on technology).

A   This contains multiple errors: incorrect coordination using *both*; omission of *for* in the second coordinated element; and a misplaced modifier *especially if focusing on technology*.

B   Correct. This sentence correctly uses the idiom *both … and* to coordinate two prepositional phrases and uses a well-structured participial phrase to identify a subclass of the class of general consumer magazines.

C   The position of *for*, preceding rather than following *both*, is incorrect. This misleadingly suggests that just two business journals are being referred to and fails by incorrectly coordinating two structurally dissimilar elements, i.e., a noun phrase (*both business journals*) and a prepositional phrase (*for general consumer magazines*). The phrase *especially when focused …* seems to modify the sentence subject, but in context that reading fails to capture the intended meaning.

D   The phrase *especially if focused …* seems to modify the sentence subject, but in context that reading fails to capture the intended meaning. The simple-past verb *reduced* instead of the past-perfect form *has reduced* does not go well with the reference to a "current" economic downturn. The past-perfect form indicates a past action that is carrying over to the present, and this meaning would be more appropriate.

E   This variant makes it appear that just two unnamed business journals are being referred to, contrary to the clearly intended meaning of the sentence. The simple-past verb *reduced* instead of the past-perfect form *has reduced* does not go well with the reference to a "current" economic downturn.

The correct answer is B.

SC01002

281. The reason many people consider the Mediterranean island to be ungovernable is because that the inhabitants long ago learned to distrust and neutralize all written laws.

(A) is because that the inhabitants long ago learned to distrust and neutralize

(B) is the inhabitants long ago learned distrusting and neutralizing

(C) was because of the inhabitants long ago learning to distrust and to be neutralizing

(D) is that the inhabitants long ago learned to distrust and to neutralize

(E) was on account of the inhabitants long ago learning to distrust and neutralize

Verb Form; Grammatical Construction

The sentence provides a reason for why "many people" consider a certain Mediterranean island to be "ungovernable." It has the form *X is Y*, with *X* a noun phrase that refers to the reason in terms of what is being explained. *Y* provides the explanation.

A   This sentence has two words next to one another that would each, by itself, have the same function. Each of *because* and *that* could serve alone to introduce the explanation and is provided by portion *Y*. Furthermore, in addition to introducing a redundancy, the two words together make the sentence ungrammatical. Removing any one of these words would resolve this issue.

B   If the word *that* were inserted between *is* and *the*, then it would be more immediately clear, when reading this sentence, where the explanation begins (immediately after the word *that*). Furthermore, *learned distrusting*

and neutralizing all written laws should be *learned to distrust and to neutralize all written laws.*

C   In this sentence, the verb *consider* needs to agree with *was*. As it stands, *consider* pertains to the present while *was* pertains to the past.

D   Correct. This sentence follows recommendations made in connection with answer choice A.

E   As in answer choice C, the verb *consider* needs to agree with *was*.

The correct answer is D.

SC28801.01

282. Though there is some overlap with the two concepts *market economy* and *laissez faire,* several important differences between them must be borne in mind.

(A) with the two concepts *market economy* and *laissez faire,* several important differences between them must be borne in mind

(B) between the two concepts *market economy* and *laissez faire,* several important differences must be borne in mind

(C) spanning the two concepts *market economy* and *laissez faire,* one must bear several important differences between them in mind

(D) among the two concepts of *market economy* and *laissez faire,* there are several important differences among them that must be borne in mind

(E) with the two concepts of *market economy* and *laissez faire,* one must bear in mind several important differences

Idiom; Rhetorical Construction

The sentence's unidiomatic use of *there is some overlap with the two concepts* misleadingly sets up the expectation that there is some third thing that overlaps with the concepts *market economy* and *laissez faire,* whereas the sentence is merely intending to say that those two concepts overlap with one another. The sentence would be clearer and more idiomatic if it instead said *there is some overlap between the two concepts.* Because the sentence uses *with* rather than *between* in the first clause, the sentence must indicate that the differences in question are between these two concepts by using the awkward locution *several important differences between them.*

A   The sentence should use *between* rather than *with*, allowing it to avoid having to use the awkward phrase *several important differences between them.*

B   Correct. The sentence uses the idiomatic phrase *overlap between the two*; the second clause is well expressed.

C   The use of *overlap spanning the two* is unidiomatic; *one must bear several important differences between them in mind* is awkward.

D   When talking of just two things, *between* rather than *among* should be used; *there are several important differences among them that must be borne in mind* is awkward and wordy.

E   *Between* rather than *with* should be used; the use of *with* improperly sets up an expectation that the sentence is discussing an overlap between the two concepts *market economy* and *laissez faire* and some third thing.

The correct answer is B.

SC71061.01

283. Because of the erratic pattern of sales increases this year, retailers and analysts hesitate to predict five-year trends in retail sales during the months that have historically been the most profitable.

(A)   Because of the erratic pattern of sales increases this year, retailers and analysts hesitate to predict

(B)   With the erratic pattern of this year's sales increases, retailers and analysts are hesitant in predicting

(C)   This year, due to the erratic pattern of increasing sales, there is some hesitation among retailers and analysts in predicting

(D)   The erratic pattern of sales increases have made retailers and analysts hesitate this year to predict

(E)   This year's erratic pattern of increasing sales have made retailers and analysts hesitate to predict

Diction; Idiom; Agreement

The intended idea of the sentence is that this year's erratic pattern of sales increases has made retailers and analysts hesitant to make any prediction regarding a particular trend. This idea is well expressed by using *because of.* Furthermore, the correct answer, unlike some of the other answer choices, uses the appropriate idiom *hesitant to* rather than *hesitant in* and has no agreement error between subject and verb.

A   Correct. The sentence's use of *Because of* appropriately conveys the idea that the erratic pattern of sales increases explains why the retailers and analysts are hesitant to make a prediction. The sentence uses the correct idiom *hesitate to* and has no agreement errors.

B   The use of *with* is less effective than *because of* in the correct answer; the meaning is conveyed less clearly than in answer choice A. Also, *hesitant in predicting* is awkward and unidiomatic.

C   *Due to* effectively communicates that the erratic pattern of increasing sales helps explain the retailers' and analysts' hesitation to make a prediction, but the sentence employs the awkward, wordy, and unidiomatic *hesitation … in predicting.*

D   *The erratic pattern …* is singular, so the verb should be *has.* The placement of the adverbial phrase *this year* would be more appropriate immediately following *increases.*

E   *The erratic pattern …* is singular, so the verb should be *has.*

The correct answer is A.

SC89941.01

284. Proceeding without a definite plan for upcoming labor negotiations, like the firm had agreed to last year, it would surely have proven to be a disaster in the face of the skilled and resolute opposition involved this time.

(A)   Proceeding without a definite plan for upcoming labor negotiations, like the firm had agreed to last year, it would surely have proven to be a disaster

(B) Proceeding without a definite plan for upcoming labor negotiations, as the firm agreed last year to do, would surely have proven to be a disaster

(C) Going ahead without the presence of a definite plan for upcoming labor negotiations, like the firm had agreed last year to do, would surely have proven disastrous

(D) To proceed without the presence of a definite plan for upcoming labor negotiations, as the firm had agreed to last year, would surely have proven disastrous

(E) Going ahead without their having a definite plan for upcoming labor negotiations, as they agreed to last year, it would surely have proven to be a disaster for the firm

Diction; Rhetorical Construction; Logical Predication

Although in informal speech and writing, *like* is sometimes used as a conjunction as it is here, this use in more formal writing is controversial and is generally frowned on; using *as* instead of *like* would be preferable in this sentence. The phrase *proceeding without a definite plan for the upcoming labor negotiations* can function either as a gerund phrase, in which case it functions as a noun, or as a participle phrase, in which case it functions as an adjective. As worded here, the phrase may seem to function as an adjective, modifying *it*. However, what is meant by the sentence is that the act of proceeding without a definite plan would have proven to be a disaster, in which case the word *it* should be removed and the phrase in question should be taken to be a gerund phrase that acts as the subject for the verb *would have proven*.

A The sentence is flawed in the ways explained above.

B **Correct.** This version correctly uses *as* rather than *like*, and concisely uses the phrase beginning with *proceeding* as the subject of the sentence.

C *Without the presence of a definite plan* is wordier than necessary; *without a definite plan* would be preferable. *As* would be preferable to *like*.

D *Without the presence of a definite plan* is wordier than necessary; *without a definite plan* would be preferable.

E *Without their having a definite plan* is wordy; *without a definite plan* would be preferable. The word *it* should be removed as described in connection with answer choice A.

The correct answer is B.

SC03916

285. Because the collagen fibers in skin line up in the direction of tension, surgical cuts made along these so-called Langer's lines sever fewer fibers and is less likely to leave an unsightly scar.

(A) Because the collagen fibers in skin line up in the direction of tension, surgical cuts made along these so-called Langer's lines sever fewer

(B) Because the collagen fibers in skin line up in the direction of tension, a surgical cut having been made along these so-called Langer's lines severs less

(C) Because the collagen fibers in skin line up in the direction of tension, a surgical cut made along these so-called Langer's lines severs fewer

(D) With the collagen fibers in skin lining up in the direction of tension, surgical cuts made along these so-called Langer's lines sever less

(E) With the collagen fibers in skin lining up in the direction of tension, a surgical cut made along these so-called Langer's lines sever fewer

Agreement; Diction

This sentence explains a causal connection between the alignment of collagen fibers and the impact of a particular type of surgical cut. *Because* is appropriate to express that causal relationship. The singular verb in the phrase *is less likely to leave* requires a singular subject (*cut*) and must be coordinated with another singular verb (*severs*). Because *fibers* are countable, the correct modifier is *fewer* rather than *less*.

A The plural subject *cuts* does not agree with the singular verb *is*.

B The verb form *having been made* is inconsistent with the present tense verb *severs*; *less* inappropriately modifies countable *fibers*.

C **Correct.** The adverbial conjunction *because* accurately captures the causal relationship expressed by the sentence. The singular

461

subject *cut* agrees with the singular verbs *severs* and *is*, and *fewer* appropriately modifies countable *fibers*.

D   The preposition *with* does not capture the causal relationship expressed by the sentence; the plural subject *cuts* does not agree with the singular verbs (*severs* and *is*); and *less* is an inappropriate modifier for countable *fibers*.

E   As in answer choice D, the preposition *with* fails to capture the causal relationship between alignment of fibers and scarring. The plural verb *sever* does not agree with the singular subject *cut* and the subsequent singular verb *is*.

The correct answer is C.

SC01639
286. The completion in 1925 of the Holland Tunnel, linking Manhattan with New Jersey's highways, which permitted 2,000 cars to pass through each tube every hour and was hailed as the decade's $48 million engineering masterpiece.

(A)   Tunnel, linking Manhattan with New Jersey's highways, which permitted 2,000 cars to pass through each tube every hour and

(B)   Tunnel, linking Manhattan with New Jersey's highways and permitting 2,000 cars to pass through each tube every hour, it

(C)   Tunnel, linking Manhattan with New Jersey's highways and permitting 2,000 cars to pass through each tube every hour,

(D)   Tunnel linked Manhattan with New Jersey's highways, which permitted 2,000 cars to pass through each tube every hour and

(E)   Tunnel linked Manhattan with New Jersey's highways, permitting 2,000 cars to pass through each tube every hour,

Grammatical Construction; Parallelism

The sentence (not a properly grammatical sentence as it stands) reports that the completion of the Holland Tunnel was hailed as an engineering masterpiece. Parenthetically, it seeks to describe characteristics of the tunnel that made it useful and perhaps help explain its enthusiastic reception. Questions to consider include: what

is the proper antecedent of the relative pronoun *which*? And how would the tunnel's two major characteristics be best described?

A   The relative pronoun *which* is adjacent to *New Jersey's highways*, but contextually, *the completion of the Holland Tunnel* (or perhaps *the Holland Tunnel*) seems to be the pronoun's antecedent. The relative clause has two verbal phrases *permitted ... and *was hailed ...* coordinated with *and*. However, there is no properly grammatical sentence here, since there is no independent clause.

B   The participial phrases *linking ... highways* and *permitting ... hour* are parallel and coordinated by *and*. This portion is correct and describes two characteristics of the tunnel. However, the addition of the pronoun *it* makes what precedes it into a mere sentence fragment, so there is no properly grammatical sentence here.

C   **Correct.** The complex phrase *linking ... hour* correctly exhibits parallelism between two participial phrases and modifies *the Holland Tunnel*. The phrase functions parenthetically, and the sentence as a whole has a coherent grammatical structure.

D   The antecedent of the relative pronoun *which* is unclear and makes this version fail. Is it *New Jersey's highways*, the whole preceding clause, or *the completion of the Holland Tunnel*? The relative pronoun is the subject both of *permitted* and of *was hailed* in the complex relative clause and must have the same antecedent in both cases. As the subject of *was hailed*, the pronoun's antecedent is *the completion of the Holland Tunnel*. As the subject of *permitted*, the pronoun cannot grammatically have that as its antecedent. Thus the complex relative clause *which permitted ... masterpiece* is grammatically incoherent.

E   This version makes *was hailed ... masterpiece* into a mere sentence fragment, not properly coordinated with the remainder of the sentence.

The correct answer is C.

SC03315

287. The World Wildlife Fund has declared that global warming, a phenomenon that most scientists agree is caused by human beings' burning of fossil fuels, will create havoc among migratory birds <u>by harming their habitats as a result of altering the environment.</u>

(A) by harming their habitats as a result of altering the environment

(B) by altering the environment to the extent of it harming their habitats

(C) by altering the environment in ways harmful to their habitats

(D) from the fact that their habitats will be harmed by the environment being altered

(E) from the fact that the environment will be altered and this will harm their habitats

Logical Predication; Rhetorical Construction

The sentence describes a declaration by the World Wildlife Fund that global warming will "create havoc" among migratory birds in certain respects, which are specified in the underlined portion. The underlined portion thus needs to specify, in a clear and focused fashion, how, according to the World Wildlife Fund, global warming will create havoc for the birds.

A   The description in this answer choice of the effects of global warming among migratory birds is convoluted and confusing. First, the sentence as written does not specify who or what is altering the environment. Second, given the reasonable guess that it is global warming that is or will harm the environment, the order of the listing of the causal elements is confusing. According to the sentence, global warming will alter the environment and then this altering will harm the habitat of birds. However, although this sentence accurately describes what causes what, the elements are listed in an order that does not correspond to the order of causation ("global warming" is followed by "harming the habitats," which is followed by "altering the environment").

B   This sentence uses the word *extent*, followed by a condition, *it harming their habitats*, intended to imply a certain level of *extent*. The extent is great enough to harm the habitat of the birds. However, as worded, the sentence does not provide a clear condition on the level of extent. For example, in *it harming their habitat*, it is not clear what *it* refers to. The word *it* could refer to the environment or to the extent of change to the environment.

C   **Correct.** This sentence clearly specifies how global warming will "create havoc" for the birds.

D   This sentence, like answer choice A, is convoluted and confusing, in part because, when reading the sentence, it is unnecessarily difficult to understand what is supposed to be causing what. Note that, although the meaning of this answer choice is more or less the same as that of answer choice C, this sentence in answer choice D is much more difficult to process.

E   This sentence is unnecessarily wordy and difficult to process. Answer choice C is a much better choice.

The correct answer is C.

SC05244

288. Tropical bats play an important role in the rain forest ecosystem, aiding in the dispersal of cashew, date, and fig seeds; <u>pollinating banana, breadfruit, and mango trees; and indirectly help the producing of</u> tequila by pollinating agave plants.

(A) pollinating banana, breadfruit, and mango trees; and indirectly help the producing of

(B) pollinating banana, breadfruit, and mango trees; and indirectly helping to produce

(C) pollinating banana, breadfruit, and mango trees; and they indirectly help to produce

(D) they pollinate banana, breadfruit, and mango trees; and indirectly help producing

(E) they pollinate banana, breadfruit, and mango trees; indirectly helping the producing of

Parallelism; Diction

The sentence indicates three ways in which tropical bats play an important role in the rainforest ecosystem, but it does not express these three ways by using appropriately parallel grammatical constructions. The first two ways mentioned—*aiding in the dispersal of cashew, date, and fig seeds* and *pollinating banana, breadfruit, and mango trees*—are expressed using participial phrases (which function as adjectives), whereas the third is expressed as part of a compound predicate—*and indirectly help the producing of tequila by pollinating agave plants* (also note that *the producing of* involves a poor choice of words, and would be better expressed by writing *to produce* or perhaps *with the production of*).

A   The phrases beginning with *aiding*, *pollinating*, and *help* are not appropriately parallel grammatical constructions. Also *the producing of* is awkward and would be better worded as *to produce* or *with the production of.*

B   **Correct.** This sentence has an appropriate grammatical parallelism and involves no questionable word choices.

C   The construction of the sentence is not appropriately parallel.

D   The construction of the sentence is not appropriately parallel and *producing* is a questionable choice of words (*to produce* would be better).

E   The construction of the sentence is not appropriately parallel and *the producing of* is a questionable choice of words (*to produce* or perhaps *with the production of* would be better).

The correct answer is B.

SC04346

289. A recent court decision has qualified a 1998 ruling that workers cannot be laid off if they have been given reason to believe that their jobs will be safe, provided that their performance remains satisfactory.

(A)   if they have been given reason to believe that their jobs will

(B)   if they are given reason for believing that their jobs would still

(C)   having been given reason for believing that their jobs would

(D)   having been given reason to believe their jobs to

(E)   given reason to believe that their jobs will still

Verb Form; Idiom

This sentence asserts that a court decision has qualified a 1998 ruling. It then goes on to explain the series of conditions stipulated by that ruling: workers cannot be laid off if they have been given (prior) reason to believe that continued satisfactory job performance will (always) ensure that their jobs are safe. To express these complicated temporal relationships, the present tense passive verb *cannot be laid off* describes the assurance provided by the ruling; the present-perfect, passive verb describes the prior condition *have been given …*, and the future tense verb *will be* describes the outcome the workers can expect. The idiom *reason to believe* succinctly describes the assurance given to workers.

A   **Correct.** The sequence of conditions makes sense, and the idiom is correct.

B   The present tense *are given* fails to clarify that the assurance of job security must precede the workers' confidence that they cannot be laid off. The phrase *reason for believing* (singular, with no article) is unidiomatic and in this context is inappropriate.

C   This version appears to be presenting *having been given reason …* as a restrictive modifier of *laid off.* This makes the sentence very awkward and hard to make sense of, and it obscures the requisite nature of the condition (that workers had been given prior reason to think their jobs were safe). *Reason for believing* is unidiomatic.

D   Without a comma after *off*, it is unclear what *having been given reason …* modifies; the string of infinitive phrases is awkward and confusing.

E   As in answer choice D, it is unclear what the participial phrase (in this case, *given reason to believe*) is supposed to modify.

The correct answer is A.

SC04874

290. Of all the record companies involved in early jazz, the three most prominent were Columbia, Victor, and OKeh.

(A) Of all the record companies involved in early jazz, the three most prominent were Columbia, Victor, and OKeh.

(B) Three most prominent record companies of all the ones that were involved in early jazz were Columbia, Victor, and OKeh.

(C) Columbia, Victor, and OKeh were, of all the record companies involved in early jazz, the three of them that were most prominent.

(D) Columbia, Victor, and OKeh were three most prominent of all the record companies involved in early jazz.

(E) Out of all the record companies that were involved in early jazz, three of them that were the most prominent were Columbia, Victor, and OKeh.

Diction; Rhetorical Construction

This sentence aims to emphasize the special prominence of just three specific companies, as opposed to all other companies. Where *three most prominent companies* is not preceded by a definite article, it is unidiomatic. To indicate that these three were more prominent than any others, it should say *the three most prominent companies*. If the intention were, instead, to indicate that these companies were merely among a number of highly prominent ones, it should say *three of the most prominent companies*. Also, in general, one should avoid relative clause constructions when simple adjectives can express the same idea more simply.

A **Correct.** *The three ...* is used, and *prominent* modifies the understood *companies* in a concise way.

B *The* is omitted before *three*, and *of all the ones that were involved* is inferior to a simpler expression such as *of all the ones involved*.

C *The three of them that were most prominent* is long and awkward; *the three most prominent* is shorter and simpler.

D *The* is omitted before *three*.

E Not only is *the* omitted, but *three of them that were the most prominent* is too long and complex, compared to *the three most prominent*.

The correct answer is A.

SC01451

291. Since 1992, in an attempt to build up the Atlantic salmon population in each of the seven rivers in which salmon still spawn, state officials in Maine have stocked them with fry raised in hatcheries from eggs produced by wild fish found in that particular river.

(A) them

(B) the river

(C) the rivers

(D) each river

(E) that river

Rhetorical Construction; Diction

The meaning that the sentence was intended to convey is clear, but because the plural *them* is discordant with the singulars *each* and *that particular river*, the sentence fails to express its intended meaning coherently.

A The earlier part of the sentence uses the phrase *each of the seven rivers*, so the plural *them* is inappropriate.

B The phrase *the river* is singular but can refer only to a particular river, whereas *each* refers to the individual rivers in the group of seven.

C The plural *the rivers* does not match the singular *each* in the earlier part of the sentence.

D **Correct.** The phrase *each river* is consistent with the earlier reference to "each of the seven rivers."

E Although *that river* is singular, it can only refer to a particular river, but no particular river is referred to in the earlier part of the sentence.

The correct answer is D.

SC02382
292. On the tournament roster are listed several tennis students, <u>most all of which play as good</u> as their instructors.

    (A)   most all of which play as good

    (B)   most all of whom play as good

    (C)   almost all of which play as well

    (D)   almost all of whom play as good

    (E)   almost all of whom play as well

Idiom; Diction

The standard formal, written word to express a quantity just short of everything is *almost*, not *most*. With animate entities such as people, *who(m)* is preferred over *which*. For all but a few exceptional verbs, adverbial modifiers (*well*) are correct as opposed to adjectival ones (*good*).

A   None of *most*, *which*, or *good* are the preferred forms.

B   *Most* and *good* are not the correct standard forms.

C   Although *almost* and *well* are fine, *which* is not.

D   Although *almost* and *whom* are fine, *good* is not.

E   **Correct.** All of *almost*, *whom*, and *well* are correct.

The correct answer is E.

SC07143
293. In 1974 a large area of the surface of Mercury was photographed from varying distances, <u>which revealed a degree of cratering similar to that of the Moon's.</u>

    (A)   which revealed a degree of cratering similar to that of the Moon's

    (B)   to reveal a degree of cratering similar to the Moon

    (C)   revealing a degree of cratering similar to that of the Moon

    (D)   and revealed cratering similar in degree to the Moon

    (E)   that revealed cratering similar in degree to that of the Moon

Logical Predication; Parallelism

This sentence's second clause, expressing what the imaging of Mercury showed, must be linked to the first clause in a grammatically correct way.

This is best done either by an appositive relative clause (requiring the relative marker *which*), or by a clause starting with a nonfinite verb (*to reveal* or *revealing*). Also, whatever is said to be similar to a degree of cratering (on Mercury) should also be a degree of cratering (on the Moon); this must be expressed clearly.

A   The use of *which* is correct, but *that of the Moon's* is inferior to *that of the Moon*, because the possessive *'s* and *that of the* redundantly express the same idea. *That of the Moon's* appears to refer, illogically, to cratering of some unspecified thing that belongs to the Moon, not cratering of the Moon itself.

B   *To reveal* is acceptable, but *to the Moon* incorrectly compares a physical entity (the Moon) to a degree of cratering.

C   **Correct.** *Revealing* is a good way to start the second clause, and *to that of the Moon* properly contrasts two degrees of cratering.

D   *And* is incorrect as a way to introduce the second clause; *to the Moon* makes the wrong sort of comparison.

E   *That* is not the correct way to introduce an appositive relative clause. *That* is typically used restrictively, whereas the comma preceding it makes the ensuing clause nonrestrictive. This leaves the meaning unclear.

The correct answer is C.

SC46270.02
294. The survival of a rare New Zealand species of mistletoe that produces spectacular sprays of scarlet flowers <u>is threatened both because their leaves are extremely tasty to a voracious opossum species and also because their</u> flowers are pollinated by two species of birds whose populations are in decline.

    (A)   is threatened both because their leaves are extremely tasty to a voracious opossum species and also because their

    (B)   is threatened both because its leaves are extremely tasty to a voracious opossum species and because its

    (C)   is threatened both because its leaves are extremely tasty to a voracious opossum species and also its

(D)   are threatened both because its leaves are extremely tasty to a voracious opossum species and its

(E)   are threatened both because their leaves are extremely tasty to a voracious opossum species and because their

Idiom; Agreement

The antecedent of *their* is *a rare New Zealand species of mistletoe*, which is singular. Therefore, *their*, which is a plural pronoun, is incorrect. *Its* would be the appropriate pronoun to use here. An additional problem with this sentence is that *both . . . and also* is unidiomatic. Either *both* or *also* should be deleted.

A   As explained above, *their* is incorrect. Because the antecedent is the singular noun phrase *a rare New Zealand species of mistletoe*, the appropriate possessive pronoun is *its*. Furthermore, *both because . . . and also because* is unidiomatic.

B   Correct. This version correctly uses *its* to agree in number with the singular noun phrase *a rare New Zealand species of mistletoe*, and uses the appropriate idiom, *both because . . . and because.*

C   This version's *both because . . . and also* is unidiomatic. *Also* should be replaced with *because.*

D   The plural verb *are* does not agree with the singular subject, *the survival of a rare New Zealand species of mistletoe.* Furthermore, this version is unidiomatic. The appropriate idiom is *both because . . . and because.* This version lacks the second occurrence of *because.*

E   This version has two agreement problems: First, *The survival of a rare New Zealand species of mistletoe* is the subject and is singular, and so the verb *are*, which should be used only with a plural subject, is inappropriate; *is* would be the correct pronoun to use here. Second, *their* is incorrect. The antecedent is the singular noun phrase *a rare New Zealand species of mistletoe*; the appropriate possessive pronoun to use would be *its.*

The correct answer is B.

SC05894

295. The computer company reported strong second-quarter earnings that surpassed Wall Street's estimates and announced the first in a series of price cuts intended to increase sales further.

(A)   The computer company reported strong second-quarter earnings that surpassed Wall Street's estimates and announced the first in a series of price cuts intended to increase sales further.

(B)   The report of the computer company showed strong second-quarter earnings, surpassing Wall Street's estimates, and they announced the first in a series of price cuts that they intend to increase sales further.

(C)   Surpassing Wall Street's estimates, the report of the computer company showed strong second-quarter earnings, and, for the purpose of increasing sales further, they announced the first in a series of price cuts.

(D)   The computer company reported strong second-quarter earnings, surpassing Wall Street's estimates, and announcing the first in a series of price cuts for the purpose of further increasing sales.

(E)   The computer company, surpassing Wall Street's estimates, reported strong second-quarter earnings, while announcing that to increase sales further there would be the first in a series of price cuts.

Logical Predication; Idiom

The point of the sentence is to describe two actions of the computer company: its earnings report and its announcement of a price cut. To present this information most efficiently, the sentence requires a singular subject "the computer company" and compound verbs (*reported* and *announced*). To indicate that it is the company's earnings and not the report that surpassed Wall Street's estimates, the relative clause *that surpassed . . .* must immediately follow *earnings.*

A   **Correct.** The sentence makes clear that the company is responsible for reporting its earnings and announcing its sales plan; the placement of the relative clause *that surpassed . . .* makes it clear that the company's earnings, not the report, surpassed Wall Street's estimate.

B   Because this compound sentence opens the first clause with the subject *the report*, and relegates the computer company to the position of object of a preposition, the referent of the subject of the second clause *they* is obscured—particularly since *they* is plural and the intended referent *company* is singular. The function of *that* in the final clause is ambiguous and confusing.

C   The placement of the opening modifier *surpassing …* makes it modify *report* rather than *estimate*. The plural pronoun *they* does not agree with its intended antecedent, *company*.

D   *Surpassing …* and the parallel phrase *announcing …* both appear to modify the entire opening clause, representing parallel functions of the company's report of its earnings.

E   The placement of *surpassing …* makes that phrase modify *reported* …. The conjunction *while* indicates that the announcement and the report occurred simultaneously. The phrase *there would be …* introduces unnecessary wordiness and indirection.

The correct answer is A.

SC01562

296. Long overshadowed by the Maya and Aztec civilizations, historians are now exploring the more ancient Olmec culture for the legacy it had for succeeding Mesoamerican societies.

(A)   historians are now exploring the more ancient Olmec culture for the legacy it had for succeeding Mesoamerican societies

(B)   historians' exploration is now of the more ancient Olmec culture's legacy to the Mesoamerican societies succeeding them

(C)   the legacy of the more ancient Olmec culture to the Mesoamerican societies that succeeded them is what historians are now exploring

(D)   the more ancient Olmec culture is now being explored by historians for its legacy to succeeding Mesoamerican societies

(E)   the Olmec culture is more ancient and had a legacy to succeeding Mesoamerican societies that historians are now exploring

Logical Predication; Idiom

The sentence notes that historians are exploring the contributions of the ancient Olmec culture to societies that came after it. The sentence structure is flawed, however.

A   The sentence's initial phrase is, nonsensically, predicated of *historians* rather than of *Olmec culture*. The wording *for the legacy it had for* is verbose, the repetition of *for* is awkward, and the second *for* is unidiomatic with *legacy*.

B   The sentence's initial phrase *long … civilizations* is, nonsensically, predicated of *exploration*. The wording *is now of* is unnecessarily awkward (for example, the phrase *now focuses on* would not be so).

C   The context suggests that the sentence's initial phrase *long … civilizations* is more likely meant to be predicated of a noun phrase referring to another civilization (or culture), thus making *the legacy* be the subject of the sentence (as opposed to *the more ancient Olmec culture*). The relative *what* and its antecedent are too widely separated from each other; also, the construction *is what … is* unnecessarily awkward.

D   **Correct.** This version is logically and structurally correct. Making *the more ancient Olmec culture* the subject of the main clause—the most logical subject, given the initial modifying phrase referring to civilizations—has required a change in the verb form, from active to passive. The preposition *to* following *legacy* is idiomatic.

E   This shifts the emphasis, compared with the given sentence, to how far back in time the Olmec culture existed. Unlike the given sentence, it makes the historians' current preoccupation with the Olmec culture seem secondary. The wording *had a legacy to* is unnecessarily awkward.

The correct answer is D.

SC02370

297. The bank holds $3 billion in loans that are seriously delinquent or in such trouble that <u>they do not expect payments when</u> due.

    (A)   they do not expect payments when

    (B)   it does not expect payments when it is

    (C)   it does not expect payments to be made when they are

    (D)   payments are not to be expected to be paid when

    (E)   payments are not expected to be paid when they will be

Agreement; Logical Predication; Verb Form

The plural pronoun *they* cannot be used to refer to the singular noun *bank*. The structure of *they do not expect payments when due* is awkward and unclear.

A   *Bank* requires the singular pronoun *it*, not the plural pronoun *they*. The structure of *when due* creates ambiguity in meaning.

B   *Payments* is a plural noun, so the singular *it is* is incorrect.

C   **Correct.** The pronouns and their referents agree, as do subjects and their verbs. The addition of the modifying phrase *to be made* clarifies the meaning of the sentence.

D   The active voice is preferable here, since the passive voice leaves it unclear who does not expect the payments to be made. *Payments … to be paid* is redundant. *Are not to be* incorrectly suggests that the writer is prescribing that the payments not be expected.

E   The active voice is preferable here, since the passive voice leaves it unclear who does not expect the payments to be made. *Payments … to be paid* is redundant. *Will be* is not the correct verb form.

The correct answer is C.

SC01435

298. <u>A researcher claims that a tornado of a given size and strength is likely to cause more deaths, both proportionately and in absolute numbers, in the southeastern region of the United States than in the northeastern.</u>

    (A)   A researcher claims that a tornado of a given size and strength is likely to cause more deaths, both proportionately and in absolute numbers, in the southeastern region of the United States than in the northeastern.

    (B)   A researcher claims that a tornado, if of a given size and strength, is likely both proportionately and in absolute numbers to cause more deaths in the southeastern region of the United States than in the northeastern.

    (C)   A researcher claims that, with a tornado of a given size and strength, it is likely to cause more death, both proportionately and in absolute numbers, in the southeastern rather than in the northeastern region of the United States.

    (D)   If a tornado is of a given size and strength, a researcher claims, it is more likely, both proportionately and in absolute numbers, to cause death if it is in the southeastern region of the United States rather than in the northeastern region.

    (E)   Both proportionately and in absolute numbers, a researcher claims that a tornado of a given size and strength is likely to cause more deaths in the southeastern region of the United States rather than in the northeastern.

Grammatical Construction; Diction

The sentence clearly and correctly reports a researcher's claim about the relative incidence of fatalities from a tornado of any given size in two different regions of the United States. It states that the incidence of fatalities in the southeastern region would be greater both in number and as a percentage of the affected population than would the incidence in the northeastern region. Some issues to note about the erroneous sentences are: use of *rather than* instead of simply *than*; use of the singular *death* instead of the plural; the placement of the adverbial phrase *both proportionately … numbers*; and the use of *if*-statements.

A   **Correct.** This sentence expresses a complex thought clearly and coherently while avoiding errors related to the issues mentioned.

B   The researcher's claim is not that a tornado of a certain magnitude is likely to cause more fatalities in the southeastern than in the northeastern region; rather the claim is that a tornado of any given magnitude will cause more deaths in the southeastern region than in the northeastern.

C   This sentence is unnecessarily awkward because of the adverbial phrase beginning *with* and the use of *it* to refer to *a tornado*. The singular *death* does not go well with the mention of numbers, which indicates the counting of individual deaths. The number of deaths in one region is being compared with the number in another; for that purpose, *rather than* is unidiomatic, as opposed to *than*.

D   Beginning the sentence with this *if*-clause suggests that the claimed likelihood of variation in regional incidence of fatalities is conditional on the tornado being of a certain minimum size and strength. Nothing suggests that this is the claim that the given sentence meant to attribute to the researcher. Also, the matter at issue is not whether there would be any death (singular) but rather what the incidence of fatalities (plural) would be in each of two different regions. Another error is that the placement of the adverbial phrase *both proportionately . . . numbers* makes it function as a modifier of the verbal phrase *is more likely*.

E   The placement of the adverbial phrase *both proportionately . . . numbers* seems nonsensically to make it modify the verb *claims*, and does not reflect the intended meaning of the given sentence. The use of *rather than* instead of *than* is an incorrect usage for the comparison intended.

The correct answer is A.

SC04603
299. Heirloom tomatoes, grown from seeds saved from the previous year, only look less appetizing than their round and red supermarket cousins, often green and striped, or have plenty of bumps and bruises, but are more flavorful.

(A)   cousins, often green and striped, or have plenty of bumps and bruises, but are

(B)   cousins, often green and striped, or with plenty of bumps and bruises, although

(C)   cousins, often green and striped, or they have plenty of bumps and bruises, although they are

(D)   cousins; they are often green and striped, or with plenty of bumps and bruises, although

(E)   cousins; they are often green and striped, or have plenty of bumps and bruises, but they are

Logical Predication; Grammatical Construction

The sentence is intended to say that, although heirloom tomatoes may appear to be less appetizing than the round, red supermarket variety, the often green and striped or bumpy and bruised heirloom tomatoes actually are more flavorful. Any version of the sentence in which *green and striped*, *have bumps and bruises*, or *are more flavorful* appear to modify *round and red supermarket cousins* is ill-formed.

A   In this version of the sentence, *often green and striped*, *have plenty of bumps and bruises*, and *are more flavorful* all illogically appear to modify *round and red supermarket cousins* rather than *heirloom tomatoes*.

B   In this version of the sentence as well, *often green and striped*, *with plenty of bumps and bruises*, and *although more flavorful* all illogically appear to modify *round and red supermarket cousins* rather than *heirloom tomatoes*.

C   In this version of the sentence, *often green and striped* illogically appears to modify *round and red supermarket cousins* rather than *heirloom tomatoes*.

D   Although in this version *green and striped* and *with plenty of bumps and bruises* clearly, and correctly, modify *heirloom tomatoes*, the *or* in *they are often green and striped, or with*

plenty of bumps and bruises is unnecessary and awkward. Furthermore, the final clause is ungrammatical and should say *although they are more flavorful*.

E   **Correct.** In this version of the sentence, *green and striped, with plenty of bumps and bruises*, and *are more flavorful* clearly, and correctly, modify *heirloom tomatoes*, and the phrases in the sentence are appropriately parallel with one another.

The correct answer is E.

SC05381

300. In the textbook publishing business, the second quarter is historically weak, because revenues are low and marketing expenses are high as companies prepare for the coming school year.

(A)   low and marketing expenses are high as companies prepare

(B)   low and their marketing expenses are high as they prepare

(C)   low with higher marketing expenses in preparation

(D)   low, while marketing expenses are higher to prepare

(E)   low, while their marketing expenses are higher in preparation

Parallelism; Logical Predication

This sentence is correctly written. It uses parallel structure to give two reasons why textbook publishers have weak second quarters: *revenues are low* and *expenses are high*. The construction *as companies prepare for the coming school year* is clear, as opposed to the awkward constructions using the ambiguous plural pronouns *they* and *their*.

A   **Correct.** This sentence uses the parallel forms *are low … are high* and employs the unambiguous *companies* as the subject of *prepare*.

B   *Their* seems illogically to refer to *revenues*. The subject of *prepare* is the ambiguous *they*.

C   *Higher* is not parallel to *low*, and it gives no indication of what the comparison is supposed to be (Higher than what?). This construction makes it appear, illogically, that

the low revenues have higher marketing expenses.

D   *Higher* is not parallel to *low* and is illogical. The infinitive construction *to prepare …* is awkward.

E   *Higher* is not parallel to *low* and is illogical since no comparison is being made; *their* has no clear referent.

The correct answer is A.

SC01485

301. Because of the sharp increases in the price of gold and silver, the value of Monica Taylor's portfolio rose as her daughter-in-law's dropped.

(A)   as her daughter-in-law's dropped

(B)   while her daughter-in-law's has dropped

(C)   as there was a drop in her daughter-in-law's

(D)   while that of her daughter-in-law's dropped

(E)   as it dropped for her daughter-in-law's

Parallelism; Rhetorical Construction

The sentence attempts to explain two opposing trends in portfolio value: the value of one person's portfolio rose as the value of another person's portfolio dropped. Note, however, that the sentence as given here refers to a rise in value and a drop in a portfolio: this indicates a failure in required parallelism. The comparison, properly expressed, would mention *the value of Monica Taylor's portfolio* and *the value of her daughter-in-law's portfolio*.

A   This is incorrect because it refers to the daughter-in-law's portfolio, not to the value of her portfolio.

B   The conjunction *while* is appropriate here, but the sentence lacks the parallelism needed to clearly compare the opposing trends in portfolio value.

C   This is wordy and lacks the required parallelism already mentioned.

D   **Correct.** The phrase *that of her daughter-in-law's* is a way of referring to the value of her daughter-in-law's portfolio. The antecedent of *that* is *the value*. The phrase *Monica Taylor's portfolio* is parallel to *her daughter-in-law's portfolio*; each involves a noun with a possessive that functions adjectivally. The word *portfolio* is understood, not explicit.

E   Lacking the parallelism noted, this is unnecessarily awkward. Structurally, the pronoun *it* can logically have as antecedent either *the value of Monica Taylor's portfolio* or *Monica Taylor's portfolio*, but neither of these readings yields a correct sentence.

The correct answer is D.

SC02791

302. Ms. Chambers is among the forecasters who predict that the rate of addition to arable lands will drop while those of loss rise.

(A)   those of loss rise

(B)   it rises for loss

(C)   those of losses rise

(D)   the rate of loss rises

(E)   there are rises for the rate of loss

Logical Predication; Parallelism

The forecaster is making predictions about two different rates. The forecast changes in the rates can be compared using the construction *the rate of x will drop while the rate of y rises*; *x* and *y* should be parallel.

A   There is no referent for *those*.

B   *It* refers *to the rate of addition*, creating a nonsensical statement.

C   There is no referent for *those*. *Of losses* should be singular to parallel *of addition*.

D   **Correct.** This sentence uses a construction that clearly states the predicted changes in the rates; the rates are expressed in parallel ways.

E   *There are rises for* is wordy and unidiomatic.

The correct answer is D.

SC00987

303. In keeping with her commitment to her Christian faith, Sojourner Truth demonstrated as a public speaker a dedication both to the nonviolent abolition of slavery as well as for women to be emancipated.

(A)   a dedication both to the nonviolent abolition of slavery as well as for women to be emancipated

(B)   her being dedicated to both the nonviolent abolishing of slavery as well as for women's emancipation

(C)   a dedication to both the nonviolent abolition of slavery and the emancipation of women

(D)   that she was dedicated both to abolishing slavery nonviolently and to emancipate women

(E)   her dedication both to the nonviolent abolition of slavery and emancipation of women

Parallelism; Rhetorical Construction

The sentence describes Sojourner Truth's dedication, as a public speaker, to the nonviolent abolition of slavery and to the emancipation of women. It thus provides a list of two things that Sojourner Truth was dedicated to: the nonviolent abolition of slavery and the emancipation of women. Although there are various ways of describing this list, the two elements need to be described in a parallel fashion.

A   This sentence begins the description of the list with the beginning of the construction *both to … and to*. If implemented properly, this construction will describe the elements of the list in parallel. However, as the sentence is written, the second element of the list, *as for women to be emancipated*, is not parallel to the first element, *to the nonviolent abolition of slavery*.

B   This sentence, with *to* before *both*, begins the description of the list with a somewhat different construction than answer choice A does. In this case, *the nonviolent abolishing of slavery* needs to be made parallel with *for women's emancipation*. As written, the sentence presents a severe case of lack of parallelism.

C   **Correct.** This sentence correctly implements the construction *to both … and ….* In particular, *the nonviolent abolition of slavery* is parallel to *the emancipation of women*.

D   This sentence begins the description of the list with the same construction as in answer choice A, *both to … and to ….* In this case, *abolishing slavery nonviolently* is not parallel to *emancipate women*.

E   This sentence uses the same construction as answer choices A and D: *both to ... and to ....*. In this case, *to the nonviolent abolition of slavery* is not parallel to *emancipation of women*. If *to the* were inserted immediately before *emancipation of women*, then the parallelism issue would be resolved.

The correct answer is C.

Questions 304 to 348 - Difficulty: **Hard**

SC01972

304. Less than 400 Sumatran rhinos survive on the Malay peninsula and on the islands of Sumatra and Borneo, and they occupy a small fraction of the species' former range.

(A) Less than 400 Sumatran rhinos survive on the Malay peninsula and on the islands of Sumatra and Borneo, and they occupy a small fraction of the species' former range.

(B) Less than 400 Sumatran rhinos, surviving on the Malay peninsula and on the islands of Sumatra and Borneo, occupy a small fraction of the species' former range.

(C) Occupying a small fraction of the species' former range, the Malay peninsula and the islands of Sumatra and Borneo are where fewer than 400 Sumatran rhinos survive.

(D) Occupying a small fraction of the species' former range, fewer than 400 Sumatran rhinos survive on the Malay peninsula and on the islands of Sumatra and Borneo.

(E) Surviving on the Malay peninsula and on the islands of Sumatra and Borneo, less than 400 Sumatran rhinos occupy a small fraction of the species' former range.

Diction; Logical Predication

Because the number of Sumatran rhinos has been given, the comparative term *fewer* rather than *less* should be used to account for their numbers. In order to clarify that habitat currently occupied by the rhinos is but a small fraction of their former range, the information about their dwindling habitat is most efficiently presented in an opening participial phrase describing the rhinos, followed by a main clause in which the number of surviving rhinos is the subject, with the predicate explaining where

the rhinos currently live. By presenting the information about the population and range of rhinos in two separate independent clauses, the sentence as written does not clarify that the former range of the rhinos once extended beyond the peninsula and the islands.

A   *Less* is inappropriate for describing the specific number of surviving Sumatran rhinos. The separate independent clauses obscure the fact that the rhinos' range used to extend beyond the peninsula and the two islands. The referent of *they* is unclear.

B   *Less* is inappropriate for describing the specific number of surviving Sumatran rhinos. By using a nonrestrictive phrase *surviving ...*, the sentence suggests that fewer than 400 rhinos—perhaps only a portion of the total number—occupy a small fraction of the species' former range.

C   The opening participial phrase somewhat illogically modifies *peninsula and ... islands* rather than the rhinos.

D   Correct. The opening participial phrase correctly modifies *fewer than 400 ... rhinos*, a phrase that uses the correct comparative term.

E   The comparative term *less* is inappropriate for describing the number of rhinos.

The correct answer is D.

SC11068

305. Certain pesticides can become ineffective if used repeatedly in the same place; one reason is suggested by the finding that there are much larger populations of pesticide-degrading microbes in soils with a relatively long history of pesticide use than in soils that are free of such chemicals.

(A) Certain pesticides can become ineffective if used repeatedly in the same place; one reason is suggested by the finding that there are much larger populations of pesticide-degrading microbes in soils with a relatively long history of pesticide use than in soils that are free of such chemicals.

(B) If used repeatedly in the same place, one reason that certain pesticides can become ineffective is suggested by the finding that there are much larger populations of pesticide-degrading microbes in soils with a relatively long history of pesticide use than in soils that are free of such chemicals.

(C)   If used repeatedly in the same place, one reason certain pesticides can become ineffective is suggested by the finding that much larger populations of pesticide-degrading microbes are found in soils with a relatively long history of pesticide use than those that are free of such chemicals.

(D)   The finding that there are much larger populations of pesticide-degrading microbes in soils with a relatively long history of pesticide use than in soils that are free of such chemicals is suggestive of one reason, if used repeatedly in the same place, certain pesticides can become ineffective.

(E)   The finding of much larger populations of pesticide-degrading microbes in soils with a relatively long history of pesticide use than in those that are free of such chemicals suggests one reason certain pesticides can become ineffective if used repeatedly in the same place.

Logical Predication; Rhetorical Construction

The sentence is correctly constructed; it has two independent clauses connected by a semicolon. *If used repeatedly in the same place* clearly and correctly modifies *certain pesticides.*

A   Correct. The sentence is correctly constructed; the modifier *if used repeatedly in the same place* is correctly placed.

B   *If used repeatedly in the same place* modifies *one reason* when it should modify *certain pesticides.*

C   *If used repeatedly in the same place* modifies *one reason* when it should modify *certain pesticides.* The absence of *in* in the phrase *than those ...* makes the comparison unclear.

D   *If used repeatedly in the same place* ambiguously modifies *one reason* when it should clearly modify *certain pesticides.*

E   The comparison *the finding of much larger populations ... than in those that ...* is improperly constructed in a way that makes *the finding* appear to refer awkwardly to a discovery of larger populations rather than to a research conclusion about the presence of such populations.

The correct answer is A.

SC11854
306. While some academicians believe that business ethics should be integrated into every business course, others say that students will take ethics seriously <u>only if it would be taught as a separately required course.</u>

(A)   only if it would be taught as a separately required course

(B)   only if it is taught as a separate, required course

(C)   if it is taught only as a course required separately

(D)   if it was taught only as a separate and required course

(E)   if it would only be taught as a required course, separately

Rhetorical Construction; Verb Form; Diction

Conditional constructions require specific verb tenses. For a present condition, like this debate between academicians, the subordinate clause introduced by *if* uses the present indicative, and the main clause uses the future tense: *y will happen* (main clause) *only if x happens* (subordinate clause). Logically, the *course* is to be both *separate* and *required*, so the two adjectives should equally modify the noun and thus be separated by a comma: *separate, required course.*

A   The verb tense in the *if* clause is incorrect. The adverb *separately* should be the adjective *separate.*

B   Correct. This sentence has the correct verb tense, and the two adjectives equally modify the noun.

C   The placement of *only* distorts the meaning; it should precede *if. A course required separately* is unclear.

D   The verb tense in the *if* clause is incorrect. The placement of *only* distorts the meaning.

E   The verb tense in the *if* clause is incorrect. The placement of *only* distorts the meaning. The adjective *separate* should be used instead of the adverb *separately* and should precede the noun.

The correct answer is B.

SC08272

307. Whether they will scale back their orders to pre-2003 levels or stop doing business with us altogether depends on whether the changes that their management has proposed will be fully implemented.

- (A) Whether they will scale back their orders to pre-2003 levels or stop doing business with us altogether depends on whether the changes that their management has proposed will be fully implemented.

- (B) Whether they scale back their orders to pre-2003 levels or whether they discontinue their business with us altogether depends on the changes their management has proposed, if fully implemented or not.

- (C) Their either scaling back their orders in the future to pre-2003 levels, or their outright termination of business with us, depends on their management's proposed changes being fully implemented or not.

- (D) Whether they will scale back their orders to pre-2003 levels or stop doing business with us altogether depends if the changes that their management has proposed become fully implemented.

- (E) They will either scale back their orders to pre-2003 levels, or they will stop doing business with us altogether dependent on whether the changes their management has proposed will be fully implemented, or not.

Rhetorical Construction; Diction

This sentence expresses a dependency between two sets of options: the first is scaling back orders versus stopping all business, and the second is fully implementing changes versus not fully implementing changes. In each case, the most succinct way to express the two options is the *whether X (or Y)* construction, which immediately and clearly signals the presence of two opposed options. In linking the two sets of options, *depend* or *dependent* requires the preposition *on*.

A **Correct.** Each set of options is expressed concisely with a single *whether*, and *depend* is followed by *on*.

B The first set of options is expressed by means of a second, redundant and illogical *whether*; the second set is expressed in an unclear way,

unnecessarily delaying the identification of the two options until the very end. *Depends on the changes … if fully implemented or not* makes the meaning unclear. This could be an awkward way of trying to say that the outcome depends on whether the changes will be made, but it could just as plausibly be an attempt to say that the outcome depends on the changes, regardless of whether the changes will be fully implemented.

C Both sets of options are expressed without *whether*, and the first set does not even explicitly say that there is such an option. As a result, the existence of two dependent sets of options is unclear until the end of the sentence.

D The first set of options is correctly expressed with *whether*, but the second is not; also, *depend* lacks a following preposition *on*.

E Both sets of options are expressed without *whether*, and the first set does not even explicitly signal the existence of options, so the existence of two dependent sets of options is unclear until the end of the sentence.

The correct answer is A.

SC00975

308. Until 1868 and Disraeli, Great Britain had no prime ministers not coming from a landed family.

- (A) Until 1868 and Disraeli, Great Britain had no prime ministers not coming

- (B) Until 1868 and Disraeli, Great Britain had had no prime ministers who have not come

- (C) Until Disraeli in 1868, there were no prime ministers in Great Britain who have not come

- (D) It was not until 1868 that Great Britain had a prime minister—Disraeli—who did not come

- (E) It was only in 1868 and Disraeli that Great Britain had one of its prime ministers not coming

Verb Form; Idiom

This sentence explains how Disraeli marked a turning point in British history: he was the first prime minister who did not come from the landed gentry. The placement of the double negative is crucial. While *no prime ministers not coming from …* is hard to untangle, *[n]ot until … that Great Britain had a prime minister who did not come ...* separates the negatives into separate clauses, making them easier to decode. An appropriate way to express the temporal relationship is to use the idiomatic phrase *not until ... that.*

A The phrase *no prime ministers not coming* is unnecessarily confusing. It is also confusing to follow the preposition *until* with two very different types of objects—a date and a person.

B As in answer choice A, the double negative and unlike objects of the prepositional phrase starting with *until* are confusing. Additionally, the verb form *have not come,* which is the present-perfect tense, is inappropriate following the past perfect *had had* in this context.

C The present-perfect tense (*have not come*) is inappropriate after the past tense *were* in this context. *Until Disraeli* is imprecise and incomplete. *Before Disraeli's term in 1868 ...* or *Until Disraeli became prime minster in 1868* would work.

D **Correct.** This version correctly uses the idiomatic construction *not until ... that,* and it correctly uses past tense throughout.

E While it makes sense to say that a historical change occurred *in 1868,* it does not make sense to say that it occurred *in Disraeli.* It is unidiomatic to say *had one of its prime ministers not coming.*

The correct answer is D.

SC02011

309. Around 1900, fishermen in the Chesapeake Bay area landed more than seventeen million pounds of shad in a single year, but by 1920, overfishing and the proliferation of milldams and culverts that have blocked shad migrations up their spawning streams had reduced landings to less than four million pounds.

(A) that have blocked shad migrations up their spawning streams had reduced landings to less

(B) that blocked shad from migrating up their spawning streams had reduced landings to less

(C) that blocked shad from migrating up their spawning streams reduced landings to a lower amount

(D) having blocked shad from migrating up their spawning streams reduced landings to less

(E) having blocked shad migrations up their spawning streams had reduced landings to an amount lower

Diction; Verb Form

The point of this sentence is to explain how overfishing and interference with shad spawning streams affected the size of shad landings. The sentence makes this point by comparing the sizes of annual landings before and after 1920. The sentence most efficiently compares the poundage of pre- and post-1920 landings with the comparative form [*from*] *more than ... to less than ....*

A The present-perfect tense of *have blocked* inappropriately describes an event that caused something to happen before 1920. In addition, *migrations up their spawning streams* is incorrect.

B **Correct.** The comparison of poundage is efficiently explained, and the sequence of tenses makes sense. Despite a possible superficial appearance of a comparison between countable things (pounds), *less* is more appropriate than *fewer* for the comparison. The fishermen landed different amounts of fish; they did not land the number of pounds in terms of which those amounts are measured.

C The comparative expression *to a lower amount* is unnecessarily wordy. The past-perfect form *had reduced* would make the temporal relationships somewhat clearer than does the past tense *reduced.*

D The present-perfect participial phrase, *having blocked ... streams,* should be set off in commas; as it stands, it does not make sense. The past-perfect form *had reduced* would make the temporal relationships somewhat clearer than does the past tense *reduced.*

E The present-perfect participial phrase must be set off with commas; the pronoun *their,* which is also in answer choice A, nonsensically refers to *migrations,* and the comparative expression *to an amount lower* is unnecessarily wordy.

The correct answer is B.

SC04492

310. By offering lower prices and a menu of personal communications options, such as caller identification and voice mail, the new telecommunications company has not only captured customers from other phone companies but also forced them to offer competitive prices.

(A) has not only captured customers from other phone companies but also forced them

(B) has not only captured customers from other phone companies, but it also forced them

(C) has not only captured customers from other phone companies but also forced these companies

(D) not only has captured customers from other phone companies but also these companies have been forced

(E) not only captured customers from other phone companies, but it also has forced them

Parallelism; Verb Form

The sentence intends to show the effect of the new telecommunications company on the other phone companies. In the original sentence, however, the antecedent of the pronoun *them* is unclear; it may refer to *companies* or to *customers*. If it refers to *customers*, the sentence structure illogically has the new company forcing customers to offer competitive prices.

A The referent of *them* is unclear.

B The referent of *them* is unclear, and the use of *it* is redundant.

C **Correct.** The verbs are parallel in this sentence, and *these companies* is clearly the object of the verb *forced*.

D The sentence does not maintain parallelism, unnecessarily changing from active voice (*has captured*) to passive voice (*have been forced*).

E The referent of *them* is unclear. *Captured* and *has forced* are not parallel in verb tense, and the use of *it* is redundant.

The correct answer is C.

SC06132

311. After suffering $2 billion in losses and 25,000 layoffs, the nation's semiconductor industry, which makes chips that run everything from computers and spy satellites to dishwashers, appears to have made a long-awaited recovery.

(A) computers and spy satellites to dishwashers, appears to have

(B) computers, spy satellites, and dishwashers, appears having

(C) computers, spy satellites, and dishwashers, appears that it has

(D) computers and spy satellites to dishwashers, appears that it has

(E) computers and spy satellites as well as dishwashers, appears to have

Idiom; Grammatical Construction; Verb Form

This sentence correctly makes use of the idiomatic expression *from ... to ...* to describe the range of products made by the semiconductor industry. The main verb *appears* is intransitive and is most efficiently followed by the infinitive form *to have made*, which introduces a description of the subject, *the semiconductor industry*.

A **Correct.** The sentence is grammatically correct and uses the idiomatic expression correctly.

B The phrase *everything from* anticipates idiomatic completion with the second preposition *to*; without the *to* it could refer to components coming from the listed items, but this reading is unlikely; *appears having* is an incorrect verb form and makes the clause ungrammatical.

C This version is unidiomatic because *from* is not completed by *to*; *appears that it has* is an awkward and incorrect verb form.

D *Appears that it has* is an incorrect verb form.

E *As well as* is awkward and imprecise here; it is the wrong completion for the idiomatic expression *from ... to ....*

The correct answer is A.

SC04588
312. Over a range of frequencies from 100 to 5,000 hertz, monkeys and marmosets have a hearing sensitivity remarkably similar to humans, above which the sensitivity begins to differ.

(A) Over a range of frequencies from 100 to 5,000 hertz, monkeys and marmosets have a hearing sensitivity remarkably similar to humans

(B) Compared to humans, the hearing sensitivity of monkeys and marmosets are remarkably similar over a range of frequencies from 100 to 5,000 hertz

(C) Compared to humans over a range of frequencies from 100 to 5,000 hertz, the hearing sensitivity of monkeys and marmosets is remarkably similar

(D) The hearing sensitivity of monkeys and marmosets, when compared to humans over a range of frequencies from 100 to 5,000 hertz, is remarkably similar

(E) The hearing sensitivity of monkeys, marmosets, and humans is remarkably similar over a range of frequencies from 100 to 5,000 hertz

Logical Predication; Agreement

This sentence expresses two ideas: the similarity in monkey, marmoset, and human hearing in the stated frequency range, and the divergence in hearing sensitivity above that range. The second idea is introduced by *above which. Above which* should be immediately preceded by the antecedent of *which*, that is, the 100–5,000 Hz range. Also, the subject and verb must agree in number.

A   In this construction, *above which …* illogically modifies either *humans* or *a hearing sensitivity remarkably similar to humans*, rather than the frequency range.

B   The singular subject in this version, *the hearing sensitivity …*, is not accompanied by the correct singular verb form (*is*).

C   *Above which* is incorrectly preceded by *similar*, rather than by the expression of the frequency range. The sentence appears, illogically, to compare *humans over a range of frequencies* with monkeys' and marmosets' hearing sensitivity.

D   *Above which* is incorrectly preceded by *similar*, rather than by the expression of

the frequency range. The sentence appears, illogically, to compare *humans over a range of frequencies* with monkeys' and marmosets' hearing sensitivity.

E   **Correct.** *Above which* is correctly preceded by *a range of frequencies …*, and the verb *is* is in its proper singular form.

The correct answer is E.

SC03998
313. The computer company has announced that it will purchase the color-printing division of a rival company for $950 million, which is part of a deal that will make it the largest manufacturer in the office color-printing market.

(A) million, which is part of a deal that will make

(B) million, a part of a deal that makes

(C) million, a part of a deal making

(D) million as a part of a deal to make

(E) million as part of a deal that will make

Rhetorical Construction; Verb Form

The relative pronoun *which* requires a clear antecedent, but none appears in the original version of the sentence. The company's announcement is entirely geared to the future—it *will* purchase the division as part of a deal that *will* make it the largest manufacturer.

A   There is no antecedent for the relative pronoun *which*.

B   Like a relative pronoun, the appositive phrase (*a part …*) must have a noun or noun phrase as a clear antecedent; the verb *makes* should be future tense.

C   The appositive phrase requires a clear antecedent; *making* does not indicate future tense.

D   This sentence is a little awkward (the article *a* in *a part* is unnecessary) and says something rather different; *as a part of a deal to make* suggests that the deal itself includes making the company the *largest manufacturer* rather than its being the outcome of the deal.

E   **Correct.** The future tense is used throughout and the sentence structure is clear.

The correct answer is E.

SC03289

314. Kudzu, an Asian vine that has grown rampantly in the southern United States since introducing it in the 1920s to thwart soil erosion, has overrun many houses and countless acres of roadside.

(A) that has grown rampantly in the southern United States since introducing it in the 1920s to thwart

(B) that has grown rampantly in the southern United States, since it was introduced in the 1920s for thwarting

(C) that has grown rampant in the southern United States since it was introduced in the 1920s to thwart

(D) growing rampant in the southern United States since introducing it in the 1920s for thwarting

(E) growing rampantly in the southern United States, since it was introduced in the 1920s to thwart

Idiom; Logical Predication

The sentence describes the destructive, out-of-control growth of the invasive vine kudzu in the southern United States. Because the sentence does not indicate who introduced the vine to that region, the passive construction *it was introduced* should be used instead of *introducing it.*

A There is no clear subject for the verb *introducing.* This construction appears to indicate that kudzu introduced itself or some other, unspecified thing.

B The adverbial clause *since it was introduced in the 1920s* should not be set off from *has grown rampantly,* which it modifies. Also, *introduced … for thwarting* is not idiomatic. *Introduced … to thwart* is the correct idiom.

C **Correct.** The sentence correctly uses the passive construction *it was introduced* and the idiom *was introduced … to thwart.*

D *Since introducing it* illogically indicates that the vine introduced itself. *Introducing … for thwarting* is unidiomatic.

E The adverbial clause *since it was introduced in the 1920s* should not be set off from *has grown rampantly,* which it modifies.

The correct answer is C.

SC01712

315. Unable to build nests or care for their young, a female cowbird lays up to 40 eggs a year in the nests of other birds, including warblers, vireos, flycatchers, and thrushes.

(A) a female cowbird lays up to 40 eggs a year in the nests of other birds, including

(B) a female cowbird will use the nests of other birds to lay up to 40 eggs a year, including those of

(C) female cowbirds use the nests of other birds to lay up to 40 eggs a year, including those of

(D) female cowbirds lay up to 40 eggs a year in the nests of other birds, including

(E) up to 40 eggs a year are laid by female cowbirds in the nests of other birds, including

Agreement; Logical Predication

This sentence describes the behavior of female cowbirds, but it begins by referring to the birds in plural (*their young*) and then shifts unexpectedly to singular (*a female cowbird*). The best construction refers to the birds consistently in plural and places modifiers near the words they modify.

A The sentence shifts unexpectedly from the plural *their young* to the singular *a female cowbird.*

B The sentence shifts unexpectedly from the plural *their young* to the singular *a female cowbird.* The participial phrase *including those of* incorrectly modifies *eggs,* illogically indicating that cowbirds lay the eggs of other birds.

C The participial phrase *including those of* incorrectly modifies *eggs,* illogically indicating that cowbirds lay the eggs of other birds.

D **Correct.** The sentence consistently refers to *cowbirds* in the plural and places modifiers in the correct location.

E The modifier *Unable … young* incorrectly modifies *eggs.*

The correct answer is D.

SC01954

316. Bluegrass musician Bill Monroe, whose repertory, views on musical collaboration, and vocal style <u>were influential on generations of bluegrass artists, was also an inspiration to many musicians, that included Elvis Presley and Jerry Garcia, whose music differed significantly from</u> his own.

   (A) were influential on generations of bluegrass artists, was also an inspiration to many musicians, that included Elvis Presley and Jerry Garcia, whose music differed significantly from

   (B) influenced generations of bluegrass artists, also inspired many musicians, including Elvis Presley and Jerry Garcia, whose music differed significantly from

   (C) was influential to generations of bluegrass artists, was also inspirational to many musicians, that included Elvis Presley and Jerry Garcia, whose music was different significantly in comparison to

   (D) was influential to generations of bluegrass artists, also inspired many musicians, who included Elvis Presley and Jerry Garcia, the music of whom differed significantly when compared to

   (E) were an influence on generations of bluegrass artists, was also an inspiration to many musicians, including Elvis Presley and Jerry Garcia, whose music was significantly different from that of

Agreement; Rhetorical Construction; Grammatical Construction

The original sentence logically intends to explain that Monroe's work influenced generations of artists in his own musical field and that he inspired many musicians in other musical fields. Who or what influenced or inspired whom must be more clearly stated. Additionally, the original sentence lacks precision, being overly wordy and using phrases that are not idiomatic. Concise and consistent verb forms, as well as the use of subordinate phrases rather than clauses, improve the precision of the sentence.

A   The phrase *were influential on* is wordy and is not idiomatic; the use of verb forms *were* (the predicate of *repertory*, *views*, and *style*) and *was* (the predicate of *Monroe*) is confusing.

B   **Correct.** The use of the concise verb forms of *influenced* and *inspired* simplifies and clarifies the sentence. The concise use of *including* avoids the pronoun error and unnecessary wordiness.

C   The subject and verb do not agree in *repertory*, *views*, and *style … was* (compound subject with singular verb). *Was influential to* and *different … in comparison to* are unnecessarily wordy.

D   There is incorrect subject-verb agreement in *repertory*, *views*, and *style … was* (compound subject with singular verb). *Was influential to* and in *when compared to* are unnecessarily wordy. *The music of whom* is cumbersome and stilted.

E   The phrase *were an influence on* is wordy and not idiomatic. The phrases *was also an inspiration to* and *was significantly different* are unnecessarily wordy. The phrase *from that of* is unclear and confusing.

The correct answer is B.

SC12645

317. In many of the world's regions, increasing pressure on water resources has resulted <u>both from expanding development, changes in climate, and from pollution, so that the future supply in some of the more arid areas is a concern going forward.</u>

   (A) both from expanding development, changes in climate, and from pollution, so that the future supply in some of the more arid areas is a concern going forward

   (B) both from expanding development or changes in climate, and pollution, so that future supplies in some of the more arid areas are a concern

   (C) from expanding development, changes in climate, and also from pollution, so that the future supply in some of the more arid areas is a matter of concern going forward

   (D) from expanding development, changes in climate, and pollution, so that future supplies in some of the more arid areas are a concern

   (E) from expansion of development, changes in climate, and from pollution, so that supplies in some of the more arid areas are a future concern

Parallelism; Rhetorical Construction

The sentence lists three factors that have increased pressure on water resources and expresses concern for future water supplies in arid regions. The preposition *both* creates confusion since it indicates two factors, when the sentence actually lists three. If *expanding development* and *changes in climate* are supposed to be grouped together—implausibly—as a single factor, they should be conjoined by *and*, not separated by commas. The sentence could be constructed most clearly by listing all three factors in parallel form as objects of the preposition *from*: *from expanding development, changes in climate, and pollution*.

A   The preposition *both* creates confusion since it indicates two factors, when the sentence actually lists three.

B   *Both* indicates that there are two factors. If the entire disjunction *expanding development or changes in climate* is intended—somewhat implausibly—to be the first of the two factors, the comma before *and pollution* makes its relationship to the preceding portion of the sentence unclear.

C   Repetition of the preposition *from* disrupts the parallelism of the list and makes the meaning unclear.

D   **Correct**. The three factors are listed in parallel form as objects of the preposition *from*.

E   Repetition of the preposition *from* disrupts the parallelism of the list and makes the meaning unclear. *Future* somewhat implausibly modifies *concern* rather than *supplies*.

The correct answer is D.

SC01747

318. The computer company's present troubles are a result of technological stagnation, marketing missteps, and managerial blunders so that several attempts to revise corporate strategies have failed to correct it.

(A)   so that several attempts to revise corporate strategies have failed to correct it

(B)   so that several attempts at revising corporate strategies have failed to correct

(C)   in that several attempts at revising corporate strategies have failed to correct them

(D)   that several attempts to revise corporate strategies have failed to correct

(E)   that several attempts at revising corporate strategies have failed to correct them

Agreement; Rhetorical Construction

This sentence lists three causes of the company's troubles and asserts that strategies to correct the causes of the problems have failed. The clearest, most efficient way to explain this is to refer to the causes with the relative pronoun *that*, positioning it as an object of the verb *failed to correct*.

A   The singular pronoun *it* has no clear antecedent; the conjunction *so* typically indicates that a consequence will follow, but this is not the case.

B   The conjunction *so* is inappropriate because no consequences are given; the verb *correct* has no object.

C   *In that* is an inappropriate connector because it is not followed by an indication of how the company's troubles result from the three problems listed in the first part of the sentence.

D   **Correct**. The sentence is clearly and efficiently worded, and the referent of the pronoun *that* is clear.

E   Because *attempts* is the subject of the final clause, and *that* is the object of its verb (*have failed to correct*), the pronoun *them* has no function.

The correct answer is D.

SC11880

319. The root systems of most flowering perennials either become too crowded, which results in loss in vigor, and spread too far outward, producing a bare center.

(A)   which results in loss in vigor, and spread

(B)   resulting in loss in vigor, or spreading

(C)   with the result of loss of vigor, or spreading

(D)   resulting in loss of vigor, or spread

(E)   with a resulting loss of vigor, and spread

Idiom; Parallelism

This sentence uses the construction *either x or y*; *x* and *y* must be grammatically parallel. In this

481

case, *and spread* must be *or spread*. The antecedent of *which* is unclear; replacing *which results* with *resulting* clarifies the meaning.

A   *Either* is incorrectly followed by *and*; *which* has no clear referent.

B   *Or spreading* is not parallel to *either become*.

C   *With the result of* is wordy and awkward. *Or spreading* is not parallel to *either become*.

D   **Correct.** The phrase *resulting in loss of vigor* concisely modifies the first clause; the either/or construction is correct and parallel in this sentence.

E   *Either* is incorrectly followed by *and*; *with a resulting loss* is wordy.

The correct answer is D.

SC11910

320. In theory, international civil servants at the United Nations are prohibited from continuing to draw salaries from their own governments; in practice, however, some governments merely substitute living allowances for their employees' paychecks, assigned by them to the United Nations.

(A)   for their employees' paychecks, assigned by them

(B)   for the paychecks of their employees who have been assigned

(C)   for the paychecks of their employees, having been assigned

(D)   in place of their employees' paychecks, for those of them assigned

(E)   in place of the paychecks of their employees to have been assigned by them

Logical Predication; Rhetorical Construction

It is difficult to tell which parts of this sentence go together because of errors and confusion in the underlined portion. *Living allowances* is the counterpart of *paychecks*, so it is better to say *governments … substitute living allowances for the paychecks of their employees* because it makes the substitution clearer. This change also makes it easier to correct the modification error that appears in the phrase *assigned by them*, which incorrectly modifies *paychecks* rather than *employees*. The modifying

clause *who have been assigned* clearly describes *employees* and fits into the remaining part of the sentence, *to the United Nations*.

A   *Assigned by them* incorrectly and illogically modifies *paychecks*.

B   **Correct.** In this sentence, the meaning is clearer, because *paychecks* is separated from *employees*. The relative clause clearly modifies *employees*.

C   *Having been assigned* illogically modifies *governments*.

D   The correct construction is *substitutes x for y*, not *substitutes x in place of y*. The construction following *paychecks* is wordy and awkward.

E   The correct construction is *substitutes x for y*, not *substitutes x in place of y*. The construction following *employees* is wordy and awkward.

The correct answer is B.

SC05216

321. Industry analysts said that the recent rise in fuel prices may be an early signal of the possibility of gasoline and heating oil prices staying higher than usually through the end of the year.

(A)   of the possibility of gasoline and heating oil prices staying higher than usually through

(B)   of the possibility that gasoline and heating oil prices could stay higher than usual throughout

(C)   of prices of gasoline and heating oil possibly staying higher than usually through

(D)   that prices of gasoline and heating oil could stay higher than they usually are throughout

(E)   that prices of gasoline and heating oil will stay higher than usual through

Verb Form; Idiom

This sentence describes analysts' prediction about prices for gasoline and heating oil. The speculative nature of the analysts' comments is communicated through the modal verb *may be*, so there is no need to reiterate that idea with the wordy phrase *of the possibility of*. The correct idiom to contrast prices with the norm is *higher than usual*—not *usually*, as written. The correct idiom to indicate the span of time from the present to the end of the year is *through the end of the year*. A simple future tense verb would concisely communicate the analysts' prediction: prices *will stay higher than usual through the end of the year.*

A   The unnecessary phrase *of the possibility of* makes the sentence wordy; *higher than usually* is not a proper idiom.

B   The unnecessary phrase *of the possibility that* makes the sentence wordy; *throughout the end of the year* is not a proper idiom.

C   *Possibly* is redundant with *may* and is not needed to indicate the speculative nature of the prediction; *higher than usually* is not a proper idiom.

D   The conditional verb tense *could stay* is incorrect since the modal verb *may* has already introduced the concept of possibility; *throughout the end of the year* is not a proper idiom.

E   **Correct**. The simple future tense verb *will stay* expresses the analysts' prediction, and idioms are used correctly.

The correct answer is E.

SC07141

322. The Anasazi settlements at Chaco Canyon were built on a spectacular scale, with more than 75 carefully engineered structures, of up to 600 rooms each, were connected by a complex regional system of roads.

(A)   scale, with more than 75 carefully engineered structures, of up to 600 rooms each, were

(B)   scale, with more than 75 carefully engineered structures, of up to 600 rooms each,

(C)   scale of more than 75 carefully engineered structures of up to 600 rooms, each that had been

(D)   scale of more than 75 carefully engineered structures of up to 600 rooms and with each

(E)   scale of more than 75 carefully engineered structures of up to 600 rooms, each had been

Logical Predication; Grammatical Construction

This sentence makes a claim about the scale (size, extent) of the Anasazi settlements and then illustrates that claim with a description of the settlements' structures. The second part

of the sentence, introduced by the preposition *with*, describes the structures first in terms of their rooms and then in terms of the roads that connect them together. To describe the noun *structures*, the participial form *connected* should be used, turning the verb into an adjective.

A   The verb *were connected* has no subject, since *structures* is the object of the preposition *with*.

B   **Correct**. The sentence is logically coherent and grammatically correct.

C   The comma preceding *each* makes *each* a subject, but it has no verb, since *that* is the subject of *had been connected*.

D   This sentence suggests that the scale or size of the settlements is made up of structures, rather than uses the structures as an example of the settlements' grand scale; it also nonsensically indicates that each room is connected by a complex system of roads.

E   This run-on sentence suffers from a comma splice, as the phrase following the comma is a main clause; the referent of the pronoun *each* is ambiguous.

The correct answer is B.

SC07066

323. Even though the overall consumer price index did not change in April, indicating the absence of any general inflation or deflation, prices in several categories of merchandise have fallen over the last several months.

(A)   April, indicating the absence of any general inflation or deflation, prices in several categories of merchandise have fallen

(B)   April, indicating that any general inflation or deflation were absent, prices in several categories of merchandise fell

(C)   April and indicated that absence of any general inflation or deflation, prices in several categories of merchandise fell

(D)   April, having indicated the absence of any general inflation or deflation, prices in several categories of merchandise fell

(E)   April, which indicated that any general inflation or deflation were absent, prices in several categories of merchandise have fallen

Rhetorical Construction; Agreement

Coordinated noun phrases in which singular nouns are linked by *or* are considered singular, so when the phrase *any general inflation or deflation* is a subject, it requires a singular verb. One of the answer choices incorrectly uses the word *that*. Another phrasing problem is with *indicating/indicated*. *Indicating* works well as a verb form in the options where it occurs.

A **Correct.** *Any general inflation or deflation* is not a subject (it functions as the object of the preposition *of*), so there is no potential agreement problem.

B *Were* is incorrect as the agreeing form of *be*; it should be *is*.

C If *that* is taken as a demonstrative adjective modifying *absence*, it is inappropriate (the word *the* is required); if it is meant as a subordinating conjunction, it is incorrect because it is not followed by a clause.

D *Having indicated* is unclear and unnecessarily long. It appears to say, somewhat illogically, that the indication occurred at some unspecified time prior to the lack of change in April. *Indicating* works well alone and would be a preferable verb form here.

E *Were* here could only be meant either as a plural past-tense verb or as a singular subjunctive-mood verb (appropriate only in certain conditional contexts); in either case it is incorrect. Also, *indicating* works well, and the *which*-clause is unnecessary.

The correct answer is A.

SC12460

324. Despite Japan's relative isolation from world trade at the time, the prolonged peace during the Tokugawa shogunate produced an almost explosive expansion of commerce.

(A) Japan's relative isolation from world trade at the time, the prolonged peace during the Tokugawa shogunate

(B) the relative isolation of Japan from world trade at the time and the Tokugawa shogunate's prolonged peace, it

(C) being relatively isolated from world trade at the time, the prolonged peace during Japan's Tokugawa shogunate

(D) Japan's relative isolation from world trade at the time during the Tokugawa shogunate, prolonged peace

(E) its relative isolation from world trade then, prolonged peace in Japan during the Tokugawa shogunate

Logical Predication; Rhetorical Construction

All predicates must have a clear subject; in this sentence, the logical subject of the verb *produced* is *the prolonged peace*. *During* is a concise way to introduce the relevant time period of this peace (the period of the Tokugawa shogunate); the phrase *at the time* clearly refers to the same time period.

A **Correct.** The subject of *produced* is clearly and logically identified; *during* succinctly provides the time frame.

B The phrase *at the time* leaves it uncertain what time is being referred to. The subject *it* of *produced* does not clearly identify this verb's logical subject, since it is singular yet seems to be intended to refer to two situations previously mentioned, *isolation* and *prolonged peace*.

C *Being relatively isolated* is most likely meant to refer to Japan's isolation, but since grammatically it must modify *the prolonged peace* (the subject of the main clause), the sentence would have an illogical and unintended meaning.

D If *at the time* is to be used instead of *during*, it should be followed by *of*; the better choice is to simply use *during* by itself.

E The use of *then* after *world trade* is awkward and redundant, because *during* later in the sentence supplies the time frame for both Japan's isolation and the period of peace. The structure of the sentence leaves *it(s)* without a clear referent.

The correct answer is A.

SC02333

325. Government officials announced that <u>restrictions on the use of water would continue because no appreciative increase in the level of the river</u> resulted from the intermittent showers that had fallen throughout the area the day before.

(A) restrictions on the use of water would continue because no appreciative increase in the level of the river

(B) restricting the use of water would continue because there had not been any appreciative increase in the river's level that

(C) the use of water would continue to be restricted because not any appreciable increase in the river's level had

(D) restrictions on the use of water would continue because no appreciable increase in the level of the river had

(E) using water would continue being restricted because not any appreciable increase in the level of the river

Rhetorical Construction; Logical Predication; Verb Form

This sentence explains the rationale behind a governmental announcement made at some point in the past. The most efficient way to express the meaning of the announcement is to use *restrictions* as the subject of the clause introduced by *that* and to use a negative subject (*no appreciable increase*) and a positive verb in the subordinate clause that follows.

A   It makes no sense to say that a hypothetical increase in river level is *appreciative*. The past tense of the verb *resulted* in this context does not as clearly express the temporal relationships between the announcement and the other events as would the past perfect *had resulted*.

B   The use of *there* and the negative verb make the dependent clause unnecessarily wordy and indirect; the relative pronoun *that* appears to refer nonsensically to *level*. It makes no sense to say that a hypothetical increase in river level is *appreciative*.

C   By making *use of water* instead of *restrictions* the subject of the *that* clause, this version of

the sentence necessitates the use of a wordy and indirect passive infinitive phrase *to be restricted*. The sentence becomes even more wordy and convoluted with the introduction of an awkward, unidiomatic negative subject (*not any appreciable increase*) of the dependent clause.

D   **Correct.** The sentence is direct and efficient, and the past-perfect verb *had resulted* appropriately expresses the sequence of events.

E   The phrase *using water ... being restricted* is wordy and imprecise, and the unidiomatic negative subject (*not any appreciable increase*) of the dependent clause introduces further indirection and wordiness. The past tense of the verb *resulted* in this context does not as clearly express the temporal relationships between the announcement and the other events as would the past perfect *had resulted*.

The correct answer is D.

SC04732

326. According to United States census data, <u>while there was about one-third of mothers with young children working outside the home in 1975, in 2000, almost two-thirds of those mothers were employed outside the home.</u>

(A) while there was about one-third of mothers with young children working outside the home in 1975, in 2000, almost two-thirds of those mothers were employed outside the home

(B) there were about one-third of mothers with young children who worked outside the home in 1975; in 2000, almost two-thirds of those mothers were employed outside the home

(C) in 1975 about one-third of mothers with young children worked outside the home; in 2000, almost two-thirds of such mothers were employed outside the home

(D) even though in 1975 there were about one-third of mothers with young children who worked outside the home, almost two-thirds of such mothers were employed outside the home in 2000

(E) with about one-third of mothers with young children working outside the home in 1975, almost two-thirds of such mothers were employed outside the home in 2000

Idiom; Logical Predication

The sentence presents two pieces of data, one from the 1975 census and one from the 2000 census. It does not attempt to explain a logical relationship beyond the numerical difference. The incorrect versions of the sentence attempt but fail to make a logical connection between the two data (*while ...*, *even though ...*, and *with ...*) and/or introduce unnecessary wordiness with the phrase *there was* or *there were*. The most efficient way to present the two data for reader comparison is in two parallel independent clauses joined by a semicolon. To avoid the confusion of misplaced or *squinting* modifiers, these clauses are best structured with subjects designating percentage of mothers with children, followed by participial phrases that indicate that these mothers *worked* or *were employed* outside the home.

A   The phrase *there was* introduces unnecessary wordiness, and the singular verb *was* does not agree with the plural predicate nominative *one-third of mothers with children*. The placement of the modifier *working outside the home* immediately after children suggests that the children rather than the mothers were externally employed.

B   *There were* introduces unnecessary wordiness; because of its placement, the relative clause *who worked outside the home* appears to describe children rather than mothers.

C   **Correct.** The two pieces of data are presented in parallel independent clauses, joined by a semicolon, allowing the reader to note the numerical difference.

D   The introductory phrase *even though* suggests a relationship between the two pieces of data that the sentence does not support; *there were* introduces unnecessary wordiness; *who worked outside the home* appears to describe *young children*.

E   The introductory word *with* nonsensically suggests the simultaneity of the two pieces of data; the placement of the modifier *working outside the home* attaches it to *young children* rather than *mothers*.

The correct answer is C.

SC04672

327. Clouds are formed from the evaporation of the oceans' water that is warmed by the sun and rises high into the atmosphere, condensing in tiny droplets on minute particles of dust.

(A)   Clouds are formed from the evaporation of the oceans' water that is warmed by the sun and rises high into the atmosphere, condensing in tiny droplets on minute particles of dust.

(B)   Clouds form by the sun's warmth evaporating the water in the oceans, which rises high into the atmosphere, condensing in tiny droplets on minute particles of dust.

(C)   Warmed by the sun, ocean water evaporates, rises high into the atmosphere, and condenses in tiny droplets on minute particles of dust to form clouds.

(D)   The water in the oceans evaporates, warmed by the sun, rises high into the atmosphere, and condenses in tiny droplets on minute particles of dust, which forms clouds.

(E)   Ocean water, warmed by the sun, evaporates and rises high into the atmosphere, which then condenses in tiny droplets on minute particles of dust to form as clouds.

Rhetorical Construction; Logical Predication

This sentence describes a multistep process by which ocean water is transformed into clouds. These steps are most clearly presented in chronological order, with *ocean water* as the main subject of the sentence.

A   This sentence provides no sense of steps and illogically suggests that the oceans' water evaporates after it rises high into the atmosphere.

B   The antecedent for the relative pronoun *which* is ambiguous, again suggesting that oceans rise high.

C   **Correct.** The sequence of steps in a cloud's formation is clear.

D   The nonchronological order of the steps by which clouds are produced is confusing, suggesting that dust forms clouds.

E   The relative pronoun *which* grammatically refers to *atmosphere*, creating a nonsensical claim that the atmosphere, rather than the water, condenses.

The correct answer is C.

SC02664

328. Schistosomiasis, a disease caused by a parasitic worm, is prevalent in hot, humid climates, and it has become more widespread as irrigation projects have enlarged the habitat of the freshwater snails that are the parasite's hosts for part of its life cycle.

(A)   the freshwater snails that are the parasite's hosts for part of its life cycle

(B)   the freshwater snails that are the parasite's hosts in part of their life cycle

(C)   freshwater snails which become the parasite's hosts for part of its life cycles

(D)   freshwater snails which become the hosts of the parasite during the parasite's life cycles

(E)   parasite's hosts, freshwater snails which become their hosts during their life cycles

Rhetorical Construction; Agreement

This sentence explains the increased incidence of schistosomiasis as a consequence of the enlarged habitat of the kind of freshwater snails that host the parasitic worm responsible for the disease. The definite article is necessary before *freshwater snails* because the sentence identifies a particular type of snail, namely, those that host the parasite. The correct preposition to express duration in combination with *host* is *for*, not *in*. As the parasite is referred to as singular, the possessive pronoun in the final phrase must also be singular.

A   **Correct.** The sentence is clear with all pronouns and verbs in agreement.

B   The preposition *in* is inappropriate for expressing duration; the plural possessive pronoun *their* does not agree with the singular antecedent *parasite*.

C   A definite article should precede *freshwater snails* to identify a particular type of snail; the plural *cycles* is inappropriate because *its* refers to a singular parasite, which only has one life cycle.

D   A definite article is needed before *freshwater snails*; repetition of the word *parasite* makes the final phrase unnecessarily wordy; *cycles* should be singular.

E   The repetition of *hosts* makes the final phrase unnecessarily wordy; *cycles* should be singular; *their hosts* should be *its hosts*; the referent for the second appearance of *their* is unclear—does it refer to *snails* or the *parasite*?

The correct answer is A.

SC07754

329. Sor Juana Inés de la Cruz was making the case for women's equality long before the cause had a name: Born in the mid-seventeenth century in San Miguel Nepantla, Mexico, the convent was the perfect environment for Sor Juana to pursue intellectual pursuits, achieving renown as a mathematician, poet, philosopher, and playwright.

(A)   the convent was the perfect environment for Sor Juana to pursue intellectual pursuits, achieving

(B)   Sor Juana found the convent provided the perfect environment for intellectual pursuits, and she went on to achieve

(C)   the convent provided the perfect environment for intellectual pursuits for Sor Juana; going on to achieve

(D)   Sor Juana found the convent provided the perfect environment for intellectual pursuits; achieving

(E)   the convent was, Sor Juana found, the perfect environment for intellectual pursuits, and she went on to achieve

Logical Predication; Grammatical Construction

This sentence focuses on Sor Juana Inés de la Cruz, but the subject of its second clause is *the convent*. This causes a problem because the predicates *born* and *achieving*, which have only understood subjects, are grammatically paired with *the convent*, an illogical subject. Also, normally where a semicolon is used to mark the end of an independent clause (as in some of the answer choices), it should be followed by another independent clause.

A   *The convent* is the subject of the second clause, so both *born* and *achieving* are illogically forced to take it as their subject.

B   Correct. *Sor Juana* provides the correct logical subject for *born* and *went on to achieve*; the second clause is correctly introduced by *and*, and is constructed as a full clause with a subject and tensed verb.

C   As *the convent* is the subject of the second clause, *born* is illogically forced to take that phrase as its subject. Also, the clause after the semicolon is not an independent full clause with a subject and a tensed verb; *she went on* is required instead of *going on*.

D   The clause after the semicolon is not an independent full clause with a subject and a tensed verb: *she achieved* is required instead of *achieving*.

E   Since *the convent* is the subject of the second clause, *born* must illogically take that phrase as its subject.

The correct answer is B.

SC14406

330. By devising an instrument made from a rod, wire, and lead balls, and employing uncommonly precise measurements, in 1797–1798 Henry Cavendish's apparatus enabled him to arrive at an astonishingly accurate figure for the weight of the earth.

(A)   By devising an instrument made from a rod, wire, and lead balls, and employing uncommonly precise measurements, in 1797–1798 Henry Cavendish's apparatus enabled him

(B)   In 1797–1798, by devising an instrument made from a rod, wire, and lead balls, and employing uncommonly precise measurements, Henry Cavendish's apparatus enabled him

(C)   Henry Cavendish devised an instrument made from a rod, wire, and lead balls, and employed uncommonly precise measurements, and in 1797–1798 was able

(D)   Having devised an instrument from a rod, wire, and lead balls, and employment of uncommonly precise measurements, Henry Cavendish in 1797–1798 was able

(E)   By devising an instrument made from a rod, wire, and lead balls, and employing uncommonly precise measurements, Henry Cavendish was able in 1797–1798

Logical Predication; Rhetorical Construction

The core of this sentence's idea is either the verb *enable*, which must have its logically correct subject *Henry Cavendish's apparatus*, or *be able*, with the subject *Henry Cavendish*; these subjects must also be able to supply the correct subjects for any other verbs that have understood subjects. The sentence should also clearly express the two things that enabled Cavendish's accomplishment (devising the instrument and employing precise measurement).

A   *Devising* needs a subject supplied from elsewhere in the sentence, but the only available subject is the illogical *Henry Cavendish's apparatus* (an apparatus does not "devise" anything).

B   *Devising* needs a subject supplied from elsewhere in the sentence, but the only option is the illogical *Henry Cavendish's apparatus*.

C   Connecting the three parts of the sentence with two occurrences of *and* is awkward; the first two parts are best connected by *and*, but the final portion expressing what Cavendish achieved would be better expressed, for example, as a new sentence beginning, *In 1797–1798, he employed*.

D   This variant seems to suggest, illogically, that Cavendish devised an instrument from several objects plus employment; using *employed* instead of *employment of* would be one way of correctly pairing his two actions.

E   Correct. The verbs *devising, employing*, and *was able* have their correct logical subject (*Henry Cavendish*), and the actions of devising and employing are paired clearly, with *by* understood before *employing*.

The correct answer is E.

SC08285

331. The growth projected for these storms in different computerized weather models varies widely.

(A) projected for these storms in different computerized weather models varies widely

(B) for these storms is projected in different computerized models of weather to vary widely

(C) of these storms, projected in different computerized weather models, vary widely

(D) projected for these storms, which vary widely in different computerized weather models

(E) that varies widely for these storms are projected in different computerized weather models

Logical Predication; Agreement

The point of the sentence is that there is great variation in projections of how the storms that it refers to will grow. The structure of the sentence makes it clear that the variation is in the computer models' projections.

A Correct. The sentence explains concisely that *growth projected* in different weather models *varies widely*.

B *Growth for these storms* is unidiomatic and unclear. The construction *growth … is projected … to vary* makes it unclear whether the models project widely varying growth or vary in how much growth they project.

C The construction *growth … vary widely* places the variation in the growth of the storms rather than in the projections. The plural verb *vary* does not agree with the singular subject *growth*.

D If *growth projected for these storms* is taken as the subject of the sentence, the subject is not paired with a verb and the sentence is grammatically incomplete.

E The phrase *growth that varies widely* indicates that the variation is in the growth of the storms rather than in the projections. The plural verb *are projected* does not agree with the singular subject *growth*.

The correct answer is A.

SC02131

332. By using a process called echolocation to analyze the echoes of the high-pitched sounds they produce, bats can determine not only the distance to an object, but they also can determine its shape and size and the direction in which it is moving.

(A) can determine not only the distance to an object, but they also can determine

(B) not only can determine the distance to an object but also

(C) can determine not only the distance to an object but also

(D) not only can determine its distance from an object but also

(E) can determine not only their distance from an object, but they can also determine

Parallelism; Logical Predication

This sentence explains that bats' echolocation allows them to determine both the distance to an object and other pieces of information. The correct way to construct this sentence using a correlative conjunction is to follow *not only* and *but also* with the same parts of speech. Using nouns to indicate all the kinds of information bats gain through echolocation provides parallel grammatical structure and concise wording: *not only distance, but also shape, size, and direction.*

A Introducing the second main clause *they also can determine* makes the sentence wordy and disrupts the correct formation of the correlative conjunction *not only, but also.*

B The correlative conjunction is used incorrectly because *not only* is followed by a verb, while *but also* is followed by a list of nouns.

C Correct. This sentence concisely uses *not only, but also* to connect a series of nouns.

D The correlative conjunction is used incorrectly because *not only* is followed by a verb, while *but also* is followed by a list of nouns. *Its* most plausibly refers to bats, but on that interpretation the singular pronoun does not agree with its plural antecedent, and the sentence indicates, somewhat implausibly, that the bats use echolocation to determine their own shape, size, and direction of movement. Alternatively, *its* could refer to some other thing that is not named in the sentence, but it is implausible and confusing to say that the bats determine the distance of that unnamed thing from an unspecified object.

E   Introducing the second main clause *they also can determine* makes the sentence wordy and disrupts the correct construction to be used with the correlative conjunction: *not only* is followed by a noun, while *but also* is followed by a verb.

The correct answer is C.

SC06205

333. Carbon dioxide, which traps heat in the atmosphere and helps regulate the planet's surface temperature, is constantly being <u>exchanged between the atmosphere on the one hand and the oceans and terrestrial plants on the other.</u>

(A)   exchanged between the atmosphere on the one hand and the oceans and terrestrial plants on the other

(B)   exchanged, on the one hand, between the atmosphere and the oceans and terrestrial plants, on the other

(C)   exchanged between, on the one hand, the atmosphere, with the oceans and terrestrial plants, on the other

(D)   exchanged, on the one hand, among the oceans and terrestrial plants, and the atmosphere, on the other

(E)   exchanged among the oceans and terrestrial plants on the one hand and the atmosphere on the other

Parallelism; Idiom

This sentence describes an exchange between the atmosphere and the Earth's surface using the paired phrases *on the one hand* and *on the other*. Preceding both phrases with nouns creates a parallel grammatical structure: *the atmosphere on the one hand and the oceans and terrestrial plants on the other*. Although three locations are mentioned, *between* is the correct preposition to describe the exchange since *the oceans and terrestrial plants* are treated as a set, both members of which are located on the Earth's surface.

A   **Correct.** The exchange between the atmosphere and the Earth's surface is expressed using parallel nouns and the paired phrases *on the one hand* and *on the other*.

B   The placement of all three nouns between the paired phrases *on the one hand* and *on the other* obscures the nature of the exchange and makes it unclear whether the exchange is among all three of the locations, between the first one and the last two, or between the first two and the last one. *On the one hand* appears to encompass all three of the locations, leaving *on the other* dangling.

C   The preposition *with* disrupts the expression of an exchange *between* two locations; the construction *on the one hand* and *on the other* is not in parallel form.

D   The preposition *among*, the placement of *and the atmosphere* between commas, and the lack of parallelism make the meaning of this sentence unclear.

E   If the relationship is supposed to be among all three of the locations mentioned, the binary relationship indicator (*on the one hand … on the other*) makes no sense. Alternatively, *among* could appear to distribute, implicitly, to both sides of the comparison (*among the oceans and terrestrial plants on the one hand and* (among) *the atmosphere on the other*). On that interpretation, *among the atmosphere* makes no sense, because *among* signals a relationship involving multiple entities, but *atmosphere* is a singular noun and is not normally construed as either plural or collective.

The correct answer is A.

SC01990

334. Floating in the waters of the equatorial Pacific, an array of buoys collects and transmits data on long-term interactions between the ocean and the <u>atmosphere, interactions that affect</u> global climate.

    (A) atmosphere, interactions that affect
    (B) atmosphere, with interactions affecting
    (C) atmosphere that affects
    (D) atmosphere that is affecting
    (E) atmosphere as affects

Grammatical Construction; Agreement

The underlined portion of the sentence is an appositive, a terminal noun phrase restating the kind of data being collected and providing additional information about it. This is a clear and economical way to provide the extra information.

A   Correct. The sentence is grammatically correct and logically coherent.

B   The prepositional phrase *with* ... has no clear noun or noun phrase to attach to and is therefore ungrammatical.

C   Using the restrictive *that* after *atmosphere* illogically suggests that there are many atmospheres to differentiate from and the one in question in this sentence is the one affecting global climate.

D   The restrictive *that* also follows *atmosphere* as in answer choice C.

E   The phrase *as affects global climate* functions as an adverb, but there is no verb for it to modify.

The correct answer is A.

SC04344

335. Sixty-five million years ago, according to some scientists, an asteroid bigger than Mount Everest slammed into North America, <u>which, causing plant and animal extinctions, marks</u> the end of the geologic era known as the Cretaceous Period.

    (A) which, causing plant and animal extinctions, marks
    (B) which caused the plant and animal extinctions and marks
    (C) and causing plant and animal extinctions that mark

    (D) an event that caused plant and animal extinctions, which marks
    (E) an event that caused the plant and animal extinctions that mark

Logical Predication; Agreement

This sentence describes a two-part sequence of events, the second of which has led to a particular categorization of geological time. In order to clarify that it is not the first event (asteroid strike) that produced the time division (end of the Cretaceous Period), but the first event's consequences (biological extinctions), the sentence needs an appositive form to restate the content of the main clause (*an event*), followed by a two-part chain of relative clauses (*that caused ... that mark ...*).

A   The antecedent for the relative pronoun *which* is ambiguous; it is therefore unclear what *marks* the end of the Cretaceous Period.

B   The antecedent of *which* is unclear; the compound verbs *caused* and *marks* fail to indicate that the extinctions, not the asteroid strike, are significant markers of geological time.

C   Following the conjunction *and* with a participial rather than a main verb is grammatically incorrect because it violates parallelism and produces a fragment at the end of the sentence.

D   *Which*, referring to *extinctions*, should be followed by a plural verb.

E   Correct. The sentence is unambiguous, and the verbs agree with their subjects.

The correct answer is E.

SC02338

336. <u>Although the first pulsar, or rapidly spinning collapsed star, to be sighted was in the summer of 1967 by graduate student Jocelyn Bell, it had not been announced until February 1968.</u>

    (A) Although the first pulsar, or rapidly spinning collapsed star, to be sighted was in the summer of 1967 by graduate student Jocelyn Bell, it had not been announced until February 1968.

(B)   Although not announced until February 1968, in the summer of 1967 graduate student Jocelyn Bell observed the first pulsar, or rapidly spinning collapsed star, to be sighted.

(C)   Although observed by graduate student Jocelyn Bell in the summer of 1967, the discovery of the first sighted pulsar, or rapidly spinning collapsed star, had not been announced before February 1968.

(D)   The first pulsar, or rapidly spinning collapsed star, to be sighted was observed in the summer of 1967 by graduate student Jocelyn Bell, but the discovery was not announced until February 1968.

(E)   The first sighted pulsar, or rapidly spinning collapsed star, was not announced until February 1968, while it was observed in the summer of 1967 by graduate student Jocelyn Bell.

Verb Form; Logical Predication; Rhetorical Construction

This sentence presents conditions that are followed by an unexpected outcome: a delayed announcement of the discovery of a pulsar. A compound sentence using a coordinating conjunction *but* is an effective way to present the conditions of the first pulsar sighting and then information about the subsequent announcement of the discovery. The sentence must clarify that it is not about *the first pulsar*, but *the first pulsar … to be sighted*. The verbs in the sentence must all be in past tense; using a past-perfect verb to present information about the announcement of the discovery indicates that this announcement illogically took place before the pulsar was first sighted.

A   The subject of the opening dependent clause is *pulsar*, and the verb is *was*. The clause needs to indicate not just that the pulsar existed but that it was observed by Bell; the past-perfect verb tense is inappropriate in the concluding clause.

B   The opening participial phrase functions as an adjective, but it has no logical noun or noun phrase to attach to; Bell herself was not announced in 1968.

C   Grammatically, the opening participial phrase describes the first noun that follows, but it makes no sense to say that *the*

discovery of the pulsar was *observed*; *discovery of the first sighted pulsar* is also imprecise; one does not discover a first sighting.

D   Correct. The sentence presents the sequence of events clearly and in the past tense.

E   This sentence presents events in a way that is confusing; as a conjunction, *while* indicates simultaneous events, but this sentence is about events that occurred in a sequence.

The correct answer is D.

SC02766

337.   Sound can travel through water for enormous distances, <u>prevented from dissipating its acoustic energy as a result of</u> boundaries in the ocean created by water layers of different temperatures and densities.

(A)   prevented from dissipating its acoustic energy as a result of

(B)   prevented from having its acoustic energy dissipated by

(C)   its acoustic energy prevented from dissipating by

(D)   its acoustic energy prevented from being dissipated as a result of

(E)   preventing its acoustic energy from dissipating by

Logical Predication; Rhetorical Construction

This sentence opens with a statement that sound can travel long distances through water and then explains why that is so: water layers in the ocean prevent acoustic energy from dissipating. Because *dissipating* is an intransitive verb, *acoustic energy* cannot be its object.

A   *Dissipating* is not a transitive verb, so *acoustic energy* cannot function as its object.

B   This version of the sentence is wordy, awkward, and indirect; *from having … by* erroneously suggests that the boundaries in the ocean are attempting to dissipate sound energy.

C   Correct. Here, *acoustic energy* is effectively modified by the participial *prevented from dissipating …*.

D   This version of the sentence is wordy, awkward, and indirect; *being dissipated as a result of* makes it unclear whether the boundaries contribute to energy loss or prevent it.

E   This version of the sentence nonsensically explains that sound prevents the dissipation of its own energy.

The correct answer is C.

SC10996

338. Last year, land values in most parts of the pinelands rose almost <u>so fast, and in some parts even faster than what they did</u> outside the pinelands.

(A)   so fast, and in some parts even faster than what they did

(B)   so fast, and in some parts even faster than, those

(C)   as fast, and in some parts even faster than, those

(D)   as fast as, and in some parts even faster than, those

(E)   as fast as, and in some parts even faster than what they did

Idiom; Parallelism

This sentence says *x* rose *almost so fast y*, which is not a correct idiomatic construction; *x* rose *almost as fast as y* is the correct idiom for this comparison. The two elements being compared, *x* and *y*, must be parallel, but the noun *land values* (*x*) is not parallel to *what they did* (*y*). *Land values* in the pinelands (*x*) must be compared with *those* (the pronoun correctly replacing *land values*) outside the pinelands (*y*).

A   *So fast* is used instead of *as fast*. *What they did* is not parallel to *land values*.

B   *So fast* is not the correct idiom for comparison.

C   *As fast* must be followed by *as* in this comparison.

D   **Correct.** *As fast as* is the correct comparative conjunction used in this sentence; *those* is parallel to *land values*.

E   *What they did* is not parallel to *land values*.

The correct answer is D.

SC03010

339. The North American <u>moose's long legs enable it to move quickly through the woods, stepping easily over downed trees, but predators pursuing it must leap or go around them.</u>

(A)   moose's long legs enable it to move quickly through the woods, stepping easily over downed trees, but predators pursuing it must leap or go around them

(B)   moose's long legs enable it to move quickly through the woods, stepping easily over downed trees while predators pursuing them must leap or go around

(C)   moose's long legs enable it to move quickly through the woods and to step easily over downed trees, but predators pursuing them must leap over or go around them

(D)   moose has long legs, enabling it to move quickly through the woods and to step easily over downed trees while predators pursuing them must leap or go around

(E)   moose has long legs that enable it to move quickly through the woods, stepping easily over downed trees while predators pursuing it must leap over or go around them

Logical Predication; Agreement

This sentence explains the advantages of long legs to the North American moose. Since the sentence contains multiple relationships among pronouns, nouns, and modifiers, it is important that the various elements be clearly connected. The structure of the sentence makes it unclear whether *stepping easily over downed trees* is intended to modify the main subject, *the North American moose's long legs*, or the pronoun *it*. Although *it* presumably refers to *the North American moose*, it does so only obliquely, because *moose* does not appear in noun form in the sentence. The best way to construct this sentence is to make *moose* the subject of the main clause so that both occurrences of *it* have a clear antecedent. Because *stepping easily over them* is set off by commas from the preceding and ensuing clauses and because the apparently intransitive verb *leap* intervenes between *downed trees* and *them*, it is unclear whether *them* refers to the moose's legs or the downed trees. The phrase *leap or go around them* should say *leap over*, because the

493

point is that the predators must either leap over the downed trees (or go around them), not merely that the predators leap in the air or else go around the trees.

A   The function of *stepping easily over downed trees* is unclear in relation to the rest of the sentence. The pronoun *it* refers only obliquely and unclearly to *moose*, because only the possessive form *moose's* appears in the sentence. Furthermore, the final phrase should say *leap over*, not merely *leap*.

B   The function of *stepping easily over downed trees* is unclear in relation to the rest of the sentence. The pronoun *it* refers only obliquely and unclearly to *moose*, because only the possessive form *moose's* appears in the sentence. The plural pronoun *them* has no logical plural antecedent (surely the predators are not pursuing the moose's legs, but the moose itself; nor are the predators pursuing the downed trees). Furthermore, the final phrase should say *leap over*, not merely *leap*.

C   The plural pronoun *them* in *pursuing them* has no logical plural antecedent.

D   The plural pronoun *them* has no logical plural antecedent (*moose* can be used as a plural, but because in this sentence the singular verb *has* is used, *moose* must be construed as being singular here). Furthermore, the final phrase should say *leap over*, not merely *leap*.

E   **Correct.** The pronoun *it* refers to *moose*, and the pronoun *them* refers to *trees*. Also, the final phrase correctly says *leap over or go around them*.

The correct answer is E.

SC07885

340. Early administrative decisions in China's Ming Dynasty eventually caused a drastic fall in tax revenues, a reduction in military preparedness, <u>the collapse of the currency system, and failed</u> to make sufficient investment in vital transportation infrastructure.

(A)   the collapse of the currency system, and failed

(B)   the collapse of the currency system, and failing

(C)   and the collapse of the currency system, also failed

(D)   the collapse of the currency system, as well as failing

(E)   and the collapse of the currency system, as well as a failure

Parallelism; Grammatical Construction; Rhetorical Construction

The sentence provides a list of effects stemming from administrative decisions in the Ming Dynasty. To make the meaning clear, all items in the list should be in parallel grammatical form. The first three are noun phrases—*a drastic fall, a reduction*, and *the collapse*—but the final item, *failed*, is a verb. To preserve parallel structure, the fourth item should also be a noun phrase: *a failure*. An alternative interpretation might take *failed* as parallel with *caused*, so that *decisions* is the subject of both verbs, but it is illogical to say that the *decisions* failed to make sufficient investments.

A   The list of effects is not parallel since the first three items are noun phrases but the fourth is the verb *failed*. An alternative interpretation might take *failed* as parallel with *caused*, so that *decisions* is the subject of both verbs, but it is illogical to say that the *decisions* failed to make sufficient investments.

B   The list of effects is not parallel since the first three items are noun phrases but the fourth is the participle *failing*.

C   The list of three effects is followed by the verb *failed*, which lacks a subject, thus making the sentence ungrammatical.

D   The list of effects is not parallel since the first three items are noun phrases but the fourth is the participle *failing*.

E   **Correct.** The list of four effects is expressed in parallel grammatical form using noun phrases, including *a failure*.

The correct answer is E.

SC11017

341. Seismologists studying the earthquake that struck northern California in October 1989 are still investigating some of its mysteries: the unexpected power of the seismic waves, <u>the upward thrust that threw one man straight into the air, and the strange electromagnetic signals detected hours before the temblor.</u>

(A) the upward thrust that threw one man straight into the air, and the strange electromagnetic signals detected hours before the temblor

(B) the upward thrust that threw one man straight into the air, and strange electromagnetic signals were detected hours before the temblor

(C) the upward thrust threw one man straight into the air, and hours before the temblor strange electromagnetic signals were detected

(D) one man was thrown straight into the air by the upward thrust, and hours before the temblor strange electromagnetic signals were detected

(E) one man who was thrown straight into the air by the upward thrust, and strange electromagnetic signals that were detected hours before the temblor

Parallelism; Grammatical Construction

Some of the earthquake's *mysteries* are described in a series of three correctly parallel elements: (1) *the unexpected power* …, (2) *the upward thrust* …, and (3) *the strange electromagnetic signals* …. Each of the three elements begins with an article (*the*), a modifier, and a noun. This parallelism is crucial, but each mystery is allowed the further modification most appropriate to it, whether a prepositional phrase (1), a clause (2), or a participial phrase (3).

A **Correct.** This sentence correctly provides a parallel series of three mysteries.

B *The* is omitted before *strange*. The verb *were detected* makes the last element not parallel to the previous two.

C Because they use complete independent clauses, the last two elements are not parallel to the first, and the sentence is ungrammatical.

D The constructions beginning *one man* and *hours before* are not parallel to the construction beginning *the unexpected power*.

E The grammatical constructions describing the mysteries are not parallel.

The correct answer is A.

SC10878

342. The type of behavior exhibited when an animal recognizes itself in a mirror comes within the domain <u>of "theory of mind," thus is best</u> studied as part of the field of animal cognition.

(A) of "theory of mind," thus is best

(B) "theory of mind," and so is best to be

(C) of a "theory of mind," thus it is best

(D) of "theory of mind" and thus is best

(E) of the "theory of mind," and so it is best to be

Grammatical Construction; Idiom

This sentence links two independent clauses; in such sentences, the clauses must normally be set off from each other (by a semicolon, for example), or else the second clause must be introduced by *and* or some other conjunction, not merely an adverb like *thus*. Also, a noun like *domain* normally is followed by the preposition *of* immediately preceding the noun phrase describing the domain.

A The second clause incorrectly lacks an introducing conjunction.

B The phrasing *is best to be studied* is awkwardly unusual and unidiomatic; *is best studied* is a better choice.

C The second clause incorrectly lacks an introducing conjunction. The phrase *a "theory of mind"* would refer to one particular theory rather than (as intended) to a theoretical domain.

D **Correct.** *And* introduces the second clause, which uses the concise wording *best studied*.

E The beginning of the second clause is redundant and wordy: the word *and* is unnecessary because the conjunction *so* is used, and *best to be studied* is unidiomatic.

The correct answer is D.

SC11054

343. Unlike the United States, where farmers can usually <u>depend on rain or snow all year long, the rains in most parts of Sri Lanka</u> are concentrated in the monsoon months, June to September, and the skies are generally clear for the rest of the year.

(A) Unlike the United States, where farmers can usually depend on rain or snow all year long, the rains in most parts of Sri Lanka

(B) Unlike the United States farmers who can usually depend on rain or snow all year long, the rains in most parts of Sri Lanka

(C) Unlike those of the United States, where farmers can usually depend on rain or snow all year long, most parts of Sri Lanka's rains

(D) In comparison with the United States, whose farmers can usually depend on rain or snow all year long, the rains in most parts of Sri Lanka

(E) In the United States, farmers can usually depend on rain or snow all year long, but in most parts of Sri Lanka, the rains

Logical Predication; Rhetorical Construction

The intent of the sentence is to compare seasonal rainfall patterns in the United States and Sri Lanka. There are many ways to set up such comparisons: *unlike x, y; in comparison with x, y; compared to x, y;* and so on. The *x* and *y* being compared must be grammatically and logically parallel. An alternative way of stating the comparison is the use of two independent clauses connected by *but*. The original sentence compares *the United States* to *the rains in most parts of Sri Lanka*; this illogical comparison cannot convey the writer's intention.

A This sentence illogically compares *the United States* to *the rains in most parts of Sri Lanka.*

B Comparing *United States farmers* to *the rains in most parts of Sri Lanka* is not logical.

C The sentence awkwardly and illogically seems to be comparing most parts of the United States with *most parts of Sri Lanka's rains.*

D This sentence compares *the United States* and *the rains in most parts of Sri Lanka.*

E **Correct.** This sentence uses two independent clauses to make the comparison. The first clause describes conditions in the United States, and the second clause describes conditions in Sri Lanka. The comparison is clear and logical.

The correct answer is E.

SC01564

344. <u>In preparation for the prediction of a major earthquake that will hit the state, a satellite-based computer network is being built by the California Office of Emergency Services for identifying</u> earthquake damage and to pinpoint the most affected areas within two hours of the event.

(A) In preparation for the prediction of a major earthquake that will hit the state, a satellite-based computer network is being built by the California Office of Emergency Services for identifying

(B) In preparing for the prediction that a major earthquake will hit the state, the California Office of Emergency Services is building a satellite-based computer network that will identify

(C) In preparing for a major earthquake that is predicted to hit the state, the California Office of Emergency Services is building a satellite-based computer network to identify

(D) To prepare for the prediction of a major earthquake hitting the state, a satellite-based computer network is being built by the California Office of Emergency Services to identify

(E) To prepare for a major earthquake that is predicted to hit the state, the California Office of Emergency Services is building a satellite-based computer network that will identify

Logical Predication; Parallelism

This sentence explains what the California Office of Emergency Services is doing to prepare for an earthquake that has been predicted for the state, but the sentence appears to claim that the California Office is doing these things to prepare for the prediction. The two purposes of these preparations should be presented in parallel form, but the sentence as written presents one as a prepositional phrase (*for identifying*) and the other as an infinitive (*to pinpoint*).

A   The opening phrase illogically claims that the California Office is preparing for a prediction, but later in the sentence it becomes clear that the preparations are targeted to the aftermath of a possible earthquake, not its prediction. The two purposes of the preparations are not presented in parallel form.

B   Like answer choice A, this identifies preparations for a prediction rather than an earthquake; the two purposes of the preparations are not presented in parallel form.

C   **Correct.** The preparations are correctly presented as being for an earthquake, and the two purposes of the preparations are presented in parallel form (*to identify* and *to pinpoint*).

D   As in answer choices A and B, the beginning of this sentence is inconsistent with the rest of it. The opening phrase claims to describe preparations for a prediction, whereas the latter part of the sentence indicates that the preparations are for a predicted earthquake.

E   Like answer choices A and B, this does not present the two purposes of the preparations in parallel form.

The correct answer is C.

SC06727

345.   Once numbering in the millions worldwide, it is estimated that the wolf has declined to 200,000 in 57 countries, some 11,000 of them to be found in the lower 48 United States and Alaska.

(A)   it is estimated that the wolf has declined to 200,000 in 57 countries, some

(B)   the wolf is estimated to have declined to 200,000 in 57 countries, with approximately

(C)   the wolf has declined to an estimate of 200,000 in 57 countries, some

(D)   wolves have declined to an estimate of 200,000 in 57 countries, with approximately

(E)   wolves have declined to an estimated 200,000 in 57 countries, some

Logical Predication; Idiom

The predicate *numbered* must have its logically correct subject, which is *wolves*. Although *the wolf* can be used to refer collectively to wolves as a category, the noun should be plural in this case since the sentence refers to numbers of them and since agreement is needed between the noun and the plural pronoun *them*. Given the plural subject, the verb in the independent clause should be *have declined*. The object of *decline to* should be a word or phrase naming a number or estimated number (e.g., a phrase such as *an estimated 200,000*), not the phrase *an estimate*.

A   The subject of the main clause (*it*) seems to supply the subject of *numbering*, so the latter does not have its correct logical subject, which should be a word or phrase referring to wolves.

B   *The wolf* cannot correctly be taken as the subject of *numbering*, as it is singular and in disagreement with *them* occurring later in the sentence.

C   *The wolf* cannot correctly be taken as the subject of *numbering*, as it is singular and disagrees with the later *them*; also, a decline is strictly speaking to a number, not to *an estimate*.

D   Although *wolves* is a correct subject for *numbering*, a decline should be to a number, not to *an estimate*.

E   **Correct.** *Wolves* is a proper subject for *numbering* and agrees with the later *them*. The decline is correctly said to be to a number, *an estimated 200,000*.

The correct answer is E.

SC11926

346.   As business grows more complex, students majoring in specialized areas like those of finance and marketing have been becoming increasingly successful in the job market.

(A)   majoring in specialized areas like those of finance and marketing have been becoming increasingly

(B)   who major in such specialized areas as finance and marketing are becoming more and more

(C) who majored in specialized areas such as those of finance and marketing are being increasingly

(D) who major in specialized areas like those of finance and marketing have been becoming more and more

(E) having majored in such specialized areas as finance and marketing are being increasingly

Verb Form; Diction

The subordinate clause *as business grows more complex* uses the present-tense verb *grows* to describe an ongoing situation. The main clause describes an effect of this growing complexity; the verbs in the main clause should also use present-tense verbs. The present perfect progressive *have been becoming* is incorrect. The preferred way to introduce examples is with the phrase *such as*, rather than with the word *like*, which suggests a comparison.

A *Like* should be replaced by *such as*. *Have been becoming* is an incorrect verb tense.

B **Correct.** In this sentence, *major* and *are becoming* are present-tense verbs; *such … as* is the preferred form for introducing examples.

C *Majored* is a past-tense verb; *those of* is unnecessary and awkward. *Becoming* is preferable to *being* for describing an unfolding pattern of events.

D *Like* should be replaced by *such as*. *Those of* is unnecessary and awkward. *Have been becoming* is an incorrect verb tense.

E *Having majored* is an awkward past participle. *Becoming* is preferable to *being* for describing an unfolding pattern of events.

The correct answer is B.

SC04682

347. Created in 1945 to reduce poverty and stabilize foreign currency markets, the World Bank and the International Monetary Fund have, according to some critics, <u>continually struggled to meet the expectations of their major shareholders—a group comprising many of the world's rich nations—but neglected</u> their intended beneficiaries in the developing world.

(A) continually struggled to meet the expectations of their major shareholders—a group comprising many of the world's rich nations—but neglected

(B) continually struggled as they try to meet the expectations of their major shareholders—a group comprising many of the world's rich nations—while neglecting that of

(C) continually struggled to meet their major shareholders' expectations—a group comprising many of the world's rich nations—but neglected that of

(D) had to struggle continually in trying to meet the expectations of their major shareholders—a group comprising many of the world's rich nations—while neglecting that of

(E) struggled continually in trying to meet their major shareholders' expectations—a group comprising many of the world's rich nations—and neglecting

Idiom; Verb Form

This sentence describes a contradiction some critics have ascribed to the actions and policies of both the World Bank and the International Monetary Fund: although they were created to address poverty in the developing world, they struggled to meet their major shareholders' expectations and neglected their intended beneficiaries. The contradiction is best expressed by joining the two past-tense verbs *struggled to meet …* and *neglected …* with the contrasting conjunction *but*. The appositive phrase set off with dashes must immediately follow the noun it defines (*shareholders*).

A **Correct.** The conjunction *but* accurately describes the contradiction between what the organizations did for their major shareholders and what they did not do for their intended beneficiaries, and the appositive clearly defines the immediately preceding noun, *shareholders*.

B The present tense of *as they try to meet* is inconsistent with the rest of the verbs in the sentence. The pronoun *that* seems to have no referent in the phrase *while neglecting that of …* since the only likely antecedent *expectations* is plural.

C The appositive grammatically but nonsensically describes expectations rather than shareholders; as in answer choice B, the pronoun *that* does not agree in number with its likely antecedent *expectations*.

D   Like answer choice B, this version is unnecessarily wordy, and like answer choice C, it introduces the pronoun *that*, which disagrees in number with the antecedent *expectations*.

E   As in answer choice C, the appositive seems to define *expectations* rather than *shareholders*, and the conjunction *and* fails to capture the contradictory relationship between the organizations' actions toward their shareholders and their intended beneficiaries.

The correct answer is A.

SC11934

348. Unlike auto insurance, the frequency of claims does not affect the premiums for personal property coverage, but if the insurance company is able to prove excessive loss due to owner negligence, it may decline to renew the policy.

(A)   Unlike auto insurance, the frequency of claims does not affect the premiums for personal property coverage,

(B)   Unlike with auto insurance, the frequency of claims do not affect the premiums for personal property coverage,

(C)   Unlike the frequency of claims for auto insurance, the premiums for personal property coverage are not affected by the frequency of claims,

(D)   Unlike the premiums for auto insurance, the premiums for personal property coverage are not affected by the frequency of claims,

(E)   Unlike with the premiums for auto insurance, the premiums for personal property coverage is not affected by the frequency of claims,

Logical Predication; Agreement

The sentence has been written so that *auto insurance* is contrasted with *the frequency of claims*. The correct contrast is between *the premiums for auto insurance and the premiums for personal property coverage*.

A   *Auto insurance* is illogically contrasted with *the frequency of claims*.

B   *Unlike with* is an incorrect idiom; *auto insurance* is contrasted with *the frequency of claims*; the singular subject *frequency* does not agree with the plural verb *do*.

C   *The frequency of claims* is contrasted with *the premiums for personal property coverage*.

D   Correct. The contrast between *the premiums for auto insurance* and *the premiums for personal property coverage* is clearly and correctly stated in this sentence.

E   *Unlike with* is an incorrect idiom; the plural subject *premiums* does not agree with the singular verb *is not affected*.

The correct answer is D.

7.0   GMAT™ Official Guide Verbal Review
Question Index

7.0 GMAT™ Official Guide Verbal Review Question Index

The Official Guide Verbal Review Question Index is organized by GMAT™ section, difficulty level, and then by mathematical or verbal concept. The question number, page number, and answer explanation page number are listed so that questions within the book can be quickly located.

To locate a question from the online question bank in the book—Every question in the online question bank has a unique ID, called the Practice Question Identifier or PQID, which appears above the question number. Look up the PQID in the table to find its problem number and page number in the book.

Verbal Review

Difficulty	Concept	Question #	Page	Answer Explanation Page	PQID
Easy	Argument Construction	1	20	21	CR63800.03
Easy	Evaluation of a Plan	4	25	25	CR96370.03
Easy	Evaluation of a Plan	5	27	27	CR03570.03
Easy	Idiom; Rhetorical Construction	24	76	77	SC92120.03
Easy	Inference	8	29	31	RC73100-05.03
Easy	Logical Predication; Parallelism	23	75	75	SC74010.03
Easy	Main Idea	9	29	31	RC73100-06.03
Easy	Supporting Idea	6	29	29	RC73100-01.03
Easy	Supporting Idea	7	29	30	RC73100-03.03
Easy	Verb Form; Diction	18	59	60	SC93410.03
Medium	Argument Evaluation	2	20	21	CR32900.03
Medium	Evaluation	13	41	43	RC43000-04.03
Medium	Inference	12	41	42	RC43000-03.03
Medium	Inference	14	41	43	RC43000-07.03
Medium	Logical Predication; Grammatical Construction	22	72	73	SC50620.03

(Continued)

Difficulty	Concept	Question #	Page	Answer Explanation Page	PQID
Medium	Main Idea	11	40	41	RC43000-01.03
Medium	Rhetorical Construction; Parallelism	25	76	77	CR09351.03
Medium	Verb Form; Rhetorical Construction	20	66	66	SC75420.03
Hard	Argument Evaluation	10	34	34	CR51800.03
Hard	Argument Evaluation	3	23	23	CR49110.03
Hard	Argument Evaluation	15	45	46	CR28310.03
Hard	Argument Evaluation	16	50	51	CR88310.03
Hard	Argument Evaluation	17	53	54	CR13750.03
Hard	Grammatical Construction; Logical Predication	21	70	70	SC95430.03
Hard	Rhetorical Construction; Parallelism	19	64	64	SC11910.03

Reading Comprehension

Difficulty	Concept	Question #	Page	Answer Explanation Page	PQID
Easy	Application	2	90	130	RC00184-02
Easy	Evaluation	21	97	141	RC00492-05
Easy	Evaluation	26	98	144	RC00222-03
Easy	Evaluation	28	99	145	RC00222-05.02
Easy	Evaluation	30	100	147	RC38000-02.02

Difficulty	Concept	Question #	Page	Answer Explanation Page	PQID
Easy	Evaluation	32	101	148	RC38000-04.02
Easy	Inference	7	93	133	RC00144-05
Easy	Inference	13	95	137	RC00113-03
Easy	Inference	15	95	138	RC00113-05
Easy	Inference	17	96	139	RC00492-01
Easy	Inference	19	97	140	RC00492-03
Easy	Inference	20	97	141	RC00492-04
Easy	Inference	22	97	142	RC00492-06
Easy	Inference	23	97	143	RC00492-07
Easy	Inference	24	98	143	RC00222-01
Easy	Inference	31	100	148	RC38000-03.02
Easy	Inference	33	101	149	RC38000-05.02
Easy	Inference	35	101	150	RC38000-07.02
Easy	Main Idea	4	91	131	RC00184-04
Easy	Main Idea	9	93	134	RC00144-07
Easy	Main Idea	11	94	136	RC00113-01
Easy	Main Idea	29	100	146	RC38000-01.02
Easy	Supporting Idea	1	90	130	RC00184-01
Easy	Supporting Idea	3	91	131	RC00184-03
Easy	Supporting Idea	5	92	132	RC00144-03
Easy	Supporting Idea	6	92	133	RC00144-04
Easy	Supporting Idea	8	93	134	RC00144-06
Easy	Supporting Idea	10	93	135	RC00144-08
Easy	Supporting Idea	12	95	136	RC00113-02
Easy	Supporting Idea	14	95	137	RC00113-04
Easy	Supporting Idea	16	95	138	RC00113-07
Easy	Supporting Idea	18	97	140	RC00492-02
Easy	Supporting Idea	25	98	144	RC00222-02
Easy	Supporting Idea	27	99	145	RC00222-04
Easy	Supporting Idea	34	101	149	RC38000-06.02

(Continued)

Difficulty	Concept	Question #	Page	Answer Explanation Page	PQID
Easy	Supporting Idea	36	101	151	RC38000-08.02
Medium	Application	42	104	154	RC00141-04
Medium	Application	44	104	156	RC00141-06
Medium	Application	60	109	165	RC00322-02
Medium	Application	61	109	166	RC00322-05
Medium	Application	65	111	168	RC22661-04.01
Medium	Application	80	115	176	RC00097-06
Medium	Evaluation	39	102	152	RC00267-03
Medium	Evaluation	43	104	155	RC00141-05
Medium	Evaluation	48	105	158	RC00204-03
Medium	Evaluation	49	106	159	RC00204-04
Medium	Evaluation	56	107	163	RC00201-03
Medium	Evaluation	58	108	164	RC00201-05
Medium	Evaluation	63	110	167	RC22661-02.01
Medium	Evaluation	69	112	170	RC32661-01.01
Medium	Evaluation	71	113	171	RC32661-03.01
Medium	Evaluation	73	113	172	RC32661-05.01
Medium	Evaluation	77	114	175	RC00097-03
Medium	Evaluation	78	115	175	RC00097-04
Medium	Inference	38	102	152	RC00267-02
Medium	Inference	45	104	157	RC00141-07
Medium	Inference	47	105	158	RC00204-02
Medium	Inference	50	106	159	RC00204-05
Medium	Inference	51	106	160	RC00204-06
Medium	Inference	52	106	161	RC00204-07
Medium	Inference	53	106	161	RC00204-08
Medium	Inference	54	106	162	RC00204-09
Medium	Inference	57	108	163	RC00201-04
Medium	Inference	66	111	169	RC22661-05.01
Medium	Inference	67	111	169	RC22661-06.01

Difficulty	Concept	Question #	Page	Answer Explanation Page	PQID
Medium	Inference	70	112	171	RC32661-02.01
Medium	Inference	74	113	173	RC32661-06.01
Medium	Inference	79	115	176	RC00097-05
Medium	Main Idea	37	102	151	RC00267-01
Medium	Main Idea	40	103	153	RC00141-01
Medium	Main Idea	55	107	162	RC00201-01
Medium	Main Idea	59	109	165	RC00322-01
Medium	Main Idea	68	111	170	RC22661-07.01
Medium	Main Idea	72	113	172	RC32661-04.01
Medium	Supporting Idea	41	103	154	RC00141-02
Medium	Supporting Idea	46	105	157	RC00204-01
Medium	Supporting Idea	62	110	166	RC22661-01.01
Medium	Supporting Idea	64	110	167	RC22661-03.01
Medium	Supporting Idea	75	113	174	RC32661-07.01
Medium	Supporting Idea	76	114	174	RC00097-02
Hard	Application	96	121	185	RC00548-04
Hard	Evaluation	85	117	179	RC00054-05
Hard	Evaluation	97	121	186	RC00548-05
Hard	Evaluation	108	126	192	RC00613-10
Hard	Evaluation	111	128	194	RC00512-05
Hard	Inference	82	116	177	RC00054-02
Hard	Inference	83	116	178	RC00054-03
Hard	Inference	84	117	178	RC00054-04
Hard	Inference	86	117	180	RC00054-06
Hard	Inference	90	118	182	RC11238-03
Hard	Inference	91	119	182	RC11238-04
Hard	Inference	98	122	186	RC00533-03
Hard	Inference	100	123	187	RC00533-05
Hard	Inference	102	124	188	RC00613-02
Hard	Inference	103	125	189	RC00613-03

(Continued)

Difficulty	Concept	Question #	Page	Answer Explanation Page	PQID
Hard	Inference	104	125	190	RC00613-04
Hard	Inference	105	125	190	RC00613-05
Hard	Inference	106	125	191	RC00613-08
Hard	Inference	110	127	194	RC00512-03
Hard	Inference	112	128	195	RC00512-07
Hard	Logical Structure	92	119	183	RC11238-05
Hard	Logical Structure	93	119	183	RC11238-06
Hard	Main Idea	87	117	180	RC00054-07
Hard	Main Idea	88	118	181	RC11238-01
Hard	Main Idea	94	120	184	RC00548-01.02
Hard	Main Idea	107	126	192	RC00613-09.02
Hard	Main Idea	109	127	193	RC00512-01
Hard	Supporting Idea	81	116	177	RC00054-01
Hard	Supporting Idea	89	118	181	RC11238-02
Hard	Supporting Idea	95	120	184	RC00548-03
Hard	Supporting Idea	99	122	187	RC00533-04
Hard	Supporting Idea	101	124	188	RC00613-01

Critical Reasoning

Difficulty	Concept	Question #	Page	Answer Explanation Page	PQID
Easy	Argument Construction	117	203	260	CR00701
Easy	Argument Construction	118	204	261	CR04192
Easy	Argument Construction	125	206	268	CR07618
Easy	Argument Construction	126	207	269	CR02958
Easy	Argument Construction	129	208	272	CR06018
Easy	Argument Construction	133	210	276	CR07547
Easy	Argument Construction	135	211	278	CR01298
Easy	Argument Construction	136	211	279	CR07589

Difficulty	Concept	Question #	Page	Answer Explanation Page	PQID
Easy	Argument Construction	139	212	282	CR03826
Easy	Argument Construction	143	214	286	CR02851
Easy	Argument Construction	145	215	288	CR02704
Easy	Argument Construction	146	215	289	CR03659
Easy	Argument Construction	148	216	291	CR08756
Easy	Argument Construction	151	217	294	CR80661.01
Easy	Argument Evaluation	113	202	256	CR14249
Easy	Argument Evaluation	114	202	257	CR12701.02
Easy	Argument Evaluation	115	203	258	CR12721.02
Easy	Argument Evaluation	116	203	259	CR07612
Easy	Argument Evaluation	119	204	262	CR52441.01
Easy	Argument Evaluation	120	205	263	CR03129
Easy	Argument Evaluation	121	205	264	CR59590.02
Easy	Argument Evaluation	122	205	265	CR20531.01
Easy	Argument Evaluation	123	206	266	CR00828
Easy	Argument Evaluation	124	206	267	CR10639
Easy	Argument Evaluation	127	207	270	CR75231.01
Easy	Argument Evaluation	128	208	271	CR04073
Easy	Argument Evaluation	130	209	273	CR28931.01
Easy	Argument Evaluation	131	209	274	CR04738
Easy	Argument Evaluation	132	210	275	CR91131.02
Easy	Argument Evaluation	134	210	277	CR02270
Easy	Argument Evaluation	137	211	280	CR07785
Easy	Argument Evaluation	138	212	281	CR03535
Easy	Argument Evaluation	140	213	283	CR01430
Easy	Argument Evaluation	141	213	284	CR04180
Easy	Argument Evaluation	142	214	285	CR05096
Easy	Argument Evaluation	144	214	287	CR06331
Easy	Argument Evaluation	147	216	290	CR02518
Easy	Argument Evaluation	149	217	292	CR00780

(*Continued*)

Difficulty	Concept	Question #	Page	Answer Explanation Page	PQID
Easy	Argument Evaluation	150	217	293	CR70661.01
Easy	Argument Evaluation	152	218	295	CR01661.01
Easy	Argument Evaluation	153	218	296	CR11661.01
Easy	Argument Evaluation	154	218	297	CR41661.01
Medium	Argument Construction	161	221	304	CR06795
Medium	Argument Construction	162	222	305	CR02865
Medium	Argument Construction	163	222	306	CR00693
Medium	Argument Construction	164	223	307	CR06845
Medium	Argument Construction	165	223	308	CR10106
Medium	Argument Construction	169	225	312	CR10731
Medium	Argument Construction	170	226	313	CR09120
Medium	Argument Construction	172	227	315	CR04532
Medium	Argument Construction	174	228	317	CR06831
Medium	Argument Construction	175	228	318	CR03697
Medium	Argument Construction	176	229	319	CR05438
Medium	Argument Construction	177	229	320	CR00663
Medium	Argument Construction	180	230	323	CR05431
Medium	Argument Construction	182	231	325	CR01101
Medium	Argument Construction	184	232	327	CR01355
Medium	Argument Construction	187	234	330	CR06152
Medium	Argument Evaluation	167	224	310	CR00783
Medium	Argument Evaluation	168	225	311	CR05590
Medium	Argument Evaluation	171	226	314	CR05065
Medium	Argument Evaluation	173	227	316	CR01353
Medium	Argument Evaluation	178	230	321	CR00677
Medium	Argument Evaluation	179	230	322	CR00726
Medium	Argument Evaluation	181	231	324	CR05750
Medium	Argument Evaluation	183	232	326	CR13093
Medium	Argument Evaluation	186	233	329	CR05079
Medium	Argument Evaluation	188	234	331	CR09046

Difficulty	Concept	Question #	Page	Answer Explanation Page	PQID
Medium	Evaluation of a Plan	155	219	298	CR90661.01
Medium	Evaluation of a Plan	156	219	299	CR21661.01
Medium	Evaluation of a Plan	157	219	300	CR31661.01
Medium	Evaluation of a Plan	158	220	301	CR91661.01
Medium	Evaluation of a Plan	159	220	302	CR02661.01
Medium	Evaluation of a Plan	160	221	303	CR12661.01
Medium	Evaluation of a Plan	166	224	309	CR01392
Medium	Evaluation of a Plan	185	233	328	CR05418
Hard	Argument Construction	189	234	332	CR66900.02
Hard	Argument Construction	190	235	333	CR59820.02
Hard	Argument Construction	193	236	336	CR08540.02
Hard	Argument Construction	195	237	338	CR09740.02
Hard	Argument Construction	197	238	340	CR11050.02
Hard	Argument Construction	201	240	344	CR28001.02
Hard	Argument Construction	204	241	347	CR14448
Hard	Argument Construction	205	242	348	CR09085
Hard	Argument Construction	208	243	351	CR37090.02
Hard	Argument Construction	209	244	352	CR03416
Hard	Argument Construction	212	245	355	CR07562
Hard	Argument Construction	214	246	357	CR01338
Hard	Argument Construction	220	248	363	CR01140
Hard	Argument Construction	221	249	364	CR06422
Hard	Argument Construction	223	250	366	CR06826
Hard	Argument Construction	224	250	367	CR05554
Hard	Argument Construction	228	252	371	CR67850.02
Hard	Argument Construction	230	253	373	CR05656
Hard	Argument Evaluation	192	236	335	CR55030.02
Hard	Argument Evaluation	198	239	341	CR55190.02
Hard	Argument Evaluation	199	239	342	CR11080.02
Hard	Argument Evaluation	203	241	346	CR04999

(Continued)

Difficulty	Concept	Question #	Page	Answer Explanation Page	PQID
Hard	Argument Evaluation	206	242	349	CR01766
Hard	Argument Evaluation	207	243	350	CR12567
Hard	Argument Evaluation	210	244	353	CR03867
Hard	Argument Evaluation	211	245	354	CR01903
Hard	Argument Evaluation	213	246	356	CR07676
Hard	Argument Evaluation	215	247	358	CR09592
Hard	Argument Evaluation	216	247	359	CR10678
Hard	Argument Evaluation	217	247	360	CR05665
Hard	Argument Evaluation	218	248	361	CR01173
Hard	Argument Evaluation	219	248	362	CR03331
Hard	Argument Evaluation	222	249	365	CR07793
Hard	Argument Evaluation	225	251	368	CR05625
Hard	Argument Evaluation	226	251	369	CR04930
Hard	Argument Evaluation	227	252	370	CR09969
Hard	Evaluation of a Plan	191	235	334	CR89820.02
Hard	Evaluation of a Plan	194	237	337	CR62740.02
Hard	Evaluation of a Plan	196	238	339	CR29940.02
Hard	Evaluation of a Plan	200	240	343	CR63780.02
Hard	Evaluation of a Plan	202	240	345	CR01887
Hard	Evaluation of a Plan	229	253	372	CR20190.02
Hard	Evaluation of a Plan	231	253	374	CR56601.02
Hard	Evaluation of a Plan	232	254	375	CR50611.02
Hard	Evaluation of a Plan	233	254	376	CR98001.02

Sentence Correction

Difficulty	Concept	Question #	Page	Answer Explanation Page	PQID
Easy	Agreement; Grammatical Construction	247	404	437	SC01482
Easy	Agreement; Grammatical Construction	252	405	440	SC01543

Difficulty	Concept	Question #	Page	Answer Explanation Page	PQID
Easy	Agreement; Idiom	245	404	436	SC01579
Easy	Agreement; Logical Predication	249	405	438	SC01069
Easy	Agreement; Rhetorical Construction	236	404	431	SC14890
Easy	Agreement; Rhetorical Construction	253	406	441	SC06613
Easy	Diction; Logical Predication	243	404	435	SC01594
Easy	Diction; Verb Form	264	408	447	SC02241
Easy	Grammatical Construction; Diction	263	408	447	SC06935
Easy	Grammatical Construction; Logical Predication	238	403	432	SC01519
Easy	Grammatical Construction; Logical Predication	240	403	433	SC05367
Easy	Grammatical Construction; Parallelism	241	403	434	SC03552
Easy	Grammatical Construction; Parallelism	248	405	438	SC01481
Easy	Grammatical Construction; Rhetorical Construction	250	405	439	SC02628
Easy	Grammatical Construction; Verb Form	259	407	445	SC03779
Easy	Idiom; Agreement	266	408	449	SC61661.01
Easy	Idiom; Logical Predication	265	408	448	SC51661.01
Easy	Idiom; Rhetorical Construction	256	406	443	SC05787
Easy	Idiom; Verb Form	239	403	433	SC02548
Easy	Logical Predication; Diction	235	402	430	SC07435
Easy	Logical Predication; Grammatical Construction	255	406	442	SC01596
Easy	Logical Predication; Parallelism	254	406	442	SC06012
Easy	Logical Predication; Rhetorical Construction	242	404	435	SC04083

(Continued)

Difficulty	Concept	Question #	Page	Answer Explanation Page	PQID
Easy	Logical Predication; Rhetorical Construction	244	404	436	SC04652
Easy	Logical Predication; Rhetorical Construction	246	404	437	SC04026
Easy	Logical Predication; Rhetorical Construction	268	409	450	SC94920.02
Easy	Parallelism; Agreement	260	407	445	SC03146
Easy	Parallelism; Grammatical Construction	258	407	444	SC01600
Easy	Parallelism; Rhetorical Construction	237	402	431	SC02940
Easy	Parallelism; Rhetorical Construction	251	405	439	SC04198
Easy	Parallelism; Rhetorical Construction	262	407	446	SC01915
Easy	Rhetorical Construction; Agreement	261	407	446	SC12367
Easy	Rhetorical Construction; Logical Predication	257	407	443	SC03724
Easy	Rhetorical Construction; Parallel Construction	234	402	430	SC01545
Easy	Verb Agreement; Parallelism	267	408	449	SC81661.01
Medium	Agreement; Diction	285	413	461	SC03916
Medium	Agreement; Logical Predication; Verb Form	297	416	469	SC02370
Medium	Diction; Agreement; Rhetorical Construction	272	410	452	SC62661.01
Medium	Diction; Agreement; Rhetorical Construction	275	410	455	SC92661.01
Medium	Diction; Idiom; Agreement	283	413	460	SC71061.01
Medium	Diction; Rhetorical Construction	271	409	452	SC52661.01
Medium	Diction; Rhetorical Construction	290	414	465	SC04874

Difficulty	Concept	Question #	Page	Answer Explanation Page	PQID
Medium	Diction; Rhetorical Construction; Logical Predication	284	413	460	SC89941.01
Medium	Grammatical Construction; Diction	278	411	456	SC99250.01
Medium	Grammatical Construction; Diction	298	416	469	SC01435
Medium	Grammatical Construction; Parallelism	286	413	462	SC01639
Medium	Grammatical Construction; Verb Form	277	411	456	SC37620.01
Medium	Idiom; Agreement	294	415	466	SC46270.02
Medium	Idiom; Diction	292	414	466	SC02382
Medium	Idiom; Grammatical Construction; Parallelism	280	412	458	SC60440.01
Medium	Idiom; Parallelism	276	411	455	SC03661.01
Medium	Idiom; Rhetorical Construction	282	412	459	SC28801.01
Medium	Logical Predication; Grammatical Construction	299	416	470	SC04603
Medium	Logical Predication; Idiom	295	415	467	SC05894
Medium	Logical Predication; Idiom	296	415	468	SC01562
Medium	Logical Predication; Parallelism	293	415	466	SC07143
Medium	Logical Predication; Parallelism	302	417	472	SC02791
Medium	Logical Predication; Parallelism; Grammatical Construction	279	412	457	SC04215
Medium	Logical Predication; Rhetorical Construction	287	414	463	SC03315
Medium	Logical Predication; Verb Form	270	409	451	SC42661.01
Medium	Parallelism Diction	288	414	463	SC05244

(*Continued*)

Difficulty	Concept	Question #	Page	Answer Explanation Page	PQID
Medium	Parallelism Diction; Rhetorical Construction; Logical Predication	273	410	453	SC72661.01
Medium	Parallelism; Logical Predication	300	416	471	SC05381
Medium	Parallelism; Rhetorical Construction	301	416	471	SC01485
Medium	Parallelism; Rhetorical Construction	303	417	472	SC00987
Medium	Rhetorical Construction Diction	291	414	465	SC01451
Medium	Rhetorical Construction; Agreement; Logical Predication	269	409	451	SC71661.01
Medium	Verb Form; Diction	274	410	454	SC82661.01
Medium	Verb Form; Grammatical Construction	281	412	459	SC01002
Medium	Verb Form; Idiom	289	414	464	SC04346
Hard	Agreement; Logical Predication	315	420	479	SC01712
Hard	Agreement; Rhetorical Construction	318	421	481	SC01747
Hard	Agreement; Rhetorical Construction; Grammatical Construction	316	420	480	SC01954
Hard	Diction; Logical Predication	304	417	473	SC01972
Hard	Diction; Verb Form	309	419	476	SC02011
Hard	Grammatical Construction; Agreement	334	424	491	SC01990
Hard	Grammatical Construction; Idiom	342	426	495	SC10878
Hard	Idiom; Grammatical; Verb Form	311	419	477	SC06132
Hard	Idiom; Logical Predication	314	420	479	SC03289
Hard	Idiom; Logical Predication	326	423	485	SC04732
Hard	Idiom; Parallelism	319	421	481	SC11880

(Continued)

Difficulty	Concept	Question #	Page	Answer Explanation Page	PQID
Hard	Parallelism; Idiom	333	424	490	SC06205
Hard	Parallelism; Logical Predication	332	424	489	SC02131
Hard	Parallelism; Rhetorical Construction	317	421	480	SC12645
Hard	Parallelism; Verb Form	310	419	477	SC04492
Hard	Rhetorical Construction; Agreement	323	422	483	SC07066
Hard	Rhetorical Construction; Agreement	328	423	487	SC02664
Hard	Rhetorical Construction; Diction	307	418	475	SC08272
Hard	Rhetorical Construction; Logical Predication	327	423	486	SC04672
Hard	Rhetorical Construction; Logical Predication; Verb Form	325	422	485	SC02333
Hard	Rhetorical Construction; Verb Form	313	420	478	SC03998
Hard	Rhetorical Construction; Verb Form; Diction	306	418	474	SC11854
Hard	Verb Form; Diction	346	427	497	SC11926
Hard	Verb Form; Idiom	308	419	475	SC00975
Hard	Verb Form; Idiom	321	421	482	SC05216
Hard	Verb Form; Logical Predication; Rhetorical Construction	336	425	491	SC02338

Appendix A   Answer Sheets

Reading Comprehension Answer Sheet

1.	24.	47.	70.	93.
2.	25.	48.	71.	94.
3.	26.	49.	72.	95.
4.	27.	50.	73.	96.
5.	28.	51.	74.	97.
6.	29.	52.	75.	98.
7.	30.	53.	76.	99.
8.	31.	54.	77.	100.
9.	32.	55.	78.	101.
10.	33.	56.	79.	102.
11.	34.	57.	80.	103.
12.	35.	58.	81.	104.
13.	36.	59.	82.	105.
14.	37.	60.	83.	106.
15.	38.	61.	84.	107.
16.	39.	62.	85.	108.
17.	40.	63.	86.	109.
18.	41.	64.	87.	110.
19.	42.	65.	88.	111.
20.	43.	66.	89.	112.
21.	44.	67.	90.	
22.	45.	68.	91.	
23.	46.	69.	92.	

Critical Reasoning Answer Sheet

113.	138.	163.	188.	213.
114.	139.	164.	189.	214.
115.	140.	165.	190.	215.
116.	141.	166.	191.	216.
117.	142.	167.	192.	217.
118.	143.	168.	193.	218.
119.	144.	169.	194.	219.
120.	145.	170.	195.	220.
121.	146.	171.	196.	221.
122.	147.	172.	197.	222.
123.	148.	173.	198.	223.
124.	149.	174.	199.	224.
125.	150.	175.	200.	225.
126.	151.	176.	201.	226.
127.	152.	177.	202.	227.
128.	153.	178.	203.	228.
129.	154.	179.	204.	229.
130.	155.	180.	205.	230.
131.	156.	181.	206.	231.
132.	157.	182.	207.	232.
133.	158.	183.	208.	233.
134.	159.	184.	209.	
135.	160.	185.	210.	
136.	161.	186.	211.	
137.	162.	187.	212.	

Sentence Correction Answer Sheet

234.	257.	280.	303.	326.
235.	258.	281.	304.	327.
236.	259.	282.	305.	328.
237.	260.	283.	306.	329.
238.	261.	284.	307.	330.
239.	262.	285.	308.	331.
240.	263.	286.	309.	332.
241.	264.	287.	310.	333.
242.	265.	288.	311.	334.
243.	266.	289.	312.	335.
244.	267.	290.	313.	336.
245.	268.	291.	314.	337.
246.	269.	292.	315.	338.
247.	270.	293.	316.	339.
248.	271.	294.	317.	340.
249.	272.	295.	318.	341.
250.	273.	296.	319.	342.
251.	274.	297.	320.	343.
252.	275.	298.	321.	344.
253.	276.	299.	322.	345.
254.	277.	300.	323.	346.
255.	278.	301.	324.	347.
256.	279.	302.	325.	348.

Notes

Notes

Notes

1 test.
2 ways.
The choice is yours.

The GMAT™ exam is available everyday. Online & in-person.

[🖱 gmat.com]

Compare.

Download the **free comparison grid** to see which format is best for you.

ONLINE **&** TEST CENTER

[gmat.com/compare]

Learn.

Listen to **Inside the GMAT™** official podcast to become a GMAT insider.

[insidethegmat.com]